Emerging Advancements in AI and Big Data Technologies in Business and Society

Jingyuan Zhao
University of Toronto, Canada

Joseph Richards
California State University, Sacramento, USA

V. Vinoth Kumar
Vellore Institute of Technology, India

A volume in the Advances in Computational
Intelligence and Robotics (ACIR) Book Series

Published in the United States of America by
IGI Global
Engineering Science Reference (an imprint of IGI Global)
701 E. Chocolate Avenue
Hershey PA, USA 17033
Tel: 717-533-8845
Fax: 717-533-8661
E-mail: cust@igi-global.com
Web site: http://www.igi-global.com

Library of Congress Cataloging-in-Publication Data

Library of Congress Cataloging-in-Publication Data

Names: Zhao, Jingyuan, 1968- editor. | Richards, Joseph, 1966- editor. |
  Kumar, V. Vinoth, 1988- editor.
Title: Emerging advancements in AI and big data technologies in business
  and society / edited by: Jingyuan Zhao, Joseph Richards, Vinoth Kumar V.

Description: Hershey PA : Engineering Science Reference, [2024] | Includes
  bibliographical references. | Summary: "The book presents a full
  understanding on recent advancements in AI and Big Data technologies,
  with a focus on state-of-the-art approaches, methodologies, and systems
  for the design, development, deployment, and innovative use of those
  technologies. It provides insight for how to develop AI and Big Data
  technologies to meet smart business and society development demands"--
  Provided by publisher.
Identifiers: LCCN 2023037133 (print) | LCCN 2023037134 (ebook) | ISBN
  9798369306833 (hardcover) | ISBN 9798369306840 (paperback) | ISBN
  9798369306857 (ebook)
Subjects: LCSH: Artificial intelligence--Industrial applications. | Big
  data--Industrial applications.
Classification: LCC TA347.A78 .E434 2024 (print) | LCC TA347.A78 (ebook)
  | DDC 670.285/63--dc23/eng/20240125
LC record available at https://lccn.loc.gov/2023037133
LC ebook record available at https://lccn.loc.gov/2023037134

British Cataloguing in Publication Data
A Cataloguing in Publication record for this book is available from the British Library.

The views expressed in this book are those of the authors, but not necessarily of the publisher.

For electronic access to this publication, please contact: eresources@igi-global.com.

Advances in Computational Intelligence and Robotics (ACIR) Book Series

Ivan Giannoccaro
University of Salento, Italy

ISSN:2327-0411
EISSN:2327-042X

Mission

While intelligence is traditionally a term applied to humans and human cognition, technology has progressed in such a way to allow for the development of intelligent systems able to simulate many human traits. With this new era of simulated and artificial intelligence, much research is needed in order to continue to advance the field and also to evaluate the ethical and societal concerns of the existence of artificial life and machine learning.

The **Advances in Computational Intelligence and Robotics (ACIR) Book Series** encourages scholarly discourse on all topics pertaining to evolutionary computing, artificial life, computational intelligence, machine learning, and robotics. ACIR presents the latest research being conducted on diverse topics in intelligence technologies with the goal of advancing knowledge and applications in this rapidly evolving field.

Coverage

- Evolutionary Computing
- Robotics
- Adaptive and Complex Systems
- Computer Vision
- Artificial Intelligence
- Computational Intelligence
- Neural Networks
- Fuzzy Systems
- Brain Simulation
- Algorithmic Learning

IGI Global is currently accepting manuscripts for publication within this series. To submit a proposal for a volume in this series, please contact our Acquisition Editors at Acquisitions@igi-global.com or visit: http://www.igi-global.com/publish/.

Titles in this Series

For a list of additional titles in this series, please visit: www.igi-global.com/book-series

Cross-Industry AI Applications
P. Paramasivan (Dhaanish Ahmed College of Engineering, India) S. Suman Rajest (Dhaanish Ahmed College of Engineering, India) Karthikeyan Chinnusamy (Veritas, USA) R. Regin (SRM Institute of Science and Technology, India) and Ferdin Joe John Joseph (Thai-Nichi Institute of Technology, Thailand)
Engineering Science Reference • copyright 2024 • 389pp • H/C (ISBN: 9798369359518) • US $415.00 (our price)

Harnessing Artificial Emotional Intelligence for Improved Human-Computer Interactions
Nitendra Kumar (Amity Business School, Amity University, Noida, India) Surya Kant Pal (Sharda University, Greater Noida, India) Priyanka Agarwal (Amity Business School, Amity University, Noida, India) Joanna Rosak-Szyrocka (Częstochowa University of Technology, Poland) and Vishal Jain (Sharda University, Greater Noida, India)
Engineering Science Reference • copyright 2024 • 300pp • H/C (ISBN: 9798369327944) • US $335.00 (our price)

Applied AI and Humanoid Robotics for the Ultra-Smart Cyberspace
Eduard Babulak (National Science Foundation, USA)
Engineering Science Reference • copyright 2024 • 287pp • H/C (ISBN: 9798369323991) • US $305.00 (our price)

AI Algorithms and ChatGPT for Student Engagement in Online Learning
Rohit Bansal (Vaish College of Engineering, India) Aziza Chakir (Faculty of Law, Economics, and Social Sciences, Hassan II University, Casablanca, Morocco) Abdul Hafaz Ngah (Faculty of Business Economics and Social Development, Universiti Malaysia, Terengganu, Malaysia) Fazla Rabby (Stanford Institute of Management and Technology, Australia) and Ajay Jain (Shri Cloth Market Kanya Vanijya Mahavidyalaya, Indore, India)
Information Science Reference • copyright 2024 • 292pp • H/C (ISBN: 9798369342688) • US $265.00 (our price)

Applications, Challenges, and the Future of ChatGPT
Priyanka Sharma (Swami Keshvanand Institute of Technology, Management, and Gramothan, Jaipur, India) Monika Jyotiyana (Manipal University Jaipur, India) and A.V. Senthil Kumar (Hindusthan College of Arts and Sciences, India)
Engineering Science Reference • copyright 2024 • 309pp • H/C (ISBN: 9798369368244) • US $365.00 (our price)

Modeling, Simulation, and Control of AI Robotics and Autonomous Systems
Tanupriya Choudhury (Graphic Era University, India) Anitha Mary X. (Karunya Institute of Technology and Sciences, India) Subrata Chowdhury (Sreenivasa Institute of Technology and Management Studies, India) C. Karthik (Jyothi Engineering College, India) and C. Suganthi Evangeline (Sri Eshwar College of Engineering, India)

701 East Chocolate Avenue, Hershey, PA 17033, USA
Tel: 717-533-8845 x100 • Fax: 717-533-8661
E-Mail: cust@igi-global.com • www.igi-global.com

Titles in this Series

For a list of additional titles in this series, please visit: www.igi-global.com/book-series

Engineering Science Reference ● copyright 2024 ● 295pp ● H/C (ISBN: 9798369319628) ● US $300.00 (our price)

701 East Chocolate Avenue, Hershey, PA 17033, USA
Tel: 717-533-8845 x100 ● Fax: 717-533-8661
E-Mail: cust@igi-global.com ● www.igi-global.com

Table of Contents

Detailed Table of Contents

Chapter 1

Hulya Kocyigit, Icahn School of Medicine at Mount Sinai, USA & Karamanoglu Mehmetbey University, Turkey

Machine learning (ML), a subfield of artificial intelligence (AI), has been rapidly expanding both conceptually and in its various applications. Over the years, organizations across different business sectors have increasingly adopted modern machine-learning approaches. This chapter outlines the fundamentals of ML in business analytics. Special attention is given to the most prominent techniques of supervised learning, such as decision trees, random forests, k-nearest neighbors (KNN), and Naive Bayes. Additionally, the chapter explores significant theoretical examples that demonstrate the core principles of machine learning and its practical applications, aiming to foster an understanding of more technical explanations throughout.

Chapter 2

Aditya Pai H., Jain University, India
Mahesh T. R., Jain University, India
Jyoti Agarwal, Graphic Era University, India
Vinoth Kumar V., Vellore Institute of Technology University, India
Sharon Christa, School of Computing, MIT ADT University, India
A. Suresh Kumar, Independent Researcher, India

Industries follow the reactive approach in finding the errors and threats in the development process and mitigating them. In the chapter, an IT industry of small and medium levels is taken as a part of the case study. In small and medium level enterprises (SMEs), the predictive maintenance technique is used rather than the reactive approach. The transition from reactive to predictive was essential for the SMEs to help the managers and the development team anticipate future problems based on past data. An SME has been taken as a case study. The study uses a data set of 6 months for the prediction. The dataset generates the software development process and rules matrix. The matrix is used for analyzing and predicting the accuracy of the software development results of the project. Here, three AI algorithms are used for the prediction. After getting the result, comparative analyses are done between the three AI algorithms to select the best among the three. The chosen algorithm will be used in the development process to improve the business prospects of the enterprise.

Chapter 3

Giulio Ferrigno, Scuola Superiore Sant'Anna, Pisa, Italy
Valentina Cucino, Scuola Superiore Sant'Anna, Pisa, Italy & Lumsa University, Rome

Industry 4.0, the Fourth Industrial Revolution, has fundamentally transformed manufacturing by integrating advanced digital technologies like IoT, AI, big data, and the cloud, creating intelligent, interconnected environments. Developed nations have embraced this revolution to enhance efficiency and productivity. However, the adoption of Industry 4.0 is equally vital for developing countries. This study examines how Industry 4.0 can promote economic growth in developing nations, focusing on Costa Rica's successful implementation as a case study. Factors contributing to Costa Rica's success include a skilled workforce, infrastructure investment, and a conducive business environment. The analysis explores Costa Rica's Industry 4.0 readiness, highlighting government initiatives, key benefiting sectors, and preparedness factors. The findings inform policy recommendations for other emerging economies, underscoring Industry 4.0's potential to bridge development gaps and foster sustainable growth.

Chapter 4

N. Krishnamoorthy, Vellore Institute of Technology, India
V. Vinoth Kumar, Vellore Institute of Technology, India
Chinchu Nair, Dr. MGR Educational and Research Institute, India
A. Maheswari, Dr. MGR Educational and Research Institute, India
Sonali Mishra, Vellore Institute of Technology, India
Ayush Sinha, Vellore Institute of Technology, India

The high rate of staff turnover in knowledge-based organizations is a key challenge. Invaluable tacit information, which is frequently the source of a company's competitive advantage, is often taken with departing personnel. If a company wants to keep a better competitive edge over its competitors, it should prioritize lowering staff churn. By forecasting attrition based on demographic and job-related factors, this study finds employee traits that aid in predicting employee turnover in organizations. With an IBM dataset of 14,999 samples and 10 features, up-sampling techniques and various machine learning algorithms are employed to find the best predictive model. Data visualization and analysis reveal significant factors and correlations. Further, the authors have used models to predict and analyze employee attrition and turnover. Using classifiers like k-nearest neighbors (KNN), support vector machine (SVM), decision trees (DT), and random forest classifiers (RF), four main tests were run on the IBM dataset to predict employee attrition.

Chapter 5

Emmanuel Ifeduba, Redeemer's University, Nigeria

Digital technologies have impacted all aspects of magazine publishing, and emerging technologies such as artificial intelligence (AI) promise to make even greater impacts. Notwithstanding, the rapidity of their introduction has made the empirical tracking and classification of trending e-collaboration and e-marketing innovations difficult. This study, therefore, explores e-marking and e-collaboration innovations employed by digital magazines available online, with the aim of identifying and classifying trending e-marketing and e-collaboration innovations; and illustrating publisher relations with content creators and marketing collaborators, to guide future research, e-commerce and AI adoption. Analysis indicated that 10 promotional, 10 e-pricing, 9 e-distribution, 7 e-commerce, and 19 e-collaboration innovations are trending, and adapting them to complement AI would enable e-magazines to perform, especially if they would adopt e-collaboration rather than e-competition.

Chapter 6

Amandeep Dhaliwal, Manav Rachna International Institute of Research and Studies, India

The upcoming sixth-generation (6G) networks are envisioned as offering ultra-low latency, high bandwidth, and improved quality of service, which aims to facilitate effective communication among network nodes. Integration of this cutting-edge technology in healthcare facilities can support intelligent diagnosis, patient-centric treatment, and various healthcare services, both within hospitals and remotely. Thus, the expanding healthcare sector, wherein an increasing array of applications is integrated into the network, yields diverse data in terms of shapes and sizes would facilitate enhanced personalized and remote healthcare services. The trajectory of future intelligent healthcare thus involves the synergistic integration of 6G to address prevailing constraints associated with cellular coverage, network performance, and security concerns. This chapter endeavors to elucidate the features, prospects, challenges, and future directions pertinent to this evolving futuristics healthcare landscape.

The improving medical instrumentation thru hyper spectral imaging for sustainable medical care (IMITH-SM) project is a research initiative that seeks to develop and boost hyperspectral imaging (HSI) technologies to correctly and as it should be screen, diagnose, and deal with clinically associated conditions in the clinical discipline. More particularly, this venture pursuits to discover and expand using HSI and its software to enhance the accuracy and range of medical examinations, diagnoses, treatments, and decisions. By leveraging the benefits of HSI, the IMITH-SM mission seeks to enhance clinical instrumentation and patient care by providing greater dependable, quicker, and simpler-to-recognize imaging and diagnostic records. Specifically, these targets include exploring how HSI may be used as a diagnostic device for commonplace illnesses such as cancer and cardiovascular illnesses and figuring out capability programs for HSI-enabled scientific robotics.

This chapter has studies that attempt to assess the detection of neuroblastoma and pediatric cancer via time series evaluation. The look took a retrospective method using five patient datasets, combining gadget learning and traditional statistical techniques to detect chance tiers of tumors inside the datasets. The machine-getting-to-know techniques include random forests, decision trees, assist vector machines, k-nearest friends, and convolutional neural nets. Statistical strategies used included co-occurrence matrix evaluation, principal element evaluation, and Shannon entropy. The observation outcomes demonstrate that time series analysis can offer high accuracy in predicting cancer threat levels and may be carried out on diverse cancers for well-timed and reliable prognosis. Eventually, the chapter offers various hints to enhance detection, incorporating extra statistics capabilities and designing a custom reference index.

Tharun Ashwin B., Vellore Institute of Technology, Chennai, India
Bhuvaneswari Amma N. G., Vellore Institute of Technology, Chennai, India

Heart and blood vessel problems are collectively referred to as cardiovascular diseases. Fatty deposits build up inside an artery, generating a blood clot, which causes the artery to harden and constrict, reducing blood flow to the body, brain, or heart. In the study, a comparative analysis between nine machine learning classifiers has been made. Also, in the study, the authors are training and testing the data set under different split ratio to analyze the difference in the result that the authors obtain after executing those set of data. The split ratio includes a 60:40 split ratio, 70:30 split ratio, 80:20 split ratio, and 90:10 split ratio. They analyzed the performance of the classifiers with respect to various metrics. They concluded by saying the proposed model yields the best accuracy when they use a random forest classifier with an accuracy of 99.26% for the split ratio of 60:40.

Chapter 10

Bharanidharan N., School of Computer Science Engineering and Information Systems,
Vellore Institute of Technology, Vellore, India
Sannasi Chakravarthy S. R., Department of Electronics and Communication Engineering,
Bannari Amman Institute of Technology, Sathyamangalam, India
Vinoth Kumar V., School of Computer Science Engineering and Information Systems, Vellore
Institute of Technology, Vellore, India
Pratham Aggarwal, School of Computer Science Engineering and Information Systems,
Vellore Institute of Technology, Vellore, India
Harikumar Rajaguru, Department of Electronics and Communication Engineering, Bannari
Amman Institute of Technology, Sathyamangalam, India

Renal cancer is among the top 10 cancers in both genders. Microarray gene expression data is one of the effective modalities to diagnose renal cancer. The main objective of this work is to label the gene expression sample as either normal or clear cell renal cell carcinoma. To improve the classification performance and reduce the training time of the above-mentioned supervised classifiers, various feature selection and dimensionality reduction techniques are investigated. Feature selection techniques, namely variance filter, chi-square test, ANOVA test, and mutual information filter, are tested. In addition, principal component analysis, independent component analysis, and linear discriminant analysis are evaluated as dimensionality reduction techniques. Highest balanced accuracy score of 91.6% is attained for support vector machine classifier while it was increased to 94.4% through the usage appropriate dimensionality reduction or feature selection technique.

    S. Niranjan, Karunya Institute of Technology and Sciences, India
    Samson Arun Raj, Karunya Institute of Technology and Sciences, India
    T. Jemima Jebaseeli, Karunya Institute of Technology and Sciences, India
    S. Marshal, Karunya Institute of Technology and Sciences, India
    S. S. Ashik, Karunya Institute of Technology and Sciences, India

A timely and precise diagnosis is essential for effective treatment of epilepsy, a neurological condition characterized by recurrent seizures. Because of their capacity to capture cerebral processes, electroencephalogram (EEG) data are crucial in the diagnosis of epilepsy. The proposed system gives a detailed comparison of EEG signal processing strategies for epilepsy detection utilizing ensemble techniques and investigates the usefulness of ensemble algorithms such as gradient boosting, AdaBoost, XGBoost, and bagging classifier in improving epilepsy detection. Through the use of these ensemble approaches, the system preprocesses the EEG data, extracts features, and classifies them. Accuracy, precision, recall, and F1-score are performance indicators that are used to assess each ensemble approach's efficiency. The results were obtained through extensive testing on a well-curated dataset. The finding of the proposed system clarifies the positive impacts and regulates each ensemble technique for determining the presence of epilepsy.

    V. Muthukumaran, SRM Institute of Science and Technology, India
    R. Udhayakumar, Vellore Institute of Technology, India
    *B. Vennila, College of Engineering and Technology, SRM Institute of Science and
        Technology, India*
    Joseph P. Bindu, Dayananda Sagar College of Engineering, Bangalore, India
    Meram Munirathnam, Rajiv Gandhi University of Knowledge Technologies, India
    N. Thillaiarasu, REVA University, India

Smart cities aim to sustainably increase urbanization, lower energy consumption, improve inhabitants' economic and quality of life, and protect the environment. The idea of smart cities revolves around ICT since it makes it easier to formulate policies, make decisions, execution, and ultimately the supply of helpful offerings. In addition to utilizing digital technologies, the concept of the "smart city" is a response to the political, social, and economic issues that post-industrial civilizations are facing at the beginning of the new millennium. In this chapter, the authors discuss several IoT-based machine learning techniques that are applied, among other things, in the aforementioned domains. Furthermore, a review of the assessments and a report on the lessons learned are presented, with an emphasis on the fundamental role that machine learning techniques should play in internet of things networks.

Chapter 13

Dharmesh Dhabliya, Vishwakarma Institute of Information Technology, India
Ankur Gupta, Vaish College of Engineering, India
Sukhvinder Singh Dari, Symbiosis International University, India
Ritika Dhabliya, Yashika Journal Publications Pvt. Ltd., India
Anishkumar Dhablia, Altimetrik India Pvt. Ltd., India
Nitin N. Sakhare, Vishwakarma Institute of Information Technology, India
Sabyasachi Pramanik, Haldia Institute of Technology, India

Subterranean water pipes deteriorate due to a variety of physical, mechanical, environmental, and social factors. Accurate pipe failure prediction is a prerequisite for a rational administrative approach to the water supply network (WSN) and is a challenge for the conventional physics-dependent model. The enormous water supply network's past maintenance data history was utilized by the study to anticipate water pipe breaks using data-directed machine learning methodologies. In order to include many factors that contribute to the deterioration of subsurface pipes, an initial multi-source data-aggregation system was created. The framework outlined the conditions for merging many datasets, including the soil type, population count, geographic, and meteorological datasets as well as the conventional pipe leaking dataset. Based on the data, five machine learning (ML) techniques—LightGBM, ANN, logistic regression, K-NN, and SVM algorithm—are developed to forecast pipe failure. It was found that LightGBM provided the optimum performance. Five criteria were used to analyze the relative importance of the main contributing factors to the water pipe breakdowns: calculation time, accuracy, effect of categorical variables, and interpretation. LightGBM, the model with the second-lowest training time, performed the best. Given the severe skewness of the dataset, it has been shown that the receiver operating characteristics (ROC) measure is too optimistic using the precision-recall curve (PRC) metric. It's noteworthy to note that socioeconomic factors within a community have been shown to have an impact on pipe failure probability. This study implies that data-directed analysis, which combines ML techniques with the proposed data aggregation architecture, may enhance reliable decision-making in WSN administration.

    B. Swapna, Dr. MGR Educational and Research Institute, India

    M. Kamalahasan, Dr. MGR Educational and Research Institute, India

    G. Kavitha, Dr. MGR Educational and Research Institute, India

    M. Sujitha, Dr. MGR Educational and Research Institute, India

    S. Reshma Chandran, Dr. MGR Educational and Research Institute, India

    D. Surendiran Muthukumar, Kalasalingam Academy of Research and Education, India

    S. Bhuvaneswari, S.A. Engineering College, India

AUVs are robotic submarines that are a part of the emerging field of autonomous and unmanned vehicles. This project shows the design implementation of an AUV as a miniature size and its test bed platform for a variety of research in underwater technologies especially involving small-scale, surface water, and low-cost underwater robots. The general design and its consideration are well discussed in this chapter. The AUV prototype has been developed by SolidWorks. It will have a fixed mechanical system and body, having a modular electronic system that allows the development of various controllers. The controller and motors have been tested in small-scale surface water, and the result is encouraging. Some factors affecting AUV performance are also elaborated for future research in this area. Underwater robots can explore areas of the ocean that are too dangerous or too difficult for humans to go.

    Archana Reddy R., SR University, India

    Aruna S., SRM Institute of Science and Technology, Kattankulathur, India

    Saranya A., SRM Institute of Science and Technology, Kattankulathur, India

    Boobalan J., Kumaraguru College of Technology, India

    Sujatha M., Koneru Lakshmaiah Education Foundation, India

    Prabu S., Mahendra Institute of Technology, India

Ensemble Kalman filters (EnKFs) is a statistics assimilation technique extensively used for the most influential kingdom estimation and forecasting. This chapter investigates the potential of ensemble Kalman filters for area networks and their use within the international optimization of network overall performance. It highlights the advantages of using ensemble Kalman filters in phrases of higher overall performance, quicker convergence, and progressed robustness with admiration to local optimization schemes. Moreover, the chapter gives an easy yet effective option to the problem of model error and uncertainty that is usually located when handling massive-scale networks. Subsequently, it validates the proposed method by comparing its outcomes with the ones acquired with local optimization methods. The results of this comparison show that ensemble Kalman filters outperform neighborhood optimization schemes in terms of network overall performance, scalability, and robustness.

Chapter 16

B. Jothi, SRM Institute of Science and Technology, India
J. Jeyasudha, SRM Institute of Science and Technology, India
M. Sujatha, Koneru Lakshmaiah Education Foundation, India
M. Jayalakshmi, Kalasalingam Academy of Research and Education, India
Nagendar Yamsani, SR University, India
C. Aarthi, Sengunthar Engineering College, India

This chapter compares Markov autoregressive (MAR) models and ARIMAX models for network overall performance optimization. The fashions' inherent skills, in addition to their respective traits and underlying assumptions, are in comparison. Each model kind's accuracy and predictive capability are assessed using simulations based on randomly generated information. The conclusions drawn from this observation advocate that MAR models are ideal for predicting community overall performance because of their capability to capture the dynamic nature of community traffic correctly. Additionally, the need to specify a further coefficient within the ARIMAX overestimates anticipated values and decreases overall performance prediction accuracy. Further research is warranted to investigate the differences between the two forms of models more excellent very well.

Chapter 17

Prasanna Ranjith Christodoss, University of Technology and Applied Sciences, Shinas,
*   Oman*
Thamarai Selvi Vaidhyanathan, Sohar University, Oman
Vaidhyanathan Pandian, University of Technology and Applied Sciences, Shinas, Oman
S. Syed Khaja Mohideen, University of Technology and Applied Sciences, Salalah, Oman
T. Karthikeyan, University of Technology and Applied Sciences, Salalah, Oman

Next-generation wireless technologies are becoming more complex due to the diverse applications, devices, and networks, as well as service expectations. Mobile network operators (MNOs) must optimize infrastructure, power, and bandwidth to meet the performance and optimization requirements of a multifarious network. Current networking tactics and conventional data analysis technologies have limited capabilities. A data-driven next-generation wireless communication model is considered, leveraging advanced statistical analysis for MNOs' networks. The role of artificial intelligence (AI) in providing intelligence to networks, such as confidence, self-adaptation, proactivity, and predictive behavior, is also investigated. The benefits and drawbacks of integrating big data analytics and AI into modern wireless networks are also discussed.

Chapter 18

    Aruna S., Department of Computational Intelligence, SRM Institute of Science and
        Technology, Kattankulathur, India
    Maheswari M., Department of Computational Intelligence, SRM Institute of Science and
        Technology, Kattankulathur, India
    Charulatha G., Selvam College of Technology, India
    Lekashri S., King Engineering College, India
    Nivedha M., Arasu Engineering College, India
    Vijayalakshmi A., Vels Institute of Science, Technology, and Advanced Studies, India

Lower back propagation-based algorithms (BPBA) use supervised gaining knowledge to understand items in photos. BPBAs are frequently called convolutional neural networks (CNNs) because they utilize filters to extract dense functions from input photos and construct larger, extra-strong models of objects. In this chapter, the authors discuss evaluating BPBAs for item reputation obligations. They compare BPBA models to conventional machine studying techniques (such as aid vector machines) and compare their overall performance. They use metrics that include accuracy, precision, recall, and F1 score to compare the fashions. The findings advise that BPBAs outperform traditional gadget-mastering procedures for object recognition obligations and impart advanced accuracy in photograph classification tasks. Additionally, they display that BPBAs have a bonus over traditional methods in that they require drastically less education time. Eventually, BPBAs represent a possible alternative to conventional methods for object popularity and other computer vision duties.

    Razika Lounas, LIMOSE Laboratory, Faculty of Sciences, University of M'Hamed Bougara
        of Boumerdes, Algeria
    Rachid Djerbi, LIMOSE Laboratory, Faculty of Sciences, University of M'Hamed Bougara of
        Boumerdes, Algeria
    Hocine Mokrani, LIMOSE Laboratory, Faculty of Sciences, University of M'Hamed Bougara
        of Boumerdes, Algeria
    Mohamed Tahar Bennai, LIMOSE Laboratory, Faculty of Sciences, University of M'Hamed
        Bougara of Boumerdes, Algeria

This chapter explores the transformative impact of information and communication technology (ICT) on pedagogy, specifically focusing on the integration of collaboration tools in final year projects (FYPs). Final year projects (FYPs) represent the ultimate activity in the student's curriculum. They are designed to use, test, and enhance the knowledge students have gained over the years by confronting them with real-world projects. Despite existing systems for FYPs, the chapter identifies gaps, particularly in covering the entire FYP process and in addressing different collaborative aspects. With a focus on the rise of machine learning-based FYPs, this research aims to propose a comprehensive solution based on a proposed collaboration architecture in response to various needs such as communication, coordination, production, and resource sharing. The application is designed for multiple user roles, including students, advisors, and administrative staff, each allocated a personalized workspace. The novelty of the proposed system is its comprehensive coverage of all collaborative aspects mentioned throughout the FYP process, including proposal processing, project assignment, project completion, and evaluation. The research contributes to fostering innovation in machine learning projects by effectively managing and sharing datasets through collaboration tools. The results indicate good scores in improving collaborative aspects with a score of 98% for virtualization in coordination and 96% for communication. The results also showed that surveyed users are positively inclined to use the system as their final year project (FYP) management system, with an attention-to-use score of 90% of advisors and 92.8% of students.

    N. Krishnamoorthy, Vellore Institute of Technology, India
    Vinoth Kumar Venkatesan, Vellore Institute of Technology, India
    B. Swapna, Dr. MGR Educational and Research Institute, India
    Deepakshi Rawal, Vellore Institute of Technology, India
    Dakshita Dutta, Vellore Institute of Technology, India
    S. Sushil, Vellore Institute of Technology, India

The personality indicator uses machine learning techniques to assess each person's personality in both the personal and professional lives. There are various types of indicators, but the two commonly used ones are Myers-Briggs type indicator (MTBI) and big five personality traits model. This work used MBTI personality indicator, and it can offer valuable insights. It attempted to use SVD, naive bayes, random forest, and logistic regression machine learning approaches for personality prediction. This model makes it simple for users to identify their personalities and technical abilities. This personality indicator is based on MBTI that categorizes individuals into one of 16 personality types. This approach has the potential to provide a more objective and scalable way of assessing personality, compared to traditional self-report measures. The use of MBTI type based on their online activity, such as their social media posts and communication habits, has gained popularity in recent years.

Preface

The world was awakened to the promise of artificial intelligence (AI) with the release of ChatGPT in November 2022. This application empowers users to ask a wide range of questions and receive instant and intelligent answers. Users were surprised by the seeming expert nature by which many of the answers were constructed. Millions of users signed up within a few days, and now today ChatGPT boasts of hundreds of millions of monthly users who are finding that they now have a tool that could revolutionize the way they work and play. Major technology companies like Google, Meta, and Microsoft, among others, are rapidly introducing products and services based on AI technology. In short, the AI revolution is underway, and by all accounts, it is anticipated to bring about profound consequences for both the business world and society at large.

A classical definition of AI dates to the 1950s, all including the concept that AI can enable computers to accomplish intelligent tasks and activities, i.e., requiring human-level intelligence. Given the difficulties in defining human intelligence, a more operational definition refers to the abilities and capabilities AI aims to automatize: communication, perception, knowledge, planning, and reasoning. As all these are interconnected, so are the corresponding subfields of AI research: problem-solving, intelligent agents, natural language processing (NLP), speech recognition, computer vision, robotics, knowledge representation, and machine learning. Today AI is considered to be the fourth industrial revolution. Despite its ups and downs, the use of AI technologies and systems has become so widespread that discussions about their applications, performances, and impact are quotidian.

Most readers would not recognize the fact that AI technologies have been part of our daily lives for quite sometime now. When a credit card company automatically detects fraudulent activity on your credit card or when calls to an airline complaining about your travel experience are routed automatically based on your prospective value to the airline, in all these situations the AI and Big Data technologies are working in the background to optimize the outcomes for the user as well as for the provider.

The promise of AI and Big Data seems boundless now, with potential applications in every field concerning our daily lives. We sketch out some application areas briefly here for the needed context. For instance, Big Data with AI can create personalized experiences for customers through targeted handling of customer service requests and through that enhancing customer satisfaction and engagement. Vast amounts of data can be used to train machine learning algorithms thereby enabling the development of models for image and video recognition, real time speech recognition, and natural language processing. AI, combined with Big Data, could allow businesses to predict trends and patterns by analyzing historical and real-time data. This is beneficial in the areas of marketing and finance for making informed decisions when huge amounts of data need to be analyzed on the fly. We can analyze large medical datasets that are now buried in patient records and in research hospitals, and such analysis facilitates disease diagnosis and prognosis, discover efficacy of drugs and drug interactions. A direct to consumer marketer could employ AI technologies to forecast demand, manage inventory, and optimize logistics, leading to cost reduction and improved efficiency. A digital marketer could analyze large volumes of textual data from social media postings, user reviews, and discussion forums to determine user sentiment for real-time fine tuning of marketing communications. City planners can employ AI tools to optimize traffic management and infrastructure development. Non-profits can fine tune their advocacy strategies based on the large troves of data that could be potentially collected and analyzed specific to their interest areas. In short, the scope of AI and big data technologies is almost limitless.

Today AI with the help of Big Data is transforming diverse industries around the world and is revolutionizing business and society. AI and Big Data technologies are increasingly employed to accelerate business growth in emerging economies. However, despite its great promise, the AI and data revolution is yet to yield tangible dividends for most developing countries. More often than not, these countries do not have all the prerequisites in place in order to collect sufficient data to utilize AI algorithms for development. Furthermore, existing data often remain unused because they are not recorded at all or not collected in a systematic manner, and even when they are collected data often are not available in digital format or lack the level of granularity needed for decision-making and local innovation.

Technologies are all about the creation of tools and methods to achieve goals in more efficient ways for today's economic, business, and social needs. For example, COVID-19, the most recent pandemic that is ravaging many parts of the world with untold human loss and suffering has resulted in an unprecedented global economic upheaval, rejigging of global supply chains, and prompted social and political changes in many societies. The COVID-19 pandemic has put a major emphasis on the essential impact that AI and Big Data technologies play in smart healthcare services. More importantly, the AI and Big Data revolution by itself is becoming the catalyst for seismic changes in all areas of human endeavour, and accordingly, we can rightly term this development as the fourth industrial revolution. This book is a collection of high-quality research on the recent development of tools and methods based on AI and Big Data technologies with a focus on those technologies and applications to advance business and society in emerging economies. Below, we provide a brief summary of all the papers included in this reference book.

Chapter 1 (The Foundations of AI And ML in Business) describes the fundamentals of ML in business analytics. The most salient techniques of supervised learning will be the subject of special attention such as the decision tree family, random forest, K-Nearest Neighbor (KNN), and Naive Bayes. In addition, the author looks at some important theoretical examples that illustrate the essence of machine learning and how it is applied in application with emphasis on developing awareness for more technical explanations throughout the chapter.

Chapter 2 (AI and Its Impact on Business and Society) uses a data set of 6 months for the prediction. The dataset generates the software development process and rules matrix. The matrix is used for analyzing and predicting the accuracy of the software development results of the project. Here three AI algorithms are used for the prediction. After getting the result, comparative analyses are done between the three AI algorithms to select the best among them. The chosen algorithm will be used in the development process to improve the business prospects of the enterprise.

Chapter 3 (Industry 4.0 Technologies in a Developing Country: The Case of Costa Rica) examines how Industry 4.0 can promote economic growth in developing nations, focusing on Costa Rica's successful implementation as a case study. The study explores Costa Rica's Industry 4.0 readiness, highlighting government initiatives, key benefiting sectors, and preparedness factors. The findings inform policy recommendations for other emerging economies, underscoring Industry 4.0's potential to bridge development gaps and foster sustainable growth.

Chapter 4 (HR Analytics and Employee Attrition Prediction Using Machine Learning) finds employee traits that aid in predicting employee turnover in organizations by forecasting attrition based on demographic and job-related factors. Further, authors use models to predict and analyze employee attrition and turnover. Using classifiers like K-nearest neighbors (KNN), Support Vector Machine (SVM), Decision Trees (DT) and Random Forest classifiers (RF) four main tests were run on the IBM dataset to predict employee attrition.

Chapter 5 (Taxonomy of E-Magazine Marketing and Collaboration Trends) explores e-marking and e-collaboration innovations employed by digital magazines available online, with the aim of identifying and classifying trending e-marketing and e-collaboration innovations; and illustrating publisher relations with content creators and marketing collaborators, to guide future research, e-commerce and AI adoption.

Chapter 6 (6G for Intelligent Healthcare: The Potential Impact and the Challenges) claims that the trajectory of future intelligent healthcare involves the synergistic integration of 6G to address prevailing constraints associated with cellular coverage, network performance, and security concerns. This research article endeavors to elucidate the features, prospects, challenges, and future directions pertinent to this evolving futuristics Healthcare landscape.

Chapter 7 (Diagnostic Device for Sustainable Medical Care Using Hyperspectral Imaging) finds that, by leveraging the benefits of HSI, the IMITH-SM mission seeks to enhance clinical instrumentation and patient care by providing greater dependable, quicker, and simpler-to-recognize imaging and diagnostic records. These targets include exploring how HSI may be used as a diagnostic device for commonplace illnesses such as cancer and cardiovascular illnesses and figuring out capability programs for HSI-enabled scientific robotics.

Chapter 8 (Identification of Neuroblastoma and Pediatric Cancer Using Time Series Analysis) attempts to assess the detection of neuroblastoma, and pediatric cancer, via time series evaluation. The observation outcomes demonstrate that time series analysis can offer high accuracy in predicting cancer threat levels and may be carried out on diverse cancers for well-timed and reliable prognosis. Eventually, the chapter offers various hints to enhance detection, incorporating extra statistics capabilities and designing a custom reference index.

Chapter 9 (Comparative Analysis of Machine Learning Techniques for Classifying the Risk of Cardiovascular Diseases) studies the data set under different split ratio to analyze the difference in the result that authors obtain after executing those set of data. Authors analyzed the performance of the classifiers with respect to various metrics and concluded by saying the proposed model yields the best accuracy when authors use a random forest classifier with an accuracy of 99.26% for the split ratio of 60:40.

Chapter 10 (Investigation of Various Dimensionality Reduction and Feature Selection Techniques in Microarray Gene Data for Renal Cancer Diagnosis) aims to label the gene expression sample as either Normal or Clear Cell Renal Cell Carcinoma. To improve the classification performance and reduce the training time of the above-mentioned supervised classifiers, various feature selection and dimensionality reduction techniques are investigated. Feature selection techniques namely Variance filter, Chi-square test, ANOVA test, and Mutual Information filter are tested.

Chapter 11 (Comparative Analysis of Electroencephalogram Signals Using Ensemble Methods for Epilepsy Detection) proposes a system that gives a detailed comparison of EEG signal processing strategies for epilepsy detection utilizing ensemble techniques and investigates the usefulness of ensemble algorithms such as Gradient Boosting, AdaBoost, XGBoost, and Bagging Classifier in improving epilepsy detection. The finding of the proposed system clarifies the positive impacts and regulates each ensemble technique for determining the presence of epilepsy.

Chapter 12 (IoT for Smart Cities Intelligent Healthcare Using Machine Learning Techniques) discusses several IoT-based machine learning techniques that are applied, among other things, in the aforementioned domains. Furthermore, a review of the assessments and a report on the lessons learned are presented, with an emphasis on the fundamental role that machine learning techniques should play in Internet of Things networks.

Chapter 13 (The Effects of Socioeconomic Status, Geological, Engineering, and Climate Factors on Machine Learning-dependent Forecast of Water Pipe Failure) develops an initial multi-source data-aggregation system. The framework outlined the conditions for merging many datasets, including the soil type, population count, geographic, and meteorological datasets as well as the conventional pipe leaking dataset. Based on the data, five machine learning (ML) techniques were developed to forecast pipe failure. It was found that LightGBM provided the optimum performance.

Chapter 14 (Design and Development of Autonomous and Unmanned Vehicle for Submarine Applications) presents the AUV prototype that was developed by SolidWorks. In the study, the controller and motors have been tested in small-scale surface water and the result is encouraging. Some factors affecting AUV performance are also elaborated for future research in this area. Underwater robots can explore areas of the ocean that are too dangerous or too difficult for humans to go.

Chapter 15 (Performance Improvement and Optimization in Network Using Ensemble Kalman Filters) investigates the potential of Ensemble Kalman Filters for area Networks and their use within the international optimization of network overall performance. The results of this comparison show that Ensemble Kalman Filters outperform neighborhood optimization schemes in terms of network overall performance, scalability, and robustness.

Chapter 16 (Analysis of Network Performance Using Markov Autoregressive and ARIMAX Models Using Optimization) compares Markov Autoregressive (MAR) models and ARIMAX models for network overall performance optimization. The conclusions drawn from this observation advocate that MAR models are ideal for predicting community overall performance because of their capability to capture the dynamic nature of community traffic correctly. Additionally, the need to specify a further coefficient within the ARIMAX overestimates anticipated values and decreases overall performance prediction accuracy.

Chapter 17 (Artificial Intelligence and Big Data Analytics Contemporary-Generation Wireless Network) discusses a data-driven next-generation wireless communication model for leveraging advanced statistical analysis for MNOs' networks. The role of Artificial Intelligence (AI) in providing intelligence to networks, such as confidence, self-adaptation, proactivity, and predictive behavior, is also investigated. The benefits and drawbacks of integrating big data analytics and AI into modern wireless networks are also discussed.

Chapter 18 (Analysis of Object Recognition Using Back Propagation-Based Algorithms) advises that BPBAs outperform traditional gadget-mastering procedures for object recognition obligations and impart advanced accuracy in photograph classification tasks. Additionally, authors display that BPBAs have a bonus over traditional methods in that they require drastically less education time. Eventually, BPBAs represent a possible alternative to conventional methods for object popularity and other computer vision duties.

Chapter 19 (A Collaborative System for Machine Learning- Based Final Year Projects With Enhanced Dataset Accessibility) examines machine learning - based final year projects and proposes a collaborative system that provides tools in response to various needs such as communication, coordination, production, and resource sharing. The results indicate good scores in improving collaborative aspects, improved process efficiency, and that users are positively inclined to use the system as their FYP management platform.

Chapter 20 (Personality Prediction Based on Myers-Briggs Type Indicator Using Machine Learning) uses MBTI personality indicator for valuable insights. This model makes it simple for users to identify their personalities and technical abilities. This approach has the potential to provide a more objective and scalable way of assessing personality, compared to traditional self-report measures. The use of MBTI type based on their online activity, such as their social media posts and communication habits, has gained popularity in recent years.

Jingyuan Zhao
University of Toronto, Canada

Joseph Richards
California State University, Sacramento, USA

V. Vinoth Kumar
Vellore Institute of Technology, India
2024 January

Chapter 1
The Foundations of AI and ML in Business

Hulya Kocyigit

Icahn School of Medicine at Mount Sinai, USA & Karamanoglu Mehmetbey University, Turkey

ABSTRACT

Machine learning (ML), a subfield of artificial intelligence (AI), has been rapidly expanding both conceptually and in its various applications. Over the years, organizations across different business sectors have increasingly adopted modern machine-learning approaches. This chapter outlines the fundamentals of ML in business analytics. Special attention is given to the most prominent techniques of supervised learning, such as decision trees, random forests, k-nearest neighbors (KNN), and Naive Bayes. Additionally, the chapter explores significant theoretical examples that demonstrate the core principles of machine learning and its practical applications, aiming to foster an understanding of more technical explanations throughout.

1. INTRODUCTION

In the digital age, businesses have demanded reduced waiting times due to the rapidly changing market environment. This perspective has driven many companies to adopt innovative technologies aimed at enhancing performance and gaining a competitive edge. Artificial intelligence (AI) has emerged as a significant advancement, capturing the attention of both academics and industry leaders. AI encompasses the study of intelligent machine learning, primarily through sophisticated computer programs that produce outcomes similar to human cognition. This process typically involves data collection, developing effective mechanisms for utilizing that data, presenting precise or approximate findings, and making self-corrections and adjustments. AI is often employed to analyze machine learning and mimic human cognitive functions. AI might be used to conduct analyses that are more precise and to achieve helpful interpretation. According to this viewpoint, AI technology combines computer intelligence with a variety of practical statistical models (Raza et al.,2022). In terms of the present and future growth of our communities and businesses, AI has been seen to be a confluence of new technologies, procedures, and

DOI: 10.4018/979-8-3693-0683-3.ch001

methodologies. Currently, AI is used in many different industries, including financial services, vehicle autonomous driving, optical character recognition, and medical diagnostics.

Recent developments in AI technology have led to a significant expansion of machine learning (ML) research in the business analytics field. In particular, the creation of novel ML applications has the potential to have an enormous effect on the discipline of business analytics. These applications address existing business problems such as triage and disposition, early identification of financial risk and its outcomes in merchant banks, bankruptcy intervention in operations, recognizing and confirming customer behavior, and promptly and effectively responding to cyberattacks. It might be extremely beneficial for financiers, bosses, or enterprising to comprehend computational approaches like ML that can meaningfully analyze massive amounts of complex data due to the growing availability of business data.

By the end of this chapter, readers should feel confident in their understanding of major AI and machine learning concepts. The chapter will explain the approach and limitations of machine learning, the main algorithms, the value and necessity of data, and how to assess the effectiveness of such systems. While unsupervised learning, reinforcement learning, and semi-supervised learning are important topics, this chapter will not delve into them in detail. Instead, it will focus extensively on supervised learning techniques, including decision trees, random forests, k-nearest neighbors (KNN), and Naive Bayes.

1.1. History of Artificial Intelligence

The history of AI has been evaluated using the metaphor of the four seasons (i.e., spring, summer, fall, and winter) in literature. This approach helps to assess the progress made in this field. Researchers first examine the past to understand how far AI has advanced, then analyze the present to identify the current challenges businesses face, and finally, look ahead to help everyone prepare for future obstacles (Haenlein and Kaplan, 2019). In the field of artificial intelligence, research objectives have evolved over time. When the computer was first created in the 1940s, people quickly recognized that it could do much more than just perform mathematical calculations and that it could be used to perform a variety of intellectual tasks that are typically thought to require human intelligence. British mathematician Alan Turing was an innovator in modern computer science and artificial intelligence (1950). His idea of intelligent behavior in a computer—later referred to as the "Turing test"—was the ability to do cognitive activities at a level that is comparable to that of a person. Alan Turing proposed that it would be feasible to establish if a computer is intelligent based on its capacity to display intelligent conduct that is indiscernible from an intelligent human's behavior. In 1956, John McCarthy and Marvin Minsky, who hosted the roughly eight-week-long Dartmouth Summer Research Project on Artificial Intelligence (DSRPAI) at Dartmouth College in New Hampshire, formally developed the term "artificial intelligence." The well-known ELIZA computer software, launched by Joseph Weizenbaum at MIT between 1964 and 1966, is a primary example of software. One of the earliest algorithms to try to pass the aforementioned Turing Test was ELIZA, which was able to simulate human conversation utilizing pattern matching and replacement methodology employing natural language processing, which served as the basis for future chatterbots. Another important AI achievement was the General Problem Solver program, which was developed by Nobel Prize winner Herbert Simon, and the researchers Cliff Shaw and Allen Newell of the RAND Corporation. This computer was able to automatically solve various sorts of simple problems. These uplifting success tales led to significant funding being given to AI research, resulting in an increase in initiatives. However, everything did not go to well as the researchers' expectations. This issue, unfortunately, led to stopped/ decreased funding of artificial intelligence (AI) research in the U.S.

and England governments even though the U.S. DARPA increased funds in response to the Japanese government's 1980s decision to significantly support AI research. However, no more developments were made in the years that followed. Thus, this period is called the "AI winter/summer" term. The beginning of the golden age, known as the harvest period of artificial intelligence, corresponds to the beginning of the 2000s. In other words, this period is referred to as the "AI fall" in literature. Contrary to the years of the 1970s-2000s, AI research at the beginning of the 2000s has led to the start of milestone steps that can be groundbreaking such as invitations of deep learning, IBM's DeepQA technology, Google's AlphaGo program, speech recognition algorithms by Facebook, Apple's virtual assistant (i.e., Siri) and Amazon's virtual assistant (i.e., Alexa) (Haenlein and Kaplan, 2019; Kaul et. al,2020; Williamson and Eynon,2020).

1.2. History of Machine Learning

One of the most frequently asked questions is whether deep learning (DL) and/or machine learning (ML) belong to artificial intelligence (AI) and what distinguishes them from one another. Deep learning is a subset of both ML and AI; thus, ML is also a part of AI, as illustrated in Figure 1. Although AI and machine learning techniques are sometimes used interchangeably, there is a nuanced distinction between them. According to Aziz and Dowling (2019), AI is generally understood as intelligence exhibited by machines, with intelligence defined in terms of human-like capabilities. In essence, machine learning is a crucial AI technique that involves learning from data, but AI often encompasses additional methods and criteria.

Figure 1. The Relation Between Artificial Intelligence vs. Machine Learning vs. Deep Learning

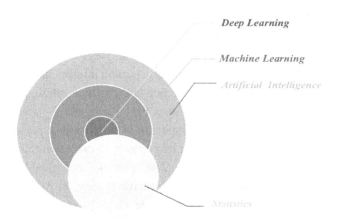

The phrase "machine learning" is attributed to Arthur Samuel of IBM, who in 1959 suggested that it would be able to educate computers to learn what they must comprehend about the environment and how to do jobs for themselves. As seen in Figure 2, the following four groups can be defined to properly categorize machine learning algorithms: Supervised Learning, Unsupervised Learning, Reinforcement Learning, and Semi-Supervised Learning. The aforementioned groups are determined by the type of data used for training, the manner in which the data are utilized, and the intended use of the trained model. The simplest out-of-the-box application of a particular algorithm will typically fall into one category.

However, in solving real-world problems, most algorithms offer a wide range of capabilities, some of which may belong to different categories or meet the requirements of multiple groups.

Figure 2. The Main Types of Machine Learning

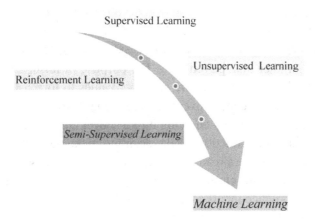

Supervised learning called a machine learning paradigm uses a set of paired input-output training samples to gather knowledge about the input-output relationships of an object (Liu et al., 2000). When learning is being done under supervision, a pair of data—a training set and a test set—are provided to the learner, who is often a computer software. The goal is for the learner to "learn" from a collection of labeled examples in the training set in order to identify unlabeled instances in the test set as accurately as possible. In other words, the learner's objective is to create a rule, a program, or a method that categorizes new examples at the test set by investigating samples that have already been assigned a class label (Learned-Miller,2014). The learned mapping determines how the input data is classified if the output accepts a limited number of discrete values that represent the input's class labels. A regression of the input occurs if the output only accepts continuous numbers. Information about the input-output relationship is commonly modeled using learning-model parameters. When these parameters cannot be obtained directly from training samples, a learning system must perform an estimating method to get these parameters (Liu et al., 2000). Two kinds underlie supervised learning: discriminative and generative models. A discriminative model learns the line of demarcation between the categories and intuitively learns how the output distribution changes depending on the input. In generative models, the joint distribution of the input and output is directly learned (Dixon et al.,2020). Before we become familiar with how supervised machine learning operates and its methodologies, let us examine the pros and cons of supervised learning. The following list highlights the main benefits of supervised machine learning: (*i*) Data can be simply gathered or produced using previous experience. (*ii*) assists easily in addressing computing issues in the real world. (*iii*) provides experience-based guidance that will enable you to maximize performance criteria. (*iv*) be very beneficial in categorization problems. (*v*) having precise knowledge of (*vi*) the training data's class number. (*vii*) easier to comprehend method than other learning classes. However, there are some substantial drawbacks, including the following: (a) Some of the more complex machine learning tasks can't be handled. (b) Big data might be challenging to categorize. (c) A lot of computation time is required. Lastly, there are well-known types of supervised learning algorithms: Decision tree, random forest, logistics regression, support vector, naïve bayes, various regression methods, etc. are preferred to use in modeling and estimating in business analytics.

Unsupervised learning, in opposition, refers to the slightly more difficult circumstance in which we see a vector of independent variables x_i but no associated dependent variable y_i for each individual $i = 1$, …, n. Since there is no dependent variable to predict, a linear regression model cannot be fit. As a result of the absence of a dependent variable that can oversee our study, we are in a sense operating blindly in this circumstance, which is why it is commonly described as unsupervised. Due to the lack of labels in the data, unsupervised learning differs from supervised learning. That is to say, the sole elements of the data are input vectors rather than paired data. The purpose of unsupervised learning differs from supervised learning typically because there are no target values to forecast. As opposed to supervised learning, where the user has more control over what the model learns, unsupervised learning generally involves feeding the model raw data and enabling it to discover connections or relevant information in the input. In addition, dimension reduction, or the desire to make the data less complex, is one of our main goals. Many research fields are already familiar with several of these methodologies, such as principal component analysis (PCA) and cluster analysis. As we previously indicated, unsupervised machine learning can be utilized to produce inputs for supervised learning.

Reinforcement learning (RL) is the study of how natural and artificial systems may acquire the ability to predict the effects of their actions and maximize their behavior in situations where behaviors might change their state or condition, result in rewards or penalties, or both. These are closed-loop issues, as the learning system's actions impact its subsequent inputs. Unlike many other forms of machine learning, the learner in RL is not explicitly told which actions to take; instead, they must experiment to discover which actions yield the highest rewards. In the most complex and challenging situations, decisions can affect not only the immediate reward but also the subsequent state and, consequently, all future rewards. The three most crucial characteristics that set reinforcement learning problems apart from other types of problems are their essential closed-loop nature, the lack of explicit instructions regarding what actions to take, and the fact that the effects of behaviors, involving reward signals, take a long time to manifest.

A subfield of machine learning called *semi-supervised learning* combines supervised learning and unsupervised learning. Semi-supervised learning techniques frequently make use of data usually associated with the other assignment to help one of these two (i.e., classification or clustering) execute better. In fact, the cluster and classification assumptions, which both have to do with data distribution, are the two fundamental presumptions in semi-supervised learning. The earlier model presupposes that data have an innate cluster structure and that instances belonging to the same cluster have the same class label. The latter presupposes that the data are distributed throughout a manifold and that close examples would forecast similarly. When the assumption matches the innate structure of the data, semi-supervised learning is helpful. In other words, semi-supervised learning algorithms would not function as intended by the user when they were damaged. These techniques address the issue of a dearth of labeled training examples and a sizable number of unlabeled samples. In such a situation, Semi-supervised learning techniques are more suited to practical applications because labeled instances are frequently difficult, expensive, and time-consuming to gather whereas unlabeled data are easily accessible. Semi-supervised learning might create superior classifiers that make up for the absence of labeled training data.

1.3. Machine Learning in Business

Recent advancements in information-based development have significantly expanded the features and applications of computers. Traditionally, computers were primarily used for processing and storing numerical data. However, to simulate and analyze intellectual data, we need to develop new computational techniques and hardware capable of mimicking learning, retention, and reasoning processes (Gopal, 2019). Creating intelligent choices relying on what has been learned is how machine learning algorithms achieve this. This is an inductive strategy whereby statistical techniques are used to identify decision rules based on the gathered data (Enholm,2022). Those datasets can be collected by governments, foundations, non-profit institutions, or companies. Especially, businesses frequently keep records of every transaction for as long as possible, and an industrial process can have thousands of sensors whose values are recorded at least once each minute. As a result, we now have the chance to employ this data to comprehend the processes and to develop brand-new data-driven apps that may not have been feasible a decade ago.

Companies have needed to change the manner in which they conduct business as robots and sensor-activated equipment will replace employees. It is important to highlight that machine learning-driven trends in global industrial operations are expanding dramatically, which suggests that machine learning is already a top concern for many firms throughout the world or has done so recently. Machine learning delivers accurate and trustworthy forecasting parameters that help businesses enhance their spending in terms of buying and order processing since it can keep, evaluate, and—more importantly—forecast data continuously. Additionally, it describes tendencies and processes that support the development of better merchandising as well as manufacturing techniques. In other words, a company, referred to as the upstream strengthening selected for requirement disparity, frequently experiences ambiguity or data bias in many decisions. It can be tough to prepare each person specifically. A business strategy might be used in several production activities, including procurement, shipping, marketing, etc. Numerous strategies, like continuous resupply, co-marketing, etc., are put into practice using algorithms, statistics, modeling, and simulation as solution techniques. Nowadays, academics and specialists have figured out how to effectively handle the data and use it to get more reliable conclusions (Ghazal et al.,2021). For example, both customers and third parties can fall victim to credit card fraud. Several strategies have been developed to prevent such fraud, and if scams do occur, methods can be devised to identify the improperly executed transactions. Numerous innovative and distinctive machine learning algorithms can be employed to protect digital data transfers against unauthorized access (Dileep et al., 2021).

2. DECISION TREE

Decision Trees, which are presented by Breiman et al. (1984), have emerged as a well-known branch and a recognizable choice among nonparametric methods. A branching representation of decisions and their results is achieved using the modeling technique of decision trees. Decision trees can be employed to evaluate the probability of several decision paths leading to the accomplishment of a given objective in predictive modeling. A decision tree's nodes represent the many stages of the decision-making process. The basic idea behind a decision tree is to use a flowchart-like structure resembling a tree to generate predictions, where each branch reflects a decision between many feature alternatives in the internal nodes and finally leads to a conclusion in the leaf node. A method that separates data into smaller components and uses those segments for predicting events by finding patterns. In other words, a greedy method called Decision Tree Induction uses the split and conquer strategy to iteratively build a tree from the top down.

Figure 3 depicts the decision tree's characteristic form. In this case, a target field of data is recursively subset based on the values of related fields to produce segments and related descendent data subsets (nodes) that, at any given level of the tree, include the desired values that are continually similar within nodes and progressively different between nodes. In this case, a bank plans to decide on whether customers' credit card limits increase considering the many cases. A test on a feature value is represented by each nonterminal node. The root node (seen as the top node in Figure 3) of the example decision tree determines if the example to be categorized is based on the customer's having real estate which is evaluated under the "yes" and "no" options. The categorization that will be returned if we get there is stored in a leaf node. In this example, if the customer does not own any real estate, we disregard the values of further attributes and assume that the person will default if their credit card limit is increased. Next, we reach a nonterminal node that checks whether the average daily income balance is more than $400 or if the monthly income exceeds $5000 (assuming these thresholds are determined by the bank's financial risk office). If either condition is met, we proceed along the left branch to the income node, anticipating that the customer will not miss a credit card payment. If neither condition is met, we anticipate that the customer will default.

Figure 3. The shape of the decision tree to decide on increasing credit card limit

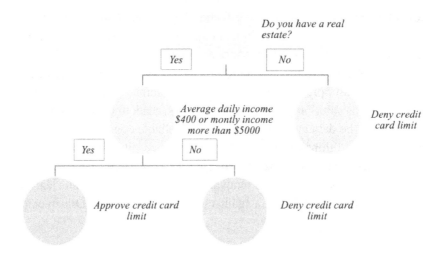

When stratifying the data so that there is little variation within each stratum, a good query will divide an array of items with heterogeneous class labels into nodes with relatively homogenous class labels. A variety of metrics have been developed to assess the level of impurity or inhomogeneity in a group of items. In decision trees, feature selection is a key topic that is addressed by methods like the Entropy, Gini index, Information Gain, and G-statistics. Assume that we are utilizing a collection of training elements E to categorize things into N classes. Let pi ($i = 1,...,n$) represent the proportion of E items that are categorized under class i. Then, Entropy can be expressed computationally as

$$E = -\sum_{i=1}^{n} p_i \log p_i$$

The Gini Index is calculated as follows:

$$\sum_{i=1}^{n} p_i(1 - p_i) = 1 - \sum_{i=1}^{n} p_i^2$$

Example 1 illustrates good example of how decision tree structure is built.

Example 1: Table 4.1 involves three independent covariates (x_1, x_2, x_3), and a dependent variable (company status, y).

Table 1. Raw dataset

x_1	x_2	x_3	y
1	6	1	Bankruptcy
2	8	7	Bankruptcy
4	7	2	Ok
1	2	6	Bankruptcy
3	9	2	Ok
7	4	1	Bankruptcy
5	6	3	Bankruptcy

As illustrated in Table 1, the dependent variable is divided by "Bankruptcy" and "Ok". The dependent variable's entropy is calculated without adjusting for any covariates:

$$E(outcome) = -\left(\frac{5}{7}\right)\log_2\frac{5}{7} - \frac{2}{7}\log_2\frac{2}{7}$$

$=0.863$ (1)

Thus, we find the entropy of the dependent variable from Eq. (1) is 0.6934. The average value of the factors may be used to determine whether to divide a Decision Tree depending on that variable. We would divide the Decision Tree based on whether x_1 was larger than 3 or less than/equal to 3 because the average for x1 is slightly above 3. We can create Table 2 for x_1 variable based on Table 1. As seen in Table 2, the probability of "bankruptcy" is 5/7 while the probability of "ok" is 2/7. In other words, there are three results for x_1 greater than three and four results for x_1 variable less than 3 in Table 2. Moreover, the probability of "bankruptcy" is 2/3 while the probability of "ok" is 1/3 when x_1 was larger than 3 as illustrated in Table 3. Then, the probability of "bankruptcy" is ¾ while the probability of "ok" is ¼ when x_1 was less than 3 as illustrated in Table 4.

Table 2. Decision trees for x_1

x_1	Bankruptcy	Ok
>3	2	1
≤3	3	1

Table 3. Decision trees rely on x_1>3

x_1	x_2	x_3	y	Probability
4	7	2	Ok	1/3
7	4	1	Bankruptcy	2/3
5	6	3		

Table 4. Decision trees rely on x_1 ≤3

x_1	x_2	x_3	y	Probability
1	6	1	Bankruptcy	3/4
2	8	7		
1	2	6		
3	9	2	Ok	1/4

Given Table 3 and Table 4 that we could compute the entropy of x_1 variable in Eq (3) and Eq. (4), which are performed in the following that:

$$E(x_1 > 3) =$$

$$-\left(\frac{1}{3}\right) log_2 \frac{1}{3} - \frac{2}{3} log_2 \frac{2}{3} = 0.918 \tag{3}$$

and

$$E(x_1 \leq 3) =$$

$$-\left(\tfrac{3}{4}\right)log_2\tfrac{3}{4} - \tfrac{1}{4}log_2\tfrac{1}{4}$$

$$= 0.811 \tag{4}$$

We perform entropy value using Eq. (1) corresponding values weighted from Eq. (2) and Eq. (3) for a decision split with x_1 at the mean value of x_1:

$$E_{(x_1)} = \left(\tfrac{3}{7}\right)*0.918 + \left(\tfrac{4}{7}\right)*0.811 = 0.856 \tag{5}$$

Similarly, we can compute the entropy values of x_2 and x_3, respectively. Splitting at > 6 and ≤ 6 is used to calculate the entropy of the x_2 variable meanwhile, the entropy value of the x_3 variable is computed by dividing at > 3 and ≤ 3 in following that.

Table 5. Decision trees for x_2

x_2	Bankruptcy	Ok
>6	1	2
≤ 6	4	0

Table 6. Decision trees rely on x_2>6

x_1	x_2	x_3	y	Probability
2	8	7	Bankruptcy	1/3
4	7	2	Ok	2/3
3	9	2	Ok	

Table 7. Decision trees rely on x_2 ≤6

x_1	x_2	x_3	y	Probability
1	6	1	Bankruptcy	1
1	2	6	Bankruptcy	
7	4	1	Bankruptcy	
5	6	3	Bankruptcy	

Entropy value is computed in Eq. (6) based on the company status where x_2 has a value greater than 6, while Eq. (7) is used to calculate entropy when x_2 variable is less than 6.

$$E\left(x_2 > 6\right) =$$

$$-\left(\frac{1}{3}\right)log_2\frac{1}{3} - \frac{2}{3}log_2\frac{2}{3} = 0.918 \tag{6}$$

and

$$E\left(x_2 \leq 6\right) =$$

$$-\left(\frac{4}{4}\right)log_2 1 - \frac{0}{4}log_2\frac{0}{4} = 0 \tag{7}$$

Similarly, we perform entropy value using Eq. (1) corresponding values weighted from Eq. (6) and Eq. (7) for a decision split with x_2 at the mean value of x_2:

$$E(x_2) = \left(\frac{3}{7}\right)*0.918 + 0 = 0.393 \tag{8}$$

Table 8. Decision trees for x_3

x_1		Bankruptcy	Ok
	>3	2	0
≤ 3		3	2

Table 9. Decision trees rely on x_3>3

x_1	x_2	x_3	y	Probability
2	8	7	Bankruptcy	1
1	2	6	Bankruptcy	

Table 10. Decision trees rely on $x_3 \leq 3$

x_1	x_2	x_3	y	Probability
1	6	1	Bankruptcy	3/5
7	4	1	Bankruptcy	
5	6	3	Bankruptcy	
4	7	2	Ok	2/5
3	9	2	Ok	

$$E(x_3 > 3) = -\left(\tfrac{2}{2}\right)log_2 1 - \tfrac{0}{2}log_2\tfrac{0}{2} = 0 \tag{9}$$

and

$$E(x_3 \leq 3) = -\left(\tfrac{3}{5}\right)log_2\tfrac{3}{5} - \tfrac{2}{5}log_2\tfrac{2}{5} = 0.970 \tag{10}$$

We perform entropy value using Eq. (1) corresponding values weighted from Eq. (9) and Eq. (10) for a decision split with x_2 at the mean value of x_2:

$$E(x_3) = \left(\tfrac{5}{7}\right)*0.970 + 0 = 0.692 \tag{11}$$

In the next step, it is straightforward to calculate the information gain for x_1, x_2 and x_3 variables as seen Eqs. (12), (13) and (14) with E (dependent variable) calculated in Eq. (2), respectively.

Informationgain$_1$

=

$E(outcome) - E(x_1)$

=0.863-0.856=0.007   (12)

Informationgain$_2$

=

$E(outcome) - E(x_2)$

=0.863-0.393=0.47 (13)

Informationgain₃

Information gain$_3$

=

E(outcome) − E(x₃)

$E(outcome) - E_{(x_3)}$

=0.863-0.692=0.171 (14)

According to information gain values from Eq.'s (12), (13), and (13), we could select x_2 variable with split at a value larger than 6 because of having larger information gain value among all information gain values. The right side in Figure 4 has zero entropy value, which means that there is no information. That's why we will continue to split for building the decision tree with x_2 variable greater than 6 in the next steps.

Figure 4. Decision Tree with entropy estimates based on the x_2 variable

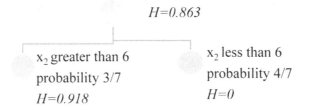

H=0.863

x_2 greater than 6
probability 3/7
H=0.918

x_2 less than 6
probability 4/7
H=0

Table 11. Decision trees for x_1

x_1	Bankruptcy	Ok
>3	0	1
≤3	1	1

Table 12. Decision trees rely on x_1>3

x_1	x_2	x_3	y	Probability
4	7	2	Ok	1

Table 13. Decision trees rely on x_1 ≤3

x_1	x_2	x_3	y	Probability
2	8	7	Bankruptcy	1/2
3	9	2	Ok	1/2

According to supported Table 12 and Table 13, let's compute the entropy of x_1 variable in Eq (15) and Eq. (16), which are computed in the following:

$$E(x_1 > 3) =$$

$$-\left(\frac{1}{1}\right)log_2\frac{1}{1} - \frac{0}{1}log_2\frac{0}{1} = 0 \tag{15}$$

and

$$E(x_1 \le 3) =$$

$$-\left(\frac{1}{2}\right)log_2\frac{1}{2} - \frac{1}{2}log_2\frac{1}{2}$$

$$= 1 \tag{16}$$

Using Eq. (1) might be used to compute the entropy value corresponding to values weighted from Eq. (15) and Eq. (16) for a decision split with x_1 at the mean value of x_1:

$$E(x_1) = \left(\frac{2}{3}\right)*1 + \left(\frac{1}{3}\right)*0 = 0.666 \tag{17}$$

Table 14. Decision trees for x_3

x_1	Bankruptcy	Ok
>4	1	0
≤4	0	2

Table 15. Decision trees rely on x_3>4

x_1	x_2	x_3	y	Probability
2	8	7	Bankruptcy	1

Table 16. Decision trees rely on x_3 ≤4

x_1	x_2	x_3	y	Probability
4	7	2	Ok	1
3	9	2	Ok	

Based on Table 14 and Table 15, we calculate the entropy of x_3 variable in Eq (18) and Eq. (19) in the following:

$$E\left(x_3 > 4\right) =$$

$$-\left(\frac{1}{1}\right)log_2\frac{1}{1} - \frac{0}{1}log_2\frac{0}{1} = 0 \tag{18}$$

and

$$E\left(x_3 \leq 4\right) =$$

$$-\left(\frac{2}{2}\right)log_2\frac{2}{2} - \frac{0}{2}log_2\frac{0}{2}$$

$$= 0 \qquad\qquad\qquad (19)$$

Then, we perform weighted entropy with decision split using x_3 as shown in Eq. (20)

$$E_{(x_3)} = \left(\tfrac{1}{3}\right)*0 + \left(\tfrac{2}{3}\right)*0 = 0 \qquad\qquad (20)$$

Eq.'s (21) and (22) have provided the information gain for x_1 and x_3 variables, respectively.

Informationgain$_1$

$$=$$

$$E(outcome) - E_{(x_1)}$$

$$=0.918\text{-}0.666= 0.252 \qquad\qquad (21)$$

Informationgain$_3$

$$=$$

$$E(outcome) - E_{(x_3)}$$

$$=0.918\text{-}0 =0.918 \qquad\qquad (22)$$

According to the results of information gain values for x_1 and x_3 variables, we should select the information gain value of x_3 variable, which provides the highest value. However, we did not select x_3 variable with split at 4 values because of its having zero for entropy value with split at value >4 and value ≤ 4. So, we could not continue to build decision trees in the next step. That's why we will proceed using x_3 to build decision trees as seen in Figure 5.

Figure 5. Decision trees with entropy estimates based on the x_1 and x_2 variables

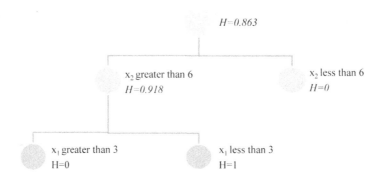

Figure 6 illustrates the outcome of the decision to divide on x_1 after further dividing data on the third branch with values for x_1 greater than 2 or less than 2.

Figure 6. Build final decision trees

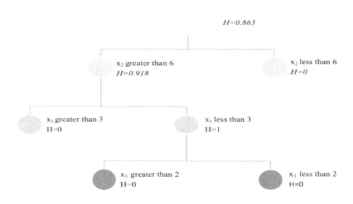

Widely used techniques under the umbrella of decision trees include ID3 (Iterative Dichotomiser 3), C4.5, C5.0, Classification and Regression Trees (CART or CRT), Chi-squared Automatic Interaction Detector (CHAID), and Quick, Unbiased, Efficient, Statistical Trees (QUEST). This tree-based approach has gained popularity in the business community because of its capacity to generate straightforward business decision criteria allowing experts to quickly categorize new customers as low or high risk.

Classification and Regression Trees (CART), proposed by Breiman et. all in 1984, is regarded as a key turning point in the development of ML and non-parametric statistics. CART is used non-parametric statistical method and can be classified as either a classification tree (CT) or a regression tree (RT) depending on whether the exploratory variable is qualitative or quantitative. The process begins at the root node, where the data are divided into two child nodes. Each child node is then further divided into grandchild nodes. Without the application of a stopping rule, the tree continues to grow until it reaches its maximum size, which occurs when no further divisions are feasible due to insufficient data. The unique cost-complexity pruning technique is then used to trim the maximally large tree back to the root.

The split that contributes the least to the overall effectiveness of the tree on training data is the next split to be trimmed. CART relies on purity metrics like entropy or Gini index to choose which characteristics to divide and where to divide it. In regression trees, the output characteristic lacks classes, hence the objective is to estimate the value of the output variable rather than the class to which a record belongs. Every characteristic in the dataset is divided into a number of points, the difference between the estimated and real value is determined, and the dividing point with the lowest sum of squared errors is selected as the root node. This procedure is repeated until all attributes have been divided into two. This tree-based approach has gained popularity in the business community because of its capacity to generate straightforward business decision criteria allowing experts to quickly categorize new customers as low or high risk (Zacharis,2017).

ID3 (Iterative Dichotomiser) technique, is one of the traditional decision tree classification methods, which was introduced by Ross Quinlan in 1986. ID3 is frequently employed in the fields of natural language processing and machine learning. It classifies objects according to those values by comparing the values of the characteristics. It starts with a collection of objects and a description of their properties and generates a decision tree for the supplied data top-down. The target set is divided relying on the results of testing a single attribute at each node of the tree using the principles of maximizing information gain and minimizing entropy (Yang et al.,2018; Adhatrao et al.,2013).

A decision tree can be created using the widely used algorithm *C4.5*. It is a modification of the ID3 algorithm to get over its drawbacks. The C4.5 approach sometimes goes by the name "statistical classifier" since it can produce decision trees that can be employed for categorization. The C4.5 algorithm evaluates all potential tests that could divide the data and chooses the test that provides the best information gain. The bias against broad decision trees in ID3 is eliminated by this test. One test is utilized for each discrete attribute to yield as many outcomes as there are discrete values for the characteristic. Data is arranged for each continuous property before the entropy gain is determined for each individual value using binary cuts in a single scan of the sorted data. A dataset's characteristics may be numerical or nominal, and their output formats differ. Each outcome for a numerical property creates a value in the default condition, however, optional elements may allow merging at least two groups as an output. (Singh and Gupta,2021; Adhatrao et al.,2013; Wu et al.,2009).

The C5.0 method, a modified variant of C4.5, can be implemented either by creating a decision tree or by applying a set of rules. The gain ratio, which modifies information gain, is the C5.0 criterion. A C5.0 DT algorithm divides the samples depending on the attribute with the maximum Information Gain (IG). Every subsample defined by the initial split is subsequently split multiple times until they become inseparable relying on the IG characteristic that follows. After reviewing the lowest level divides, the splits that provide little or no contribution to the model are pruned. C5.0 has the advantages of significantly lower error rates, minimal memory usage, and high optimization. This makes the C5.0 algorithm considerably faster and more precise. C5.0 builds decision trees using the "divide and rule" method, prunes the original decision tree, and has tree-like structures. Additionally, the boosting approach has seen the largest development in C5.0 (Tian and Zhang,2022; Saeed et al.,2020).

CHAID, also known as CHi-squared Automatic Interaction Detection, is employed for prediction and classification. Regression trees will be produced by CART and CHAID if the outcome variable is numerical or categorical. Additionally, the methods used to divide the trees into branches and sub-branches differ throughout the various tree-based systems. CART uses the Gini metric to divide a tree into branches for categorical variables while the Chi-square test, which is the main tool used by CHAID, is a categorization technique. The CHAID method often involves examining the correlation between the dependent variable and a number of independent variables. Iteratively, the independent variables utilized in the classification are examined one at a time, and they are then arranged according to their level of importance (Ngo et al.,2015; Fitrianto et al.,2022).

3. RANDOM FOREST

The Random Forest (RF) approach, which consists of an ensemble learning technique and naturally integrates feature selection and interactions in the learning procedure, is a well-liked option in the field of finance. RF offers great prediction reliability for several different forms of datasets, which is nonparametric, interpretable, and efficient. RF has been used more recently in computational studies based on finance due to its special benefits in handling some limitations such as limited sample sizes, high-dimensional feature spaces, and complex data structures. So, the remarkable question arises as to why linear regression performs worse on prediction challenges than a random forest. Although the concept is made simple to understand by this premise, it frequently lacks the predictability necessary. In other words, random forest appears to be estimated more precisely than linear regression because random forest might immediately adapt to nonlinearities in the data. More specially, medium to large-sized datasets are well-suited for ensemble learning techniques like random forest. The linear methods (i.e., linear regression and logistic regression) will not operate when the number of independent variables is greater than the number of observations since there are more variables that need to be predicted than there are data. Not all predictor variables are employed altogether in a random forest, which makes it effective.

Random Forest Algorithm:

1. For $B_i, i = 1,...,B$
    i. Generate a bootstrap sample M of size N from training data.
    ii. By utilizing the bootstrapped data, to create random-forest trees,T_b, as far as we can iteratively follow the sub-algorithm to find the minimum terminal node size,n_{min} .
    iii. Pick ν parameters at random from all sets of parameters, $\mathcal{V}$.
    iv. Then, we need to determine the best-split point from the ν parameters.
    v. Split the terminal node into two sub-branches.
2. Thus, created random forest trees as $\{T_b\}$
3. Finally, evaluate the model or prediction of the random forest model under the regression and classification part, respectively:

Obtain the regression: $\hat{g}^B(x) = \frac{1}{B}\sum_{b=1}^{B} T_b(x)$

Obtain classification based on the using majority voting of $\widehat{C}_b(x)$.

Figure 7. The processes of the random forest algorithm

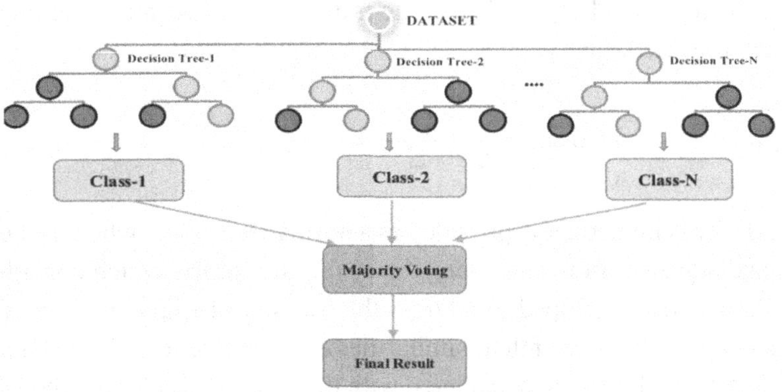

Random forest is preferred over the other ML methods because of the underlying benefits:

- It effectively operates on big data sets and is unrivaled in precision among existing techniques.
- It can properly correct faults in imbalanced data sets for the class population.
- It provides an efficient technique for predicting missing data, which can retain precision even when a significant portion of the data is missing.

There are some drawbacks to employing RF models:

- Random forests may overfit the data when there are numerous categorical variables with high cardinality.
- Moreover, Random Forests offer a discrete predictive model. Only in different values are achievable through prediction if the dependent variables are continuous variables. It might be possible to predict continuous data using other regression algorithms.
- Random Forests struggle to accommodate incremental learning. They need to be reevaluated with new info.
- Decision trees are straightforward and simple to understand, yet random forests frequently have a lot of noise. Different splits and even new models can result from even small alterations in the data.
- Like with other regression prediction models, Random Forests also tend to be slower, especially when there are more trees and a greater depth of trees.

4. K-NEAREST NEIGHBOR (KNN)

KNN was created by Evelyn Fix and Joseph Hodges in 1951 and was later expanded by Cover and Hart in 1967. KNN is one of the non-parametric and supervised learning techniques. The KNN technique is applicable to both classification and regression issues. Finding the K nearest neighbors for a given data point is a pretty straightforward idea. It is assumed that related products are located close to one another.

Here, "close" refers to a distance measurement between two places that can be as straightforward as their Euclidean distance. You can determine that the test data refers to a class by locating the largest class of things that are like the test data. Let x and y denote n-dimensional vectors. The Euclidean distance and cosine similarity are provided:

$$\text{Euclidean} = \sqrt{\sum_i^n (x_i - y_i)^2} \text{ and Cosine} = \frac{2\sum_i^n x_i y_i}{\sum_i^n x_i^2 + \sum_i^n y_i^2} = \frac{2xy}{\| x \| + \| y \|}$$

The cosine similarity is immediately provided as a normalized value, whereas the Euclidean distance must be reversed and adjusted. In recent years, the cosine similarity, which considers both feature and feature value similarity, was developed to address the fragility of sparse vectors. We need to order by increasing the order of their distance or their similarities after we calculate the distances or similarities. In other words, the nearest neighbors are considered with the greatest similarity when the cosine similarity equation is used and the smallest distance when Euclidean distance is preferred. Moreover, the average of the label values can be considered while solving regression problems. This is written as

$$\hat{y} = \frac{\left(\sum_i^k y_i\right)}{k}$$

where y and k notations denote output values and i*th* nearest neighbor. Sometimes, Mahalanobis distance might be preferred to compute the distance between neighbors. Mahalanobis distance is formularized as

$$d(x,y) = \sqrt{(x-y)^T \Sigma (x-y)}$$

where let x and y denote vectors of the dataset whereas Σ is the covariance matrix of the dataset. Thus, we can interpret that the size of a feature can have an excessive effect on these distance measurements. Moreover, the limitations are that prediction is remarkably slow with large data, algorithm is very sensitive to both relevant features and the size of the data. It is susceptible to outliers.

5. NAÏVE BAYES

Another extremely straightforward approach for classification is the Naive Bayes algorithm which uses the Bayes theorem and a strong independent assumption. A Naive Bayes classifier, in its most basic form, presupposes that the existence of one characteristic in a class is independent of the existence of any other characteristic. Even if the fundamental premise is false, the Naive Bayes classifier still works admirably. Bayes theorem is written as

$$P(c|x) = \frac{P(x|c)P(c)}{P(x)}$$

where let x and c denote all variables and given class. So, $P(c)$ is the probability of a class, $P(x)$ is the probability of variables, $P(x|c)$ is the probability of variable, x given the class, c and $P(c|x)$ is called posterior probability that means the probability of a class, c in given the variable, x.

Let's consider a scenario where the human resources department of a company wants to hire a senior researcher from among job applicants who either have or do not have a Ph.D. The HR department plans to make decisions based on a single variable—gender, categorized as female or male. We define the probability of a Ph.D. degree among female applicants as follows:

1) Pr(Ph.D.) is the probability of having a Ph.D. degree, calculated as the number of applicants with a Ph.D. divided by the total number of applicants for the position.

2) P(women| Ph.D.) is the probability of an applicant being a woman given they have a Ph.D., calculated as the number of women with a Ph.D. divided by the total number of applicants with a Ph.D.

3) P(women|not-Ph.D.) is the probability of an applicant being a woman given they do not have a Ph.D., calculated as the number of women without a Ph.D. divided by the total number of applicants without a Ph.D. Therefore, P(Ph.D.|women) can be formulated as follows:

$$(Ph.D.|women) = \frac{P(Ph.D.) \times P(women|Ph.D.)}{P(Ph.D.) \times P(women|Ph.D.) + P(non-Ph.D.) \times P(women|not-Ph.D.)}$$

Unfortunately, there could be many factors in reality. At this point, we should assume that all factors are independent when Naïve Bayes is used.

REFERENCES

Adhatrao, K., Gaykar, A., Dhawan, A., Jha, R., & Honrao, V. (2013). Predicting students' performance using ID3 and C4. 5 classification algorithms. arXiv preprint arXiv:1310.2071.

Aziz, S., & Dowling, M. (2019). Machine learning and AI for risk management. *Disrupting finance: FinTech and strategy in the 21st century*, 33-50. 10.1007/978-3-030-02330-0_3

Breiman, L., Friedman, J., Olshen, R., & Stone, C. (1984). *Cart. Classification and regression trees*. .10.1201/9781315139470

Cover, T., & Hart, P. (1967). Nearest neighbor pattern classification. *IEEE Transactions on Information Theory*, 13(1), 21–27. 10.1109/TIT.1967.1053964

Dileep, M. R., Navaneeth, A. V., & Abhishek, M. (2021, February). A novel approach for credit card fraud detection using decision tree and random forest algorithms. In *2021 Third International Conference on Intelligent Communication Technologies and Virtual Mobile Networks (ICICV)* (pp. 1025-1028). IEEE. 10.1109/ICICV50876.2021.9388431

Dixon, M. F., Halperin, I., & Bilokon, P. (2020). *Machine learning in finance* (Vol. 1170). Springer International Publishing. 10.1007/978-3-030-41068-1

Enholm, I. M., Papagiannidis, E., Mikalef, P., & Krogstie, J. (2022). Artificial intelligence and business value: A literature review. *Information Systems Frontiers*, 24(5), 1709–1734. 10.1007/s10796-021-10186-w

Fitrianto, A., Muhamad, W. Z. A. W., & Susetyo, B. (2022). Development of direct marketing strategy for the banking industry: The use of a Chi-squared Automatic Interaction Detector (CHAID) in deposit subscription classification. *Journal of Socioeconomics and Development*, 5(1), 64–75. 10.31328/jsed.v5i1.3420

Fix, E., & Hodges, J. L. (1951). *Discriminatory analysis, nonparametric discrimination: consistency properties*. US Air Force School of Aviation Medicine. Technical Report 4, (3).

Ghazal, T. M., & Alzoubi, H. M. (2021). Modeling supply chain information collaboration empowered with machine learning technique. *Intelligent Automation & Soft Computing*, 29(3), 243–257. 10.32604/iasc.2021.018983

Gopal, M. (2019). Applied machine learning. McGraw-Hill Education.

Haenlein, M., & Kaplan, A. (2019). A brief history of artificial intelligence: On the past, present, and future of artificial intelligence. *California Management Review*, 61(4), 5–14. 10.1177/0008125619864925

Kaul, V., Enslin, S., & Gross, S. A. (2020). History of artificial intelligence in medicine. *Gastrointestinal Endoscopy*, 92(4), 807–812. 10.1016/j.gie.2020.06.04032565184

Learned-Miller, E. G. (2014). *Introduction to supervised learning*. Department of Computer Science, University of Massachusetts.

Liu, Q., Levinson, S., Wu, Y., & Huang, T. (2000, February). Interactive and incremental learning via a mixture of supervised and unsupervised learning strategies. In *Proceedings of the Fifth Joint Conference on Information Sciences* (Vol. 1, pp. 555-558). Academic Press.

Ngo, F. T., Govindu, R., & Agarwal, A. (2015). Assessing the predictive utility of logistic regression, classification, and regression tree, chi-squared automatic interaction detection, and neural network models in predicting inmate misconduct. *American Journal of Criminal Justice*, 40(1), 47–74. 10.1007/s12103-014-9246-6

Quinlan, J. R. (1996). Improved use of continuous attributes in C4. 5. *Journal of Artificial Intelligence Research*, 4, 77–90. 10.1613/jair.279

Quinlan, J. R. (2014). *C4. 5: programs for machine learning*. Elsevier. 10.1016/j.procs.2016.04.224

Raza, M. A., Aziz, S., Noreen, M., Saeed, A., Anjum, I., Ahmed, M., & Raza, S. M. (2022). Artificial Intelligence (AI) in Pharmacy: An Overview of Innovations. *Innovations in Pharmacy*, 13(2), 13. Advance online publication. 10.24926/iip.v13i2.483936654703

Samuel, A. L. (1959). Some studies in machine learning using the game of checkers. *IBM Journal of Research and Development*, 3(3), 210–229. 10.1147/rd.33.0210

Steinberg, D., & Colla, P. (2009). CART: classification and regression trees. *The top ten algorithms in data mining, 9*, 179.

Tian, J. X., & Zhang, J. (2022). Breast cancer diagnosis using feature extraction and boosted C5. 0 decision tree algorithm with penalty factor. *Mathematical Biosciences and Engineering*, 19(3), 2193–2205. 10.3934/mbe.202210235240781

Williamson, B., & Eynon, R. (2020). Historical threads, missing links, and future directions in AI in education. *Learning, Media and Technology*, 45(3), 223–235. 10.1080/17439884.2020.1798995

Wu, G., Li, H., Hu, X., Bi, Y., Zhang, J., & Wu, X. (2009, August). MReC4. 5: C4. 5 ensemble classification with MapReduce. In *2009 fourth ChinaGrid annual conference* (pp. 249-255). IEEE. 10.1109/ChinaGrid.2009.39

Yang, S., Guo, J. Z., & Jin, J. W. (2018). An improved Id3 algorithm for medical data classification. *Computers & Electrical Engineering*, 65, 474–487. 10.1016/j.compeleceng.2017.08.005

Zacharis, N. Z. (2018). Classification and regression trees (CART) for predictive modeling in blended learning. *International Journal of Intelligent Systems and Applications*, 3(3), 1–9. 10.5815/ijisa.2018.03.01

Chapter 2
AI and Its Impact on Business and Society

Aditya Pai H.
http://orcid.org/0000-0002-8186-2467
Jain University, India

Mahesh T. R.
Jain University, India

Jyoti Agarwal
Graphic Era University, India

Vinoth Kumar V.
http://orcid.org/0000-0003-1070-3212
Vellore Institute of Technology University, India

Sharon Christa
http://orcid.org/0000-0001-6717-2200
School of Computing, MIT ADT University, India

A. Suresh Kumar
http://orcid.org/0000-0001-7145-6337
Independent Researcher, India

ABSTRACT

Industries follow the reactive approach in finding the errors and threats in the development process and mitigating them. In the chapter, an IT industry of small and medium levels is taken as a part of the case study. In small and medium level enterprises (SMEs), the predictive maintenance technique is used rather than the reactive approach. The transition from reactive to predictive was essential for the SMEs to help the managers and the development team anticipate future problems based on past data. An SME has been taken as a case study. The study uses a data set of 6 months for the prediction. The dataset generates the software development process and rules matrix. The matrix is used for analyzing and predicting the accuracy of the software development results of the project. Here, three AI algorithms are used for the prediction. After getting the result, comparative analyses are done between the three AI algorithms to select the best among the three. The chosen algorithm will be used in the development process to improve the business prospects of the enterprise.

INTRODUCTION

Lead time is the time taken from placing an order or requesting services by the customers to the delivery of the products or services by the enterprises. Following the lead time is essential in this competitive era. The delivery of the product or services is always decided by the customer. The enterprises must ensure

DOI: 10.4018/979-8-3693-0683-3.ch002

the strict time in delivering services to them else leading to the longer lead time. If an enterprise takes longer lead time, then the consequences faced by them are immensely bad. The enterprises will have a hit on the goodwill and hence will have a bad name in the market. Secondly, the more the lead time taken the chances of losing clients or customers are more. Thirdly, delay in the delivery of the product and services also leads to enterprises spending on the resources from their own funds rather than from the client funds. This will keep the enterprises in a jittery state financially, especially for the SMEs.

The causes behind the longer lead time are due to the various reasons. The list of the reason behind the SMEs lags behind in following the lead time is as follows:

- Lack of communication or lack of transparency shown within the team in the organization and also across various hierarchies can create confusion and causes the delay in the development approach.
- The lack of the proper environment for the development team to create and test the software features is the following issue encountered throughout the software development process. Here, it alludes to the necessity of software version control for the developers to keep track of multiple programme versions.
- The testing of the programme is another issue the development team is dealing with. This stage typically takes longer than is necessary. because it includes a variety of testing, including smoke testing and user acceptance testing.
- The delay in the software's deployment is the main issue in this situation. The software and hardware environment in the customer's environment is not adequate enough for the software developer to install, among other things, might be one of the causes of this. As a result, the software developer must also solve this issue.

In this chapter we discuss about the reason for the delay in the software development process, and how AI helps in improving the same. The significance of using different AI algorithms is learnt here to check how it impact the business and society in the positive direction. Thus, in the chapter a new algorithm is proposed to find whether the software development processes followed by a SME is ideal or not. Another two AI algorithms used are Convolution Neural Network (CNN) and Naïve Bayes. To carry out the research nine software development rules (SDR_{1-9}) are proposed along with the seven software development processes (SDP_{1-7}). For the field work study, the example of Embitel Technologies is used. Two projects are used for the research study purpose namely Telenetrix and EngiNX solutions. The research data was carried out in the Embitel Technologies in the period of 6 months, December 2022. The motivation behind the study is to provide an optimal development process for SMEs like Embitel Technologies by bringing Artificial Intelligence approach to the software development process and thus improving the overall business of the organization.

The paper is divided into following sections, Section 2 is the Related Works, Section 3 is the Research Methodology that shows the flow of research carried, Section 4 is Results and Discussions where the study of the software development processes following the software development rules are carried out by using three AI algorithms namely proposed algorithm, second one is CNN and the third one is Naïve Bayes algorithm, the ANOVA analysis and graph comparison is done to verify the find the best algorithm among the three proposed technique. The best algorithm chosen is the one which will be used for improving the software development processes. Thus, having positive impact on the businesses of the mentioned SME. The Section 5 is the Conclusion part which summarizes how Artificial Intelligence has impacted on the business and society.

RELATED WORKS

Over the past few decades, "data mining and analytics have played a significant role in knowledge discovery and decision making in the process industry" (Dogan A & Birant D, 2021). Data mining and analytics employ machine learning as a computational engine to extract information, identify patterns in data (Wijaya DR, 2020) and make predictions (Pangestu A & Wijaya DR, 2020). Machine learning approaches have been used successfully to forecast things like rainfall amounts (Liyew CM & Melese HA, 2021), poverty levels (Aulia TF & Wijaya DR, 2020), alumni incomes (Gomez-Cravioto DA & Diaz-Ramos RE, 2022), and COVID-19-related instances (Budiharto W., 2021), among other things (Hssayeni MD & Chala A, 2021). Operational business processes can be streamlined using techniques to predictive modelling in business process management (Breuker D & Matzner M, 2016). Process mining may be used to identify or diagnose fact-based issues (Cho S, 2021), as well as learn about the company's process workflows, activity activities, and machine mechanisms (Faizan M & Zuhairi MF, 2020). Process mining investigates the disparity between event data, or actual behaviour, and process model predictions in order to identify anomalies, conduct compliance checks, forecast delays, aid in decision-making, and propose process redesigns (Faizan M & Zuhairi MF, 2020). However, machine learning algorithms might be used into process mining techniques to create models and predictive analyses.

The focus of the fourth industrial revolution is on utilising technology to enhance manufacturing operations. This initiative has drawn a lot of academic researchers and industry professionals to concentrate on using machine learning in production operations for machine maintenance and fault diagnostics (Dalzochio J & Kunst R, 2020) The existing literature has used a variety of machine learning techniques to predict production delay, and this study has used four machine learning techniques: Decision Tree, Neural Network, Random Forest, and Nave Bayes. These techniques outperformed other supervised learning algorithms. Algorithms like decision trees and random forests are frequently employed in defect diagnosis and are regarded as classification methods. Random forest algorithm generates a number of decision trees, and the final prediction is based on the voting of the outcomes from each decision tree, whereas decision tree algorithm builds one ideal decision tree model for forecasting the target (Gong S & Wu X, 2020). The effectiveness of these two approaches varies depending on the dataset and variables utilised, with decision tree outperforming random forest (Zhang C & Hu C, 2021) and vice versa (Tsai MF & Chu YC, 2021). On the other hand, the artificial neural network (ANN) technology is renowned for its noise tolerance and is capable of identifying a specific issue type. In the manufacturing sector, ANN has been utilised for fault detection in the die-casting sector (Lee J, 2021), to forecast failures in a blade pitch system (Cho S, 2021), and many other applications. Because of its effectiveness and ability to perform well with a short training dataset, the Nave Bayes algorithm is one of the most used machine learning techniques in predictive models (Truong D., 2021). In the paper, new Machine Learning algorithm is proposed, along with Convolution Neural Network (CNN) and Naive Bayes Algorithm.

To summarise from the related work, the artificial intelligence approaches play an important role in various sectors of the industries. In this paper, impact of using artificial intelligence approaches to the small and medium level enterprises are being studied through a field work carried out in Embitel Technologies.

RESEARCH METHODOLOGY

As discussed in the Section 1 – Introduction, it is always necessary to maintain the lead time. Hence the methodology followed in the proposed chapter are the three AI techniques – one is the proposed machine learning algorithm used to find whether the software development processes and the development rules followed are ideal or not. Second one is the Convolution Neural Network algorithm being used to check the same and finally the Naïve Bayes algorithm is used. The comparative analysis of these 3 algorithms is done to check the best algorithm among the three. The comparison is done by graphical comparison and also by carrying out the ANOVA test. This comparison test is necessary to find the best algorithm between the three Machine learning algorithm including the proposed machine learning algorithm technique. If there is a need for the change in any software development processes or development rules, the process will be repeated. The proposed research methodology is mentioned in the (Figure 1) below.

Figure 1. Research methodology used for the proposed study

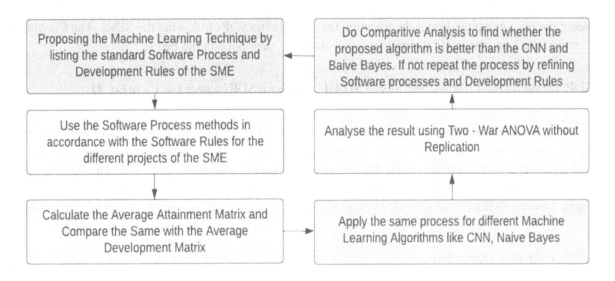

RESULTS AND DISCUSSIONS

Proposed Technique for Finding the Problem in the Software Development Process

As discussed in the methodology, in the first step - the Artificial Intelligence (Machine Learning Models) are used for which the software development rules and processes are required to be defined. The second step is to map the software processes with the software development rules for the identified projects. Third step is to calculate the attainment matrix and the same is required to be compared with the average development matrix. Fourth Step is to - use the same approach for other AI approaches like CNN and Naïve Bayes. In the Fifth Step – analyse the result using Two-War ANOVA without replication for comparing the results of different AI approaches. In the Sixth Step after the comparing different AI algorithms with the proposed AI Approach. If the proposes approach is found better than the different mentioned AI algorithms, then the same approach will be utilized for the software development processes for optimal results. If there is contrasting results then the proposed approach will be reframed till it gives the better results.

The Artificial Intelligence Model (Machine Learning Model) is used for Predicting the delay in the Lead Time for the SME named 'Embitel Technologies Private Ltd'. During the field work study two projects were taken Telenetrix and EngiNX Solutions. To carry out these projects different Software Development Processes (SDP $_{[1-7]}$) were used. These SDPs must follow the guidelines mentioned in the Software Development Rule (SDR $_{[1-9]}$). The SDRs help in carry out the tasks of the project in the standard manner. The following (Table 1) and (Table 2) are the examples of the two mentioned project for the SME 'Embitel Technologies Private Ltd.' As shown in the (Table 1) and (Table 2), the articulation matrix mapping the two corresponding parameters. This signifies that whether each SDPs are following SDRs are not. If the mapping rate is 3 then it is said to be good mapping, 2 is satisfactory mapping and 1 being the poor mapping. Better the mapping the better is the SDPs following the SDRs. The Congenial between the 2 parameters in the matrix is calculated as mentioned in the Eq. 1,

$$SDPi \text{ for each } i = 1 .. n = \text{Cong}[SDP, \quad SDR]\binom{3}{0} \text{for each } SDRi \text{ where } i = 1 .. n \textbf{\textit{(Eq. 1)}}$$

Here as per the acronym mentioned in the Eq. 2 are SDP which stands for the Software Development Process. SDR stands for the Development Rules. Cong stands for congenial between the SDP and SDR. The Congenial checks for the compatibility between the SDP and SDR. The compatibility or congenial mappings in the matrix are on the basis of estimation based on the previous experiences carried by the SMEs.

Table 1. Project – Telenetrix

Software Development Rules	SDR$_1$	SDR$_2$	SDR$_3$	SDR$_4$	SDR$_5$	SDR$_6$	SDR$_7$	SDR$_8$	SDR$_9$
Software Development Process									
SDP$_1$	2	3	2	2	3	3	3	3	3
SDP$_2$	3	1	2	1	2	2	2	2	1
SDP$_3$	3	3	2	2	2	3	3	2	2
SDP$_4$	2	3	2	2	3	2	2	3	2
SDP$_5$	1	2	2	3	3	3	2	2	2
SDP$_6$	2	2	3	2	3	2	3	2	1
SDP$_7$	3	2	3	2	3	2	2	3	2
ASDP$_{IA}$	2.29	2.29	2.29	2	2.71	2.43	2.43	2.43	1.86

Table 2. Project -EngiNX Solutions

Software Development Rules	SDR$_1$	SDR$_2$	SDR$_3$	SDR$_4$	SDR$_5$	SDR$_6$	SDR$_7$	SDR$_8$	SDR$_9$
Software Development Process									
SDP$_1$	2	2	2	3	2	2	2	2	2
SDP$_2$	3	3	2	3	3	3	3	2	3
SDP$_3$	3	3	3	3	3	3	3	3	3
SDP$_4$	2	3	2	2	2	2	2	2	2
SDP$_5$	2	2	2	2	3	2	2	3	3
SDP$_6$	2	2	3	2	3	3	3	2	2
SDP$_7$	3	2	3	2	3	3	3	3	2
ASDP$_{IIA}$	2.43	2.43	2.43	2.43	2.71	2.57	2.57	2.43	2.43

Next the actual outcome of the Projects mentioned in (Table 1) and (Table 2) are checked. For this the listing of different SDPs are mentioned below:

- SDP1 – For assessing the right software requirements
- SDP2 - To build the methodology
- SDP3 – To gather the requirements
- SDP4 – To design Software Requirement specifications like Use Cases, ER Diagrams
- SDP5 – To create user stories
- SDP6 – Using the agile methodology
- SDP7 – Deployment and Maintenance

Each SDPs are mapped with the subsequent SDRs. These SDRs are nothing but the rules that are required to be followed during SDPs. The listing of SDR is mentioned below:

- SDR1 – Using Proper Software Engineering Rules
- SDR2 – Designing and Developing the solutions based on the clients
- SDR3 – Finding and Solving the complexities in the problem
- SDR4 – Usage of the modern tool
- SDR5 – Requirement of the sustainable development
- SDR6 – Working as an individual and as a team
- SDR7 – Using ethics
- SDR8 – Documentation
- SDR9 – Proper project management

The outcome of the Software Development Processes of the Telenetrix and EngiNX Solutions project is found out.

Figure 2. Outcome after evaluating the SDP of Telenetrix

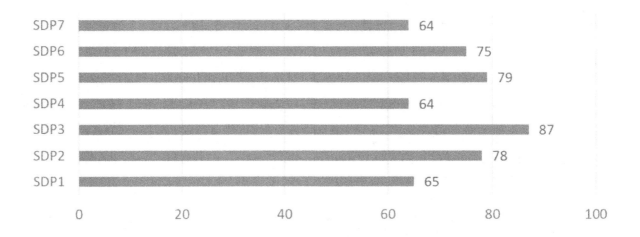

Figure 3. Outcome after evaluating the SDP of EngiNX solutions

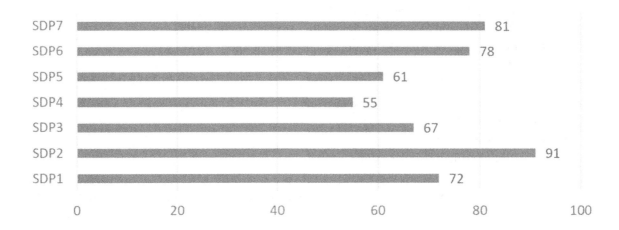

As shown in the (Figure 2) and (Figure 3) the actual outcome of the two projects after evaluating is shown. As mentioned in the graph, the SDP outcome between 70 -100 falls under 3 category, SDP outcome between 40 – 69 falls under 2 category and less than 40 comes under 1 category. The same is described in (Table 3).

Table 3. SDP Outcome of Telenetrix and EngiNX Solutions

SDP #	SDP Outcome of Telenetrix	SDP Outcome of EngiNX Solutions
SDP1	2	3
SDP2	3	3
SDP3	3	2
SDP4	2	2
SDP5	3	2
SDP6	3	3
SDP7	2	3

The mapping for the congenial between the multiplied Software Development Process (mSDP) and SDR is calculated. The mSDP is the matrix elements of SDP multiplied with the SDP outcome. The same is explained in the Eq. 2:

$$mSDPi \text{ for every } i = 1 .. n = OuDP*\left[Cong[SDP, \quad SDR]\binom{3}{0}\text{for each SPR}i \text{ where } i = 1 .. n\right] \textbf{(Eq.2)}$$

The outcome of the Eq.1 has been applied to the (Table 1) and (Table 2) for the projects Telenetrix and EngiNX respectively. In the equation (Eq. 2) OuDP is multiplied to that mentioned in the Eq.1 to attain the matrix mentioned in the (Table 4) and (Table 5).

Table 4. Updated Matrix of Telenetrix

Development Rules	SDR_1	SDR_2	SDR_3	SDR_4	SDR_5	SDR_6	SDR_7	SDR_8	SDR_9
Development Process									
$mSDP_1$	4	6	4	4	6	6	6	6	6
$mSDP_2$	9	3	6	3	6	6	6	6	3
$mSDP_3$	9	9	6	6	6	9	9	6	6
$mSDP_4$	4	6	4	4	6	4	4	6	4
$mSDP_5$	3	6	6	9	9	9	6	6	6
$mSDP_6$	6	6	9	6	9	6	9	6	3
$mSDP_7$	6	4	6	4	6	4	4	6	4
$mASDP_{IA}$	5.86	5.71	5.86	5.14	6.86	6.29	6.29	6	4.57

Table 5. Updated Matrix of EngiNX Solutions

Development Rules	SDR_1	SDR_2	SDR_3	SDR_4	SDR_5	SDR_6	SDR_7	SDR_8	SDR_9
Development Process									
$mSDP_1$	6	6	6	9	6	6	6	6	6
$mSDP_2$	9	9	6	9	9	9	9	6	9
$mSDP_3$	6	6	6	6	6	6	6	6	6
$mSDP_4$	4	6	4	4	4	4	4	4	4
$mSDP_5$	4	4	4	4	6	4	4	6	6
$mSDP_6$	6	6	9	6	9	9	9	6	6
$mSDP_7$	9	6	9	6	9	9	9	9	6
mASDPII	6.286	6.143	6.286	6.286	7	6.714	6.714	6.143	6.143

(Table 4) and (Table 5) are the updated matrix of the projects – Telenetrix and EngiNX Solutions respectively. In this matrix the outcomes attained listed in the (Table 3) is multiplied to each matrix elements of (Table 1) and (Table 2). Hence resulting the product matrix between the actual outcome and the estimated outcome for the projects. $mASDP_I$ and $mASDP_{II}$ in the (Table 4) and (Table 5) are the average of the sum of product elements in the matrix.

For every matrix m, the Average Attainment Matrix mentioned in the Eq. 3 is the division between the sum of the squares of multiplied Software Development Matrix (Table 4, Table 5) and the sum of the Software Development Matrix (Table 1, Table 2) as shown in (Table 6).

$$\text{Average Attainment Matrix} = \frac{\text{Average of multiplied Software Development Matrix}}{\text{Average of Software Development Matrix}} \; (\textbf{\textit{Eq}}. 3)$$

Table 6. Average of Attainment Matrix

Projects	SDR_1	SDR_2	SDR_3	SDR_4	SDR_5	SDR_6	SDR_7	SDR_8	SDR_9
Telenetrix (SDPs)	2.56	2.49	2.56	2.57	2.53	2.59	2.59	2.47	2.46
EngiNX Solutions (SDPs)	2.59	2.53	2.59	2.59	2.58	2.61	2.61	2.53	2.53
Average of Attainment Matrix	2.58	2.51	2.58	2.58	2.56	2.6	2.6	2.5	2.5

In (Table 7), the averages mentioned in the (Table 1) and (Table 2) are listed as the elements in the matrix. Here the average of those averages is taken

Table 7. Average of Development Process

Projects	SDR_1	SDR_2	SDR_3	SDR_4	SDR_5	SDR_6	SDR_7	SDR_8	SDR_9
Telenetrix (SDPs)	2.29	2.29	2.29	2	2.71	2.43	2.43	2.43	1.86
EngiNX Solutions (SDPs)	2.43	2.43	2.43	2.43	2.71	2.57	2.57	2.43	2.43
Average of Development Process Matrix	2.36	2.36	2.36	2.22	2.71	2.5	2.5	2.43	2.15

Next, the average of attainment matrix is compared with the average of development process matrix. If the value of the average of development process matrix is more than the average of attainment matrix then it is proved that the Software Development Processes defined for the project doesn't require any modification. If anyone parameter is found to be lesser value when compared to the attainment matrix. Then there is a need to redefine the Software Development Rule for the Software Development Processes. Here it shows that SDPS following SDR_5 has the requirement to be redefined. The reason for this is due to the SDP value for the Average Attainment Matrix is less than the SDP value for the Average of Development Matrix at SDR5. Hence there is a need to use effective Machine Learning algorithm to get the efficient result. The comparative analysis graph is shown in the (Figure 4) below.

Figure 4. Comparative Analysis Using the Proposed Machine Learning Algorithm

COMPARITVE RESULTS BASED ON THE PROPOSED PREDICTION ALGORITHM

| SDR1 | SDR2 | SDR3 | SDR4 | SDR5 | SDR6 | SDR7 | SDR8 | SDR9 |

— —Average of Attainment Matrix   — —Average of Development Matrix

Using Other Machine Learning Algorithms

Convolution Neural Network (CNN)

Among the other proposed algorithms, Convolution Neural Network (CNN) is the first algorithm chosen. The algorithm consists of various inputs leading to the single output. Between the input and the output there are 3 different hidden layers. These hidden layers are used to pass the data between the network of nodes. Once the data is sent from the input to the output, the three hidden layers are activated and the data is passed. The representation of the same is shown in the (Figure 5). The concept of the same is used in the current research technique.

Figure 5. Convolution Neural Network

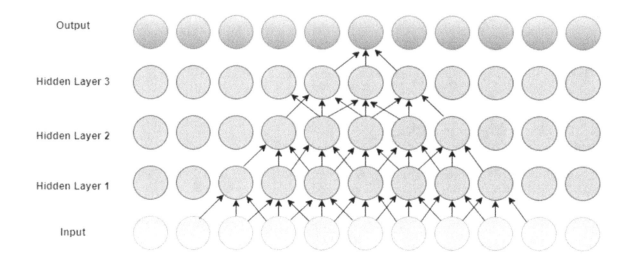

The result of the same is mentioned in the (Table 8) below, where the average attainment matrix of the CNN is calculated. The average of attainment matrix in (Table 8) is now compared with the average of development matrix in (Table 7). The comparative graph showing the comparison between average attainment matrix using CNN and the average of development matrix is shown in the (Figure 6) below.

Table 8. Average of Attainment Matrix Using CNN

Projects	DR1	DR2	DR3	DR4	DR5	DR6	DR7	DR8	DR9
Telenetrix (SDPs)	2	3	3	2	3	3	3	2	3
EngiNX Solutions (SDPs)	6	9	6	4	6	9	9	6	6
Average of Attainment Matrix	3	3	2	2	2	3	3	3	2

Figure 6. Comparative Analysis Using Convolution Neural Network

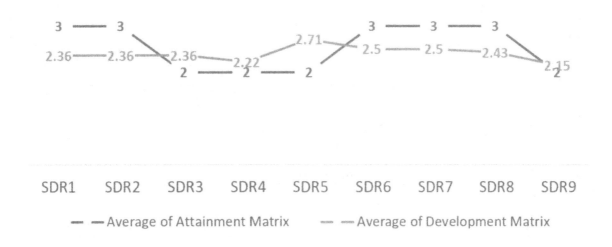

The (Figure 6) shows the comparative analysis of the average attainment matrix using Convolution Neural Network (CNN) with the Average of Development Matrix. As shown in the (Figure 6), for the SDR_1, SDR_2, SDR_6, SDR_7 and SDR_8 the Average of Attainment Matrix is more than the Average of Development Matrix. Whereas for the SDR_3, SDR_4, SDR_5 and SDR_9, the Average of Development Matrix is more than the Average Attainment Matrix. Hence as per the given algorithm SDR_3, SDR_4, SDR_5 and SDR_9 rules are required to be redefined along with the SDPs.

Naïve Bayes

The third proposed algorithm is the Naïve Bayes algorithm for the project Telenetrix and EngiNX Solutions. The Naïve Bayes algorithm is the AI algorithm which is used for classifying the assumption of a particular feature in a class that is present in another feature. In this chapter we are finding whether the attainment elements in the matrix is different from the development matrix. The formula used for the Naïve Bayes for the given study is mentioned in the Eq.4, Eq. 5 and Eq. 6. At first, we find the frequency of the occurrences of 3, 2, 1 for the given Software Development Rules in the (Table 9) and (Table 10) respectively. These tables are known as Frequency Table. Next, the likelihood of 3, 2, 1 are found out by finding the average likely of each possibility in the respective Software Development Rules. The likelihood is found for the two mentioned projects. The same is shown in the (Table 11) and (Table 12).

Table 9. Project – Telenetrix (Frequency Table)

Frequencies	3	2	1
Software Development Rules			
SDR_1	3	3	1
SDR_2	3	3	1
SDR_3	2	5	
SDR_4	1	5	1
SDR_5	5	2	
SDR_6	3	4	
SDR_7	3	4	
SDR_8	3	4	
SDR_9	1	4	2

Table 10. Project – EngiNX Solutions (Frequency Table)

Frequencies	3	2	1
Software Development Rules			
SDR_1	3	4	
SDR_2	3	4	
SDR_3	3	4	
SDR_4	3	4	
SDR_5	5	2	
SDR_6	4	3	
SDR_7	4	3	
SDR_8	3	4	
SDR_9	3	4	

Table 11. Project – Telenetrix (Likelihood Table)

Frequencies	3	2	1	Average Likely of SDR	
Software Development Rules					
SDR_1	3	3	1	=3/3	1
SDR_2	3	3	1	=3/3	1
SDR_3	2	5		=2/3	0.66
SDR_4	1	5	1	=3/3	1
SDR_5	5	2		=2/3	0.66
SDR_6	3	4		=2/3	0.66
SDR_7	3	4		=2/3	0.66

continued on following page

Table 11. Continued

Frequencies	3	2	1	Average Likely of SDR	
Software Development Rules					
SDR$_8$	3	4		=2/3	0.66
SDR$_9$	1	4	2	=3/3	1
Average Likely Of [3,2,1]	2.67	3.78	0.56		

Table 12. Project – EngiNX Solutions (Likelihood Table)

Frequencies	3	2	1	Average Likely of SDR	
Software Development Rules					
SDR$_1$	3	4		=2/3	0.66
SDR$_2$	3	4		=2/3	0.66
SDR$_3$	3	4		=2/3	0.66
SDR$_4$	3	4		=2/3	0.66
SDR$_5$	5	2		=2/3	0.66
SDR$_6$	4	3		=2/3	0.66
SDR$_7$	4	3		=2/3	0.66
SDR$_8$	3	4		=2/3	0.66
SDR$_9$	3	4		=2/3	0.66
Average Likely Of [3,2,1]	3.44	3.56	0		

In the (Table 13) for the Telenetrix project, the Eq. 4 is used for calculation. For the $P(SDR_1|3)$ the value $P(3|SDR_1)$ is divided with $P(SDR_1)$ i.e., 2.67 / 1 = 2.67. The next value for $P(SDR_2|3)$ is calculated by dividing $P(3|SDR_2)$ with $P(SDR_2)$ i.e., 2.67 / 1 = 2.67. The same way other probabilities are checked for $P(SDR_3|3)$, $P(SDR_4|3)$, $P(SDR_5|3)$, $P(SDR_6|3)$, $P(SDR_7|3)$, $P(SDR_8|3)$ and $P(SDR_9|3)$ to get the following values 4.045455, 2.67, 4.045455, 4.045455, 4.045455, 4.045455 and 2.67 respectively.

Table 13. Telenetrix - Probability of SDRn with outcome as 3

	P(3|SDRn)	P(SDRn)	P(3|SDRn) / P(SDRn)
P(SDR1|3)	2.67	1	2.67
P(SDR2|3)	2.67	1	2.67
P(SDR3|3)	2.67	0.66	4.045455
P(SDR4|3)	2.67	1	2.67
P(SDR5|3)	2.67	0.66	4.045455
P(SDR6|3)	2.67	0.66	4.045455
P(SDR7|3)	2.67	0.66	4.045455

continued on following page

Table 13. Continued

	P(3|SDRn)	P(SDRn)	P(3|SDRn) / P(SDRn)
P(SDR8|3)	2.67	0.66	4.045455
P(SDR9|3)	2.67	1	2.67

For the same Telenetrix project, in the (Table 14), the Eq. 5 is used for calculation. For the $P(SDR_1|2)$ the value $P(2|SDR_1)$ is divided with $P(SDR_1)$ i.e., 3.78 / 1 = 3.78. The next value for $P(SDR_2|2)$ is calculated by dividing $P(2|SDR_2)$ with $P(SDR_2)$ i.e., 3.78 / 1 = 3.78. The same way other probabilities are checked for $P(SDR_3|2)$, $P(SDR_4|2)$, $P(SDR_5|2)$, $P(SDR_6|2)$, $P(SDR_7|2)$, $P(SDR_8|2)$ and $P(SDR_9|2)$ to get the following values 5.727273, 3.78, 5.727273, 5.727273, 5.727273, 5.727273 and 3.78 respectively.

Table 14. Telenetrix - Probability of SDRn with outcome as 2

	P(2|SDRn)	P(SDRn)	P(2|SDRn) / P(SDRn)
P(SDR1|2)	3.78	1	3.78
P(SDR2|2)	3.78	1	3.78
P(SDR3|2)	3.78	0.66	5.727273
P(SDR4|2)	3.78	1	3.78
P(SDR5|2)	3.78	0.66	5.727273
P(SDR6|2)	3.78	0.66	5.727273
P(SDR7|2)	3.78	0.66	5.727273
P(SDR8|2)	3.78	0.66	5.727273
P(SDR9|2)	3.78	1	3.78

Then in the (Table 15), the Eq. 6 is used for calculation of Probability of 1 for the Telenetrix project. For the $P(SDR_1|1)$ the value $P(1|SDR_1)$ is divided with $P(SDR_1)$ i.e., 0.56 / 1 = 0.56. The next value for $P(SDR_2|1)$ is calculated by dividing $P(1|SDR_2)$ with $P(SDR_2)$ i.e., 0.56 / 1 = 0.56. The same way other probabilities are checked for $P(SDR_3|1)$, $P(SDR_4|1)$, $P(SDR_5|1)$, $P(SDR_6|1)$, $P(SDR_7|1)$, $P(SDR_8|1)$ and $P(SDR_9|1)$ to get the following values 0.848485, 0.56, 0.848485, 0.848485, 0.848485, 0.848485 and 0.56 respectively.

Table 15. Telenetrix - Probability of SDRn with outcome as 1

	P(1|SDRn)	P(SDRn)	P(1|SDRn) / P(SDRn)
P(SDR1|1)	0.56	1	0.56
P(SDR2|1)	0.56	1	0.56
P(SDR3|1)	0.56	0.66	0.848485
P(SDR4|1)	0.56	1	0.56
P(SDR5|1)	0.56	0.66	0.848485
P(SDR6|1)	0.56	0.66	0.848485
P(SDR7|1)	0.56	0.66	0.848485
P(SDR8|1)	0.56	0.66	0.848485
P(SDR9|1)	0.56	1	0.56

In the (Table 16), the Average Cumulative Probability Outcomes of Telenetrix project of 3, 2 and 1 for the SDR_1, SDR_2, SDR_3, SDR_4, SDR_5, SDR_6, SDR_7, SDR_8 and SDR_9 are 2.34, 2.34, 3.54, 2.34, 3.54, 3.54, 3.54, 3.54 and 2.34 respectively.

Table 16. Telenetrix – Cumulative Outcome of 3, 2, 1 for the Probabilities of SDRn

	SDR1	SDR2	SDR3	SDR4	SDR5	SDR6	SDR7	SDR8	SDR9
3	2.67	2.67	4.05	2.67	4.05	4.05	4.05	4.05	2.67
2	3.78	3.78	5.73	3.78	5.73	5.73	5.73	5.73	3.78
1	0.56	0.56	0.85	0.56	0.85	0.85	0.85	0.85	0.56
Average	2.34	2.34	3.54	2.34	3.54	3.54	3.54	3.54	2.34

In the (Table 17) for the EngiNX Solutions project, the Eq. 4 is used for calculation. For the $P(SDR_1|3)$ the value $P(3|SDR_1)$ is divided with $P(SDR_1)$ i.e., $3.44 / 0.66 = 5.212121$. The next value for $P(SDR_2|3)$ is calculated by dividing $P(3|SDR_2)$ with $P(SDR_2)$ i.e., $3.44 / 0.66 = 5.212121$. The same way other probabilities are checked for $P(SDR_3|3)$, $P(SDR_4|3)$, $P(SDR_5|3)$, $P(SDR_6|3)$, $P(SDR_7|3)$, $P(SDR_8|3)$ and $P(SDR_9|3)$ to get the following values 5.212121, 5.212121, 5.212121, 5.212121, 5.212121, 5.212121 and 5.212121 respectively.

Table 17. EngiNX Solutions - Probability of SDRn with outcome as 3

	P(3|SDRn)	P(SDRn)	P(3|SDRn) / P(SDRn)
P(SDR1|3)	3.44	0.66	5.212121
P(SDR2|3)	3.44	0.66	5.212121
P(SDR3|3)	3.44	0.66	5.212121
P(SDR4|3)	3.44	0.66	5.212121
P(SDR5|3)	3.44	0.66	5.212121
P(SDR6|3)	3.44	0.66	5.212121
P(SDR7|3)	3.44	0.66	5.212121
P(SDR8|3)	3.44	0.66	5.212121
P(SDR9|3)	3.44	0.66	5.212121

In the (Table 18) for the same EngiNX Solutions project, the Eq. 5 is used for calculation. For the $P(SDR_1|2)$ the value $P(2|SDR_1)$ is divided with $P(SDR_1)$ i.e., $3.56 / 0.66 = 5.393939$. The next value for $P(SDR_2|2)$ is calculated by dividing $P(2|SDR_2)$ with $P(SDR_2)$ i.e., $3.56 / 0.66 = 5.393939$. The same way other probabilities are checked for $P(SDR_3|2)$, $P(SDR_4|2)$, $P(SDR_5|2)$, $P(SDR_6|2)$, $P(SDR_7|2)$, $P(SDR_8|2)$ and $P(SDR_9|2)$ to get the following values 5.393939, 5.393939, 5.393939, 5.393939, 5.393939, 5.393939 and 5.393939 respectively.

Table 18. EngiNX Solutions - Probability of SDRn with outcome as 2

	P(2|SDRn)	P(SDRn)	P(2|SDRn) / P(SDRn)
P(SDR1|2)	3.56	0.66	5.393939
P(SDR2|2)	3.56	0.66	5.393939
P(SDR3|2)	3.56	0.66	5.393939
P(SDR4|2)	3.56	0.66	5.393939
P(SDR5|2)	3.56	0.66	5.393939
P(SDR6|2)	3.56	0.66	5.393939
P(SDR7|2)	3.56	0.66	5.393939
P(SDR8|2)	3.56	0.66	5.393939
P(SDR9|2)	3.56	0.66	5.393939

Then in the (Table 19), the Eq. 6 is used for calculation of Probability of 1 for the EngiNX Solutions project. For the $P(SDR_1|1)$ the value $P(1|SDR_1)$ is divided with $P(SDR_1)$ i.e., 0 / 0.66 = 0. The next value for $P(SDR_2|1)$ is calculated by dividing $P(1|SDR_2)$ with $P(SDR_2)$ i.e., 0 / 0.66 = 0. The same way other probabilities are checked for $P(SDR_3|1)$, $P(SDR_4|1)$, $P(SDR_5|1)$, $P(SDR_6|1)$, $P(SDR_7|1)$, $P(SDR_8|1)$ and $P(SDR_9|1)$ to get the following values 0, 0, 0, 0, 0 ,0 and 0 respectively.

Table 19. EngiNX Solutions - Probability of SDRn with outcome as 1

	P(1|SDRn)	P(SDRn)	P(1|SDRn) / P(SDRn)
P(SDR1|1)	0	0.66	0
P(SDR2|1)	0	0.66	0
P(SDR3|1)	0	0.66	0
P(SDR4|1)	0	0.66	0
P(SDR5|1)	0	0.66	0
P(SDR6|1)	0	0.66	0
P(SDR7|1)	0	0.66	0
P(SDR8|1)	0	0.66	0
P(SDR9|1)	0	0.66	0

In the (Table 20), the Average Cumulative Probability Outcomes of EngiNX Solutions project of 3, 2 and 1 for the SDR_1, SDR_2, SDR_3, SDR_4, SDR_5, SDR_6, SDR_7, SDR_8 and SDR_9 are 3.53, 3.53, 3.53, 3.53, 3.53, 3.53, 3.53, 3.53 and 3.53 respectively respectively.

Table 20. EngiNX Solutions – Cumulative Outcome of 3, 2, 1 for the Probabilities of SDRn

	SDR1	SDR2	SDR3	SDR4	SDR5	SDR6	SDR7	SDR8	SDR9
3	5.21	5.21	5.21	5.21	5.21	5.21	5.21	5.21	5.21
2	5.39	5.39	5.39	5.39	5.39	5.39	5.39	5.39	5.39
1	0	0	0	0	0	0	0	0	0
Average	3.53	3.53	3.53	3.53	3.53	3.53	3.53	3.53	3.53

The (Table 21) lists all the average of probability of all SDRs for the Telenetrix and EngiNX Solutions.

Table 21. Average of Probability of SDRn for Telenetrix and EngiNX Solutions

Projects	SDR1	SDR2	SDR3	SDR4	SDR5	SDR6	SDR7	SDR8	SDR9
Telenetrix	5.21	5.21	5.21	5.21	5.21	5.21	5.21	5.21	5.21
EngiNX Solutions	5.39	5.39	5.39	5.39	5.39	5.39	5.39	5.39	5.39

Now divide the average values of Telenetrix and EngiNX solutions in the (Table 21) with the values mentioned in (Table 1) and (Table 2) respectively as shown in the (Table 22) to get the Average Attainment Matrix using Naïve Bayes.

Table 22. Average of Attainment Matrix Using Naïve Bayes

Projects	SDR1	SDR2	SDR3	SDR4	SDR5	SDR6	SDR7	SDR8	SDR9
Telenetrix	1.02	1.02	1.55	1.17	1.31	1.46	1.46	1.46	1.26
EngiNX Solutions	1.45	1.45	1.45	1.45	1.30	1.37	1.37	1.45	1.45
Average of Attainment Matrix	1.24	1.24	1.50	1.31	1.31	1.42	1.42	1.46	1.36

The (Figure 7) below shows the comparative analysis of the average attainment matrix using Naïve Bayes with the Average of Development Matrix. As shown in the Figure 7, for the SDRs -SDR_1, SDR_2, SDR_3, SDR_4, SDR_5, SDR_6, SDR_7, SDR_8 and SDR_9 the Average of Attainment Matrix is more than the Average of Development Matrix. Hence as per the given algorithm all the SDR rules are required to be redefined along with the SDPs.

Figure 7. Comparative Analysis Using Naïve Bayes

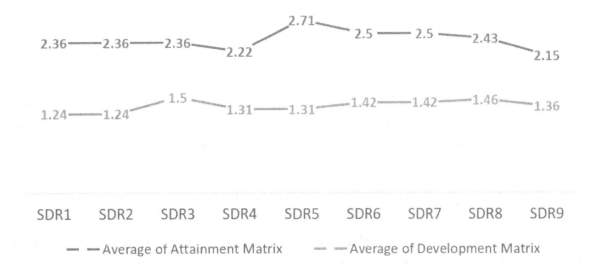

ANOVA Analysis on the Machine Learning Algorithm

For the given study, the NULL hypothesis proposed is

H_0: There is a no significant difference between the SDRs of Average Attainment Matrix and Average of Development Matrix.

H_A: There is significant difference between the SDRs of Average Attainment Matrix and Average of Development Matrix.

As shown in the (Table 23) below the Two-Way ANOVA without replication is carried out to get the conclusive evidence of the comparative result for the proposed machine learning algorithm.

Table 23. ANOVA: Two-Factor Without Replication for the proposed Machine Learning Algorithm

SUMMARY	Count	Sum	Average	Variance
Average of Attainment Matrix	9	23.01	2.556667	0.00175
Average of Development Process Matrix	9	21.59	2.398889	0.027086
SDR1	2	4.94	2.47	0.0242
SDR2	2	4.87	2.435	0.01125
SDR3	2	4.94	2.47	0.0242
SDR4	2	4.8	2.4	0.0648
SDR5	2	5.27	2.635	0.01125
SDR6	2	5.1	2.55	0.005
SDR7	2	5.1	2.55	0.005
SDR8	2	4.93	2.465	0.00245
SDR9	2	4.65	2.325	0.06125

As shown in the (Table 23) the Average of Attainment Matrix for the proposed Machine Learning Algorithm is greater and with the sum of 5.27 and average of 2.635 the variance is 0.01125. Also, SDR5 is said to be poor.

Table 24. ANOVA for the proposed Machine Learning Algorithm

Source of Variation	SS	Df	MS	F	P-value	F crit
Rows	0.112022	1	0.112022	9.203104	0.016219	5.317655
Columns	0.133311	8	0.016664	1.36901	0.333705	3.438101
Error	0.097378	8	0.012172			
Total	0.342711	17				

As per the (Table 24) the F.critical values of the rows is less than the F value with P-value less than 0.05 which means there is no significant difference between SDRs and thus rejecting the NULL hypothesis .

As shown in the (Table 25) below the Two-Way ANOVA without replication is carried out to get the conclusive evidence of the comparative result for the proposed machine learning algorithm. As shown in the (Table 25) the Average of Attainment Matrix for the CNN Algorithm is greater and with the sum of 23 and average of 2.555556 the variance is 0.277778. Even here, SDR5 is said to be poor.

Table 25. ANOVA: Two-Factor Without Replication for the Convolution Neural Network Algorithm

SUMMARY	Count	Sum	Average	Variance
Average of Attainment Matrix	9	23	2.555556	0.277778
Average of Development Process Matrix	9	21.59	2.398889	0.027086
SDR1	2	5.36	2.68	0.2048
SDR2	2	5.36	2.68	0.2048
SDR3	2	4.36	2.18	0.0648
SDR4	2	4.22	2.11	0.0242
SDR5	2	4.71	2.355	0.25205
SDR6	2	5.5	2.75	0.125
SDR7	2	5.5	2.75	0.125
SDR8	2	5.43	2.715	0.16245
SDR9	2	4.15	2.075	0.01125

As per the (Table 26) the F.critical values of the rows here is greater than the F value with P-value greater than 0.05 which means there is a significant difference between SDRs, thus accepting the NULL hypothesis.

Table 26. ANOVA for the Convolution Neural Network Algorithm

Source of Variation	SS	df	MS	F	P-value	F crit
Rows	0.11045	1	0.11045	0.830529	0.388755	5.317655
Columns	1.375011	8	0.171876	1.292425	0.362728	3.438101
Error	1.0639	8	0.132988			
Total	2.549361	17				

As shown in the (Table 27) below the Two-Way ANOVA without replication is carried out to get the conclusive evidence of the comparative result for the proposed machine learning algorithm. As shown in the (Table 27) the Average of Attainment Matrix for the Naïve Bayes Algorithm is lesser than Average of Development Process Matrix, with the sum of 21.59 and average of 2.398889 the variance is 0.027086. Even here, SDR5 is said to be poor.

Table 27. ANOVA: Two-Factor Without Replication for Naïve Bayes Algorithm

SUMMARY	Count	Sum	Average	Variance
Average of Attainment Matrix	9	12.26	1.362222	0.008819
Average of Development Process Matrix	9	21.59	2.398889	0.027086
SDR1	2	3.6	1.8	0.6272
SDR2	2	3.6	1.8	0.6272
SDR3	2	3.86	1.93	0.3698
SDR4	2	3.53	1.765	0.41405
SDR5	2	4.02	2.01	0.98
SDR6	2	3.92	1.96	0.5832
SDR7	2	3.92	1.96	0.5832
SDR8	2	3.89	1.945	0.47045
SDR9	2	3.51	1.755	0.31205

As per the (Table 28) the F.critical values of the rows here is greater than the F value with P-value very greater than 0.05 which means there is a significant difference between SDRs, thus accepting the NULL hypothesis.

Table 28. ANOVA for Naïve Bayes Algorithm

Source of Variation	SS	df	MS	F	P-value	F crit
Rows	4.83605	1	4.83605	295.106	1.34E-07	5.317655
Columns	0.156144	8	0.019518	1.191033	0.405359	3.438101
Error	0.1311	8	0.016388			
Total	5.123294	17				

Summary of the Result

Table 29. Summary of the Result

Source of Variation	F	P-value	F crit	Hypothesis Accepted
Rows (between SDRs) – Proposed Algorithm	9.203104	0.016219	5.317655	Alternate Hypothesis
Rows (between SDRs) – CNN	0.830529	0.388755	5.317655	Null Hypothesis
Rows (between SDRs) – Naïve Bayes	295.106	1.34E-07	5.317655	Null Hypothesis

Hence with the results from (Table 24), (Table 26) and (Table 28) it is conclusive that the proposed algorithm is rejecting the NULL hypothesis and the other two algorithms CNN and Naïve Bayes algorithms used accept the NULL hypothesis. Hence, we choose the one with alternate hypothesis that is the proposed algorithm. (Table 29) summarizes the same. Also, by comparing the (Figure 4), (Figure 6) and (Figure

7) we can see that the comparative graphs between the SDRs of proposed algorithm, CNN and Naïve Bayes it is conclusive that there is no significant difference between SDRs for the proposed algorithm.

CONCLUSION

The goal of the book chapter is to find how the Artificial Intelligence plays an important role in business and society. In this article, the case study of Small and Medium Level Enterprise (SME) is taken as an example for carrying out the research, where the 2 projects are taken for study to find out how the standard software development process and the software development rules plays an important role in carrying out the task. To analyse and predict the results from these projects a machine learning algorithm was proposed. Along with this two other AI algorithms CNN and Naïve Bayes were used. These algorithms were used to compare the results obtained during the development process and the results attained from the AI algorithms have any significant difference or not. From the study it is found that the proposed ML algorithm has only minimal significant difference, whereas the other 2 algorithms showed major differences between the attained result and development process result. Thus, it can be easily said that the proposed ML algorithm is ideally used for the software development process and also with the analysis there is a need for the change for the 5th rule of Software Development Rules. Here we can infer with the right choice of AI approach we can improve the business prospects of a SME and thus providing benefit to the society involved in this cluster including the software developers, clients, investors, managers, users etc.

REFERENCES

Aulia, T. F., & Wijaya, D. R. (2020). Poverty level prediction based on E-commerce data using K-nearest neighbor and information-theoretical-based feature selection. *ICOIACT*, 2020, 28–33.

Breuker, D., & Matzner, M. (2016). Comprehensible predictive models for business processes. *Manag Inf Syst Q*.https://aisel.aisnet.org/misq/vol40/iss4/12

Budiharto W. (2021). Data science approach to stock prices forecasting in Indonesia during Covid-19 using Long Short-Term Memory (LSTM). *J Big Data*, 1–9.

Cho, S. (2021). Fault detection and diagnosis of a blade pitch system in a floating wind turbine based on Kalman flters and artifcial neural networks. *Renewable Energy*, 169, 1–13.

Dalzochio, J., & Kunst, R. (2020). Machine learning and reasoning for predictive maintenance in Industry 4.0: Current status and challenges. *Computers in Industry*.

Dogan, A., & Birant, D. (2021). Machine learning and data mining in manufacturing. *Expert Systems with Applications*, 166, 114060.

Faizan, M., & Zuhairi, M. F. (2020). *Challenges and use cases of process discovery in process mining* (Vol. 9). Int J Adv Trends Comput Sci Eng.

Gomez-Cravioto, D. A., & Diaz-Ramos, R. E. (2022). Supervised machine learning predictive analytics for alumni income. *Journal of Big Data*, 9(1), 1–31.

Gong, S., & Wu, X. (2020). Research on Fault Diagnosis Method of Photovoltaic Array Based on Random Forest Algorithm. *Chinese Control Conference CCC, IEEE.*,https://ieeexplore.ieee.org/document/9362559/

Hssayeni, M. D., & Chala, A. (2021). The forecast of COVID-19 spread risk at the county level. *Journal of Big Data*, 8, 1–16.

Lee, J. (2021). Migration from the traditional to the smart factory in the die-casting industry: Novel process data acquisition and fault detection based on artifcial neural network. *Journal of Materials Processing Technology*.

Liyew, C. M., & Melese, H. A. (2021). Machine learning techniques to predict daily rainfall amount. *Journal of Big Data*, 8(1), 1–11.

Pangestu, A., & Wijaya, D. R. (2020). *Wrapper feature selection for poverty level prediction based on E-commerce dataset, ICoDSA*. IEEE.

Truong, D. (2021). *Using causal machine learning for predicting the risk of flight delays in air transportation*. JATM.

Tsai, M. F., & Chu, Y. C. (2021). *Smart machinery monitoring system with reduced information transmission and fault prediction methods using industrial internet of things* (Vol. 9). MDPI AG. https://www.mdpi.com/2227-7390/9/1/3

Wijaya, D. R., & Paramita, N. L. P. S. P. (2020). *Estimating city-level poverty rate based on e-commerce data with machine learning*. ECR.

Zhang, C., & Hu, C. (2021). Research on the application of Decision Tree and Random Forest Algorithm in the main transformer fault evaluation. *JPCS*. https://doi.org/10.1088/1742-6596/1732/1/012086

Chapter 3
Industry 4.0 Technologies in a Developing Country:
The Case of Costa Rica

Giulio Ferrigno

Scuola Superiore Sant'Anna, Pisa, Italy

Valentina Cucino

Scuola Superiore Sant'Anna, Pisa, Italy & Lumsa University, Rome

ABSTRACT

Industry 4.0, the Fourth Industrial Revolution, has fundamentally transformed manufacturing by integrating advanced digital technologies like IoT, AI, big data, and the cloud, creating intelligent, interconnected environments. Developed nations have embraced this revolution to enhance efficiency and productivity. However, the adoption of Industry 4.0 is equally vital for developing countries. This study examines how Industry 4.0 can promote economic growth in developing nations, focusing on Costa Rica's successful implementation as a case study. Factors contributing to Costa Rica's success include a skilled workforce, infrastructure investment, and a conducive business environment. The analysis explores Costa Rica's Industry 4.0 readiness, highlighting government initiatives, key benefiting sectors, and preparedness factors. The findings inform policy recommendations for other emerging economies, underscoring Industry 4.0's potential to bridge development gaps and foster sustainable growth.

1. INTRODUCTION

Industry 4.0, otherwise known as the Fourth Industrial Revolution, is defined by the paradigm shift in the manufacturing sector (Eberl, 2021; Gebhardt et al., 2022; Lasi et al. 2014). It is characterized by integrating advanced digital technologies – such as the Internet of Things, Artificial Intelligence, Big data and Analytics, and the Cloud - into industrial processes, creating an intelligent and interconnected environment (Ferrigno, Del Sarto, Piccaluga, Baroncelli, 2023).

Existing literature has underscored that Industry 4.0 increases efficiency and productivity in many developed countries (Martinelli, Mina, & Moggi, 2021). Moreover, Industry 4.0 is revolutionizing manufacturing processes, technological innovations, and the overall industrial landscape of developed countries

DOI: 10.4018/979-8-3693-0683-3.ch003

(Dalenogare et al., 2018; Ferrigno, Del Sarto, Piccaluga, Baroncelli, 2023). However, scholarly works have not investigated how Industry 4.0 can be effectively implemented in developing countries. With the exception of few studies (i.e., Cucino & Ferrigno, 2023; Yüksel, 2020), we lack a comprehensive overview of Industry 4.0 in developing countries. Understanding this issue is particularly important. In fact, these countries, often characterized by underdeveloped industrial sectors and lower HDI, must strive to develop the necessary infrastructure and skills required to close the gap between themselves and developed nations (Bag et al., 2021). Additionally, underdeveloped countries must work to seize the opportunities offered by Industry 4.0 while mitigating the threats posed by these technologies to achieve sustainable growth and development of their economies (Ferrigno, Crupi, Di Minin, & Ritala, 2023). Therefore, this new era of technological innovation presents opportunities and difficulties for developing countries that require an adequate examination (Cucino, Dagnino, Ferrigno, Kaplan, Ritala, Higgins, & Liang, 2024). As such, in this book chapter we aim to examine the following research question: *"how Industry 4.0 technologies can be effectively adopted and implemented to promote economic growth of developing countries?"*

To tackle this research question, we firstly review what are the most important enabling technologies that characterize Industry 4.0 (Ferrigno, Del Sarto, Piccaluga, & Baroncelli, 2023; Martinelli, Mina, & Moggi, 2021). After providing this understanding, we develop the idea that these Industry 4.0 technologies can be particularly important also in developing countries. We also investigate this idea empirically by examining the case of Costa Rica, a paradigmatic example of a developing country that has effectively implemented Industry 4.0 technologies to promote economic growth and position itself as a leader. The choice of studying the adoption of Industry 4.0 in a developing country such as Costa Rica can be justified for many reasons. Studying how a developing economy can efficiently embrace the power of Industry 4.0 technologies offers valuable insight into the obstacles and opportunities faced by such nations. Nevertheless, Costa Rica stands out as a notable success story since it has many factors that have led to its success, including its highly skilled workforce, investment in infrastructure, and favorable business environment.

In particular, we begin with an overview of Costa Rica's current state of Industry 4.0 adoption, highlighting government initiatives, public and private partnerships, and key sectors benefiting from the adoption of enabling technologies. In addition, we examine Costa Rica's readiness for these technologies, considering factors such as skills and education, infrastructure, and data privacy and cybersecurity. Lastly, we also analyze Costa Rica's standing based on the Government AI Readiness Index and the Global Competitiveness Report.

Drawing on the findings that will emerge from this exploratory analysis, this book chapter will encompass numerous objectives it seeks to achieve. Firstly, it offers a timely evaluation of Industry 4.0 adoption in Costa Rica, including its readiness to adopt these technologies (Treviño-Elizondo, & García-Reyes, 2020). Secondly, it identifies the key industries that benefit from Industry 4.0 era and the impact on the economic development of the country (Raj et al., 2021). Additionally, it analyzes the implications for developing nations in terms of competitiveness, job creation, and economic expansion. Lastly, based on the findings provided by this analysis, this book chapter provides several policy recommendations to leverage the power of Industry 4.0 in other emerging countries.

The book chapter will be structured as it follows. In Section 1, we provide an overview of Industry 4.0 and its enabling technologies. Additionally, we analyze the country's current economic state and emphasizes the importance of this new era for developing nations. In Section 2 we review the relevant literature, examining Costa Rica's progress in embracing the power of Industry 4.0. Nevertheless, we explore the key industries that benefit from Industry 4.0 technologies as well as the readiness of Costa Rica to leverage the opportunities of this new era of technological change. In Section 3, we offer a discussion of findings by examining opportunities and threats. Lastly, in Section 4, we discuss the implications of the book chapter as well as we propose some policy recommendations to further enhance Costa Rica's performance.

2. THEORETICAL BACKGROUND

This section provides a theoretical background on Industry 4.0 and its enabling technologies. Industry 4.0 has been shaped by the three precedent revolutions, each of which has contributed to this new era (Martinelli, Mina, & Moggi, 2021).

2.1. An overview of Industry 4.0 Technologies

The term Industry 4.0. originated in Germany at the Hannover Fair in 2011 (Kalnoskas, 2017). Since the concept was introduced, Industry 4.0 in Germany has become a widely discussed topic. Germany has positioned itself as a leader in the manufacturing industry and is considered one of the most influential countries in automotive manufacturing (Rojko, 2017). The German government has also played a key role in the development of smart manufacturing, they launched a program, "Industrie 4.0," to integrate digital technologies and digitalize manufacturing processes (Klitou, Conrads, Rasmussen, Probst, & Pedersen, 2017). Nevertheless, the state has sponsored numerous research programs to position the country as a leader in the industry (Huda, 2023).

Industry 4.0. is creating a bridge between the physical and digital worlds (Ferrigno, Del Sarto, Piccaluga, Baroncelli, 2023), differently from what is happening in the context of Industry 5.0 (Celenta, Cucino, Feola, & Parente, 2024). It is characterized by massive amounts of data, increased connectivity between systems, and rapid growth of computing power (I-Scoop, 2023). Industry 4.0 has built upon previous advancements and harnessed the power of digital technologies to create a smarter, more interconnected world (Martinelli, Mina, & Moggi, 2021).

Existing studies have grouped Industry 4.0's technologies into nine enabling technologies: Advanced Manufacturing solutions, Additive manufacturing, Augmented Reality, Simulation, Horizontal and Vertical Integration, Industrial Internet, Cloud Computing, Big Data and Analytics, and Cybersecurity (Ferrigno, Del Sarto, Piccaluga, Baroncelli, 2023; Martinelli, Mina, & Moggi, 2021). These nine transformative technologies are reshaping industries and presenting remarkable opportunities for business model innovation (Ferrigno, Del Sarto, Piccaluga, Baroncelli, 2023). In this new era of digital transformation, understanding the potential of these technologies can allow organizations to achieve organizational efficiency and thrive in today's dynamic environment (Erboz, 2017). Below we briefly discuss them.

Advanced manufacturing solutions lie at the forefront of Industry 4.0. These solutions apply cutting-edge technologies for product improvement, product development, and production tasks that build on product quality (Huang et al., 2013). It includes real-time monitoring of operations, automation, and robotics. Robots are designed to be self-sufficient and collaborate with humans rather than just work as tools (Ministero delle Imprese, 2016).

Additive manufacturing, otherwise referred to as 3D printing, is a process where three-dimensional objects are built by layering materials (Kozolanka, 2018). In contrast to traditional manufacturing, this process adds different materials, e.g., composite material, resin, and plastic, in a controlled manner, allowing for numerous advantages such as flexibility of design, complex shapes, and the ability to quickly bring prototypes to life (Shahrubudin, Lee, & Ramlan, 2019).

Augmented Reality is a technology that combines the real world with computer-generated content, enhancing the user's interaction with their surroundings (Erboz, 2017). In contrast to Virtual Reality, which is completely virtual, augmented reality overlaps the physical world with the digital one. Augmented Reality can be applied to different industries and provide numerous advantages. For instance, it minimizes errors and improves accuracy since it provides a real-time guide to workers (Moore, 2019).

Simulation, on the other hand, creates models to recreate real-world situations that enable virtual testing (Hu et al., 2023). It allows users to predict how events will unfold and assess the impact of changes in design before creating the actual product. Industries can leverage simulation by predicting outcomes and ensuring that models are efficient before bringing to life design (NRTC Alabama, 2022).

Horizontal and Vertical Integration play a pivotal role in Industry 4.0, as it allows for manufacturing processes to be seamlessly connected within the value chain (McLaughlin, 2022). Horizontal Integration involves different processes or systems at the same level of the industry; on the other hand, Vertical Integration focuses on different stages within the same value chain (Martinelli, Mina, & Moggi, 2021). Both processes are essential as they improve efficiency within the supply chain and enable communication and coordination between different stakeholders (McLaughlin, 2022).

The industrial Internet (IioT), a subcategory of the Internet of Things (IoT), consists of interconnected equipment that collects and processes data (Del Sarto et al., 2022). By analyzing the data, these devices can communicate with each other and make informed decisions about operations (Erboz, 2017). The Industrial Internet is becoming an essential part of many industries, e.g., healthcare, agriculture, and even retailing sectors, as it allows these to achieve operational agility and enhance operational efficiency (Varistor Technologies, 2019).

Cloud computing, another key technology in Industry 4.0, is composed of servers connected to the internet and accessed via data centers (Ferrigno, Del Sarto, Piccaluga, Baroncelli, 2023). Users and different industries can leverage the cloud since instead of accessing data locally, they can access files on demand (Yang et al., 2017). The cloud provides numerous benefits as it allows for easy accessibility, the process of large volumes of data, and collaboration among different users at a relatively low cost (Red Reply, 2018).

In today's modern world, data is growing at an ever-increasing rate. Around 328.77 million terabytes are created daily (Duarte, 2023). In the face of immense volumes of data being generated by industries, leveraging Big Data and Analytics has become paramount for achieving success (Ferrigno, Del Sarto, Piccaluga, Baroncelli, 2023). Data can come from numerous sources, e.g., social media, sensors, and associated equipment, and it can be structured or unstructured (Del Vecchio et al., 2018). On the other hand, Analytics processes and interprets valuable data to make decisions and gain valuable insights (Martinelli, Mina, & Moggi, 2021).

Finally, it is important to understand the importance *Cyber Security* as one of the enabling technologies of Industry 4.0 (Kaur & Ramkumar, 2022). As cyberattacks become increasingly frequent and industrial systems grow more complex, industries must integrate cybersecurity measures (Tonge et al., 2013). Cybersecurity measures allow companies from all sectors to maintain privacy, safeguard their infrastructure, protect intellectual property, and mitigate financial losses (Tonge et al., 2013). Therefore, by prioritizing data protection, industries can mitigate risks and ensure operational efficiency (Erboz, 2017).

2.2. Industry 4.0 Technologies in Developing Countries

There are numerous interpretations of what constitutes a developing country; however, the most common consensus is that a nation can be considered developing if it has a lower standard of living in comparison to others (Asghar et al., 2020). A developing country is typically dependent on the agricultural industry as a primary economic source and is underdeveloped in the industrial sector (Kuepper, 2022). Most developing countries have a lower per capita income, lower human development index (HDI), and poor infrastructures.

In this era of technological innovation, developing countries must seize the opportunities presented by this wave of change. Since the first Industrial Revolution, each wave of technological change has been marked by creating increased inequalities between countries (Martinelli, Mina, & Moggi, 2021). Successful development has been typically associated with a shift from low value-added activities, e.g., agriculture, towards higher value-added activities, e.g., industry and services (Erboz, 2017). However, lower-income countries have traditionally experienced a shift from agricultural activities to service activities, neglecting industrialization in some cases. Nevertheless, since the 1990s, foreign direct investment trends have been rapidly increasing. Multinational companies from developed nations have been investing in developing countries given decreased communication expenses and lower labor costs (United Nations, 2022). Today, there are significant gaps in productivity between developed and developing nations. Many developing countries are still predominantly agriculturally based and have informal economies, all of which are indications of unproductivity (IMF Press Center, 2021).

In this book chapter we argue that technological advancements brought by Industry 4.0 can offer developing countries opportunities and threats to diversify their economies. For instance, by embracing Industry 4.0 technologies, developing countries can enjoy numerous advantages such as increasing productivity, promoting economic growth, creating job opportunities, and adopting sustainable practices. Moreover, when replacing traditional manufacturing with smart manufacturing, increased productivity can be achieved. Smart factories can reduce downtime, eliminate waste, and optimize processes (Ferrigno, Del Sarto, Piccaluga, Baroncelli, 2023). As a result, industries in developing countries can achieve higher outputs and meet the demands of markets. On the other hand, underdeveloped nations can benefit from economic growth resulting from faster development in the manufacturing sector. This, in turn, can lead to demand for new jobs and traditional jobs might disappear. Nevertheless, the digitalization of manufacturing processes can enable developing industries to adopt more sustainable practices. For instance, it can enable resource efficiency and conservation, and minimize the use of energy which can allow industries to reduce their carbon footprint (United Nations, 2022).

Despite underdeveloped countries can take advantage of many opportunities by leveraging Industry 4.0 technologies, these advancements are not without risks. For instance, governments must address several underlying issues such as underdeveloped infrastructure, unskilled workers, preparedness of industries, and support institutions (Raj et al., 2020). In addition, the digitalization of industries poses threats such as job displacement, digital divide, and loss of competitive advantage (Anshari et al., 2022). Moreover, a big concern arising from implementing Industry 4.0 technologies is the loss of jobs primarily in developing countries, which have more routine jobs and unskilled workers (Asghar et al., 2020). Most developing economies tend to lack two important drivers: high-technology sectors and high-skilled jobs. Given this, it is harder for developing nations to diffuse and implement technologies, which further leads to inequalities between countries (Raj et al., 2020). This can impact developing economies as it could minimize investment from thriving economies that were originally incentivized by cheap labor (United Nations, 2022).

As a net result, Industry 4.0 technologies can offer both opportunities and challenges to developing countries (Ferrigno, Del Sarto, Piccaluga, Baroncelli, 2023; Raj et al., 2020). However, existing studies have fallen short to discuss how these technologies can be effectively implemented in these countries. In this book chapter, we aim to understand this issue by conducting an exploratory analysis of the usage of Industry 4.0 technologies in Costa Rica.

3. METHODOLOGY: THE CASE OF COSTA RICA

3.1. Research Design

To empirically examine how Industry 4.0 technologies can be effectively implemented in a developing country, we decided to use real cases (Eisenhardt, 1989; Siggelkow, 2007). In this perspective, we conducted a thorough examination of an individual case, as advocated by Eisenhardt and Graebner (2007) and Siggelkow (2007). This decision is motivated by several factors. Firstly, scrutinizing a solitary case serves as a distinctive and crucial instance for assessing a well-defined theory, as emphasized by Yin (2009). Secondly, given the limited theoretical understanding of Industry 4.0 technologies in developin countries, an inductive research approach that allows theory to emerge from the data proves to be a valuable initial approach (Siggelkow, 2007). Thirdly, the researchers have gained access to a situation that was previously beyond the purview of scientific observation, aligning with Yin's rationale (2009). Therefore, it appears that a single case study can be viewed as an illuminating example for delving into the effective usage of Industry 4.0 in developing countries.

3.2. Theoretical Sampling

The selection of the case is based on the basic principles of theoretical sampling (Pettigrew, 1990). Several reasons have led us to study the case of Costa Rica. First, Costa Rica is a paradigmatic example of developing country that has effectively implemented Industry 4.0 technologies. It is a small nation located at the heart of Central America. While the country only accounts for 0.03% of the Earth's surface, it contains nearly 6% of the planet's biodiversity, offering remarkable potential for economic development (MINAE, 2018). It abolished its army nearly seven decades ago and has since relieved the country of military expenditures (Hernandez, 2022). Nevertheless, Costa Rica has a literacy rate of 98%, given the high government expenditure on education (UNESCO, 2021). Over the years, the economy has had significant growth despite the recent global challenges. Overall, Costa Rica's potential for economic growth, along with its high educational investment, environmental preservation, and democratic rule, position the nation as a pioneer among Latin American countries.

Second, the economy of Costa Rica thrives from a balanced framework of the primary, secondary, and tertiary sectors. The primary sector is predominantly composed of agriculture, fishing, forestry, and livestock. The agricultural industry makes up around 70% of the sector and it is composed mainly of bananas, pineapple, and coffee, respectively. On the other hand, livestock makes up about 20% of the primary sector, with cow milk production being the strongest activity. Nevertheless, fishing accounts for 2% of the sector and forestry for 3% (Oficina Económica y Comercial de España en Panamá, 2021). Despite Costa Rica not being considered an industrialized country, the secondary sector made up 19.3% of the country's GDP in 2020, positioning the country well above other Latin American regions (see Figure 1). The secondary sector is primarily focused on food production; however, due to the newly established Free Economic Zones, high-tech industries have experienced significant growth (Oficina Económica y Comercial de España en Panamá, 2021). Medical equipment such as orthopedic devices and surgical instruments make up the country's biggest export (Comercio Exterior, 2022). Since 2014, when Intel closed its biggest manufacturing plant, the country has experienced a shift from the manufacturing of electric components towards a focus on the service sector (Murillo, 2014).

Figure 1. Distribution of GDP by Sectors of Activity (%)

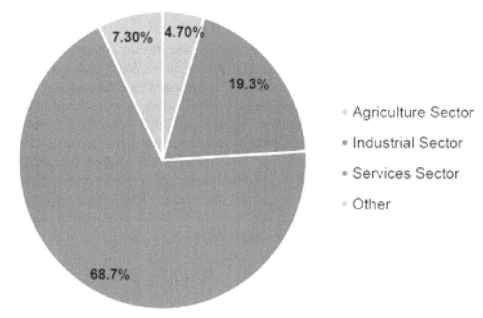

Source: Authors' elaboration from Oficina Económica y Comercial de España en Panamá (2011)

The service, or tertiary sector, represented 68.7% of Costa Rica's GDP in 2020, making it the most important for the economy (see Figure 1) (Oficina Económica y Comercial de España en Panamá, 2021). The service industry is primarily composed of education, health, commercial, and financial activities. However, tourism is one of the economy's most important drivers (EFE, 2018). In 2020, revenues from the tourism sector were highly impacted due to lockdowns happening across the globe.

Third, Costa Rica has become a very favorable destination for foreign investments. Its strategic location between the Pacific Ocean and the Caribbean Sea, political stability, high labor productivity, skilled workforce, and Free Trade Zones have made it a sought-out investment destination in Central America (Cordero & Paus, 2008). According to the latest data published by COMEX, the Foreign Direct Investment (FDI) in Costa Rica, increased by 16% in 2019 with an investment of $2,598 million. Additionally, Costa Rica's main partner and investor is the United States of America, making it highly dependent on its economic welfare. This affiliation represents 40% of Costa Rica's exports, 40% of its imports, 75% of its stock investments, and 40% of its tourists Nevertheless, other important investors are Colombia, Mexico, and Spain. In addition, the manufacturing sector has been experiencing the most significant investments, with up to $1,503 million in 2018 (Oficina Económica y Comercial de España en Panamá, 2021).

In conclusion, Costa Rica's economy shows remarkable potential for development and prosperity. Its unique features distinguish the nation from Latin American countries and place it as an attractive investment for investors. Nevertheless, the country must develop strict economic policies to address its fiscal deficit, growing public debt, and exorbitant public spending (Cerdas, 2023). Despite facing economic challenges during recent years, the country remains optimistic about economic stability over the next years.

4. FINDINGS

4.1. A Snapshot of Industry 4.0 Adoption in Costa Rica

As technological changes are unfolding, countries around the globe are embracing the transformative power of digital technologies to promote economic growth and competitiveness. Costa Rica, as a developing nation, has recognized the potential of Industry 4.0 and the implications it has for various sectors of the economy. The government has played an essential role as it has implemented numerous programs, policies, and initiatives to facilitate the adoption of these technologies. Moreover, public and private partnerships have served as a catalyst for the promotion of Industry 4.0 adoption in the country. The collaboration between the government, industry, and academia is essential to maintain the country as a regional benchmark in innovation (Jiménez, 2019).

Costa Rica's government is committed to harnessing the opportunities offered by the Fourth Industrial Revolution by promoting innovation and digital transformation in different sectors of the economy. The state has developed initiatives supporting the adoption of these revolutionary technologies in collaboration with public entities. For instance, in 2018, the government alongside the Ministry of Science, Technology, and Telecommunications developed a 5-year strategy, known as the Digital Transformation Strategy towards Costa Rica of the Bicentennial 4.0, intending to accelerate the competitiveness and productivity of industries through inclusive socio-economic growth. Ultimately, the goal of this strategy is to use transformative technologies to enhance the government-citizen relationship, improve quality of life, and ensure businesses are ready to transition to Industry 4.0 (MICITT, 2022). Nevertheless, the plan is composed of six strategic pillars, as illustrated in Figure 2.

Figure 2. Lines of Action for Costa Rica's Digital Transformation Towards the Bicentennial 4.0

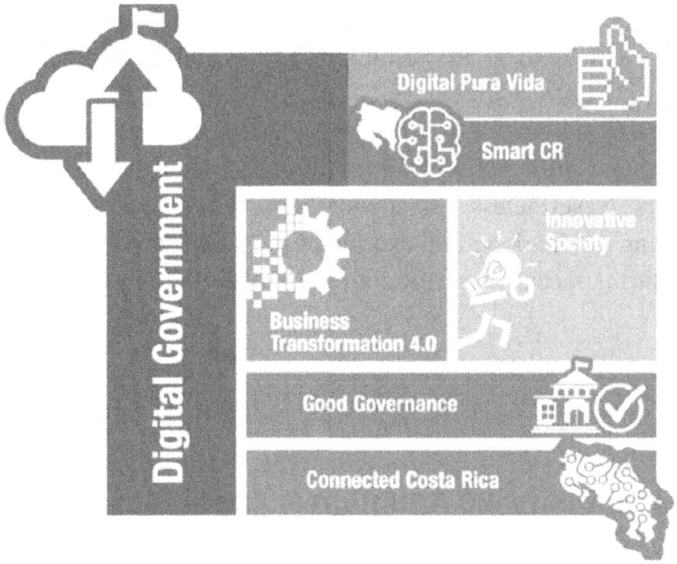

Source: MICITT (2022)

The first pillar, or *Digital Pura Vida*, aims to implement digital technologies in government institutions to efficiently respond to the needs of citizens transparently and inclusively. Pura Vida Digital has four main objectives: develop digital services for citizens' health, create a system of smart transportation, implement a digital governmental portal, and digitalize the platform of municipal services. The second pillar, *Smart CR*, aims to apply transformative technologies to make intelligent decisions in public institutions. It aims to enact a National Code for digital technologies, create a digital profile for each citizen, design an interconnected platform for public services, and develop a strategy for the state's cybersecurity. Additionally, the third pillar, *Business Transformation 4.0*, is directed toward industries; it aims to develop the necessary mechanisms to implement transformative technologies and make it easier for businesses to employ them to increase productivity. This pillar also has four strategies: develop digital capabilities and culture for Industry 4.0, transform the agricultural sector, implement digital technologies for tourism, and strengthen digital-based entrepreneurship. The fourth pillar, *Innovative Society* is focused on empowering Costa Rican citizens by promoting innovation and the use of the digital technologies of Industry 4.0. This pillar focuses on achieving three goals: strengthen the existing mechanisms to create an efficient environment that promotes collaboration, enhance the skills and abilities of citizens to promote digital literacy, and develop the capabilities required for the jobs and businesses of the future. Nevertheless, the fifth pillar, known as *Good Governance*, seeks to ensure good governance through community involvement and government transparency. Its goals are to promote the use of data analysis to make informed decisions and mitigate risks, establish an Open State that allows for digital citizen involvement, implement regulations to protect data, and revise laws and regulations to ensure an updated legal framework with new technological advancements. Lastly, the sixth pillar, Connected Costa Rica, focuses on developing a telecommunications infrastructure that ensures inclusivity and access. To achieve this, this pillar aims to improve internet access throughout the entire country, develop a fifth-generation (5G) network infrastructure that will enhance data transmission, create smart regions that maximize the use of technologies, and finally provide the education sector with broadband to improve learning and teaching (MICITT, 2022).

On the other hand, Costa Rica's government has set in place numerous tax incentives to encourage and persuade the implementation of Industry 4.0 technologies across all industries. For instance, the Law for the Promotion of Scientific and Technological Development, initially enacted in 1990 but recently updated in 2021, has been established to promote scientific research and technological development among private and public institutions. This law encompasses a range of objectives; for instance, technology-based companies in Costa Rica are granted a deduction from their income tax during the first years for investments in technological infrastructure, technical training, and research and development projects. In addition, the law states that the government must create programs and offer scholarships to encourage high-achieving students to pursue STEM degrees in collaboration with the National Council for Scientific and Technological Research (CONICIT) and the National Council of Rectors (CONARE). Nevertheless, the Ministry of Science and Technology must partner with the Incentives Commission every year to provide financing for new or established companies seeking technological innovations. Furthermore, the law declares that the state must offer all types of incentives to encourage the creation of technology parks in collaboration with private companies and institutions of higher education. These parks will aim to foster the growth of technology-based companies to improve and modernize innovation in the country (Asamblea Legislativa, 2021).

The creation of Free Trade Zones in Costa Rica by the government has served as a strategic initiative to attract technology-driven foreign direct investment (FDI) and stimulate economic growth (Chaves, Gamboa, Hernández, & Sánchez, 2006). According to law No. 7210, the Law of Free Trade Zone Regime, the State will offer a series of incentives and benefits to companies investing in the country, subject to a series of obligations and regulations (Asamblea Legislativa, 2022). For instance, companies that operate under the regime will be able to benefit from tax exemption on purchases for goods necessary for the operation of the company, exception on remittance taxes, exemption of all profits-related taxes or any other taxes based on gross or net profits, exemption on taxes for municipal patents for 10 years, and many other immunities (Esencial Costa Rica; Procomer, 2022).

Free Trade Zones in Costa Rica offer numerous advantages, especially in the context of embracing Industry 4.0 technologies. Companies established in these regimes benefit from contributions that go beyond economic means. Free Trade Zones attract foreign investment, provide access to new markets, introduce cutting-edge production technologies, improve working practices, and boost environmental and safety standards. Nevertheless, these have had an immense impact on job creation around the country. For instance, they have created around 200,000 job positions, both direct and indirect. These markets have also attracted the presence of industry-leading companies such as Intel, Hospira, and Amazon, which have helped position Costa Rica as a center for investment in advanced manufacturing and technology. As a result of Free Trade Zones, Costa Rica has been able to not only promote economic development but also drive the country toward becoming a technologically driven and advanced manufacturer (Artavia, 2021).

In Costa Rica, public and private partnerships have played a crucial role in driving the adoption of Industry 4.0's transformative technologies. These relationships emphasize the importance of collaboration between the public and private sectors to develop an environment that fosters technical advancement and economic expansion. One prominent example is the collaboration between the Costa Rican Investment Promotion Agency (CINDE) and the government. CINDE, a private and non-profit institution, oversees attracting and guiding direct foreign investment in industries such as health, smart manufacturing, and knowledge-intensive services (Soto, 2023). The agency partnered alongside the Ministry of Science, Technology, and Telecommunication (MICITT) to promote education in high-tech industries. These two organizations developed a scholarship program to help citizens gain the skills and knowledge required to succeed in the digital age by providing training and certification in fields linked to information and communication technologies (ICTs). By providing scholarships, this initiative aims to enable the country's workforce to acquire the essential capabilities needed to successfully integrate Costa Rica into the Fourth Industrial Revolution (La Rebública, 2020).

In addition to the government's efforts, Costa Rica has made significant progress in adopting the Internet of Things (IoT) as a lever for the development of the economy. According to a study conducted by Deloitte, Costa Rica is ranked second among Latin America for its degree of IoT adoption in the business sector (Deloitte, 2018). The study analyzed six different factors, as evidenced in Figure 3, that reflected the country's readiness to implement IoT solutions. The report's findings come as no surprise, given that Costa Rica possesses some of the most advanced ITC infrastructures, benefits from political stability, and has advanced legislation concerning data protection. Furthermore, the IoT sector is essential for the country's economy, as an estimated 46% of companies specializing in Industry 4.0 in Costa Rica also focus on IoT offerings (PROCOMER, 2020).

Figure 3. Degree of IoT Adoption and Country Scores in the Index of Interest

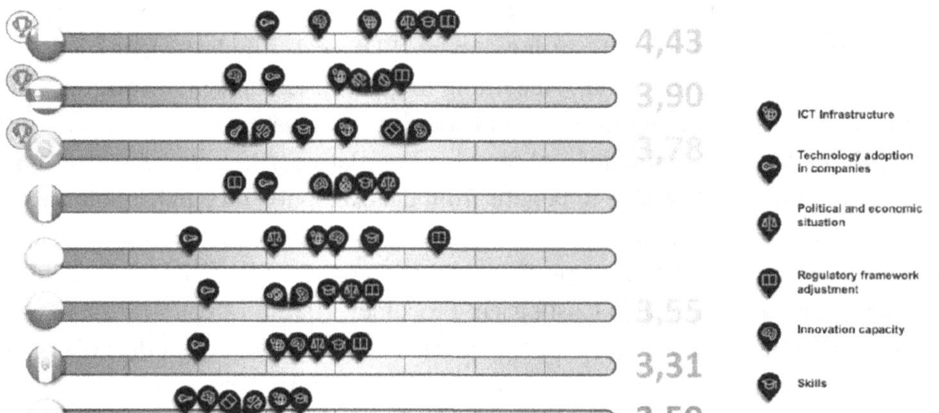

Source: Deloitte (2018)

4.2. Key Industries That Benefit From Industry 4.0 Technologies in Costa Rica

Costa Rica has a range of industries that stand to benefit from the application of Industry 4.0 technologies. As the country seeks to promote economic growth and strengthen its position among developing countries, it is crucial to identify the sectors that can leverage the application of these advanced technologies.

The *agriculture sector* is gradually embracing the enabling technologies of Industry 4.0 to enhance productivity, increase efficiency, and boost production. For instance, precision agriculture techniques are being implemented for the harvest of pineapples, which holds significant importance since Costa Rica stands as the biggest exporter of pineapple in the global market[1]. Precision agriculture integrates agricultural practices with technology to collect and interpret data, enabling the prediction and informed decision-making required to increase. Additionally, it uses drones, sensors, satellites, and cameras to optimize the use of resources. For instance, precision agriculture assists farmers in making informed decisions about when and how much fertilizers are required, irrigation schedules, and pest control methods. Furthermore, this technique acts as an early warning system that alerts farmers of potential health issues with crops and provides timely solutions (Morales, 2022). Additionally, the current shipping container crisis, which has risen the price of containers substantially, along with the rising costs of fertilizers and carton boxes has made it essential that farmers optimize resources to minimize costs and reach international markets (Moral, 2022). By combining real-time data and advanced technologies, this technique is empowering Costa Rican farmers to improve agricultural efficiency. The agriculture sector is also embracing the use of artificial intelligence to monitor livestock. Farmers are using smart artificial intelligence collars, which have a cost ranging from €125,000 to €175,000, to observe the health of cows, pigs, and other animals. These collars help detect early health problems with livestock as well as digestion patterns. Nevertheless, they are particularly important for milk production, as they track data and automatically remove milking cups to prevent excessive milking. However, the adoption of these collars has created a divide between farmers who have access to these technologies and those who do not due to cost barriers. To address this challenge and help smaller-scale farmers, the Ministry of Agriculture and Livestock, in collaboration with the government, is developing programs, granting subsidies, and providing other incentives to promote the use of these technologies and enhance livestock production (Siles, 2022).

The *medicine and healthcare sector* in Costa Rica is also a key industry that benefits from Industry 4.0 technologies as it has revolutionized medical procedures and improved patient care. Three-Dimensional printing, for example, has been increasingly used in the medical field. For example, the National Institute of Learning (INA) in collaboration with the Costa Rican Social Security Fund (CCSS) is currently working on the development of a 3D-printed cranial prosthesis. The initial phase focuses on creating a prosthesis for 35 patients with cranial defects at Hospital Mexico. These prostheses are created using a medical polymer that is compatible with human cells, which ensures compatibility with the patient and minimizes the risks of side effects (Castro, 2022). On the other hand, numerous hospitals in Costa Rica have witnessed a surge in robotic assistance. In 2021 Costa Rica became the first Central American country to use the assistance of a robot in a surgical procedure. The robot ROSA (Robotic Surgical Assistant) was used to assist orthopedic surgeons during a knee replacement by collecting data before and throughout the surgery. It provided the surgeons with anatomical details, allowing for the doctors to optimize the implant adjustment and resulting in a better patient outcome. Overall, both artificial intelligence and 3D printing technologies have made significant contributions to improving patient care in Costa Rica[2].

The *manufacturing sector* has also benefited from the advancements brought about by Industry 4.0 technologies. Costa Rica is recognized by the World Economic Forum as a key leader in Latin America for its production process, as it has been able to leverage advanced technologies for manufacturing processes. With a well-established intelligent manufacturing Industry, Costa Rica operates at a high level of complexity, offering a diverse range of products, and contributing to the country's dynamic economic growth (Manufactura Inteligente, 2023).

Numerous renowned international companies have established their manufacturing plants in Costa Rica to leverage the educated workforce, incentives from Free Trade Zones, and strategic location. One example is Panduit Costa Rica, which harnesses the power of advanced analytics to interpret the data collected from its processes to create predictive models and enable the company to make efficient decisions. In addition, another significant player in the manufacturing sector is Boston Scientific, the largest medical equipment company in Costa Rica. The company utilizes the Internet of Things to track and trace products throughout its manufacturing processes to ensure quality control and compliance with standards (Comex, 2019). Nevertheless, other important companies include Philips, Align Technologies, Baxter Healthcare, and Pfizer. By implementing digitalization, automation, data analytics, and other important technologies, these companies have enhanced operational effectiveness, product quality, and overall competitiveness (Manufactura Inteligente, 2023).

4.3. Costa Rica's Readiness for Industry 4.0 Technologies

In the era of Industry 4.0, the industrial environment has experienced a rapid shift driven by advanced technologies. Developing nations have been compelled to join the wave of technological change to effectively embrace these innovations. To better understand Costa Rica's readiness to adopt Industry 4.0 technologies, in this subsection we analyze the country's education, infrastructure, and data privacy and cybersecurity. In addition, we consider Costa Rica's global perspective, as reflected by the Government AI Readiness Index and the Global Competitiveness Report. These dimensions will provide a comprehensive understanding of the country's strengths, weaknesses, and prospects in adopting the enabling technologies of this new era.

The successful adoption of Industry 4.0 technologies in Costa Rica requires an educated workforce that possesses digital and technical skills. Costa Rica has positioned itself as a leader in Latin America for its human talent, which has been a key factor in attracting foreign investors[3]. According to the World Bank, 6.7% of the nation's GDP was allocated to education in 2020, demonstrating the government's commitment to providing its citizens with accessible and high-quality education required for the development of digital competencies[4].

Public and private partnerships have been key drivers to promote education and support digital skill development. For instance, the Ministry of Education collaborated with the Quirós Tanzi Foundation to create the project "Conectándonos," which aims to offer a technological education program to students from public schools. The main objective of this project is to provide each student with a laptop to use both at home and at school, thereby offering better opportunities for digital social inclusion, as evidenced in recent studies addressing the impact of technology for society (Cucino, Lungu, De Rosis, & Piccaluga, 2023). The project aims to ensure that their learning process is comprehensive by leveraging the potential of technologies in various educational settings (Muñoz, 2014).

On the other hand, there have also been joint efforts between private and public institutions to offer educational opportunities to individuals of all ages, including adults who can benefit from acquiring new skills for their jobs. For instance, Coursera, a leading education platform, collaborated with the Ministry of Labor, the Ministry of Foreign Affairs, and CINDE to launch a free program to train 50,000 people to provide the technical abilities required for Industry 4.0 (Coursera, 2020). The program provides different study plans that focus on numerous skills such as programming, cybersecurity, blockchain, artificial intelligence, data science, and many more[5].

While Costa Rica has showcased many strengths in its education system, it is still faced with the persistent digital divide among its population. The term "digital divide" is used to describe the gap that exists between individuals and communities that have access to Information and Communication Technologies (ICTs) and those who do not, as well as between those who have access but lack the knowledge or skills to effectively use them (Ministerio de Ciencias, Tecnología y Telecomunicaciones, 2019). The problem is persistently more dominant in rural areas. For instance, according to a study conducted by the Telecommunications Directorate, the regions in the center, which are the most highly populated and developed, experienced lower rates of digital divide compared to the border and coastal areas (Muñoz, 2014).

To better understand Costa Rica's readiness for Industry 4.0 technologies, it is essential to examine the country's infrastructure. The development of Costa Rica's digital infrastructure has advanced significantly. According to a study conducted by the Superintendence of Telecommunications (SUETEL), the country has experienced notable growth in fiber optic internet, with an expansion rate of 183% from 2018 to 2020[6].In addition, Costa Rica is ranked among the top five countries in Latin America with the best-fixed broadband internet connection, with an average download speed of 51.85 Megabits per second (Mbps) (Castro, 2022). Nevertheless, Costa Rica is leading the market among Central American countries with its data centers. Currently, the nation has over 14 certified data centers. The ICE Data Center, for example, stands out as one of the most robust facilities in the country. This development is boosting access to cloud services and providing a competitive advantage to Costa Rica (Castro, 2018).

Although the country has made significant improvements in its networking and data transmission, there are still areas for improvement. A study conducted by Uswitch highlighted the average cost of broadband per month in OCDE countries, in which Costa Rica ranked as the second least affordable country. The study exposed an average monthly cost of 42.32€, accounting for 4.72% of the average income (Hiley, 2022). In addition, there are concerns regarding Costa Rica's adoption of 5G technology, as its implementation has been delayed and is now expected to be installed as late as 2024[7].

Moreover, to gain insight into the country's readiness for Industry 4.0 technologies, cybersecurity, and data privacy policies should be studied. Overall, in comparison to other Latin American countries, Costa Rica has implemented robust regulations for data protection (Deloitte, 2018). Law No. 8968, the Law on Personal Data Protection, establishes the main regulatory foundation for personal data protection in Costa Rica (OECD, 2020). This law is applied to both private and public entities and is regulated by the Data Protection Agency of Inhabitants (PRODHAB). The law regulates organizations that collect and process personal data and ensures that they implement the necessary security measures to obtain and get consent from individuals for data processing purposes (Asamblea Legislativa, 2011).

Nevertheless, international cooperation has been a key aspect of Costa Rica's cybersecurity efforts. The country actively participates in numerous international initiatives, such as the Ibero-American Data Protection Network. In addition, it recently ratified the "Convention of Cybercrime," otherwise known as the Budapest Convention, which seeks to address the country's efforts to combat fraudulent and deceptive commercial practices (OCDE, 2020). Furthermore, Costa Rica is planning on joining other international efforts to strengthen cybersecurity measures. For instance, the country is working on becoming a member of the Convention for the Protection of Individuals as well as the Global Privacy Enforcement Network (GPEN). Through these international efforts, Costa Rica is showcasing its commitment to strengthening its cybersecurity and aligning with the international framework.

Finally, to fully assess Costa Rica's readiness for Industry 4.0 technologies, it is essential to analyze its performance from a global standing. The Government AI Readiness Index, for instance, evaluates how ready the government is to integrate Artificial Intelligence (AI) into public services. The index measures three main pillars Government Pillar, Technology Sector Pillar, and Data and Infrastructure Pillar. In these pillars, Costa Rica scored 40.37, 33.02, and 61.51 respectively, resulting in a total score of 44.97, as illustrated in Figure 4. Nevertheless, this index placed the country at 78th out of the 181 countries analyzed. In comparison to other countries, Costa Rica has relatively lower scores, which suggests that there are still areas for improvement. For example, the country is doing worse in areas of data and infrastructure. This comes as no surprise given that it has not been able to successfully implement 5G technologies around the country. Nevertheless, the government does not possess the strong internal digital capacity required to succeed (Rogerson, Hankins, Fuentes, & Rahim, 2022).

Figure 4. AI Government Readiness in Latin America and the Caribbean

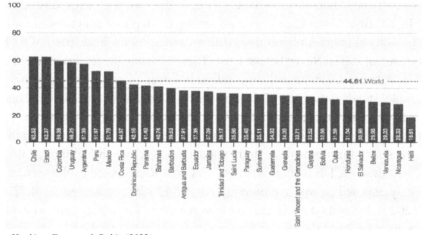

Source: Rogerson, Hankins, Fuentes, & Rahin (2022)

On the other hand, another important index to consider when analyzing Costa Rica's global standing is the Global Competitive Index. This score provides a comprehensive assessment of a nation's performance in the era of the Fourth Industrial Revolution. It provides a broad perspective on the factors that influence productivity, growth, and human development. According to the most recent report, which was published in 2019, Costa Rica ranked 62 out of 141 economies analyzed. However, it is important to consider that within this ranking, developed nations with larger economies are also taken into consideration. As illustrated in Figure 5, Costa Rica is ranked fifth within Latin America and the Caribbean.

Figure 5. The Global Competitiveness Index 4.0 2019 Rankings for Latin America and the Caribbean

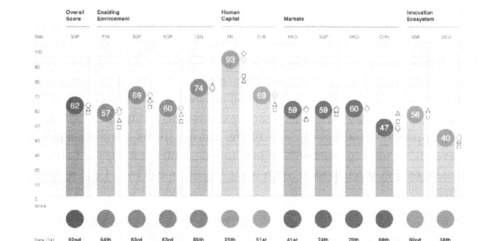

Source: Authors' elaboration from Schwab (2019)

Nevertheless, as seen in Figure 6, Costa Rica has done significant improvements in areas of inno-vation capability (Schwab, 2019). However, despite these strengths, Costa Rica is facing considerable challenges in leveraging the technologies of Industry 4.0. For instance, it is facing challenges with ICT adoption given the few subscriptions to fiber optic internet and fixed broadband. In addition, Costa Rica's financial system is struggling with the low financing of SMEs due to the underdeveloped capi-tal market (Esquivel, 2019). The Global Competitive Index provides key statistics for analyzing Costa Rica's position in the global market. This index can guide policymakers and stakeholders to formulate strategies to enhance the nation's competitiveness in the digital era.

Figure 6. Costa Rica's Performance Overview

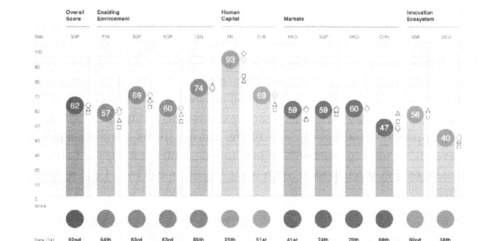

Source: Schwab (2019)

5. DISCUSSION OF FINDINGS

In this section we provide an interpretation of the analysis conducted so far. To achieve this aim, we delve into the implications of Industry 4.0 adoption for Costa Rica's economic growth and development. In addition, after a careful analysis, we offer some policy recommendations to the government as well as key stakeholders for the effective implementation and adoption of these technologies. Lastly, we examine a broader perspective by analyzing the impacts of this era on developing countries.

5.1. Implications for Costa Rica's Economic Growth and Development

The development and adoption of Industry 4.0 technologies in Costa Rica has significant implications for the country in terms of economic growth and development. By leveraging the power of these technologies, Costa Rica has been able to reshape its economy, create job opportunities, and attract foreign investment.

The adoption of digital technologies has led to a diversification of the economy, with a significant shift from traditional sectors to more advanced manufacturing. Several companies in Costa Rica are associated with Industry 4.0, composing 22% of the country's ICT business ecosystem. The rapid transformation driven by digitalization is reshaping the economy in terms of production, consumption, trade, and work. This shift towards digital technologies has had an immense impact on the economy, especially regarding exports. In 2021, companies in the technology sector recorded $11.4 million in international sales. However, the local market remained the biggest consumer of Industry 4.0 technologies, representing 64% of sales, or $19.5 million, in the same year (PROCOMER, 2022). The openness of the local demand in Costa Rica presents significant opportunities for collaboration among local businesses. By strengthening these local linkages, the economy has proven to be more self-sufficient and less dependent on the external market.

As Costa Rica continues its adoption of Industry 4.0 technologies, the labor market is faced with challenges and opportunities. For instance, automation poses a significant threat to the development of the country, as it puts thousands of citizens at risk of job displacement. According to a study conducted by Fernández, jobs that require lower levels of skills and preparation are more susceptible to automation. As illustrated in Table 1, six economic sectors stand out for having a higher proportion of workers at risk of automation: accommodation and food services activities, construction, administrative and support services, transportation and storage, agriculture, forestry, fishing, and manufacturing industries. Altogether, these six sectors represent 46% of jobs in the country, and they are all characterized by a lower requirement for job specialization, meaning a higher probability of disappearing in the future (Fernández, 2020).

Table 1. Distribution of Workers by the Level of Automation Risk in Their Jobs

Activity Sector	Total workers	Workers at high-risk level	%
Wholesale and retail trade; repair of vehicles	341,494	129,197	37.8%
Agriculture, forestry, and fishing	261,580	176,264	67.4%
Manufacturing industries	225,079	116,727	51.9%

continued on following page

Table 1. Continued

Activity Sector	Total workers	Workers at high-risk level	%
Activities of households as employers	158,794	12,578	7.9%
Education	157,770	31,539	20.0%
Accommodation and food service activities	140,604	117,325	83.4%
Construction	134,742	103,843	77.1%
Transportation and storage	114,080	79,138	69.4%
Administrative and support service activities	112,889	87,579	77.6%
Other service activities	95,753	42,769	44.7%
Public administration and social security	94,045	34,365	36.5%
Human health and social work activities	85,448	26,040	30.5%
Others	236,131	100,556	42.6%
Total	**2,158,409**	**1,057,920**	**49.0%**

Source: Authors' elaboration from Fernández (2022)

5.2. Policy Recommendations for Industry 4.0 Promotion in Costa Rica

Despite being a small economy, Costa Rica has emerged as regional leader in various sectors. While the country has made significant progress in promoting technological development and innovation, it still faces challenges that must be addressed. The current legal mechanisms lack the necessary structure to fully leverage the enabling technologies of Industry 4.0. Consequently, Costa Rica must develop a regulatory framework that fosters innovation, collaboration, and development. By setting a strong foundation and developing better policies, Costa Rica will be able to sustain economic growth, attract investment, and capitalize on the advantages brought by Industry 4.0 technologies.

Firstly, Costa Rica should prioritize the implementation of measures that aim to promote *free competition and eliminate monopolies*. Currently, the generation and distribution of electricity in the country are solely controlled by the National Company of Power and Light (CNFL). There is a law in the country, law No. 7472, Law on Promotion of Competition and Effective Consumer Protection, that protects the interests of consumers, promotes free competition, and prohibits monopolies (Asamblea Legislativa, 2012). However, despite the existence of this law, the government of Costa Rica, being the sole distributor of electricity in the country, is exempted from its directives, resulting in the monopolization of the electricity service nationwide (OECD, 2020). The existing electricity monopoly is impacting Costa Rica's ability to implement Industry 4.0 technologies. It is creating barriers for businesses resulting from unfair competition, rising prices, and hindering innovation. To overcome these obstacles, Costa Rica should extend the current law to encompass all market participants and allow other companies to enter the electricity sector.

To further enhance the promotion of Industry 4.0 in Costa Rica, the country must address the challenges posed by the *large state apparatus and bureaucratic processes* (GSMA, 2021). The government's lack of agility often results in delays and inefficiencies, which impedes progress. Currently, many pending bills remain inactive due to slow bureaucratic procedures (Barquero, 2018). Therefore, as a policy recommendation, Costa Rica should simplify and digitalize procedures, facilitating the implementation of

Industry 4.0. policies. By fostering an environment characterized by agility, flexibility, and efficiency, Costa Rica can improve the responsiveness required to jump in the wave of digitalization.

On another hand, Costa Rica is in urgent need of a comprehensive strategy that addresses the *lack of cybersecurity awareness among SMEs*. The small nation is confronted with a significant challenge due to the lack of investment and awareness in cybersecurity, posing a significant threat to the well-being of SMEs. The issue is that small and medium companies have limited resources and consequently they are unable to afford IT consulting services, making their websites vulnerable to hacking. To address this, the government should launch programs that educate companies on the dangers of cyber-attacks and provide free training initiatives that guide business owners on how to protect their property. Nevertheless, they should promote updated antivirus programs, firewalls, and other robust mechanisms (Siles, 2022). By educating SMEs on the importance of cybersecurity, Costa Rica can minimize the possibility of attacks and foster the growth of the small business sector.

Industry 4.0 is an era of technological development, characterized by rapid change. Although it promotes innovation, it can also pose threats, especially to those who are already marginalized. According to a study conducted by Frey and Osborne, "In Costa Rica, the commerce sector employs approximately 18% of the workforce, and out of these jobs, an average of 57% has a high probability of automation" (Asamblea Legislativa, 2021). Considering this, Costa Rica must *develop policies of social inclusion* to protect the interests of those who are most vulnerable in the face of automatization during the Firth Industrial Revolution. The government should establish policies that protect low-qualified workers. In fact, according to a study conducted by the OCDE, automation will most likely displace workers with jobs requiring few qualifications. To address this, the government should first identify which jobs are at risk of getting substituted by digital technologies. Second, it should support funding for training programs as well as education initiatives. Nevertheless, policymakers should draft guidelines to regulate the automation of jobs. Lastly, the state should try to diversify Costa Rica's economy and try to shift towards industries that are less prone to be replaced by automation.

Finally, to promote the adoption of Industry 4.0 in Costa Rica, it is key to address the *digital divide* between the country's rural and metropolitan areas. Currently, the metropolitan region is more developed and better prepared for the adoption of Industry 4.0 than the rest of the country (Samper & González, 2020). Therefore, to promote the adoption of the enabling technologies of this new era, the government should set in place a comprehensive policy framework that will create a bridge between these areas. For instance, the state should invest in the IT infrastructure of underdeveloped coastal areas. Additionally, it should prioritize education initiatives in rural areas to develop the digital skills required for the era of innovation. Furthermore, the government should create incentives for big companies to invest in these rural regions, thereby promoting economic growth in the country. By addressing the digital divide, Costa Rica will promote inclusive development and accelerate the adoption of Industry 4.0 technologies.

5.3. Opportunities and Challenges for Industry 4.0 Technologies in Developing Countries

This book chapter has examined the current state of Industry 4.0 adoption in Costa Rica, analyzing its readiness and identifying key industries that benefit from these technologies. However, to fully comprehend this next phase of technological development, it is essential to analyze the challenges and opportunities it presents to developing countries.

As the new era of Industry 4.0 unfolds, a new opportunity for collaboration between countries is emerging, creating connections like never seen before (United Nations, 2018). With the application of advanced technologies and interconnected systems, nations can seamlessly connect, allowing a transfer of knowledge and cooperation. This has resulted in successful cases of collaboration between developing and developed nations. For instance, Argentina and Spain are working to develop a digitalized tool to help small and medium-sized enterprises (SMEs) leverage investments. Additionally, this collaboration aims to reestablish the transatlantic link and promote collaboration within the entire region (Gobierno de Argentina, 2022). The era of Industry 4.0 has allowed nations to come together, eliminating boundaries and embracing the opportunities provided by the enabling technologies of this era.

Despite the possibilities offered by the implementation of Industry 4.0 in developing countries, it is not without challenges. The adoption of Industry 4.0 technologies will create a structural shift in the global economy, resulting in a new distribution of work. As new technologies are implemented, certain outsourcing practices will become unnecessary, leading to a rise in insourcing trends. Consequently, developing nations will face the challenge of reduced job opportunities. In addition, the implementation of these technologies will require increased digital skills and higher levels of education, which the workforce in developing countries lacks. These challenges will further increase the gap between the existing inequalities between countries (United Nations, 2018).

Additionally, another barrier faced by developing countries is the lack of knowledge regarding Industry 4.0 (Raj, Dwivedi, Sharma, & Lopes, 2021). In these economies SMEs have a lack of understanding of the strategic importance of implementing digital technologies to achieve efficiency (Asghar, Rextina, Ahmed, & Tamimy, 2020). The lack of knowledge and awareness regarding the Fourth Industrial Revolution presents a significant obstacle for developing nations, as these cannot leverage the power of digital technologies to optimize productivity, improve operational efficiency, and optimize resource allocation. This knowledge gap has become particularly evident in the case of developing nations like Malaysia. For instance, a study conducted revealed that only about 12% of the population was aware of the term "Industry 4.0" (Petaling, 2017). Consequently, this lack of awareness is a setback for Malaysia, as companies are hesitant to invest in the necessary infrastructure and skills required to harness the opportunities of this new era.

Additionally, the lack of capital and investment available in developing economies poses a challenge to the adoption of Industry 4.0 technologies. Developing nations lack the investments and infrastructure required to develop and implement Industry 4.0. However, these economies have more pressing issues to address, such as the lack of financial resources needed to establish technology-based companies. Furthermore, these countries already struggle with informal economies that must prioritize immediate concerns like high levels of poverty, unemployment, and underdeveloped infrastructure. For instance, in the case of Tanzania, the country relies on an informal economy that is primarily dependent on trade. Unfortunately, Tanzania doesn't have the necessary capital to invest in essential elements for the adoption of Industry 4.0, including infrastructure, an educated workforce, and innovation (Asghar, Rextina, Ahmed, & Tamimy, 2020).

In conclusion, the adoption of Industry 4.0 technologies presents numerous opportunities and challenges for developing countries. Through collaboration and capital investment, countries will be able to harness the power of the enabling technologies. However, addressing the challenges is essential to narrow the gap between developed and developing nations. By overcoming these challenges, developing countries can achieve economic growth and position themselves as competitive forces in the global economy.

6. CONCLUSION

In conclusion, after careful consideration, it can be asserted that Costa Rica has been able to successfully adopt the enabling technologies of Industry 4.0 to promote economic growth and establish itself as a pioneer among developing nations. Costa Rica has leveraged its unique features, such as being a biodiverse country, politically stable, and having a highly educated workforce to achieve remarkable success. Although there is still room for economic progress, the nation has successfully gained a competitive advantage by leveraging these features.

This book chapter set out to achieve numerous objectives, which have been accomplished. We comprehensively analyzed Costa Rica's current state of Industry 4.0, focusing on government initiatives and private-public collaborations. In addition, we delved into the key industries benefiting Industry 4.0 technologies, such as the agriculture, healthcare, and manufacturing sector. Nevertheless, we thoroughly examined the implications for developing economies by considering the opportunities and threats brought by this transformative era.

While Costa Rica has undoubtedly made significant progress and stands out among developing countries, specifically in the region, it still faces a long way to go. To fully harness the power of these technologies, the country must still overcome numerous obstacles. Specifically, policymakers and key stakeholders must address the problems in rural areas and tackle issues related to infrastructure, education, and research in those areas.

Costa Rica has made remarkable progress in leveraging the power of the digital technologies of this new era. By capitalizing on its strengths and successfully promoting foreign investment, the country has become an attractive destination for Industry 4.0 initiatives by major industries. Analyzing the successful case of this developing nation provides valuable insights that can serve as a guide for other countries seeking to enhance their state of Industry 4.0 adoption.

ACKNOWLEDGMENT

This research was funded under the EU research and innovation program Horizon2020. Funding Agreement No. 871042, SoBigData-PlusPlus.

REFERENCES

Alabama, N. R. T. C. (2022, February 22). Industry 4.0: Simulations, IOT, and AR in manufacturing - NRTC automation. From NRTC Automation: https://nrtcautomation.com/blog/industry-40-simulations -iot-and-ar-in-manufacturing

Alfaro, J. (2023, January 8). https://www.elfinancierocr.com/economia-y-politica/inversion- extranjer a-directa-como-se-compara-costa/CPMMPU5HIZBORISU47VQZVMXCI/story/

Anshari, M., Syafrudin, M., & Fitriyani, N. L. (2022). Fourth industrial revolution between knowledge management and digital humanities. *Information (Basel)*, 13(6), 292. 10.3390/info13060292

Artavia, R. (2021, January 25). La verdad sobre las zonas francas. From Delfino: https://delfino.cr/2021/ 01/la-verdad-sobre-las-zonas-francas

Asghar, R., & Tamimy. (2020). The Fourth Industrial Revolution in the Developing Nations: Challenges and Road Map. South Centre, 4-33.

Bag, S., Yadav, G., Dhamija, P., & Kataria, K. K. (2021). Key resources for industry 4.0 adoption and its effect on sustainable production and circular economy: An empirical study. *Journal of Cleaner Production*, 281, 125233. 10.1016/j.jclepro.2020.125233

Banco Central de Costa Rica. (2023). Banco Central mantiene en 2,7% la proyección de crecimiento del PIB para el 2023 y para el 2024 lo estima en 3,5%. Comunicado de Prensa, 1-5.

Barquero, M. (2018, April 18). Atraso en aprobación de seis proyectos de ley frena acceso de Costa Rica a la OCDE. From La Nación: https://www.nacion.com/economia/politica- economica/atraso-en-aprobacio n-de-seis-proyectos-de- ley/2GAQFYKWRNAKJE6MTPP424VXYQ/story/

Castro, D. (2022, March 22). INA desarrollará prótesis craneales para pacientes del Hospital México. From Telediario: https://www.telediario.cr/nacional/ina-desarrollara-protesis- craneales-paciente s-hospital-mexico

Castro, J. (2022, April 28). Costa Rica subió tres puestos en ranking mundial de velocidades fijas a Internet. From La República: https://www.larepublica.net/noticia/costa-rica-subio-tres-puestos-en-ranking -mundial-de-velocidades-fijas-a-internet

Castro. (2018, May 8). Costa Rica lidera mercado de datacenters en el istmo. From La República: https:// www.larepublica.net/noticia/costa-rica-lidera-mercado-de-datacenters-en-el-istmo

Celenta, R., Cucino, V., Feola, R., & Parente, R. (2024). Towards Innovation 5.0: The Role of Corporate Entrepreneurship. In *The International Research & Innovation Forum* (pp. 451–463). Springer.

Cerdas, M. (2023, April 12). Inflación de Costa Rica se aproxima a la meta, variación interanual de marzo fue de 4,42%. From El Financiero: https://www.elfinancierocr.com/finanzas/inflacion-de-costa-rica-se-aproxima-a-la- meta/SRQGG3NGJV AK5PL2Y4PTQXL73A/story/

Chaves, Gamboa, Hernández, & Sánchez. (2006). Balance de las Zonas Francas: Beneficio Neto del Régimen para Costa Rica. 2-111.

Comex. (2019, August 21). Boston Scientific se convierte en la empresa de dispositivos médicos más grande de Costa Rica. From Comercio Exterior Costa Rica: https://www.comex.go.cr/sala-de-prensa/comunicados/2019/agosto/cp-2401-boston- scientific-se-convierte-en-la-empresa-de-dispositivos-m%C3%A9dicos-m%C3%A1s- grande-de-costa-rica/

Cordero & Paus (2008). Foreign Investment and Economic Development in Costa Rica: The Unrealized Potential. Working Group on Development and Environment in the Americas, 1-29.

Costa Rica's commitment to developing talent in industry 4.0. (2022, August 31). From Investment Monitor: https://www.investmentmonitor.ai/sponsored/costa-ricas-commitment-to-developing-talent-in-industry-4-0/

Coursera. (2020). Coursera Impact Report. 2-25. From Coursera.

Coursera and Costa Rica Launch a Joint Program to Strengthen Industry 4.0 Skills and Train - Free of Charge - 50,000 People to Confront the COVID-19 Crisis. (2020, June 15). From CINDE Invest in Costa Rica: https://www.cinde.org/en/essential-news/coursera-and-costa-rica-launch-a-joint-program-to-strengthen-industry-40-skills-and-train-free- of-charge-50000-people-to-confront-the-covid19-crisis

Cucino, V., Dagnino, G. B., Ferrigno, G., Kaplan, A., Ritala, P., Higgins, C., & Liang, C. H. E. N. (2024). Special Issue Call for Papers NEW TECHNOLOGIES FOR BUSINESS AND SOCIETY: ACHIEVING MULTIPLE GOALS WITH MULTIPLE TYPES OF ORGANIZATIONS. Business & Society.

Cucino, V., Lungu, D. A., De Rosis, S., & Piccaluga, A. (2023). Creating value from purpose-based innovation: Starting from frailty. *Journal of Social Entrepreneurship*, ●●●, 1–29.

Dalenogare, L. S., Benitez, G. B., Ayala, N. F., & Frank, A. G. (2018). The expected contribution of Industry 4.0 technologies for industrial performance. *International Journal of Production Economics*, 204, 383–394. 10.1016/j.ijpe.2018.08.019

Del Sarto, N., Cesaroni, F., Di Minin, A., & Piccaluga, A. (2022). One size does not fit all. Business models heterogeneity among Internet of Things architecture layers. *Technology Analysis and Strategic Management*, 34(7), 787–802. 10.1080/09537325.2021.1921138

Del Vecchio, P., Di Minin, A., Petruzzelli, A. M., Panniello, U., & Pirri, S. (2018). Big Data For Open Innovation In Smes And Large Corporations: Trends, Opportunities, And Challenges. *Creativity and Innovation Management*, 27(1), 6–22. 10.1111/caim.12224

Deloitte. (2018). IoT para el Sector Empresarial en América Latina. cet. la, 1-249. ¿Hay buena cobertura de Internet de fibra óptica en Costa Rica? https://www.marketeroslatam.com/hay-buena-cobertura-de-internet-de-fibra-optica-en-costa-rica/

Duarte, F. (2023, April 3). Amount of Data Created Daily. From Exploding Topics: https://explodingtopics.com/blog/data-generated-per-day

Eberl, M. (2021, May 25). What is Industry 4.0? From Customodal: https://customodal.com/blog/what-is-industry-4-0/

EFE. (2018, November 15). Turismo aporta 8.2% del pib de forma directa e indirecta en costa rica. From El Economista: https://www.eleconomista.net/actualidad/Turismo-aporta- 8.2-del- PIB-de-forma-directa-e-indirecta-en-Costa-Rica-20181115-0032.html

Eisenhardt, K. M. (1989). Building theories from case study research. *Academy of Management Review*, 14(4), 532–550. 10.2307/258557

Eisenhardt, K. M., & Graebner, M. E. (2007). Theory building from cases: Opportunities and challenges. *Academy of Management Journal*, 50(1), 25–32. 10.5465/amj.2007.24160888

Erboz, G. (2017). How to Define Industry 4.0: The Main Pillars Of Industry 4.0. Managerial Trends in the Development of Enterprises in Globalization Era, 761-767.

Esencial Costa Rica. (2022). *Procomer*. Guía Régimen Zonas Francas.

Esquivel, M. (2019, October 10). Costa Rica ranks 62 according to the Global Competitiveness Report. From INCAE: https://en.incae.edu/en/node/95858

Exterior, C. (2022, November 25). Exportaciones de costa rica crecieron 26,25% en 2021. From INEC: https://inec.cr/noticias/exportaciones-costa-rica-crecieron-2625- 2021

Factory, S. What is smart Manufacturing? (2022, December 7). From Team Viewer: https://www.teamviewer.com/en/info/what-is-smart-factory/

Fernández, A. (2020). Retos de la cuarta revolución industrial sobre el mercado laboral costarricense. 4-92.

Ferrigno, G., Crupi, A., Di Minin, A., & Ritala, P. (2023). 50+ years of R&D Management: a retrospective synthesis and new research trajectories. *R&D Management*.

Ferrigno, G., & Cucino, V. (2023). AI technologies and hospital blood delivery in peripheral regions: insights from zipline international. In *Impact of Artificial Intelligence in Business and Society. Opportunities and challenges*. Routledge.

Ferrigno, G., Del Sarto, N., Piccaluga, A., & Baroncelli, A. (2023). Industry 4.0 base technologies and business models: A bibliometric analysis. *European Journal of Innovation Management*, 26(7), 502–526. 10.1108/EJIM-02-2023-0107

Ferrigno, G., Zordan, A., & Di Minin, A. (2022). The emergence of dominant design in the early automotive industry: An historical analysis of Ford's technological experimentation from 1896 to 1906. *Technology Analysis and Strategic Management*, 1–12.

Gasto público en educación, total (% del PIB) - Costa Rica. (2020). From Banco Mundial: https://datos.bancomundial.org/indicator/SE.XPD.TOTL.GD.ZS?locations=CR

Gebhardt, M., Kopyto, M., Birkel, H., & Hartmann, E. (2022). Industry 4.0 technologies as enablers of collaboration in circular supply chains: A systematic literature review. *International Journal of Production Research*, 60(23), 6967–6995. 10.1080/00207543.2021.1999521

Gobierno de Argentina. (2022, November 8). Argentina y España sellan acuerdo productivo estratégico para el desarrollo de la Industria 4.0. From Argentina. gob.ar: https://www.argentina.gob.ar/noticias/ argentina-y-espana-sellan-acuerdo-productivo-estrategico-para-el-desarrollo-de-la-industria.

GSMA. (2021). *El camino hacia una Costa Rica digital*. GSMA Latin America.

Gutiérrez, T. (2023, February 9). Empresas multinacionales generaron 22 mil nuevos empleos en 2022. From La República: https://www.larepublica.net/noticia/empresas-multinacionales-generaron-22-mil -empleos-nuevos-el-ano-pasado

Hernandez, D. (2022, December 2). Costa Rica, el país que lleva 74 años sin ejército. From Voz de América: https://www.vozdeamerica.com/a/costa-rica-el-pa%C3%ADs-que- lleva-74-a%C3%B1os-d e-vivir-sin-ej%C3%A9rcito/6860180.html#:~:text=Costa%20Rica%2C%20el%20pa%C3%ADs%20 que%20lleva %2074%20a%C3%B1os%20sin%20ej%C3%A9rcito

Hiley, C. (2022, March 10). Global Broadband Index. From Uswitch: https://www.uswitch.com/broadband/ studies/global-broadband-index/

Hu, X., Li, S., Huang, T., Tang, B., Huai, R., & Chen, L. (2023). How Simulation Helps Autonomous Driving: A Survey of Sim2real, Digital Twins, and Parallel Intelligence. *IEEE Transactions on Intelligent Vehicles*.

Huang, S. H., Liu, P., Mokasdar, A., & Hou, L. (2013). Additive manufacturing and its societal impact: A literature review. *International Journal of Advanced Manufacturing Technology*, 67(5-8), 1191–1203. 10.1007/s00170-012-4558-5

Huda, N. (2023, February 16). The Rise of Industry 4.0 in Germany: A Journey of Innovation and Transformation. From Linkedin: https://www.linkedin.com/pulse/rise-industry-40- germany-journe y-innovation-nazmul-huda#:~:text=The%20German%20government%20has%20also,partnerships%20 between%20industry%20and%20academia

I-Scoop. (2023, April 11). Industry 4.0 and the fourth industrial revolution explained. From I- Scoop: https://www.i-scoop.eu/industry-4-0/

IMF Press Center. (2021, July 28). Five Things to Know about the Informal Economy. From International Monetary Fund: https://www.imf.org/en/News/Articles/2021/07/28/na- 072821-five-things-to-kn ow-about-the-informal-economy#:~:text=The%20informal%20economy%20consists%20of,lights%20 all%20 over%20the%20world

Inteligente, M. (2023). From CINDE: https://www.cinde.org/es/sectores/manufactura-inteligente/ manufactura

Jiménez, G. (2019, November 13). Empresas, gobierno y academia: actores esenciales para implementar la industria 4.0 en Costa Rica. From Tecnológico de Costa Rica: https://www.tec.ac.cr/hoyeneltec/2019/ 11/13/empresas-gobierno-academia-actores- esenciales-implementar-industria-40-costa-rica

Kalnoskas, A. (2017, August 1). Industry 4.0: Interweaving Manufacturing and Technology for a Smart Factory. From EE World: https://www.eeworldonline.com/industry-4-0- interweaving-manufacturing-technology-smart-factory/

Kaur, J., & Ramkumar, K. R. (2022). The recent trends in cyber security: A review. *Journal of King Saud University. Computer and Information Sciences*, 34(8), 5766–5781. 10.1016/j.jksuci.2021.01.018

Klitou, D., Conrads, J., Rasmussen, M., Probst, L., & Pedersen, B. (2017). Germany: Industrie 4.0. Digital Transformation Monitor, 2-7.

Kozolanka, K. (2018, May 25). Think in three dimensions: Innovative Design and manufacturing find a home at IDEAWORKS. Mohawk College. From Mohawk College:http://web.archive.org/web/20210920082530/https:/www.mohawkcollege.ca/about/ne ws/blogs/think-three-dimensions-innovativ e-design-and-manufacturing-finds-a-home- at-0

Kuepper, J. (2022, May 5). What Is a Developing Country? From The Balance: https://www.thebalancemoney .com/what-is-a-developing-country-1978982

Lasi, H., Fettke, P., Kemper, H. G., Feld, T., & Hoffmann, M. (2014). Industry 4.0. *Business & Information Systems Engineering*, 6(4), 239–242. 10.1007/s12599-014-0334-4

Legislativa, A. (2011). *Ley de protección de la persona frente al tratamiento de sus datos personales*. La Gaceta.

Asamblea Legislativa. (2012). Ley de Promoción de la Competencia y Defensa Efectiva del Consumidor.

Asamblea Legislativa. (2021). Ley de Promoción del Desarrollo Científico y Tecnológico.

Asamblea Legislativa. (2021). Ley para el fortalecimiento de la formación profesional para la empleabilidad, la inclusión social y la productividad de cara a la Revolución Industrial 4.0 y el empleo del futuro.

Asamblea Legislativa. (2022). Ley de Régimen de Zonas Francas.

Martinelli, Mina, & Moggi. (2021). The enabling technologies of industry 4.0: examining the seeds of the fourth industrial revolution. *Oxford University Press*.

McLaughlin, S. (2022, August 17). Horizontal and Vertical Integration in Industry 4.0 for Pharmaceutical and Medical Device Manufacturers. From SL Controls: https://slcontrols.com/en/horizontal-and-vertical -integration-in-industry-4-0-for- pharmaceutical-and-medical-device-manufacturers/

MICITT. (2022). Estrategia de Transformación Digital hacia la Costa Rica del Bicentenario 4.0. 1-54.

MINAE. (2018). Resumen del Sexto Informe Nacional al Convenio de Diversidad Biológica NACIONAL COSTA RICA de Costa Rica. Programa de Naciones Unidas para el Desarrollo, 1-66.

Ministerio de Ciencias. (2019). *Tecnología y Telecomunicaciones*. Indice de Brecha Digital.

Ministerio delle Imprese. (2016). Piano Nazionale Industria 4.0. 2-18.

Mohajan, H. (2019). The First Industrial Revolution Brings Global Development. *Journal of Social Sciences and Humanities*, 2–27.

Mohajan, H. (2021). Third Industrial Revolution Brings Global Development. *Journal of Social Sciences and Humanities*, 2–33.

Monge, R. (2023, June 1). Preparación laboral para triunfar en la era de la automatización. From Academia de Centroamérica: https://www.academiaca.or.cr/opinion/preparacion- laboral-para-triunfar-en-la-era-de-la-automatizacion/

Moore, L. (2019, April 19). Augmented reality vs. virtual reality vs. mixed reality. From Tech Target: https://www.techtarget.com/searcherp/feature/AR-vs-VR-vs-MR-Differences-similarities-and -manufacturing-uses

Moral, M. (2022, June 8). La agricultura de precisión nos ha permitido ser más eficientes en la gestión de los envíos de piña en estos momentos complicados. From Fresh Plaza: https://www.freshplaza.es/article/ 9433882/la-agricultura-de-precision-nos-ha- permitido-ser-mas-eficientes-en-la-gestion-de-los-envios-de-pina-en-estos-momentos- complicados/

Morales, A. A. (2022, June 2). Panorama. Retrieved from https://www.panoramadigital.co.cr/la-agricultura -de-precision-en-costa-rica-el-futuro- ya-llego/

Muñoz, D. (2014). Un acercamiento a la brecha digital en Costa Rica desde el punto de vista del acceso, la conectividad y la alfabetización digital. E-Ciencias de la Información, 1- 29.

Murillo, A. (2014, April 9). Intel deja a costa rica sin su mayor fábrica exportadora. From El País: https:// elpais.com/economia/2014/04/09/actualidad/1397005915_851656.html

5G. no llegaría a Costa Rica antes de fines de 2024. (2022, August 20). From BN Americas: https://www .bnamericas.com/es/noticias/5g-no-llegaria-a-costa-rica-antes-de-fines-de-2024

OCDE. (2020). *Estudios Económicos de la OCDE: Costa Rica*, 2020, 2–66.

OECD. (2020). Costa Rica: Assessment and Competition of Law and Policy 2020.

OECD. (2020). Digital Economy Policy in Costa Rica. 2-75.

OECD. (2022). Recommendation of the Council on Information and Communication Technologies and the Environment. OECD Legal Instruments, 3-6.

OECD. (n.d.). Growth in Latin America. From OECD: https://www.oecd.org/countries/ecuador/growth -in-latin-america.htm/

Oficina Económica y Comercial de España en Panamá. (2021). Informe Económico y Social: Costa Rica. Secretaria de estado de Comercio, 1-45.

Pérez, J. C. (2022, October 17). Pymes del sector tecnología en Costa Rica y cuarta revolución industrial. From Disruptiva: https://www.disruptiva.media/pymes-del-sector-tecnologia-en-costa-rica-y-cuarta -revolucion-industrial

Petaling, J. (2017, October 12). Low awareness, and adoption of Industry 4.0 among Malaysian Manufacturers. From Sun Daily: https://www.thesundaily.my/archive/low-awareness-adoption-industry-40 -among-malaysian-manufacturers-FTARCH492369

Pettigrew, A. M. (1990). Longitudinal field research on change: Theory and practice. *Organization Science*, 1(3), 267–292. 10.1287/orsc.1.3.267

Prococomer; Esencial Costa Rica. (2022). Guía Régimen Zona Franca. 4-25.

PROCOMER. (2020). Costa Rica and Industry 4.0. Business Intelligence Department, 3-12.

PROCOMER. (2022, March 3). 22% del parque empresarial TIC de Costa Rica ofrece tecnologías vinculadas a la cuarta revolución industrial. From Esencial Costa Rica & PROCOMER: https://www.procomer.com/noticia/exportador-noticia/22-del-parque- empresarial-tic-de-costa-rica-ofrece-tecnolog ias-vinculadas-a-la-cuarta-revolucion- industrial/

Producción mundial de piña por país. (2021). From Atlas Big: https://www.atlasbig.com/es- es/paises-por-produccion-de-pina

Raj, A., Dwivedi, G., Sharma, A., de Sousa Jabbour, A. B. L., & Rajak, S. (2020). Barriers to the adoption of industry 4.0 technologies in the manufacturing sector: An inter-country comparative perspective. *International Journal of Production Economics*, 224, 107546. 10.1016/j.ijpe.2019.107546

Rebública, L. (2020, May 6). Nuevas becas para capacitación y certificación en áreas tecnológicas. From La República: https://www.larepublica.net/noticia/nuevas-becas-para-capacitacion-y-certificacion-en -areas-tecnologicas

Red Reply. (2018). How to Take Advantage of Cloud Computing for Industrie 4.0 and Enterprise 4.0. International Journal of Interactive Mobile Technologies, 3-14.

Robot asiste a ortopedistas en cirugía de reemplazo de rodilla. (2021, June 21). From El País: https://www.elpais.cr/2021/06/21/robot-asiste-a-ortopedistas-en-cirugia-de-reemplazo- de-rodilla/

Rogerson, Hankins, Fuentes, & Rahim. (2022). Government AI Readiness Index 2022. Oxford Insights, 3-59.

Rojko, A. (2017). Industry 4.0 Concept: Background and Overview. ECPE European Center for Power Electronics, 77-90.

Samper, & González. (2020). Caracterización de los espacios rurales en Costa Rica y propuestas de alternativas metodológicas para su medición. Documentos de proyectos, 3-79.

Schwab, K. (2019). The Global Competitiveness Report 2019. World Economic Forum.

Shahrubudin, Lee, & Ramlan. (2019). An Overview on 3D Printing Technology: Technological, Materials, and Applications An Overview on 3D Printing Technology: T. *Procedia Manufacturing*, 1287–1296.

Siggelkow, N. (2007). Persuasion with case studies. *Academy of Management Journal*, 50(1), 20–24. 10.5465/amj.2007.24160882

Siles, A. (2022, December 7). Falta de inversión y desconocimiento ponen en jaque a Pymes ante ciber-ataques. From DPL News: https://dplnews.com/costa-rica-falta-de-inversion- y-desconocimiento-pone n-en-jaque-a-pymes-ante-ciberataques/

Siles, A. (2022, October 13). Costa Rica | IA lleva a ganaderos ticos a un nuevo nivel. From DPL News: https://dplnews.com/costa-rica-ia-lleva-a-ganaderos-ticos-a-un-nuevo- nivel/

Soto, T. (2023, May 3). Cinde: qué es y para qué sirve la coalición con la que rompió el gobierno de Rodrigo Chaves. From El Financiero: https://www.elfinancierocr.com/economia-y-politica/cinde-que-es -y-para-que-sirve-la-coalicion-conla/R5IN5DOJZFHMXOCO3YQNZTHPMY/story/

Technologies, V. (2019, May 13). Integrating IoT into Healthcare, Agriculture and Transportation Applications. From IoT For All: https://www.iotforall.com/integrating- machine-learning-ml-iot-applications

Tonge, A. M., Kasture, S. S., & Chaudhari, S. R. (2013). Cyber security: Challenges for society-literature review. *IOSR Journal of Computer Engineering*, 2(12), 67–75. 10.9790/0661-1226775

Treviño-Elizondo, B. L., & García-Reyes, H. (2020). Industry 4.0 Adoption in Latin America: A Systematic Literature Review. In IIE Annual Conference. Proceedings (pp. 174-179). Institute of Industrial and Systems Engineers (IISE).

UNESCO. (2021). Tasa de alfabetización, total de adultos (% de personas de 15 años o más) - Costa Rica. From Banco Mundial: https://datos.bancomundial.org/indicator/SE.ADT.LITR.ZS?locations=CR

United Nations. (2018). Industry 4.0 – the opportunities behind the challenge. Department of Trade, Investment, and Innovation (TII), 2-31.

United Nations. (2022). Industry 4.0 for inclusive development. Commission on Science and Technology for Development, 2-18.

Yang, C., Huang, Q., Li, Z., Liu, K., & Hu, F. (2017). Big Data and cloud computing: Innovation opportunities and challenges. *International Journal of Digital Earth*, 10(1), 13–53. 10.1080/17538947.2016.1239771

Yin, R. K. (2009). How to do better case studies. The SAGE handbook of applied social research methods, 2(254-282).

Yüksel, H. (2020). An empirical evaluation of industry 4.0 applications of companies in Turkey: The case of a developing country. *Technology in Society*, 63, 101364. 10.1016/j.techsoc.2020.101364

KEY TERMS AND DEFINITIONS

Costa Rica: Is a nation located in Central America, bordered to the north by Nicaragua and to the south by Panama. With relatively stable politics and economy in the region, Costa Rica is known for its rich biodiversity, national parks, and ecological commitment. The country has also attracted investments, fostering sectors such as technology, tourism, and sustainable practices.

Developing Countries: Also known as less developed or underdeveloped countries, are nations undergoing an economic and industrial transition with the goal of improving the living conditions of their citizens. These countries may face challenges such as poverty, lack of developed infrastructure, and limited access to resources. Efforts to stimulate economic development in these countries often involve investments in key sectors such as education, healthcare, infrastructure, and sustainability.

Economic Growth: It refers to the sustained increase in the production and consumption of goods and services within an economy over time. It is commonly measured by the rise in a country's Gross Domestic Product (GDP), which encompasses the total value of all goods and services produced within its borders. Economic growth is a key indicator of a nation's prosperity and development.

Industry 4.0: Also known as the fourth industrial revolution, represents a paradigm shift in digital transformation within the manufacturing sector aiming to create intelligent and highly automated production environments. This technological evolution promises to improve operational efficiency, optimize supply chain management, and enable more flexible and personalized production.

Technologies: They refer to a set of knowledge, skills, tools, and methodologies used to develop practical solutions and solve problems. In the contemporary context, the term is often associated with innovations in the fields of information technology, electronics, and communications. Emerging technologies include artificial intelligence, the Internet of Things, blockchain, biotechnology, and many others, influencing various sectors such as health, industry, education, and the environment.

ENDNOTES

[1] Producción mundial de piña por país, 2021.

[2] Robot asiste a ortopedistas en cirugía de reemplazo de rodilla, 2021.

[3] Costa Rica's commitment to developing talent in industry 4.0, 2022.

[4] Gasto público en educación, total (% del PIB) - Costa Rica, 2020.

[5] Coursera and Costa Rica Launch a Joint Program to Strengthen Industry 4.0 Skills and Train - Free of Charge - 50,000 People to Confront the COVID-19 Crisis, 2020.

[6] Hay buena cobertura de Internet de fibra óptica en Costa Rica?, 2023.

[7] 5G no llegaría a Costa Rica antes de fines de 2024, 2022.

Chapter 4
HR Analytics and Employee Attrition Prediction Using Machine Learning

N. Krishnamoorthy
Vellore Institute of Technology, India

V. Vinoth Kumar
Vellore Institute of Technology, India

Chinchu Nair
Dr. MGR Educational and Research Institute, India

A. Maheswari
http://orcid.org/0009-0002-2578-5265
Dr. MGR Educational and Research Institute, India

Sonali Mishra
Vellore Institute of Technology, India

Ayush Sinha
Vellore Institute of Technology, India

ABSTRACT

The high rate of staff turnover in knowledge-based organizations is a key challenge. Invaluable tacit information, which is frequently the source of a company's competitive advantage, is often taken with departing personnel. If a company wants to keep a better competitive edge over its competitors, it should prioritize lowering staff churn. By forecasting attrition based on demographic and job-related factors, this study finds employee traits that aid in predicting employee turnover in organizations. With an IBM dataset of 14,999 samples and 10 features, up-sampling techniques and various machine learning algorithms are employed to find the best predictive model. Data visualization and analysis reveal significant factors and correlations. Further, the authors have used models to predict and analyze employee attrition and turnover. Using classifiers like k-nearest neighbors (KNN), support vector machine (SVM), decision trees (DT), and random forest classifiers (RF), four main tests were run on the IBM dataset to predict employee attrition.

DOI: 10.4018/979-8-3693-0683-3.ch004

I. INTRODUCTION

The pace at which employees depart from an organization is referred to as employee attrition, also known as turnover. It can be caused by various factors such as job dissatisfaction, lack of advancement opportunities, poor leadership, or better job offers elsewhere. High attrition rates can be costly for businesses due to the expenses associated with recruiting and training new employees (Kumar, D et al., 2021). Employee attrition prediction involves using data analysis and predictive modeling techniques to estimate the likelihood of employees leaving an organization (Basheer, S at al., 2020). By analyzing various data sources, organizations can identify patterns and factors contributing to attrition and implement proactive strategies to retain valuable employees. This can lead to higher retention, employee satisfaction, and cost savings for the company (Maithili, K at al., 2018).

II. LITERATURE SURVEY

(Joseph, R et al., 2021) proposed a model taking into account a variety of factors and has a prediction accuracy of 86.0% (Random Forest Classifier) for attrition and mental health for a specific employee. (Rajeswari G. R et al., 2022) proposed four machine learning models by getting the best accuracy of 90% in logistic regression model. (Yedida, R et al., 2018) proposed a method in which the impact of voluntary attrition on organizations was discussed, along with the significance of foreseeing it with an accuracy of 94.32%. (Jain R., & Nayyar A, 2018) constructed a ML model utilizing the XGBoost strategy with the accuracy of 89%. On the IBM USA dataset, (Bhuva, K., & Srivastava, K, 2018) applied a variety of classification algorithms, including logistic regression model, DT, LDA, ridge classification, and RF, to make predictions about the departure of employees for a variety of reasons. The purpose of (Fallucchi, F et al., 2020) was to better anticipate employee attrition by identifying the contributing components and root reasons. With an accuracy of 82.5%, the Naive Bayes model was the highest accurate model. (George, S et al, 2022) compared the performance of four ML models, ETC, SVM, Logistic regression, and DTC, for predicting employee attrition When the dataset was multiplied by ten times, the SVM, LR, DTC, and ETC achieved accuracy scores of 88%, 74%, 84%, and 93%, respectively. (Mohbey, K. K, 2020, pp. 121-128) using the HR dataset proposed the effectiveness of several machine learning algorithms is assessed in this study. For this dataset, logistic regression worked well based on the accuracy measurement. Using models like SVM, Random forest, and decision tree, (Yadav, S., Jain, A., & Singh, D, 2018) provided a model that concluded that salary and additional financial considerations, such as promotions, are not among the primary causes of employee attrition. (Jain, P. K., Jain, M., & Pamula, R, 2020) and (Krishnamoorthy, N & Parameswari, V. L, 2018) proposed a method in which HR data has been subjected to predictive analysis approaches. Predictive models like SVM, DT, and RF were then applied to the cleaned data to determine best model for the dataset.

III. PROBLEM DESCRIPTION

Employee attrition prediction refers to the process of analyzing data related to employees in an organization to identify those who are likely to leave their jobs voluntarily or involuntarily. This problem is important for organizations to address, as high levels of employee turnover can lead to reduced productivity, increased costs, and loss of valuable knowledge and skills. To predict staff turnover and various attributes are considered like employee fulfillment level, job evaluation, work performance and external factors like the economy or job market. The data can be collected through surveys, performance evaluations, and employee records (Karthikeyan, T et al., 2019).The issue of employee attrition prediction must be resolved before developing a machine learning model to forecast employee attrition from the available data (Krishnamoorthy, N et al., 2022). The model applied to new data to forecast which employees are most likely to leave after being trained on historical data of employees who have left or stayed with the company.

Employee attrition prediction's ultimate objective is to give organizations insights into the factors that affect employee turnover and assist them in creating retention strategies for their valuable employees.

Limitations

After analyzing these research papers, we found that the accuracy of algorithms used in most papers was around 80% with a very few touching 90%. We have chosen the most suitable algorithms that will surely give high performance based upon our dataset from Kaggle. We aimed for around 95% accuracy or more with our dataset and four algorithms that are RF, DT, KNN and SVM and we will also do a comparative analysis amongst them. Then, we will focus both on performance of our models and data exploration using Correlation Matrix and Heatmap and various Distribution Plots comparing the most important features contributing to Employee Attrition to find out the most important factor why the Employees are leaving the organization(Dhiman, G et al., 2021).

IV. PROPOSED WORK

The proposed system uses machine learning models to predict and analyze employee attrition. Using classifiers like KNN, SVM, DT, RF classifiers, and Multilayer Perceptron (MLP), five main tests were run on the IBM dataset to predict employee attrition.

The process begins with importing the necessary libraries and the dataset. After cleaning and exploring the dataset, results with be analyzed with the help of Correlation Matrix and Heatmap through which we will find the correlation between features (Krishnamoorthy, N et al., 2021). It allows us to respond to a number of queries, such as which features have a high link with one another and similarly, which features have an impact on our target variable (turnover). We will further analyze our features using distribution plots visually to find the reasons of employee attrition.

Further, Feature importance will be done and we will create train and test datasets too. Then, we will contrast all four algorithms—RF, DT, KNN, and SVM—to observe which one of them operates the best for our data and offers the greatest degree of accuracy when it comes to of forecasting employee attrition.

We will also use logistic regression coefficients and three most important features – satisfaction, evaluation and years at company to develop an equation and calculate the employee turnover score.

Figure 1. Employee retention form the dataset

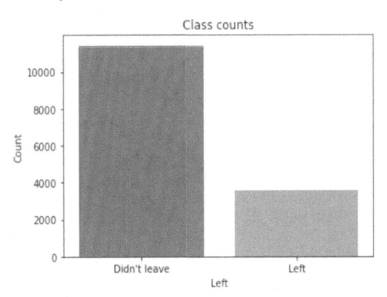

V. DATA COLLECTION

This dataset comprises 14,999 samples and ten traits, encompassing satisfaction level, recent assessment, quantity of tasks, median monthly hours performed, time employed for an organisation, workplace accident, left promotions in the last five years, sales, and salary from the Figure 1. None of the variable column's values are null or missing. Random examples for unidentified cases were used to test the dataset Figure 2. The minority class's size would then rise while the majority class's size would fall.

Figure 2. Features considered from the dataset

```
# Check the type of our features.
df.dtypes

turnover                        int64
satisfaction                    float64
evaluation                      float64
projectCount                    int64
averageMonthlyHours             int64
yearsAtCompany                  int64
workAccident                    int64
promotion                       int64
department                      object
salary                          object
dtype: object
```

VI. DATA PREPROCESSING AND ANALYZING

Data collection, exploration is the primary task which is to be done to verify the data and analyze the data at some extent like in this dataset it is found that employees having less satisfaction (<0.50) have a high rate of turnover as it can be easily seen in the graph below (Figure 3). The x-axis represents the turnover (0 or 1) based on the satisfaction level and the y-axis shows the number of employees. Figure 4 shows the total turnover count of the employees while Figure 5 shows the correlation (strong or weak) between various attributes.

Figure 3. Turnover vs. satisfaction rate

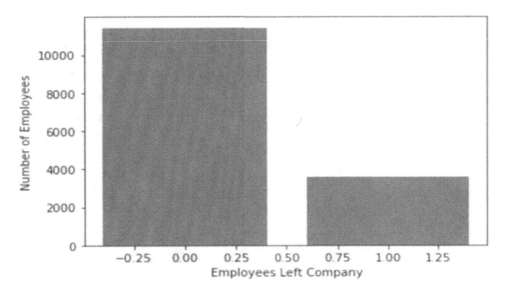

Figure 4. Turnover rate

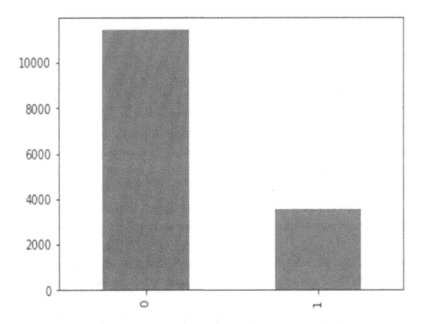

Figure 5. Correlation between attributes

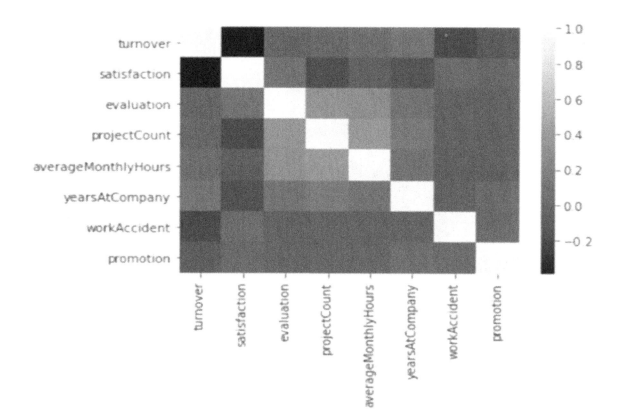

Statistical Test for Correlation

One-Sample T-Test (Determining Level of Satisfaction) –

One-sample t-tests serve for assessing whether sample means and population means are different. We examined whether there was a difference in the median level of satisfaction between employees who experienced a turnover and those who did not, considering that employee satisfaction had the greatest correlation to our dependent variable turnover.

Testing the hypothesis: Is there a discernible difference between the means of employee satisfaction among those who experienced a turnover and those who did not?

- Null Hypothesis: (H0: pTS = pES) The null hypothesis asserts there is no disparity between employees who left their current positions and those who stayed when it comes to of employee satisfaction.

- Alternate Hypothesis: (HA: pTS != pES) The alternative hypothesis postulates that those who quit their employment versus those who stayed experienced different levels of job satisfaction.

The test result "t" equals -51.33, so there seemed to be a statistically significant distinction among the average satisfaction of workers, who had undergone a turnover and the overall employee population, as determined by the statistical evaluation using a one sample t-test.

VII. CLASSIFICATION TECHNIQUES

- Random forest - Numerous decision trees are generated by the algorithm for supervised learning random forest. When arriving at the final selection, the vast majority of the decision-making tree is used. One of the most significant ensemble classification methods integrates multiple decision trees pursuant to the bagging principle to enhance the accuracy of predictions. Every pupil gets independent bagging training. Each hierarchy of decisions is trained using a distinct set of data, and replacement is utilized to generate multiple random portions derived from the original dataset. Additionally, while establishing the tree, features are selected at random. By combining many trees, a prediction is made by a majority vote.

Decision trees and Random Forests are comparable. It creates a forest of trees, each one composed of a random assortment of attributes drawn from the entire set. These uncorrelated trees can be averaged to reduce variation, resulting in a less complex and more stable output.

- Decision Tree performs at a high level with little effort and time. In order to classify, categorize, and generalize a set of data, decision trees are one type of data mining technique that incorporates mathematical and computational techniques. Making a decision tree where each data point has a class attribute assigned to it.

By splitting the source set into segments according to a test of attribute values, a tree might be "learned" using the information provided.

The method that repeatedly takes place on each subset is referred to simply recursive partitioning.

The Decision Tree performs at a high level with little effort and time. In order to classify, categories, and generalize a set of data, decision trees are one sort of data mining strategy that involves mathematical and computer methodologies. Constructing a decision tree where each data point has a class attribute added to it.

A tree could be "learned "by segmenting the source set into subsets based on an attribute value test. Recursive partitioning is the name of the process that repeats on each subset repeatedly.

- K-Nearest Neighbor - is an algorithm for supervised machine learning. In essence, it compares newly discovered cases and data to those already known, classifying them as being the most similar to existing cases. Regression and classification are its main applications.

The technique for finding the nearest k generally uses the Euclidean distance formula. Here is the Euclidean distance formula in the KNN algorithm.

Where dis = Euclidean Distance; xi = the x variable's value in the sample data; yi = the sample data's value for the y variable; and n = amount of data.

For each sample X_test in the TS set, the KNN algorithm searches the TR set for the K closest samples. As a result, the KNN uses either Manhattan distance or the most popular distance measure for this task, Euclidean distance, to calculate the distances between all of TR's samples and X_test. The effectiveness and noise tolerance of the method can be affected by the k value picked.

• Support Vector Machine is a machine learning method for supervised learning that can be applied to address issues with regression or classification. Text classification is one classification challenge where it is frequently used. The strategy known as SVM portrays each data point like in a space of "n" dimensions (n representing the number of features you have), with the corresponding value of every attribute being the value of its specific coordinate. .The best hyper-plane for splitting the two classes will then be found and classification is subsequently finished (Mahesh, T. R et al., 2023).

SVM: By varying the spacing between the data points, a hyper-plane is created, effectively isolating the classes. Assume that N represents the overall number of vectors that were trained using the separable sample sets (x_i, y_i), $1 \leq i \leq N$. D is the input space dimension where $x_i \in R^D$, and the input vectors x_i are the training vectors.

The hyperplane separation is calculated using the equation w. x + b = 0, where w stands for the vector's weight, the dot (.) for the inner product, and the letter b for the bias expression.

VIII. DETAILED DESIGN

The design process starts with collecting the data and preprocessing it followed by exploration, feature extraction and applying the four classification techniques like Random Forest, Decision Tree, KNN and SVM. Employee attrition prediction is done at last. The entire process of the detailed design is shown in the Figure 6. Entire flow of the process is given the Figure 7.

Figure 6. Detailed design

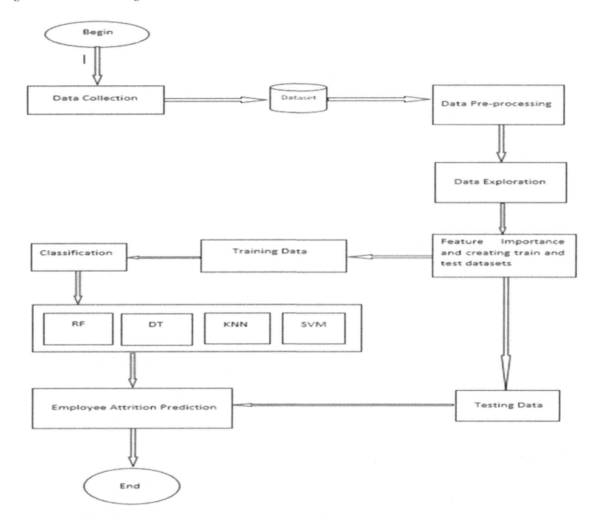

Figure 7. Process flow

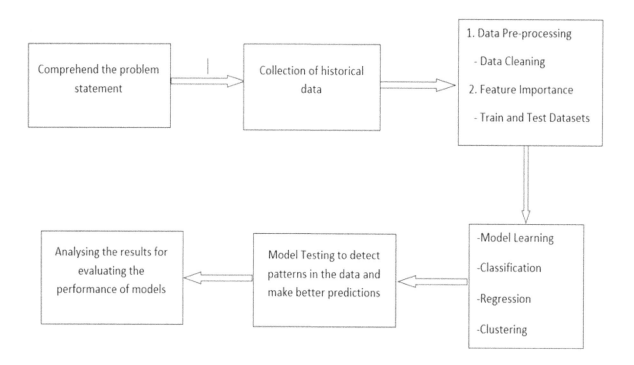

IX. RESULT AND DISCUSSION

This study shows how to predict employee attrition rates in an organisation using a variety of classification algorithms, including Support Vector Machines (SVM), Decision Tree Classifier (DT), Random Forest Classifier (RF), and KNeighbors (KNN).

A comparative analysis of all four algorithms was done to find the best performing algorithm by comparing their accuracies after they had all been trained is shown in the Table 1. The ROC curve is used to measure the total analytical enactment of a test and to link the concert of two or more analytical tests is shown in the Figure 8.

Table 1. Comparative Analysis

Models	Accuracy
Random Forest	98%
Decision Tree	95%
KNN	98%
SVM	91%

Figure 8. Receiver Operating Characteristic (ROC) curve

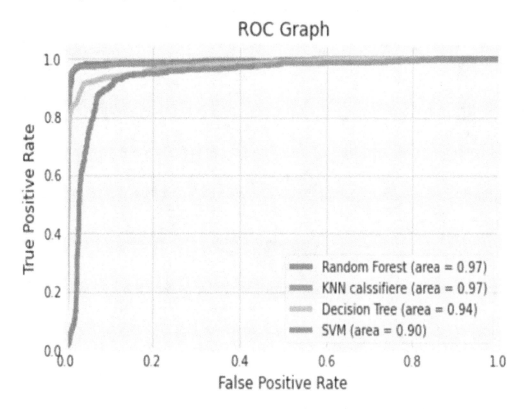

If these employee numbers were to be incorporated into the equation:

Satisfaction: 0.7, Evaluation: 0.8, YearsAtCompany: 3

Score on employee turnover equals $(0.7)(-3.769) + (0.8)(0.) + (3)(0.170) + 0.181 = 0.14 = 14\%$ The likelihood of this staff leaving the company is 14%. Our retention strategy can then be created using this information.

Figure 9. Cluster of Employee Turnover

Cluster 1 (Blue): Hard-working and Sad Employees
Cluster 2 (Green): Bad and Sad Employee
Cluster 3 (Red): Hard-working and Happy Employee

It was feasible to rank the features implemented for the prediction through the use of a decision tree classifier shown in Figure 9. Employee happiness, YearsAtCompany, and evaluation were the top three features. As a result, when we use minimal traits in our model formulation for logistic regression, it will be simpler to figure out how it operates.

Top 3 Features identification from the Figure 10:

1- Satisfaction
2- YearsAtCompany
3- Evaluation

Figure 10. Important Features form DT

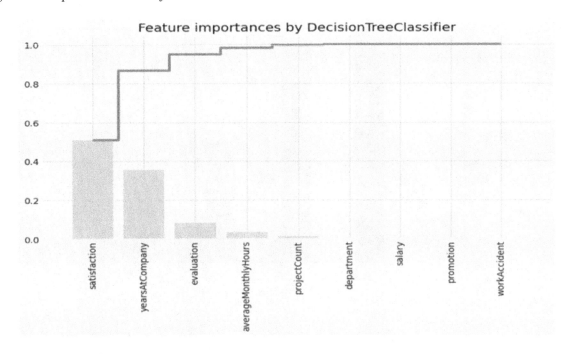

Figure 11. Employee Satisfaction Distribution

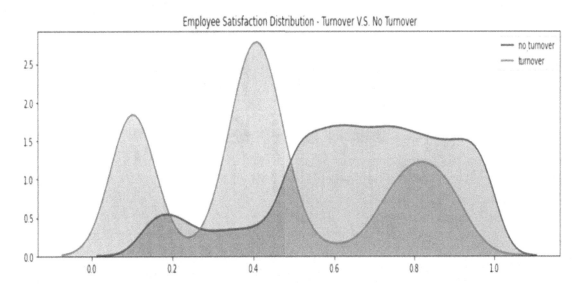

Figure 12. Employee Turnover

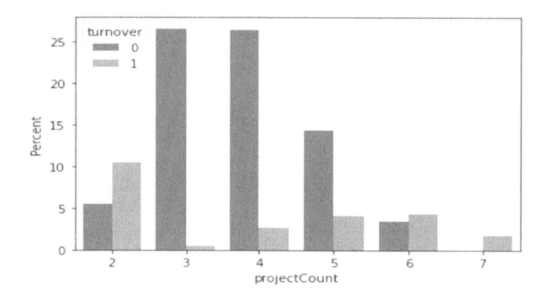

Figure 13. Employee Evaluation

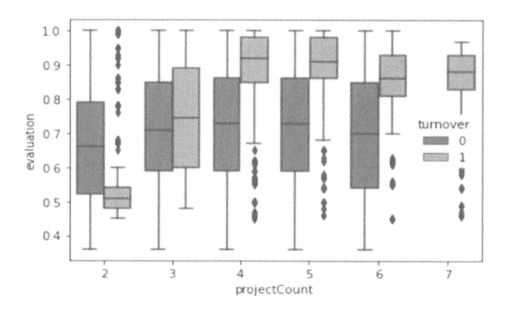

X. INTERPRETING THE DATA

With all of this knowledge, we now know these reasons why workers leave their employers -

* Employees who work too little (less than 150 working hours per month or six office hours per day) frequently quit their employment.
* When employees work too much (greater than ten hours each day or over 250 hours per month), they frequently quit their employment.
* Employees with either extraordinarily high or bad ratings should be considered when determining the high turnover rate. The majority of turnover among employees is among those making low to moderate salaries.
* Employees with a total of 2, 6 or 7 assignments were subject to a possible dismissal by the employer.
* Employee happiness is the best indicator of employee turnover.

Employee's satisfaction distribution, Turnover and Evaluation are explained the Figure 11, Figure 12 and Figure 13.

Potential Solution

* We can allocate a constrained incentive budget to the cases with the highest likelihood by rating employees according to their likelihood of quitting, or we can use the probability of turnover to allocate our incentive budget to the cases with the biggest projected loss.
* Create managerial education programmes. Then use analytics to gauge their productivity and monitor progress.

XI. CONCLUSION

Based on the results of our analysis, we can conclude that Random Forest and SVM were the best models for Employee Attrition Prediction among all the four models (RF, DT, KNN and SVM) with an accuracy of 98%. Organizations can use employee attrition prediction to improve retention efforts, cut costs, plan for succession, and make knowledgeable talent management decisions. It encourages a more stable and engaged workforce and gives businesses the power to be proactive in addressing attrition risks.

We also did feature importance with the help of decision tree classifier to find the most important reasons why the employee are leaving the organization and further using the logistic regression coefficient, we found the probability of the employee turnover.

REFERENCES

Basheer, S., Anbarasi, M., Sakshi, D. G., & Vinoth Kumar, V. (2020). Efficient text summarization method for blind people using text mining techniques. *International Journal of Speech Technology*, 23(4), 713–725. 10.1007/s10772-020-09712-z

Bhuva, K., & Srivastava, K. (2018). Comparative study of the machine learning techniques for predicting the employee attrition. [IJRAR]. *IJRAR-International Journal of Research and Analytical Reviews*, 5(3), 568–577.

Dhiman, G., Vinoth Kumar, V., Kaur, A., & Sharma, A. (2021). Don: Deep learning and optimization-based framework for detection of novel coronavirus disease using x-ray images. *Interdisciplinary Sciences, Computational Life Sciences*, 13(2), 260–272. 10.1007/s12539-021-00418-733587262

Fallucchi, F., Coladangelo, M., Giuliano, R., & William De Luca, E. (2020). Predicting employee attrition using machine learning techniques. *Computers*, 9(4), 86. 10.3390/computers9040086

George, S., Lakshmi, K. A., & Thomas, K. T. (2022, December). Predicting Employee Attrition Using Machine Learning Algorithms. In *2022 4th International Conference on Advances in Computing, Communication Control and Networking (ICAC3N)* (pp. 700-705). IEEE. 10.1109/ICAC3N56670.2022.10074131

Jain, P. K., Jain, M., & Pamula, R. (2020). Explaining and predicting employees' attrition: A machine learning approach. *SN Applied Sciences*, 2(4), 1–11. 10.1007/s42452-020-2519-4

Jain, R., & Nayyar, A. (2018, November). *Predicting employee attrition using xgboost machine learning approach. In 2018 international conference on system modeling & advancement in research trends (smart)*. IEEE.

Joseph, R., Udupa, S., Jangale, S., Kotkar, K., & Pawar, P. (2021, May). Employee attrition using machine learning and depression analysis. In *2021 5th International Conference on Intelligent Computing and Control Systems (ICICCS)* (pp. 1000-1005). IEEE. 10.1109/ICICCS51141.2021.9432259

Karthikeyan, T., Sekaran, K., Ranjith, D., & Balajee, J. M. (2019). Personalized content extraction and text classification using effective web scraping techniques. [IJWP]. *International Journal of Web Portals*, 11(2), 41–52. 10.4018/IJWP.2019070103

Krishnamoorthy, N., Nirmaladevi, K., Kumaravel, T., Nithish, K. S., Sarathkumar, S., & Sarveshwaran, M. (2022, April). Diagnosis of Pneumonia Using Deep Learning Techniques. In *2022 Second International Conference on Advances in Electrical, Computing, Communication and Sustainable Technologies (ICAECT)* (pp. 1-5). IEEE. 10.1109/ICAECT54875.2022.9807954

Krishnamoorthy, N., Nirmaladevi, K., Shanth, S., & Karthikeyan, N. (2021, November). Investigation and comparison of different CNN architectures on tomato leaf disease prediction using deep learning. In *AIP Conference Proceedings* (Vol. 2387, No. 1). AIP Publishing. 10.1063/5.0068638

Krishnamoorthy, N., & Parameswari, V. L. (2018). Rice leaf disease detection via deep neural networks with transfer learning for early identification. *Turkish Journal of Physiotherapy and Rehabilitation, 32*, 2.s (ICAECT) (pp. 1-5). IEEE.

Kumar, D., Swathi, P., Jahangir, A., Sah, N. K., & Vinothkumar, V. (2021). Intelligent speech processing technique for suspicious voice call identification using adaptive machine learning approach. In Handbook of Research on Innovations and Applications of AI, IoT, and Cognitive Technologies (pp. 372-380). IGI Global. 10.4018/978-1-7998-6870-5.ch025

Mahesh, T. R., Sivakami, R., Manimozhi, I., Krishnamoorthy, N., & Swapna, B. (2023). Early Predictive Model for Detection of Plant Leaf Diseases Using MobileNetV2 Architecture. *International Journal of Intelligent Systems and Applications in Engineering*, 11(2), 46–54.

Maithili, K., Vinothkumar, V., & Latha, P. (2018). Analyzing the security mechanisms to prevent unauthorized access in cloud and network security. *Journal of Computational and Theoretical Nanoscience*, 15(6-7), 2059–2063. 10.1166/jctn.2018.7407

Mohbey, K. K. (2020). Employee's attrition prediction using machine learning approaches. In *Machine Learning and Deep Learning in Real-Time Applications* (pp. 121–128). IGI Global. 10.4018/978-1-7998-3095-5.ch005

Rajeswari, G. R., Murugesan, R., Aruna, R., Jayakrishnan, B., & Nilavathy, K. (2022, October). Predicting Employee Attrition through Machine Learning. In *2022 3rd International Conference on Smart Electronics and Communication (ICOSEC)* (pp. 1370-1379). IEEE. 10.1109/ICOSEC54921.2022.9952020

Yadav, S., Jain, A., & Singh, D. (2018, December). Early prediction of employee attrition using data mining techniques. In *2018 IEEE 8th international advance computing conference (IACC)* (pp. 349-354). IEEE. 10.1109/IADCC.2018.8692137

Yedida, R., Reddy, R., Vahi, R., & Jana, R. GV, A., & Kulkarni, D. (2018). Employee attrition prediction. *arXiv preprint arXiv:1806.10480*.

Chapter 5
Taxonomy of E–Magazine Marketing and Collaboration Trends

Emmanuel Ifeduba
https://orcid.org/0000-0002-7121-3279
Redeemer's University, Nigeria

ABSTRACT

Digital technologies have impacted all aspects of magazine publishing, and emerging technologies such as artificial intelligence (AI) promise to make even greater impacts. Notwithstanding, the rapidity of their introduction has made the empirical tracking and classification of trending e-collaboration and e-marketing innovations difficult. This study, therefore, explores e-marking and e-collaboration innovations employed by digital magazines available online, with the aim of identifying and classifying trending e-marketing and e-collaboration innovations; and illustrating publisher relations with content creators and marketing collaborators, to guide future research, e-commerce and AI adoption. Analysis indicated that 10 promotional, 10 e-pricing, 9 e-distribution, 7 e-commerce, and 19 e-collaboration innovations are trending, and adapting them to complement AI would enable e-magazines to perform, especially if they would adopt e-collaboration rather than e-competition.

INTRODUCTION

With the coming of the Internet, there have been predictions that magazine titles that failed to go digital might not survive for long. Magazine publishers are, therefore, adopting and deploying digital technologies in content creation and marketing. And the very nature of the Internet environment has induced many of them to also seek a variety of online collaborations necessary for survival and profitability (Santos-Silva, 2012).

As this flurry of innovative activities unfolds, studies have examined various dimensions of digital magazine publishing, including the history of e-publishing and adoption of various innovations. Many of the findings suggest that instead of extinction, many magazines have found a new vitality in the digital environment. But hardly has any study taken stock of the progression or made a compilation of a comprehensive list of e-marketing and e-collaboration innovations deployed by magazine publishers

DOI: 10.4018/979-8-3693-0683-3.ch005

to keep afloat. Yet, after about twenty years of massive adoption of digital marketing innovations, it makes sense that a search for a standard digital formula for success should begin with an exploration of the progression of trending marketing and collaboration variables (Magplus, 2019).

This study, therefore, aims to explore the progression of e-magazine publishing from the perspective of e-marketing and e-collaboration innovations with a view to compiling and describing in one document the various tested as well as evolving strategies that have served as keys to success for early adopters seeking to give a long tail to their titles. Besides updating history and adding to the understanding of this phenomenon, start-up publishers should find it as an innovation-guide document (Rowlands, 2013). To achieve this research objective, therefore, the study answers the following questions: What is the progress made in e-content creation innovations? What strategies are trending in the e-promotion of digital magazines? What strategies are trending in the e-pricing of digital magazines? What strategies are trending in the e-distribution of digital magazines? What strategies are trending in e-commerce on digital magazines? What collaboration strategies are trending in the marketing of digital magazines?

REVIEW OF LITERATURE

Origin and Features of Digital Magazines: Foleon publishers stated that digital magazines did not start with online magazines as some studies suggest. The study noted that the first digital magazines were actually produced in the 1980s as Diskzines or diskmags, and were generally distributed on floppy disks to consumers by post to be read on desktop computers. These early digital native magazines could be described as executable programs that often contained music, animation, and various forms of multimedia (Foleon, 2022). On the other hand, online magazines sometimes referred to as e-zines, e-magazines or webzines, are digital magazines that are hosted online, distributed online and read online. *Acorn User* pioneered the use of these electronic tools in the magazine industry as early as 1982. In that same year, a publishing company in the United Kingdom (Redwood) introduced the Econet system based on this new technology from Acorn (Quinn, 2011).

From the emergence of the first e-magazine publishing websites in the 1990s, initially to complement traditional print editions, to the release of iPad in 2010, the magazine sub-sector of the mass media industry has seen many opportunities presented by new technologies of various descriptions. And it has been predicted that in 2022 digital magazines would represent 30% of the magazine market and 75% of all periodical markets by 2032 (Santos-Silva, 2012). In terms of typology, Tingson (2015) categorizes them into online magazines, online magazine archives or libraries, digital magazine Apps and digital-only Apps. Digital magazine Apps are further sub-divided into digital replica, replica-plus and reflow plus (Tingson, 2015) while Ed Coburn classifies e-magazines into seven: PDF edition (simple replica) Flipbook-style replica edition, App magazine edition, Apple newsstand edition, Google newsstand edition, Kindle newsstand edition and Web edition (Coburn, 2015).

Currently, the industry is awash with magazines that are interactive and many that are created from scratch to digital platforms such as the Internet, iPad, mobile phones, private networks and other devices. And studies indicate that digital magazines are increasingly attracting the attention of advertisers due to their ability to draw away readers from print through interactive content, low costs of production and low cost of distribution (Krishen and Tillett, 2011). Main features of a digital magazine also include having a beginning, middle and end; being edited and curated to specific editorial standards, being divided into prior established sections, having an appealing aesthetic treatment being a periodical with established weekly, monthly or quarterly frequency of publication. In addition, magazine contents should appear with some consistency in a section. Owing to this description, some scholars argue that many e-magazines do not fit into the standard definition (Santos-Silva, 2012).

Since magazines are traditionally perceived as containers for the curated content of words, images and designs, the lifestyle an e-magazine portrays could be as important a factor in a purchase decision as the actual information it conveys. And these features are likely to continue since many are replicas of the print version while others are born digital (Audit Bureau of Circulations, 2011). The launch of the e-reader has added impetus to the diffusion of e-magazines as publishers explore ways to draw magazine readers to the digital environment where shelves and smartphone apps also appeal to digital content consumers. Also, the fact that tablets are becoming very durable to withstand wear and tear has become an important factor in deciding whether to read digital magazines (Drake, 2015).

To compete for the attention of online readers, digital magazine pages are formatted to be viewed on computer screen with larger type, embedded video and flash animations for better user experiences such as comments, completing a surveys, click-to-play content, click-to-download (additional) content, membership registration and magazine sharing on social media. etc.; they contain ads that readers can interact with They also include links, more high-resolution images, embedded audio and web animations (Gordon 2011).

E-magazine Audience Engagement Modes: There are several ways of engaging with magazine consumers, depending on readership, budget, marketing strategy, and business model. One way to accomplish this is to build a community around it, and scholars believe that when an active community is created on a magazine blog, forum, or social media pages, it gives readers a shared sense of belonging (Renee, 2018). However, publishers rushing to create digital versions of their print magazines often start their digitizing process by embedding PDF file in a website, resulting to a flip-book style copy of a print magazine, or a link to a PDF file. But PDF magazine formats have many limitations. Others engage consumers by building a magazine app. Also, to entice users of devices such as iphones, ipads, and android devices, they introduce built-in distribution though the App Store and Google Play Store. Many print magazine publishers have also opted to distribute electronic versions of their magazines using the Kindle news stand, thereby making their content easy to read on Kindle devices, for a better reading experience, especially for those tired of reading on brightly-lit screens (Greard, 2017).

One of the simplest options to achieve digital engagement is to use an existing Content Management System (CMS) to publish each post to a unique URL path on which a landing page would present that magazine's 'table of contents' and cover. Publishers wishing to engage readers with stories that have a distraction-free visual presentation, high-resolution media and advanced visual storytelling techniques, such as scroll-based animation, resort to digital publication of visually immersive digital stories. In terms of content, digital magazines engage consumers with content that satisfy their surveillance, correlation, entertainment, and purchase needs. They specialize in an aspect of life to gain a defined audience, increase consumer loyalty and have a stable clientele. They also emphasize that reading it anywhere and anytime is important and create stories not as long as the ones in print (Sujlana, 2018; Foleon, 2022). Furthermore, they increase access to each article through the social media, sometimes causing such articles to go viral on social media, while brand magazines resort to immersive brand storytelling to educate and entertain potential consumers.

Digital Magazine Marketing Trends: The online promotional mix is an extension of the offline, but with some significant differences. Online promotion can be tracked, measured and targeted in a far more sophisticated way. Promoting digital magazine and the service online is concerned with a number of issues. Having a recognizable domain name is the first stage towards e-promotion. The Internet, as an information and entertainment medium, naturally lends itself to being used to promote products (Shanthakumari and Priyadarsini, 2013). And magazine publishers do this by placing banner advertisements on other web pages, engaging in web public relations (WPR), sending out WPR articles to review sites for consumers to read, direct e-mails, e-leaflets, by Sending Persistent Annoying e-Mails, (Spam Mail), advertising in the print media and on their websites (Shanthakumari and Priyadarsini, 2013). They also use a mix of promotions, unique logo or brands and run short stories that provide complementary content on your website (Neves de Carvalho, 2014).

Pricing of digital magazines online could be a complex exercise and requires both a test-and-learn mentality and an intuitive view of how one would like one's digital magazine to be perceived. And such perceptions could make site visitors exit to another website or patronize the publisher. Thus, publishers engage in it by offering free content to the subscribers, hoping to make profit through advertising incomes (Strauss, Frost and Sinha, 2014). Due to the fact that the internet gives consumers the power to click around for the best deal without leaving their homes, online pricing has become very competitive. Some websites compare the prices of digital magazines to inform consumers of where the best deals exist, and by so doing they build traffic on their own sites, making e-pricing even more competitive. The growth of online auctions, reward of repeat visitors and constant rewards to loyal customers by some firms also help consumers to dictate price, thereby making e-pricing even more difficult and unstable (McCormick, 2017).

E-distribution is the type of distribution that is begun and completed online by downloading from the Internet to the consumer's electronic device. Sometimes publishers accomplish this by using indirect channels managed by intermediaries because it makes their products more accessible to a large number of customers and afford them an opportunity to make their marketing more cost effective. One major advantage of this is that all orders can be immediately acted upon, and considerable overhead is reduced, giving the seller more control within a short time. Other advantages include the extensive market reach capability and less need for manpower as sellers have direct communication with their buyers. With these largely efficient and secure payment systems, e-distribution can reduce or eliminate lead times and possible shortages towards a more profitable business (Michael, 2014). The role of online product review by consumers, or word of mouth in reaching out to consumers in this digital age has also been interrogated as a new element of marketing communication mix by Chen and Xie (2008).

E-distribution is an important component of e-commerce since the creation of content and community is a powerful combination, especially where there is evidence of quality. Without quality content, site visitors and community members would naturally lose the desire to share it. When this strategy is aligned to the use of a combination of several media channels to offer information in multiple formats, the chances of reaching the target audience is far greater (Michael, 2014). Another means of distribution is instant sharing, whereby the publisher immediately shares the content on social media. It is not out of place also for the publisher to create a website from which subscribers can print the magazine if need be (Krishen, 2015).

E-commerce refers to the marketing techniques affording publishers and other marketers the opportunity to use electronic media (PC, software, databases and networks), and mainly the Internet and new media in general to sell their products. Sometimes they make sales by offering basic services or basic downloadable digital products for free and charge them for advanced or special features. This is increasingly referred to as "freemium" selling, coined from the two words "free" and "premium" which characterise this business model. The advertising model refers to the practice of giving free contents and getting their revenue from advertising only (Gerard, 2017; Foleon, 2022). Then there is also a model that is called the affiliate model. The affiliate model is a business model, which makes money by driving traffic, leads, or sales to another website. One general challenge facing the non-advertising models, however, is that web users are not used to paying and do not want to start doing so (The Nielsen Company, 2010).

E-collaboration Innovation Trends: E-collaboration is the use of electronic technologies in collaboration among firms, individuals or groups engaged in a common task or related tasks. Magazine publishers use of blogs, wikis, portals, groupware, calendar sharing, discussion boards, document synchronization, cloud storage, video conferencing, white boards and instant messaging in collaborating with or among in-house teams. These tools help them to collectively author, edit, and review materials in a group work space irrespective of distance or location, while supporting easy management of projects and exchange of workflows in the haste to meet deadlines (Malik, 2021). Publishers are also increasingly deploying easy-to-use solutions such as IBM Workplace, Slack or Box Asana and Atlassian Confluence, thereby allowing organizations to maximize employee productivity by offering either a complete or a customized collaboration platform (Genius Project.com, 2022).

E-collaboration tools and applications are increasingly becoming important in all walks of life including collaborative and distributive publishing research (International Resources Management Association, 2018; Juan, A.A. et al., 2012) crisis management communication (Zhao, 2022) and for gaining competitive advantage in challenging times such the world has seen since 2019 (Zhao, 2021). E-magazine publishers, therefore, seek e-collaboration solutions for content creation, content supplies and new product development among others (Hall, 2020). Studies suggest that publishers and their intermediaries collaboratively aggregate supply and demand in ways that streamline the market for providers and consumers (O'Leary, 2014) implying that the range of activities requiring e-collaboration is gradually getting wider, all to the benefit of publishers.

Theoretical Perspectives: This study is anchored on two theories—the Long Tail Publishing Theory and the Diffusion of Innovations Theory.

The Long Tail Publishing Theory has its roots in traditional print publishing. In conventional publishing, when the sales of some books come to a peak, they soon go out of print, having become unviable whereas others record reduced sales but continue to attract a profitable number of buyers for many more years. And the term "long tail" is used to describe such books that continue to sell for a long time after reaching their peak. But in 2004 Chris Anderson, a magazine publisher, adapted and popularized the term for online marketers. Thus, the theory assumes that online magazines and similar publications, benefitting from fragmentation, unlimited shelf space and niche marketing that characterize the digital environment, when distributed through numerous online channels, could collectively earn a market share exceeding that of the high-volume products sold through a few channels (Baradell, 2018). In those niche markets, little quantities are sold on each site, suggesting a short tail, but when sales from numerous internet-enabled fragments are summed up, they amount to a high volume or a long tail for the brand (Brynjolfsson; Yu and Simester, 2011). In relation to this study, magazines do not only thrive on niche marketing, they are migrating online for survival, implying that use of multiple channels could give a magazine brand a long tail at the end of the day.

Diffusion of Innovations Theory: The diffusion of innovations theory emphasizes that adoption of innovation generally involves five major steps–knowledge, persuasion, decision, implementation and confirmation. Some studies suggest that persuasion is the most critical step in explaining individuals decision to adopt an innovation while others report contradicting results on this (Abukhzam and Lee, 2010; Boston University School of Public Health, 2013). But several studies support the claim that relative advantage consistently and positively correlates with adoption of innovations in organizations including publishing firms (Al-Gaith, Sanzogni and Sandhu, 2010). Advantages that correlate with adoption of technology include expediency, cost-saving, profit, time-saving and convenience. Firms also adopt digital, collaborative innovations for promotion, competition, customer relations, new business opportunities and customer interaction though findings vary from industry to industry and often depend on the nature of products and services as well as environments. The collaboration trends reported in this study are only those that have been implemented. Below is a graphic presentation of the collaborative relationship between e-magazine publishers and content creators on the one hand and e-magazine publishers and e-marketers on the other for the achievement of transactional, functional, exploratory and entrepreneurial objectives: Details are presented in figure 1:

Figure 1. Publisher Relations with Content Creation and Marketing Collaborators

With adaptations from Hall, 2020, two-way arrows represent two-way collaboration while one way arrow points to publishers' collaboration objectives.

METHODS

Content analysis method was employed for data collection and analysis because it is a technique for systematically describing written, spoken and visual communication. It provides both quantitative and qualitative primary data usually from newspapers, books, magazines, television, video, web pages and documents (Wimmer and Dominick, 2011). The research population is made up of all digital magazine websites available on the World Wide Web, accessible through Google, Yahoo, Bing and WebCrawler. A preliminary search through these search engines produced 838 magazine websites. A total of 40 magazine websites which had maintained a consistent online presence for three or more years, and had Alexa or bestseller ranking, was purposively selected for data collection. The selected magazines are presented in Table 1:

Table 1. Selected Magazines and their Alexa Rankings

SN	Magazine	Alexa Ranking (Category)	Alexa Ranking (Global)
1	Time	#75	#3,376
2	Esquire	#104	#2,566
3	GQ	#323	#16,045
4	Men's journal	#206	#8,926
5	Golf Digest	#4	#11696
6	Men'shealth	#2	#1790
7	Prevention	NA	# 17,775
8	Salon	#48	#8,694
9	Bloomberg	#30	#831
10	Ebony	#2093	#151,638
11	People	#15	#493
12	National Geographic	#91	#6500
13	Vogue	#131	#3950
14	Tell	# 4221	#858,552
15	Mechanics	#363	#11136
16	Maxim	#1359	#48418
17	Glamour	#253	#10272
18	Pitchfork	#26	#5232
19	Backpage Football	#299	#1776436
20	Playboy	NA	#49139
21	Jezebel,	#78	#15086
22	Grist	#17	#102799
23	Wired	#71	#31933
24	Road and Track	#205*	NA
25	Artist	#334	#328371
26	Good Housekeeping	#2	#1352

continued on following page

Table 1. Continued

SN	Magazine	Alexa Ranking (Category)	Alexa Ranking (Global)
27	Kiplinger	NA	#23743
28	OK Magazine	#129	# #34426
29	Entrepreneur	#10	#11472
30	Chatelaine	#36	#54821
31	Soap Opera Digest	#2,424,735*	NA
32	Cosmopolitan	#54	#1183
33	New Yorker	#96	#4705
34	FHM	#23	#96368
35	Harvard Art Museum	# #3,732,302*	NA
36	India Today	#18	#1065
37	Cereal	#6,762,622*	NA
38	Colours	#39	#953568
39	The CEO Magazine	# 1888	#121043
40	Findit.com	#26988	NA

*Bestseller ranking

On each website, available data were categorized in line with the research questions. The Delphi expert validation method involving four scholars and three publishers was used to validate the variables. The procedures were in three stages: In the first phase, participants were intimated of the purpose of the research and were asked to suggest additions to a short list of e-magazine marketing and e-collaboration tools and strategies presented to them; or suggest the removal of any irrelevant entry. In phase two, all suggestions were made available to every participant for discussion. In phase three, suggestions were harmonized by the researcher and rationales were presented for such decisions. On the whole, the participants validated the initial variables and suggested seven additional variables (Bundle pricing, Charm Pricing, Free promotional gifts on own site, Free samples, Online bartering, E-subscription and Syndication distribution). Participants also made suggestions that ensured that categories under e-promotion, e-distribution and e-commerce were mutually exclusive. The procedure lasted four weeks.

Unit of Analysis and Content Categories: Text and illustrations on home pages and adjoining pages constituted unit of analysis (Wimmer and Dominick, 2011). For content categorisation and delineation, e-marketing content was operationalized in terms of e-promotion, e-pricing, e-distribution and e-commerce content while e-collaboration was operationalized in terms of collaborative blogs, wikis, portals, groupware, calendar sharing, discussion boards, document synchronization, cloud storage, video conferencing, white boards and instant messaging, asynchronous collaboration, distributed workforce, AI and machine learning for collaboration, VR and AR adoption, huddle rooms, corporate social networking, smart meeting rooms. Details are presented in Tables 2 and 3:

Table 2. E-Marketing Content Categories

SN	E-Promotion Content Categories	E-Pricing Content Categories	E-Distribution Content Categories	E-Commerce Content Categories
1	Advertising on other sites	Cost-Plus Pricing	Print on demand distribution	Online product display
2	Promotion on blog sites	Target Return Pricing	E-subscription	Online payment
3	Google trends promotion	Value-Based Pricing	Instant download from website	Online store
4	Search engine optimization	Competitive Pricing	Multiple network channel distribution	Online bartering
5	Push notification or public alert	Lead Generation Model	Licensing distribution	Online shopping carts
6	Promoting a magazine site off-line	Cost-based pricing	Digital magazine rentals	Online collaboration
7	Free promotional gifts on own site	Consumer-oriented pricing	Syndication distribution	Online ordering
8	Email promotion	Charm Pricing	Content sharing on social media	
9	Hyperlinks on other sites	Rational vs. Emotional Pricing	Mobile application distribution	
10	Social media marketing	Bundle pricing	Widgets and gadgets	
11	Free samples			

The rapidity of innovation in e-collaboration has resulted in so many bits of e-collaboration in publishing. In this study, e-collaboration contents were categorized into 19 classes. Details are presented in Table 3:

Table 3. **E-Collaboration Content Categories**

SN	E-Collaboration	SN	E-Collaboration
1	Blogs	11	Document synchronization
2	Wikis	12	Cloud storage
3	Portals	13	Video conferencing
4	Groupware	14	White boards
5	Calendar sharing	15	Instant messaging
6	Discussion boards	16	File sharing tools
7	Asynchronous Collaboration	17	Huddle Rooms
8	Distributed Workforce	18	Corporate Social Networking
9	AI and Machine Learning for Collaboration	19	Smart Meeting Rooms
10	VR and AR Adoption		

The instrument for data collection was a three-column, fifty-row coding sheet. While column one presented content categories, columns two and three were for availability and non-availability values. The 50 rows were for the 50 content categories as presented in tables 2 and 3. Textual contents were assigned values to enable the researcher sort the information into quantitative categories.

Two researchers independently coded the contents and inter-coder reliability was computed with Holsti's formula as recommended by Bernard and Ryan (2010). Reliability coefficients ranged from .857-.921. Data collected were classified and tabulated in line with the research questions. Totals were calculated and their percentages computed. Results are presented under the section on data presentation and analysis.

DATA PRESENTATION AND ANALYSIS

The websites were analysed in search of e-marketing and e-collaboration strategies. Findings are presented beginning with e-marketing trends encompassing e-promotion, e-pricing, e-distribution and e-commerce. The results for e-promotion indicate that Search Engine Optimization (SEO) and social media promotion are the most commonly adopted e-promotion strategies (100% each) followed by the use of blogs (77.5%) and push notifications (55%). Each of the other strategies was deployed by less than 50% of the sampled sites. Details are presented in Table 4:

Table 4. E-Promotion Trends

SN	E-Promotion strategy	Frequency	Percent
1	Advertising on other sites	17	42.5
2	Blogs	31	77.5
3	Google Trends promotion	15	37.5
4	Search Engine Optimization	40	100
5	Push notification/publication alert Promotion	22	55
6	Promoting site off-line	9	22.5
7	Gifts on own site	12	30
8	Email promotion	16	40
9	Hyperlinks to other sites	14	35
10	Social media promotion	40	100
	Total	**40**	

The findings indicate that value-based pricing, competitive pricing and cost-plus pricing were trending in over 87%, 67% and 65% of the websites respectively. Charm pricing and consumer-oriented pricing were least evident on the sites. Details are presented in Table 5:

Table 5. E-Pricing Trends

SN	E-Pricing Strategies	Frequency	Percentage
1	Cost-Plus Pricing	25	62.5
2	Target Return Pricing	14	35
3	Value-Based Pricing	35	87.5
4	Competitive Pricing	27	67.5
5	Lead Generation Model	12	30
6	Cost-based pricing	5	12.5
7	Consumer-oriented pricing	6	15

continued on following page

Table 5. Continued

SN	E-Pricing Strategies	Frequency	Percentage
8	Charm Pricing	3	7.5
9	Rational /Emotional Pricing	13	32.5
10	Bundle pricing	10	25
	Total	40	

Indicators of instant download from site, e-subscription and multiple network channel distribution were evident on all the sites whereas distribution by mobile application was evident on 92.5% and content sharing on social media on 85.5% of the sites. Details are presented in Table 6:

Table 6. E-Distribution Trends

SN	E-Distribution strategies	Frequency	Percentage
1	Print on demand	4	10
2	E-subscription	40	100
3	Instant download from site	40	100
4	Multiple network channel distribution	40	100
5	Licensing distribution	9	22.5
6	Digital magazine rentals	12	30
7	Syndication distribution	13	32.5
8	Content sharing on social media	35	87.5
9	Mobile application distribution	37	92.5
	Total	**40**	

Almost all the content categories under e-commerce were trending on the observed sites with the exception of online bartering which was evident only in 10% and online collaborative e-commerce which was evident on 37.5% of the observed websites. Details are presented in Table 7:

Table 7. E-Commerce Trends

SN	Ecommerce strategies	Frequency	Percent
1	Online displays	40	100
2	Online payments	40	100
3	Online store	40	100
4	Online bartering	4	10
5	Shopping carts	40	100
6	Online collaboration	15	37.5
7	Online ordering	40	100
	Total	**40**	

Findings indicate that use of blogs for collaboration, instant messaging, file sharing and document synchronization and video conferencing are trending in that order among the publishers as against collaborative cloud storage, groupware and calendar sharing which trailed other collaboration strategies. Details are presented in Table 8:

Table 8. E-Collaboration Trends

SN	E-collaboration Strategies	Frequency	Percent
1	Blogs	36	90
2	Wikis	17	31
3	Portals	16	40
4	Groupware	12	30
5	Calendar sharing	12	30
6	Discussion boards	13	32.5
7	Document synchronization	32	80
8	Cloud storage	10	25
9	Video conferencing	29	72.5
10	White boards	14	35
11	Instant messaging	34	85
12	File sharing tools	33	82.5
13	Asynchronous Collaboration	12	30
14	AI and Machine Learning for Collaboration	12	30
15	VR and AR Adoption	13	32.5
16	Smart Meeting Rooms	32	80
17	Corporate Social Networking	10	25
18	Distributed Workforce	29	72.5
19	Huddle Rooms	14	35
	Total		

DISCUSSION OF FINDINGS

The findings showing that search engine optimization, use of blogs, social media promotion and push notifications are the most commonly adopted e-promotion strategies support the ever increasing propensity of publishers to make their publications discoverable. This is consistent with previous studies showing that search engine optimization could help organizations to compete more profitably, improve a search engine's ranking quality and increase the satisfaction of website visitors (Berman, and Katona, 2013). It also supports previous studies presenting evidence that search engine optimization increases traffic on websites (Jakub, 2015). This finding is also consistent with studies indicating that city magazines use social media to reach out to their readers and actually make a difference (Sivek, 2013).

The findings indicate that value-based pricing, competitive pricing and cost-plus pricing were trending in most of the websites whereas charm pricing and consumer-oriented pricing were least evident on the sites. These findings seem to support previous conclusions indicating that there is a correlation between e-pricing and online buying as well as e-pricing and higher purchase rate (Joshi, 2017). Hence more publishers adopt those pricing strategies that give them competitive edge such as competitive pricing. Although a study (Maass and Schefer, 2004) had stated that a possible strategy to solve the problem of selling information goods at a price higher than the marginal cost without resorting to price differentiation is the bundling of information goods, this study, in contrast, shows that bundling information was available in only about 25% of the sites, implying that its popularity among magazine publishers may be declining.

Indicators of instant download from site, e-subscription and multiple network channel distribution were evident on all the sites whereas distribution by mobile application was evident on 92.5% and content sharing on social media evident on 85.5% of the sites. These strategies target diverse segments and suggest that these distribution strategies are trending among magazine publishers, probably because publishers may generally have their eyes on achieving long tails for their brands. One e-magazine that seems to emphasize social media distribution and e-mailing on its website is *FIDO-Friendly*, a pet market magazine which claims a regular circulation figure of 160, 000.

There was evidence of e-commerce indicators trending on most of the observed sites. This is expected of e-magazines since their abilities to attract and hold readers' patronage is essential and depends largely on their websites. However, online bartering was evident only on 10% of the sites, and this is consistent with the unpopularity of this strategy even in the marketing of other types of products. It is also remarkable that activities such as bargain hunting and comparative shopping which Krishen, Kachen and Haniff (2014) describe as commonplace on magazine websites were not evident on the sites.

For e-collaboration, use of blogs, instant messaging, file sharing and document synchronization as well as video conferencing are trending in that order. This finding is consistent with previous studies stating that 43% of employees want workplaces that promote collaboration, according to the Gensler US Workplace Survey, and a similar study by Capital One indicating that over 75% of employees perform better in collaborative work environments (Financeonline.com, 2022). With all the debilitating effects of COVID-19 pandemic considered, this trend is likely to continue, especially the collaborative strategies enabling people to work from different locations. However, brand competition has been a major setback to inter-organisation e-collaboration.

RECOMMENDATIONS

1. Working online and from remote locations has been trending since 2020, after COVID-19 lockdowns. This implies that magazines leveraging on e-marketing and e-collaboration innovations may wish to save cost on office rental on the one hand. On the other hand, magazine reporters and editors now stand a chance of earning additional income by working for several publications from the same remote location using collaborative tools.

2. E-collaboration could come with huge cost advantages. Therefore, publishers should strive for more collaboration and less competition. Increase in specialization and brand differentiation in terms of content is bound to minimize competitive activities, thereby paving way for more collaborative activities among magazine publishers.

FUTURE RESEARCH DIRECTIONS

Studies on collaborative publishing are few and far between. Therefore, time is auspicious for studies aimed at examining cost-effective ways of leveraging on collaborative e-marketing to make struggling magazines more profitable and sustainable. Also, more studies are needed for the purpose of gaining deeper understanding of e-subscription and e-distribution dynamics.

CONCLUSION

Over twenty-five e-marketing and e-collaboration strategies are trending online, and there is no doubt that e-magazine marketing strategies are only evolving. Thus, a strategy trending today may not trend in future, but the current trends point to the fact that e-magazines will surely hold their own in the emerging and growing digital environment. As fragmentation which is a hallmark of digital publishing evolves, e-promotion, e-pricing, e-distribution and e-commerce are bound to do better by e-collaboration rather than competition.

REFERENCES

Abukhzam, M., & Lee, A. (2010). Workforce attitude on technology adoption and Diffusion, *The Built & Human. Environmental Reviews*, 3, 60–72. https://www.semanticscholar.org/paper/

Al-Ghaith, W., Sanzogni, L., & Sandhu, K. (2010). Factors influencing the adoption and usage of online services in Saudi Arabia. *The Electric Journal on Information Systems in Developing Countries*, 40. https://citeseerx.ist.psu.edu/viewdoc/download?

Baradell, S. (2018) Understanding the long tail theory in media, marketing and E-commerce. *Idea Grove.* https://www.ideagrove.com/blog/understanding-the-long-tail-theory-of-media-fragmentation

Berman, R., & Katona, Z. (2013). The Role of Search Engine Optimization in Search Marketing. *Marketing Science*, 32(4), 644–651. Advance online publication. 10.1287/mksc.2013.0783

Bernard, H. R., & Ryan, G. W. (2010). *Analyzing qualitative data: Systematic approaches.* Sage Publications.

Brynjolfsson, E., Yu, J. H., & Simester, D. (2011). Goodbye Pareto Principle, Hello Long Tail: The Effect of Search Costs on the Concentration of Product Sales. *Management Science*, 57(8), 1373–1386. Advance online publication. 10.1287/mnsc.1110.1371

Chen, Y., & Xie, J. (2008). Online consumer review: Word-of-mouth as a new element of marketing communication mix. *Management Science*, 54(3), 477–491. 10.1287/mnsc.1070.0810

Coburn, E. (2015) The 7 Types of Digital Magazines, *Linkedin*, https://www.linkedin.com/pulse/7-types-digital-magazines-ed-coburn

Drake, M. G. (2015) Past drive subscribers' attitudes and usage behaviors in regard to the publication's digital outlets: Thesis submitted to the Faculty of the Graduate College of the Oklahoma State University in partial fulfillment of the requirements for the Degree of Master of Science, https://shareok.org/bitstream/handle/

Financeonline.com. (2022) 8 Future Collaboration Trends & Forecasts for 2022 – A Look into What's Next, *Financeonline.com*, https://financesonline.com/collaboration-trends/

Foleon.com. (2022) How to start your own online magazine in 2022, *Foleon.com*, https://www.foleon.com/topics/how-to-start-your-own-online-magazine-from-scratch

Geniusproject.com. (2022) Types of Collaboration Tools, https://www.geniusproject.com/guide/project-collaboration-tools/types-collaboration-tools

Gerard, J. (2017) How to Publish a Magazine on a Kindle, *Pen and the Paper,* https://penandthepad.com/publish-magazine-kindle-8296149.html

Gordon, J. (2011). The Case for Advertising in Interactive Digital Magazines: How the Next Generation of Digital Magazines is Succeeding as an Advertising Platform: Nextbook Media and VIVmag, http://pages.nxtbook.com/nxtbooks/NXTbook/

Hall, F. (2020) Creative Digital Collaboration in Publishing: How do digital collaborative partnerships work and how publishing companies adapt to facilitate them? A Doctoral thesis (Ph.D), Submitted to the University College London, https://discovery.ucl.ac.uk/id/eprint/10110283/

Information Resources Management Association. (2018) E-Planning and Collaboration: Concepts, Methodologies, Tools, and Applications (3 Volumes). https://www.igi-global.com/book/collaborative-distributed-research/5827210.4018/978-1-5225-5646-6

Jakub, Z. (2015) Search Engine Optimization, *CBU International Conference Proceedings*, 3. 10.12955/cbup.v3.645

Joshi, M. (2017) A Study of Online Buying Behavior among Adults in Pune City, *SIES Journal of Management*, 13(1), 29-37. https://web.s.ebscohost.com/abstract

Juan, A. A. (2012) Collaborative and Distributed E-Research: Innovations in Technologies, Strategies and Applications. https://www.igi-global.com/book/collaborative-distributed-research/5827210.4018/978-1-4666-0125-3

Krishen, A., Kachen, S., & Haniff, Z. (2014) Are we Locked in Print? Exploring Consumer Perceptions of Digital Versus Print Magazines, *Developments in Marketing Science: Proceedings of the Academy of Marketing Science book series* (DMSPAMS) https://link.springer.com/chapter/10.1007/978-3-319-10951-0_102

Magplus (2019) Ten Benefits of Publishing Digital Magazines, https://www.magplus.com/blog/ten-benefits-of-publishing-digital-magazines/

Malik, A. (2021) Instagram rolls out new tools for creators to collaborate and partner with brands. https://techcrunch.com/2021/10/22/

McCormick, M. (2017) Ecommerce: How to Effectively Price your Products, *BlackCurve,* https://blog.blackcurve.com/ecommerce-how-to-effectively-price-your-products

Michael, G. (2014), *4 Important Digital Marketing Channels You Should Know About*, from https://www.digitaldoughnut.com/articles/2014/november/4-important-digital-marketing-channels-you-should/

Neves de Carvalho, T. A. (2014) Effects of Message Design and Content on the Performance of Email Marketing Campaigns: Dissertation submitted in partial fulfillment of the requirements for the degree of MSc in Business Administration at Católica-Lisbon School of Business & Economics, https://repositorio.ucp.pt/bitstream/10400.14/18224/1/Thesis%20Teresa%20%20Carvalho.pdf

O'Leary, B. (2014). An architecture of collaboration. *Publishing Research Quarterly*, 30(3). www.researchgate.net

Quinn, A. (2016) A History of British Magazine Design, https://www.amazon.com/History-British-Magazine-Design/dp/1851777865

Renee, K. (2018) How to start a magazine online in 15 steps, *Lucidpress.com,* https://www.lucidpress.com/blog/how-to-start-magazine-online

Rowland, B. (2013) The fall and rise of magazines from print to digital, *The Guardian,* https://www.theguardian.com/media-network/media-network-blog/2013/mar/07/fall-rise-magazines-print-digital

Santos-Silva, D. (2012) The future of digital magazine publishing· Presented at 16th International Conference on Electronic Publishing – ELPUB 2012 – Social Shaping of Digital Publishing: Exploring the Interplay between Culture and Technology, https://content.iospress.com/articles/information-services-and-use/isu661

Shanthakumari, S., & Priyadarsini, K. (2013) A study on E- Promotional strategies for e-marketing *International Journal of scientific research and management, Volume1 Issue 8 Pages 426-434* www.ijsrm.in

Shorthand.com. (2022) The definitive guide to making a digital magazine, *Shorthand.com,* https://shorthand.com/the-craft/how-to-make-a-digital-magazine/index.html

Sivek, S. C. (2013). City Magazines and Social Media: Moving Beyond the Monthly. *Journal of Magazine Media*, 14(2). Advance online publication. https://muse.jhu.edu/article/773658/pdf. 10.1353/jmm.2013.0001

Stahl, F., Maass, W., & Schefer, M. (2004) Strategies for Selling Paid Content on Newspaper and Magazine Websites: An Empirical Analysis of Bundling and Splitting of News and Magazine Articles, https://www.tandfonline.com/doi/abs/10.1080/14241277.2004.9669382

Strauss, J., Frost, R., & Sinha, N. (2014) *E-marketing*, Upper Saddle River, NJ: Pearson, https://www.scirp.org/

Sujlana, A. (2018). 10 Reasons to Create a digital magazine, https://www.clavistechnologies.com/blog/

The Nielsen Company. (2010). *Changing Models: A Global Perspective on Paying for Content Online.* Available: http://blog.nielsen.com/nielsenwire/global/

Tingson, A. (2015) 7 Content Marketing Trends You Need To Focus On This 2015, https://www.linkedin.com/pulse/7-content-marketing-trends-you-need-focus-2015-arlene-tingson-mba?trk=portfolio_article-card_title

Wimmer, R., & Dominick, T. (2011). *Mass Media Research: An Introduction.* Wadsworth Cengage Learning.

Zhao, J., & Kumar, V. (2022) Technologies and Systems for E-Collaboration during Global Crises. www.researchgate.net10.4018/978-1-7998-9640-1

Zhao, J., & Richards, J. (2021) E-Collaboration Technologies and Strategies for Competitive Advantage amid Challenging Times. www.researchgate.net10.4018/978-1-7998-7764-6

ADDITIONAL READING

Santos-Silva, D. (2012) The future of digital magazine publishing· Presented at 16th International Conference on Electronic Publishing – ELPUB 2012 – Social Shaping of Digital Publishing: Exploring the Interplay between Culture and Technology, https://content.iospress.com/articles/information-services-and-use/isu661

Shorthand.com. (2022) The definitive guide to making a digital magazine, *Shorthand.com,* https://shorthand.com/the-craft/how-to-make-a-digital-magazine/index.html

Sivek, S. C. (2013). City Magazines and Social Media: Moving Beyond the Monthly. *Journal of Magazine Media*, 14(2). Advance online publication. https://muse.jhu.edu/article/773658/pdf. 10.1353/jmm.2013.0001

Chapter 6
6G for Intelligent Healthcare:
The Potential Impact and the Challenges

Amandeep Dhaliwal

Manav Rachna International Institute of Research and Studies, India

ABSTRACT

The upcoming sixth-generation (6G) networks are envisioned as offering ultra-low latency, high bandwidth, and improved quality of service, which aims to facilitate effective communication among network nodes. Integration of this cutting-edge technology in healthcare facilities can support intelligent diagnosis, patient-centric treatment, and various healthcare services, both within hospitals and remotely. Thus, the expanding healthcare sector, wherein an increasing array of applications is integrated into the network, yields diverse data in terms of shapes and sizes would facilitate enhanced personalized and remote healthcare services. The trajectory of future intelligent healthcare thus involves the synergistic integration of 6G to address prevailing constraints associated with cellular coverage, network performance, and security concerns. This chapter endeavors to elucidate the features, prospects, challenges, and future directions pertinent to this evolving futuristics healthcare landscape.

I. INTRODUCTION

In spite of recent technological strides, the management of disasters poses persistent challenges, particularly when they directly imperil human health, as exemplified by the recent COVID-19 pandemic. Owing to unpreparedness, healthcare facilities struggled to accommodate the surge in patient numbers, resulting in a global inadequacy of essential medical care post-pandemic declaration. The COVID-19 crisis underscored that escalating patient volumes, insufficient medical services, failure to prevent infections, and delayed responses collectively precipitated the collapse of healthcare systems. Even in the most developed nations, healthcare infrastructures geared towards delivering expeditious and secure medical services for both staff and patients grappled with mitigating the ramifications.

Moreover, the COVID-19 pandemic has elucidated the advantages of telemedicine, diminishing the risk of virus transmission associated with hospital visits and fostering treatment delivery by qualified specialists. The imminent transition into an era characterized by intelligent and interconnected smart healthcare is discernible, where sensors are either externally or internally affixed to the human body. Smart healthcare entails the provisioning of healthcare services through smart devices, such as smart-

DOI: 10.4018/979-8-3693-0683-3.ch006

phones, smartwatches, wireless smart glucometers, and wireless blood pressure monitors, along with networks such as the Body Area Network (Chaudhary et al., 2022).

These smart devices process health information derived from diverse sources encompassing sensors, bodily implants, and biomedical systems. In essence, smart healthcare facilitates access to pertinent information and optimal solutions for individuals from various backgrounds, including medical professionals, patients, caretakers, and family members, with the overarching goal of minimizing medical errors and reducing costs. The proliferation of connected healthcare applications and devices is anticipated to generate data of varying magnitudes and formats, potentially enhancing human well-being, playing a crucial role in addressing future pandemics and diseases, and facilitating early diagnoses.

However, supporting such a vast array of healthcare devices and sensor-based applications in hospitals necessitates the implementation of a dependable and scalable communication network infrastructure. This network must meet stringent requirements concerning bandwidth, data rate, latency, and other parameters. Additionally, emerging use cases such as remote surgeries and tactile Internet are expected to intensify the demand for ultra-reliable and low-latency communications.

Future 6G-enabled Internet of Things (IoT) networks are envisaged to cater to smart healthcare applications by offering ultra-low latency, high throughput, ultra-high reliability, high density, and energy efficiency. Preliminary efforts toward the development of 6G networks, services, and requirements are already underway. During the standardization of 5G technology, three primary areas were examined: massive machine-type communications (mMTC), improved mobile broadband, ultra-reliable and low-latency communications (URLLC), and Enhanced Mobile Broadband (eMBB) (Mughees et al., n.d.). Despite introducing various advantages, 5G networks still grapple with significant limitations in mobile traffic capabilities, device density, and latency, which are crucial for healthcare and other applications.

A comparative analysis between the capabilities, enabling technologies, and use cases of 5G and anticipated 6G networks is delineated in Table I.

Table 1. Comparison between 6G and 5G.

FEATURE	6G	5G
Mobility Support	Up to 1000 km h^{-1}	Up to 500 km h^{-1}
Spectral Efficiency	100 bps Hz^{-1}	30 bps Hz^{-1}
Frequency	1000GHz (1 THz)	3–300 GHz
End to End Latency	<1 ms	1–5 ms
Peak Data Rate	1 Tbps	20 Gbps
Healthcare Applications	Connected Robotics and Autonomous Systems, Remote surgery, Brain-computer Interface, Intelligent Wearable Devices, Hospital-to-Home (H$_2$H) services	Drone, Virtual Reality (VR), Augmented Reality (AR),
Enabling Technologies	Blockchain, Machine learning and Deep Neural Networks, Reflective intelligent surfaces, Edge Intelligence, Visible Light Communication, and Cell-free smart surfaces.	mmWave, NOMA, Fog, Edge Computing, Software-defined networking, Network Function virtualisation, dense net- works

6G networks are anticipated to build upon the trajectory set by 5G, expanding the scope and capabilities with an emphasis on massive URLLC, connectivity, and coverage for smart devices (Wang et al., 2022). The unique requirements of 6G for IoT are poised to furnish a novel echelon of network services.

1. Facilitating mobile traffic up to a rate of 1 Gb s^{-1}/m^2 to address the demanding requirements for superlative data rates and extensive device density within a specified geographic area.
2. Attaining exceedingly low network latencies (10–100 µs) is imperative to fulfill the requisites of haptic applications, notably in domains such as e-health and remote surgery.
3. Delivering exceptionally elevated data rates, reaching up to 1 Tb/s, to accommodate data-intensive applications, including but not limited to ultra-high definition videos and applications related to Augmented and Virtual Reality (AR/VR).
4. Realizing a notably high device connectivity density of 10^7 devices/km^2, a parameter instrumental in facilitating the implementation of remarkably dense Internet of Things (IoT) networks.

II. THE ROLE OF 6G IN THE HEALTHCARE

The prospective 6G architecture for Internet of Things (IoT) networks is envisioned as a comprehensive and unified network, facilitating broader and more diverse access across various communication modalities, including terrestrial, satellite, short-range device-to-device, among others. The adoption of 6G technology has engendered a significant advancement in the biomedical and healthcare engineering sector. Foreseen as a revolutionary force, this technology is anticipated to reshape the sector, spanning from remote activity surveillance to the execution of remote robotic surgery with optimal efficiency .

Intelligent technology plays a pivotal role in facilitating real-time decision-making processes. Within the framework of the 6G network, operations related to networking, data processing, resource management, and service-based communication are intricately driven by Artificial Intelligence (AI), enabling tailored functionality across diverse environments to enhance service provision (Nguyen et al., 2022; Nova et al., 2021). The confluence of technical advancements and escalating data requirements in healthcare has led to the foundational underpinnings of 6G. This iteration is poised to capitalize on prevailing technological trends and emergent needs, thereby fostering the evolution and establishment of wireless communication ecosystems within the healthcare domain.

The application of 6G robotics stands out as an innovative means to conduct remote surgeries, enabling distant physicians to manage procedures through robotic devices with millisecond latency and high dependability (Nayak & Patgiri, 2021). The intelligent network underpinned by 6G is expected to substantially enhance telemedicine services and technologies such as Ambient Assisted Living (AAL), particularly in monitoring elderly individuals and delivering timely treatment (Srinivasu et al., 2022). The scope of healthcare applications has expanded beyond catering solely to patients or those with illnesses; it now encompasses services geared towards elevating the overall living standards of individuals (Hakeem & Hussein, 2022). Notable services include Emergency services, Intelligent Wearable Devices (IWD), Hospital-to-Home services, remote pharmacy services, surgeries performed by physicians, insurance services, and ambulance services.

IWD, as a featured service, stands to significantly benefit patients by providing vital information such as cardiac rate, health metrics, blood test results, blood pressure, body weight, and dietary intake. Consequently, IWD is anticipated to enhance patient convenience, reduce the frequency of hospital visits, and enable prolonged periods of stay at home (Noor-A-Rahim et al., 2022). The integration of healthcare applications over the 6G technology landscape is illustrated in Figure 1.

Moreover, Wireless Body Area Networks (WBANs) contribute to enhancing device performance (Mucchi et al., 2020). WBANs are mandated to prolong network life, ensuring the delivery of emergency data with recognized reliability to augment overall performance (Saeidi et al., 2020). Additionally, services such as remote robotic surgery demand minimal latency (<1 ms) (Khan et al., 2019), emphasizing the requisite for networks characterized by exceptionally high reliability in data exchange, data accuracy, and rapid transfer rates for information sharing among remote health centers.

The nature of healthcare networks should transcend the characteristics of conventional wireless networks to meet the exigencies of Quality of Service (QoS). This mandates a framework characterized by mobility, substantial compliance support, extremely low latency (<1 ms), environmentally sustainable communication for patient security, and continuous connectivity. Technological possibilities such as the Internet of Medical Things (Kumar et al., 2022) and the Internet of Nano Things (Sahin et al., 2021) for body-level communication are strategically considered to cater to patient-centric services.

Given these stringent requirements, 6G emerges as the most suitable choice for hosting healthcare networks, poised to usher in transformative changes within the healthcare industry. As a robust competitor, 6G is anticipated to provide essential support in terms of dependability, mobility, capacity, and security (Hussein & Abd El-Kader, 2017).

To fulfill stringent requirements, 6G is anticipated to operate at higher frequencies, encompassing visible light, Terahertz, and mmWave (Chen et al., 2022), as depicted in Figure 1.

Figure 1. 6G enabled-IoT for future smart healthcare (Source: Ahad & Tahir, 2023)

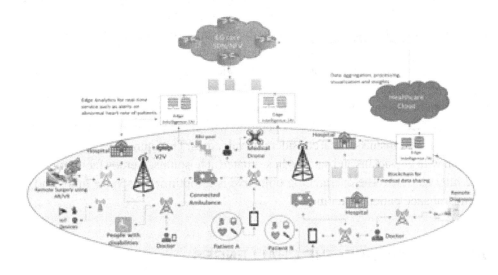

The envisaged 6G framework is poised to support a ubiquitous intelligent mobile society by generating substantial volumes of data through the Internet of Everything (IoE). This data will be seamlessly integrated with cutting-edge technologies such as Artificial Intelligence (AI), Blockchains, cloud/edge/fog computing, and reflective intelligent surfaces (RIS).

A notable application benefiting from the high throughput capabilities of 6G is holographic communication, akin to the role played by virtual and augmented reality (AR/VR) in the context of 5G. In the healthcare domain, the implementation of 6G is expected to enhance virtual and augmented reality experiences by facilitating the communication of additional sensory information encompassing audio, visual, somatosensory, and haptic modalities (Katz & Ahmed, 2020). This enhancement will enable real-time interaction and precise presentation of three-dimensional images of virtual and tangible objects (Strinati et al., 2019). Consequently, remote medical examinations, particularly of specific body areas, will be significantly improved, providing enhanced visibility and proving invaluable in instances of intricate surgical procedures with elevated risk factors. The advent of the Intelligent Internet of Medical Things (IIoMT) is anticipated to contribute to the optimization of surgical procedures, ultimately reducing associated risks (Akhtar et al., 2020).

In order to facilitate the provision of medical assistance across remote locations, the Intelligent Internet of Medical Things (IIoMT) is poised to incorporate holographic and tactile communication, alongside augmented and virtual reality technologies. This strategic integration aims to enable distant physicians to engage in collaborative healthcare efforts with heightened efficacy (Akhtar et al., 2020). Furthermore, the implementation of 6G robotics holds promise for executing remote surgical procedures, wherein remote doctors can orchestrate interventions through robotic devices characterized by millisecond latency and ultrahigh reliability.

Unmanned Aerial Vehicles (UAVs) emerge as a solution to counteract delayed healthcare response rates, particularly in emergency scenarios. These UAVs are adept at expeditiously transporting crucial healthcare supplies, such as surgical tools and medications, from medical facilities situated in disparate geographical regions (Ahad et al., 2020). This mitigates the impact of road traffic delays and ensures timely assistance. Notably, implants and on-body sensors are instrumental in facilitating real-time communication and data transfer with an unparalleled degree of reliability and availability. Such data is subsequently relayed to edge devices or cloud centers for comprehensive short- and long-term medical analysis (Gupta et al., 2021).

The integration of 6G-enabled Internet of Things (IoT) networks into ambulance systems establishes a novel paradigm. Networked ambulances, operating within the ambit of 6G-IoT, have the capacity to stream real-time video transmissions at considerable velocities. This innovative approach ensures seamless communication with physicians and paramedics situated at hospitals, thereby facilitating prompt medical support and interventions. The overarching objective is to optimize response times and, ultimately, to safeguard and enhance patient outcomes.

III. 6G AND HEALTHCARE: THE CHALLENGES

To ensure the success of healthcare in the future, several formidable challenges must be addressed within the framework of 6G-enabled Internet of Things (IoT) networks. Notable obstacles encompass the management of vast datasets, power supply concerns, limitations associated with Internet of Things (IoT) devices, and various facets of hardware development.

Security and privacy – One of the biggest concerns that loom large as the integration of healthcare devices into 6G-enabled IoT networks is that of security and privacy. 6g enabled networks exposes these healthcare devices to wireless interface attacks, including unauthorized data access, risks to integrity, and Denial of Service (DoS) incidents targeting healthcare applications and data centers. Other network considerations encompass information processing, threat intelligence and identification, network monitoring, traffic analysis, and the formulation of data encryption strategies As the number of device connections proliferates, so does the susceptibility to security and privacy risks.

Data communication and management centers are particularly susceptible to a spectrum of attacks, such as DoS, hijacking, spoofing, and eavesdropping, thereby necessitating robust risk mitigation measures to uphold high standards of security and privacy for 6G-IoT. To safeguard the confidentiality and integrity of sensitive healthcare data, the implementation of blockchain, distributed ledger technologies, and Quantum security capabilities is crucial. Quantum Machine Learning algorithms have the potential to enhance network privacy and security, as evidenced in recent research (Kumar et al., 2022). The Blockchain paradigm also emerges as a pertinent solution in the 6G era, given the decentralized and distributed nature of IoT networks, aligning seamlessly with Blockchain's decentralization attributes while concurrently providing security features such as anonymity and integrity (McGhin et al., 2019).

Network Latency Issues - Minimizing computational delays is imperative for the effective functioning of devices and sensors within the healthcare domain. Collaboration between networking components and smart healthcare devices is particularly crucial in applications such as remote surgeries, robotic-assisted medication, and ambient-assisted environments. The aspiration for 6G technology is to deliver ultra-low latency in comparison to preceding generations, thereby enhancing the network's capability to efficiently and promptly manage and respond to external stimuli (Alfian et al., 2018).

Low power and low-cost communication - Addressing the challenge of low power and low-cost communication is paramount, especially for IoT devices in the realm of smart healthcare with compact footprints connected to multiple sensors. The continuous power requirement poses substantial cost and battery life challenges. To overcome these issues, energy-efficient algorithms are imperative to facilitate communication among devices while minimizing energy consumption. Developments in microelectronics, wireless communication, and energy harvesting are viable avenues. For instance, sensors embedded in the body can harness solar energy for healthcare monitoring using Bluetooth-enabled low-energy modules enclosed in transparent silicon (Wu et al., 2018). Furthermore, innovative materials like MXenes-based intelligent biosensors can revolutionize implants by detecting diverse biomarkers/pathogens related to fatal and infectious diseases without external power requirements (Bhansali et al., 2022).

Network Bandwidth Issues - The proliferation of wireless technology-dependent devices continues to expand, emphasizing the necessity for sustainable bandwidth to facilitate uninterrupted communication. The goal is to augment smart healthcare applications within the 6G paradigm through the integration of machine intelligence and edge technologies (Sodhro et al., 2021). This integration aims to enhance the efficient utilization of heterogeneous networks, incorporating extensive antennas equipped with intelligent channel allocation mechanisms and wider bandwidth to cater to a diverse array of services (Sarieddeen et al., 2020).

Resource constraints of IoT devices – The constraints of IOT devices are a significant concern for edge intelligence and Ultra-Reliable Low Latency Communication (URLLC) data transmission. Wearable sensors, intelligent healthcare devices, and mobile devices need the capability to perform Artificial Intelligence (AI) tasks. Some IoT sensors and implants face challenges in meeting computational requirements due to limitations in hardware, memory, and power resources. Hence, hardware-based AI training solutions on nano IoT devices and integrated wearables are imperative for the evolution of intelligent 6G-enabled IoT networks, particularly in the context of intelligent-enhanced life assistance services (Fafoutis et al., 2018).

Network Openness - The network device should enable the interoperability of disparate end-systems and the adaptable scheduling of distributed network segments. In the context of 6G, there will be a focus on service-driven heterogeneous network management, providing the capability for network operators and specialized industries to expeditiously deploy novel services. The openness of the connecting interface is leveraged to enhance the seamless interconnection and interoperability of multiple networking devices. This aspect is pivotal for the consolidation of infrastructure facilities and the evolution of the mobile network ecosystem, as underscored by existing literature (Zhou et al., 2020).

Healthcare data analytics- pose another challenge as smart healthcare, with its billions of connected devices, generates vast amounts of data requiring analysis. This data may encompass private information about individual users (e.g., patient data) and information about the local environment (e.g., ECG, Heart Rate monitoring). To address this, intelligent algorithms and procedures are essential to safeguard user privacy and confidentiality while deriving valuable insights for various use cases. Federated learning algorithms, for instance, can effectively analyze data generated by locally linked devices (Rieke, n.d.).

Cellular Coverage - Owing to various considerations, the imperative for uninterrupted coverage and connectivity is paramount across diverse scenarios within healthcare systems. The intricate spatial configuration of hospitals, coupled with the presence of attached devices, poses limitations on network coverage. In addressing this challenge, aerial networks, particularly Unmanned Aerial Vehicles (UAVs), High Altitude Platforms (HAPs), and satellites, emerge as highly promising avenues for the expansion of coverage. These networks have the potential to enhance coverage by functioning as base stations or relay transceivers, as elucidated in pertinent literature (Janjua et al., 2020).

Estimation and channel modelling of THz communication- The estimation and channel modeling of Terahertz (THz) communication constitute a pivotal aspect, necessitating the development of reliable channel models for effective wireless communication systems in the THz range. Simulating a THz channel requires consideration of factors such as spatial non-stationarity over ultra-massive antenna arrays, near-field effects, mutual coupling effects, and highly frequency-selective path loss due to the absorption loss of oxygen and water-vapor molecules. Consequently, channel estimation algorithms requiring minimal computational resources for THz communication systems with large antenna arrays are highly desirable.

Localization And Precise Positioning - The indoor and outdoor locations assumes critical importance in facilitating prompt responses during emergency scenarios, particularly in the context of natural catastrophes. While outdoor tracking and localization are conventionally addressed by the Global Positioning System (GPS), its efficacy diminishes within complex electromagnetic propagation environments, rendering it unreliable for indoor location determination (Säily et al., 2021). This limitation becomes particularly pronounced when hospitals experience an influx of individuals following a crisis, exacerbating the challenges associated with locating physicians, medical personnel, and patients. Addressing this issue involves the implementation of a real-time location system over the 6G architecture, offering real-time coordination and swift responses, especially for critical patients, as expounded in pertinent literature (Mogyorósi et al., 2022).

Intelligent spectrum sharing - It is a critical consideration, involving technologies such as device-to-device communication, in-band full-duplex communication, non-orthogonal multiple access, and spectrum sharing in unlicensed space within 6G-enabled IoT networks. Effective interference avoidance/mitigation strategies are crucial to enhance system performance while managing a large number of connections in 6G applications. The potential efficacy of blockchain technology and deep learning as approaches for flexible spectrum sharing is an attractive proposition. Therefore, the development of new frameworks and protocols for intelligent spectrum sharing assumes paramount importance.

Data ownership and ethical concerns – These concerns emerge prominently due to the sensitive and personal nature of healthcare data. Despite the potential improvements in quality of life facilitated by smart healthcare devices, apprehensions surrounding data ownership persist. For example, a digital pill with embedded sensors may provide caretakers and clinicians access to information about medication adherence via a web-based interface. While these assists medical professionals in treatment plan evaluation, concerns arise regarding the potential for insurance companies to monitor and potentially deny coverage based on patient adherence data (Chowdhury et al., 2020). Addressing these concerns at the policy-making level requires careful consideration of the type and frequency of data collection, user informed consent, and mechanisms for users to decline data collection or prohibit the sale of their data.

Edge Intelligence And Fog Computing - Within the healthcare domain, pertinent information concerning stakeholders, including patients and physicians, is remotely stored on cloud platforms. Intelligent devices generate data, which is subsequently transmitted to the cloud for storage, thereby utilizing channel access and bandwidth resources. The forthcoming 6G technology asserts its capability to accommodate a substantial capacity, facilitating seamless service provision to a myriad of smart devices. Notably, 6G places reliance on Edge technology to furnish expeditious and uninterrupted internet access to intelligent devices, a facet deemed critical within healthcare settings. In the realm of Edge technology, information pertaining to healthcare is gathered, computed, and analyzed in real-time within its Edge nodes, as elucidated in existing literature (Mao et al., 2020).

While the evolutionary stages of 5G and advanced 5G technologies, such as 5G+, have introduced notable enhancements in areas like coverage, device mobility, and device intelligence, challenges persist. These challenges encompass factors like data rate, latency, spectrum limitations, and bandwidth constraints, particularly impacting time-sensitive and resource-aware services within the healthcare sector (You et al., 2020).

IV. CONCLUSION

Prospective healthcare networks are poised to enable real-time collaboration among medical professionals through advanced technologies such as holographic communication, facilitating remote surgeries, and analyzing data from intelligent Internet of Things (IoT) devices for enhanced diagnostic capabilities and patient care. The extant communication technologies face challenges in meeting the intricate and dynamic demands posed by a diverse array of intelligent healthcare applications.

At the same time 6G technology exhibits potential limitations, including concerns related to the security and privacy aspects associated with the network, the substantial costs involved in the establishment and maintenance of the network, and the potential health impacts on individuals. The emergence of 6G technology is anticipated to introduce a heightened diversity of service and application requirements compared to previous technological iterations. Meeting these diverse needs necessitates a comprehensive understanding and adaptability within the technological framework. Similarly, the enhancement of user experiences requires the dynamic orchestration and configuration of end-to-end networks to cater to on-demand, customized, and personalized services. This responsiveness is integral to delivering an immersive and tailored user experience. Also the convergence of communication, computation, and sensing capabilities is identified as a critical factor augmenting the quality of services and fostering diverse business cases. This integrative approach represents a departure from conventional paradigms, emphasizing a synergistic utilization of these technological components.

The nascent stage of development for 6G-IoT networks and applications underscores an ongoing process. It is anticipated that the advent of 6G will bring about a revolutionary transformation in existing IoT infrastructures, introducing unprecedented levels of service quality, improvements in quality of living, and enhanced user experiences in forthcoming healthcare applications. This paper has undertaken an exploration of the fundamental technologies and domains within 6G-enabled IoT networks, while also delineating potential avenues for future research.

REFERENCES

Ahad, A., Tahir, M., Sheikh, M. A., Ahmed, K. I., Mughees, A., & Numani, A. (2020). Technologies trend towards 5g network for smart healthcare using IoT: A review. *Sensors (Basel)*, 20(14), 4047. 10.3390/s2014404732708139

Akhtar, M. W., Hassan, S. A., Ghaffar, R., Jung, H., Garg, S., & Hossain, M. S. (2020). The shift to 6g communications: Vision and requirements. *Human-centric Computing and Information Sciences.*, 10(1), 1. 10.1186/s13673-020-00258-2

Alfian, G., Syafrudin, M., Ijaz, M. F., Syaekhoni, M. A., Fitriyani, N. L., & Rhee, J. (2018). A Personalized Healthcare Monitoring System for Diabetic Patients by Utilizing BLE-Based Sensors and Real-Time Data Processing. *Sensors (Basel)*, 18(7), 2183. 10.3390/s1807218329986473

Bhansali, S., Li, C.Z., & Kaushik, A. (2022). Towards hospital-on-chip supported by 2D MXenes-based 5th generation intelligent biosensors. *Biosens. Bioelectron.*, 220, 114847.

Chaudhary, V., Khanna, V., Awan, H. T. A., Singh, K., Khalid, M., & Mishra, Y. (2022). Towards hospital-on-chip supported by 2D MXenes-based 5th generation intelligent biosensors. *Biosensors & Bioelectronics*.36335709

Chen, S., Liang, Y. C., Sun, S., Kang, S., Cheng, W., & Peng, M. (2022). Vision, requirements, and technology trend of 6g: How to tackle the challenges of system coverage, capacity, user data-rate and movement speed. *IEEE Wireless Communications*, 217.

Chowdhury, M. Z., Shahjalal, M., Ahmed, S., & Jang, Y. M. (2020). 6G Wireless Communication Systems: Applications, Requirements, Technologies, Challenges, and Research Directions. *IEEE Open Journal of the Communications Society*, 1, 957–975. 10.1109/OJCOMS.2020.3010270

Fafoutis, X., Marchegiani, L., Elsts, A., Pope, J., Piechocki, R., & Craddock, I. (2018). Extending the battery lifetime of wearable sensors with embedded machine learning. *Proc. IEEE 4th World Forum Internet Things*. 10.1109/WF-IoT.2018.8355116

Gupta, A., Fernando, X., & Das, O. (2021). *Reliability and Availability Modeling Techniques in 6G IoT Networks: A Taxonomy and Survey. In 2021 International Wireless Communications and Mobile Computing*. IWCMC. 10.1109/IWCMC51323.2021.9498628

Hakeem, A. A., & Hussein, H. H. (2022, June). Hyung won, K.: Vision and research directions of 6G technologies and applications. *Journal of King Saud University. Computer and Information Sciences*, 34(6), 2419–2442. 10.1016/j.jksuci.2022.03.019

Hussein, H. H., & Abd El-Kader, S. M. (2017). Enhancing signal to noise interference ratio for device to device technology in 5G applying mode selection technique. In *2017 Intl Conf on Advanced Control Circuits Systems (ACCS) Systems & 2017 Intl Conf on New Paradigms in Electronics & Information Technology (PEIT)*.10.1109/ACCS-PEIT.2017.8303040

Janjua, M.B., Duranay, A.E., & Arslan, H. (2020). Role of Wireless Communication in Healthcare System to Cater Disaster Situations Under 6G Vision. *Frontiers in Communications and Networks, 1.*

Katz, M., & Ahmed, I. (2020). *Opportunities and challenges for visible light commu- nications in 6g. 2020 2nd 6G wireless summit (6G SUMMIT.*

Khan, W., Rehman, M. H., Zangoti, H. M., Afzal, M. K., Armi, N., & Salah, K. (2019). Industrial Internet of Things: Recent Advances, Enabling Technologies, and Open Challenges. *Computers & Electrical Engineering*, 81, 106522. Advance online publication. 10.1016/j.compeleceng.2019.106522

Kumar, M., Kavita, , Verma, S., Kumar, A., Ijaz, M. F., & Rawat, D. B. (2022). ANAF-IoMT: A Novel Architectural Framework for IoMT-Enabled Smart Healthcare System by Enhancing Security Based on RECC-VC. *IEEE Transactions on Industrial Informatics*, 18(12), 8936–8943. 10.1109/TII.2022.3181614

Mao, B., Kawamoto, Y., & Kato, N. (2020). AI-Based Joint Optimization of QoS and Security for 6G Energy Harvesting Internet of Things. *IEEE Internet of Things Journal*, 7(8), 7032–7042. 10.1109/JIOT.2020.2982417

McGhin, T., Kim-Kwang, R. C., Charles, Z. L., & He, H. D. (2019). Blockchain in healthcare applications: Research challenges and opportunities. *Journal of Network and Computer Applications*, 135, 62–75. 10.1016/j.jnca.2019.02.027

Mogyorósi, F., Revisnyei, P., Pašić, A., Papp, Z., Törös, I., Varga, P., & Pašić, A. (2022). Positioning in 5G and 6G Networks—A Survey. *Sensors (Basel)*, 22(13), 4757. 10.3390/s2213475735808254

Mucchi, L., Jayousi, S., Caputo, S., Paoletti, E., Zoppi, P., Geli, S., & Dioniso, P. (2020). *How 6G Technology Can Change the Future Wireless Healthcare. In 2020 2nd 6G Wireless Summit (6G SUMMIT).*, 10.1109/6GSUMMIT49458.2020.9083916

Mughees, A., Tahir, M., Sheikh, M.A., & Ahad, A. (n.d.). *Energy-efficient ultra-dense 5G networks: recent advances, taxonomy and future research directions.* IEEE.

Nayak, S., & Patgiri, R. (2021). *6G Communication Technology: A Vision on Intelligent Healthcare.* 10.1007/978-981-15-9735-0_1

Nguyen, D. C., Ding, M., Pathirana, P. N., Seneviratne, A., Li, J., Niyato, D., Dobre, O., & Poor, H. V. (2022). 6G Internet of Things: A Comprehensive Survey. *IEEE Internet of Things Journal*, 9(1), 359–383. 10.1109/JIOT.2021.3103320

Noor-A-Rahim, M., Liu, Z., Lee, H., Khyam, M. O., He, J., Pesch, D., Moessner, K., Saad, W., & Poor, H. V. (2022). 6G for Vehicle-to-Everything (V2X) Communications: Enabling Technologies, Challenges, and Opportunities. *Proceedings of the IEEE*, 110(6), 712–734. 10.1109/JPROC.2022.3173031

Nova, S.N., Rahman, M.S., & Chakraborty, C. (2021). Patients' Health Surveillance Model Using IoT and 6G Technology. *Green Technological Innovation for Sustainable Smart Societies: Post Pandemic Era*, 191–209.

Rieke, N. (n.d.). The future of digital health with federated learning. *NPJ Digital.* 10.1038/s41746-020-00323-1

Saeidi, T., Mahmood, S. N., Alani, S., Ali, S. M., Ismail, I., & Alhawari, A. R. H. (2020). Sub-6G Metamaterial-Based Flexible Wearable UWB Antenna for IoT and WBAN. *Proceedings - IEEE 18th International Conference on Dependable, Autonomic and Secure Computing, IEEE 18th International Conference on Pervasive Intelligence and Computing, IEEE 6th International Conference on Cloud and Big Data Computing and IEEE 5th Cybe*, 7–13.

Sahin, E., Dagdeviren, O., & Akkas, M. A. (2021). An Evaluation of Internet of Nano-Things Simulators. *2021 6th International Conference on Computer Science and Engineering (UBMK)*, 670–675. 10.1109/UBMK52708.2021.9558990

Säily, M., Yilmaz, O. N. C., Michalopoulos, D. S., Pérez, E., Keating, R., & Schaepperle, J. (2021). Positioning Technology Trends and Solutions Toward 6G. *2021 IEEE 32nd Annual International Symposium on Personal, Indoor and Mobile Radio Communications (PIMRC)*, 1–7. 10.1109/PIM-RC50174.2021.9569341

Sarieddeen, H., Saeed, N., Al-Naffouri, T. Y., & Alouini, M.-S. (2020). Next Generation Terahertz Communications: A Rendezvous of Sensing, Imaging, and Localization. *IEEE Communications Magazine*, 58(5), 69–75. 10.1109/MCOM.001.1900698

Sodhro, A. H., Pirbhulal, S., Luo, Z., Muhammad, K., & Zahid, N. Z. (2021). Towards 6G Architecture for Energy Efficient Communication in IoT-Enabled Smart Automation Systems. *IEEE Internet of Things Journal*, 8(7), 5141–5148. 10.1109/JIOT.2020.3024715

Srinivasu, P. N., JayaLakshmi, G., Jhaveri, R. H., & Praveen, S. P. (2022). JayaLakshmi, G., Jhaveri, R.H., Praveen, S.P.: Ambient Assistive Living for Monitoring the Physical Activity of Diabetic Adults through Body Area Networks. *Mobile Information Systems*, 2022, e3169927. 10.1155/2022/3169927

Strinati, E. C., Barbarossa, S., Gonzalez-Jimenez, J. L., Ktenas, D., & Cassiau, N. (2019). 6g: the next frontier: from holographic messaging to artificial intelligence using subterahertz and visible light communication. *IEEE Vehicular Technology Magazine*, 14.

Wang, Z., Du, Y., Wei, K., Han, K., Xu, X., Wei, G., Tong, W., Zhu, P., Ma, J., Wang, J., Wang, G., Yan, X., Xiang, J., Huang, H., Li, R., Wang, X., Wang, Y., Sun, S., Suo, S., & Su, X. (2022). Vision, application scenarios, and key technology trends for 6G mobile communications. *Science China. Information Sciences*, 65(5), 1. 10.1007/s11432-021-3351-5

Wu, T., Redoute, J.-M., & Yuce, M. R. (2018). A wireless implantable sensor design with subcutaneous energy harvesting for long-term IoT healthcare applications. *IEEE Access : Practical Innovations, Open Solutions*, 6, 35801–35808. 10.1109/ACCESS.2018.2851940

You, X., Wang, C.-X., Huang, J., Gao, X., Zhang, Z., Wang, M., Huang, Y., Zhang, C., Jiang, Y., Wang, J., Zhu, M., Sheng, B., Wang, D., Pan, Z., Zhu, P., Yang, Y., Liu, Z., Zhang, P., Tao, X., & Ma, X. (2020). Towards 6G wireless communication networks: vision, enabling technologies, and new paradigm shifts. *Science China. Information Sciences*, 64(1), 110301. 10.1007/s11432-020-2955-6

Zhou, Y., Ling, L., Wang, L., Hui, N., Cui, X., Wu, J., Peng, Y., Qi, Y., & Xing, C. (2020). Service aware 6G: An intelligent and open network based on convergence of communication, computing and caching. *Digital Communications and Networks*, 6(3), 253–260. Advance online publication. 10.1016/j. dcan.2020.05.003

Chapter 7
Diagnostic Device for Sustainable Medical Care Using Hyperspectral Imaging

G. Vinuja

https://orcid.org/0000-0001-8109-988X

Saveetha School of Engineering, Saveetha Institute of Medical and Technical Sciences, India

V. Saravanan

Saveetha School of Engineering, Saveetha Institute of Medical and Technical Sciences, India

K. Maharajan

Saveetha School of Engineering, Saveetha Institute of Medical and Technical Sciences, India

V. Jayasudha

Saveetha School of Engineering, Saveetha Institute of Medical and Technical Sciences, India

R. Ramya

Saveetha School of Engineering, Saveetha Institute of Medical and Technical Sciences, India

S. Jothi Arunachalam

Saveetha School of Engineering, Saveetha Institute of Medical and Technical Sciences, India

ABSTRACT

The improving medical instrumentation thru hyper spectral imaging for sustainable medical care (IMITH-SM) project is a research initiative that seeks to develop and boost hyperspectral imaging (HSI) technologies to correctly and as it should be screen, diagnose, and deal with clinically associated conditions in the clinical discipline. More particularly, this venture pursuits to discover and expand using HSI and its software to enhance the accuracy and range of medical examinations, diagnoses, treatments, and decisions. By leveraging the benefits of HSI, the IMITH-SM mission seeks to enhance clinical instrumentation and patient care by providing greater dependable, quicker, and simpler-to-recognize imaging and diagnostic records. Specifically, these targets include exploring how HSI may be used as a diagnostic device for commonplace illnesses such as cancer and cardiovascular illnesses and figuring out capability programs for HSI-enabled scientific robotics.

DOI: 10.4018/979-8-3693-0683-3.ch007

I. INTRODUCTION

In recent years, the scientific field has seen remarkable advances in generation and instrumentation. Hyper Spectral Imaging (HSI) is one of the latest innovations in clinical instrumentation that could offer an extra sustainable and cost-effective hospital treatment method (Bonifazi et al., 2023). HSI involves shooting light from diverse areas of the electromagnetic spectrum and reading the facts to create an in-depth picture. HSI can be used to analyze and remedy illnesses, detect tumors, and monitor remedy reactions.HSI offers some blessings over traditional imaging techniques. For instance, HSI can offer more fantastic particular images by appropriately taking pictures of extraordinary tiers of light from the complete electromagnetic spectrum (Zhang et al., 2023; Puustinen et al., 2023). It affects higher-resolution images, making diagnosing diseases, locating tumors, or displaying treatment responses more challenging. The HSI can be used for preventive medicinal drugs by presenting more excellent and accurate readings of medical statistics while not having to carry out high-priced scans or biopsies. HSI additionally offers notably decreased radiation publicity in comparison to traditional imaging techniques (Studier-Fischer et al., 2023). Using HSI for medical instrumentation can also help lessen expenses by imparting a non-invasive way to diagnose diseases, come across tumors, and monitor treatment response. HSI technology is likewise more cost-powerful than traditional imaging techniques because of decreased running costs and the ability to reuse the outcomes of scans more than once (Mishra et al., 2023). That allows you to capitalize on the benefits of HSI for medical instrumentation ultimately and to ensure the maximum sustainable and fee-powerful approach to hospital treatment; extra research and improvement are needed to tailor HSI structures to shape extraordinary needs (Rodrigues & Hemmer., 2022; (Thatcher et al., 2023)). Artificial intelligence and deep getting-to-know abilities also can assist in maximizing the performance and fee-effectiveness of HSI structures (Okamoto et al., 2022).HSI can revolutionize hospital therapy and offer extra correct and sustainable results than traditional strategies. With further studies and development, HSI structures may want to provide doctors with the correct prognosis and treatment facts for patients while reducing expenses and radiation publicity (Martinez-Vega et al., 2022; Pruitt et al., 2023). As the usage of HSI keeps developing, it will now enable the scientific discipline to offer better, extra sustainable care and enhance our information and expertise of the human frame, leading to better treatments (Ma et al., 2022; Li et al., 2022; Mahmoud & El-Sharkawy., 2023). The venture also ambitions to develop HSI software solutions to facilitate the combination of HSI in present medical gadgets and facilitate conversation between medical teams of workers and patients (Yin et al., 2022; Shitharth et al., 2022). The assignment utilizes a multi-disciplinary method that entails a vast range of experts, from generations of specialists to medical practitioners. These experts are running collectively to broaden HSI hardware specific to scientific instrument programs and create server-facet software answers to streamline statistics usage and facilitate communiqué (Felli et al., 2022; Cui et al., 2022). If successful, the IMITH-SM task will offer healthcare professionals stepped-forward imaging and diagnostic abilities and enable quicker and more correct analysis, remedy, and decisions. Ultimately, this assignment seeks to improve the sustainability of hospital therapy by assisting in lessening medical charges and enhancing medical results (Karim et al., 2023). The main contribution of the research has the following,

- Discount of optical distortion and stepped forward spectral resolution: HSI can lessen optical distortion and considerably improve the spectral resolution of clinical instruments, taking into account more excellent correct analysis of clinical snapshots.

- Progressed sensitivity and specificity: Using leveraging HSI techniques, medical professionals can better understand a person's medical situation, enabling them to make extra correctly informed and localized selections while supplying hospital therapy.
- Step forward accuracy of scientific diagnosis: With HSI, scientific specialists can make higher diagnosis selections, mainly to better-affected person outcomes. HSI enables scientific professionals to perceive certain kinds of tissue and other functions within an image that might, in any other case, be difficult to hit upon. Its progressed accuracy allows ensuring scientific specialists to provide first-class care to their sufferers.

II. RELATED WORKS

Hyperspectral imaging implemented to WEEE (waste electric and digital gadget) plastic recycling is a new and rising generation for helping facilitate the green extraction of critical materials from WEEE recycling streams (Bonifazi et al., 2023). This approach entails using an imaging scanner to capture light in numerous exceptional wavelengths that could be used to differentiate and pick out diverse varieties of plastic, even when they may be blended collectively. This imaging can significantly lessen the time spent trying to identify plastics from waste streams. Moreover, it may reduce the guide labor associated with sorting and segregating substances. This generation is a promising device for WEEE experts to assist them higher manipulate their plastic waste streams more efficiently, fee-powerfully, and ecologically sustainable.

Near-infrared II hyperspectral imaging (NIR-II HSI) is a spectral imaging technology that uses near-infrared (NIR) mild to document spectral information approximately a pattern (Zhang et al., 2023). NIR-II HSI technology has a wide range of programs inside the medical subject, together with pathology. By reading the spectral information collected by the imaging system, it is far more feasible to perceive the sort of cells and tissues found in a tissue sample and come across any symptoms of disorder or abnormality. This pretty touchy technology can enhance the accuracy of pathological sampling for multiple varieties of most cancers, which includes cancer and lung cancer. NIR-II HSI can stumble on minimal changes in the absorbance spectra of those varieties of most cancer cells, which can be used to locate subtle variations among benign and cancerous tissues. This improved accuracy can assist medical personnel higher become aware of and diagnosing cancers inside the early ranges, leading to more successful remedies and higher survival charges.

Hyperspectral Imaging, in Mind Tumor surgical procedure, is a new application of machine learning for diagnostic guidance (Puustinen et al., 2023). The method uses hyperspectral imaging to capture brain information, which has been analyzed for tumor traits and used for manual surgical navigation. System-gaining knowledge of algorithms can be used to assess the tumor functions for quicker prognosis and remedy planning. This system may reduce the time wished for the guide evaluation of pattern tissues and growth the accuracy of surgical techniques. Hyperspectral imaging may enhance surgical navigation by imparting the identity of areas with a higher probability of tumor recurrence.

HeiPorSPECTRAL is a public database governing the spectrometric research of regular porcine organs gathered from a slaughterhouse (Studier-Fischer et al., 2023). It consists of 20 not-unusual physiological organs of the pig, which include numerous muscle mass, connective tissue, skin, fats, and mind count. The dataset consists of HyperSPECTRAL imaging data (HCIs) captured from an ASD FieldSpec 4 Hi-Res

HyperSPECTRAL imaging spectroradiometer spanning the entire seen spectrum (four hundred-900nm) and the near-infrared spectrum (900-2500nm). The dataset helps studies into more substantial processing and evaluation of HyperSPECTRAL imaging statistics.

Comparing meals pleasant of agro produce involves figuring out the first-class agricultural merchandise, including meals that are grown and harvested (Mishra et al., 2023). Excellent can be evaluated by trying out the product's chemical, bodily, and biological properties, as well as its protection and shelf lifestyles. Opinions involve assessing whether or not and how outside factors, inclusive of climate, pests, and agricultural practices, may affect the fine of the product. The assessment can assist in making certain great agro products for the meals supply and help determine the satisfactory approaches to keep, system, deliver and distribute those goods. Acceptable evaluation may be completed using a ramification of strategies and techniques, chemical test methods, sensory organoleptic exams, and bodily testing. Through carrying out excellent reviews, it is far possible to make sure that all agro-produce is safe, wholesome, and of a regular exceptional. The comprehensive analysis has shown in the following table.1

Table 1. Comprehensive analysis

Model	Technology	Advantage	Drawbacks
Development, Symptoms and Diagnosis.	Computer-Assisted Differentiation	Hyperspectral imaging implemented to WEEE (waste electric and digital gadget) plastic recycling is a new and rising generation for helping facilitate the green extraction of critical materials from WEEE recycling streams	Moreover, it may reduce the guide labor associated with sorting and segregating substances
Complete mesocolic excision versus conventional surgery for colon cancer	Meta-analysis	NIR-II HSI technology has a wide range of programs inside the medical subject, together with pathology.	NIR-II HSI can stumble on minimal changes in the absorbance spectra of those varieties of most cancer cells, which can be used to locate subtle variations among benign and cancerous tissues.
non-complete mesocolic excision in patients with colon cancer:	Meta-analysis	The method uses hyperspectral imaging to capture brain information, which has been analyzed for tumor traits and used for manual surgical navigation.	Hyperspectral imaging may enhance surgical navigation by imparting the identity of areas with a higher probability of tumor recurrence
Surgical technique and survival in patients having a curative resection for colon cancer.	Computer-Assisted Differentiation	HeiPorSPECTRAL is a public database governing the spectrometric research of regular porcine organs gathered from a slaughterhouse	The dataset helps studies into more substantial processing and evaluation of HyperSPECTRAL imaging statistics.
Impact of D3 lymph node dissection on survival for patients with T3 and T4 colon cancer.	meta-analysis	Excellent can be evaluated by trying out the product's chemical, bodily, and biological properties, as well as its protection and shelf lifestyles	The assessment can assist in making certain great agro products for the meals supply and help determine the satisfactory approaches to keep, system, deliver and distribute those goods

III. PROPOSED MODEL

Hyper-spectral imaging can revolutionize clinical instrumentation for more accurate and value-effective healthcare. Hyper-spectral imaging consists of capturing electromagnetic radiation from illness-associated tissues, then analyzing and quantifying disease parameters in the sample. By studying the sample composition, medical experts can acquire an in-intensity prognosis approximately the state of a patient's fitness. Technology may be used for a massive kind of hospital therapy, ranging from dermatology to ophthalmology to radiography. In dermatology, hyper-spectral imaging may be used to detect skin most cancers cells and classify and diagnose several pores and skin sicknesses. This technology can be used in ophthalmology for early detection and analysis of retinal sicknesses, including age-related macular degeneration and diabetic retinopathy. In radiography, imaging gadgets, including computed tomography (CT) and Magnetic Resonance Imaging (MRI), are used to set up an affected person's frame composition and diagnose numerous kinds of hemorrhages, including worrying brain and spinal wire injuries.in order to enhance medical instrumentation with hyper-spectral imaging, some upgrades want to be made. First, scientific specialists must ensure that the hyper-spectral photos produced are of the highest first-rate and may be reliably interpreted. Second, the technology wishes to be price-powerful, so it is far available to scientific experts in rural and aid-restrained settings. 1/3 of healthcare companies want to study how to use the gadgets efficiently and correctly interpret the images they produce. Fig.1 shows the Synthetic RGB, Ground truth and Overlap.

Figure 1. Synthetic RGB, ground truth, and overlap

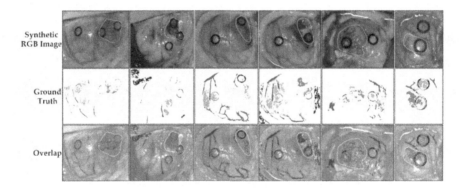

The software program wishes to evolve to automate the method of measuring, quantifying, and deciphering the snapshots produced through hyper-spectral imaging. Through these upgrades, hyper-spectral imaging becomes an essential device for clinical specialists to apply an excellent way to provide greater correct and value-powerful healthcare for everyone. In addition, patient statistics and records become easier to shop and get the right of entry to, and healthcare structures become more efficient and streamlined. All in all, these upgrades will lead to greater affected person pleasure and improved get admission to hospital therapy.

A. Colon Results

Hyper Spectral Imaging (HSI) may be used to come across and examine modifications in tissues because of pathological or physiological methods. It facilitates doctors and scientists to check the progress of sicknesses and health challenges and recommend treatments.HSI is ideally suited to inspecting and comparing the colon due to its non-invasive, actual-time properties. HSI-aided colonoscopy improves consolation for patients and safety for clinicians by notably lowering the danger of headaches. Hyper Spectral Imaging can discover and identify minute adjustments in the structure and composition of the colon, which could imply the presence of colorectal tumors and polyps in their early ranges. It could also spot changes in blood vessels, vascular networks, and cells. It allows doctors more as it should verify their location, speed, and course's gives an extra specific prognosis of disease inside the colon and can detect and measure subtle modifications in the colon's molecular and mobile composition, permitting doctors to devise focused remedies more excellently.HSI can also identify dietary residences and monitor metabolic techniques that create and disturb the colon. It, in turn, helps doctors to apprehend how metabolic disorders, allergic reactions, and pressure affect the colon and how they contribute to developing colorectal cancer. Hyper Spectral Imaging enables hit-upon physiological adjustments inclusive of cell malignancy, malformation, and apoptosis in near real-time, so doctors can respond quickly and increase treatments for lengthy-time period care. Medical doctors can also use HSI to hit upon and monitor the consequences of remedies along with chemotherapy on the colon and evaluate the recuperation rate.in addition to assessing ailment, HSI can also be used to locate strange changes inside the colon's microbiota, helping doctors modify dietary plans (along with probiotics and prebiotics) to prevent and control colorectal diseases.Fig.2 shows the regularly occurring processing-chain block diagram for category the use of ML and DL models.

Figure 2. Regularly occurring processing-chain block diagram for category the use of ML and DL models

B. Esophagogastric Results

Hyperspectral imaging (HSI) is a non-invasive imaging generation used to come across and diagnose diseases and problems of the gastrointestinal tract. It uses excessive-strength, excessive-resolution imaging equipment to capture precise structural, purposeful, and chemical facts from the tissues underneath research. The results of HSI can be used to guide the control of a massive range of gastrointestinal illnesses, including inflammatory bowel diseases, Barrett's esophagus, and neoplastic lesions.HSI may be used to locate diffused adjustments in tissue structure and composition that can suggest a sickness or ailment, altered infection, multiplied epithelial cell turnover, improved mucosal goblet mobile numbers, or epithelial hyper proliferation. Additionally, HSI can degree the tiers of certain materials, such as nitrates and proteins, that may be used to detect infection and adjust organ features. HSI can also be hired to screen the presence or absence of specific viruses or microorganisms related to disease onset or progression. It could also help diagnose and analyze sicknesses of the esophagus and belly. Fig.3 shows the Steps of the pre processing chain block diagram.

Figure 3. Steps of the pre processing chain block diagram

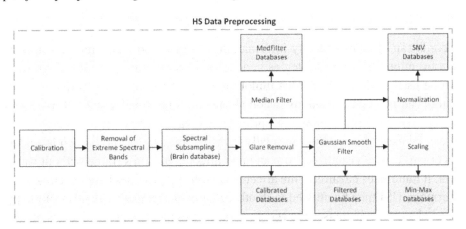

HSI can be used to evaluate the presence and interest of Helicobacter pylori, which is the causative agent of some gastric and duodenal ulcers. It may also be used to assess the presence of reflux esophagitis due to infiltrating inflammatory cells. In hospital treatment, HSI can be used as an accessory to standard imaging modalities, including conventional endoscopy and computed tomography. It may provide additional statistics about an affected person's sickness status and assist in guiding and telling the most suitable treatment selections. HSI can also be used in screening packages to pick out individuals vulnerable to growing positive gastrointestinal problems and to display the efficacy of treatments that can be employed. Using HSI in hospital therapy is a rising field; similar studies are wanted to apprehend its complete capacity and programs. With improved usage of this era, it is expected that its benefits for sustainable hospital therapy will become more apparent.

C. Brain Results

Hyperspectral imaging (HSI) is a modern imaging technology that permits researchers to seize some distance extra specific medical photographs than ever before. HSI captures pics of particular parts of the electromagnetic spectrum, resulting in a more comprehensive view of tissues and organs. This generation is beneficial for the clinical enterprise, taking into account more significant correct analysis and better-affected person care's offers clinical professionals insight into more than one characteristic of an organ or tissue, such as shape, composition, temperature, electric homes, and plenty extra.

$$X = 100 \cdot \frac{\beta - Y_{ref}}{W_{ref} - D_{ref}} \tag{1}$$

$$X_{Mim-Max}' = \frac{C_i - \min(X)}{\max(X) - \min(X)} \tag{2}$$

$$X_{i,j}^{SNV} = \frac{(X_{i,j} - X_i)}{\sqrt{\frac{\sum_{j=1}^{L}(X_{i,j} - X_i)^2}{L-1}}}$$

(3)

These records can offer in-intensity information on shape and characteristics now not previously viable with conventional imaging strategies.in addition to presenting precious diagnostic information, HSI also can be used to detect cancerous tumors in actual time, allowing active remedy. Using HSI, medical doctors can perceive variations inside tissues on a far smaller scale. It permits them to goal particular areas rather than performing high-priced and invasive surgeries to get admission to the entire place's also can be used to carry out minimally-invasive imaging methods such as endoscopies. With HSI, various organs can be visualized from an inner affected person's frame without wanting a surgical establishment. It minimizes hazards to the affected person and provides better accuracy and faster prognosis. Furthermore, HSI may be utilized with other diagnostic exams to identify subtle tissue structure or composition changes. It increases the accuracy of the prognosis and lets doctors make decisions.

D. Performance Visualization

Hyperspectral imaging (HSI) is a method used to visualize the spectral signatures of numerous substances. It is used in scientific imaging to pick out and classify tissue texture, which may provide treasured statistics approximately the stage and evolution of the disease. HSI enables clinical specialists to view various tissue properties and identify diffused modifications within the tissue texture's generates an image with a massive variety of spectral bands or channels. The spectral bands are then processed to provide a picture with a distinctive pixel resolution level. The resulting image is used to visualize various tissue features throughout the complete region of the hobby. HSI can decide the distinct varieties of tissue found in a place, the proportion of these tissues, and their relative concentrations. Performance visualization of HSI entails studying and deciphering the results of the pics produced through the machine. It includes the assessment of the feel of the tissues, and the relative concentrations of diverse varieties of tissues across the vicinity scanned. The evaluation can display capabilities consisting of regions of cellular systems, microorganisms' presence, and tissue shade gradation. The overall performance of HSI may be assessed by studying the outcomes of numerous programs, which consist of sickness diagnostics, quantitative imaging, and tissue engineering. Overall performance visualization of HSI also may be used to evaluate HSI's general performance based on total image processing strategies. It will include techniques including noise discount, photograph segmentation, and class algorithms.

IV. RESULTS AND DISCUSSION

The approach can provide an in-depth map of an organ or tissue, which may be used to detect subtle modifications inside the structure or feature of the item. HSI can also be used to track materials or markers in the body, detect the presence of most cancer cells, or track the tiers of a selected drug or hormone. Table.2 shows the details of CNN architecture.

Table 2. Details of CNN architecture

Layer	Filter Shape	Number of Output Channel	Stride	Number of Trainable Parameters
Conv 1	(4.4.4)	30	(2.2.2)	660
Relu	/	/	/	/
Pool 1	(4.2.2)	30	(3.2.2)	1320
Conv 2	(4.4.4)	45	(2.2.2)	19,035
Relu	/	/	/	/
Pool 2	(4.2.2)	45	(3.2.2)	3810
Conv3	(4.2.2)	45	(2.2.2)	3810
Relu	/	/	/	/
Pool 3	(3.2.2)	45	(3.2.2)	2495
Relu	/	/	/	/
Fc	(455.3.1)	3	/	922

A. Sensitivity

Hyper Spectral Imaging (HSI) is a faraway sensing era that captures and methods nearly the electromagnetic spectrum straight away, from ultraviolet to thermal infrared. This wide range of wavelengths allows the generation to provide distinctive environmental information from an unmarried photograph. In medical care, HSI can be utilized in various programs, from diagnostics to drug delivery. In diagnostics, HSI can be used to locate tissue color, length, and texture modifications. For instance, it can discover diffused differences in light absorbance in tissue that may indicate particular scientific situations along with inflammation or tumors. HSI also can be used to perceive cancerous cells in a tissue or hit upon changes in blood float. In drug shipping, HSI can come across specific molecules that could indicate the presence of precise pills and the attention of the medication in a particular vicinity. It could help to guide the transport of a drug to the perfect cell or tissue kind, thereby improving drug efficacy. The sensitivity of HSI is such that even minor adjustments in spectral features may be detected. It makes the generation touchy sufficient to discover minimal concentrations of substances, permitting doctors to correctly perceive and diagnose scientific situations with extra accuracy and precision.

B. Prevalence

Hyper spectral imaging (HSI) is a technique used in medical imaging that combines the power of both spectroscopy and imaging to obtain detailed spectral information about an object. The technique is widely used in medical diagnosis, tissue imaging, surgical guidance, and cancer detection. Unlike traditional imaging techniques, such as CT or MRI, HSI relies on the spectral properties of a substance in order to analyze a sample. It manner that HSI can discover even small changes in the chemical composition of a sample and may be used to offer distinctive information about an object, which includes its chemical composition and structure. As a result, it may be used to diagnose various conditions and assist are expecting remedy effects. HSI can be used to scientifically have a look at physiological and biochemical approaches inside the frame, along with detecting and identifying biomolecules and different markers associated with sickness.

C. Accuracy

Hyper Spectral Imaging (HSI) is a hastily emerging field in scientific imaging, imparting an excellent capacity for detecting and remedying a comprehensive form of scientific conditions. HSI offers immoderate-decision snapshots of organic and human tissue, presenting essential data approximately disorder development and pathology. The era can potentially revolutionize scientific practice, imparting more excellent correct evaluations and extra brilliant, powerful remedy alternatives. HSI has a diffusion of applications in medical imaging, from analyzing most cancers and infections to detecting and diagnosing outstanding tissue structure. The accuracy of HSI photos depends upon a variety of factors, including the exceptional system used, the precise imaging parameters selected, and the operator's information. In general, modern-day HSI structures can provide photos with an accuracy of zero.1-zero.5mm. This accuracy is similar to different imaging modalities, MRI and CT scans, and represents a giant improvement over the accuracy of different clinical imaging technologies. Moreover, using HSI permits clinicians to detect and diagnose diffused modifications in tissue shape and characteristics, resulting in more correct diagnoses and more effective treatments. Table.3 shows the Mean and standard deviation values of the quantitative metrics obtained.

Table 3. Mean and standard deviation values of the quantitative metrics obtained

	Models	**TT**	**CT**	**AUC**	**MCC**
SVM	Calibrated	0.47~ 0.37	0.15~ 0.23	0.71~ 0.37	0.38~ 0.34
	Filtered	0.38 ~ 0.28	0.87 ~ 0.25	0.68 ~ 0.27	0.22 ~ 0.27
	Min-Max	0.31 ~ 0. 26	0.97 ~ 0.03	0.71 ~ 0.23	0.19 ~ 0.21
	SNV	0.32 ~ 0.21	0.97 ~ 0.03	0.74 ~ 0.18	0.19 ~ 0.21
	Med-Filter	0.43 ~ 0. 28	0.98 ~ 0.03	0.84 ~ 0.15	0.36 ~ 0.27
3DCNN	Calibrated	0.52 ~ 0.21	0.90 ~ 0.11	0.94 ~ 0.06	0.50 ~ 0.19
	Filtered	0.46 ~ 0.26	0.88 ~ 0.11	0.96 ~ 0.03	0.48 ~ 0.22
	Min-Max	0.38 ~ 0.26	0.85 ~ 0.12	0.93 ~ 0.08	0.37 ~ 0.22
	SNV	0.45 ~ 0.22	0.87 ~ 0.13	0.90 ~ 0.08	0.44 ~ 0.20
	Med-Filter	0.52 ~ 0.23	0.91 ~ 0.08	0.94 ~ 0.08	0.52 ~ 0.20

The belief of this examination turned out that Hyper Spectral Imaging (HSI) technology has the potential to revolutionize clinical instrumentation and facilitate sustainable hospital treatment. HSI technology improves the accuracy, speed, and value-performance of scientific analysis and could permit clinicians to become aware of even the slightest abnormalities in an affected person's physiological situation. With HSI technology, scientific practitioners can perceive anomalies in tissue shape and shape-characteristic relationships.

$$F_1 - Score = \frac{2AZ}{2AZ + 2FZ + FN} \tag{4}$$

$$MCC = \frac{AZ.AN - FZ.FN}{\sqrt{(AZ + FZ).(AZ + FN).(AN + FZ).(AN + FN)}} \tag{5}$$

Figure 4. Calibrated preprocessing technique

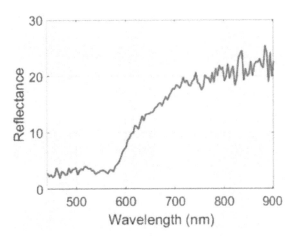

Figure 5. Filtered preprocessing technique

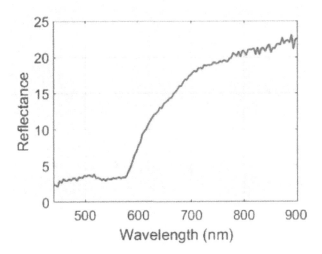

Figure 6. Min-Max preprocessing technique

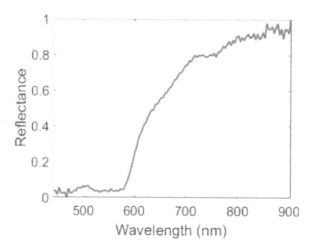

Figure 7. Med Filter preprocessing technique

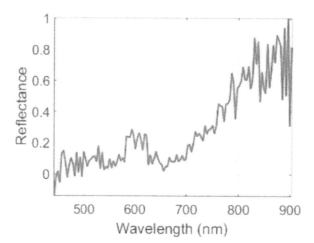

Furthermore, this generation has enabled practitioners to hit upon and diagnose medical situations more fast and appropriately, even by minimizing patients' radiation exposure. This era also benefits biomedicine studies by giving researchers access to worthwhile imaging facts inside the body. As HSI technology keeps expanding, the capacity for more excellent knowledgeable clinical decision-making will extend and enhance patient care.

VI. CONCLUSION

The capability programs of hyperspectral imaging in clinical instrumentation are several. By using this era, physicians can quickly and correctly locate diseases in a patient without the need for costly and time-eating laboratory tests. Further, the high decision of hyperspectral imaging can locate diffused modifications in tissue composition that could suggest the presence of a disorder. This generation can also be used to screen the progress of remedies, offer certain records approximately the form and shape of organs, or even discover ordinary cells. Soon, hyperspectral imaging can assist clinical professionals in discovering new and progressed methods to diagnose and deal with diverse situations. As an example, hyperspectral imaging can enhance the accuracy of cancer diagnosis by supplying exact information about the shape of the tumor cells, which can assist physicians in determining excellent remedy alternatives. It could also permit docs to detect sickness in areas that cannot be seen with conventional imaging techniques. As hyperspectral imaging progresses, it turns into increasingly important in the practice of sustainable hospital therapy. By allowing clinical experts to come across sickness earlier and provide extra correct prognosis and remedy, hyperspectral imaging will reduce the time and price required to deal with ailments. It will enable fitness care companies to offer more excellent, efficient, and effective care and improve the health of sufferers worldwide.

REFERENCES

Bonifazi, G., Fiore, L., Gasbarrone, R., Palmieri, R., & Serranti, S. (2023). Hyperspectral Imaging Applied to WEEE Plastic Recycling: A Methodological Approach. *Sustainability (Basel)*, 15(14), 11345. 10.3390/su151411345

Cui, Q., Yang, B., Liu, B., Li, Y., & Ning, J. (2022). Tea Category Identification Using Wavelet Signal Reconstruction of Hyperspectral Imagery and Machine Learning. *Agriculture*, 12(8), 1085. 10.3390/agriculture12081085

Felli, E., Cinelli, L., Bannone, E., Giannone, F., Muttillo, E. M., Barberio, M., Keller, D. S., Rodríguez-Luna, M. R., Okamoto, N., Collins, T., Hostettler, A., Schuster, C., Mutter, D., Pessaux, P., Marescaux, J., Gioux, S., Felli, E., & Diana, M. (2022). Hyperspectral imaging in major hepatectomies: Preliminary results from the ex-machyna trial. *Cancers (Basel)*, 14(22), 5591. 10.3390/cancers1422559136428685

Karim, S., Qadir, A., Farooq, U., Shakir, M., & Laghari, A. A. (2023). Hyperspectral imaging: A review and trends towards medical imaging. *Current Medical Imaging*, 19(5), 417–427. 10.2174/1573405618 66622051914435835598236

Li, N., Xue, J., & Jia, S. (2022, January). Spectral context-aware transformer for cholangiocarcinoma hyperspectral image segmentation. In *Proceedings of the 2022 5th International Conference on Image and Graphics Processing* (pp. 209-213). 10.1145/3512388.3512419

Ma, L., Little, J. V., Chen, A. Y., Myers, L., Sumer, B. D., & Fei, B. (2022). Automatic detection of head and neck squamous cell carcinoma on histologic slides using hyperspectral microscopic imaging. *Journal of Biomedical Optics*, 27(4), 046501–046501. 10.1117/1.JBO.27.4.04650135484692

Mahmoud, A., & El-Sharkawy, Y. H. (2023). Quantitative phase analysis and hyperspectral imaging for the automatic identification of veins and blood perfusion maps. *Photodiagnosis and Photodynamic Therapy*, 42, 103307. 10.1016/j.pdpdt.2023.10330736709016

Martinez-Vega, B., Tkachenko, M., Matkabi, M., Ortega, S., Fabelo, H., Balea-Fernandez, F., La Salvia, M., Torti, E., Leporati, F., Callico, G. M., & Chalopin, C. (2022). Evaluation of preprocessing methods on independent medical hyperspectral databases to improve analysis. *Sensors (Basel)*, 22(22), 8917. 10.3390/s2222891736433516

Mishra, N., Patel, D. P., & Jain, S. K. (n.d.). Hyperspectral imaging technique: A brief introduction for evaluating food quality of agro produce. *Exploration and Development of Agriculture in India*, 88.

Okamoto, N., Rodríguez-Luna, M. R., Bencteux, V., Al-Taher, M., Cinelli, L., Felli, E., Urade, T., Nkusi, R., Mutter, D., Marescaux, J., Hostettler, A., Collins, T., & Diana, M. (2022). Computer-assisted differentiation between colon-mesocolon and retroperitoneum using hyperspectral imaging (HSI) technology. *Diagnostics (Basel)*, 12(9), 2225. 10.3390/diagnostics1209222536140626

Pruitt, K., Johnson, B., Gahan, J., Ma, L., & Fei, B. (2023, April). A high-speed hyperspectral laparoscopic imaging system. *Image-Guided Procedures, Robotic Interventions, and Modeling*, 12466, 49–61.

Puustinen, S., Vrzáková, H., Hyttinen, J., Rauramaa, T., Fält, P., Hauta-Kasari, M., Bednarik, R., Koivisto, T., Rantala, S., von und zu Fraunberg, M., Jääskeläinen, J. E., & Elomaa, A. P. (2023). Hyperspectral Imaging in Brain Tumor Surgery—Evidence of Machine Learning-Based Performance. *World Neurosurgery*, 175, e614–e635. 10.1016/j.wneu.2023.03.14937030483

Rodrigues, E. M., & Hemmer, E. (2022). Trends in hyperspectral imaging: From environmental and health sensing to structure-property and nano-bio interaction studies. *Analytical and Bioanalytical Chemistry*, 414(15), 4269–4279. 10.1007/s00216-022-03959-y35175390

Shitharth, S., Manoharan, H., Alshareef, A. M., Yafoz, A., Alkhiri, H., & Mirza, O. M. (2022). Hyper spectral image classifications for monitoring harvests in agriculture using fly optimization algorithm. *Computers & Electrical Engineering*, 103, 108400. 10.1016/j.compeleceng.2022.108400

Studier-Fischer, A., Seidlitz, S., Sellner, J., Bressan, M., Özdemir, B., Ayala, L., Odenthal, J., Knoedler, S., Kowalewski, K.-F., Haney, C. M., Salg, G., Dietrich, M., Kenngott, H., Gockel, I., Hackert, T., Müller-Stich, B. P., Maier-Hein, L., & Nickel, F. (2023). HeiPorSPECTRAL - the Heidelberg Porcine HyperSPECTRAL Imaging Dataset of 20 Physiological Organs. *Scientific Data*, 10(1), 414. 10.1038/s41597-023-02315-837355750

Thatcher, J. E., Yi, F., Nussbaum, A. E., DiMaio, J. M., Dwight, J., Plant, K., Carter, J. E., & Holmes, J. H.IV. (2023). Clinical Investigation of a Rapid Non-invasive Multispectral Imaging Device Utilizing an Artificial Intelligence Algorithm for Improved Burn Assessment. *Journal of Burn Care & Research; Official Publication of the American Burn Association*, 44(4), 969–981. 10.1093/jbcr/irad05137082889

Yin, H., Li, B., Zhang, F., Su, C. T., & Ou-Yang, A. G. (2022). Detection of early bruises on loquat using hyperspectral imaging technology coupled with band ratio and improved Otsu method. *Spectrochimica Acta. Part A: Molecular and Biomolecular Spectroscopy*, 283, 121775. 10.1016/j.saa.2022.12177536007346

Zhang, L., Liao, J., Wang, H., Zhang, M., Liu, Y., Jiang, C., Han, D., Jia, Z., Qin, C., Niu, S. Y., Bu, H., Yao, J., & Liu, Y. (2023). Near-infrared II hyperspectral imaging improves the accuracy of pathological sampling of multiple cancer types. *Laboratory Investigation*, 103(10), 100212. 10.1016/j.labinv.2023.10021237442199

Chapter 8
Identification of Neuro–Blastoma and Pediatric Cancer Using Time Series Analysis

Sujatha Moorthy
Koneru Lakshmaiah Education Foundation, India

S. Nazrin Salma
Thamirabharani Engineering College, India

J. Boobalan
Kumaraguru College of Technology, India

G. Charulatha
Selvam College of Technology, India

M. Nivedha
Arasu Engineering College, India

A. Niyas Ahamed
Thamirabharani Engineering College, India

ABSTRACT

This chapter has studies that attempt to assess the detection of neuroblastoma and pediatric cancer via time series evaluation. The look took a retrospective method using five patient datasets, combining gadget learning and traditional statistical techniques to detect chance tiers of tumors inside the datasets. The machine-getting-to-know techniques include random forests, decision trees, assist vector machines, k-nearest friends, and convolutional neural nets. Statistical strategies used included co-occurrence matrix evaluation, principal element evaluation, and Shannon entropy. The observation outcomes demonstrate that time series analysis can offer high accuracy in predicting cancer threat levels and may be carried out on diverse cancers for well-timed and reliable prognosis. Eventually, the chapter offers various hints to enhance detection, incorporating extra statistics capabilities and designing a custom reference index.

I. INTRODUCTION

Neuroblastoma is an extraordinary shape of cancer that influences babies because of the fast development of their medullary nervous system. The 5-yr survival fee for this form of most cancers has been predicted to be around 45%. However, the price can range depending on the level at which the disease is identified (Hesko et al., 2023). Given the capability severity and recurrence of neuroblastoma, the potential to locate and accurately assess it in a well-timed way is of extreme significance. This essay will explore how time series evaluation may be used to help examine the detection of neuroblastoma. Time

DOI: 10.4018/979-8-3693-0683-3.ch008

series analysis includes developing styles over a time frame (Wear et al., 2023; Cole et al., 2023). Via this technique, traits and adjustments in information may be detected and monitored for any anomalies which can imply the early stages of an ailment, together with neuroblastoma. The first step in utilizing time collection analysis for assessing the detection of neuroblastoma is to collect the applicable scientific records. IT would encompass exams, including blood assessments, scans, imaging, genetic statistics, and other fitness records that may be collected through the years (Inoue et al., 2023; Kholodenko et al., 2023). Those statistical factors may be used to broaden a baseline of everyday fitness for a patient or a populace of sufferers. As the arena advances in medical innovation and generation, new studies, methods, and analysis while assessing most cancers were made for medical practitioners to help come across, screen, and manage the progression of most cancers (Wear et al., 2023). It can discuss the current advances in neuroblastoma detection and its evaluation through time collection analysis of gene expression statistics. Neuroblastoma is a crucial kind of pediatric cancer that outcomes in extra than 50,000 deaths annually worldwide (Dhunmati et al., 2022). Early detection and remedy of this cancer is paramount, leading to improved clinical consequences. Time series analysis has been used to examine the expressions of several genes associated with cancer progression (Ghanem et al., 2022). Information from these genes presents insights closer to the early detection and control of most cancers. Time series evaluation of gene expression information is an increasingly popular device for studying the improvement of most cancers (Stein et al., 2023). By analyzing the time series of gene expression information, designers can better identify gene-expression patterns indicative of most cancers' development. Through the analysis, researchers can decide which genes are most influential over the years in cancer development, allowing them to develop individualized remedies. Studying the changes among time points can also offer valuable insights into the magnitude of genetic changes indicative of cancer progression (Świętoń et al., 2022; Hesko et al., 2023). Neuroblastoma is an aggressive sort of cancer in children that requires early and accurate detection for a hit treatment. Fortuitously, new techniques within the subject of time series analysis have recently been developed that have proven capacity for enhancing the detection and assessment of neuroblastoma (Natale et al., 2023). Time series analysis is a method of looking at a series of statistical factors over a selected period to discover patterns, trends, and other traits. By analysing time series data, researchers can perceive patterns that can provide greater correct and efficient tests of neuroblastoma progression. Time series evaluation has been used in many areas of study. However, its software to examine neuroblastoma is fantastically current (Furman et al., 2022). For this purpose, researchers practice autocorrelation, which helps track adjustments inside the depth of most cancers over time. This approach gives insight into tumour growth over the years and enables clinicians to decide the first-class path of remedy (Cole et al., 2023). By analysing records from the diffusion of assets, including affected person files, scans, and other scientific statistics, clinicians can identify, and song tumour increase and hit upon changes in tumour conduct earlier than they turn out to be massive sufficient to motivate signs. Further, time collection analysis also can offer a higher understanding of the underlying genetic and environmental elements that contribute to improving neuroblastoma (Vural et al., 2023). By reading an affected person's genetic profile and environmental history, researchers can pick out chance factors for a person growing the sickness. This advanced understanding can then inform treatment selections or expand new remedies (Daniel et al., 2022). Universal time collection evaluation has become a more and more vital tool in assessing and detecting neuroblastoma. This method can provide extra correct and reliable exams of the ailment, in addition to better information on the genetic and environmental factors that result in the improvement of neuroblastoma (Stein & VanHouwelingen

2023). With this step forward expertise, clinicians can provide better and more powerful treatment plans for sufferers, central to better outcomes and improved survival prices.

- Evolved a green gadget getting to know the model as it should assess and detect neuroblastoma.
- Statistical pre-processing strategies were used to eliminate redundant data and deny the time series information.
- Random wooded area and Adobos algorithms were hired to construct a classifier for neuroblastoma prognosis.
- Analyzing the scientific statistics yields vital insights regarding affected person management, outcome prediction, and informative biomarker choice.

II. RELATED WORKS

Neurocognitive results in grownup neuroblastoma survivors is an essential study topic as neuroblastoma is one of the most commonplace pediatric cancers. Long-lasting physical and mental consequences afflict folks that live on frequently. Cognitive deficits are a first-rate subject as they can have lengthy-term implications on the affected person's bodily, intellectual, and social functioning. This file from the youth most cancers Survivor examination provides records of the cognitive talents of grownup survivors of neuroblastoma compared to those without a record of most cancers. It assesses a selection of cognitive domains, together with executive functioning, memory, and motor abilities, and explores the impact of neuroblastoma on each of those domains. Moreover, it discusses capacity risk elements associated with terrible cognitive results and identifies areas where interventions may benefit (Hesko et al., 2023).

Autophagy inhibition thru hydroxychloroquine or three-methyl adenine enhances chemotherapy-caused apoptosis in neuroblastoma and glioblastoma cells because it limits the survival and unfolding of these cancer cells. Autophagy is mainly used as a defense mechanism with the aid of cells to protect themselves from cell loss of life and degrade mobile additives; if hormones that stimulate autophagy are gifted, autophagy is elevated. Inhibition of autophagy forces most cancer cells to end up more significantly depending on the apoptosis process, making them more excellent and responsive to chemotherapy-precipitated apoptosis. It gives the therapy a higher threat of succeeding in casting off the cancer cells (Wear et al., 2023).

Pediatric phase 2 trials are designed to decide the protection and efficacy of recent remedies and treatment plans for disease situations affecting pediatric populations. Especially in the Pediatric segment, two clinical trials of a WEE1 inhibitor (AZD1775) and irinotecan for relapsed neuroblastoma, medulloblastoma, and rhabdomyosarcoma are being carried out to assess the tolerability and efficacy of this experimental aggregate drug remedy for the treatment of these pediatric cancers. Many times, in the relapsed placing, current remedies are not practical, and there's a need for brand new remedies, consisting of a mixture of drug treatment plans, to target most cancer cells more efficiently. This trial aims to assess this experimental mixture remedy in a scientific place and determine if it can offer a viable therapeutic alternative for youngsters unable to reply to present treatments (Cole et al., 2023).

Minimum residual ailment (MRD) is described because microscopic quantities of tumor cells are final within the body after treatment. Higher degrees of MRD in peripheral blood compared to bone marrow may indicate an extra aggressive form of the sickness. It could signal relapse or regrowth of the tumor and might advise a poorer diagnosis. The case mentioned in this file indicates that the patient had excessive-hazard neuroblastoma, which is known to be an extraordinarily competitive most cancers and may have a pessimistic analysis. Better stages of MRD in peripheral blood compared to bone marrow could be a sign of a more competitive shape of the sickness and reflect the aggressive nature of the tumor (Inoue et al., 2023).

Reversing pathological cell states is a promising vicinity of studies in medication. This approach, known as the "opposite engineering" of biological tactics, entails figuring out the molecular and cell adjustments that cause pathological cell states and deriving new remedies that restore the cells to their everyday physiology. This method is particularly vital for illnesses wherein direct therapeutic interventions may not be available. By unraveling the complex molecular and cellular pathways and characterizing the character additives, scientists and clinicians can design remedies that might be extra particular to a character patient, main to progressed consequences. Such customized remedies can target diseased cells without affecting normal ones, boosting the remedy's efficacy, and reducing side results. Moreover, this technique can lead to the identity of new therapeutic targets, which might also cause novel remedies for diseases for which healing procedures are not presently available. Table 1 shows the comprehensive Patient characteristics (Kholodenko et al., 2023).

Table 1. Comprehensive patient characteristics

Model	Technology	Advantage	Drawbacks
recurrent neural networks considering maintenance	Neural network	Recurrent neural networks can be used to predict urban road performance in Beijing, China by considering maintenance.	This would be beneficial to the local authorities, helping them plan maintenance for urban roads more efficiently and cost-effectively while delivering better urban road performance.
Predictability of stock returns using neural networks	Neural network	It's far more challenging to do than it should be expecting stock returns because of the marketplace's tremendously complex and dynamic nature.	This approach includes building a machine based totally on expert knowledge using algorithms that may be used to research records relationships, stumble on developments and patterns, and ultimately generate forecasts.
Optimizing Traffic Flow in Smart Cities	Long term	This approach to optimizing visitor flow is based totally on recurrent neural networks (RNNs), an artificial neural network.	This method allows cities to plan better and optimize their site visitor systems to lessen congestion and make them more efficient and sustainable.
Long-term missing value imputation,	Neural network	Long-term lacking value imputation for time series data using deep neural networks (DNNs) involves using a recurrent neural community (RNN) structure.	This method is particularly beneficial for time series records with lengthy-time period correlations because a DNN can seize such correlations accurately.
Nonlinear inflation forecasting with recurrent neural networks	Long term	The recurrent neural networks, blended with cutting-edge deep learning techniques, can extract beneficial patterns from raw statistics and output a sequence of correct and statistically considerable inflation forecasts.	Incorporating domain information into the community architecture can enhance forecasting performance.

III. PROPOSED MODEL

The proposed version seeks to develop a device to evaluate the detection of neuroblastoma (a variety of cancer) in patients over time through time collection analysis. The model will use patient facts accrued over a specific period to discover any styles within neuroblastoma development with an appreciation for the affected person's health situation. The device will use superior time collection analysis strategies like exponential smoothing, transferring average, and autoregressive, including transferring common to music, and predicting neuroblastoma development in sufferers. Fig.1 shows the expression of neuroblastoma cell traces.

Figure 1. Expression of neuroblastoma cell traces

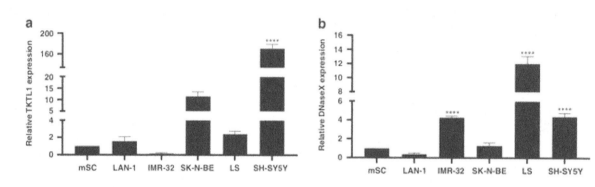

The device will even examine the possibility of neuroblastoma progression inside the patient through leveraging predictive analytics methods like logistic regression and assist vector machines. Furthermore, the proposed version will permit evaluating the effectiveness of remedy options like chemotherapy or immunotherapy to deal with neuroblastoma. This information can also be used to make choices regarding the remedy alternative. Additionally, the tool can verify the chance of relapse after the remedy. The version will provide clinicians or scientific professionals with the required records to expand customized treatment plans for neuroblastoma. Fig.2 shows the Uptake through the years measured by way of dynamic puppy scanning. Table.2 shows the patient characteristics.

Table 2. Patient characteristics

Characteristics	Number of Patients in % (n=40)	Number of Healthy Individuals in % (n=39)	P Value
Age (months)			
Mean	70 (range 34-178)	172(range 70-214)	0.1112
Gender			
M	34(73.2%)	44(74.9%)	0.2102
F	24(46.9%)	23(45.2%)	0.2102
Stage			

continued on following page

Table 2. Continued

Characteristics	Number of Patients in % (n=40)	Number of Healthy Individuals in % (n=39)	P Value
I	2	4	0.3654
II	2	5	0.4112
III	20	26	0.6894
IV	32	34	0.8123
NMYC status			
neg	44	36	0.8454
pos	6	14	0.2356
Choromosome 2 (p46)			
neg	8	16	0.7413
pos	4	18	0.5478

Where, n-sample size, no- number, M – male, F – female, neg –negative, pos_ positive

Figure 2. Uptake through the years measured by way of dynamic puppy scanning

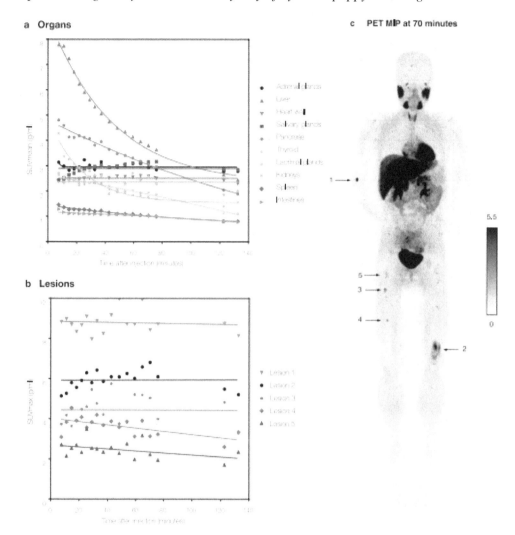

A. Construction

Neuroblastoma is a cancer that bureaucracy in nerve tissue, generally within the adrenal glands or around the backbone. *Time collection analysis* is a technique used to analyse statistics gathered over time. It could be used to become aware of developments in statistics, expect destiny values, and locate underlying styles and correlations. With time collection analysis, researchers can track modifications within the improvement of neuroblastoma over time, together with ailment progression and reaction to remedy. This evaluation can help physicians decide their sufferers' excellent course of action. Additionally, time collection evaluation can perceive biomarkers that can provide helpful perception into the reason for neuroblastoma and potential remedies. Fig.3 shows the similar physiological and pathological distribution.

Figure 3. Similar physiological and pathological distribution

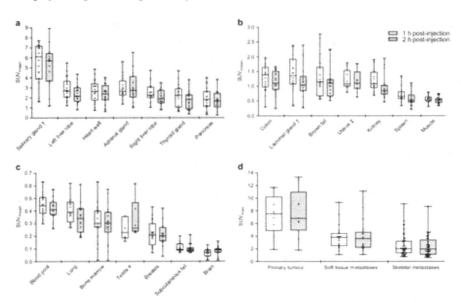

B. Operating Principle

Neuroblastoma through Time collection evaluation (NTSA) is an information-driven AI technique used to predict the development of neuroblastoma (a type of cancer) in sufferers through the years. NTSA combines system-getting-to-know algorithms with temporal analysis to analyse styles that screen how the path of the sickness will progress over the years. It uses numerical values inclusive of tumour size, age at prognosis, and gene expression profiles to generate a prediction that may be used to guide remedy. NTSA is vital for improving neuroblastoma studies and care, ensuring a set-off and powerful remedy for this competitive form of paediatric cancer.

C. Functional Working

Neuroblastoma is the most cancer that impacts the anxious machine and is especially widespread in children. It is a fast-developing and competitive form of cancer and one of the leading reasons for death among young youngsters. Time series evaluation is an essential and powerful way of tracking neuroblastoma progression through the years. This form of analysis enables researchers to look at the increase of most cancers more comprehensively and better understand the underlying dynamics of the disease. Time collection analysis is predicated on reading record points collected over time. As an example, maximum datasets are gathered for neuroblastoma from sufferers who have been recognized with the ailment.

D. Proposed Algorithm

These datasets can encompass medical data such as age, analysis, treatments, and tumour size; by plotting these records factors on a graph, it is possible to study the progression of the ailment over the years. It helps researchers see modifications in tumour growth, the impact of remedies, and the efficacy of the various treatments used. The construction of the proposed algorithm has shown in the following Table 3.

Table 3. Time series analysis algorithm

N←length of w1
M←length of w2
Elements of matrix dp[N][M] with 0
For i←1 to N;
For j←1 to M;
If w1[i]==w2[j];
V1←dp[i-1][j-1]
V1←dp[i-1][j-1]+1
V2←1+dp[i-1][j]
V3←1+dp[i][j-1]
V4←infinity
For S in sublist;
p←length of Sx
q←length of Sy
If w2[i-p+1: i]=Sx and w2[j-q+1: j]=Sy;
V4←min(v4, g(Sf) + dp[i-p][j-q])
Dp[i][j]←min(v1,v2,v3,v4)
OP:MED(w1,w2)=dp[N][M]

The datasets also can be used to pick out specific patterns or tendencies that are probably visible within the data. For example, it can be viable to perceive part of the sickness progression that has no longer been identified or explain why specific treatments have been more successful than others. It may additionally be a helpful resource in predicting destiny developments in the ailment and provide researchers a better understanding of enhancing treatments inside the destiny.

IV. RESULTS AND DISCUSSION

This technique has a few advantages over conventional histomorphology, as the quantitative evaluation of imaging datasets allows for the popularity and assessment of temporal changes concerning the evolution of the tumor. The technique is used to help physicians and oncologists recognize a tumor's behavior in time and may consequently cause more accurate diagnostics and improved prognostics. Table 4 shows the Normal organ absorbed radiation doses.

Table 4. Normal organs absorb radiation doses

Organ	Dynamic Scan 1 (Scan 6)	Dynamic Scan 2 (Scan 15)
Adrenals	0.0050	0.0030
Brain	0.004	0.004
Breasts	0.008	0.007
Gallbladder wall	0.018	0.018
Lowest large intestine wall	0.013	0.014
stomach wall	0.013	0.014
Upper large intestine wall	0.012	0.012
Heart wall	0.012	0.014
Kidneys	0.048	0.038
Liver	0.025	0.052
Lungs	0.014	0.008
Muscle	0.013	0.046
Ovaries	0.025	0.052
Pancreas	0.016	0.008
Red bone marrow	0.010	0.046
Osteogenic cells	0.014	0.009
Skin	0.016	0.013
Spleen	0.045	0.008
Testes	0.011	0.018
Thymus	0.010	0.009
Thyroid	0.029	0.145
Urinary bladder wall	0.018	0.011

A. True Positive Rate

The genuine, effective rate of Neuro-blastoma through Time series evaluation is calculated by dividing the number of genuine positives (identifying an actual instance of a cancerous boom) through the whole variety of actual and fake positives. The accurate excellent charge is a trademark of the accuracy of a diagnostic approach, in this example, the time series evaluation. Fig 4a shows the EDIM scores of patients Apo10 EDIM scores.

Figure 4a. EDIM scores of patients Apo10 EDIM scores

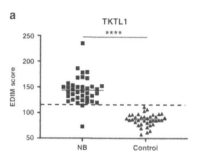

The higher the genuine favorable fee, the more correct the analysis. It is vital to apply multiple analysis strategies, including genetic analysis, histology, and imaging. The actual favorable price of Neuroblastoma through Time collection evaluation can differ dependent on the records used and the configuration of the evaluation.

B. Specificity

The particular approach utilized in Neuro-blastoma thru Time series evaluation is based on the application of unsupervised gadgets to gain knowledge of fashions that classify and quantify biomarkers that might be acquired from medical imaging (such as ultrasound, pet scans, MRI pix, and X-Ray pix). These fashions can automatically extract quantitative features and classify the snapshots in keeping with their inherent temporal behavior. Features extracted include a region of involvement, tumor length, and adjustments in tumor dimensions during time. The analysis also measures the accumulation of metabolites over the path of the remedy and the presence of infiltrating cells at one-of-a-kind ranges of the tumor increase. Fig 4b shows the EDIM scores of patients combined with EDIM score.

Figure 4b. EDIM scores of patients combined EDIM score

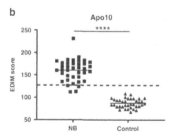

Usually talking, accurate bad quotes vary depending on the model's accuracy. Fig 5a shows the GD2-positive macrophages of patients.

Figure 5. a) GD2-positive macrophages of patients, b) GD2 abundance of macrophages sensitivity

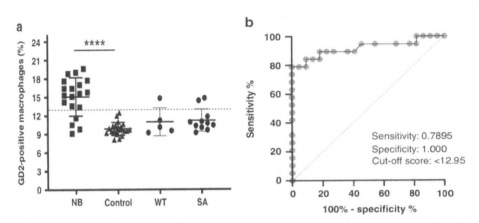

The accuracy of time collection evaluation models is generally evaluated via diagnostic assessments along with the location underneath the receiver operating function curve (AUROC). Fig 5b shows the GD2 abundance of macrophages sensitivity.

It is crucial to note, however, that the AUROC is the most straightforward measure of the overall performance of the version and does not necessarily imply the truly terrible price of the version.

C. True Negative Rate

The actual poor charge (additionally known as the specificity) of neuroblastoma via time collection evaluation is commonly reported as the price of efficiently identified actual bad instances (i.e., sufferers who did now not have the ailment). This price is generally calculated as the proportion of negatives effectively identified out of all the cases that were, in truth, poor. This fee is crucial to recollect because it may assist clinicians in determining whether or not or no longer the version is offering correct prognostic facts for sufferers who do not have neuroblastoma. As is well known, the accurate terrible price of neuroblastoma thru time collection analysis is usually pronounced as being extra than 90%. This charge may be similarly advanced with model optimization strategies consisting of hyperparameter tuning.

V. CONCLUSION

The conclusion of Assessing the Detection of Neuroblastoma via Time series evaluation changed into that while the traditional strategies of evaluating the analysis of neuroblastoma with laboratory checks gave significant consequences, using time collection analysis furnished a good extra accurate and dependable technique in detecting the disease in kids. The combination of functions extracted from the time collection analysis of the ultrasounds of the sufferers had been capable of effectively offering very high accuracy in the prognosis. Furthermore, using synthetic neural networks during function extraction and transformation became capable of providing a fair better accuracy than previous methods. Indicates the aggregate of time series analysis and deep getting-to-know ought to provide an effective technique for analysing neuroblastoma in children.

REFERENCES

Cole, K. A., Ijaz, H., Surrey, L. F., Santi, M., Liu, X., Minard, C. G., ... Weigel, B. J. (2023). *Pediatric phase 2 trial of a WEE1 inhibitor, adavosertib (AZD1775), and irinotecan for relapsed neuroblastoma, medulloblastoma, and rhabdomyosarcoma.* Cancer.

Daniel, P., Sun, C., Koptyra, M., Drinkwater, C., Chew, N., Bradshaw, G., Loi, M., Shi, C., Tourchi, M., Parackal, S., Chong, W. C., Fernando, D., Adjumain, S., Nguyen, H., Habarakada, D., Sooraj, D., Crombie, D., Zhukova, N., Jones, C., & Firestein, R. (2022). MODL-17. The Childhood Brain Cancer Cell Line Atlas: A Resource for Biomarker Identification and Therapeutic Development. *Neuro-Oncology*, 24(Supplement_1), i172–i172. 10.1093/neuonc/noac079.640

Dhunmati, K., Nalini, C. N., Ramalakshmi, N., Niraimathi, V., & Amuthalakshmi, S. (2022). Synthesis, Molecular Docking and Invitro Evaluation of Nipecotic Acid-Flavone Hybrids as Anti Alzheimer Agents.–A Multi Target Directed Ligand Approach. *Journal of Pharmaceutical Negative Results*, 229–238.

Furman, W. L., McCarville, B., Shulkin, B. L., Davidoff, A., Krasin, M., Hsu, C. W., Pan, H., Wu, J., Brennan, R., Bishop, M. W., Helmig, S., Stewart, E., Navid, F., Triplett, B., Santana, V., Santiago, T., Hank, J. A., Gillies, S. D., Yu, A., & Federico, S. M. (2022). Improved outcome in children with newly diagnosed high-risk neuroblastoma treated with chemoimmunotherapy: Updated results of a phase II study using hu14. 18K322A. *Journal of Clinical Oncology*, 40(4), 335–344. 10.1200/JCO.21.0137534871104

Ghanem, S. S., Majbour, N. K., Vaikath, N. N., Ardah, M. T., Erskine, D., Jensen, N. M., Fayyad, M., Sudhakaran, I. P., Vasili, E., Melachroinou, K., Abdi, I. Y., Poggiolini, I., Santos, P., Dorn, A., Carloni, P., Vekrellis, K., Attems, J., McKeith, I., Outeiro, T. F., & El-Agnaf, O. M. (2022). α-Synuclein phosphorylation at serine 129 occurs after initial protein deposition and inhibits seeded fibril formation and toxicity. *Proceedings of the National Academy of Sciences of the United States of America*, 119(15), e2109617119. 10.1073/pnas.210961711935353605

Hesko, C., Liu, W., Srivastava, D. K., Brinkman, T. M., Diller, L., Gibson, T. M., Oeffinger, K. C., Leisenring, W. M., Howell, R., Armstrong, G. T., Krull, K. R., & Henderson, T. O. (2023). Neurocognitive outcomes in adult survivors of neuroblastoma: A report from the Childhood Cancer Survivor Study. *Cancer*, 129(18), 2904–2914. 10.1002/cncr.3484737199722

Inoue, S., Nay Win, K. H., Mon, C. Y., Fujikawa, T., Hyodo, S., Uemura, S., Ishida, T., Mori, T., Hasegawa, D., Kosaka, Y., Nishimura, A., Nakatani, N., Nino, N., Tamura, A., Yamamoto, N., Nozu, K., & Nishimura, N. (2023). Higher levels of minimal residual disease in peripheral blood than bone marrow before 1st and 2nd relapse/regrowth in a patient with high-risk neuroblastoma: A case report. *Oncology Letters*, 26(3), 1–5. 10.3892/ol.2023.1395537559575

Kholodenko, B. N., Kolch, W., & Rukhlenko, O. S. (2023). Reversing pathological cell states: The road less travelled can extend the therapeutic horizon. *Trends in Cell Biology*, 33(11), 913–923. 10.1016/j.tcb.2023.04.00437263821

Natale, G., Forte, S., Messina, G., Leonardi, B., Mirra, R., Leone, F., Di Filippo, V., Pica, D. G., Capasso, F., Bove, M., Noro, A., Opromolla, G., Martone, M., De Angelis, S., & Fiorelli, A. (2023). Intrathoracic neurogenic tumors (ITNs): Management of solid and cystic lesions. *Thoracic Cancer*, 14(19), 1824–1830. 10.1111/1759-7714.1492737201908

Stein, N. R., & VanHouwelingen, L. (2023). Making good use of ultrasound for abdominal tumors in children. *Jornal de Pediatria, 99*, 1-3.

Świętoń, D., Szarmach, A., & Kosiak, W. (2022). Contrast-enhanced ultrasound of adrenal hemorrhage: A helpful problem solving tool. *Medical Ultrasonography*, 24(3), 284–289.35437529

Vural, O., Aydos, U., Okur, A., Pinarli, F. G., & Atay, L. Ö. (2023). Prognostic Values of Primary Tumor Textural Heterogeneity and Blood Biomarkers in High-risk Neuroblastoma. *Journal of Pediatric Hematology/Oncology*, 45(7), 10–1097. 10.1097/MPH.0000000000002662237027243

Wear, D., Bhagirath, E., Balachandar, A., Vegh, C., & Pandey, S. (2023). Autophagy Inhibition via Hydroxychloroquine or 3-Methyladenine Enhances Chemotherapy-Induced Apoptosis in Neuro-Blastoma and Glioblastoma. *International Journal of Molecular Sciences*, 24(15), 12052. 10.3390/ijms24151205237569432

Chapter 9
Comparative Analysis of Machine Learning Techniques for Classifying the Risk of Cardiovascular Diseases

Tharun Ashwin B.

Vellore Institute of Technology, Chennai, India

Bhuvaneswari Amma N. G.

http://orcid.org/0000-0003-3660-380X

Vellore Institute of Technology, Chennai, India

ABSTRACT

Heart and blood vessel problems are collectively referred to as cardiovascular diseases. Fatty deposits build up inside an artery, generating a blood clot, which causes the artery to harden and constrict, reducing blood flow to the body, brain, or heart. In the study, a comparative analysis between nine machine learning classifiers has been made. Also, in the study, the authors are training and testing the data set under different split ratio to analyze the difference in the result that the authors obtain after executing those set of data. The split ratio includes a 60:40 split ratio, 70:30 split ratio, 80:20 split ratio, and 90:10 split ratio. They analyzed the performance of the classifiers with respect to various metrics. They concluded by saying the proposed model yields the best accuracy when they use a random forest classifier with an accuracy of 99.26% for the split ratio of 60:40.

1. INTRODUCTION

The most severe and fatal illness affecting humans has long been thought to be cardiovascular disease (CVD). The prevalence of cardiovascular illnesses, which have a high death rate, is increasing the danger to and burden on the global healthcare systems (Dinesh et al., 2018). The majority of heart disease deaths take place under-developed countries. In 2019, noncommunicable illnesses caused 17 million deaths before the age of 70, with 38% of those fatalities being related to CVDs. Most cardiovascular diseases can be avoided by addressing behavioral danger elements like unhealthy life-style such as smoking,

DOI: 10.4018/979-8-3693-0683-3.ch009

improper diet habits, obesity, lack of physical activity, and excessive alcohol use (Nadakinamani et al., 2022; Shah et al., 2020).

Early detection of cardiovascular disease is necessary to start counselling, psychotherapy, and treatment. A viable strategy is to find risk variables using machine learning algorithms. We would want to provide a model that combines many approaches to get more precise cardiac disease prediction (Jindal et al., 2021). We have successfully created improved data for the training model using effective approaches for record collection, pre-processing, and record transformation. It's critical to assess the influence of risk factors that fit three criteria, including large prevalence in the majority of people, a considerable heart effect disease independently, and the ability to be managed or treated to lower the risks. In modeling the predictors for CVD, several studies have added varying risk variables or characteristics. Age, gender, exercise-induced angina (exang), ST depression induced by exercise relative to rest (oldpeak), slope, number of major vessels coloured by fluoroscopy (ca), heart status (thal), maximum heart rate achieved (thalach), poor diet, and family history are some of the factors that can contribute to chest pain are the important attributes taken into the development of heart disease prediction models (Weng et al., 2017).

According to recent studies, the forecast must have a minimum of 14 qualities to be accurate and dependable (Anuar et al., 2020). In order to accurately forecast cardiac disease, researchers are currently having trouble combining these variables with the right machine learning models. The best machine learning models are those that have been trained on the right datasets (Guarneros-Nolasco et al., 2021). AdaBoost (AB), Support Vector Classifier (SVC), Logistic Regression (LR), Random Forest (RF), SGD-Classifier, Decision Tree (DT), K-Nearest Neighbors (KNN), Gaussian Naive Bayes (GNB) and XGB-Classifiers were just a few of the supervised models used in this work. The final results obtained from all of these classifiers are compared with each other and their accuracy, precision, recall, F1- score, AUC- score are taken into account to find the best classifier for our proposed model.

2. RELATED WORKS

Due to increased forecast accuracy and efficiency, the use of artificial intelligence and machine learning algorithms has grown significantly in recent years. The potential to create and choose models with the maximum accuracy and efficiency is what makes this study so important (Krishnani et al., 2019; Mohan et al., 2019). A potential method for illness prediction is to use hybrid models, which combine several machine learning models with information systems (Nikhar & Karandikar, 2016). In contrast to Motarwar et al.'s simulation result of 47.54%, the suggested work's simulation result utilizing the MLP method is 82.47% (Motarwar et al., 2020). When results are examined, it is clear that the MLP algorithm offers more accuracy (82.47%) than Naive Bayes (69.11%) and Decision tree (78.57%, 80.68%). Therefore, when compared to other ML algorithms, the proposed MLP model is more effective at predicting CVD. We enhance the accuracy of the MLP model by increasing the number of hidden layer nodes and applying a 10-fold cross-validation method.

Padmanabhan et al. examined the effectiveness of different well-known ML approaches for coronary artery disease identification in the literature (Padmanabhan et al., 2019). Kumar et al. presented an ensemble approach to improve the accuracy of weak classifiers by 7.26% (Kumar et al., 2020). Using random forest, Maiga et al. presented a heart disease risk-prediction model with a 94.9% accuracy (Maiga & Hungilo, 2019). Alaa et al. used R-Studio and Rapid Miner to examine the performance of several ML algorithms based on the Framingham heart database to predict coronary heart disease, and a support vector machine technique yielded the greatest AUC value of 0.75 (Alaa et al., 2019). Using an artificial neural network to predict the survival rate of wounded patients, Marbaniang et al. acquired a 0.89 AUC rating (Marbaniang et al., 2020). Abdeldjouad et al. published a heart disease risk-prediction model with 86.9% accuracy, 90.6% sensitivity, and 82.7% specificity by using the random forest algorithm (Abdeldjouad et al., 2020), while Krittanawong et al. published a cardiac illness risk-prediction system with 86.9% accuracy, 90.6% sensitivity, and 82.7% specifically by using the K-NN method (Krittanawong et al., 2020). In this work, K-NN and MLP, two ML methods for cardiovascular disease estimation, are compared. In comparison to K-NN, which has a success rate of 73.77%, MLP offers greater accuracy (82.47%). For the MLP and K-NN algorithms, detection rates were found to be 86.41 and 86.21%, respectively (Louridi et al., 2019). The diagnostic process for CVD is time and money-consuming in the medical industry (Anbuselvan, 2020). According to the suggested method, ML may be used clinically to identify CVD and will be especially helpful to doctors in cases of incorrect diagnoses.

In comparison to the previous methods described, the developed MLP model gives constant accuracy and can also predict additional illnesses (Katarya & Meena, 2021). In this work, a method of exploratory data evaluation was used to exclude characteristics with null values, and more nodes in the hidden layer were added to increase the accuracy of the model. The proposed strategy is anticipated to help the medical field continue to advance. Other long-term conditions such as thyroid, liver, diabetes mellitus, and breast cancer can also be categorized using the suggested technique. IoT and cloud computing approaches may be used to forecast chronic illnesses utilizing the created models on massive data sets (Krishnan & Geetha, 2019). According to the research above, the use of ML approaches will significantly help in reducing deaths and support medical professionals' attempts to combat the prevalence of CVD across every patient classification from various age groups, genders, and social and economic statuses. If put into practice, this would be a classic example of modern technology being used for the greater good.

3. PROPOSED METHODOLOGY

The process of creating a sophisticated machine-learning platform using a collection of records of chronic heart disease is presented in general terms. It is a part of the framework. The proposed models' procedure is shown in Figure 1. The merged dataset is examined during data preparation to look for any missing values, which are then filled up using the K-Nearest Neighbors imputation method.

3.1 Application of the Proposed Model

Analyzed the performance of classifiers using both the features chosen by these approaches and the original features. The dataset is divided into training and testing when features are chosen. 80% of the data are designated for the training phase and the remaining 20% is chosen for the testing phase based on model learning rates.

3.2 Performance Measure Indices

Performance indicators can be used to assess the machine learning technique's efficacy and accuracy. When a person is identified as having CVD, positive categorization takes place. A person is given a negative categorization when they are not identified as having CVD (Shameer et al., 2018). To obtain all of this, the formula from (1) to (7) has been used.

A = Let A be the True Positive (when the model correctly Identified as having CVD).

B = True Negative (when the model correctly identified
the opposite class, such as patients truly having no heart issues).

C = False Positive (when the model incorrectly identified CVD patients i.e., identifying non-CVD patients as CVD patients)

D = False Negative (when the model incorrectly identified the opposite class, such as CVD patients as normal patients).

Accuracy (Acc) =

$$\frac{(A + B)}{(A + B + C + D)} \tag{1}$$

Precision =

$$\frac{(A)}{(A + C)} \tag{2}$$

Recall or Sensitivity (Sen) =

$$\frac{(A)}{(A + D)} \tag{3}$$

F1-score =

$$\frac{2(Precision * Recall)}{(Precison + Recall)} \tag{4}$$

False Positive Rate =

$$\frac{(C)}{(C + B)} \tag{5}$$

False Negative Rate =

$$\frac{(D)}{(A + D)} \tag{6}$$

Negative predictive value =

$$\frac{(B)}{(B + D)} \tag{7}$$

3.3 Approach of the Proposed Model

The creation of this special system and the ability to meet the problems of the actual world both depend on having an appropriate application of the suggested model. This section provides examples of the procedures

1. Gathering of report in the database.
2. We select the attribute from the dataset as an input to train the model.
3. Those chosen fields are processed in trained model.
4. The end result is produced in the form of 0 and 1.

   - 0 = person is less prone to CVDs.
   - 1 = person is prone to CVDs.

5. If the result says '1' then notify the person to visit a physician.
6. Values are loaded to table is used to build prepared model and with that model we find the accuracy and choose the model which best fit our dataset.

4. IMPLEMENTATION

The model proposed is executed using Jupyter Notebook's Python programming language using various libraries like Numpy, Pandas, Pyplot, Mplot3d, xgboost, Seaborn and Scikit-learn. Collection of data is must for us to use machine learning techniques to obtain the best results. So, let's take a look how the values in the data are related with each other. In our Dataset he had 1025 cases which are collected along with 13 fields of these are taken as diagnosis inputs, and the 'target' field is selected as output.

Correlation matrix is used to describe the large set of data and find the pattern and based on it makes a decision which is shown in Figure 2. From this technique we can see that which attributes has the most correlation to which attribute and visualize the result best of our view, this correlation matrix shows us the final result in the form rows and columns. Here to plot this correlation matrix we took age, resting blood pressure (trestbps), cholesterol (chol), maximum heart rate achieved (thalach), ST depression induced by exercise relative to rest (oldpeak), target. A scatterplot uses two-dimensional points to show

how much one variable is influenced by another, or how they are related. In that they employ horizontal and vertical axes to depict data points, scatter charts and line charts are extremely similar to one another. The scatterplot for the heart disease dataset is shown in the Figure 3.

In the present day, a lot of data may be gained through surveys, experiments, the internet, and other means (Sajja et al., 2021; Singh et al., 2017). Yet, the data that must be used frequently have missing values, noise, and distortions. Also, the pooled dataset utilized for this study includes null or missing values. To cope with missing values, various well-liked strategies may be utilized, including imputation and deletion. K-Nearest Neighbors imputation is used in our dataset to tackle this issue. Data must also be normalized or standardized before machine learning techniques may be used (Ward et al., 2020). The machine learning techniques utilized in this study to create an intelligent heart disease prediction system are covered in this part. Here we use various classifier to find which has the best accuracy.

4.1 Adaboost Classifier

An AdaBoost classifier, a type of meta-estimator, begins by fitting a classifier to the initial dataset. The same dataset is then used to fit more copies of the classifier with the weights of instances that were mistakenly categorized modified so that subsequent classifiers would focus more on difficult situations. The AdaBoost-SAMME algorithm is implemented by this class. The parameter which we passed in the Adaboost is the largest estimate size at which boosting is terminated is n_estimators. The learning process ends sooner when everything fits perfectly. Values must fall between the [1, inf] range. Adaboost's core principle is to train the data sample and modify the classifier weights in order to produce precise predictions of unusual occurrences. The foundation classifier may be any machine learning technique that accepts weights from the training set.

4.2 Support Vector Classifier

SVM provides a very high accuracy compared to other classifiers like decision trees and logistic regression (Haq et al., 2018). It handles nonlinear input spaces using a well-known kernel technique. It is utilized in many different applications, including handwriting recognition, intrusion detection, categorization of genes, classification of emails, news items, and web pages. Although support vector machines are frequently associated with classification, they may be applied to both classification- and regression-related problems. It is possible to handle several continuous and categorical variables with ease. In order to divide numerous classes, SVM creates a hyperplane in multidimensional space. To reduce inaccuracy, SVM repeatedly builds an ideal hyperplane. Finding a maximum marginal hyperplane (MMH) that optimally classifies the dataset is the primary goal of SVM.

4.3 Decision Tree

The most effective and well-liked technique for categorization and prediction is the decision tree (Khan et al., 2023). A supervised learning method may be used to solve classification and regression issues, but it is often favored for doing so. It is a tree-structured classifier, where internal nodes stand in for a dataset's characteristics, branches for the decision-making process, and each leaf node for the classification result. A decision tree is a type of tree structure that resembles a flowchart, where each internal node represents a test on an attribute, each branch a test result, and each leaf node (terminal node) a class label. The Decision Node and Leaf Node are the two nodes of a decision tree. Whereas Leaf nodes are the results of decisions and do not have any more branches, Decision nodes are used to create decisions and have numerous branches.

In a decision tree, the algorithm begins at the root node and works its way up to forecast the class of the provided dataset. This algorithm follows the branch and jumps to the following node by comparing the values of the root attribute with those of the record (real dataset) attribute. The algorithm verifies the attribute value with the other sub-nodes once again for the following node before continuing. It keeps doing this until it reaches the tree's leaf node.

The fundamental problem that emerges while developing a decision tree is how to choose the optimal attribute for the root node and for sub-nodes (Li et al., 2020). Thus, a method known as attribute selection measure, or ASM, can be used to tackle these issues. By using this measurement, we can choose the ideal characteristic for the tree nodes with ease. There are two widely used ASM approaches, which are as follows:

$$\text{Information Gain} = \text{Entropy}(S) - [(\text{Weighted Avg}) * \text{Entropy (each feature)}] \tag{8}$$

Entropy is a metric to measure the impurity in a given attribute. It specifies randomness in data. Entropy can be calculated as:

$$\text{Entropy}(s) = -P(\text{yes})\log2\ P(\text{yes}) - P(\text{no})\ \log2\ P(\text{no}) \tag{9}$$

Where,
S= Total number of samples
P(yes)= probability of yes
P(no)= probability of no
When using the CART (Classification and Regression Tree) technique to create a decision tree, the Gini index is a purity or impurity indicator. It is preferable to have an attribute with a low Gini index than one with a high Gini value. It only generates binary splits, whereas the CART method generates binary splits using the Gini index.

The following formula may be used to get the Gini index:

$$\text{Gini Index} = 1 - \sum_j P_j^2 \tag{10}$$

4.4 Logistic Regression

One of the most often used Machine Learning algorithms, within the category of Supervised Learning, is logistic regression (El-Hasnony et al., 2022). With a predetermined set of independent factors, it is used to predict the categorical dependent variable. With a categorical dependent variable, the output is predicted via logistic regression.

As a result, the result must be a discrete or categorical value. Rather than providing the precise values of 0 and 1, it provides the probabilistic values that fall between 0 and 1. It can be either Yes or No, 0 or 1, true or false, etc. With the exception of how they are applied, logistic regression and linear regression are very similar. Whereas logistic regression is used to solve classification difficulties, linear regression is used to solve regression problems.

Since it can classify new data using both continuous and discrete datasets, logistic regression is a key machine-learning approach. When classifying observations using various sources of data, logistic regression may be used to quickly identify the factors that will work well. The linear regression equation yields the logistic regression equation.

- We are aware that the equation for a straight line is:

$$Y = b_0 x_0 + b_1 x_1 + b_2 x_2 + b_3 x_3 + b_4 x_4 + \ldots\ldots + b_n x_n \qquad (11)$$

- Let's divide the preceding equation by (1-y) because y in Logistic Regression can only be between 0 and 1 in order to account for this:

$\frac{y}{1-y}$; gives 0 when y=0 and gives infinity when y=1

- Nevertheless, we want a range between -[infinity] and +[infinity]. If we take the equation's logarithm, it becomes:

$$log \left[\frac{y}{1-y} \right] = b_0 + b_1 x_1 + b_2 x_2 + b_3 x_3 + \ldots\ldots + b_n x_n \qquad (12)$$

4.5 Random Forest

Like its name suggests, a random forest is made up of several independent decision trees that work together as an ensemble. The class with the highest votes becomes the prediction made by our model. The random forest's individual trees each spit forth a class prediction (Sitar-tăut et al., 2009).

Maximum accuracy and overfitting are minimized by the larger number of trees in the forest. Some decision trees may predict the proper output, while others may not, since the random forest mixes numerous trees to forecast the class of the dataset. Yet when all the trees are combined, they forecast the right result. Hence, the following two presumptions for an improved Random Forest classifier:

- For the dataset's feature variable to predict true outcomes rather than a speculated result, there should be some real values in the dataset.
- Each tree's predictions must have extremely low correlations.

4.6 Stochastic Gradient Descent

To determine the parameters or coefficients of functions that minimize a cost function, one can use the straightforward yet effective optimization process known as stochastic gradient descent (SGD). To put it another way, it is employed in the discriminative learning of linear classifiers under convex loss functions, including SVM and logistic regression.

If a standard Gradient Descent optimization approach is used and the dataset contains a million samples, you will need to use all one million samples to complete one iteration of the Gradient Descent. This process must be repeated until the minima are achieved. As a result, performing it becomes exceedingly expensive computationally.

With stochastic gradient descent, this issue is resolved. SGD does each iteration using a single sample, or a batch size of one. The sample is chosen and randomly shuffled in order to carry out the iteration.

How well the model fits the training data is shown by the loss function, which is also known as the cost function. The cost function should be minimized as much as possible to improve model fit.

4.7 K-Nearest Neighbors

A supervised machine learning model is the kNN algorithm. In other words, it makes predictions about a target variable based on one or more independent factors. The K-NN method makes the assumption that the new case and the existing cases are comparable, and it places the new instance in the category that is most like the existing categories (Dalal et al., 2023).

A new data point is classified using the K-NN algorithm based on similarity after all the existing data has been stored. This means that utilizing the K-NN method, fresh data may be quickly and accurately sorted into a suitable category. As K-NN is a non-parametric technique, it makes no assumptions about the underlying data. It is also known as a lazy learner algorithm since it saves the training dataset rather than learning from it immediately. Instead, it uses the dataset to execute an action when classifying data.

The key functionality of kNN is if there are two categories, Category A and Category B, and we have a new data point, x1, which category does this data point belong in? We require a K-NN method to address this kind of issue. K-NN makes it simple to determine the category or class of a given dataset.

Here will look into the working algorithm of kNN Classifier:

* Choose the k- number of the neighbor.
* Find the Euclidean distance between K neighbors.
* Choose the K nearest neighbor from the obtained Euclidean distance.
* Out of the chosen K neighbor find the count of data points in each category.
* Now update the data points to the category where the neighbor count is at it's highest.

Euclidean distance between two points is calculated using the formula:

$ED =$

$$\sqrt{(X2 - X1)2 + (Y2 - Y1)2} \tag{13}$$

In the above formula,

A and B are the two points of the neighbor and their coordinates are (X1, Y1) and (X2, Y2) respectively.

This classifier is easy to implement and one of the successful classifiers for noisy training data. Its maximum utility can be obtained if the training data is large.

4.8 Gaussian Naive Bayes

A statistical classification method based on the Bayes Theorem is called naive Bayes. One of the easiest supervised learning methods is this one. The quick, accurate, and dependable approach is the naive Bayes classifier (Nikhar & Karandikar, 2016). For big datasets, naive Bayes classifiers perform quickly and accurately.

Naive The Bayes classifier makes the assumption that an individual feature's impact on a class is unrelated to the effects of other characteristics. For instance, a loan applicant's suitability depends on factors including their income, history of loans and transactions, age, and geography. These traits are nonetheless taken into account separately even though they are interconnected. This assumption is regarded as naïve since it makes calculation easier. The term "class conditional independence" refers to this presumption.

$$P(m|N) =$$

$$\frac{P(N|m)P(m)}{P(N)} \tag{14}$$

In the above formula,

- P(m): is the probability if the hypothesis 'm' being true (irrespective of the date). It is also called a prior probability of 'm'.
- P(N): is the probability of the data 'N' (irrespective of the hypothesis). It is also called as the prior probability.
- P(m|N): is the probability of the hypothesis 'm' given the data 'N'. It is also called as posterior probability.
- P(N|m): is the probability of the data 'N' given that the hypothesis 'm' was true. It is also called as posterior probability.

4.9 Extreme Gradient Boosting

A gradient boosting framework is offered by the open-source Python module XGBoost. It aids in creating a model that is very effective, adaptable, and portable. XGBoost performs better at making predictions than other algorithms or machine learning frameworks (Krishnan & Geetha, 2019).

This is as a result of its improved performance and precision. To fix the mistakes produced by earlier models, it merges numerous models into one. This AI technique is used, among other things, in classification and regression assignments. It presents an expectation model as a group of mediocre decision trees for forecasting. A loss function should be improved, which entails making it smaller than the outcome.

Weak learners are employed in the model to set expectations. In this, decision trees are used in a jealous manner, which refers to choosing the best-divided targets in light of Gini Impurity and other factors or to restrict the loss function. The loss function is constrained by combining all of the fragile models using the additive model. Each tree is added, making sure that no already existing trees in the decision tree are modified. The ideal hyper bounds are regularly discovered using the angle plummet procedure, after which more loads are renewed.

In order to allow models to be treated like classifiers or regressors in the scikit-learn system, XGBoost provides a covering class.

This indicates that the scikit-learn library can be fully utilized by the XGBoost models. The XG-Boost model for grouping is known as XGBClassifier. Making and fitting it to our preparation datasets is possible. The scikit-learn API and the model are used to fit the models.fit() perform.

Boundaries can be supplied to the model in the constructor's parameter list to prepare it. Thus, we use logical defaults in this case. Also, we may view the data of the trained XGBoost model by printing the model.

It is simple to construct an XGBoost classifier; all that has to be changed is the goal function. The two most well-liked categorization goals are:

- Binary: logistic - binary classification
- multi: softprob - multi-class classification

here in the XGBoost performing both the primary and multi-class classification is nearly the same, which mean we don't find any significant difference between those two classifications. The main distinction is that we use Sklearn' s Ordinal Encoder to encode the text classes in the target because XGBoost only takes numbers in the target.

The above were the set of classifiers which are used to implement our dataset, from those set of classifiers we find the accuracy, precision, re-call, F1- score, AUC- score. We also implemented our data set using different train and test ratio.

5. RESULTS AND DISCUSSIONS

For a visual representation of a binary classifier's performance, utilize the ROC, or Receiver Operating Characteristic plot. For various categorization criteria, it reveals the trade-off between the True Positive Rate (X) and the False Positive Rate (Y).

True Positive Rate is the alternative term of recall and the formula using which we calculate X is:

$$X=$$

$$\frac{A}{A+D} \tag{15}$$

The formula using which we calculated Y is:

Y=

$$\frac{D}{A+D} \qquad (16)$$

From the above formula,

A= True Positive

D= False Negative

We have carried our implementation using various split ratio, here the size of the test data and train data varies and based on that the accuracy result also varies. As we already know when we carry out the same Implementation using different split ratio our accuracy varies and this could help us understand the relationship between the split ratio and accuracy. To look into various output result.

Following split ration taken into consideration for implementing the dataset:

* 60:40 ratio (60% of the data is passed to train the model and 20% to test the data).
* 70:30 ratio (70% of the data is passed to train the model and 30% to test the data).
* 80:20 ratio (80% of the data is passed to train the model and 20% to test the data).
* 90:10 ratio (90% of the data is passed to train the model and 10% to test the data).

5.1 ROC Plot for 60-40 Ratio

From the above ROC- plot in the Figure 4, we can see that the AUC-score obtained for all the classifiers used for the 60:40 ratio, where 60% of data is used to train the data and 40% to test the data. The AUC- score of the classifiers are 0.8611 for AdaBoost Classifier, 0.8048 for Support Vector Classifier, 0.9657 for Decision Tree, 0.8465 for Linear Regression, 0.9926 for Random Forest, 0.7619 for Stochastic Gradient Descent Classifier, 0.8391 for the k- Nearest Neighbors, 0.8342 for Gaussian Naive Bayes Classifier, 0.9853 for Extreme Gradient Boosting Classifier. We know that ROC- plot signifies the performance of the classifier, from the values listed above we can conclude that Random Forest whose AUC- score is found to be 0.9926 which produces the best result out of all the classifiers used for the split ratio of 90:10.

5.2 ROC Plot for 70-30 Ratio

From the Figure 5, ROC- plot we can see that the AUC-score obtained for all the classifiers used for the 70:30 ratio, where 70% of data is used to train the data and 30% to test the data. The AUC- score of the classifiers are 0.8445 for AdaBoost Classifier, 0.7985 for Support Vector Classifier, 1.0 for Decision Tree, 0.8578 for Linear Regression, 0.9901 for Random Forest, 0.8516 for Stochastic Gradient Descent Classifier, 0.8344 for the k- Nearest Neighbors, 0.8249 for Gaussian Naive Bayes Classifier, 0.9901 for Extreme Gradient Boosting Classifier. We know that ROC- plot signifies the performance of the classifier, from the values listed above we can conclude that Decision Tree whose AUC- score is found to be 1.0 which produces the best result out of all the classifiers used for the split ratio of 70:30.

5.3 ROC Plot for 80-20 Ratio

From the Figure 6, ROC- plot we can see that the AUC-score obtained for all the classifiers used for the 80:20 ratio, where 80% of data is used to train the data and 20% to test the data. The AUC- score of the classifiers are 0.8504 for AdaBoost Classifier, 0.7696 for Support Vector Classifier, 1.0 for Decision Tree, 0.8517 for Linear Regression, 1.0 for Random Forest, 0.8203 for Stochastic Gradient Descent Classifier, 0.8534 for the k- Nearest Neighbors, 0.8164 for Gaussian Naive Bayes Classifier, 1.0 for Extreme Gradient Boosting Classifier. We know that ROC- plot signifies the performance of the classifier, from the values listed above we can conclude that Decision Tree, Random Forest and Extreme Gradient Boosting whose AUC- score is found to be 1.0 which produces the best result out of all the classifiers used for the split ratio of 80:20.

5.4 ROC Plot for 90-10 Ratio

From the Figure 7, ROC- plot we can see that the AUC-score obtained for all the classifiers used for the 90:10 ratio, where 90% of data is used to train the data and 10% to test the data. The AUC- score of the classifiers are 0.8920 for AdaBoost Classifier, 0.7907 for Support Vector Classifier, 1.0 for Decision Tree, 0.8530 for Linear Regression, 1.0 for Random Forest, 0.8477 for Stochastic Gradient Descent Classifier, 0.8670 for the k- Nearest Neighbors, 0.8466 for Gaussian Naive Bayes Classifier, 1.0 for Extreme Gradient Boosting Classifier. We know that ROC- plot signifies the performance of the classifier, from the values listed above we can conclude that Decision Tree, Random Forest and Extreme Gradient Boosting whose AUC- score is found to be 1.0 which produces the best result out of all the classifiers used for the split ratio of 90:10.

5.5 Performance Analysis

From Table 1, we can see various reading listed when we use different machine learning algorithm under different test ratios. From the table we can see importance of choosing the test-train split ratio while training the model. Also choosing the algorithm which yield us with maximum accuracy is very important. Let's look into the output which we got.

For the train-test split ratio is 60-40 let's look into the metrics we got. When the algorithm used is AdaBoost Classifier, we get accuracy: 0.861, precision: 0.84, recall: 0.89, f1-score: 0.86 and auc-score: 0.8611. When the algorithm used is Support Vector Classifier, we get accuracy: 0.805, precision: 0.81, recall: 0.79, f1-score: 0.80 and auc-score: 0.8048. When the algorithm used is Decision Tree, we get accuracy: 0.966, precision: 0.98, recall: 0.95, f1-score: 0.96 and auc-score: 0.9657. When the algorithm used is Logistic Regression, we get accuracy: 0.846, precision: 0.82, recall: 0.88, f1-score: 0.85 and auc-score: 0.8465. When the algorithm used is Random Forest, we get accuracy: 0.993, precision: 1.00, recall: 0.99, f1-score: 0.99 and auc-score: 0.9926. When the algorithm used is Stochastic Gradient Descent, we get accuracy: 0.761, precision: 0.69, recall: 0.96, f1-score: 0.80 and auc-score: 0.7619. When the algorithm used is k- Nearest Neighbors, we get accuracy: 0.84, precision: 0.83, recall: 0.85, f1-score: 0.84 and auc-score: 0.8391. When the algorithm used is Gaussian Naive Bayes Classifier, we get accuracy: 0.834, precision: 0.83, recall: 0.84, f1-score: 0.83 and auc-score: 0.8342.

When the algorithm used is Extreme Gradient Boosting Classifier, we get accuracy: 0.985, precision: 1.00, recall: 0.97, f1-score: 0.99 and auc-score: 0.9853. So, we can conclude by saying when our test-train split ratio is 60:40 Random Forest algorithm provide us with maximum accuracy.

For the train-test split ratio is 70-30 let's look into the metrics we got. When the algorithm used is AdaBoost Classifier, we get accuracy: 0.844, precision: 0.82, recall: 0.88, f1-score: 0.85 and auc-score: 0.8445. When the algorithm used is Support Vector Classifier, we get accuracy: 0.798, precision: 0.80, recall: 0.79, f1-score: 0.79 and auc-score: 0.7985. When the algorithm used is Decision Tree, we get accuracy: 1.00, precision: 1.00, recall: 1.00, f1-score: 1.00 and auc-score: 1.00. When the algorithm used is Logistic Regression, we get accuracy: 0.857, precision: 0.82, recall: 0.91, f1-score: 0.86 and auc-score: 0.8578. When the algorithm used is Random Forest, we get accuracy: 0.990, precision: 1.00, recall: 0.98, f1-score: 0.99 and auc-score: 0.9901. When the algorithm used is Stochastic Gradient Descent, we get accuracy: 0.851, precision: 0.8, recall: 0.93, f1-score: 0.86 and auc-score: 0.8516. When the algorithm used is k- Nearest Neighbors, we get accuracy: 0.834, precision: 0.83, recall: 0.84, f1-score: 0.83 and auc-score: 0.8344. When the algorithm used is Gaussian Naive Bayes Classifier, we get accuracy: 0.825, precision: 0.81, recall: 0.85, f1-score: 0.83 and auc-score: 0.8249. When the algorithm used is Extreme Gradient Boosting Classifier, we get accuracy: 0.99, precision: 1.00, recall: 0.98, f1-score: 0.99 and auc-score: 0.9901. So, we can conclude by saying when our test-train split ratio is 70:30 Decision Tree algorithm provide us with maximum accuracy.

For the train-test split ratio is 80-20 let's look into the metrics we got. When the algorithm used is AdaBoost Classifier, we get accuracy: 0.849, precision: 0.81, recall: 0.89, f1-score: 0.85 and auc-score: 0.8504. When the algorithm used is Support Vector Classifier, we get accuracy: 0.771, precision: 0.77, recall: 0.74, f1-score: 0.76 and auc-score: 0.7696. When the algorithm used is Decision Tree, we get accuracy: 1.00, precision: 1.00, recall: 1.00, f1-score: 1.00 and auc-score: 1.00. When the algorithm used is Logistic Regression, we get accuracy: 0.849, precision: 0.80, recall: 0.92, f1-score: 0.85 and auc-score: 0.8517. When the algorithm used is Random Forest, we get accuracy: 1.00, precision: 1.00, recall: 1.00, f1-score: 1.00 and auc-score: 1.00. When the algorithm used is Stochastic Gradient Descent, we get accuracy: 0.815, precision: 0.74, recall: 0.95, f1-score: 0.83 and auc-score: 0.8203. When the algorithm used is k- Nearest Neighbors, we get accuracy: 0.854, precision: 0.85, recall: 0.85, f1-score: 0.85 and auc-score: 0.8534. When the algorithm used is Gaussian Naive Bayes Classifier, we get accuracy: 0.815, precision: 0.78, recall: 0.86, f1-score: 0.82 and auc-score: 0.8164. When the algorithm used is Extreme Gradient Boosting Classifier, we get accuracy: 1.00, precision: 1.00, recall: 1.00, f1-score: 1.00 and auc-score: 1.00. So, we can conclude by saying when our test-train split ratio is 80:20 Decision tree, Random Forest and Extreme Gradient Boosting algorithm provide us with maximum accuracy.

For the train-test split ratio is 90-10 let's look into the metrics we got. When the algorithm used is AdaBoost Classifier, we get accuracy: 0.893, precision: 0.89, recall: 0.91, f1-score: 0.90 and auc-score: 0.8920. When the algorithm used is Support Vector Classifier, we get accuracy: 0.786, precision: 0.85, recall: 0.73, f1-score: 0.78 and auc-score: 0.7907. When the algorithm used is Decision Tree, we get accuracy: 1.00, precision: 1.00, recall: 1.00, f1-score: 1.00 and auc-score: 1.00. When the algorithm used is Logistic Regression, we get accuracy: 0.854, precision: 0.86, recall: 0.87, f1-score: 0.86 and auc-score: 0.8530. When the algorithm used is Random Forest, we get accuracy: 1.00, precision: 1.00, recall: 1.00, f1-score: 1.00 and auc-score: 1.00. When the algorithm used is Stochastic Gradient Descent, we get accuracy: 0.854, precision: 0.81, recall: 0.95, f1-score: 0.87 and auc-score: 0.8477. When the algorithm used is k- Nearest Neighbors, we get accuracy: 0.864, precision: 0.92, recall: 0.82, f1-score: 0.87 and auc-score: 0.8467. When the algorithm used is Gaussian Naive Bayes Classifier, we get accuracy: 0.845, precision: 0.88, recall: 0.82, f1-score: 0.85 and auc-score: 0.8466. When the algorithm used is Extreme Gradient Boosting Classifier, we get accuracy: 1.00, precision: 1.00, recall: 1.00, f1-score: 1.00 and auc-score: 1.00. So, we can conclude by saying when our test-train split ratio is 80:20 Decision tree, Random Forest and Extreme Gradient Boosting algorithm provide us with maximum accuracy.

6. CONCLUSION

When heart conditions worsen, they become completely out of control. Heart conditions are difficult and claim many lives each year. When the early signs of cardiovascular illness are disregarded, the patient may experience severe effects quickly. The problem has gotten worse as a result of today's world's sedentary lifestyle and excessive stress. Early illness detection allows for the management of the condition. However, it is always advisable to exercise every day and get rid of bad habits as soon as possible. Stroke and heart disease risk factors include using nicotine and eating poorly. It's a good idea to consume a minimum of 5 servings of fruits and vegetables each day. It is advised to limit salt intake for people with heart disease to one teaspoon per day. The fact that these studies have mostly focused on applying algorithms for classification to the identification of cardiovascular disease rather than researching various data cleaning and pruning approaches that may be used to prepare a dataset for mining is one of their biggest shortcomings. A contaminated dataset with values that are missing performs substantially worse than one that has been thoroughly cleaned and trimmed. The development of prediction systems that provide increased accuracy will result from the use of appropriate data cleaning procedures in conjunction with appropriate classification techniques.

In the future, an intelligent system may be created that can guide the patient with cardiovascular disease in choosing the best course of therapy. Making models that can forecast whether a patient is going to acquire heart disease or not has previously required a lot of study. Once a patient has been identified as having a specific type of heart disease, there are numerous treatment options available. By collecting information from these pertinent databases, data extraction may be a very useful tool in determining the course of therapy to be taken.

Figure 1. Block diagram of proposed methodology

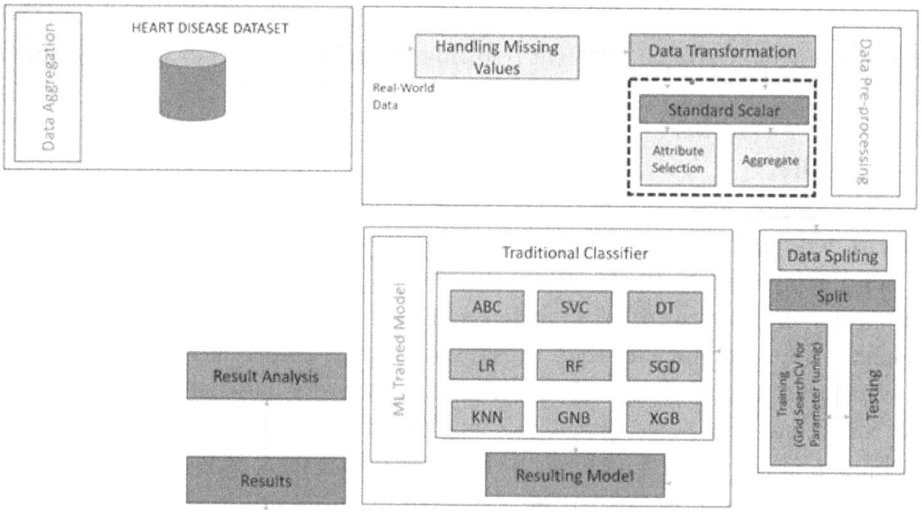

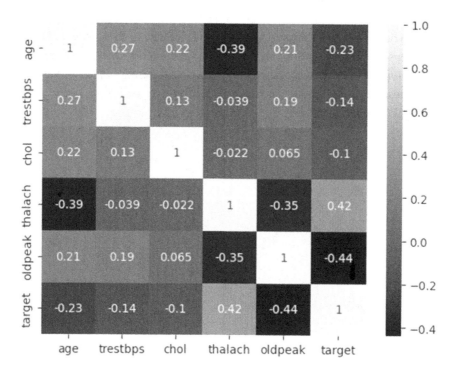

Figure 2. Correlation matrix

Figure 3. Scatter plot

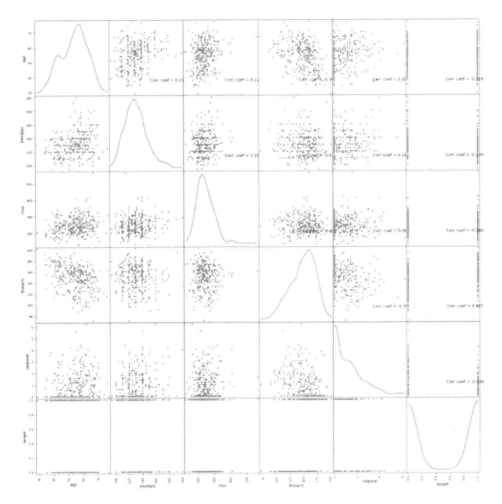

Figure 4. ROC plot for 60-40 ratio

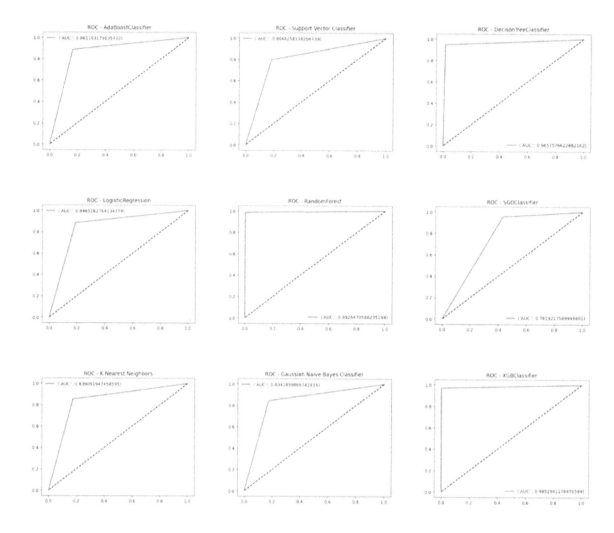

Figure 5. ROC plot for 70-30 ratio

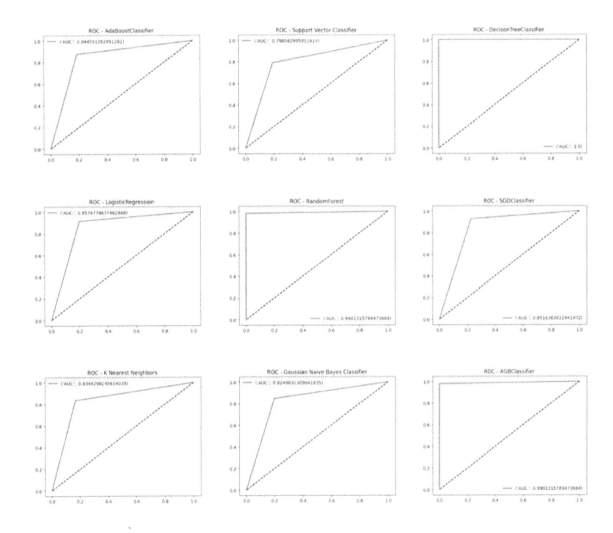

Figure 6. ROC plot for 80-20 ratio

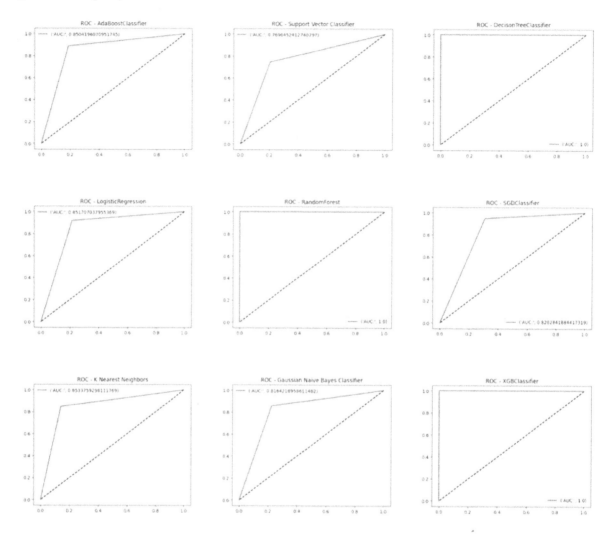

Figure 7. ROC plot for 90-10 ratio

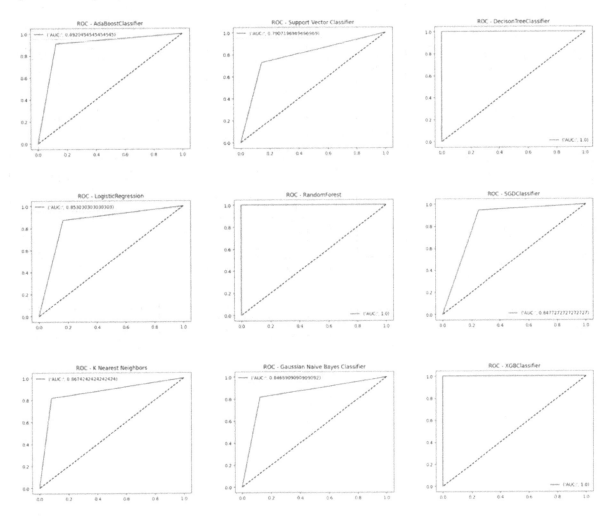

Table 1. Comparison between all the classifiers used under different train and test ratio

Split Ratio	Metrics	ABC	SVC	DT	LR	RF	SGD	KNN	GNB	XGB
60:40	Accuracy	0.861	0.805	0.966	0.846	0.993	0.761	0.84	0.834	0.985
	Precision	0.84	0.81	0.98	0.82	1.00	0.69	0.83	0.83	1.00
	Recall	0.89	0.79	0.95	0.88	0.99	0.96	0.85	0.84	0.97
	F1-Score	0.86	0.80	0.96	0.85	0.99	0.80	0.84	0.83	0.99
	AUC-score	0.8611	0.8048	0.9657	0.8465	0.9926	0.7619	0.8391	0.8342	0.9853

continued on following page

Table 1. Continued

Split Ratio	Metrics	ABC	SVC	DT	LR	RF	SGD	KNN	GNB	XGB
70:30	Accuracy	0.844	0.798	1.0	0.857	0.990	0.851	0.834	0.825	0.99
	Precision	0.82	0.8	1.0	0.82	1.0	0.8	0.83	0.81	1.00
	Recall	0.88	0.79	1.0	0.91	0.98	0.93	0.84	0.85	0.98
	F1-Score	0.85	0.79	1.0	0.86	0.99	0.86	0.83	0.83	0.99
	AUC-score	0.8445	0.7985	1.0	0.8578	0.9901	0.8516	0.8344	0.8249	0.9901
80:20	Accuracy	0.849	0.771	1.0	0.849	1.0	0.815	0.854	0.815	1.0
	Precision	0.81	0.77	1.0	0.80	1.0	0.74	0.85	0.78	1.0
	Recall	0.89	0.74	1.0	0.92	1.0	0.95	0.85	0.86	1.0
	F1-Score	0.85	0.76	1.0	0.85	1.0	0.83	0.85	0.82	1.0
	AUC-score	0.8504	0.7696	1.0	0.8517	1.0	0.8203	0.8534	0.8164	1.0
90:10	Accuracy	0.893	0.786	1.0	0.854	1.0	0.854	0.864	0.845	1.0
	Precision	0.89	0.85	1.0	0.86	1.0	0.81	0.92	0.88	1.0
	Recall	0.91	0.73	1.0	0.87	1.0	0.95	0.82	0.82	1.0
	F1-Score	0.90	0.78	1.0	0.86	1.0	0.87	0.87	0.85	1.0
	AUC-score	0.8920	0.7907	1.0	0.8530	1.0	0.8477	0.867	0.8466	1.0

REFERENCES

Abdeldjouad, F. Z., Brahami, M., & Matta, N. (2020). A hybrid approach for heart disease diagnosis and prediction using machine learning techniques. *The Impact of Digital Technologies on Public Health in Developed and Developing Countries: 18th International Conference, ICOST 2020, Hammamet, Tunisia, June 24–26, 2020Proceedings*, 18, 299–306.

Alaa, A. M., Bolton, T., Di Angelantonio, E., Rudd, J. H., & Van der Schaar, M. (2019). Cardiovascular disease risk prediction using automated machine learning: A prospective study of 423,604 UK Biobank participants. *PLoS One*, 14(5), e0213653. 10.1371/journal.pone.021365331091238

Anbuselvan, P. (2020). Heart disease prediction using machine learning techniques. *International Journal of Engineering Research & Technology (Ahmedabad)*, 9, 515–518.

Anuar, N. N., Hafifah, H., Zubir, S. M., Noraidatulakma, A., Rosmina, J., Ain, M. N., ... Rahman, A. (2020). *Cardiovascular disease prediction from electrocardiogram by using machine learning*. Academic Press.

Dalal, S., Goel, P., Onyema, E. M., Alharbi, A., Mahmoud, A., Algarni, M. A., & Awal, H. (2023). Application of Machine Learning for Cardiovascular Disease Risk Prediction. *Computational Intelligence and Neuroscience*, 2023, 2023. 10.1155/2023/9418666

Dinesh, K. G., Arumugaraj, K., Santhosh, K. D., & Mareeswari, V. (2018, March). Prediction of cardiovascular disease using machine learning algorithms. In *2018 International Conference on Current Trends towards Converging Technologies (ICCTCT)* (pp. 1-7). IEEE. 10.1109/ICCTCT.2018.8550857

El-Hasnony, I. M., Elzeki, O. M., Alshehri, A., & Salem, H. (2022). Multi-label active learning-based machine learning model for heart disease prediction. *Sensors (Basel)*, 22(3), 1184. 10.3390/s2203118435161928

Guarneros-Nolasco, L. R., Cruz-Ramos, N. A., Alor-Hernández, G., Rodríguez-Mazahua, L., & Sánchez-Cervantes, J. L. (2021). Identifying the main risk factors for cardiovascular diseases prediction using machine learning algorithms. *Mathematics*, 9(20), 2537. 10.3390/math9202537

Haq, A. U., Li, J. P., Memon, M. H., Nazir, S., & Sun, R. (2018). A hybrid intelligent system framework for the prediction of heart disease using machine learning algorithms. *Mobile Information Systems*, 2018, 1–21. 10.1155/2018/3860146

Jindal, H., Agrawal, S., Khera, R., Jain, R., & Nagrath, P. (2021). Heart disease prediction using machine learning algorithms. *IOP Conference Series. Materials Science and Engineering*, 1022(1), 012072. 10.1088/1757-899X/1022/1/012072

Katarya, R., & Meena, S. K. (2021). Machine learning techniques for heart disease prediction: A comparative study and analysis. *Health and Technology*, 11(1), 87–97. 10.1007/s12553-020-00505-7

Khan, A., Qureshi, M., Daniyal, M., & Tawiah, K. (2023). A Novel Study on Machine Learning Algorithm-Based Cardiovascular Disease Prediction. *Health & Social Care in the Community*, 2023, 2023. 10.1155/2023/1406060

Krishnan, S., & Geetha, S. (2019, April). Prediction of heart disease using machine learning algorithms. In *2019 1st international conference on innovations in information and communication technology (ICIICT)* (pp. 1-5). IEEE.

Krishnani, D., Kumari, A., Dewangan, A., Singh, A., & Naik, N. S. (2019, October). Prediction of coronary heart disease using supervised machine learning algorithms. In *TENCON 2019-2019 IEEE Region 10 Conference (TENCON)* (pp. 367-372). IEEE. 10.1109/TENCON.2019.8929434

Krittanawong, C., Virk, H. U. H., Bangalore, S., Wang, Z., Johnson, K. W., Pinotti, R., Zhang, H. J., Kaplin, S., Narasimhan, B., Kitai, T., Baber, U., Halperin, J. L., & Tang, W. W. (2020). Machine learning prediction in cardiovascular diseases: A meta-analysis. *Scientific Reports*, 10(1), 16057. 10.1038/s41598-020-72685-132994452

Kumar, N. K., Sindhu, G. S., Prashanthi, D. K., & Sulthana, A. S. (2020, March). Analysis and prediction of cardio vascular disease using machine learning classifiers. In *2020 6th International Conference on Advanced Computing and Communication Systems (ICACCS)* (pp. 15-21). IEEE. 10.1109/ICACCS48705.2020.9074183

Li, Y., Sperrin, M., Ashcroft, D. M., & Van Staa, T. P. (2020). Consistency of variety of machine learning and statistical models in predicting clinical risks of individual patients: longitudinal cohort study using cardiovascular disease as exemplar. *BMJ, 371.*

Louridi, N., Amar, M., & El Ouahidi, B. (2019, October). Identification of cardiovascular diseases using machine learning. In *2019 7th mediterranean congress of telecommunications (CMT)* (pp. 1-6). IEEE. 10.1109/CMT.2019.8931411

Maiga, J., & Hungilo, G. G. (2019, October). Comparison of machine learning models in prediction of cardiovascular disease using health record data. In *2019 International Conference on Informatics, Multimedia, Cyber and Information System (ICIMCIS)* (pp. 45-48). IEEE. 10.1109/ICIMCIS48181.2019.8985205

Marbaniang, I. A., Choudhury, N. A., & Moulik, S. (2020, December). Cardiovascular disease (CVD) prediction using machine learning algorithms. In *2020 IEEE 17th India Council International Conference (INDICON)* (pp. 1-6). IEEE.

Mohan, S., Thirumalai, C., & Srivastava, G. (2019). Effective heart disease prediction using hybrid machine learning techniques. *IEEE Access : Practical Innovations, Open Solutions*, 7, 81542–81554. 10.1109/ACCESS.2019.2923707

Motarwar, P., Duraphe, A., Suganya, G., & Premalatha, M. (2020, February). Cognitive approach for heart disease prediction using machine learning. In *2020 International Conference on Emerging Trends in Information Technology and Engineering (ic-ETITE)* (pp. 1-5). IEEE. 10.1109/ic-ETITE47903.2020.242

Nadakinamani, R. G., Reyana, A., Kautish, S., Vibith, A. S., Gupta, Y., Abdelwahab, S. F., & Mohamed, A. W. (2022). Clinical data analysis for prediction of cardiovascular disease using machine learning techniques. *Computational Intelligence and Neuroscience*, 2022, 2022. 10.1155/2022/297332435069715

Nikhar, S., & Karandikar, A. M. (2016). Prediction of heart disease using machine learning algorithms. International Journal of Advanced Engineering. *Management Science*, 2(6), 239484.

Padmanabhan, M., Yuan, P., Chada, G., & Nguyen, H. V. (2019). Physician-friendly machine learning: A case study with cardiovascular disease risk prediction. *Journal of Clinical Medicine*, 8(7), 1050. 10.3390/jcm807105031323843

Sajja, G. S., Mustafa, M., Phasinam, K., Kaliyaperumal, K., Ventayen, R. J. M., & Kassanuk, T. (2021, August). Towards application of machine learning in classification and prediction of heart disease. In *2021 Second International Conference on Electronics and Sustainable Communication Systems (ICESC)* (pp. 1664-1669). IEEE. 10.1109/ICESC51422.2021.9532940

Shah, D., Patel, S., & Bharti, S. K. (2020). Heart disease prediction using machine learning techniques. *SN Computer Science*, 1(6), 1–6. 10.1007/s42979-020-00365-y

Shameer, K., Johnson, K. W., Glicksberg, B. S., Dudley, J. T., & Sengupta, P. P. (2018). Machine learning in cardiovascular medicine: Are we there yet? *Heart (British Cardiac Society)*, 104(14), 1156–1164. 10.1136/heartjnl-2017-31119829352006

Singh, Y. K., Sinha, N., & Singh, S. K. (2017). Heart disease prediction system using random forest. In *Advances in Computing and Data Sciences:First International Conference, ICACDS 2016,Ghaziabad, India,November 11-12, 2016, Revised Selected Papers 1* (pp. 613-623). Springer Singapore. 10.1007/978-981-10-5427-3_63

Sitar-tăut, A., Zdrenghea, D., Pop, D., & Sitar-tăut, D. (2009). Using machine learning algorithms in cardiovascular disease risk evaluation. *Age (Dordrecht, Netherlands)*, 1(4), 4.

Ward, A., Sarraju, A., Chung, S., Li, J., Harrington, R., Heidenreich, P., Palaniappan, L., Scheinker, D., & Rodriguez, F. (2020). Machine learning and atherosclerotic cardiovascular disease risk prediction in a multi-ethnic population. *NPJ Digital Medicine*, 3(1), 125. 10.1038/s41746-020-00331-133043149

Weng, S. F., Reps, J., Kai, J., Garibaldi, J. M., & Qureshi, N. (2017). Can machine-learning improve cardiovascular risk prediction using routine clinical data? *PLoS One*, 12(4), e0174944. 10.1371/journal.pone.017494428376093

Chapter 10
Investigation of Various Dimensionality Reduction and Feature Selection Techniques in Microarray Gene Data for Renal Cancer Diagnosis

Bharanidharan N.

School of Computer Science Engineering and Information Systems, Vellore Institute of Technology, Vellore, India

Sannasi Chakravarthy S. R.
http://orcid.org/0000-0002-0162-7206

Department of Electronics and Communication Engineering, Bannari Amman Institute of Technology, Sathyamangalam, India

Vinoth Kumar V.

School of Computer Science Engineering and Information Systems, Vellore Institute of Technology, Vellore, India

Pratham Aggarwal

School of Computer Science Engineering and Information Systems, Vellore Institute of Technology, Vellore, India

Harikumar Rajaguru
http://orcid.org/0000-0002-2792-0945

Department of Electronics and Communication Engineering, Bannari Amman Institute of Technology, Sathyamangalam, India

ABSTRACT

Renal cancer is among the top 10 cancers in both genders. Microarray gene expression data is one of the effective modalities to diagnose renal cancer. The main objective of this work is to label the gene expression sample as either normal or clear cell renal cell carcinoma. To improve the classification

DOI: 10.4018/979-8-3693-0683-3.ch010

performance and reduce the training time of the above-mentioned supervised classifiers, various feature selection and dimensionality reduction techniques are investigated. Feature selection techniques, namely variance filter, chi-square test, ANOVA test, and mutual information filter, are tested. In addition, principal component analysis, independent component analysis, and linear discriminant analysis are evaluated as dimensionality reduction techniques. Highest balanced accuracy score of 91.6% is attained for support vector machine classifier while it was increased to 94.4% through the usage appropriate dimensionality reduction or feature selection technique.

1. INTRODUCTION

Cancer that arises in the regions of kidney is termed Renal Cancer or Renal Cell Carcinoma (RCC). In this type of cancer, usually malignant cells are developed in the regions of cortex or tubular epithelial cells of kidney. Major types of RCC are Clear Cell Renal Cell Carcinoma (ccRCC), Chromophobe Renal Cell Carcinoma, and Papillary Renal Cell Carcinoma. These cancers account for almost 85% of RCC (Hsieh et al., 2017). Each cancer type will have different behavior, genetics, and biology. RCC can arise due to several factors including genetic and acquired causes. The malfunctions of genes like Von Hippel–Lindau and protein polybromo-1 may be the reason for genetic causes. In ccRCC cases, abnormality in chromosome-3 is witnessed in most of the patients. Prolonged dialysis, smoking habits, blood pressure, diabetes, and obesity can be the reasons for acquired causes (Scandling, 2017).

Renal cancer is ranked under the top 10 types of cancer that prevail in both genders. Particularly, it is ranked as seventh widespread cancer among men. Compared with other cancers that arise due to genetic abnormalities, this RCC is ranked first in mortality proportion. According to a survey in United States, one among forty-six men may encounter renal cancer and that is around 2.02% of men while 1.03% of women may develop RCC. Globally 431,288 humans are affected due to this type of cancer in the year 2020 and around 179,368 deaths occurred (Howlader et al., 2023).

The biggest challenge in treating RCC is the fact that around sixty percent of subjects are detected incidentally and crossed the earlier stage of cancer. Renal cancer can be diagnosed using microarray gene data analysis, and through other common imaging modalities like Computed Tomography, Ultrasound Imaging, Magnetic Resonance Imaging, etc. (Padala & Kallam, 2023). Investigation of microarray gene data can be very useful in diagnosing the RCC in an efficient manner. But the curse of dimensionality could be a big challenge in using such data. Hence Computerized Detection algorithms are being developed to support the clinicians (San Segundo-Val & Sanz-Lozano, 2016).

The upcoming sections can be outlined as follows: Introduction to machine learning algorithm and its various use cases are explained in the second section. Various feature selection and dimensionality reduction techniques are elaborated in the third section. Methodology used in this work is narrated in the fourth section. Results and discussion are presented in the fifth section and the chapter is concluded in the sixth section.

2. MACHINE LEARNING ALGORITHMS

Artificial Intelligence (AI) can be used to develop such computerized diagnostic systems for renal cancer. In the past decade, the application fields of AI are tremendously increasing (Bhinder et al., 2021.). Particularly in the field of healthcare, AI has the capacity to produce very good results. Machine Learning (ML) being a sub-domain of AI is widely used for the diagnostic systems where disease prediction is involved (Cruz & Wishart, 2006). ML algorithms are widely used to solve classification and regression problems. ML can be used to predict the labels for both binary classification tasks and multi-class classification tasks. ML algorithms can be broadly classified into three categories as follows: Supervised, Unsupervised, and reinforcement learning. In supervised learning, labels are already known (Soham Patangia, 2020). Usually, the supervised algorithms are modelled with crucial parameters and these parameters learnt during the training phase. The learnt parameters are used in the ML model to classify the unseen inputs in the testing phase. In unsupervised algorithms, the labels are not known. Based on the characteristics of features, the entire data will be divided into number of clusters. Based on the reward and punishment, the learning will happen in reinforcement learning. Some of the popular supervised algorithms for classification tasks include K-Nearest Neighbor classifier, Random Forest Classifier (RFC), Stochastic Gradient Descent classifier, Decision Trees classifier (DTC), Histogram Gradient Boosting classifier, Gaussian Naïve Bayes classifier (GNB), and Support Vector machine Classifier (SVC). RFC, DTC, GNB, and SVC will be used in this work to classify the features of renal cancer.

RFC is one of the ensemble techniques and meta estimator that uses many decision trees. They will be trained on the subsets of the original dataset and the average or majority will be considered in RFC to enhance the prediction performance. It is very efficient in solving both classification and regression problems. This algorithm can handle complex and large datasets. In addition, it can eradicate the overfitting problem since it is an ensemble technique that uses many weak classifiers. Even when a large part of data is missing, RFC can deliver better classification performance (Mathew, 2022).

DTC is comparatively a straightforward model which can be used for both classification and regression tasks. In classification, a single discrete target will be used. DTC is composed of many nodes and edges. Feature inputs are tested through Boolean operations at each node and edges are marked with the numerical of that feature inputs. Feature target value is specified in all the individual leaf nodes. Based on the entropy or information gain, decisions will be taken at each node. DTC is relatively simple, but it may suffer from overfitting problem in which the model has over-learnt the training data and so failing on the new unseen data.

Probabilistic modelling and gaussian distribution are considered in the designing of GNB. It assumes that each and individual feature has a stand-alone capacity to predict the output target variable through its Gaussian modeling. It uses the prediction results of all such predictors and outputs a probability value for each target variable. Based on the higher probability value, the output target class will be predicted. GNB model can be trained relatively faster since it uses the concept of conditional probabilities. It assumes the features values as continuous and follows the Gaussian distribution. It produces better classification results when its assumption is true (Ratanamahatana & Gunopulos, 2003).

SVC is one of the popular supervised ML algorithms that can be used for classification, regression, and outlier detection. It will try to find the ideal hyperplane that can be used to separate the data points belonging to different classes. It works on N-dimensional space and the value of N depends on the number of features. The ideal hyperplane is chosen in a way that margin between the hyperplane and data points are maximum. Major types of SVC are linear SVC and non-linear SVC. Usually, the linear

SVC is very simple, and it may encounter underfitting problems while the non-linear SVC is relatively complex, and it may encounter overfitting problems (Nanglia et al., 2020).

3. FEATURE SELECTION & DIMENSIONALITY REDUCTION ALGORITHMS

In the microarray gene data, large number of dimensions and irrelevant features may lead to more training time of model and poor performance. Hence there is a need to reduce the number of dimensions or features. Either dimensionality reduction techniques or feature selection techniques can be used for this purpose in between the feature extraction and classification process. Feature selection techniques are employed to select the most significant features for classification. Usually, it will filter out the redundant features and the value of features will not change due to feature selection. On the other hand, the inner projections are learnt, and only significant projections are given as output in dimensionality reduction techniques. Generally, the value of features will be changed due to dimensionality reduction. Feature selection techniques are broadly classified into filter-based and wrapper-based methods where no estimator is involved in filter-based while an estimator is used to select the significant features in wrapper-based method. Comparatively, filter-based methods are easy to implement and require less time to select features. The most common feature selection techniques are Variance filter, Chi-square test, Analysis of Variance (ANOVA) test, Correlation filter, and Mutual Information (MI) filter. Some of the popular dimensionality reduction techniques are Principal Component Analysis (PCA), Independent Component Analysis, and Linear Discriminant Analysis, etc.

The Variance filter-based feature selection employs a threshold for variance. If the variance of a particular feature is less than a given threshold, then that feature will be dropped. The features that satisfy the variance threshold condition alone will only be selected. In this feature selection, the number of required features that need to be selected will not be explicitly mentioned. Instead, the value of variance threshold will implicitly decide the number of features to be selected. Generally, chi-square test is used to examine the dependence of two events. In feature selection, it will be used to select the features that are very much related to the target variable. When the feature and target variable are having less dependency, then the observed chi-square value will be smaller. ANOVA is a statistical approach to select the features based on the means of different groups that are substantially diverse from each other. It will compute variance among different feature sets to decide intra-class and inter-class variance. Mutual information or information gain is a statistical measure that explains the significance of information gain from each feature. The significant features will be retained, and the remaining features will be dropped.

PCA is used for variety of applications such as unsupervised learning, dimensionality reduction, exploratory data analysis, data denoising, and information compression, etc. PCA will try to compute the principal components from the original data that can represents the significant part of original data. PCA ties to find the uncorrelation while ICA tries to find the independent features. ICA will transform the original feature set into the feature set that are independent at the maximum possible level. LDA also known as Normal Discriminant Analysis or Discriminant Function Analysis is a generalized technique derived from the Fisher's linear discriminant. LDA tries to find the linear combination of features that can distinguish the data points of different classes (Liu & Wang, 2011).

4. METHODOLOGY

Curated Microarray Database (CuMiDa) is one of the popular online repositories that has microarray gene expression data belonging to different types of cancer such as breast cancer, liver cancer, pancreatic cancer, renal cancer, skin cancer, etc (Feltes et al., 2019). For this work, gene expression data related to renal cancer is collected from CuMiDa website and used. 143 subjects belonging to two different classes are considered. Among them 72 subjects are normal while the remaining 71 subjects are diagnosed with ccRCC. Each subject has 54675 genes without any missing values. The methodology used in this work is depicted in Figure 1.

The microarray gene expression data will have the target labels as either Normal or ccRCC. Using label encoder, normal is encoded as 1 while the ccRCC class is encoded as 0. Then the stratified shuffle split is used to divide the dataset into training and testing sets after shuffling. Stratified split technique will ensure same ratio of each class in original dataset, train, and test sets. 25% of data is used for testing while the remaining 75% is used for training. Then a min-max scaler is used to scale all the features to a common scale. This step will ensure the justification of each feature even if the original values are varying to a larger extent. Feature selection or dimensionality reduction techniques are used to reduce the number of features since the original number of features is too large i.e., 54675 genes. Feature selection techniques namely Variance filter, Chi-square test, ANOVA test, and Mutual Information filter are tested. In addition, Principal Component Analysis, Independent Component Analysis, and Linear Discriminant Analysis are evaluated as Dimensionality reduction techniques. Four supervised classifiers namely random forest classifier, decision tree classifier, gaussian naïve bayes classifier, and support vector machine classifier are employed to classify the input gene microarray sample into two classes: Normal & ccRCC.

Figure 1. Flowchart depicting the methodology used in this research work

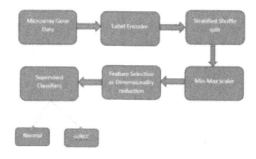

5. RESULTS AND DISCUSSION

Supervised classifiers will produce predicted labels which has to be compared with the true labels to know the performance of classification. Various performance measures like Balanced Accuracy (BAC), Precision (PREC), Recall, F1 score, Mathews Correlation Coefficient (MCC), Cohen's Kappa

Coefficient are used in this work. Out of these six metrics, except precision and recall score, all other metrics represent the overall effectiveness of classification model. Precision score is related to the exact predictions of positive labels while recall is related to the completeness of positive prediction. A good classification model should possess almost equal precision and recall values but in most of the cases, the classification model fails to achieve that. Hence F1 score is used which is computed by finding the harmonic mean between precision and recall values.

Figure 2. Balanced accuracy attained and no. of selected features for various supervised classifiers with variance filter for feature selection

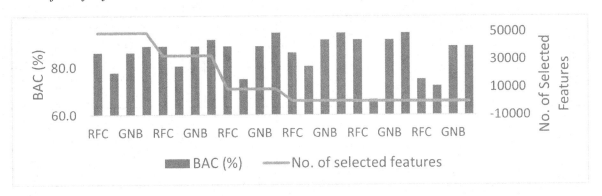

BAC attained for four supervised classifiers with variance filter for feature selection is shown in Figure 1 along with the number of selected features. Table 1 shows the performance measures of all the four examined supervised classifiers when Variance filter is used as feature selection technique. The values for variance threshold used and implicitly the number of features selected due to that threshold is also shown in Table 1. The highest BAC is attained by SVC, and it is 94.4% when the variance threshold is 0.125 and number of features is 62. For the same variance threshold value, RFC and GNB also offer the relatively higher BAC of 91.7%. But DTC requires more features and so it delivers the highest BAC of 80.6% when the variance threshold is 0.1 and number of features are 242. BAC and number of selected features when the chi-square test is used for feature selection is shown in Figure 3. Table 2 shows the various performance measures of all the four examined supervised classifiers when Chi-square test is used as feature selection technique. The highest BAC of 94.4% is attained for three different classifiers namely RFC, GNB and SVC due to chi-square test when the number of selected features is 50. But DTC requires more features to be selected and so it delivers maximum of 80.6% when 200 features are selected.

Table 1. Performance metrics of supervised classifiers with variance filter for feature selection

ML Model	Variance Threshold	No. of Selected Features	BAC	F1	PREC	RECALL	MCC	KAPPA
RFC	0.025	49138	86.1	86.5	84.2	88.9	72.3	72.2
DTC	0.025	49138	77.8	77.8	77.8	77.8	55.6	55.6
GNB	0.025	49138	86.1	86.5	84.2	88.9	72.3	72.2

continued on following page

Table 1. Continued

ML Model	Variance Threshold	No. of Selected Features	BAC	F1	PREC	RECALL	MCC	KAPPA
SVC	0.025	49138	88.9	88.9	88.9	88.9	77.8	77.8
RFC	0.035	32775	88.9	88.9	88.9	88.9	77.8	77.8
DTC	0.035	32775	80.6	80.0	82.4	77.8	61.2	61.1
GNB	0.035	32775	88.9	88.9	88.9	88.9	77.8	77.8
SVC	0.035	32775	91.7	91.4	94.1	88.9	83.5	83.3
RFC	0.05	8619	88.9	88.9	88.9	88.9	77.8	77.8
DTC	0.05	8619	75.0	74.3	76.5	72.2	50.1	50.0
GNB	0.05	8619	88.9	88.9	88.9	88.9	77.8	77.8
SVC	0.05	8619	94.4	94.1	100.0	88.9	89.4	88.9
RFC	0.1	242	86.1	86.5	84.2	88.9	72.3	72.2
DTC	0.1	242	**80.6**	**82.1**	**76.2**	**88.9**	**62.0**	**61.1**
GNB	0.1	242	91.7	91.4	94.1	88.9	83.5	83.3
SVC	0.1	242	94.4	94.1	100.0	88.9	89.4	88.9
RFC	0.125	62	**91.7**	**91.4**	**94.1**	**88.9**	**83.5**	**83.3**
DTC	0.125	62	66.7	66.7	66.7	66.7	33.3	33.3
GNB	0.125	62	**91.7**	**91.4**	**94.1**	**88.9**	**83.5**	**83.3**
SVC	0.125	62	**94.4**	**94.1**	**100.0**	**88.9**	**89.4**	**88.9**
RFC	0.15	9	75.0	74.3	76.5	72.2	50.1	50.0
DTC	0.15	9	72.2	70.6	75.0	66.7	44.7	44.4
GNB	0.15	9	88.9	88.2	93.8	83.3	78.3	77.8
SVC	0.15	9	88.9	88.2	93.8	83.3	78.3	77.8

Figure 3. Balanced accuracy attained and no. of selected features for various supervised classifiers with chi-square test for feature selection

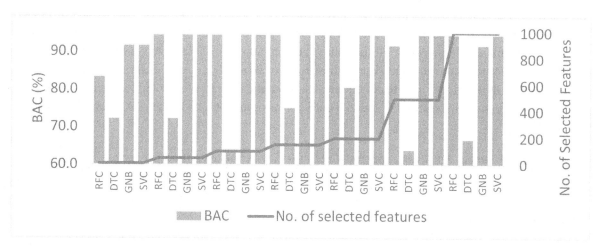

Table 2. Performance metrics of supervised classifiers with chi-square test for feature selection

ML Model	No. of Selected Features	BAC	F1	PREC	RECALL	MCC	KAPPA
RFC	10	83.3	82.4	87.5	77.8	67.1	66.7
DTC	10	72.2	72.2	72.2	72.2	44.4	44.4
GNB	10	91.7	91.4	94.1	88.9	83.5	83.3
SVC	10	91.7	91.4	94.1	88.9	83.5	83.3
RFC	50	**94.4**	**94.1**	**100.0**	**88.9**	**89.4**	**88.9**
DTC	50	72.2	73.7	70.0	77.8	44.7	44.4
GNB	50	**94.4**	**94.1**	**100.0**	**88.9**	**89.4**	**88.9**
SVC	50	**94.4**	**94.1**	**100.0**	**88.9**	**89.4**	**88.9**
RFC	100	94.4	94.1	100.0	88.9	89.4	88.9
DTC	100	63.9	62.9	64.7	61.1	27.8	27.8
GNB	100	94.4	94.1	100.0	88.9	89.4	88.9
SVC	100	94.4	94.1	100.0	88.9	89.4	88.9
RFC	150	94.4	94.1	100.0	88.9	89.4	88.9
DTC	150	75.0	66.7	100.0	50.0	57.7	50.0
GNB	150	94.4	94.1	100.0	88.9	89.4	88.9
SVC	150	94.4	94.1	100.0	88.9	89.4	88.9
RFC	200	94.4	94.1	100.0	88.9	89.4	88.9
DTC	200	**80.6**	**78.8**	**86.7**	**72.2**	**62.0**	**61.1**
GNB	200	94.4	94.1	100.0	88.9	89.4	88.9
SVC	200	94.4	94.1	100.0	88.9	89.4	88.9
RFC	500	91.7	91.4	94.1	88.9	83.5	83.3
DTC	500	63.9	64.9	63.2	66.7	27.8	27.8
GNB	500	94.4	94.1	100.0	88.9	89.4	88.9
SVC	500	94.4	94.1	100.0	88.9	89.4	88.9
RFC	1000	94.4	94.1	100.0	88.9	89.4	88.9
DTC	1000	66.7	68.4	65.0	72.2	33.5	33.3
GNB	1000	91.7	91.4	94.1	88.9	83.5	83.3
SVC	1000	94.4	94.1	100.0	88.9	89.4	88.9

BAC attained for four supervised classifiers with ANOVA test for feature selection is shown in Figure 4 along with the number of selected features. The highest BAC of 94.4% is attained for two different classifiers namely GNB and SVC due to chi-square test when the number of selected features is 15. For the same number of features, DTC offers 86.5% BAC. But 30 features are required for RFC to deliver the maximum BAC of 94.4% under this technique. Table 3 shows the other performance measures of all the four examined supervised classifiers when ANOVA test is used as feature selection technique. The number of features selected is also shown in Table 3.

Table 3. Performance metrics of supervised classifiers with ANOVA test for feature selection

ML Model	No. of Selected Features	BAC	F1	PREC	RECALL	MCC	KAPPA
RFC	10	86.1	85.7	88.2	83.3	72.3	72.2
DTC	10	80.6	81.1	78.9	83.3	61.2	61.1
GNB	10	94.4	94.1	100.0	88.9	89.4	88.9
SVC	10	94.4	94.1	100.0	88.9	89.4	88.9
RFC	15	86.1	85.7	88.2	83.3	72.3	72.2
DTC	15	**86.1**	**86.5**	**84.2**	**88.9**	**72.3**	**72.2**
GNB	15	**94.4**	**94.1**	**100.0**	**88.9**	**89.4**	**88.9**
SVC	15	**94.4**	**94.1**	**100.0**	**88.9**	**89.4**	**88.9**
RFC	30	**94.4**	**94.1**	**100.0**	**88.9**	**89.4**	**88.9**
DTC	30	69.4	71.8	66.7	77.8	39.4	38.9
GNB	30	94.4	94.1	100.0	88.9	89.4	88.9
SVC	30	94.4	94.1	100.0	88.9	89.4	88.9
RFC	50	88.9	88.9	88.9	88.9	77.8	77.8
DTC	50	66.7	70.0	63.6	77.8	34.2	33.3
GNB	50	94.4	94.1	100.0	88.9	89.4	88.9
SVC	50	94.4	94.1	100.0	88.9	89.4	88.9
RFC	100	94.4	94.1	100.0	88.9	89.4	88.9
DTC	100	77.8	77.8	77.8	77.8	55.6	55.6
GNB	100	91.7	91.4	94.1	88.9	83.5	83.3
SVC	100	94.4	94.1	100.0	88.9	89.4	88.9
RFC	200	91.7	90.9	100.0	83.3	84.5	83.3
DTC	200	77.8	78.9	75.0	83.3	55.9	55.6
GNB	200	91.7	91.4	94.1	88.9	83.5	83.3
SVC	200	94.4	94.1	100.0	88.9	89.4	88.9
RFC	500	88.9	88.2	93.8	83.3	78.3	77.8
DTC	500	69.4	68.6	70.6	66.7	38.9	38.9
GNB	500	91.7	91.4	94.1	88.9	83.5	83.3
SVC	500	94.4	94.1	100.0	88.9	89.4	88.9
RFC	1000	94.4	94.1	100.0	88.9	89.4	88.9
DTC	1000	66.7	68.4	65.0	72.2	33.5	33.3
GNB	1000	91.7	91.4	94.1	88.9	83.5	83.3
SVC	1000	94.4	94.1	100.0	88.9	89.4	88.9

Figure 4. Balanced accuracy attained and no. of selected features for various supervised classifiers with ANOVA test for feature selection

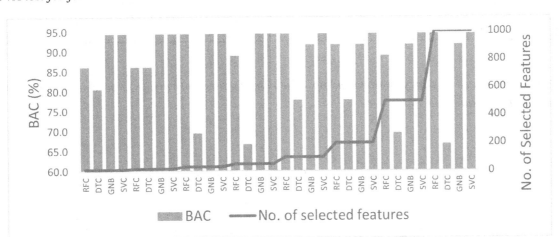

BAC attained for four supervised classifiers with MI filter for feature selection is shown in Figure 5 along with the number of selected features. SVC delivers the highest BAC of 94.4% when 30 features are selected. RFC ranks second in BAC with 91.7% but it requires 100 features to be selected. DTC and GNB are relatively underperforming with BAC of 83.3% and 88.9% respectively with number of selected features as 10. Table 4 shows all the performance measures of the four examined supervised classifiers when MI filter is used as feature selection technique.

Table 4. Performance metrics of supervised classifiers with MI filter for feature selection

ML Model	No. of Selected Features	BAC	F1	PREC	RECALL	MCC	KAPPA
RFC	10	83.3	83.3	83.3	83.3	66.7	66.7
DTC	10	**83.3**	**82.4**	**87.5**	**77.8**	**67.1**	**66.7**
GNB	10	**88.9**	**88.9**	**88.9**	**88.9**	**77.8**	**77.8**
SVC	10	91.7	91.4	94.1	88.9	83.5	83.3
RFC	30	88.9	88.9	88.9	88.9	77.8	77.8
DTC	30	80.6	80.0	82.4	77.8	61.2	61.1
GNB	30	88.9	88.9	88.9	88.9	77.8	77.8
SVC	30	**94.4**	**94.1**	**100.0**	**88.9**	**89.4**	**88.9**
RFC	100	**91.7**	**91.4**	**94.1**	**88.9**	**83.5**	**83.3**
DTC	100	75.0	78.0	69.6	88.9	52.0	50.0
GNB	100	88.9	88.9	88.9	88.9	77.8	77.8
SVC	100	94.4	94.1	100.0	88.9	89.4	88.9
RFC	500	88.9	88.9	88.9	88.9	77.8	77.8
DTC	500	69.4	71.8	66.7	77.8	39.4	38.9

continued on following page

Table 4. Continued

ML Model	No. of Selected Features	BAC	F1	PREC	RECALL	MCC	KAPPA
GNB	500	88.9	88.9	88.9	88.9	77.8	77.8
SVC	500	94.4	94.1	100.0	88.9	89.4	88.9

Figure 5. Balanced accuracy attained and no. of selected features for various supervised classifiers with MI filter for feature selection

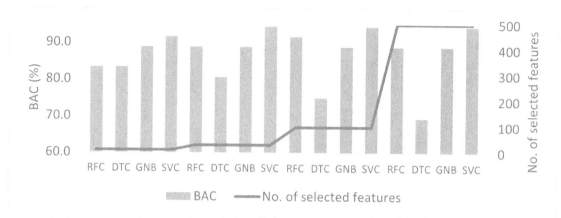

Next the results obtained by various dimensionality reduction techniques are presented in a similar manner. BAC attained for four supervised classifiers with PCA as dimensionality reduction technique is shown in Figure 6 along with the number of selected features. SVC delivers the highest BAC of 94.4% when 10 features are selected. RFC ranks second in BAC with 88.9% with the same number of features. DTC and GNB are relatively underperforming with BAC of 86.1% and 83.3% with number of selected features as 100 and 10 respectively. Table 4 shows all the performance measures of the four examined supervised classifiers when PCA as dimensionality reduction technique.

Table 5. Performance Metrics of Supervised classifiers with PCA for Dimensionality Reduction

ML Model	No. of Selected Features	BAC	F1	PREC	RECALL	MCC	KAPPA
RFC	10	**88.9**	**88.9**	**88.9**	**88.9**	**77.8**	**77.8**
DTC	10	83.3	82.4	87.5	77.8	67.1	66.7
GNB	10	**83.3**	**83.3**	**83.3**	**83.3**	**66.7**	**66.7**
SVC	10	**94.4**	**94.1**	**100.0**	**88.9**	**89.4**	**88.9**
RFC	30	83.3	82.4	87.5	77.8	67.1	66.7
DTC	30	80.6	78.8	86.7	72.2	62.0	61.1
GNB	30	50.0	10.0	50.0	5.6	0.0	0.0
SVC	30	91.7	91.4	94.1	88.9	83.5	83.3

continued on following page

Table 5. Continued

ML Model	No. of Selected Features	BAC	F1	PREC	RECALL	MCC	KAPPA
RFC	50	80.6	77.4	92.3	66.7	63.6	61.1
DTC	50	77.8	78.9	75.0	83.3	55.9	55.6
GNB	50	50.0	10.0	50.0	5.6	0.0	0.0
SVC	50	91.7	91.4	94.1	88.9	83.5	83.3
RFC	100	83.3	83.3	83.3	83.3	66.7	66.7
DTC	100	**86.1**	**86.5**	**84.2**	**88.9**	**72.3**	**72.2**
GNB	100	77.8	77.8	77.8	77.8	55.6	55.6
SVC	100	94.4	94.1	100.0	88.9	89.4	88.9

Figure 6. Balanced accuracy attained and no. of selected features for various supervised classifiers with PCA for dimensionality reduction

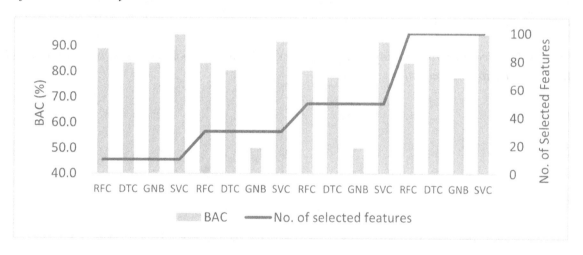

Various performance metrics of supervised classifiers when ICA is used for dimensionality reduction are shown in Table 6. In addition, BAC and no. of selected features are depicted in Figure 7. The highest BAC attained is 91.7% for RFC and SVC classifiers. DTC and GNB are offering 83.3% BAC. All the four classifiers attain the above-mentioned BAC when the number of selected features is 10.

Table 6. Performance metrics of supervised classifiers with ICA for dimensionality reduction

ML Model	No. of Selected Features	BAC	F1	PREC	RECALL	MCC	KAPPA
RFC	10	91.7	91.4	94.1	88.9	83.5	83.3
DTC	10	83.3	82.4	87.5	77.8	67.1	66.7
GNB	10	83.3	82.4	87.5	77.8	67.1	66.7
SVC	10	91.7	91.4	94.1	88.9	83.5	83.3

continued on following page

Table 6. Continued

ML Model	No. of Selected Features	BAC	F1	PREC	RECALL	MCC	KAPPA
RFC	30	77.8	75.0	85.7	66.7	57.0	55.6
DTC	30	44.4	28.6	40.0	22.2	-12.4	-11.1
GNB	30	63.9	43.5	100.0	27.8	40.2	27.8
SVC	30	88.9	88.2	93.8	83.3	78.3	77.8
RFC	50	66.7	50.0	100.0	33.3	44.7	33.3
DTC	50	58.3	51.6	61.5	44.4	17.3	16.7
GNB	50	77.8	73.3	91.7	61.1	58.9	55.6
SVC	50	61.1	36.4	100.0	22.2	35.4	22.2
RFC	100	55.6	33.3	66.7	22.2	14.9	11.1
DTC	100	50.0	35.7	50.0	27.8	0.0	0.0
GNB	100	58.3	28.6	100.0	16.7	30.2	16.7
SVC	100	72.2	61.5	100.0	44.4	53.5	44.4

Figure 7. Balanced accuracy attained and no. of selected features for various supervised classifiers with ICA for dimensionality reduction

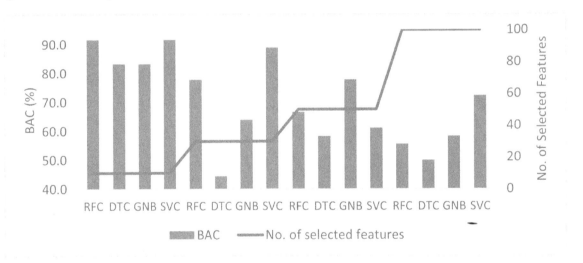

In a consolidated manner, the best attained performance metrics for each feature selection or dimensionality reduction technique are presented in Table 7. The optimal feature selection or dimensionality reduction technique should deliver higher performance metrics and use a smaller number of features. In that way, ANOVA test-based feature selection is found as best for renal cancer diagnosis since it is offering the highest BAC with minimal number of features for three tested supervised classifiers except SVC. 94.4% is the highest BAC attained for SVC, RFC, and GNB while the highest BAC is 86.1 for DTC. SVC attains 94.4% BAC with both ANOVA test and PCA. But the number of features used by PCA is 10 while ANOVA is 15 with SVC to deliver the maximum BAC. RFC requires 30 features through ANOVA feature selection to deliver the 94.4% BAC while GNB and DTC requires only 15 features through ANOVA feature selection. Hence on comparing all the supervised classifiers and feature selection or dimensionality reduction techniques, it can be stated that PCA-SVC is the optimal solution for renal cancer detection with a smaller number of features. Enhanced performance is attained for all the four tested classifiers with the ANOVA test-based feature selection. All the other investigated feature selection and dimensionality reduction techniques fail to deliver improved performance in all the four tested classifiers together. Obviously, the training time and complexity of the model will be less due to the reduced number of features.

The importance of the proposed PCA-SVC can be well understood by comparing it with the plain supervised classifiers without any feature selection or dimensionality reduction techniques. Among the four examined plain supervised classifiers, SVC produces the highest BAC of 91.7% by using 64675 features. But the proposed PCA-SVC produces 94.4% BAC by just using 10 features. Similarly better performance can be witnessed in all other classifiers with both feature selection and dimensionality reduction techniques with minimal number of features. Next the performance of classifiers with each feature selection and dimensionality reduction techniques over the plain classifiers will be discussed.

Table 7. Best attained performance metrics for each feature selection or dimensionality reduction technique

		BAC	F1	PREC	RECALL	MCC	KAPPA	Optimal Number of Features
Plain	RFC	86.1	86.5	84.2	88.9	72.3	72.2	54675
	DTC	83.3	83.3	83.3	83.3	66.7	66.7	54675
	GNB	86.1	86.5	84.2	88.9	72.3	72.2	54675
	SVC	91.7	91.4	94.1	88.9	83.5	83.3	54675
Variance Filter	RFC	91.7	91.4	94.1	88.9	83.5	83.3	62
	DTC	80.6	82.1	76.2	88.9	62.0	61.1	242
	GNB	91.7	91.4	94.1	88.9	83.5	83.3	62
	SVC	94.4	94.1	100.0	88.9	89.4	88.9	62
Chi-square	RFC	94.4	94.1	100.0	88.9	89.4	88.9	50
	DTC	80.6	78.8	86.7	72.2	62.0	61.1	200
	GNB	94.4	94.1	100.0	88.9	89.4	88.9	50
	SVC	94.4	94.1	100.0	88.9	89.4	88.9	50
ANOVA	**RFC**	**94.4**	**94.1**	**100.0**	**88.9**	**89.4**	**88.9**	**30**
	DTC	**86.1**	**86.5**	**84.2**	**88.9**	**72.3**	**72.2**	**15**
	GNB	**94.4**	**94.1**	**100.0**	**88.9**	**89.4**	**88.9**	**15**
	SVC	94.4	94.1	100.0	88.9	89.4	88.9	15
Mutual Information Filter	RFC	91.7	91.4	94.1	88.9	83.5	83.3	100
	DTC	83.3	82.4	87.5	77.8	67.1	66.7	10
	GNB	88.9	88.9	88.9	88.9	77.8	77.8	10
	SVC	94.4	94.1	100.0	88.9	89.4	88.9	30

continued on following page

Table 7. Continued

		BAC	F1	PREC	RECALL	MCC	KAPPA	Optimal Number of Features
PCA	RFC	88.9	88.9	88.9	88.9	77.8	77.8	10
	DTC	86.1	86.5	84.2	88.9	72.3	72.2	100
	GNB	83.3	83.3	83.3	83.3	66.7	66.7	10
	SVC	**94.4**	**94.1**	**100.0**	**88.9**	**89.4**	**88.9**	**10**
ICA	RFC	91.7	91.4	94.1	88.9	83.5	83.3	10
	DTC	83.3	82.4	87.5	77.8	67.1	66.7	10
	GNB	83.3	82.4	87.5	77.8	67.1	66.7	10
	SVC	91.7	91.4	94.1	88.9	83.5	83.3	10
LDA	RFC	83.3	82.4	87.5	77.8	67.1	66.7	10
	DTC	83.3	82.4	87.5	77.8	67.1	66.7	10
	GNB	91.7	90.9	100.0	83.3	84.5	83.3	10
	SVC	91.7	90.9	100.0	83.3	84.5	83.3	10

When variance-based feature selection is employed, except DTC all other three classifiers can beat the plain classifiers. For example, both plain RFC & plain GNB gives 86.1% BAC while they are enhanced to 91.7% BAC through variance-based feature selection technique. Similarly, SVC performance is also enhanced due to this feature selection technique from 91.7% to 94.4% BAC. Like variance filter, chi-square test also enhances the performance of all classifiers except DTC. Mutual information filter-based feature selection technique also delivers better performance for RFC, GNB, and SVC while DTC delivers performance similar to plain DTC. Compared to dimensionality reduction techniques, many feature selection techniques can offer the highest BAC of 94.4% while the PCA-SVC alone offers that 94.4% BAC among the examined dimensionality reduction techniques. PCA reduces the performance of GNB and boosts the performance of DTC, RFC, and SVC while ICA can improve the classification performance of only RFC and SVC. Similarly, the usage of LDA as dimensionality reduction technique enhances the performance of GNB and SVC alone.

6. CONCLUSION

Four different feature selection techniques and three different dimensionality reduction techniques are investigated on microarray gene expression analysis for renal cancer diagnosis. To get a clear view of the performance offered by these feature selection and dimensionality reduction techniques, four supervised classifiers namely RFC, SVC, GNB, and DTC are employed in this work. The highest BAC of 94.4% is offered by RFC, SVC, and GNB models with reduced number of features. Among them, the best model is PCA-SVC since it offers 94.4% BAC with just ten features. When the classification performance of all the investigated feature selection and dimensionality reduction techniques are considered, ANOVA test-based feature selection stands first. Enhanced performance is attained for all the four tested classifiers with the ANOVA test-based feature selection. All the other investigated feature selection and dimensionality reduction techniques fail to deliver improved performance in all the four tested classifiers together. Obviously, the training time and complexity of the model will be less due to the reduced number of features. The main limitation of proposed PCA-SVC is the relatively less recall score of 89.9%. Even though PCA-SVC achieves 100% precision score, the recall score is relatively less and needs to be improved. For other applications and other types of cancer diagnosis, these feature selection techniques and dimensionality reduction techniques need to be implemented and investigated in future. In addition, other supervised classifiers also need to be examined for renal cancer diagnosis through gene expression analysis. Other techniques need to be found where the balanced accuracy score reaches more than 95% in future.

REFERENCES

Bhinder, B., Gilvary, C., Madhukar, N. S., & Elemento, O. (2021). Artificial Intelligence in Cancer Research and Precision Medicine. *Cancer Discovery*, 11(4), 900–915. 10.1158/2159-8290.CD-21-009033811123

Cruz, J. A., & Wishart, D. S. (2006). Applications of Machine Learning in Cancer Prediction and Prognosis. *Cancer Informatics*, 2. 10.1177/117693510600200003019458758

Feltes, B. C., Chandelier, E. B., Grisci, B. I., & Dorn, M. (2019). CuMiDa: An Extensively Curated Microarray Database for Benchmarking and Testing of Machine Learning Approaches in Cancer Research. *Journal of Computational Biology*, 26(4), 376–386. 10.1089/cmb.2018.023830789283

Howlader, N., Noone, A. M., Krapcho, M., Miller, D., Brest, A., Yu, M., Ruhl, J., Tatalovich, Z., Mariotto, A., Lewis, D. R., Chen, H. S., Feuer, E. J., & Cronin, K. A. (2023, July 10). *SEER Cancer Statistics Review 1975-2016*. National Cancer Institute. https://seer.cancer.gov/csr/1975_2016/

Hsieh, J. J., Purdue, M. P., Signoretti, S., Swanton, C., Albiges, L., Schmidinger, M., Heng, D. Y., Larkin, J., & Ficarra, V. (2017). Renal cell carcinoma. *Nature Reviews. Disease Primers*, 3(1), 17009. Advance online publication. 10.1038/nrdp.2017.928276433

Liu, Z., & Wang, S.LIU. (2011). Improved linear discriminant analysis method. *Jisuanji Yingyong*, 31(1), 250–253. 10.3724/SP.J.1087.2011.00250

Mathew, D. (2022). An Improvised Random Forest Model for Breast Cancer Classification. *NeuroQuantology : An Interdisciplinary Journal of Neuroscience and Quantum Physics*, 20(5), 713–722. 10.14704/nq.2022.20.5.NQ22227

Nanglia, P., Kumar, S., Mahajan, A. N., Singh, P., & Rathee, D. (2021). A hybrid algorithm for lung cancer classification using SVM and Neural Networks. *ICT Express*, 7(3), 335–341. 10.1016/j.icte.2020.06.007

Padala, S. A., & Kallam, A. (2023, July 13). *Clear Cell Renal Carcinoma*. StatPearls Publishing. https://www.ncbi.nlm.nih.gov/books/NBK557644/

Patangia, S. (2020). Sales Prediction of Market using Machine Learning. *International Journal of Engineering Research & Technology (Ahmedabad)*, V9(09). Advance online publication. 10.17577/IJERTV9IS090345

Ratanamahatana, C., & Gunopulos, D. (2003). Feature selection for the naive bayesian classifier using decision trees. *Applied Artificial Intelligence*, 17(5–6), 475–487. 10.1080/713827175

San Segundo-Val, I., & Sanz-Lozano, C. S. (2016). Introduction to the Gene Expression Analysis. *Molecular Genetics of Asthma*, 29–43. 10.1007/978-1-4939-3652-6_3

Scandling, J. D. (2007). Acquired Cystic Kidney Disease and Renal Cell Cancer after Transplantation. *Clinical Journal of the American Society of Nephrology; CJASN*, 2(4), 621–622. 10.2215/CJN.0200050717699473

Chapter 11
Comparative Analysis of Electroencephalogram Signals Using Ensemble Methods for Epilepsy Detection

S. Niranjan
Karunya Institute of Technology and Sciences, India

Samson Arun Raj
Karunya Institute of Technology and Sciences, India

T. Jemima Jebaseeli
Karunya Institute of Technology and Sciences, India

S. Marshal
Karunya Institute of Technology and Sciences, India

S. S. Ashik
Karunya Institute of Technology and Sciences, India

ABSTRACT

A timely and precise diagnosis is essential for effective treatment of epilepsy, a neurological condition characterized by recurrent seizures. Because of their capacity to capture cerebral processes, electroencephalogram (EEG) data are crucial in the diagnosis of epilepsy. The proposed system gives a detailed comparison of EEG signal processing strategies for epilepsy detection utilizing ensemble techniques and investigates the usefulness of ensemble algorithms such as gradient boosting, AdaBoost, XGBoost, and bagging classifier in improving epilepsy detection. Through the use of these ensemble approaches, the system preprocesses the EEG data, extracts features, and classifies them. Accuracy, precision, recall, and F1-score are performance indicators that are used to assess each ensemble approach's efficiency. The results were obtained through extensive testing on a well-curated dataset. The finding of the proposed system clarifies the positive impacts and regulates each ensemble technique for determining the presence of epilepsy.

DOI: 10.4018/979-8-3693-0683-3.ch011

INTRODUCTION

Millions of people worldwide suffer from epilepsy, a neurological illness characterized by repeated and unexpected seizures. To provide appropriate medical care and improve the quality of life for those who have epileptic seizures, rapid and accurate identification of epileptic seizures is essential. EEG recording captures the electrical action of the central nervous system. It is shown to be an effective data for diagnosing epilepsy due to its potential to identify abnormal neural patterns associated with seizures. The incorporation of machine learning techniques into EEG analysis has produced significant progress in automating the identification procedure during recent years. Because of the enormous number of electrodes and the continual nature of the impulses, EEG recordings provide high-dimensional data. Such high-dimensional data requires complex approaches to extract relevant features and patterns. EEG readings demonstrate high inter-subject fluctuation, implying that cerebral activity patterns might differ greatly between people. This unpredictability makes creating generalized models capable of properly detecting seizures across various patients difficult. Noise in EEG signals can come from a variety of sources such as muscular activity, eye movement, and ambient interference. The removal or reduction of these sources of noise is critical for reliable epilepsy identification. It is not easy to choose the best classification method for epilepsy detection. Various algorithms respond differently to distinct sorts of patterns, therefore the selection must be adapted. This research aims to examine how ensemble techniques may be used to increase the precision and dependability of epilepsy screening using EEG data. The capacity of ensemble approaches to mixing many base models to achieve an additional robust and accurate prediction at its conclusion has gained popularity in the machine learning field. Ensemble approaches can limit overfitting, decrease bias, and capture complicated patterns in data by utilizing a variety of different models.

This study was motivated by the urgent need for precise and prompt identification of epilepsy. EEG signals provide a non-invasive and useful approach for recording cerebral activity and identifying aberrant patterns linked with seizures. The EEG signal contains several forms of noise, shown in Table 1.

Table 1. Different EEG waves and their frequency

Types of waves	Occurrences	Frequency
Delta waves	Slow-wave sleep	0.5 - 4 Hz
Theta waves	Drowsiness	4 Hz - 8Hz
Alpha waves	Relaxed wakefulness	8 Hz - 13Hz
Beta waves	Active mental state	13 Hz – 30 Hz
Gamma waves	Higher-order cognitive process	30 Hz -100 Hz

LITERATURE REVIEW

Ai et al., (2023) suggested the technique for analyzing epilepsy EEG data and obtaining interictal and preictal EEG feature maps. The CNN learns by inserting the time-frequency feature maps into it after decreasing the network parameters using a one-channel technique to minimize the range of neurons and network complexity. Hussain et al., (2022) present a classification framework that uses ensembles of sub-problems for reaching high precision with limited data. Hassan et al., (2016) suggested a single lead EEG-based controlled epileptic detection method in which EEG signal segments are deconstructed using a newly discovered signal processing strategy. Based on the theoretical foundations of the Mahalanobis distance and DWT, Song et al., (2016) introduced a novel Mahalanobis-similarity-based feature selection approach. To further enhance performance, the sample-entropy-based and Mahalanobis-similarity-based features were combined to generate a fusion feature (MS-SE-FF) and feature-fusion level. A module built on time-domain and frequency-domain characteristics is provided by Mporas et al., (2015). A seizure detection accuracy of roughly 90% was reached for all of the study subjects.

An automated seizure detection model is introduced by Raghu et al., (2019) using sigmoid entropy. The computationally efficient feature was created from discrete wavelet transformations with a non-linear SVM. Tasci et al., (2023) provided a unique hypercube-based feature extractor that creates two feature vectors and uses the Multilevel-DWT for feature extraction. A patient-specific seizure detection method is presented by Kaleem et al., (2018) utilizing hand-engineered features recovered from wavelet decomposed multi-channel EEG data. A new automated method for classifying TLE interictal and ictal epochs is introduced by Fccici et al., (2022). Li et al., (2017) provided a technique for recognizing epileptic signals. The EEG signal is split into levels of frequency using DWT and the Modified Binary Salp Swarm method (MBSSA) method, according to Ghazali et al., (2022). The technique for intuitive epilepsy identification utilizing EEG data was developed by Sunaryono et al., (2022). The Discrete Fourier Transform (DFT) and the DWT were used to process the raw EEG data. To accurately categorize the signal, an artificial neural network (ANN) is then given a new feature set that was generated via wavelet decomposition, as described by Bairagi et al., (2021). Shen et al., (2023) provided an EEG-based real-time technique for identifying epileptic seizures utilizing tunable-Q wavelet transform and CNN.

According to Gong et al.,'s (2020) methodology for recognizing intracranial electroencephalography (iEEG) seizures, iEEG data are subjected to discrete wavelet transform (DWT) analysis utilizing forward propagation and feedback neural networks. Gao et al., (2023) offer a multi-step technique for identifying signal features to recognize epilepsy. Using the best wavelet, they applied the Wavelet transform to eliminate signal noise (Dabichiz 8). To identify seizures, Kaur et al., (2023) propose a method based on transfer learning and EEG picture representations (created by applying WT at various scales and time intervals). Sharma et al., (2020) provided an automatic seizure diagnosis strategy and show the effectiveness of the method for seizure identification using deep neural network algorithms. Albaqami et al., (2023) created the multi-path seizure-type categorization deep learning network. In a comparison research with Continuous Wavelet Transform (CWT) and DWT for the classification, Gosala et al., (2023) presented the use of Wavelet Scattering Transform for neuro-disorder diagnosis.

Materials

Electroencephalogram (EEG) datasets contain individuals' recorded electroencephalogram (EEG) data. EEG datasets might differ in terms of their size, content, and specialized objectives. Typically, an overview of the EEG dataset includes the raw data, channel information, labels, preprocessed metadata, and Sample Rate. (Epileptic Seizure Recognition, Available online: https://www.kaggle.com/datasets/harunshimanto/epileptic-seizure-recognition).

System Architecture

The proposed study aims to undertake a thorough comparative review of ensemble approaches for detecting epilepsy using EEG data. The study is to investigate the efficacy of various ensemble algorithms in reliably categorizing EEG records into epileptic and non-epileptic categories. However, due to the complexity of EEG data and the difficulty in discriminating between normal and epileptic patterns, extensive data processing and classification approaches are required. The proposed idea's system design compares the existing algorithms using several tests and training models to determine the performance metrics based on a single EEG dataset.

Figure 1. System architecture for epilepsy detection

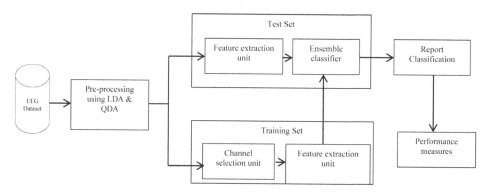

Following the extraction of the EEG dataset utilizing a tensor flow platform as a basis, pre-processing method used Linear Discriminant Analysis (LDA) and Quadratic Discriminant Analysis (QDA) is used, as shown in Fig. 1. It converts the higher dimensional quality images into lower dimensional quality images with vector matrix. It is significant to remember that LDA can be successful for some EEG signal processing tasks. Its effectiveness relies on the calibre of the data, the selection of features, and the applicability of its linear parameters for the underlying data distribution. With QDA, the assumption of identical covariance matrices for various classes is relaxed. Rather than assuming that all classes have the same covariance matrix. When the presumption of equal covariance matrices is not satisfied, QDA is very helpful. For instance, QDA can capture variability in EEG data more precisely than LDA if distinct classes have significantly distinct variability. However, it's also crucial to keep in mind that QDA might experience overfitting when there is a lack of data. The decision between LDA and QDA (or perhaps other classification methods), like with every analytic approach, relies on the features of your data and the objectives of your research. The best approach for the EEG signal categorization challenge must be chosen through extensive testing and analysis.

The dataset is divided into the test and training sets. In the test set, the dataset is examined using feature extraction, which involves picking out, transforming, and representing specific information from raw data to produce a more straightforward but informative representation that can be applied to analysis, classification, and other activities. To increase predictive accuracy, generalization, and robustness, the ensemble classifier combines several different individual models. They function by combining the results from various base models to make a final forecast based on the aggregated predictions from those models. The theory behind ensemble classifiers is that combining the advantages of various models can counteract the drawbacks of any given model and offer higher overall performance. It is especially true when several channels are available, yet not all are equally useful or pertinent to the task.

The performance of the model can be enhanced, overfitting can be decreased, and interpretability can be improved through channel selection. The outcome of the channel selection will again pass through another feature extraction unit that compares with the ensemble classifier. The ensemble classifier calculates final performance indicators including accuracy, precision, F1-score, and recall, after it has learned the algorithm's conclusion and prepared a report categorization based on the several algorithms employed for this dataset. The experimentation section lists and discusses each algorithm's advantages and disadvantages.

Taxonomy of EEG Analysis

AdaBoost

AdaBoost (Adaptive Boosting) is a machine learning algorithm that is part of the ensemble learning family. Unlike Gradient Boosting, AdaBoost adjusts the weights of data points in each iteration to focus on the ones that were misclassified in the previous iteration. The pseudo-code of the method is as follows.

Input:

- Training dataset (X_train, y_train): EEG feature vectors and corresponding labels
- Number of weak classifiers (T)
- Weak learner algorithm (e.g., decision tree)

Initialization

- Initialize sample weights $w_i = 1/N$ for each sample i, where N is the quantity of samples
- Initialize a list of weak classifiers: weak_classifiers
- Initialize a list of weak classifier weights: classifier_weights

For t = 1 to T:
Normalize sample weights: $w_i = w_i / \sum w_i$ for all i
Train a weak classifier using the training data and weights:

- Fit the weak learner algorithm on X_train using weights w_i
- Predict labels for all samples and calculate the error ε_t as the sum of w_i for misclassified samples

Calculate weak classifier weight α_t:

- Calculate $\alpha_t = 0.5 \times \ln\big((1 - \varepsilon_t)/\varepsilon_t\big)$
- Append α_t to classifier_weights list

Update sample weights w_i:

- For each sample:

- If the sample is correctly classified, $w_i = w_i \times \exp(-\alpha_t)$
- If the sample is misclassified, $w_i = w_i \times \exp(-\alpha_t)$

Store weak classifier:

- Append the trained weak classifier to weak_classifiers list
Final classification:

- Initialize an array of weighted predictions: weighted_preds = [0, 0, ..., 0] (length = number of samples) and each weak classifier at index t, add α_t prediction for each sample to weighted_preds

$$H(x) = sign\left(\sum_{t=1}^{T}\alpha_t h_t(x)\right)$$

- $h_t(x)$ is the t's weak classifier's output for input x

For each sample i:

- If weighted_preds[i] >= 0.5, classify as "epileptic"
- Otherwise, classify as "non-epileptic"

Output

- Final ensemble classifier

Multi-Layer Perceptron (MLP)

MLP architecture is commonly used for various machine learning tasks, including classification and regression. Multiple layers of linked nodes make up an MLP. It processes input data and learns to make predictions or decisions.

Random Forest

In machine learning, the widely used ensemble learning technique Random Forest is utilized for both classification and regression applications. Its foundation is the notion that several decision trees are built during training, and their results are subsequently combined to provide predictions. The term "Random Forest" refers to a group of decision trees (a forest) that have been trained using arbitrary selections of the data.

Gradient Boosting

A machine learning algorithm from the ensemble learning group is gradient boosting. Gradient Boosting involves including weak learners in the model one at a time while each one focuses on the mistakes committed by the preceding learners. The algorithm minimizes the errors of the combined model by adjusting the weights or parameters of each weak learner during each step of the process. This results in a strong predictive model that is more accurate than any individual weak learner.

XGBoost

XGBoost is a machine learning technique that works within the gradient boosting framework, which entails gradually incorporating weak learners (typically decision trees) into the model. Every new student strives to lessen the mistakes committed by the preceding ones. This method keeps on until a predetermined number of iterations have been completed or a predetermined performance measure has been reached.

Bagging Classifier

The bagging classifier belongs to the ensemble learning family. It stands for Bootstrap Aggregating, and its primary goal is to enhance the accuracy and robustness of a model by combining the predictions of multiple base learners. Bagging is particularly effective in reducing the variance and potential over-fitting of individual models.

Decision Tree

The decision Tree algorithm selects features for splitting based on impurity measures such as Gini impurity or entropy. It then recursively divides the dataset into subsets until stopping criteria, like reaching a certain depth or having a minimum number of samples, are met. To make predictions, the target variable is assigned to each leaf node with the mean value (for regression).

Support Vector Machine (SVM)

For classification and regression issues, SVM, a versatile machine learning technique, is used. It searches for the most advantageous hyperplane, or prospective determination edge, that splits many data categories.

K-Nearest Neighbors (KNN)

It is based on the resemblance among data points in a particular feature space, it provides predictions. The fundamental tenet of KNN is that comparable data points frequently share values. By locating the k closest data points in the training set and utilizing their labels (for classification) or values (for regression), it classifies or estimates a new data point.

Naïve-Bayes Classifier

A probabilistic machine learning technique used for classification problems is called the Naive Bayes Classifier. The "naïve" assumption simplifies calculations and allows the algorithm to efficiently make predictions, especially on text and high-dimensional data.

RESULT AND DISCUSSIONS

Electrodes are applied to the scalp during the test to detect and amplify brain neurons to create electrical impulses. The EEG signal may be used in a variety of medical contexts to comprehend brain activity and to inform assessments of its function using different machine learning methods.

Figure 2. Precision vs. recall against Class "0"

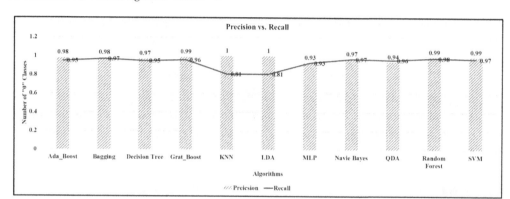

The system's training model uses AI approaches to discover patterns from large datasets and can identify seizures in real-time. Several machine learning methods may be used for the study of EEG signals. The SVM operates by locating the hyperplane that as far apart as feasible divides the data points of several classes. An artificial neural network design called an MLP may be applied to classification and regression problems. Each layer of their several layers of neurons conducts a linear change. A sort of ensemble learning method known as "random forests" combines the predictions of many decision trees. This may enable the forecasts to be more accurate. The most effective machine learning method will vary depending on the EEG signal analysis job at hand, the size and complexity of the dataset, the number of classes that need to be separated, and the level of precision that is required. SVMs and MLPs have generally been demonstrated to be efficient for EEG signal categorization applications.

Figure 3. Precision vs. recall against Class "1"

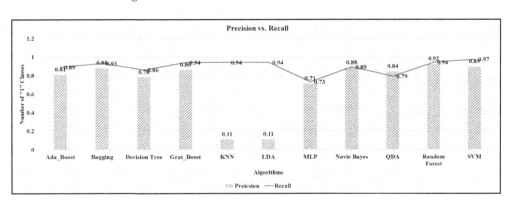

Figure 4. Accuracy comparison

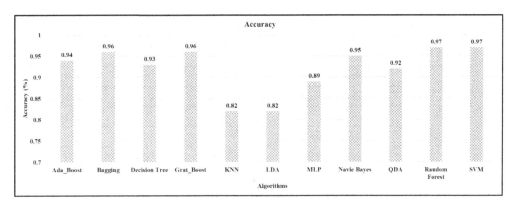

Table 2 gives the comparative analysis of various machine learning techniques that uses EEG signal for epilepsy analysis. Epileptic seizure identification entails recognizing and categorizing the many types of seizures that epileptics may experience. The implications of this knowledge may be significant for controlling and treating epilepsy as well as improving the safety and quality of life for persons who have seizures. The training model of the system can identify seizures in real time.

continued on following page

Table 2. Continued

Table 2. Comparative analysis of machine learning technique under EEG signal

Techniques	Parameters	Precision	Recall	F1-Score	Support
Ada_Boost	Number of Classes "0"	0.98	0.95	0.96	2345
	Number of Classes "1"	0.81	0.89	0.85	530
	Accuracy			0.94	2875
	Weighted Avg	0.94	0.94	0.94	2875
Bagging	Number of Classes "0"	0.98	0.97	0.98	2319
	Number of Classes "1"	0.88	0.93	0.90	556
	Accuracy			0.96	2875
	Weighted Avg	0.96	0.96	0.96	2875
Decision Tree	Number of Classes "0"	0.97	0.95	0.96	2346
	Number of Classes "1"	0.78	0.86	0.82	529
	Accuracy			0.93	2875
	Weighted Avg	0.93	0.93	0.93	2875
Grat_Boost	Number of Classes "0"	0.99	0.96	0.98	2341
	Number of Classes "1"	0.86	0.94	0.90	534
	Accuracy			0.96	2875
	Weighted Avg	0.96	0.96	0.96	2875
KNN	Number of Classes "0"	1	0.81	0.90	2804
	Number of Classes "1"	0.11	0.94	0.20	71
	Accuracy			0.82	2875
	Weighted Avg	0.98	0.82	0.88	2875
LDA	Number of Classes "0"	1	0.81	0.90	2804
	Number of Classes "1"	0.11	0.94	0.20	71
	Accuracy			0.82	2875
	Weighted Avg	0.98	0.82	0.88	2875
MLP	Number of Classes "0"	0.93	0.93	0.93	2305
	Number of Classes "1"	0.71	0.73	0.72	570
	Accuracy			0.89	2875
	Weighted Avg	0.89	0.89	0.89	2875
Naive Bayes	Number of Classes "0"	0.97	0.97	0.97	2292
	Number of Classes "1"	0.88	0.89	0.88	583
	Accuracy			0.95	2875
	Weighted Avg	0.95	0.95	0.95	2875
QDA	Number of Classes "0"	0.94	0.96	0.95	2247
	Number of Classes "1"	0.84	0.79	0.81	628
	Accuracy			0.92	2875
	Weighted Avg	0.92	0.92	0.92	2875

continued on following page

Table 2. Continued

Techniques	Parameters	Precision	Recall	F1-Score	Support
Random Forest	Number of Classes "0"	0.99	0.98	0.98	2301
	Number of Classes "1"	0.92	0.94	0.93	574
	Accuracy			0.97	2875
	Weighted Avg	0.97	0.97	0.97	2875
SVM	Number of Classes "0"	0.99	0.97	0.98	2318
	Number of Classes "1"	0.89	0.97	0.93	557
	Accuracy			0.97	2875
	Weighted Avg	0.97	0.97	0.97	2875

CONCLUSION

The performance accuracy of the current approaches shows an acceptable prediction of the seizure detection rate that ranges from 85% to 97% when the EEG dataset is used as a model for seizure classification. Additionally, the performance metric shows that by AI techniques, the medical system can be effectively trained to carry out its decision-making process and recommend the individuals who want to use such technology for research, operation, and enhancement to various medical procedures. Although these techniques and technologies show promise, it's crucial to keep in mind that they're not perfect. Based on the method and particular circumstances, seizure recognition accuracy may vary and false positives and negatives may happen. Because epilepsy therapy necessitates a complete strategy and should always be utilized under the supervision of medical professionals, any technology or method used for epileptic seizure identification should be taken into account.

REFERENCES

Ai, G., Zhang, Y., Wen, Y., Gu, M., Zhang, H., & Wang, P. (2023). Convolutional neural network-based lightweight hardware IP core design for EEG epilepsy prediction. *Microelectronics*, 137, 105810. 10.1016/j.mejo.2023.105810

Albaqami, H., Hassan, G. M., & Datta, A. (2023). MP-SeizNet: A multi-path CNN Bi-LSTM Network for seizure-type classification using EEG. *Biomedical Signal Processing and Control*, 84, 104780. 10.1016/j.bspc.2023.104780

Bairagi, R. N., Maniruzzaman, M., Pervin, S., & Sarker, A. (2021). Epileptic seizure identification in EEG signals using DWT, ANN and sequential window algorithm. *Soft Computing Letters*, 3, 100026. 10.1016/j.socl.2021.100026

Fıçıcı, C., Telatar, Z., & Eroğul, O. (2022). Automated temporal lobe epilepsy and psychogenic none-pileptic seizure patient discrimination from multichannel EEG recordings using DWT based analysis. *Biomedical Signal Processing and Control*, 77, 103755. 10.1016/j.bspc.2022.103755

Gao, Q., Omran, A. H., Baghersad, Y., Mohammadi, O., Alkhafaji, M. A., Al-Azzawi, A. K., Al-Khafaji, S. H., Emami, N., Toghraie, D., & Golkar, M. J. (2023). Electroencephalogram signal classification based on Fourier transform and Pattern Recognition Network for epilepsy diagnosis. *Engineering Applications of Artificial Intelligence*, 123, 106479. 10.1016/j.engappai.2023.106479

Ghazali, S. M., Alizadeh, M., Mazloum, J., & Baleghi, Y. (2022). Modified binary salp swarm algorithm in EEG signal classification for epilepsy seizure detection. *Biomedical Signal Processing and Control*, 78, 103858. 10.1016/j.bspc.2022.103858

Gong, C., Zhang, X., & Niu, Y. (2020). Identification of epilepsy from intracranial EEG signals by using different neural network models. *Computational Biology and Chemistry*, 87, 107310. 10.1016/j.compbiolchem.2020.10731032599460

Gosala, B., Kapgate, P. D., & Jain, P. (2023). Wavelet transforms for feature engineering in EEG data processing: An application on Schizophrenia. *Biomedical Signal Processing and Control*, 85, 104811. 10.1016/j.bspc.2023.104811

Hassan, A.R, & Subasi, A. (2016). *Automatic identification of epileptic seizures from EEG signals using linear programming boosting. computer methods and programs in biomedicine*. Academic Press.

Hussain, S. F., & Qaisar, S. M. (2022). Epileptic seizure classification using level-crossing EEG sampling and ensemble of sub-problems classifier. *Expert Systems with Applications*, 191, 116356. 10.1016/j.eswa.2021.116356

Kaleem, M., Guergachi, A., & Krishnan, S. (2018). Patient-specific seizure detection in long-term EEG using wavelet decomposition. *Biomedical Signal Processing and Control*, 46, 157–165. 10.1016/j.bspc.2018.07.006

Kaur, T, & Gandhi, T.K. (2023). Automated Diagnosis of Epileptic Seizures using EEG image representations and Deep Learning. *Neuroscience Informatics,* 100139.

Li, M., Chen, W., & Zhang, T. (2017). Classification of epilepsy EEG signals using DWT-based envelope analysis and neural network ensemble. *Biomedical Signal Processing and Control*, 31, 357–365. 10.1016/j.bspc.2016.09.008

Mporas, I., Tsirka, V., Zacharaki, E. I., Koutroumanidis, M., Richardson, M., & Megalooikonomou, V. (2015). Seizure detection using EEG and ECG signals for computer-based monitoring, analysis and management of epileptic patients. *Expert Systems with Applications*, 42(6), 3227–3233. 10.1016/j.eswa.2014.12.009

Raghu, S., Sriraam, N., Temel, Y., Rao, S. V., Hegde, A. S., & Kubben, P. L. (2019). Performance evaluation of DWT based sigmoid entropy in time and frequency domains for automated detection of epileptic seizures using SVM classifier. *Computers in Biology and Medicine*, 110, 127–143. 10.1016/j.compbiomed.2019.05.01631154257

Sharma, R., Pachori, R. B., & Sircar, P. (2020). Seizures classification based on higher order statistics and deep neural network. *Biomedical Signal Processing and Control*, 59, 101921. 10.1016/j.bspc.2020.101921

Shen, M., Wen, P., Song, B., & Li, Y. (2023). Real-time epilepsy seizure detection based on EEG using tunable-Q wavelet transform and convolutional neural network. *Biomedical Signal Processing and Control*, 82, 104566. 10.1016/j.bspc.2022.104566

Song, J. L., Hu, W., & Zhang, R. (2016). Automated detection of epileptic EEGs using a novel fusion feature and extreme learning machine. *Neurocomputing*, 175, 383–391. 10.1016/j.neucom.2015.10.070

Sunaryono, D., Sarno, R., & Siswantoro, J. (2022). Gradient boosting machines fusion for automatic epilepsy detection from EEG signals based on wavelet features. *Journal of King Saud University. Computer and Information Sciences*, 34(10), 9591–9607. 10.1016/j.jksuci.2021.11.015

Tasci, I., Tasci, B., Barua, P. D., Dogan, S., Tuncer, T., Palmer, E. E., Fujita, H., & Acharya, U. R. (2023). Epilepsy detection in 121 patient populations using hypercube pattern from EEG signals. *Information Fusion*, 96, 252–268. 10.1016/j.inffus.2023.03.022

Chapter 12
IoT for Smart Cities Intelligent Healthcare Using Machine Learning Techniques

V. Muthukumaran
http://orcid.org/0000-0002-3393-5596
SRM Institute of Science and Technology, India

R. Udhayakumar
http://orcid.org/0000-0002-7020-3466
Vellore Institute of Technology, India

B. Vennila
College of Engineering and Technology, SRM Institute of Science and Technology, India

Joseph P. Bindu
http://orcid.org/0000-0002-7033-6226
Dayananda Sagar College of Engineering, Bangalore, India

Meram Munirathnam
Rajiv Gandhi University of Knowledge Technologies, India

N. Thillaiarasu
http://orcid.org/0000-0002-7930-0748
REVA University, India

ABSTRACT

Smart cities aim to sustainably increase urbanization, lower energy consumption, improve inhabitants' economic and quality of life, and protect the environment. The idea of smart cities revolves around ICT since it makes it easier to formulate policies, make decisions, execution, and ultimately the supply of helpful offerings. In addition to utilizing digital technologies, the concept of the "smart city" is a response to the political, social, and economic issues that post-industrial civilizations are facing at the beginning of the new millennium. In this chapter, the authors discuss several IoT-based machine learning techniques that are applied, among other things, in the aforementioned domains. Furthermore, a review of the assessments and a report on the lessons learned are presented, with an emphasis on the fundamental role that machine learning techniques should play in internet of things networks.

DOI: 10.4018/979-8-3693-0683-3.ch012

1. INTRODUCTION

Nearly every industry can profit from more IT resources and self-learning computer networks, but the healthcare industry is one where AI can be applied in a variety of ways. This is because AI techniques assist medical professionals in prophylaxis and diagnosis as well as in treatment, particularly with operations. For instance, operating theatres exist in the USA where every stage of the procedure is precisely documented and where the attending physicians receive comprehensive assistance in determining the course of action, including the precise incisions to be made. Sensors incorporated within the room allow for constant tracking of the patient, resulting in best care (Muthukumaran et al., 2021).

This will have an impact on the job of specialists as well, such as radiologists. The technology is already doing remarkably well, especially with imaging procedures that are easily standardised and tested technically. It has assessed millions of instances, so it can make judgements with more precision than a treating physician can with the naked eye. The doctor will always have the last say, but with the help of artificial intelligence, he will also be able to get a second opinion that can support or expand on his own analysis.

The system's conclusions and action suggestions will be more confident the more information it has from the patient and the more cases it is aware of. As a result, it will be preferable in the future to make as much data as possible accessible and to assess it while taking all anonymization techniques into account. In general, wearable data used for routine diagnostics will help the patient and treating physician make the best choices faster and offer suggestions for next steps. For instance, a patient can make a more informed decision about whether to visit a doctor or whether the malaise will likely pass on its own during the morning if they awaken in the morning with an elevated pulse and blood pressure.

Applications for networked smart homes will be useful here as well. If the patient has symptoms, he can communicate with the attending physician by getting up in the morning and standing in front of a mirror that is fitted with cameras. He then determines in real time which actions are reasonable based on the patient data. The situation goes even further, though, as in the worst scenario, fall sensors placed in the home's carpet or on appropriate medical wearables could identify when a patient collapses and ends up on the ground or when assistance is needed for other reasons. In the context of a smart city, automation could notify the relevant control centre and dispatch an ambulance, with the appropriate hospital.

A significant portion of a nurse's limited time is spent gathering patient data. Personnel, particularly in a medical setting. Here, voice command is one way that intelligent devices can gather crucial patient data, assign it appropriately, and use big data and artificial intelligence to assess it. All of this cannot be documented employing wearables, but is frequently also derived from the perception and evaluation of the by the nursing staff to the patient. Thereby, the nursing staff would have more time to devote to the actual care and wouldn't need to capture every piece of information or even move it to an electronic patient records using a PC. In essence, this might provide a (partial) solution to the urgent situation. Figure.1 one discuses about the AI related studies

Figure 1. Types of data in AI-related studies

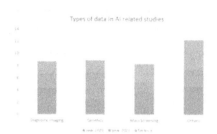

Computers could also be used for routine hospital operations like material consumption monitoring. Expanding decentralised medical care for patients who are immobile or even thousands of kilometres away is also conceivable. In areas lacking specialists and contemporary analysis tools, sending an image or a series of blood values via the internet to a computer centre and waiting for a diagnosis may soon be sufficient. This could save lives, particularly in areas with inadequate medical resources. Another significant consideration regarding smart cities is the potential drawbacks of the technology, even though there are many advantages.

Cugurullo challenges popular conceptions of smart and ecological urbanism by contending that communities that are marketed as cohesive units formed by a uniform vision of the sustainable city are, in reality, disjointed cities composed of disparate and frequently mismatched elements of the urban fabric. Cugurullo described the current level of cyberattacks on network infrastructure and services, as well as five types of vulnerabilities pertaining to smart city technologies. The understanding of urban studies and planning gained from Cugurullo's work is significant. It provides a thorough explanation of the function of cities at a time when artificial and human intelligence are irreversibly interacting with the built environment (Cugurullo et al., 2021).

2. RELATED WORK

The literature on blockchain, IoT-related AI, smart cities, smart healthcare, and IoT is reviewed in this section. Emerging trends in smart healthcare applications and significant technological advancements that directly influence these transitions were examined (Habibzadeh et al., 2020). The writers also discussed various security factors to be taken into account in smart health systems, along with their implications and protective measures. In their analysis of security and privacy concerns related to IoT applications in smart cities identified potential solutions. Since conventional approaches do not yield optimal results for security and safety critical systems, authors often turn to graph theory to rectify issues that have been highlighted (Latif et al., 2019).

Based on data collection, privacy, security, public safety, disaster management, energy consumption, and quality of life in smart cities, presented a thorough analysis of potential techniques and applications of collaborative drones with the IoT that have been used recently to enhance the smartness of smart cities (Alsamhi et al., 2019). A thorough analysis of the uses of machine learning methods for big data analysis in intelligent healthcare systems was provided (Li et al., 2021). The authors also outlined a number of the advantages and disadvantages of the current strategies, with an emphasis on the difficulties facing this area of research.

A fog computing-based model for a smart health monitoring system was presented. The suggested architecture makes the claim that it will transform the healthcare system from one that is clinic-centric to one that is smart and patient-centric by addressing its fundamental issues. A thorough analysis of published surveys utilising deep learning-based techniques for classifying brain tumours was provided. The review covered all of the key processes, such as pre-processing, feature extraction, classifications, accomplishments, and limitations. The authors also conducted in-depth experiments using transfer learning with and without data augmentation to look into cutting-edge convolutional neural network models for BTC (Vennira Selvi et al., 2022). A model for reducing traffic congestion in a smart city setting by fusing artificial intelligence and the Internet of Things. .

The benefits and drawbacks of increasing energy efficiency were discussed along with a thorough overview of the energy consumption model in the Internet of Things (Kumar et al., 2023). An OTS (one-time signature) scheme-based secure architecture for an energy-efficient Internet of Things in edge infrastructure was proposed (Singh et al., 2021). To increase the architecture's security and privacy, the authors employed a distributed network at the fog layer that was based on blockchain technology. In Table.1 discussed the review literature.

Table 1. Reviewed literature

No	Paper Title	Smart Cities	Smart Healthcare	AI/ML	Security
1	Toward uniform smart healthcare ecosystems: A survey on prospects, security, and privacy considerations(Habibzadeh et al., 2020)	N	Y	N	Y
2	A survey of security and privacy issues in IoT for smart city(Latif et al., 2017)	Y	N	N	Y
3	IoT-based smart cities: A survey(Arasteh et al., 2016)	Y	N	N	N
4	A survey on collaborative smart drones and internet of things for improving smartness of smart cities. (Alsamhi et al., 2019)	Y	N	N	N
5	A Comprehensive Survey on Machine Learning-Based Big Data Analytics for IoT-Enabled Smart Healthcare System (Li et al., 2021)	Y	N	N	N

3. SUMMARIES OF MACHINE LEARNING

The three types of machine learning techniques are supervised, unsupervised, and reinforcement learning. In the various scenarios shown in Fig. 2, the RL employs algorithms from every branch. Here, supervised and unsupervised learning are briefly explained with examples algorithms (Sharada et al., 2023). We will also go over RL and its main.

In supervised learning, an Artificial Intelligence (AI) network is trained to find a mapping function that maps input data to output using a dataset of input and target values. Regression and classification are further subcategories of supervised learning. Known instances of supervised learning include random forests, support vector machines, and linear regression.

Figure 2. General classification of machine learning algorithms

Markov Decision Process (MDP) is the foundation for the majority of RL problems. Finding the best answers to sequential decision problems (SDP) is the aim of an MDP. An MDP can assist in providing an optimal solution, or the best solution out of all the options, in the case of stochastic SDPs, but it cannot provide absolute solutions. A set of states, a set of actions, a transition model, and a reward function define an MDP model. Reward and transition rely on the situation as it is, the action that is selected, and the next state that results.

Learning with Reinforcement (RL) The RL agent's objective is to increase its long-term aggregated reward through its numerous interactions with the environment. An agent is the portion of the RL algorithm that engages in interactions and learns. This goal was accomplished by an agent using the best possible policy. An ideal policy is one that maximises the total long-term reward. A policy is a set of actions for a specific set of states. An agent's primary responsibility is to make the most of the actions that are already known to be effective while also investigating new actions that might be more profitable than the best ones currently in use.

Muthukumaran created dynamic programming (DP) in the middle of the 20th century as a mathematical and computer programming technique for solving optimisation problems. DP is a recursive technique that divides a difficult task into smaller, more manageable problems in a stepwise manner. The model-based DP technique necessitates complete observable environmental knowledge. Consequently, value iteration or the policy iteration method are used in DP to find an optimal policy in some RL problems where the given environment model is an MDP model (Muthukumaran el al., 2022).

Popular RL algorithms serve as the foundation for the actor-critic method. It is a hybrid approach that combines policy and value function. The actor modifies the policy in response to criticism from the critic, while the critic portion of the algorithm estimates the value function. This kind of approach estimates both the policy and value functions, placing it in between policy-based and value-based approaches. It holds true for both big and small action-state and state-space combinations.

4. CYBER-SECURITY

To ensure dependable and effective digital services, a smart city is designed to be comprised of interconnected sensors, actuators, and relays that are safe, secure, and dependable. These components collect, process, and transmit data. The need to address cyber-security concerns has arisen from the interconnectedness of different devices. The majority of the data is produced by cloud-based Internet of Things (IoT) devices, which are essential to many smart city applications.

Their main focus was on investigating the variety of difficult problems that come up when current communication protocols, sensors, actuators, and infrastructure are integrated. In, Muhammad et al conducted a thorough investigation and looked at the application of ML and DRL techniques from the standpoint of advanced IoT security and newly emerging security threats (Muhammad et al., 2017). The authors examined the benefits, drawbacks, and potential IoT security of ML and DRL protocols, and they suggested future research areas. They investigated numerous issues and suggested fixes for effectively utilising ML and DRL-based technologies in the cutting-edge healthcare industry.

In order to distinguish between normal and anomalous traffic, the authors of investigated the latent pattern from the training dataset using the self-taught potential and capabilities of DRL techniques (Diro et al., 2018),. Their suggested method for identifying and detecting cyberattacks in IoT applications in smart cities is based on distributed deep learning. The suggested method outperforms the shallow models-based approach in terms of efficiency. The authors of addressed the security of IoT devices in smart cities and suggested the Anomaly Detection-IoT (AD-IoT) system, an architecture based on Random Forest machine learning (Alrashdi et al., 2019). The suggested method uses machine learning-based dataset evaluation to effectively identify any suspicious activity occurring at the distributed fog nodes.

The previous model can assist in creating a variety of private and secure applications to bring the idea of a smart city to life. An ML-based secure computational offloading framework for optimising latency and energy consumption in the Fog Cloud-IoT environment was presented by the authors in .The suggested framework is built on the Neuro-Fuzzy model, which protects data at the gateway and uses Particle Swarm Optimisation (PSO) to determine which fog nodes are best for offloading computation to IoT devices (Alli et al., 2019).

5. MACHINE LEARNING AND SMART CITY HEALTHCARE

Advanced sensors, high-performance IoT devices, cloud computing, and higher data rates have all contributed to the widespread application of AI, ML, and DRL techniques in health intelligence an advanced term for health care mechanisms between 100 and 102. The aforementioned methods are essential for diagnosing diseases, predicting cures, utilising social media analytics for specific ailments, and performing medical imaging (Topol et al., 2019). The most current research trends and initiatives pertaining to health care in smart cities are briefly covered in the sections that follow.

The authors of have created a review to examine the function of 5G communication in the healthcare system, as well as the necessary methods, tools, and architecture, and to assess the main goals (Al-Turjman et al., 2019). Their main contributions centre on the architecture and components of the 5G-based health care system, a taxonomy of communication protocols and technologies, and network layer problems (such as scheduling, routing, congestion control, etc.) that are critical to IoT-based health care systems (Muthukumar et al., 2023). An extensive analysis of big data analysis using AI, ML, and DRL applications in healthcare systems was produced by the system (Al-Turjman et al., 2020). The benefits of the aforementioned techniques are examined by the authors in relation to a number of areas, including complex data analysis, diagnosis, classification, disease risk, optimal treatment, and patient survival predictions (Anbazhagu et al., 2024). In figure.3 and Figure.4 we drive the system design.

Figure 3. System design

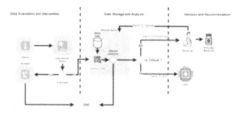

Figure 4. System model

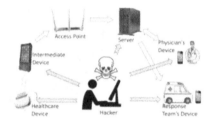

1. An IoHT implementation can be as simple as a heartbeat monitor connected to a mobile device via Bluetooth, or as complex as multiple sensors, intermediate devices, and centralized servers.
2. Generic IoHT implementation where devices communicate with each other using various protocols and servers take the appropriate actions.
3. The layered approach for describing IoHT functionalities and problems helps to identify IoHT data security and privacy issues at different layers, and what threat vectors are involved at each layer.
4. We have IoT devices have limited computational power, memory, and limited power, which makes them vulnerable to system and network attacks. Furthermore, complex encryption and authentication schemes are challenging to implement on these devices.
   1. IoHT devices come with fewer safety checks, and the firmware of these devices has security vulnerabilities. The urgency to roll out IoHT cloud platforms may result in the development of protocols having many potential security loopholes.
   2. IoT middleware platforms offer distributed system services with standard programming interfaces and protocols to minimize problems associated with heterogeneity, distribution, and scale in IoT applications development.
   3. The healthcare system has two states of data, persistent data at rest and transient data in motion. The details of each state are as follows.
   4. Healthcare devices such as sensors and actuators store event logs in the memory, and IoHT servers are the most attractive components for attackers to steal health care data from.
   5. Physicians/Response Team devices are susceptible to memory leakage attacks due to direct communication with IoHT data servers.

Tuli et al suggested a brand-new architecture dubbed Health Fog for effectively and independently analysing cardiac conditions (Tuli et al., 2020). The suggested framework is made up of edge computing devices that are able to precisely classify and manage the incoming patient data thanks to DRL protocols (Nagarajan et al., 2022). The Health Guard, a cutting-edge security system. The suggested method for identifying dubious and suspicious activity in the Smart Healthcare System (SHS) is based on machine learning protocols. In order to distinguish between the peaceful and concerning activities, the Health Guard continuously monitors the basic functions of various SHS devices and compares the vital to the changes occurring in the patient body (Newaz et al., 2019).

Zack have put forth the notion of mapping remote communities and evaluating satellite imagery using ML and DRL techniques in order to improve planning and healthcare. The authors of Zhang have created a review to investigate the effects of DRL protocols in the context of medical image analysis and to categorise different types of syndromes associated with problems with the stomach and spleen (Zhang et al., 2019). An ML-based method to evaluate patients' chances of survival following percutaneous coronary intervention was created (Zack et al., 2019). We discuss the comparison of the healthcare application in Table 2 and Table 3.

Table 2. Applications of AI, ML, and DRL in smart healthcare systems

Authors Name	Year	Approach	Summary
Tuli et al	2020	AI	Heart disease analysis using the Health Fog platform
Newaz et al	2019	ML	The Health Guard platform continuously compares and monitors the bodily conditions and operations of the connected devices.
Polu et al	2019	REST API	Using ontology rules and tele monitoring, remote patient care is provided.
Zack et al et al	2019	DRL	Communities are being mapped using DRL methods and satellite imagery to provide better healthcare.
Togaçar et al	2020	DRL	Breast cancer classified as invasive ductal carcinoma.

Table 3. Machine Learning Techniques

Technique	Pros	Cons
SPHA	Extracts psychological characteristics of users and thereby recognizes their health conditions.	Leads to improper diagnosis if false data is provided.
DLRT	Classifies genuine or fake glucose measurements.	Brings about unsuitable measurements if an intruder changes server's data.
iDispenser	Provides touchless dispensing services for minimizing infections.	Insecure as the decision is based on the Cloud.

6. PROBLEMS AND POTENTIAL AVENUES FOR FURTHER RESEARCH

The literature on smart cities currently in publication makes clear that applications based on AI, ML, and DRL have demonstrated promising outcomes. To further increase the effectiveness of smart cities, experts from academia and business can concentrate on the following open research problems that can be successfully addressed with the use of AI, ML, and DRL:

1. The efficiency of information transfer between UAVs and vehicles can be greatly increased by jointly optimising the UAV's on board capabilities (such as computing, processing, sensing, and communication resources) and its trajectory using machine learning techniques.
2. Measurement campaign in which different UAVs and vehicle velocities are used in different directions to model the vehicle-vehicle, vehicle-UAV, UAV-UAV, UAV-GBS channel, etc. in the presence of both regular and irregularly shaped infrastructure.
3. For all SGs and electric companies, the primary goal is to optimise power-down scenarios. The evaluation of communication delays is essential for creating a network that functions well. The development of strategies that allow switching between 5G communication technologies while guaranteeing a smooth power supply can be greatly aided by the application of ML and DRL based techniques.
4. Security concerns in smart cities are application-focused. A security breach at smart metres, for instance, may result in energy manipulation and inefficiency in smart grids. Therefore, in order to guarantee the cyber safety and security of smart city applications, more sophisticated and creative techniques based on big data analytics are required.

7. CONCLUSION

We investigated the usefulness of the previously mentioned protocols in order to create nearly ideal plans for a range of applications that are thought to be essential to the effectiveness of smart cities. We discussed the most recent uses of AI, ML, and DRL in smart governance design, as well as the necessity of new regulations that are both AI-assisted and AI-compatible, energy-efficient ITS, SGs, cybersecurity, and 5G and B5G communications aided by UAVs in smart cities. We gave a brief overview of the expanding role that the aforementioned methods are playing in smart health care, including their potential to help find the most convenient medication and their roles in effective diagnosis, health recovery, and the security of health-oriented IoT devices. Lastly, we discussed current research issues related to smart cities as well as upcoming research directions where earlier methods may still be very useful.

REFERENCES

Al-Turjman, F., Nawaz, M. H., & Ulusar, U. D. (2020). Intelligence in the Internet of Medical Things era: A systematic review of current and future trends. *Computer Communications*, 150, 644–660. 10.1016/j.comcom.2019.12.030

Al-Turjman, F., Zahmatkesh, H., & Mostarda, L. (2019). Quantifying uncertainty in internet of medical things and big-data services using intelligence and deep learning. *IEEE Access : Practical Innovations, Open Solutions*, 7, 115749–115759. 10.1109/ACCESS.2019.2931637

Alli, A. A., & Alam, M. M. (2019). SecOFF-FCIoT: Machine learning based secure offloading in Fog-Cloud of things for smart city applications. *Internet of Things : Engineering Cyber Physical Human Systems*, 7, 100070. 10.1016/j.iot.2019.100070

Alrashdi, I., Alqazzaz, A., Aloufi, E., Alharthi, R., Zohdy, M., & Ming, H. (2019, January). Ad-iot: Anomaly detection of iot cyberattacks in smart city using machine learning. In *2019 IEEE 9th Annual Computing and Communication Workshop and Conference (CCWC)* (pp. 305-310). IEEE.

Alsamhi, S. H., Ma, O., Ansari, M. S., & Almalki, F. A. (2019). Survey on collaborative smart drones and internet of things for improving smartness of smart cities. *IEEE Access : Practical Innovations, Open Solutions*, 7, 128125–128152. 10.1109/ACCESS.2019.2934998

Anbazhagu, U. V., Koti, M. S., Muthukumaran, V., Geetha, V., & Munrathnam, M. (2024). Multi-Criteria Decision-Making for Energy Management in Smart Homes Using Hybridized Neuro-Fuzzy Approach. *Distributed Generation & Alternative Energy Journal*, 83–110.

Arasteh, H., Hosseinnezhad, V., Loia, V., Tommasetti, A., Troisi, O., Shafie-khah, M., & Siano, P. (2016, June). Iot-based smart cities: A survey. In *2016 IEEE 16th international conference on environment and electrical engineering (EEEIC)* (pp. 1-6). IEEE. 10.1109/EEEIC.2016.7555867

Cugurullo, F. (2021). *Frankenstein urbanism: Eco, smart and autonomous cities, artificial intelligence and the end of the city*. Routledge. 10.4324/9781315652627

Diro, A. A., & Chilamkurti, N. (2018). Distributed attack detection scheme using deep learning approach for Internet of Things. *Future Generation Computer Systems*, 82, 761–768. 10.1016/j.future.2017.08.043

Habibzadeh, H., & Soyata, T. (2020). Toward uniform smart healthcare ecosystems: A survey on prospects, security, and privacy considerations. *Connected health in smart cities*, 75-112.

Kumar, S. S., Muthukumaran, V., Devi, A., Geetha, V., & Yadav, P. N. (2023). A Quantitative Approach of Purposive Sampling Techniques for Security and Privacy Issues in IoT Healthcare Applications. In *Handbook of Research on Advancements in AI and IoT Convergence Technologies* (pp. 281–299). IGI Global. 10.4018/978-1-6684-6971-2.ch016

Latif, S., & Zafar, N. A. (2017, November). A survey of security and privacy issues in IoT for smart cities. In *2017 Fifth International Conference on Aerospace Science & Engineering (ICASE)* (pp. 1-5). IEEE. 10.1109/ICASE.2017.8374288

Li, W., Chai, Y., Khan, F., Jan, S. R. U., Verma, S., Menon, V. G., Kavita, , & Li, X. (2021). A comprehensive survey on machine learning-based big data analytics for IoT-enabled smart healthcare system. *Mobile Networks and Applications*, 26(1), 234–252. 10.1007/s11036-020-01700-6

Muthukumar, V., Sivakami, R., Venkatesan, V. K., Balajee, J., Mahesh, T. R., Mohan, E., & Swapna, B. (2023). Optimizing Heterogeneity in IoT Infra Using Federated Learning and Blockchain-based Security Strategies. *International Journal of Computers, Communications & Control*, 18(6). Advance online publication. 10.15837/ijccc.2023.6.5890

Muthukumaran, V., & Manimozhi, I. (2021). Public Key Encryption With Equality Test for Industrial Internet of Things Based on Near-Ring. *International Journal of e-Collaboration*, 17(3), 25–45. 10.4018/IJeC.2021070102

Muthukumaran, V., Vinoth Kumar, V., Joseph, R. B., Munirathnam, M., Beschi, I. S., & Niveditha, V. R. (2022, November). Efficient Authenticated Key Agreement Protocol for Cloud-Based Internet of Things. *International Conference on Innovative Computing and CommunicationsProceedings of ICICC*, 3, 365–373.

Nagarajan, S. M., Deverajan, G. G., Chatterjee, P., Alnumay, W., & Muthukumaran, V. (2022). Integration of IoT based routing process for food supply chain management in sustainable smart cities. *Sustainable Cities and Society*, 76, 103448. 10.1016/j.scs.2021.103448

Newaz, A. I., Sikder, A. K., Rahman, M. A., & Uluagac, A. S. (2019, October). Healthguard: A machine learning-based security framework for smart healthcare systems. In *2019 sixth international conference on social networks analysis, management and security (SNAMS)* (pp. 389-396). IEEE. 10.1109/SNAMS.2019.8931716

Polu, S. K. (2019). Modeling of telemonitoring system for remote healthcare using ontology. *International Journal for Innovative Research in Science & Technology*, 5(9), 6–8.

Sharada, K. A., Sushma, K. S. N., Muthukumaran, V., Mahesh, T. R., Swapna, B., & Roopashree, S. (2023). High ECG diagnosis rate using novel machine learning techniques with Distributed Arithmetic (DA) based gated recurrent units. *Microprocessors and Microsystems*, 98, 104796. 10.1016/j.micpro.2023.104796

Topol, E. J. (2019). High-performance medicine: The convergence of human and artificial intelligence. *Nature Medicine*, 25(1), 44–56. 10.1038/s41591-018-0300-730617339

Tuli, S., Basumatary, N., Gill, S. S., Kahani, M., Arya, R. C., Wander, G. S., & Buyya, R. (2020). HealthFog: An ensemble deep learning based Smart Healthcare System for Automatic Diagnosis of Heart Diseases in integrated IoT and fog computing environments. *Future Generation Computer Systems*, 104, 187–200. 10.1016/j.future.2019.10.043

Vennira Selvi, G., Muthukumaran, V., Kaladevi, A. C., Satheesh Kumar, S., & Swapna, B. (2022). Integrated dominating and hit set-inspired unequal clustering-based data aggregation in wireless sensor networks. *International Journal of Intelligent Computing and Cybernetics*, 15(4), 642–655. 10.1108/IJICC-10-2021-0225

Zack, C. J., Senecal, C., Kinar, Y., Metzger, Y., Bar-Sinai, Y., Widmer, R. J., Lennon, R., Singh, M., Bell, M. R., Lerman, A., & Gulati, R. (2019). Leveraging machine learning techniques to forecast patient prognosis after percutaneous coronary intervention. *JACC: Cardiovascular Interventions*, 12(14), 1304–1311. 10.1016/j.jcin.2019.02.03531255564

Zhang, Q., Bai, C., Chen, Z., Li, P., Yu, H., Wang, S., & Gao, H. (2021). Deep learning models for diagnosing spleen and stomach diseases in smart Chinese medicine with cloud computing. *Concurrency and Computation*, 33(7), 1–1. 10.1002/cpe.5252

Chapter 13
The Effects of Socioeconomic Status, Geological, Engineering, and Climate Factors on Machine Learning–Dependent Forecast of Water Pipe Failure

Dharmesh Dhabliya
https://orcid.org/0000-0002-6340-2993
Vishwakarma Institute of Information Technology, India

Ankur Gupta
https://orcid.org/0000-0002-4651-5830
Vaish College of Engineering, India

Sukhvinder Singh Dari
https://orcid.org/0000-0002-6218-6600
Symbiosis International University, India

Ritika Dhabliya
Yashika Journal Publications Pvt. Ltd., India

Anishkumar Dhablia
Altimetrik India Pvt. Ltd., India

Nitin N. Sakhare
https://orcid.org/0000-0002-1748-799X
Vishwakarma Institute of Information Technology, India

Sabyasachi Pramanik
https://orcid.org/0000-0002-9431-8751
Haldia Institute of Technology, India

ABSTRACT

Subterranean water pipes deteriorate due to a variety of physical, mechanical, environmental, and social factors. Accurate pipe failure prediction is a prerequisite for a rational administrative approach to the water supply network (WSN) and is a challenge for the conventional physics-dependent model. The enormous water supply network's past maintenance data history was utilized by the study to anticipate water pipe breaks using data-directed machine learning methodologies. In order to include many factors that contribute to the deterioration of subsurface pipes, an initial multi-source data-aggregation system was created. The framework outlined the conditions for merging many datasets, including the soil type, population count, geographic, and meteorological datasets as well as the conventional pipe leaking dataset. Based on the data, five machine learning (ML) techniques—LightGBM, ANN, logistic regres-

DOI: 10.4018/979-8-3693-0683-3.ch013

sion, K-NN, and SVM algorithm—are developed to forecast pipe failure. It was found that LightGBM provided the optimum performance. Five criteria were used to analyze the relative importance of the main contributing factors to the water pipe breakdowns: calculation time, accuracy, effect of categorical variables, and interpretation. LightGBM, the model with the second-lowest training time, performed the best. Given the severe skewness of the dataset, it has been shown that the receiver operating characteristics (ROC) measure is too optimistic using the precision-recall curve (PRC) metric. It's noteworthy to note that socioeconomic factors within a community have been shown to have an impact on pipe failure probability. This study implies that data-directed analysis, which combines ML techniques with the proposed data aggregation architecture, may enhance reliable decision-making in WSN administration.

1. INTRODUCTION

Having a reliable and safe water supply is essential to the WSN's administration. Water distribution pipes, which move water from water treatment plants to customers, are the fundamental components of a WSN. This corrosion is especially bad for subsurface water pipes constructed in US urban centers that date back to the 19th century. The more than 700 water main breaks that happen every day in the United States and Canada result in the loss of over 2 trillion gallons of drinkable water annually. A burst water pipe may cause enormous financial losses as well as harm to the environment or society. According to US Water Service Agency projections, over the next 20 years, the replacement costs of the country's present WSNs and their anticipated expansions would come to a total of more than $1 trillion. Due to these horrible issues, management is under pressure to provide proactive support for loss reduction by adopting management practices for long-term improvement and reliable pipe failure estimate models.

The key to developing precise prediction models is to determine the significant variables—also referred to as input variables—that influence pipe failure. Several factors that might lead to pipe breaking have been assessed over the last several decades using experimental testing, finite element models, and historical data analysis. A recent review suggests that these factors may be broadly classified into three categories: physical, operational, and environmental. The physical characteristics of the pipe that are most often considered are its diameter, age, length, and material. Kettle and Goulter, for example, used statistical techniques to ascertain the relationship between pipe sizes and break likelihood.

The likelihood of longer pipes failing has been shown by Tai P. et al. (2023). The operational factor that has received the greatest research attention is the frequency of previous failures. These studies demonstrate that the probability of a pipe failing is often connected with the number of previous line failures. Water pressure is another common operational element for pipes in the WSNs. It is shown that there is a positive correlation between internal water pressure and the chance of breaking in metal and cement pipes. Pipe problems might also be caused by external factors. The factors include traffic levels, soil classifications, and climate. Furthermore, many of these details are often quite unknown. Numerous meteorological factors, such as temperature and precipitation, have been linked to pipe problems in previous studies. The results indicated that larger temperature variations may increase the risk of pipe collapse. It's critical to understand the interactions between the chance of pipe collapse and these three distinct types of contributing factors. Apart from the above mentioned elements, it is becoming evident that collaboration with diverse situations, such as social and economic concerns, has to be considered while executing forecasting for WSNs. For instance, the effects of configuration collapse and population-related data were considered in recent study on the reliability and adaptability of communities. However, these factors have seldom ever been taken into account by the pipe failure prediction model in use today. In the meanwhile, shareholders are paying close attention to how the major contributing reasons of pipe failures are interpreted in order to make well-informed decisions about the allocation of resources. This is on top of developing trustworthy and practical methods for evaluating pipe failure. Even while previous studies examined how many characteristics affected the chance of a pipe collapsing, it is still unclear what the comparative relevance—or degree of the effect—is. Thus, interpretability plays an equally important role in the development of a pipe collapse prediction model.

The existing methods for pipe collapse prediction are categorized into three groups: ML models, mathematical models, and physics-based models. The advantages and disadvantages of each strategy are briefly covered below. Physically-dependent methods use experimental or semi-empirical feature equations that account for physical factors to compare the permitted hardness of a pipe to its actual capacity. The pipe's failure probability may then be determined by comparing the pipe's current resilience and its piling using a sampling technique, such as the Monte Carlo simulation. Physics-dependent models may readily display the different inputs of the components that are considered, but this method is often computationally costly when considering the whole system. This is because a WSN comprises thousands of pipes, and a large number of samplings are required to estimate the failure probability of each pipe. Furthermore, a number of popular physics-dependent models, such as the B31G model, are too conservative. In contrast, statistical models are less expensive, particularly for niches where historical recording data is plentiful. Several statistical models may be used to anticipate pipe failures, according to earlier research. Time-dependent breakage prediction models, such as the LR model, Poisson process model, and time-exponential approach, are often described using statistical equations in statistical models. Bayesian networks have been used in recent studies to infer pipe collapse. The assumption that the collapse design won't change in the future allows for the use of these models for failure prediction as well. However, the statistical models may only include a small set of physical characteristics without revealing the physical relationship between those parameters and pipe failures. Data-directed machine learning models have recently been created as a method for pipe collapse prediction, making use of the increasing amount of accessible data. The techniques that are most popular for figuring out the complex relationship between pipe failure and other variables include ANN, GAs, LR, and neuro-fuzzy systems. These ML-dependent approaches are often criticized for their accuracy, even though they frequently have strong computational capabilities and function as "black boxes" with little to no interpretability. To get around this problem, some study used more effective explicable machine learning techniques, such the LR method and tree-dependent techniques. These methodologies may not provide a suitable degree of accuracy for water pipe failure prediction, based on the knowledge and experience of the authors. Furthermore, while certain machine learning algorithms were used to predict pipe collapse, there isn't yet a comprehensive comparison of the different ML techniques in this application area. In conclusion, even with the significant datasets maintained by water organizations and the WSN administration, accurate prediction and fair interpretation of pipe failure likely remain challenging and need more work.

We provide a multi-source data aggregation system and, in light of the previously indicated research gaps, the aim of this work is to interpret machine learning model that permits high-fidelity and efficient prediction of pipe collapse in WSNs. The proposed method was evaluated using a large WSN dataset, the largest dataset that has been studied to date, spanning over 6400 miles of water pipe.

Ecological, spatial, and population-based data are all considered during the data preparation stage. In addition to corroborated by other study, the clarification's results emphasize the important role socioeconomic factors play. Even if the consequences of the factors may vary depending on the WSN, different WSN management agencies may simply employ the provided analytical paradigm.

2. PIPE COLLAPSE PREDICTION ALGORITHMS' HISTORICAL DEVELOPMENT

Predicting pipe breakdown by treating the problem as a classification problem—that is, classifying a pipe as intact or crushed based on the given characteristics—is a common approach. Statistical learning approaches, instance-dependent learning approaches, logic-dependent approaches, perceptron-dependent methods, and SVMs are the five main groups of the current supervised machine learning techniques for classification issues. A comprehensive comparison of different machine learning algorithms is lacking, despite the fact that previous studies has used a number of machine learning approaches to predict whether or not a pipe would break based on the diversity of pipe input situations. To properly assess the performance of various machine learning classes for forecasting pipe failures, 5 well-known machine learning techniques —the LightGBM methodology, the ANN, LR, KNN, and SVC—are selected as the representative of each category. The objective of the machine learning model is to classify each pipe as either intact or collapsed based on the observed input data. A brief description of some ML methods may be found below.

LightGBM

LightGBM is a gradient boosting framework used in logic-based classification techniques. The three elements that comprise the LightGBM are Histogram and Leaf-wise Tree Growth Strategy, Exclusive Feature Bundling (EFB), and Gradient-based One-Side Sampling (GOSS). To be more specific, the GOSS is a sampling procedure that randomly samples the instances with small gradients and retains all examples with large gradients. For data instances with small gradients, a constant multiplier is used to account for the data distribution moving throughout the sampling process. Thus, performance is improved overall when these two strategies are used. EFB maximizes computing efficiency by dividing the features into fewer bundles. LightGBM uses EFB and histogram algorithms to manage category information efficiently. This has the significant benefit of eliminating the need for the conventional one-hot encoding, which is especially useful for categorical features with a high number of unique values. (Chen, Y. et al. 2023) has a wealth of knowledge and concepts.

Artificial Neural Network (ANN)

The artificial neural network, or ANN (Pramanik, S. and Bandyopadhyay, S. 2023) is a widely used perceptron that mimics how the human brain combines different inputs to get an output. The three primary components of an ANN architecture are the I/P layer, hidden layers, and O/P layer. In order to minimize the difference between the O/P and goal predictions during training, each layer's weight coefficients for its neurons are changed periodically. After calculating the weighted sum of the I/Ps from every neuron, it generates an O/P with an activation function. The mathematical expression for the interaction between I/Ps and O/Ps in each neuron is given by Eq. (1).

$$\partial = x\left(\sum_{j=1}^{m} y_r z_r + c\right) \tag{1}$$

∂ is the O/P of every neuron, f is its activation function, y_r is the weight of z_r and c is its bias.

Linear Regression (LR)

One method of statistical learning is logistic regression (LR) (Dhamodaran S, et al. 2023) which fits sample data into a logistic function. LR has thus been widely used in engineering. The ML (Ahamad, S. et al. 2023) approach in question is (1) explicable, and (2) it assigned each sample for a classification problem a value between 0 and 1, which may be regarded as the classification probability (Pandey, B. K. et al. 2023), given that each factor's weight is known after training. In mathematics, the formula for linear regression is Eq. (2).

$$j = \frac{1}{1 + e^{-(y0 + \sum_{j=1}^{k} y_j x_j)}} \tag{2}$$

where y_j is the vector sample with the ith feature, j is the O/P of each specimen, and yj denotes its weight feature that will be adjusted throughout the training process; w0 stands for constant bias. Equation illustrates how LR cannot handle categorical variables. Conversion strategies like one-hot-encoder are thus required.

Figure 1. Confusion matrix for pipe state classification

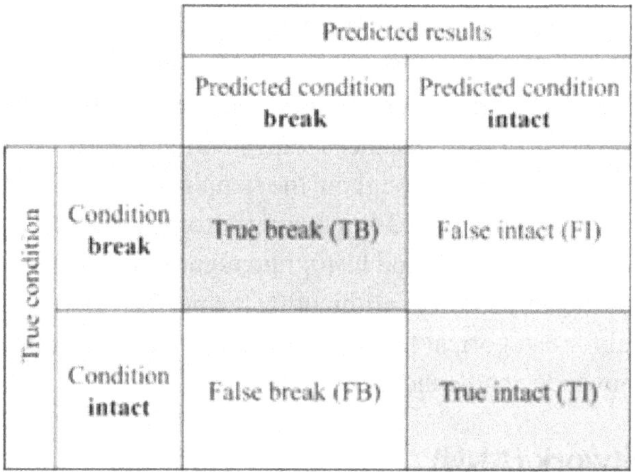

2.4 KNN

(Bhattacharya, A. et al. 2021) state that kNN is one of the most fundamental and fundamental algorithms for pattern classification. It is assumed that instances belonging to the same class are close to one another. The method used to compute the distances between instances determines how effective kNN is. Euclidean distance is the most often used distance unit. Equation (3) defines the Euclidean distance between specimens' y_i and y_j.

$$l(y_i, y_j) = \sqrt{(y_{i1} - y_{j1})^2 (y_{i2} - y_{j2})^2 (y_{i3} - y_{j3})^2 + \ldots\ldots + (y_{im} - y_{jm})^2} \tag{3}$$

yi_m represents the mth feature of the ith sample.

2.5. Classification of Support Vectors (SVC)

Support vector classification is an SVM that performs classification tasks by using the optimal hyperplane vector. According to Mandal, A. et al. (2021), the n-dimensional data points may be divided into two halves by a plane called the hyperplane. If the events are a 2D dataset, for instance, the hyperplane is a line on a 2D plane. The aim of SVC is to find the hyperplane that may maximize margins, which are the cumulative of the distances from the hyperplane to the nearest training specimens from each class. The following optimization equations are mathematically solved using SVC.

2.6. Metrics to Assess Machine Learning Models

The output of the five machine learning techniques is a continuous value between. What number between 0 and 1 indicates the probability of a pipe collapsing? This level of confidence was often interpreted as the probability of a collapse. Assuming that the ground certainty of the test dataset is a binary class (completely fine or collapsed), a common way to analyze the estimate results is to divide them into each class based on a threshold (0.5 in this example). Conversely, the sample is predicted to be broken if the output is greater than 0.5; otherwise, it is considered "intact." With the anticipated results and the real data, a confused matrix may be produced, as shown in Fig. 'True Break' and 'True Intact' denote the correctly classified samples shown in Figure 1. The term "False Intact" describes pipelines that seem to be intact but ultimately break. Based on classified prediction outcomes, accuracy, recall, and precision are used in this study to quantify the performance of ML models.

$$Accuracy = \frac{TC + TF}{TC + TF + FC + FF} \tag{4}$$

$$Recall = \frac{TC}{TC + TF} \tag{5}$$

$$Precision = \frac{TC}{TC + FC} \tag{6}$$

Here TC indicates True Collapse, TF stands for True Fine, FC stands for False Collapse and FF stands for False Fine.

Figure 2. Cleveland WDN network overview: (a) displays the pipes that the Cleveland Water Division is in charge of, (b) displays an example of repair records, (c) displays the distribution of pipe assistance over time, and (d) displays the anticipated annual maintenance cost ($)

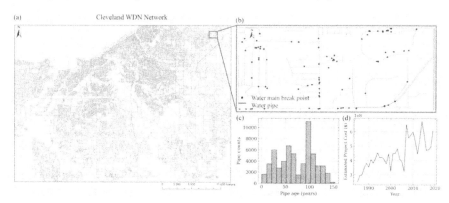

The study use three measures, namely accuracy, recall, and precision, to assess the efficacy of machine learning techniques by looking at the outcomes of categorized predictions. Equations (4) through (6) produce these measures.

3. STRUCTURE FOR GATHERING DATA FROM SEVERAL SOURCES FOR AN EXTENSIVE WSN

A critical step in data-driven machine learning algorithms is data preparation. The pipe-related dataset and historical repair records used in this study were collected by Cleveland Water Firm, which is in charge of a large WSN in the nation. The second most populous county in the US province of Ohio, Allen County, is served by 6500 miles of water main pipes that are maintained by the Cleveland Water Department. These pipes provide water to 520,000 functioning user accounts. The research area includes one of the largest cities in the Great Lakes region of North America.

The accuracy index determines the overall prediction accuracy by accounting for all anticipated outcomes. The accuracy is the ratio of all actual breaks to all anticipated breaks. The recall is defined as the ratio of each Real Break to the True Collapses. More precisely, a greater recall value means that more break cases in the testing dataset are accurately detected by the model. A greater accuracy number indicates more predicted break samples that are real break samples. Actually, a low accuracy value might lead to the improper replacement of intact pipes, increasing needless maintenance costs, while a low recall value could cause the failure pipes to be overlooked.

Previous studies indicated that accuracy (Praveenkumar, S. et al., 2023), recall (Vidya Chellam, V. et al., 2023), and precision (Mall, P. K. et al., 2023) alone would not be adequate for assessing models. The relationship between the FP rate and TP rate at different thresholds is represented by the Receiver

Operating Characteristics (ROC) curve (Mondal, D. et al. 2023), which has been widely used in previous studies to evaluate the effectiveness of different machine learning approaches. Nonetheless, the ROC curve might be misleading if it is used in situations where there is a lot of imbalanced classification. It is recommended that the reliable alternative make use of the precision-recall curve (PRC). The PRC illustrates the relationship between recall and accuracy with different thresholds. In order to demonstrate how the two indexes vary in their performance while dealing with a highly imbalanced dataset, the AUC estimations of ROC and PRC are constructed and compared in this study. Each curve has an AUC value between 0.0 and 1.0, where an estimate of 0.0 indicates no prediction, 0.6 indicates random guessing, and 1.0 indicates a superior prediction.

This area's peculiar geology causes the earth to often freeze and thaw during the winter. The system overview of the Cleveland Water Department is shown in Fig. 2. The pipe network's dispersion, which totals 55,945 pipes, is shown in 2(a). The data record includes details on the age, material, diameter, length, and other physical attributes of each pipe. Fig. 2(b) displays a record of pipe maintenance at one of the WSN's sites. The locations that have received maintenance are shown by the points. The maintenance date is also monitored by the Cleveland Water Department (CWD).

Figure 2(c) shows the distribution of pipe ages in the water delivery network. As is evident, a number of pipes have been in operation for almost a century. Assuming that every one of the damaged pipes was restored entirely, the anticipated annual cost is shown in 2(d). The estimate is based on the experience of the Cleveland Water Agency, and it is projected that the cost per foot to replace a pipe will be around $483.74. However, the actual total cost may be lower than estimated for two reasons: 1) many damages may be repaired at the same time; and 2) the care may just cause the collapse rather than fully restore the pipe. When preparing a maintenance budget, having a precise estimate of when a water pipe will rupture will be quite useful.

In order to provide a comprehensive understanding of the reasons for WSN failures and associated maintenance, data from many sources are first combined. Even if more and more data are becoming publicly accessible, it may still be difficult to combine data from several sources since they are sometimes offered by different organizations and maintained in different configurations. One of the limitations in the current use of data-directed methodologies has been noted: there are no best practices for effectively combining datasets from diverse sources. In addition to developing these guidelines, the aim of this part is to provide a multi-source data-aggregation framework. Six datasets are specifically considered in this study: (1) the WSN pipe-related dataset, (2) the prior pipe collapse dataset,

Figure 3. Schema for compiling datasets from several sources

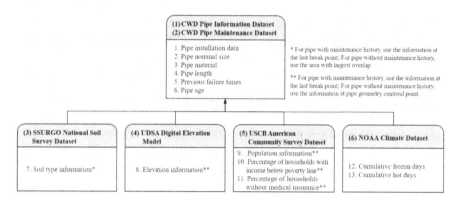

Figure 4. The data aggregation technique (Ng c, T. H. et al. 2023) involved assumptions made for a number of datasets, such as (a) the pipe collapse dataset (Reepu, et al. 2023), which relied on the proximity of the collapse point to the pipe; (b) the soil category dataset, which depended on geological data; (c) the geographical dataset, which depended on coordinates from the digital elevation technique; and (d) the population dataset, which depended on the physical coordinate of the pipe or break point to the Census block

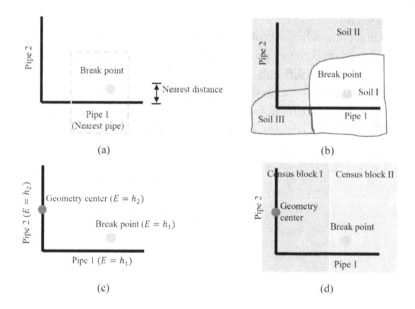

(1) and (2) come from the Cleveland Water Agency, while (3) comes from the SSURGO soil type dataset of the National Cooperative Soil Survey.

America's Community Analysis the US Agency of Agriculture provided the geographical dataset from the Digital Elevation Technique, the US Population Agency provided the 5-year data, and the Central Oceanic and Weather Agency provided the climatic dataset. To give the complete training and testing datasets, the last four publicly accessible datasets are joined with the two datasets provided by the Cleveland Water Agency. The data aggregation framework is shown in Fig. 3. More information on the presumptions and specifications for data aggregation may be found in the following.

3.1 Simplify Data Collection and Record-Keeping

For pipe information and break data in the Geographic Information System, CWD provides two distinct layer formats (Chandan, R. R. et al. 2023) according to Fig. 2 (b). "Points" represent the break-records dataset, whereas "lines" represent the pipe-information dataset.

An analysis showed that there is a little amount of overlap between these two data groups. The rationale is that pipelines are based on actual lay down, even when break locations are marked by hand or using GPS sensors that don't line up with the water pipes. According to Fig. 4(a), if the distance is less than 1 m, which is the typical resolution for GPS devices, the break records are assumed to be located at the nearest pipe for data aggregation. This makes it possible to connect the break records to the relevant water pipes. The nominal size, composition, and distance of the pipes in the original pipe information collection may be used to instantly determine the physical parameters of each pipe by assigning the failure reports to the appropriate pipe (Table 1). The pipe's nominal diameter is the standard size used in North America; no units are included. Pipes with missing data for any of these three criteria are removed. Three other components are computed or processed based on the break data: pipe age, pipe previous failure times, and interim time to last collapse.

3.2 Soil Types Grouped Together

Previous studies have shown the vital importance of the interaction between soil and pipes in pipe failures because water pipelines are often located below. Failures in the pipes specifically might be caused by the uneven ground settling. The deterioration of the pipe caused by different soil corrosivities may also have an effect on the probability of a pipe failure. Prior studies have shown that the breakdown of pipes occurs within a certain pH range. Considering the soil (Pramanik, S. 2023) categories that may be obtained from the public dataset is a more practical approach, since it is very impossible to include every soil-based factor that might influence pipe leaking. This study considers seventy-two different types of soil. These soil types are categorized by their surface texture, principal elements, slope, and other characteristics. The soil category information for each pipe is assigned based on the principal site of failure data and the majority of the soil type where the pipe is buried. According to 4(b), Pipe 1 has been assigned the soil type Soil I since it is where the break point is located. Given that Soil II contains the majority of Pipe 2 and has no break records, Soil II has been designated as the soil type.

3.3 Compiling Topographic Information

Topographical data may be utilized to make up for missing operational water pressure data in order to investigate WSN failures (Khanh, P. T. et al. 2023). Low water pressure is usually experienced by pipes located at higher altitudes. There is a wide range in elevation in the research area of the Water Supply

Network pipes in Allen County, USA, ranging from 240 to 410 meters. The topographical dataset has a resolution of 40 m and was gathered from the USDA elevation dataset using the Geospatial Data Gateway (GDG). Every location in Cuyahoga has elevation data available because to the digital elevation model. Pipe segments may vary in height, much as soil category combinations can, especially for long-distance pipelines. The breakpoint elevation is used to calculate the height of the pipe with break records, such Pipe 1, as seen in Fig. 4(c). Otherwise, the central altitude of the pipe geometry is used.

3.4 Data Acquisition for Census

Since WSN is almost often performed for localities, it seems logical to believe that community characteristics (such as user behavior and census data) may influence the probability of pipe failure. The study uses data from public censuses that include information on community characteristics to support this conclusion. The census information that was obtained from the US Census Bureau contains enormous variables that define every community block. According to the census data, Cuyahoga County is divided into 2952 community blocks. The census, poverty rate, and non-healthcare insurance rate shown in Table 2 are selected based on the availability of the information to consider community factors from several perspectives. Since a single pipe might traverse many census blocks, each pipe's population data is allocated to a representative site identified by this study. According to Fig 4(d), the breakpoint for the pipe with failure records is used as the indicative point, while the representative point for the pipe without break records is chosen as the pipe geometry centre.

3.5 Compilation of Climate Data

Previous studies have shown that the seasons have a major impact on the pipe's break (e.g., rainfall, air temperature). The findings imply that the higher incidence of pipe breaking on very hot or cold days may have been caused by the contact between the soil and the pipe. However, previous studies could not account for the temperature data needed to forecast annual pipe failures. To get past this restriction on accounting for climate effects, the study uses the total number of days that were colder and hotter to reflect the environment that each pipe encountered throughout the duration of its service life. "Cold days" are days when the temperature drops below 32 °F. Days having a high temperature over 90 degrees Fahrenheit are referred to as "hot days". A dataset provided by suppliers of climate agents is used to calculate the total number of days. From the time of installation until the selected study year, each pipe used in this study had a total number of hot and cold days.

Higher elevations often have lower water pressures. The WSN pipes under research are located in Allen County, Cleveland, Ohio, which has a broad range of altitudes, from 240 m to 410 m. The topographical dataset comes from the 30 m resolution USDA elevation dataset from the Geospatial Data Gateway (GDG). The digital elevation model (DEM) may be used to calculate the height of any location within the Cuyahoga area.

Using the existing data aggregation structure, a complete dataset that incorporates the operational conditions, geological conditions, socioeconomic elements of the community, climate, and physical characteristics of water pipes is developed and will be used.

Figure 5. Shows the ML training and interpretation procedure

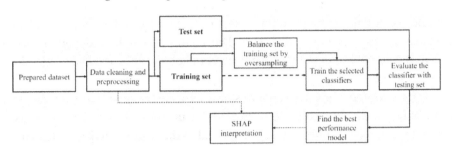

4. CASE STUDY

Figure 5 illustrates the workflow of machine learning modeling for machine learning-based pipe failure prediction. Figure 5 provides an overview of the accepted methods for water pipe break prediction. The combined dataset selected using the criteria is purified by excluding specimens that have any missing parts and outliers, as mentioned in Section 3. To improve the performance of machine learning approaches, the numerical components are standardized by removing mean values and scaling to a single unit. One-hot encoding, which uses 0s and 1s to represent categorical factors, would be used to encode the factors if the ML algorithm is unable to handle the categorical variables.

The gathered dataset was randomly split into a test set and a training set using the 8:2 ratios, which is a common technique for figuring out how well a model can predict. Since the break records only account for around 15% of the whole dataset, the imbalanced dataset for machine learning model training is a serious issue that needs to be resolved. according to Figure 5. Both balanced and unbalanced training datasets are used to train the model. In order to balance the dataset until the number of broken specimens equals the number of intact specimens, this study used an oversampling technique that involves randomly repeating the minor class of pipes. The testing dataset doesn't change. Consequently, the models trained on both balanced and unbalanced datasets were evaluated using the same testing dataset. Once the best performing ML model has been identified, the whole dataset is used for machine learning techniques using an explanation process called SHAP to understand the influence of giving components on the pipe collapse. It should be noted that the model analysis results are independent of the train-test splitting strategy since the selected model is fitted again according to the whole dataset. The steps involved in preparing data and estimating machine learning model performance are explained below.

4.2 Gathering Information and Assessing Its Attributes

4.2.1 Assembling the Dataset and Labeling It

Since the purpose of the study is to predict the pipe state at a certain time period, where the pipe status is either broken or operating good, the machine learning model is stated as a classification problem. Making a dataset that includes every year of every pipe is not feasible and might result in a highly uneven dataset. The next steps were taken to lessen the degree of imbalance and fully use the broken records by building the optimal dataset for machine learning testing and training.

1) A year is selected at random for each pipe, starting from the installation date and ending in August 2023, the latest update done before this study. During this period, time-dependent factors are discovered, such as the number of days that have been both hot and cold, the age of the pipe, and previous incidents of collapse.

2) The digits 0 for fine status or 1 for collapse status indicate the pipe status for the selected year.

3) In order to fully use the pipe collapse history, the data from the most recent break year for every pipe having a break record (or breaks) is connected to the dataset created in the earlier phases.

4) A 8:2 ratio is used to divide the final dataset into training and testing sets.

The selected data are subjected to the data aggregation process described in the preceding part of this research. The following stage, known as data cleaning, is taking out data points that have blanks in them. Following data cleaning, 40,236 pipe data specimens—32,436 fine samples and 7354 broken samples—are obtained.

Considering that the model's predicted results might be impacted by the random year selection used in Step 1. Ten random selections are performed in order to assess the model's performance, and the average estimates of the assessment criteria are applied.

Figure 6. Shows the variable histograms that were considered for the training and test sets

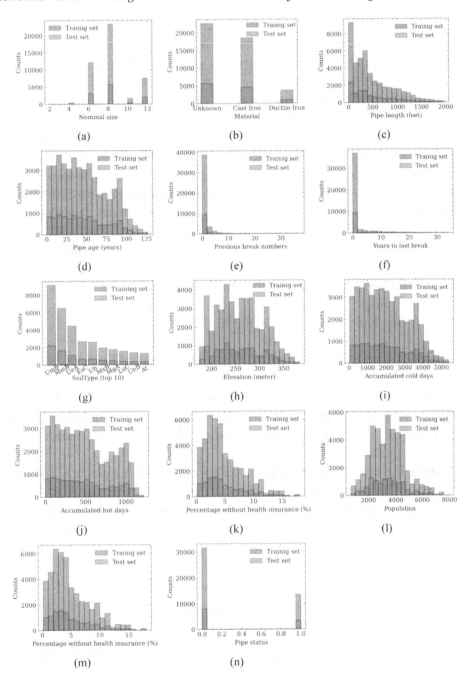

There are two category variables and eleven continuous variables totaling 13 components. These aspects fall into four fundamental categories: physical, operational, environmental, and social.

Figure 6 shows factor histograms for the training and testing datasets. Overall, the features of the testing dataset are sufficiently covered by the training dataset. A more detailed representation of the physical variable dispersion is shown in Fig. 6(a) through (d). Although many pipes have an unknown composition, cast iron and ductile iron are the most often used materials in WSN systems. In figures 6(e) and (f), the characteristics of two operational variables are shown. In 6(g) to (j), the four environmental variables are shown. For the sake of convenience of viewing, the pipes are categorized into 72 different kinds of soil. One of the climatic factors that is taken into consideration is the amount of hot and cold days throughout time. Finding out that they share traits with the pipe age distribution is fascinating and highlights the significance of climatic factors in pipe failures. The census, the percentage of people living in poverty, and the percentage of families without access to health insurance are chosen to represent the socioeconomic features of each pipe for the community they serve, as can be seen in Fig. 6(k) to (m). The population within each Census community block varies from 750 to over 8500, which is significant since Cuya-hoga County has multiple densely inhabited places, such as Cleveland City. Most community blocks have a poverty percentage of less than 40%. On the other hand, nearly 90% of the households in the poorest block earn less than the federal poverty level annually. Community blocks had a range of 0.2% to 18% of inhabitants without health insurance, which is consistent with the stated low status.

Depending on whether the pipe breaks during the selected monitoring year, the collection of pipes was divided into two groups; the class code is 1 if the pipe collapses during the monitoring year, and the code is 0 if it is OK. The results are shown in Fig. 6. (n).

4.2.2 The Relationship Between Failure State and Internal Factors

The correlation matrix may be used to show the internal connections among the factors assumed to cause pipe collapses as well as the external linkages between each component and the objective. Since the datasets include category and numeric variables, a variety of correlation indicators are used to evaluate the correlation between the variables.

The population, the percentage of the population without health insurance, and the poverty rate are a few examples of the socioeconomic variables that are related but not strongly imply that the ML model should treat them as independent variables. Moreover, no correlation has been seen between any single I/P variable and the dominant O/P variable, indicating that the pipe failure is a complex problem involving several variables.

Figure 7. The correlation measures applied to numerical and category variables are shown

	Continuous variable	Categorical variable
Continuous variable	Pearson correlation	Correlation ratio
Categorical variable	Correlation ratio	Cramer's V

The process of determining correlations between various types of data is shown in Figure 1. 7. Specifically, the correlation between two numerical variables is expressed using Pearson correlation (Samanta, D. et al. 2021), while the correlation between two categorical variables is quantified using Cramer's V coefficient. Additionally, the correlation ratio is used between numerical and category data. For category components, these indicators span from 0 to 1, and for numerical elements, they span from 1 to 1. A connection that is totally positive or negatively related is indicated by a 1, while 0 indicates that there is no association at all. A detailed description of the correlation computations is not given here due to the article length constraint. Interested readers may review the Supplementary file (Algorithm I).

Picture 8 displays the pipe failure condition (referred to as the "target" in the image) as well as the final correlation matrix among the 13 factors that were considered. The variables that have the highest link with the goal (pipe failure state) are the pipe ages, hotter days, and colder days. These imply that weather and pipe service age are two of the most important factors influencing pipe conditions. The pipe length, interval year, and previous break number are among the additional details that follow. The present research observes their behaviors in the machine learning model and clarifies the model while accounting for all of these.

4.3 Pipe Failure Prediction Based on L

4.3.1 Prediction Outcomes

The five kinds of supervised machine learning (ML) algorithms that were covered in the Background section are used to develop the pipe break classification problem. Hyperparameter optimization of each ML algorithm is done via grid-search optimization (Pramanik, S. 2023). The ANN model uses one input layer, one dropout layer, two hidden neural network layers, and one output layer. There are 68 and 132 neurons in the buried layers, respectively. The predictions made by the model after it is trained on an imbalanced dataset are shown in Fig. 9a). 9b displays the outcomes of the model's training on a balanced dataset. The recall and accuracy matrices for each class are shown on the right and bottom sides, respectively. A description of the general accuracy of the model is shown in the cell on the right-below. Regardless of whether the dataset is balanced or not, the LightGBM (Jayasingh, R. et al. 2022) and ANN models provide the best predictions in terms of accuracy, recall, and precision measures. On the other hand, while training with the balanced dataset, the KNN and SVC models often miss a large number of intact samples, and when training with the imbalanced dataset, they regularly miss a variety of broken samples. Oversampling allowed the model to detect more break samples.

To illustrate the overall performance of different models, the average Receiver Operating Characteristics (ROC), Precision-Recall Curve (PRC), area under the curve (AUC), and average training time of ten chosen datasets are calculated and shown in Fig. The LightGBM model performed better than all other models under evaluation in terms of training duration, ROC, and PRC values, regardless of whether the training sets were balanced or unbalanced. The capacity of LightGBM to manage categorical data without requiring one-hot

Figure 8. Prediction results using balanced and unbalanced training datasets ('I' denotes fine and 'B' denotes collapse)

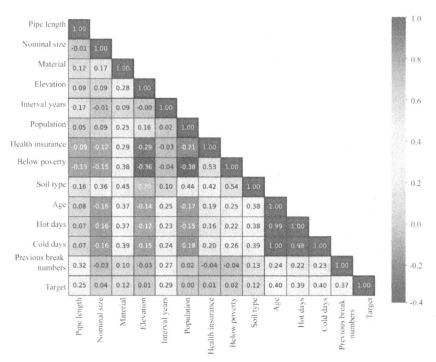

Figure 9. Prediction results using balanced and unbalanced training datasets ('I' denotes fine and 'B' denotes collapse)

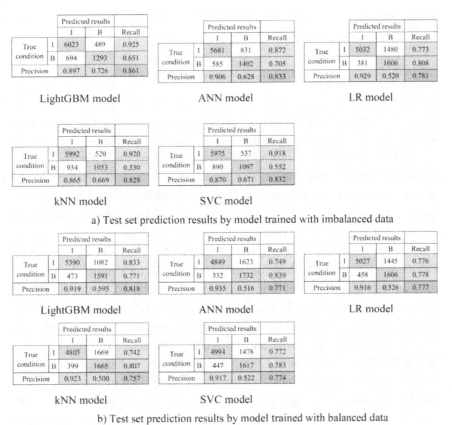

a) Test set prediction results by model trained with imbalanced data

b) Test set prediction results by model trained with balanced data

Figure 10. Comparison of several criteria for evaluating deployed machine learning models

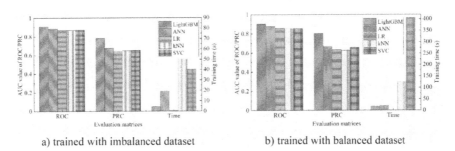

a) trained with imbalanced dataset   b) trained with balanced dataset

Table 4. summarizing the model for predicting pipe breaks

	LightGBM	Artificial Neural Network	Logistic Regression	KNN	SVC
Accuracy	○ ○ ○	○ ○	○	○	○
Learning technique speed	○ ○	○ ○	○ ○ ○	○	○
Dealing categorical values	○ ○ ○	○	○	○	○
Model Interpretability	○ ○	○	○ ○ ○	○	○

○ ○ ○ indicates a job well done.
○ Indicates the poorest effort.

The following charts describe the effects of each factor on the probability of a pipe breaking. The SHAP technique is used to compute the impact value of each variable for each sample. To show the overall effect of all the factors considered on the chance of a pipe breaking, the impact values of each element are extracted from all pipe samples. The impacts of continuous variables are colored according on how big they are. A representation is provided by the impact variables' mean values. It is conceivable to draw the following inferences from the observations. The validity of the model interpretation findings is shown by the fact that many of these results are consistent with previous studies.

1) Figure 12 illustrates how physical components work. The chance of a pipe breaking is positively impacted by each of these factors, therefore the greater the factor's value, the higher the SHAP value. Longer pipes are more likely to fail than smaller pipelines, based on the dispersion of pipe length estimates. The same findings may be made about pipe age. Older pipes have greater SHAP values, which mean they are more likely to fail than younger pipes. Furthermore, a significant correlation has been seen between the nominal size and the SHAP value, suggesting that larger nominal diameter pipes have a higher failure rate. Figure 12's right side displays each pipe material's impact separately. Despite both having low SHAP values, cast iron has a +ve SHAP effect value while ductile iron has a -ve SHAP impact value. This indicates that the likelihood of a cast iron pipe breaking is higher than that of a ductile iron pipe. This is partly because ductile iron is less fragile than cast iron.

Figure 11. The total ranking of variables taken into account for pipe failure likelihood

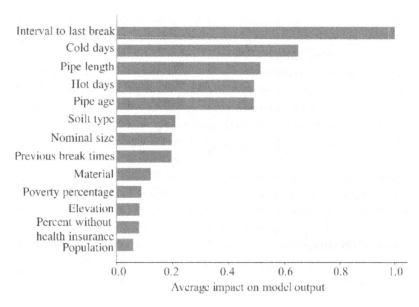

Figure 12. Effects of physical elements

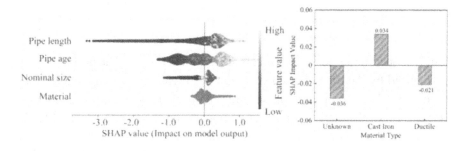

Figure 13. SHAP values shown to demonstrate how operational variables have an influence

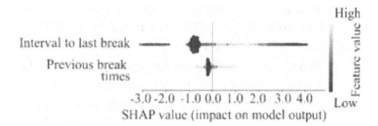

Figure 14. Influenced by environmental influences

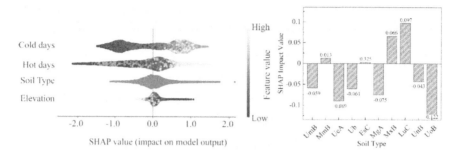

Figure 15. Impacting factors are local

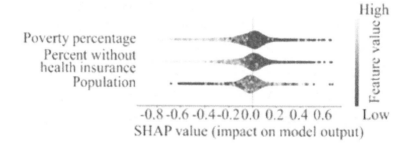

2) The outcomes of operational service elements are shown in Fig. 13. The probability of a pipe collapse is more influenced by the time elapsed since the last break than by the length of previous breaks. Longer time intervals between pipe breaks are seen to increase the failure likelihood; yet, shorter time intervals show both positive and negative impacts on the failure probability. This implies that a number of pipes suffered damage soon after installation or maintenance. This result is in line with previous studies that shown a bathtub curve in the failure rate of pipes, with a high failure probability either early in the pipe's life or when it starts to deteriorate. Furthermore, as shown by the SHAP values in Fig. 13, there is a positive correlation between the rupture probability at the pipe and the number of previous failures at the pipe. This is consistent with actual results from practitioner interviews, which show that the same locations saw a higher frequency of pipe failures.

The results indicated that the number of cold days a pipe experienced increased the risk that it would break for the environmental conditions shown in Figure 14. It could be caused by the action of soil settling as a result of soil freezing and thawing. Figure 14's right side illustrates how soil classifications have an impact. Out of the top 10 soil types, where most pipes are concealed, the LuC (Loudonville-Urban Land Complex) soil has the highest pipe rupture probability, while the UoB soil has the lowest rupture rate. Not to mention, the results indicate that pipes positioned higher up had a lower chance of bursting, which makes sense considering that lower service water pressure is experienced by pipelines at higher elevations. Consequently, the internal tension caused by the service water pressure on the pipe is minimized.

It is surprising to see that people with lower socioeconomic level or less access to healthcare had a decreased risk of having a water pipe break in relation to the sociocultural components shown in Figure 15. It's possible that the impoverished neighborhoods' lower water use or lower inspection rates are factors in the pipe's extended lifetime. More data-driven study is required for comprehensive explanations. Despite this, in the majority of pipe samples, the density of a community block does not consistently affect the likelihood of pipe failure; a densely populated area is linked to a much higher risk of water pipe breakage.

5. CONCLUSION

This project aims to examine the application of machine learning (ML) algorithms to anticipate water pipe failures based on data from a large water supply network, with the goal of understanding the effects of contributing parts. An important first step towards accounting for factors that contribute to pipe collapses, such socioeconomic factors, climate, and geology, is the design plan to integrate maintenance records from the water supply network with several public databases. Using the aggregated data, five distinct machine learning models are developed for pipe collapse estimate, each of which belongs to one of the five primary types of machine learning classification models. The models are trained on both an imbalanced training dataset (most of the data originate from intact pipes) and a balanced training dataset (the oversampling technique is used to establish balance). Results from several training datasets are compared. The learnt ML model is then interpreted using the SHAP interpolation approach. Among the main contributions of this work are:

This system provides a state-of-the-art approach to data aggregation by integrating several publically accessible datasets, resulting in the largest real-field dataset (both in size and chronology) and, therefore, the greatest number of I/P parameters for machine learning modeling in water supply networks. Consequently, this study significantly expands and deepens the communities' understanding of the impacts of technology, geology, weather, and socioeconomic concerns. To the best of our knowledge, this is the first research that assesses the role that socioeconomic features play in the collapse of water delivery networks.

1) For the purpose of implementation, five popular machine learning algorithms are carefully examined and compared based on five criteria: accuracy, processing time, influence of categorical variables, and interpretation. The model with the second-lowest training time, LightGBM, achieved the highest performance. Using the precision-recall curve (PRC) metric, it has been shown that the Receiver Operating Characteristics (ROC) measure is too optimistic in light of the dataset's extreme skew.

2) The interpretation results' agreement with past studies demonstrated the SHAP's ability to comprehend the impact of the contributing elements. The results indicate that there is a significant influence from pipe age, colder and hotter days encountered, and pipe buried time—that is, the period since the last collapse. The surroundings and the physical properties of the pipe both contribute in a way that is consistent with previous studies' conclusions. The contribution of community characteristics indicates that although areas with high population density have a larger risk of water pipe breaking, regions with significant poverty have a lower likelihood of pipe breakage (or are maintained less often). These indicate that the conditions around pipe service are significantly impacted by socioeconomic factors.

Furthermore, water pipe failure is caused by complex nonlinear interactions between different types of constituents. Owing to the model's capability and data accessibility, earlier studies often simplified the analytic procedure by considering a small number of factors. To improve the accuracy of pipe failure prediction, future research should consider including bigger datasets and more advanced machine learning techniques. Developments in a number of fields may serve as a catalyst for the shift in the decision-making process for the meticulous management of the water supply network to achieve the sustainability goal.

REFERENCES

Ahamad, S., Veeraiah, V., Ramesh, J. V. N., Rajadevi, R., Reeja, S. R., Pramanik, S., & Gupta, A. (2023). Deep Learning based Cancer Detection Technique. In *Thrust Technologies' Effect on Image Processing*. IGI Global.

Bhattacharya, A., Ghosal, A., Obaid, A. J., Krit, S., Shukla, V. K., Mandal, K., & Pramanik, S. (2021). Unsupervised Summarization Approach with Computational Statistics of Microblog Data. In Samanta, D., Althar, R. R., Pramanik, S., & Dutta, S. (Eds.), *Methodologies and Applications of Computational Statistics for Machine Learning* (pp. 23–37). IGI Global. 10.4018/978-1-7998-7701-1.ch002

Chandan, R. R., Soni, S., Raj, A., Veeraiah, V., Dhabliya, D., Pramanik, S., & Gupta, A. (2023). Genetic Algorithm and Machine Learning. In *Advanced Bioinspiration Methods for Healthcare Standards, Policies, and Reform*. IGI Global. 10.4018/978-1-6684-5656-9

Chen, Y., Jia, J., Wu, C., Ramirez-Granada, L., & Li, G. (2023). Estimation on total phosphorus of agriculture soil in China: A new sight with comparison of model learning methods. *Journal of Soils and Sediments*, 23(2), 998–1007. 10.1007/s11368-022-03374-x

Dhamodaran, S., Ahamad, S., Ramesh, J. V. N., Sathappan, S., Namdev, A., Kanse, R. R., & Pramanik, S. (2023). *Fire Detection System Utilizing an Aggregate Technique in UAV and Cloud Computing. In Thrust Technologies' Effect on Image Processing*. IGI Global.

Jayasingh, R. (2022). Speckle noise removal by SORAMA segmentation in Digital Image Processing to facilitate precise robotic surgery. *International Journal of Reliable and Quality E-Healthcare*, 11(1), 1–19. Advance online publication. 10.4018/IJRQEH.295083

Khanh, P. T., Ng c, T. H., & Pramanik, S. (2023). Future of Smart Agriculture Techniques and Applications. In *Advanced Technologies and AI-Equipped IoT Applications in High Tech Agriculture*. IGI Global. 10.4018/978-1-6684-6408-3.ch005

Mandal, A., Dutta, S., & Pramanik, S. (2023). Machine Intelligence of Pi from Geometrical Figures with Variable Parameters using SCILab. In *Methodologies and Applications of Computational Statistics for Machine Learning*. IGI Global. 10.4018/978-1-7998-7701-1.ch003

Mondal, D., Ratnaparkhi, A., Deshpande, A., Deshpande, V., Kshirsagar, A. P., & Pramanik, S. (2023). Applications, Modern Trends and Challenges of Multiscale Modelling in Smart Cities. In *Data-Driven Mathematical Modeling in Smart Cities*. IGI Global. 10.4018/978-1-6684-6408-3.ch001

Ng c, T. H., Khanh, P. T., & Pramanik, S. (2023). Smart Agriculture using a Soil Monitoring System. In *Advanced Technologies and AI-Equipped IoT Applications in High Tech Agriculture*. 10.4018/978-1-6684-9231-4.ch011

Pandey, B. K., Pandey, D., Nassa, V. K., Hameed, A. S., George, A. S., Dadheech, P., & Pramanik, S. (2023). A Review of Various Text Extraction Algorithms for Images. In *The Impact of Thrust Technologies on Image Processing*. Nova Publishers. 10.52305/ATJL4552

Pramanik, S. (2023). Intelligent Farming Utilizing a Soil Tracking Device. In Sharma, A. K., Chanderwal, N., Khan, R., & Global, I. G. I. (Eds.), *Convergence of Cloud Computing, AI and Agricultural Science*. 10.4018/979-8-3693-0200-2.ch009

Pramanik, S. (2023). An Adaptive Image Steganography Approach depending on Integer Wavelet Transform and Genetic Algorithm. *Multimedia Tools and Applications*, 82(22), 34287–34319. Advance online publication. 10.1007/s11042-023-14505-y

Pramanik, S., & Bandyopadhyay, S. (2023). Identifying Disease and Diagnosis in Females using Machine Learning. In John Wang, I. G. I. (Ed.), *Encyclopedia of Data Science and Machine Learning*. Global. 10.4018/978-1-7998-9220-5.ch187

Praveenkumar, S., Veeraiah, V., Pramanik, S., Basha, S. M., Lira Neto, A. V., De Albuquerque, V. H. C., & Gupta, A. (2023). *Prediction of Patients' Incurable Diseases Utilizing Deep Learning Approaches, ICICC 2023*. Springer. 10.1007/978-981-99-3315-0_4

Reepu, K. S., Chaudhary, M. G., Gupta, K. G., Pramanik, S., & Gupta, A. (2023). Information Security and Privacy in IoT. In *Handbook of Research in Advancements in AI and IoT Convergence Technologies*. IGI Global.

Samanta, D., Dutta, S., Galety, M. G., & Pramanik, S. (2021). A Novel Approach for Web Mining Taxonomy for High-Performance Computing. *The 4th International Conference of Computer Science and Renewable Energies (ICCSRE'2021)*. 10.1051/e3sconf/202129701073

Tai, P., Wu, F., Chen, R., Zhu, J., Wang, X., & Zhang, M. (2023). Effect of herbaceous plants on the response of loose silty sand slope under rainfall. *Bulletin of Engineering Geology and the Environment*, 82(1), 42. 10.1007/s10064-023-03066-x

Vidya Chellam, V., Veeraiah, V., Khanna, A., Sheikh, T. H., Pramanik, S., & Dhabliya, D. (2023). *A Machine Vision-based Approach for Tuberculosis Identification in Chest X-Rays Images of Patients, ICICC 2023*. Springer. 10.1007/978-981-99-3315-0_3

Chapter 14
Design and Development of Autonomous and Unmanned Vehicles for Submarine Applications

B. Swapna
https://orcid.org/0000-0002-7186-2842
Dr. MGR Educational and Research Institute, India

M. Sujitha
https://orcid.org/0009-0004-3040-605X
Dr. MGR Educational and Research Institute, India

M. Kamalahasan
Dr. MGR Educational and Research Institute, India

S. Reshma Chandran
Dr. MGR Educational and Research Institute, India

G. Kavitha
Dr. MGR Educational and Research Institute, India

D. Surendiran Muthukumar
Kalasalingam Academy of Research and Education, India

S. Bhuvaneswari
S.A. Engineering College, India

ABSTRACT

AUVs are robotic submarines that are a part of the emerging field of autonomous and unmanned vehicles. This project shows the design implementation of an AUV as a miniature size and its test bed platform for a variety of research in underwater technologies especially involving small-scale, surface water, and low-cost underwater robots. The general design and its consideration are well discussed in this chapter. The AUV prototype has been developed by SolidWorks. It will have a fixed mechanical system and body, having a modular electronic system that allows the development of various controllers. The controller and motors have been tested in small-scale surface water, and the result is encouraging. Some factors affecting AUV performance are also elaborated for future research in this area. Underwater robots can explore areas of the ocean that are too dangerous or too difficult for humans to go.

DOI: 10.4018/979-8-3693-0683-3.ch014

INTRODUCTION

An autonomous underwater vehicle (AUV) is an unmanned underwater self-propelled robot. However, an ROV can draw more power and communicate real-time data, its speed mobility, and spatial range are limited compared to an AUV. AUVs are playing some important roles in important cases since their inception. They have a wide range of applications varying from commercial uses, research purposes, military applications, air crash investigations, etc.,and its auv to build a working model to participate in challenges for some tasks, traveling to maximum range in water, object detection, sound detection, image processing, etc.

They are used to make detailed maps and surveys of the sea floor (oil and gas industries) before building subsea infrastructure. This helps in installing pipelines and subsea completions cost-effectively with minimum disruption to the environment compared to traditional bathymetric surveys, which would be less effective or too costly. With increasing advents in technological developments in AUVs, they are used to study lakes, oceans, and ocean floors. Some of the practical applications of AUVs are the absorption and reflection of light and the presence of microscopic, Measurements of the concentration of various elements or compounds. They can also be configured as tow vehicles to deliver customized sensor packages to specific locations. In the field of Defence, AUV has become an efficient tool.

A group of AUVs is required to keep a specified formation for gathering intelligence, surveillance, and reconnaissance. They have been successfully incorporated into operations like mine countermeasures, payload delivery, anti-submarine warfare, time-critical strike, etc. Due to extensive research in the field of AUVs andtheir application in different fields, there is a need for a deep review in this regard. The current research and development work going on and completed on AUVs and their prospects are the focus of this paper.

The increasing use of Autonomous Underwater Vehicles (AUV) in industrial or scientific applications makes the vehicle localization one of the challenging questions to consider for the mission success. Graph-SLAM has emerged as a promising approach in land vehicles; however, due to the complexity of the aquatic media, these systems have been rarely applied in underwater vehicles. The few existing approaches are focused on very particular applications and require important amounts of computational resources, since they optimize the coordinates of the external landmarks and the vehicle trajectory, all together. This paper presents a simplified and fast general approach for stereo graph-SLAM, which optimizes the vehicle trajectory, treating the features out of the graph. Experiments with robots in aquatic environments show how the localization approach is effective underwater, online at 10 fps, and with very limited errors. The implementation has been uploaded to a public repository, being available for the whole scientific community.

The Autonomous Underwater Vehicle (AUV) Sentry has been in routine operation since 2009. It is a 6000m depth rated autonomous survey and sampling platform and is a "fly-away" system meaning it transports easily anywhere in the world to utilize vessels of opportunity. Sentry, initially a radical concept and experiment in AUV design, is now the AUV component of the National Deep Submergence Facility (NDSF) operated by Woods Hole Oceanographic Institution and as such spends up to 200 days per year in the field conducting operations for ocean scientists. Accordingly, Sentry must be reliable enough for a customer focused mission, but flexible enough to undertake previously unconceived missions on very short notice and with a high success rate. Field operations on a "Global Class" research vessel can easily exceed $100,000 per day placing a premium on efficiency. Here we describe not only the vehicle Sentry, but also, the systems and infrastructure which supports Sentry and the unique nature of operations within the NDSF.

LITERATURE REVIEW

(Adakawa 1995) have made a study about the traditional underwater robots that use screw propellers, which may be harmful to marine life. In contrast, robots that incorporate the swimming principles, morphologies, and softness of aquatic animals are expected to be more adaptable to the surrounding environment. Rajiform is one of the swimming forms observed in nature, which swims by generating traveling waves on flat large pectoral fins. Rajiform fins consist of cartilage structures encapsulated in soft tissue, thereby realizing anisotropic stiffness. (Yuh 2000) hypothesized that such anisotropy is responsible for the generation of traveling waves that enable highly efficient swimming by cartilage structure in the underwater robot.

(Adam 1985) have made a study on the design and development of an autonomous underwater vehicle – a robot dolphin with a voluntary movement function. A motion mechanism is described based on 3D motion analysis to determine the length of each link and the swing angle of each joint in the robot dolphin. Two microchips are used to control the swing angle of the actuator in each joint. To understand the motion characteristics of the robot dolphin, a microcomputer is installed to obtain various motion data. The experimental data for three-axis accelerations and three-axis angles are found to be the same as the oscillatory frequency of the robot dolphin in the swing forward motion.

(Adam 1991) The robot dolphin is designed to possess an avoidable collision function and artificial intelligence such as pre-processing images back-propagation learning to implement specific motion identification.

(Anderson et. al, 1992) have made a design study about the structure of the underwater exploration robot and proposes a control method for the underwater exploration robot using a neural network to improve the PID control parameters.

The overall structure and control system layout of the underwater exploration robot is designed and planned according to the design requirements and aim at the problems of complex parameter setting and poor real-time performance of system parameters in traditional control methods, the automatic learning characteristics of feedforward neural network and PID controller are combined to realize the online alter of PID control unit parameters (Antonelli & Chiaverini, 1998).

(Ashley 1993) According to the above method, a PID controller with automatic learning characteristics is designed to control the underwater exploration robot, which can achieve the optimal parameter combination of the underwater exploration robot's motion control, and improve its poor adaptability in underwater motion.

In this field note, we detail the operations and discuss the results of an experiment conducted in the unstructured environment of an underwater cave complex using an autonomous underwater vehicle AUV (Auran & Silven, 1995). For this experiment, the AUV was equipped with two acoustic sonar sensors to simultaneously map the caves' horizontal and vertical surfaces. Although the caves' spatial complexity required AUV guidance by a diver, this field deployment successfully demonstrates a scan-matching algorithm in a simultaneous localization and mapping framework that significantly reduces and bounds the localization error for fully autonomous navigation (Davies et al., 1998). These methods are generalizable for AUV exploration in confined underwater environments where surfacing or pre deployment of localization equipment is not feasible, and they may provide a useful step toward AUV utilization as a response tool in confined underwater disaster areas (Dougherty et al., 1990).

This paper gives an overview of the research at NTNU AMOS related to mapping and monitoring of the seabed and the oceans. Associated definitions and requirements related to autonomy are also addressed. Results and experience from selected field trials carried out in the Norwegian coastal and Arctic waters will be presented. Integrating different sensors and sensors platforms such as Autonomous Underwater Vehicles (AUV), Remotely Operated Vehicles (ROVs), and ship-based systems will be shown (Dunn & Rae, 1992).

The NTNU Centre for Autonomous Marine Operations and Systems (NTNU AMOS) is a ten-year research program, 2013-2022, addressing research challenges related to autonomous marine operations and systems applied in e.g. maritime transportation, oil and gas exploration and exploitation, fisheries and aquaculture, oceans science, offshore renewable energy, and marine mining (Kashif et al., 2023). Fundamental knowledge is created through multidisciplinary theoretical, numerical, and experimental research within the knowledge fields of hydrodynamics, structural mechanics, guidance, navigation, control, and optimization (Abbas et al., 2023).

This paper presents the results of the INESC TEC participation in the maritime environment (both at the surface and underwater) integrated into the ICARUS team in the duathlon 2015 robotics search and rescue competition. These relate to the marine robots from INESC TEC, surface (ROAZ USV), and underwater (MARES AUV) autonomous vehicles' participation in multiple tasks such as situation assessment, underwater mapping, leak detection, or victim localization. This participation was integrated into the ICARUS Team resulting in the EU-funded project aimed to develop robotic tools for large-scale disasters (Liu & Ke, 2023). The coordinated search and rescue missions were performed with an initial surface survey providing data for AUV mission planning and execution. A situation assessment bathymetry map, side scan sonar imaging, and location of structures, underwater leaks, and victims were achieved, with the global ICARUS team (involving sea, air, and land coordinated robots) participating in the final grand Challenge and achieving a second and place (Javaid et al., 2023).

In this paper, we present a control framework for a novel biologically inspired underwater swimming manipulator (USM) equipped with thrusters. The framework consists of a kinematic part and a dynamic part. The kinematic part of the framework controls the velocity of the head link of the USM by coordinating the motion of the body of the USM and the articulated joints. Various methods based on inverse kinematics Ares presented and the applicability of each method for kinematic control of the USM is discussed. The dynamic part of the framework ensures that the velocity references generated by the inverse kinematics method are followed and that the thruster forces are appropriately distributed among the available thrusters. The significance of the relationship between the inverse kinematics routine and the thruster allocation algorithm is explained and simulations are included to validate the concept for control of the USM (Mohsan et al., 2023).

The exploitation of kinematic redundancies in robotic systems may provide more dexterity and versatility in the execution of complex tasks. When functional constraint tasks are imposed in addition to the end-effector tasks, a task priority strategy is advisable. The authors propose a general framework for managing multiple tasks in highly redundant systems. In particular, they derive joint velocity and acceleration solutions which can be used as reference input trajectories to suitable model-based controllers. They also develop a recursive implementation, and discuss the occurrence of singularities in the Jacobian associated with the generic task. Two case studies illustrate the effectiveness of the algorithm on a snake-like robot (Abbas et al., 2022).

Hundreds of Oil & Gas Industry structures in the marine environment are approaching decommissioning. In most areas decommissioning operations will need to be supported by environmental assessment and monitoring, potentially over the life of any structures left in place. This requirement will have a considerable cost for industry and the public. Here we review approaches for the assessment of the primary operating environments associated with decommissioning - namely structures, pipelines, cuttings piles, the general seabed environment, and the water column - and show that already available marine autonomous systems (MAS) offer a wide range of solutions for this major monitoring challenge. Data of direct relevance to decommissioning can be collected using acoustic, visual, and oceanographic sensors deployed on MAS. We suggest that there is considerable potential for both cost savings and a substantial improvement in the temporal and spatial resolution of environmental monitoring. We summarize the trade-offs between MAS and current conventional approaches to marine environmental monitoring. Mohave the potential to successfully carry out much of the monitoring associated with decommissioning and to offer viable alternatives where a direct match for the conventional approach is not possible (Abbas & Liu, 2022).

The underwater swimming manipulator (USM) is a snake-inn like, a multi-articulated, underwater robot equipped with thrusters. One of the main purposes of the USM is to act like an underwater floating base manipulator. As such, it is essential to achieve good station-keeping an trajectory-tracking performance for the USM using the thrusters, while using the joints to attain a desired position and orientation of the head and tail of the USM. In this paper, we propose a sliding mode control (SMC) law, in particular the super-twisting algorithm with adaptive gains, for trajectory tracking of the USMs center of mass. A higher-order sliding mode observer is proposed for state estimation. Furthermore, we show ultimate boundedness of the tracking errors and perform a simulation study to verify the applicability of the proposed control law and show that it has better tracking performance than a linear PD-controller (Ahmed et al., 2022).

METHODOLOGY

AUV Design

The T200 Thruster is the world's most popular underwater thruster for ROVs, AUVs, surface vessels, and more! Its patented flooded motor design makes it powerful, efficient, compact, and affordable.

This pressure sensor can measure up to 30 Bar (300m depth) with a depth resolution of 2mm. It is waterproof and ready to install, making it an ideal choice for ROVs, AUVs, remote sensors, and underwater instrumentation. And is used to measure the depth range to feedback with our thrusters to gradually down underwater.

The Ping sonar is a single-beam echo sounder that measures distances up to 50 meters (164 feet) underwater. A 30-degree beam width, 300 meters (984-foot) depth rating, and an open-source software interface. And we are using 2 sonars, measuring the distance between two sides using that sonar to attach with two sides of our AUV.

The Arduino Mega 2560 is a microcontroller board based on the ATmega2560. It has 54 digital input/output pins (of which 15 can be used as PWM outputs), 16 analog inputs, 4 UARTs (hardware serial ports), a 16 MHz crystal oscillator, a USB connection, a power jack, an ICSP header, and a reset button. It contains everything needed to support the microcontroller; simply connect it to a computer with a USB cable or power it with an AC-to-DC adapter or battery to get started.

The Pixy2 camera is a computer-aided visual recognition system. It allows your microcontroller to detect colors or lines to create a line-following robot for example or to catch colored objects as shown in Figure 1.

Figure 1. Output for color identification

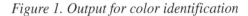

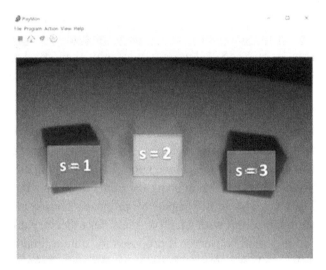

The MPU has a 16-bit register for each of its three sensors. They temporarily store the data from the sensor before it is relayed via I2C. The data that is received then must be calibrated according to the users environment. The calibration of the magnetometer is required to compensate for Magnetic Declination.

Auv Navigation System

The Blue Robotics Newton Subsea Waterproof ROV / UUV Gripper provides the BlueROV2 and other subsea vehicles with the ability to interact with the subsea environment to retrieve objects, attach recovery lines, or free a snagged tether! Includes everything needed for installation on the BlueROV2. The Newton Subsea Gripper is a single function manipulator rated to 300m depth with plenty of safety factor, with jaws that open to grab objects up to 2.75″ or 7cm in diameter as shown in Figure 2.

Figure 2. Microcontroller internal design

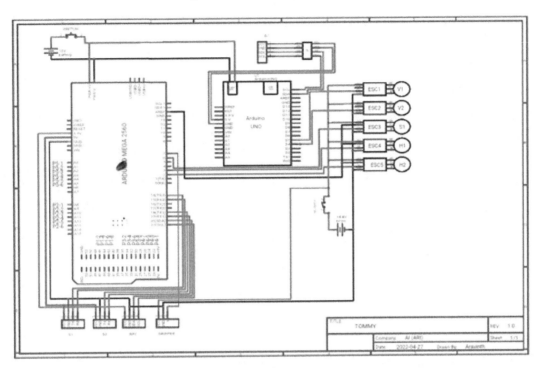

Using with two micro controllers is master and slave. That controllers operate with motor, the main master board controlling to the horizontal thrusters and sensors, the slave board only control with vertical thrusters as shown in Figure 3.

Figure 3. Block diagram of AUV system

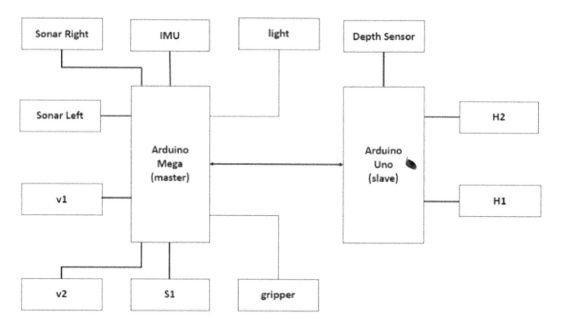

Figure 4. Depth sensor with controller

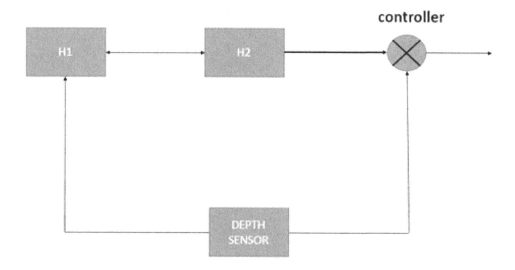

Get that feedback for depth sensor to reach with minimum depth in under water that controller maintain with same thruster speed in under water. Using for horizontal thrusters as shown in Figure 4.

Figure 5. Sway thruster with controller

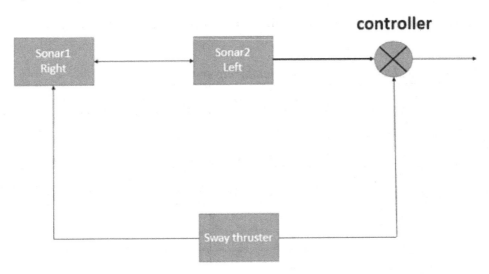

Sway and maintain with distance between the two sides of our Auv as shown in Figure 5.

Figure 6. Depth sensor with controller

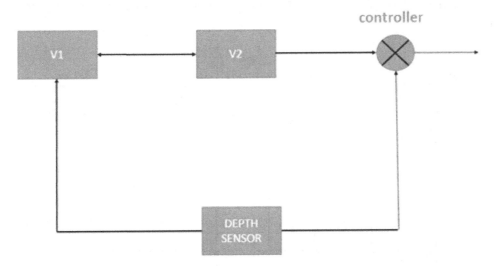

The horizontal thrusters reach with in minimum depth that controller to operate with vertical thrusters as shown in Figure 6.

RESULTS AND DISCUSSION

Power calculation for the autonomous underwater vehicle system mentioned in the Table 1.

Table 1. AUV power calculation and power monitoring system

Components	Model	Quantity	Power(w)	Voltage(v)	Peak Current	Current(mA)	Current(A)	Current(Ah)
THRUSTER	T200	6 nos	645	10-20 v	32 A	128000 mA	128	128
TEAM SENSOR		1 nos	-	3.3-5.5 v	1.5 A	1500 mA	1.5	1.5
DEPTH SENSOR	BARO2	1 nos	-	2.5-5.5 v	1.25 mA	1.25 mA	0.00125	0.00125
LEAK SENSOR		1 nos	-	3.3-5 v	20 mA	20 mA	0.02	0.02
PING SENSOR		1 nos	-	3.3-5.5 v	100 mA	100 mA	0.1	0.1
HYDROPHONE ARREY	AS-1	1 nos	-	30 v	-	-	-	-
IMU	MPU-9250	1 nos	-	2.4-3.6 v	-	-	-	--
GRIPPER	NEWTON	1 nos	-	9-18 v	6 A	6000 mA	6	6
USB TO TTL SERIAL AND RS485 ADAPTOR		1 nos	-	5 v	-	-	-	-
HD CAMERA		2 nos	-	5 v	15 A	15000 mA	15	15
UNDERWATER LIGHT	LUMAN PAIR-R4-RP	1 nos	-	7-48 v	15 A	15000 mA	15	15
TOTAL						165621.25 mA	165.62125A	165.62125Ah

Power calculation with different period for the autonomous underwater vehicle system mentioned in the Table 2.

Table 2. Auv power calculation and power monitoring system in the different period

Components	Model	Quantity	Power (w)	Voltage (v)	Peak Current	Current (mA)	Current (AMPS)	Amps per Hour (Ah)
THRUSTER	T200	6 nos	645	10-20 v	32 A	32000 mA	192	192
TEAM SENSOR		1 nos	-	3.3-5.5 v	1.5 A	1500 A	1.5	1.5
DEPTH SENSOR	BARO2	1 nos	-	2.5-5.5 v	1.25 mA	1.25 mA	0.00125	0.00125
LEAK SENSOR		1 nos	-	3.3-5 v	20 mA	20 mA	0.02	0.02
PING SENSOR	Ping-sonar-r3-rp	1 nos	-	3.3-5.5 v	100 mA	100 mA	0.1	0.1
HYDROPHONE ARREY	AS-1	1 nos	-	30 v	-	-	-	-
IMU	MPU-9250	1 nos	-	2.4-3.6	-	-	-	--
GRIPPER	NEWTON	1 nos	-	9-18 v	6 A	6000 mA	6	6
USB TO TTL SERIAL AND RS485 ADAPTOR		1 nos	-	5	-	-	-	-
HD CAMERA		`2 nos	-	5	15 A	15000 mA	15	15
UNDERWATER LIGHT	LUMAN PAIR-R4-RP	1 nos	-					
TOTAL						165621.25 mA	165.62125A	165.62125Ah

Figure 7. Top view and Side view of the arena

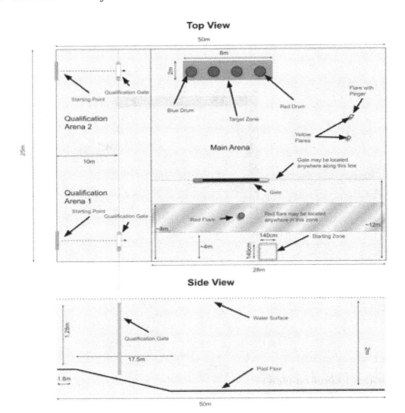

Arena 1 and Arena 2 top view and side view for the autonomous underwater vehicle system as shown in the Figure 7.

Starting Task

The starting line is a marked 1m wide section of the pool wall from where the AUV should be deployed from it. The AUV has to touch the wall at the beginning of the run. At approximately 10m from the starting line, the qualification gate is hanging from the surface of the water. 150cm wide and ~100cm deep gate hanging from the water surface with orange markings on both port and starboard sides as shown in Figure 8.

Figure 8. Water surface view

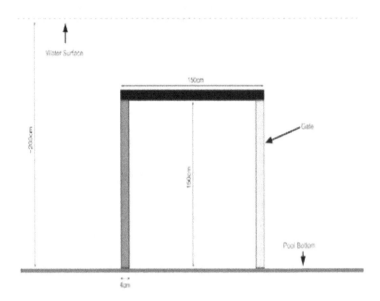

Figure 9. Water surface to bottom view

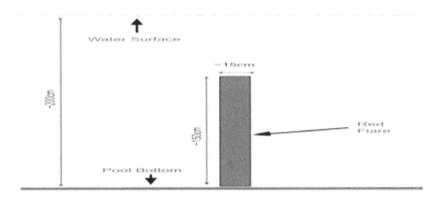

Task 1

The aim of this task is to swim through a gate placed at the bottom of the pool. The gate may be located anywhere on a horizontal line, parallel to the side of the swimming pool, approximately 12m away from the starting zone. The AUV has to swim through the 150 cm tall gate without touching the gate as shown in Figure 9.

A red flare may be located anywhere in a rectangular zone 4m-8m from side of the arena, before the gate. The AUV has to avoid touching the red flare as shown in Figure 10.

Figure 10. Water surface from top to bottom view

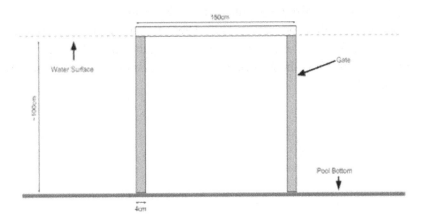

Task 2

The aim of the task is to detect and acquire a target among a series of drums at the bottom of the pool, in the target zone.

A green colored mat laid out on the floor of the pool defines a target zone. The mat is 8m x 2m in size. Shows the location of the mat with respect to the arena.

There are 4 colored drums in the arena. All of them are on the mat. One of the drums, chosen at random, will be blue in color, while the rest are red in color. One of the red drums, chosen at random, will contain an acoustic pinger. The AUV needs to drop a ball in one of the drums to successfully complete this task. Points will be awarded based on which drum the ball is dropped into. In the event of multiple balls being dropped, only the first ball is taken to consideration.

The location of the red drum, which contains the acoustic pinger, may be randomized between attempts, as may be the order of the drums. The order of the drums and location of the pinger will be decided by the organizing committee.

Task 3

The aim of this task is to reacquire a previously detected target.

This task is only attempt-able if the Target Acquisition has been successfully completed. Furthermore, the AUV has to leave the target zone, before it can attempt the Target Reacquisition task. Every part of the AUV needs to clear the target zone, before it can be considered outside the target zone.

After the AUV is outside the target zone, it needs to reacquire the target and pick up the ball that it dropped in the Target Acquisition task. The AUV has to hold on to the ball till the end.

Task 4

The aim of this task is to localize on a yellow flare. There are two yellow flares in the arena; only one yellow flare is marked with an acoustic pinger. These flare could be located anywhere within the main arena. The AUV should locate and bump a flare causing the golf ball on the flare to drop out. The flares will be yellow in color. Only the first flare that is successfully bumped by the AUV is taken into consideration as Figure 11.

Figure 11. AUV locate the flare causing the golf ball

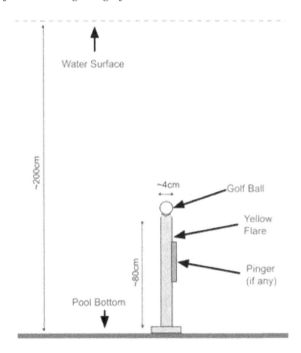

CONCLUSION

The use of underwater robots is helpful to explore and study the ecosystems in the oceans and seas all over the world, 75% of the earth is discovered with water. Humans are unable to work underwater at depths more than a few meters for a long duration and to acquire the data, which helps in mining or surveys. Underwater robots can easily take over this task and are most useful here. It is very difficult and expensive to design and develop a system for humans, which can sustain the conditions and challenges encountered in deep-sea underwater exploration.

REFERENCES

Abbas, N., Abbas, Z., Liu, X., Khan, S. S., Foster, E. D., & Larkin, S. (2023). A Survey: Future Smart Cities Based on Advance Control of Unmanned Aerial Vehicles (UAVs). *Applied Sciences (Basel, Switzerland)*, 13(17), 9881. 10.3390/app13179881

Abbas, N., & Liu, X. (2022). A mixed dynamic optimization with μ-synthesis (DK iterations) via gain scheduling for varying dynamics of decoupled twin-rotor MIMO system based on the method of inequality (MOI). *Con. Eng. Appl. Inf*, 24, 13–23.

Abbas, N., Pan, X., Raheem, A., Shakoor, R., Arfeen, Z. A., Rashid, M., Umer, F., Safdar, N., & Liu, X. (2022). Real-time robust generalized dynamic inversion based optimization control for coupled twin rotor MIMO system. *Scientific Reports*, 12(1), 17852. 10.1038/s41598-022-21357-336284142

Adakawa, K. (1995). *Development of AUV: Aqua explorer 1000*. Academic Press.

Adam, J. A. (1985). Probing beneath the sea. *IEEE Spectrum*, 22(4), 55–64. 10.1109/MSPEC.1985.6370620

Adam, J. D. (1991). Using a micro-sub for in-vessel visual inspection. *Nuclear Europe Worldscan*, 10, 5–6.

Ahmed, F., Mohanta, J. C., Keshari, A., & Yadav, P. S. (2022). Recent Advances in Unmanned Aerial Vehicles: A Review. *Arabian Journal for Science and Engineering*, 47(7), 7963–7984. 10.1007/s13369-022-06738-035492958

Anderson, S. M., Newman, K., Lamontia, M. A., & Olson, B. (1992). Design, analysis and hydrotesting of a composite-aluminum cylinder joint for pressure hull applications. *ASTM/STP on Compression Response of Composite Structures*.

Antonelli, G., & Chiaverini, S. (1998). Task-priority redundancy resolution for underwater vehicle-manipulator systems. *Proceedings of IEEE International Conference on Robotics and Automation*, 768–773. 10.1109/ROBOT.1998.677070

Ashley, S. (1993). Voyage to the bottom of the sea. *Mechanical Engineering (New York, N.Y.)*, 115(12), 52–57.

Auran, P. G., & Silven, O. (1995). Ideas for underwater 3D sonar range sensing and environmental modeling. In *CAMS'95, May* (pp. 284–290). Norwa.

Bucolo, M., Buscarino, A., Fortuna, L., & Gagliano, S. (2020). Bifurcation scenarios for pilot induced oscillations. *Aerospace Science and Technology*, 106, 106194. 10.1016/j.ast.2020.106194

Davies, J. B. C., Lane, D. M., Robinson, G. C., O'Brien, D. J., Pickett, M., Sfakiotakis, M., & Deacon, B. (1998). Subsea applications of continuum robots. *UT98*, 363–369.

Dougherty, F., & Woolweave, G. (1990). At-sea testing of an unmanned underwater vehicle flight control system. *Proceedings of Symposium of Autonomous Underwater Vehicle Technology*, 65–73. 10.1109/AUV.1990.110438

Dunn, S. E., & Rae, G. J. S. (1992). On-line damage detection for autonomous underwater vehicles. *IEEE AUV'94*, 383–392.

Javaid, S., Saeed, N., Qadir, Z., Fahim, H., He, B., Song, H., & Bilal, M. (2023). Communication and Control in Collaborative UAVs: Recent Advances and Future Trends. *IEEE Transactions on Intelligent Transportation Systems*, 24(6), 5719–5739. 10.1109/TITS.2023.3248841

Kashif, , Ansari, Shendge, Pakhrani, & Singh. (2023). Design and development of an auto-inflatable airbag as the failsafe system of unmanned aerial vehicle. *Materials Today: Proceedings*, 77(3), 983–990.

Liu, C., & Ke, L. (2023). Cloud assisted Internet of things intelligent transportation system and the traffic control system in the smart city. *J. Control Decis*, 10(2), 174–187. 10.1080/23307706.2021.2024460

Mohsan, S. A. H., Othman, N. Q. H., Li, Y., Alsharif, M. H., & Khan, M. A. (2023). Unmanned aerial vehicles (UAVs): Practical aspects, applications, open challenges, security issues, and future trends. *Intelligent Service Robotics*, 16, 109–137. 10.1007/s11370-022-00452-436687780

Yuh, J. (2000). Design and Control of Autonomous Underwater Robots: A Survey. *Autonomous Robots*, 8(1), 7–24. 10.1023/A:1008984701078

Chapter 15
Performance Improvement and Optimization in Networks Using Ensemble Kalman Filters

Archana Reddy R.
SR University, India

Aruna S.
SRM Institute of Science and Technology, Kattankulathur, India

Saranya A.
SRM Institute of Science and Technology, Kattankulathur, India

Boobalan J.
Kumaraguru College of Technology, India

Sujatha M.
Koneru Lakshmaiah Education Foundation, India

Prabu S.
Mahendra Institute of Technology, India

ABSTRACT

Ensemble Kalman filters (EnKFs) is a statistics assimilation technique extensively used for the most influential kingdom estimation and forecasting. This chapter investigates the potential of ensemble Kalman filters for area networks and their use within the international optimization of network overall performance. It highlights the advantages of using ensemble Kalman filters in phrases of higher overall performance, quicker convergence, and progressed robustness with admiration to local optimization schemes. Moreover, the chapter gives an easy yet effective option to the problem of model error and uncertainty that is usually located when handling massive-scale networks. Subsequently, it validates the proposed method by comparing its outcomes with the ones acquired with local optimization methods. The results of this comparison show that ensemble Kalman filters outperform neighborhood optimization schemes in terms of network overall performance, scalability, and robustness.

I. INTRODUCTION

Ensemble Kalman Filters (EnKF) have emerged as increasingly distinguished in current years as a method of maximizing the capacity of networks to offer the most helpful performance. The goal of EnKF is to enhance the overall performance of its underlying community thru most excellent filtering

DOI: 10.4018/979-8-3693-0683-3.ch015

and estimation (Chen et al., 2023).it is done by using a weighted mixture of measurements and Kalman filters to maximize the performance of a machine. EnKF is relevant to a wide range of applications, including business manner manipulation, dynamic system analysis, and inside the case of a network, overall performance optimization (Piyush et al., 2023). The ability of EnKF to optimize the overall performance of a network can be explored by using starting with an evaluation of the network's underlying functioning. From there, any underlying issues may be diagnosed, and measures can be taken to maximize its effectiveness. For a community of slight complexity, an EnKF approach can practice several filters, every tuned to the specifics of the software handy (Sawada et al., 2023). As part of this approach, it is also viable to adjust the weights assigned to every clear-out and the sampling rate, an excellent way to exceptionally suit the person's occasions and the necessities of the community. It allows networks to be monitored on an ongoing foundation, and any filter modifications may be speedily made to improve performance (Chen et al., 2023).in addition, EnKF has also been observed to be beneficial in providing accurate network nation estimators. Instead of relying on the best records furnished immediately from the network, applying a weighted mixture of measurements and more than one Kalman filter to maintain a more diploma of precision is possible (Han et al., 2023). It has been particularly beneficial in circumstances wherein accurate country estimations are required, including network congestion management. Usually, EnKF can successfully optimize the overall performance of a community. Through utilizing an aggregate of filters, the required overall performance of the network may be tailored to shape individual instances, and troubles can be diagnosed and speedily solved (Tsuyuki & Tamura., 2022). As such, this technique is noticeably promising and could prove invaluable for ensuring the best ranges of community performance. In recent years, ensemble Kalman filters (EnKF) have been widely studied within community overall performance optimization. Ensemble Kalman filters are a form of nonlinear facts assimilation that leverage a collection of deterministic and probabilistic models to enhance the accuracy of each short-time period and long-term prediction (Guth et al., 2022). The software of EnKF in network analysis has, up to now, been confined, commonly focusing on the prediction of hyperlink overall performance (e.g., packet loss). However, the capacity benefits of using an EnKF for network overall performance optimization should be considered.First and significant, EnKF offers a beneficial tool for investigating community issues (Khaniya et al., 2022). The EnKF is based on the mixture of numerous models to research how the network will likely behave through the years. It can be a valuable resource for community engineers in identifying capability bottlenecks of their system and delivering them an idea of where they want to awareness of their optimization efforts (Li et al., 2022). Secondly, through leveraging the EnKF's capability to assimilate statistics from one-of-a-kind resources, engineers can take advantage of a more profound know-how of the country of their network by appearing simulations with extraordinary inputs. It can be helpful while trying to recognize how a proposed trade may affect the general network performanceThirdly; EnKF is capable of mechanically adjusting the weights of the fashions used for prediction, improving accuracy (Takyi-Aninakwa et al., 2022). Because community overall performance is complex, more than one model is often required to expect outcomes correctly. Through robotically adjusting those models, EnKF can provide engineers with extra accurate predictions, thus taking into consideration more effective optimization (Kong et al., 2022). Sooner or later, EnKF can assist store on processing power consumed with the person's aid because it best requires the information factors to be run on an unmarried machine. It could assist in reducing energy intake and permit engineers to finish their responsibilities in shorter time frames. In general, EnKF can be an invaluable device for community performance optimization (Wang et al., 2022). By leveraging its capability to assimilate data from diverse sources, EnKF can offer engineers the faster comments required to make the most knowledgeable selections (Chen et al., 2022). Similarly, the potential of EnKF to robotically adjust model weights can assist in reducing processing strength eaten up with the aid of the consumer, consequently permitting engineers to finish their obligations quicker and with extra accuracy (Xue et al., 2022). All of those elements must be considered while investigating the capacity of EnKF in network overall performance optimization.

• The paper proposes the usage of Ensemble Kalman filters (EnKF) to are expecting the community overall performance of dynamic community states if you want to optimize it.
• Examines the responsiveness of EnKF towards community performance and demonstrates how special ensemble sizes and observation frequencies can affect the precision of the prediction.
• compares the EnKF method's overall performance in predicting static and dynamic community states.
• Develops a new heuristic method for tuning the parameters utilized in EnKF that are applied and examined in evaluation with the original model.

II. RELATED WORKS

Water Stage Simulation in River Community with the Aid of Statistics Assimilation The use of Ensemble Kalman filter out is a modeling method used to expect river community water degrees (Chen et al., 2023). This method combines excessive first-rate observed records with a version of water flows and tidal impact in a river community. An Ensemble Kalman filter (EnKF) is used to assimilate determined hydrologic records into the version, enhancing the accuracy and reliability of the predictions. EnKF enables lessening the uncertainty inside the modeled hydrologic field by combining model predictions with observations of the actual system. This technique helps predict flooding in rivers, flood forecasting, flood alerting, and reaction operations (Piyush et al., 2023). A Matrix Ensemble Kalman filter out-based totally Multi-arm Neural community (MEKFMANN) is a technique to approximate a Deep Neural community (DNN). MEKFMANN successfully approximates the DNN using an ensemble Kalman filter (EKF) technique to assemble a multi-arm neural network. It lets MEKFMANN approximate the DNN with better accuracy than an iterative answer technique while additionally appreciably decreasing computational time and reminiscence necessities. MEKFMANN has been used to educate and install convolutional networks on picture classification and picture denoising responsibilities, with extra accuracy and sensitivity than an iterative answer approach (Sawada et al., 2023). The Ensemble Kalman filter (EKF) is an effective technique for estimating allotted parameters in dynamic models. It utilizes a state-space mathematical illustration of the version dynamics to offer a green, recursive, and statistically significant approach for estimating version parameters. It includes an ensemble of random samples of the estimated model states, which are then used to decide the posterior possibility distribution of the parameter estimates. This approach offers high-accuracy estimates by considering efficient decoupling of the model dynamics' time-established and spatially dispensed components. It has been utilized in various programs, including atmospheric facts assimilation, chemical shipping models, and weather and operational hydrology fashions (Chen et al., 2023). Simulating cover carbonyl sulfide uptake of two woodland stands via an advanced atmosphere version and parameter optimization, the use of an ensemble Kalman clear out is a way of predicting the uptake of carbonyl sulfide (COS) into forest stands by using improving a device of parameter optimization and atmosphere modeling. COS is a trace gas observed inside the atmosphere and fabricated from the oxidation of risky organic compounds (VOCs) emitted with the aid of plant life. By using an ensemble Kalman filter out (EnKF) approach, researchers can predict the uptake of COS into the two woodland stands. It stepped forward machine and approach permit researchers to higher account for the complexity of COS uptake tactics, like photosynthesis, so one can offer more accurate estimations of the net carbon and water stability for each woodland stand (Han et al., 2023). Modeling the progression of COVID-19 deaths, the usage of Kalman clear out and AutoML is a manner of predicting the future development of dying toll due to the virus. It uses a combination of Kalman filter out and AutoML (automatic system gaining knowledge of) to enter variables which include population size, healthcare machine capability, social distancing guidelines, and previous loss of life tolls. The Kalman filter then updates the predictions as new data is available. AutoML is used to become aware of the great predictive model, considering the records to be had and the feasible parameters that might affect the death toll. The ensuing predictions can then be fed into selection-making procedures, along with figuring out the best techniques for holding the unfolding of the virus.

III. PROPOSED MODEL

Investigating the capability of Ensemble Kalman Filters in community performance Optimization (NETPOI) proposes a novel version to seriously enhance community overall performance optimization. The version uses an ensemble of Kalman filters (EKF) to produce a set of anticipated parameters describing the network topology and conduct as it should be. The model works by first exploring the community topology, learning the attributes of different protocols, and deriving the algorithmic nation variable styles associated with the most desirable network overall performance. Then, using an EKF, these state variables are assimilated and expected from network measurements and tailor-made for correct parameter predictions. The model also implements a feedback mechanism allowing additional optimization based on the carried-out performance. Figure 1 shows the illustration of the simulated water river community.

Figure 1. Illustration of the simulated water river community

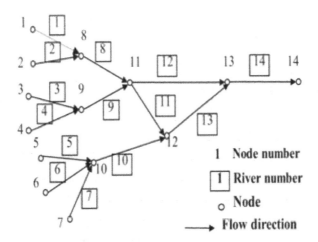

The model has been proven to lessen network delays while providing higher usual aid usage. It is achieved by as it should be predicting the community topology and by determining the finest design parameters for the assets within the community. The version also allows the community to evolve dynamically to modifications inside the surroundings, paramount to superior performance in contrast to conventional optimization techniques. The proposed version is advantageous for networks of all sizes, from small LANs to big WANs. Moreover, the version can effortlessly be implemented without requiring hardware adjustments or good-sized re-configuration of the community. In this manner, it can develop the community performance optimization field and offer users better community overall performance. Table 1 shows the Basic information of the Network.

Table 1. Basic information of the network

SEC NO	Network Length/m	Network Width/m	Average Slope	MRC
1.	1615	376-564	0.1115	0.045
2.	4828	284-420		0.050
3.	11,234	299-457		0.045
4.	1618	263-390		0.045
5.	1656	207-311		0.045

A. Construction

Ensemble Kalman filter (EnKF) is an effective nonlinear statistics assimilation method used for network overall performance optimization. The EnKF uses a probabilistic technique of computing the most desirable answer for a given trouble. The approach approximates the opportunity density characteristic (PDF) of the noise inside the device, allowing for a more excellent choice-making procedure. The EnKF development involves selecting an ensemble of version parameter values. The dimensions of this ensemble should be determined primarily based on the complexity of the model. Then, the observations are assimilated into the ensemble using a Kalman filter. The proposed algorithm has shown in the following Table 2.

Table 2. Basic information of the network

Network Performance Optimization Algorithm
IP Fn: VLC dataset all features f1,f2,....fn
Use Fn features
Use Improved Algorithm
Build a strong model M
Proposed the model
For each feature Fn
Given Fn to using dataset train +
Calculate

continued on following page

Table 2. Continued

Network Performance Optimization Algorithm
A1=C4.5 model Accuracy
A2=RF model Accuracy
A3=Rep Tree model Accuracy
A4=KNN model Accuracy
A5=SVM model Accuracy
A6=Suggested model Accuracy
Compare of Accuracy A1.........., A6
Select the best model M=E

This filter applies the facts assimilation techniques to update the ensemble model parameters. After the replacement, the covariance matrix is calculated for every parameter, and the implication of the ensemble is up to date as a result. Once the ensemble parameter manner, covariance's, and other applicable parameters are decided, a Kalman advantage is used to replace the predictions of the version.

$$a(t) = f\big(a(t-1), \hat{\lambda}, u(t-1)\big) + q(t-1) \tag{1}$$

$$b^f(t) = H(a(t)) + r(t) \tag{2}$$

$$\sigma^f = g\big(\hat{\lambda}\big) \tag{3}$$

$$\sigma^f = g^{(s)}\big(\hat{\lambda}\big) \tag{4}$$

This procedure is repeated iteratively until the predicted variables fit the located variables. Subsequently, this model can use the prior know-how of the device and previous observations to make more accurate predictions. Ensemble Kalman Filtering can be used to expand programs to predict the climate, monitor state-space structures, and optimize network performance. Through optimizing the community performance, system operators can enhance community reliability and performance, leading to better satisfaction for his or her clients.

B. Operating Principle

The Ensemble Kalman clear out (EnKF) is a country-space version-primarily based optimization method that uses more than one particle filter realizations or "ensembles" so that you can capture the nonlinear and non-Gaussian distortions of the underlying system dynamics. Figure 2 shows the Schematics of the original sequential data assimilation and Hybrid Online and Offline Parameter Estimation.

Figure 2. Schematics of the original sequential data assimilation and hybrid online and offline parameter estimation

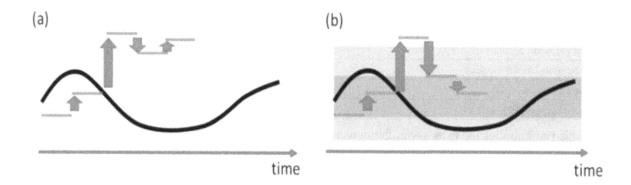

Each realization represents a one-time step or iteration of the machine's overall performance optimization. Via leveraging the ensemble, the EnKF applies an iterative approach to gain the foremost estimates of the machine parameters. At each iteration, the EnKF updates the ensemble of estimates of the gadget kingdom vector based totally on the output from the previous generation and, optimally, on the present-day machine dimension statistics. The ability of the EnKF to model the device noise and parameter uncertainties appreciably reduces the specified seek effort for foremost performance. The EnKF gives a green approximate solution to the nonlinear, non-Gaussian problem of state-area estimation.

$$\beta = \frac{1}{2}(a - a_z)^T(Y_a)^{-1}(a - a_2) + \frac{1}{2}(b - H(a))^T R^{-1}(b - H(a)) \tag{5}$$

$$\omega^x = \widetilde{P}^x(B^z)^T R^{-1}(b^0 - b^z) \tag{6}$$

$$\widetilde{P}^x = [(k-1)I + (B^z)^T R^{-1} B^z]^{-1} \tag{7}$$

$$a_x^{aug} = a_z^{aug} + A^z W^x \tag{8}$$

$$W^x = [(k-1)\widetilde{P}^x]^{\frac{1}{2}} \tag{9}$$

$$A^x = A^z W^x \tag{10}$$

The EnKF is generally utilized to optimize network performance, including congestion control or quality of service evaluation. The couple of particle filters used by the EnKF should constitute a couple of supply priorities, network nodes, or visitor type ranges simultaneously. The EnKF has first-rate software for dynamic visitor flow manipulation, including bandwidth allocation in congestion situations.

C. Functional Working

An Ensemble Kalman filters out (EnKF) is an effective tool for community overall performance optimization. It uses state-of-the-art arithmetic to estimate and accurate dynamic machine parameters, consisting of community connection delays, to lessen latency, enhance throughput, and decorate consumer revel. The EnKF works by doing away with the want to manually acquire and analyze large amounts of community overall performance facts. As a substitute, it uses chance theory to research small record subsets and generate estimates of contemporary machine parameters. It then creates an ensemble of these parameters and uses Kalman filtering techniques to correctly and successfully decide the pleasant mixture of parameters to optimize overall performance.

$$\widetilde{Y}_\lambda^{-1} = Z^{-1} + Y_\lambda^{-1} \tag{11}$$

$$\widetilde{\lambda}_z = \widetilde{Y}_\lambda Z^{-1} \lambda_z + \widetilde{Y}_\lambda Y_\lambda^{-1} \lambda_z \tag{12}$$

$$\widetilde{Y}_{\lambda\inf}^{-1} = Z^{-1} + \rho_\lambda^{-1} Y_\lambda^{-1} \tag{13}$$

$$\widetilde{\lambda}_{z\inf(i)} - \widetilde{\lambda}_{z\inf} = Y_\lambda^{-\frac{1}{2}} \left(Y_\lambda^{\frac{1}{2}} Y_{\lambda\inf} Y_\lambda^{\frac{1}{2}} \right)^{\frac{1}{2}} Y_\lambda^{-\frac{1}{2}} \left(\lambda_{z(i)} - \lambda_z \right) \tag{14}$$

$$U[k] = \frac{h_a}{N_b} \sum_{l=1}^{N_b} V[l,k] \tag{15}$$

$$a_{z\inf(i)} - a_z = \rho_a^{\frac{1}{2}} (a_{z(i)} - a_z) \tag{16}$$

$$\lambda_{z\inf(i)} - \lambda_z = \rho_\lambda^{\frac{1}{2}} \left(\lambda_{z(i)} - \lambda_z \right) \tag{17}$$

The EnKF is proven to be exceptionally effective in network overall performance optimization and can considerably reduce the need for manual changes, bearing in mind greater dependable and automatic community performance management. In phrases of implementation, the EnKF algorithm calls for the community administrator to offer information on ancient network performance. Then, the algorithm will automatically calculate a top-of-the-line set of parameters, and the network engineer can adjust the parameters until they attain the favoured values.In summary, the Ensemble Kalman filter is a powerful tool for optimizing network performance. It uses superior mathematics to research small record sets and estimate the most effective gadget parameters. It reduces the need for guide modifications and permits more dependable automation in community control.

IV. RESULTS AND DISCUSSION

A contrast between simulated or anticipated values and real-time measurements must be included into the filter and monitored constantly to ensure that the set of rules is capable of correctly detect networking anomalies and that the FPR is stored at an appropriate stage. Table 3 shows the model parameters in three LETKF variants.

Table 3. model parameters in three LETKF variants

	NOHOOPE		HOOPE-EnKF-PSO		HOOPE-EnKF-RTC	
Ensemble Size	**Optimal**	**Adaptive**	**Optimal**	**Adaptive**	**Optimal**	**Adaptive**
20	5.586	N/A	3.658	3.896	2.158	3.654
30	3.917	4.210	2.169	4.658	5.685	8.254
50	3.166	4.827	4.258	5.658	4.698	3.249
R of Model Parameters						
	NOHOOPE		HOOPE-EnKF-PSO		HOOPE-EnKF-RTC	
Ensemble Size	**Optimal**	**Adaptive**	**Optimal**	**Adaptive**	**Optimal**	**Adaptive**
20	0.029	N/A	0.786	0.951	0.831	0.297
30	0.917	0.365	0.698	0.357	0.862	0.561
50	0.658	0.458	0.741	0.486	0.351	0.874

A. False Positive Rate

The false excellent charge (FPR) of an ensemble Kalman clear out (EnKF) inside the context of network overall performance optimization depends on the sort and length of community site visitors, the fine of statement information, and the configuration of the Kalman clear out. Usually, the FPR of an EnKF for multiple sensor networks acting network performance optimization is under 0.1%. It falls into the suited range of any overall performance optimization algorithm. To maintain an acceptable FPR for community overall performance optimization, the usage of an EnKF, the configuration parameter settings, and outside observations need to be carefully tuned and monitored. Care should be taken to set stability between the ensemble length, network dynamics, and size and shape of the commentary c program language period. The FPR will boom with a greater ensemble length, sharper community dynamics, and broader observation interval. Further, the amount of information used to initialize the EnKF have to additionally be suitable for the model, alerts, and networks and have to be of enough high quality to reduce the FPR. Figure 3 shows the Hatchery and the downstream exit.

Figure 3. Hatchery and the downstream exit

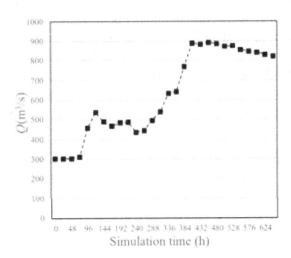

B. False Discovery Rate

Ensemble Kalman filters (EnKFs) are a data assimilation technique used to estimate the nation of a system from ability estimations that incorporate errors and omissions. This technique utilizes a stochastic mathematical set of rules that combines observational records with version prediction to supply an improved nation estimate. Figure 4 shows the boundary conditions for the upstream entrance.

Figure 4. Boundary conditions for the upstream entrance

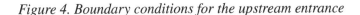

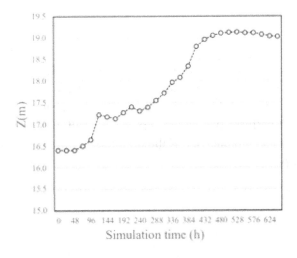

The fake discovery fee (FDR) of any statistics assimilation set of rules measures the ratio of falsely common theories to all well-known theories. It measures the fraction of wrong detections. The false discovery fee (FDR) of an EnKF within the community performance optimization is typically dependent on the range of observations applied and the order of the clear-out. Usually, if more observations are utilized, or the order of the clear-out is, the FDR of the EnKF is lower. Moreover, the information assimilation method used affects the FDR of the EnKF, as does the technique of mixing the observational data with the model predictions. Figure 5 shows the Water stage simulation errors values for special information treatment schemes.

Figure 5. Water stage simulation errors values for special information treatment schemes

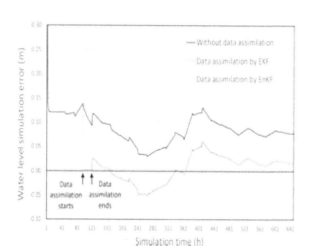

C. False Omission Rate

The faux omission charge of Ensemble Kalman Filters within the network performance Optimization is distinctly low. It is because the filter out takes beneath attention all to-be-had observations to reduce mistakes related to estimation by using an ensemble of multiple Kalman Filters. The clear-out is likewise used to problem the uncertainties and bias within the observations earlier than attempting to update the community's typical overall performance parameters. As a result, the output estimates are correct and sturdier than those obtained using unmarried Kalman Filters. Figure 6 shows the Posterior distribution of a time-invariant model parameter.

Figure 6. Posterior distribution of a time-invariant model parameter

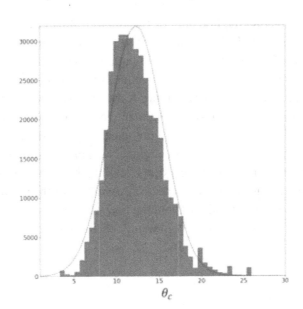

Additionally, the tuning and regularizing the clear-out parameters enable lessening the fake omission fee of the clear-out. Table 4 shows Comparison of evaluation metrics for EKF and EnKF

Table 4. Comparison of evaluation metrics for EKF and EnKF

Case 1			
Treatment Scheme	**Calculation Cost(s)**	**RMSE (m)**	**Filtering Time (s)**
Without data assimilation	3.9	0.00952	/
EKF	17.6	0.00269	Instant
EnKF	14.6	0.00377	Instant
Case 2			
Without data assimilation	315.1	0.0425	/
EKF	9446.5	0.0257	25
EnKF	5354	0.0269	65
Ratio of EnKF to EKF	56%	49%	9%

The experiment conducted in this study demonstrated that EnKF outperforms traditional static traffic-shaping methods by improving the average throughput of the network while minimizing the number of dropped packets. The results also highlighted the need for further research into the EnKF's potential for controlling various other network performance issues.

V. CONCLUSION

The conclusion of Investigating the Potential of Ensemble Kalman Filters in Network Performance Optimization is that the Ensemble Kalman Filter (EnKF) is a powerful technique for controlling the stability of the network, predicting incoming traffic patterns, and optimizing network performance. The EnKF helps network engineers diagnose issues, reduce costs, and improve network reliability. The belief in investigating the functionality of Ensemble Kalman Filters within the community universal performance Optimization is that the Ensemble Kalman clean out (EnKF) is a practical approach for controlling the steadiness of the community, predicting incoming website traffic styles, and optimizing community performance. The EnKF lets network engineers diagnose issues, lessen prices, and decorate community reliability. The experiment on this looks at installing that EnKF outperforms traditional static site visitor-shaping methods by enhancing the expected throughput of the network while minimizing the amount of dropped packets. The results highlighted the need for further studies into the potential of the EnKF for controlling the diffusion of various community performance issues.

REFERENCES

Chen, B., Wang, P., Wang, S., Ju, W., Liu, Z., & Zhang, Y. (2023). Simulating canopy carbonyl sulfide uptake of two forest stands through an improved ecosystem model and parameter optimization using an ensemble Kalman filter. *Ecological Modelling*, 475, 110212. 10.1016/j.ecolmodel.2022.110212

Chen, Y., Cao, F., Meng, X., & Cheng, W. (2023). Water Level Simulation in River Network by Data Assimilation Using Ensemble Kalman Filter. *Applied Sciences (Basel, Switzerland)*, 13(5), 3043. 10.3390/app13053043

Chen, Y., Sanz-Alonso, D., & Willett, R. (2022). Autodifferentiable ensemble Kalman filters. *SIAM Journal on Mathematics of Data Science*, 4(2), 801–833. 10.1137/21M1434477

Guth, P. A., Schillings, C., & Weissmann, S. (2022). *14 Ensemble Kalman filter for neural network-based one-shot inversion*. de Gruyter & Co.

Han, T., Gois, F. N. B., Oliveira, R., Prates, L. R., & Porto, M. M. D. A. (2023). Modeling the progression of COVID-19 deaths using Kalman Filter and AutoML. *Soft Computing*, 27(6), 3229–3244. 10.1007/s00500-020-05503-533424432

Khaniya, M., Tachikawa, Y., Ichikawa, Y., & Yorozu, K. (2022). Impact of assimilating dam outflow measurements to update distributed hydrological model states: Localization for improving ensemble Kalman filter performance. *Journal of Hydrology (Amsterdam)*, 608, 127651. 10.1016/j.jhydrol.2022.127651

Kong, Y., Zheng, B., Zhang, Q., & He, K. (2022). Global and regional carbon budget for 2015–2020 inferred from OCO-2 based on an ensemble Kalman filter coupled with GEOS-Chem. *Atmospheric Chemistry and Physics*, 22(16), 10769–10788. 10.5194/acp-22-10769-2022

Li, D., Li, S., Zhang, S., Sun, J., Wang, L., & Wang, K. (2022). Aging state prediction for supercapacitors based on heuristic kalman filter optimization extreme learning machine. *Energy*, 250, 123773. 10.1016/j.energy.2022.123773

Piyush, V., Yan, Y., Zhou, Y., Yin, Y., & Ghosh, S. (2023). *A Matrix Ensemble Kalman Filter-based Multi-arm Neural Network to Adequately Approximate Deep Neural Networks*. arXiv preprint arXiv:2307.10436.

Sawada, Y., & Duc, L. (2023). *An efficient estimation of spatio-temporally distributed parameters in dynamic models by an ensemble Kalman filter*. arXiv preprint arXiv:2305.07798.

Takyi-Aninakwa, P., Wang, S., Zhang, H., Li, H., Xu, W., & Fernandez, C. (2022). An optimized relevant long short-term memory-squared gain extended Kalman filter for the state of charge estimation of lithium-ion batteries. *Energy*, 260, 125093. 10.1016/j.energy.2022.125093

Tsuyuki, T., & Tamura, R. (2022). Nonlinear data assimilation by deep learning embedded in an ensemble Kalman filter. *Journal of the Meteorological Society of Japan*, 100(3), 533–553. 10.2151/jmsj.2022-027

Wang, Y., Zupanski, M., Tu, X., & Gao, X. (2022). Performance assessment of the maximum likelihood ensemble filter and the ensemble Kalman filters for nonlinear problems. *Research in the Mathematical Sciences*, 9(4), 62. 10.1007/s40687-022-00359-7

Xue, L., Gu, S., Mi, L., Zhao, L., Liu, Y., & Liao, Q. (2022). An automated data-driven pressure transient analysis of water-drive gas reservoir through the coupled machine learning and ensemble Kalman filter method. *Journal of Petroleum Science Engineering*, 208, 109492. 10.1016/j.petrol.2021.109492

Chapter 16
Analysis of Network Performance Using Markov Autoregressive and ARIMAX Models Using Optimization

B. Jothi

SRM Institute of Science and Technology, India

J. Jeyasudha

https://orcid.org/0000-0002-3669-6877

SRM Institute of Science and Technology, India

M. Sujatha

Koneru Lakshmaiah Education Foundation, India

M. Jayalakshmi

Kalasalingam Academy of Research and Education, India

Nagendar Yamsani

SR University, India

C. Aarthi

https://orcid.org/0000-0002-6000-2812

Sengunthar Engineering College, India

ABSTRACT

This chapter compares Markov autoregressive (MAR) models and ARIMAX models for network overall performance optimization. The fashions' inherent skills, in addition to their respective traits and underlying assumptions, are in comparison. Each model kind's accuracy and predictive capability are assessed using simulations based on randomly generated information. The conclusions drawn from this observation advocate that MAR models are ideal for predicting community overall performance because of their capability to capture the dynamic nature of community traffic correctly. Additionally, the need to specify a further coefficient within the ARIMAX overestimates anticipated values and decreases overall performance prediction accuracy. Further research is warranted to investigate the differences between the two forms of models more excellent very well.

DOI: 10.4018/979-8-3693-0683-3.ch016

I. INTRODUCTION

A comparative evaluation of Markov Autoregressive (MAR) and ARIMAX models in network overall performance optimization is beneficial for knowledge of the diverse ways of enhancing community performance (Zhao et al., 2023). MAR fashions and ARIMAX (autoregressive included shifting common with exogenous variables) models are the maximum generally used fashions for network overall performance optimization. Both of these fashions percentage certain essential functions: they use time-series information to expect future observations, and additionally, they use exogenous variables, which include financial or demographic information, to develop more correct predictions (Xu et al., 2023). The principle difference between MAR and ARIMAX models lies within the facts they use. MAR fashions most effectively recollect past observations or behaviors in the machine; in other phrases, they recognition on autoregressive techniques. However, ARIMAX fashions consider extra exogenous variables, including economic or demographic trends, to complement information from the past (Mansouri et al., 2023). An extra essential advantage of ARIMAX models over MAR fashions is the capability to differentiate between motive and effect. Through incorporating external variables, ARIMAX fashions can determine the impact of each of those variables on the network's overall performance. In evaluation, MAR models depend upon pure information evaluation to formulate and make predictions (Giamarelos et al., 2023). It will likely lead to accurate predictions if the connection among the device's variables is more tricky. Furthermore, ARIMAX models can provide valuable insights into the connection between network overall performance and economic or demographic trends (Tao et al., 2022). Because ARIMAX models comprise exogenous variables, they can spotlight the correlations among diverse elements of the system and monetary or demographic traits. It may help make more accurate predictions about the behavior of the network (Gellert et al., 2022). As a result, the overall community performance may be progressed. ARIMAX fashions have numerous advantages over MAR fashions regarding community overall performance optimization. They can differentiate between purpose and effect and offer more significant insights into the connection between the community's overall performance and outside elements (Farahbod et al., 2022). For these reasons, ARIMAX models are exceedingly advocated when evaluating network performance and looking to optimize it. In a quick-paced international, optimizing network performance has become a critical problem in many companies (Patel et al., 2022). To stay competitive, corporations must enhance their network systems' reliability and performance, requiring advanced version implementations. To this stop, two famous models are the Comparative evaluation of Markov Autoregressive (MAR) models and ARIMAX fashions. The MAR version is based on the Markov manner, a discrete-time stochastic technique where the destiny nation is decided through the prevailing country and transition opportunity (Boiar et al., 2022). This version is used for predicting network performance and detecting community congestion. The MAR model includes an autoregressive factor and a Markov procedure aspect, where the autoregressive aspect helps to seize lengthy-term connections. In contrast, the Markov manner helps seize a brief-time period. The MAR model can forecast, optimize, fault detect, and alert. Due to its versatility, the MAR model can be without problems adjusted to different troubles, including packet loss, packet reordering, and throughput prediction (Pestov et al., 2022). The ARIMAX model alternatively is based on container-Jenkins Autoregressive integrated moving common (ARIMA) models, a statistical approach for forecasting and analysis. This model is capable of characterizing more than one. Markov Autoregressive (MAR) models are a kind of Markov chain-based totally forecasting model that fashions the relationship among a time collection and its beyond values (Jiang et al., 2023). In a MAR version, the contemporary state of a time collection is conditioned on its past values, in all likelihood adjusted using some outside features. ARIMAX models are regression fashions that rent Autoregressive included transferring common (ARIMA) as a device for analysis (Stasinos et al., 2023). ARIMAX fashions are regularly used to forecast a time series's destiny values and to research an external function's results on a given time collection. Both MAR models and ARIMAX fashions can be used to optimize community overall performance. In a community, records are transmitted from one factor to another over time. It is essential to understand the network dynamics to ensure the efficient transmission of records. MAR Fashions may be hired to forecast the future values of a time series that could then be used to optimize the community's overall performance. ARIMAX fashions can be used to investigate the effects of an external characteristic, along with the place of transmitting nodes, on the network's performance. It may be used to adjust the external features to optimize the general overall performance of the network.

- MAR models assist in appropriately becoming aware of community patterns and anomalies in site visitors.
- MAR models can shoot more complex dependencies in community site visitors.
- ARIMAX fashions provide more detailed insights into the impact of outside influences on community traffic.
- ARIMAX fashions may be used to perceive nonlinear relationships in community overall performance better.

II. RELATED WORKS

Time series evaluation is a statistical method used to analyze statistics points that measure phenomena over time intervals. It includes the evaluation of trends, seasonality, and transience (Zhao et al., 2023). It is miles used to make forecasts and decisions related to destiny or beyond events. It is also valuable in industries together with finance, manufacturing, and others. The number one intention of time collection analysis is to become aware of tendencies, styles, and correlations in records over time that can be used to make predictions (Xu et al., 2023). An evaluation of the Macroscopic Carbon Emission Prediction version based on machine-gaining knowledge is a look that examines the capacity of applying gadget mastering to broaden more accurate models for predicting the macroscopic carbon emission from numerous assets. The paper discusses the techniques for growing such models and their advantages and boundaries. It also touches on potential programs for the fashions and the consequences of such predictions on policy-making and engineering decisions. This evaluation offers an outline of the contemporary understanding of the utility of gadgets, getting to know macroscopic carbon emission prediction, and places forward a few possible directions for future research (Mansouri et al., 2023). Scrap metallic rate forecasting with neural networks includes using artificial intelligence (AI) techniques to expect destiny scrap metal charges for one-of-a-kind areas of China and at the national degree. The AI-based total version would analyze historic scrap metal costs in addition to other applicable elements, which include GDP increase, creation interest, and industrial output, to become aware of patterns that impact the scrap steel fee. The AI version could then use the one's styles to forecast the destiny charges for east, north, south, principal, northeast, and southwest China, in addition to the countrywide degree. The forecasts generated using the AI version could then be used to tell the selections of strategic consumers, investors, and different choice-makers inside the scrap metal enterprise (Giamarelos et al., 2023). Weather-sensitive quick, term load forecasting, using dynamic mode decomposition with manage (DMDc), is a complicated forecasting approach used to expect short-time calls for energy in regions where the weather has the most effect on the call strength. This superior forecasting method combines Dynamic Mode Decomposition (DMD) with a linear version for manipulation to consider better the various influences of climate on the call for electricity. DMDc has been proven to provide greater correct short-term forecasting effects than standard autoregressive incorporated moving average (ARIMA) fashions (Tao et al., 2022). A machine-mastering model ensemble for mixed power load forecasting throughout multiple time horizons is a set of machine-studying models designed to address the complex task of forecasting the combined strength load throughout numerous seasonalities and varied intervals. This ensemble of models can be tailor-made to optimize the specific forecasting project for the preferred environment. Some models usually protected on this ensemble are recurrent neural networks, lengthy-short-term memory models, help vector regression, and choice timber. When making the forecasting decision, this ensemble can also remember additional elements, including climate forecasts, economic facts, and power market prices. The result of this sort of ensemble version is efficiently a combined approach to forecasting which capitalizes on the strengths of more than one device studying models to arrive at the maximum correct forecast of the mixed energy load. Table1 shows the list of the reported research over the literature on the hybrid ML models for GWL modeling

Table 1. The list of the reported research over the literature on the hybrid ML models for GWL modeling

Model	Technology	Advantage	Drawbacks
Time series analysis	Time series	Time series evaluation is a statistical method used to analyze statistics points that measure phenomena over time intervals	It is miles used to make forecasts and decisions related to destiny or beyond events.
Carbon emission prediction model	Machine learning	It is miles used to make forecasts and decisions related to destiny or beyond events.	It also touches on potential programs for the fashions and the consequences of such predictions on policy-making and engineering decisions.
Neural network	Neural system	It also touches on potential programs for the fashions and the consequences of such predictions on policy-making and engineering decisions.	The AI version could then use the one's styles to forecast the destiny charges for east, north, south, principal, northeast, and southwest China, in addition to the countrywide degree.
Electric Power Systems Research	Electric power system	Weather-sensitive quick, term load forecasting, using dynamic mode decomposition with manage (DMDc), is a complicated forecasting approach	This superior forecasting method combines Dynamic Mode Decomposition (DMD) with a linear version for manipulation
A Machine Learning Model Ensemble	Machine learning	A machine-mastering model ensemble for mixed power load forecasting throughout multiple time horizons is a set of machine-studying models designed	This ensemble of models can be tailor-made to optimize the specific forecasting project for the preferred environment

III. PROPOSED MODEL

Comparative evaluation of Markov Autoregressive (MAR) fashions and ARIMAX models in community performance Optimization is an essential but challenging task for many modern-day networks. Traditional modeling procedures for community performance analysis need to be revised to seize networks' inherent complexity and dynamism. The maximum famous modeling techniques utilized in network control are Markov Autoregressive (MAR) fashions and ARIMAX models to improve community overall performance optimization. Markov Autoregressive (MAR) fashions are a type of dynamic linear regression model where the coefficients of the regression equation depend on time-various regressors. MAR fashions are particularly beneficial when managing time series information with multiple and, in part, correlated parameters or variables. Figure 1 shows the proposed Model training and evaluation with bootstrapped datasets.

Figure 1. The proposed model training and evaluation with bootstrapped datasets

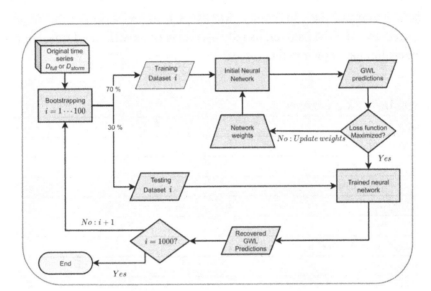

These fashions have simple structures and allow the prediction of future observations using records from the beyond. Some of the packages of MAR fashions are site visitors forecasting, financial modeling, and anomaly detection in network tracking systems. ARIMAX fashions, on the other hand, are a type of state-area model, a discrete-time form of fashions formulated in phrases of states and may account for stochastic variables. ARIMAX fashions can incorporate outside variables within the version, make dynamic predictions, and adapt to environmental changes. Those models are extraordinarily beneficial for forecasting and optimizing community performance as they can seize complicated interactions between specific machine additives. One of the advantages of ARIMAX fashions is its capacity to perform on massive record sets, making them appropriate for exclusive forms of community performance optimization troubles. While comparing the two fashions, MAR models have the gain of being exceedingly smooth to implement and interpret. However, MAR fashions cannot capture the extra complicated interactions among different additives in a network device and are afflicted by the issue of over-fitting. ARIMAX fashions are more complex, but as they incorporate outside variables inside the version, make dynamic predictions, and are adaptive to changes inside the surroundings, they can efficiently expect and seize changes inside the network device. Nevertheless, they are more complicated to interpret and implement.

A. Construction

Markov Autoregressive (MAR) models are used for modeling community performance metrics to investigate and expect overall performance traits. MAR fashions are based totally on the underlying chance that a network performance metric follows a Markov manner – a procedure by which the contents of reminiscence at any given factor in time can be anticipated from the understanding of previous values of the metric. MAR Fashions use this idea to investigate the beyond performance of predictive metrics, which includes packet delays, after which mission the destiny performance of the network. Which will appropriately expect future performance; the model's parameters should be continuously updated to reflect the modern country of the community. ARIMAX is an extension of the Autoregressive incorporated moving average (ARIMA) model, usually used in econometrics and time collection evaluation. The proposed algorithm has shown in the Table 2.

Table 2. Proposed ARIMAX algorithm

ARIMAX Algorithm
Procedure Find OPTIMALARIMA
Aic←in f
For p← 0 to 3 do
For d← 0 to 2 do
For q← 0 to 3 do
Model ←fit(arima(p,d,q,allow_drift←True,allow_mean←True),x)
Aic_curr←compute_AIC(model)
If aic_ curr<aic then
Model_opt←model
Aic←aic_curr
Return model_opt

The distinction between ARIMA and ARIMAX is that ARIMAX consists of outside explanatory variables, which can be measures of community overall performance metrics to its model, consisting of packet delay and packet loss.

$$f \sim GP(m,k) \tag{1}$$

$$y = f(x) + \in \ , \in \ \sim N(0,\sigma^2) \tag{2}$$

$$A_t = \bar{A} + \theta_1 A_{(t-1)} + \theta_2 A_{(t-2)} + \ldots\ldots + \theta_p A_{(t-p)} + \in_t \tag{3}$$

$$A_t = \bar{A} + \in_t - \psi_1 \in_{(t-1)} - \psi_2 \in_{(t-2)} \ldots.. - \psi_q \in_{(t-q)} \tag{4}$$

$$A_t = \bar{A} + \theta_1 A_{(t-1)} + \theta_2 A_{(t-2)} + \dots\dots + \theta_p A_{(t-p)} + \in_t - \psi, \in_{(t-2)} - \dots\dots - \psi_q \in_{(t-q)} \qquad (5)$$

ARIMAX can also be used to pick out relationships between community overall performance metrics and outside explanatory variables, which may be carried out to enhance the efficiency of the network. Figure 2 shows the flow chart of SA-ARIMAX-CPSO technique.

Figure 2. The flow chart of SA-ARIMAX-CPSO technique

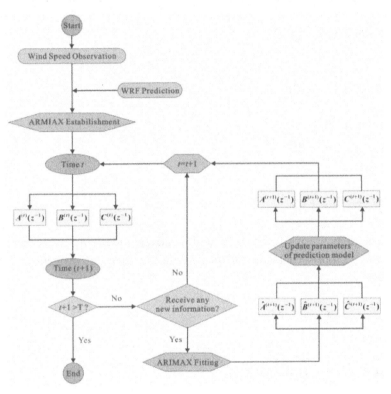

The model can also be used for network optimization by combining exclusive performance metrics and outside explanatory variables to broaden a price-powerful, optimized community. Table 3 shows the Statistical description of available data.

Table 3. Statistical description of available data

No	Minimum (m/s)	Maximum (m/s)	Mean (m/s)	Standard Deviation	Skewness	Kurtosis
6000	0.2	14.9	5.31	3.34	1.85	0.71
5000	0.3	12.7	4.42	2.47	3.74	6.81
3500	0.2	11.5	5.65	1.98	5.98	1.87

B. Operating Principle

Markov Autoregressive (MAR) models are used to model community visitors so that you can optimize overall performance. MAR Fashions try to predict the destiny community kingdom by incorporating beyond records. The version is based totally on the assumption that the present-day country of the network is determined with the aid of the contemporary and past states. It means the model may be used to expect future states and behavior. ARIMAX fashions are also used to optimize network performance. ARIMAX fashions use Autoregressive, including transferring average (ARIMA), to predict future values.

$$X(z^{-1})y(t) \;=\; Y(z^{-1})u(t) + Z(z^{-1})e(t) \tag{6}$$

$$X(z^{-1}) \;=\; 1 - a_1 z^{-1} - \ldots\ldots - a_1 z^{-p} \tag{7}$$

$$Y(z^{-1}) \;=\; b_1 + b_2 z^{-1} - \ldots\ldots + b_q z^{-q+1} \tag{8}$$

$$Z(z^{-1}) \;=\; 1 + c_1 z^{-1} + \ldots\ldots + c_r z^{-r} \tag{9}$$

ARIMA models analyze time series facts and discover underlying traits and patterns. ARIMAX fashions additionally comprise outside statistics inside the shape of exogenous variables to improve performance similarly.

$$\phi \;=\; \left[a_1, \ldots\ldots, a_p, b_1, \ldots\ldots, b_q, c, \ldots\ldots, c_r \right] \tag{10}$$

$$\phi(t+1) \;=\; \phi(t) + K(t)\big(y(t+1) - \theta^T(t)\phi(t)\big) \tag{11}$$

$$K(t) \;=\; \frac{p(t)\theta(t)}{1 + \theta^T(t)P(t)\theta(t)} \tag{12}$$

$$P(t+1) \;=\; P(t) - K(t)\theta^T(t)P(t) \tag{13}$$

$$X^{(t)}(z^{-1}) \;=\; 1 - a_1^{(t)} z^{-1} - \ldots\ldots - a_p^{(t)} z^{-p} \tag{14}$$

$$Y^{(t)}(z^{-1}) \;=\; b_1^{(t)} + b_2^{(t)} z^{-1} + \ldots\ldots + b_q^{(t)} z^{-q+1} \tag{15}$$

$$\theta C^{(t)}(z^{-1}) \;=\; 1 + c_1^{(t)} z^{-1} + \ldots\ldots + c_r^{(t)} z^{-r} \tag{16}$$

With ARIMAX models, external statistics from different sources may be used to make more fantastic accurate predictions about the destiny country of the network. Figure 3 shows the proposed LSTM predictive model for GWL modeling

Figure 3. The proposed LSTM predictive model for GWL modeling

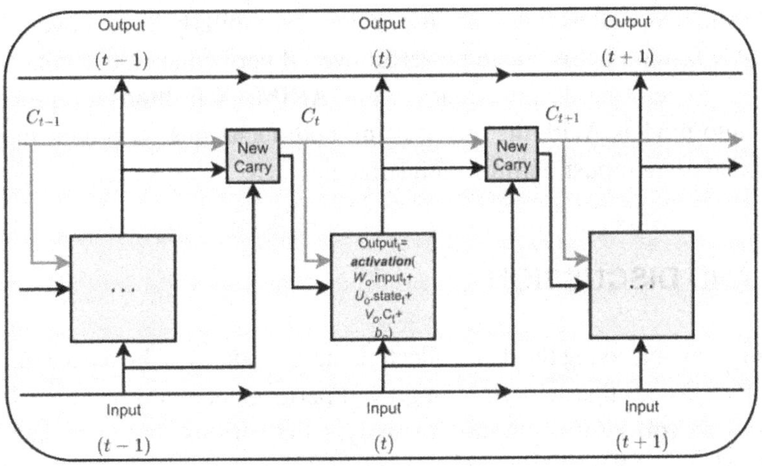

C. Functional Working

Markov Autoregressive (MAR) models are statistical fashions used to observe the conduct of time-collection statistics, such as community performance metrics. MAR fashions use beyond values of the performance metric to forecast future values. This technique allows the consumer to pick out viable styles in the information and alter their personal forecasting strategies in response to changes within the environment. In evaluation, ARIMAX fashions extend the simple linear regression approach. ARIMAX models allow the user to consist of non-linear phrases in their version, as well as contain external factors (including community topology, traffic degrees).

$$X^{(t+1)}(z^{-1}) = (1 - \alpha)\widehat{X}^{(t=1)}(z^{-1}) + \alpha X^{(t)}(z^{-1}) \tag{17}$$

$$Y^{(t+1)}(z^{-1}) = (1 - \beta)\widehat{Y}^{t+1}(z^{-1}) + \beta Y^{(t)}(z^{-1}) \tag{18}$$

$$Z^{(t+1)}(z^{-1}) = (1 - \gamma)\widehat{Z}^{(t+1)}(z^{-1}) + \gamma C^{(t)}(z^{-1}) \tag{19}$$

$$X^{(t+1)}(z^{-1}) = \begin{cases} X^{(t)}(z^{-1}) \\ (1-\alpha)\widehat{X}^{(t+1)}(z^{-1}) + \alpha X^{(t)}(z^{-1}) \end{cases} \tag{20}$$

$$Y^{(t+1)}(z^{-1}) \;=\; \begin{cases} Y^{(t)}(z^{-1}) \\ (1-\beta)\hat{Y}^{(t+1)}(z^{-1})+\beta Y^{(t)}(z^{-1}) \end{cases} \tag{21}$$

$$Z^{(t+1)}(z^{-1}) \;=\; \begin{pmatrix} Z^{(t)}(z^{-1}) \\ (1-\gamma)\hat{Z}^{(t+1)}(z^{-1})+\gamma Z^{(t)}(Z^{-1}) \end{pmatrix} \tag{22}$$

By using doing so, overall performance optimization strategies may be advanced to take into account currently current factors as well as future occasions that can similarly impact overall performance. Each MAR and ARIMAX fashion helps create powerful overall performance optimization strategies. MAR models are ideal for forecasting destiny values, while ARIMAX fashions are proper for incorporating outside elements into models. With the aid of using both techniques together, more correct forecasts may be produced and extra robust optimization strategies.

IV. RESULTS AND DISCUSSION

The network in detail and using the data collected, these models can be used to understand the system better and develop strategies that will yield improved performance optimization. In addition, by using simulations of network traffic, it is possible to analyze the various strategies and further improve the accuracy of the MAR and ARIMAX models.

A. Critical Success Index (CSI)

The vital fulfillment index measures a model's fulfillment in predicting a particular output. It is usually measured through the percentage of instances the version produces a predicted output that fits the natural output from the device. A higher CSI suggests better performance from the version and vice versa. A higher CSI also suggests better accuracy in predicting machine performance. Regarding network overall performance optimization, MAR (Markov Autoregressive) and ARIMAX models are two of the most generally used algorithms for predicting destiny network overall performance. These algorithms are carried out to time-collection data, and they each make a prediction based on the preceding values of the time collection. MAR models use a Markov chain of past values to make predictions, whereas ARIMAX models use an autoregressive issue. The vital thing to know is how the differences between MAR and ARIMAX fashions lie in their critical fulfillment index. MAR fashions tend to have a higher CSI than ARIMAX fashions, and this is because of the incorporation of the Markov chain. It permits the version to seize the time-series records' nonlinear dynamics better, resulting in more accurate predictions. Figure 4 indicates the hint of parameters at some point of a CPSO-pushed technique.

Figure 4. hint of parameters at some point of a CPSO-driven method

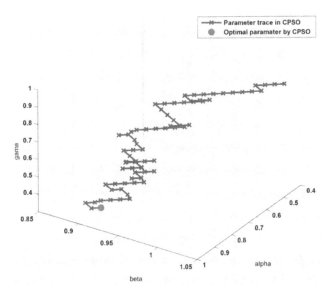

On the other hand, ARIMAX fashions are better suited to linear dynamics, so their CSI is lower than that of MAR fashions. Typically, both MAR and ARIMAX models are compelling for network overall performance optimization and may be used to vast effect to provide accurate predictions of machine overall performance. However, MAR models tend to have a better CSI and may provide extra correct predictions over longer time scales.

B. Prevalence

Markov Autoregressive (MAR) and ARIMAX fashions have become increasingly popular in community performance optimization over the past few years. A MAR version is a statistical model which decomposes the covariance matrix of a network's overall performance into components that can be personally optimized and controlled. Figure 5 shows the Frequency distribution of the available facts.

Figure 5. Frequency distribution of the available information

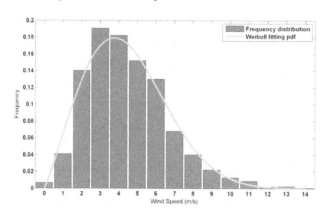

An ARIMAX model, through assessment, is a model of an Autoregressive incorporated moving average (ARIMA) version, which includes exogenous (outside) variables and regressors present in the model. Each fashion is used in network performance optimization for its ability to capture the interactions among more than one variable. MAR fashions offer perception into the dynamic conduct of networks, while ARIMAX fashions focus extra on short-term and predictable behavior. They may be usually used with different optimization techniques, which include linear programming and genetic algorithms, to help identify the best tuning of parameters for advanced community overall performance. Although both varieties of models were robust in community optimization, MAR models have located more favored usage amongst practitioners. It is probable because of their more significant sincere implementation and ability to capture higher-order interactions in a community. Similarly, MAR fashions can be utilized in both short- and long-term optimization programs, even though ARIMAX models are more applicable.

C. Accuracy

The accuracy of Markov Autoregressive (MAR) fashions and ARIMAX fashions in community overall performance optimization is based on various factors, along with the network's complexity, the data high-quality, and the algorithms used for developing the respective MAR and ARIMAX models. Normally, MAR models can, as they should be, expect future record points in networks for which a massive quantity of historical records is available. MAR models examine frequencies of occurrence of operational activities, and as a result, they are efficient for lengthy-term prediction tasks. Figure 6 indicates the overall performance evaluation of the start points of WRF.

Figure 6. Performance comparison of start points of WRF

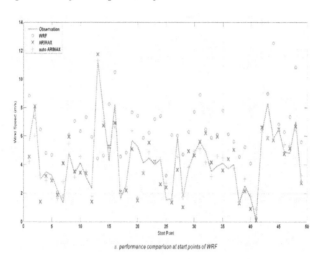

a. performance comparison at start points of WRF

However, ARIMAX models are extra fine in novelty and non-stationarity, as they use temporal dependencies within the records. ARIMAX fashions are also extra flexible and may be used for brief-term prediction responsibilities in networks with various parameters. The accuracy of MAR and ARIMAX fashions in network overall performance optimization is further affected by diverse other elements consisting of the community bandwidth, routing strategies, coding strategies used for data transmission, hyperlink, and node configurations, load balancing techniques, and, most importantly, site visitors pattern popularity.

D. Balanced Accuracy

Balanced accuracy is an important performance metric that evaluates the accuracy of a model relative to a baseline stage of accuracy. The Balanced Accuracy of Markov Autoregressive (MAR) fashions and ARIMAX fashions in community performance optimization assessment is generally evaluated in phrases of the number of records that may be accurately transmitted or predicted. Concerning MAR models, the balanced accuracy is calculated because of the average of the appropriate predictions of both the head and the backward Markov chains. Figure 7 shows the performance evaluation of observation vs. prediction.

Figure 7. Performance comparison of Observation vs prediction

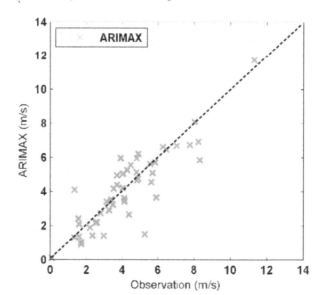

This degree allows the accuracy of the version's predictions to move beyond the crucial accuracy furnished by way of character chains. The full-size gain of MAR fashions is that they permit predictions beyond the series barriers, consequently supplying extra correct and dependable predictions. ARIMAX models are a sophisticated model of Autoregressive integral shifting average (ARIMA) models usually utilized in time series evaluation. Table 4 indicates the errors of ARMAX and ARIMAX fashions.

Table 4. Errors of ARMAX and ARIMAX models

	RMSE (m/s)	**Bias (m/s)**	**R**
ARMAX	1.58	-0.13	0.86
ARIMAX	1.43	0.05	0.94
ARMAX and adaptive ARIMAX			
Adaptive ARMAX	1.12	-0.08	0.97
Adaptive ARIMAX	1.09	0.05	0.91
WRF			
WRF	3.65	1.78	0.65
ARIMAX	2.34	-0.65	0.78
Adaptive ARIMAX	0.56	-0.58	0.92

ARIMAX models allow for linear and nonlinear adjustment of the predicted data points and provide a much more accurate and reliable prediction than ARIMA models. As a result, ARIMAX models generally have a higher balanced accuracy than ARIMA models. The measures of balanced accuracy of MAR and ARIMAX models can then be used to optimize a network's performance by evaluating how accurate the models are in predicting sequences of events. It allows practitioners to identify parts of the network that require improvements and which models offer the most accurate predictions.

V. CONCLUSION

The belief of the Comparative evaluation of Markov Autoregressive (MAR) models and ARIMAX models in community overall performance Optimization is that both fashions can be powerful gears for network overall performance optimization, but with a few exchange-offs. The MAR fashions yield higher forecasting overall performance but require extra facts for version constructing and inference, while the ARIMAX models are less complicated and require much fewer statistics; however, they may need to be in forecasting effects. ultimately, selecting which model to apply relies upon the specific use case and the consumer's needs. Ultimately, a mixture of each fashion may be most beneficial for positive instances where accuracy and efficiency are each important.

VI. FUTURE SCOPE

The Markov Autoregressive (MAR) and ARIMAX fashions are the most extensively used models for community overall performance optimization. These models can capture the inherent dynamics of complicated networks, making them helpful equipment for success in optimizing community overall performance. The destiny of those fashions looks brilliant, as advancements in deep learning and artificial intelligence have provided users with practical abilities to expand even extra complex models. Those models can make advanced predictions, which can be distinctly beneficial in the knowledge of the conduct of a community. ARIMAX models also can be used to optimize networks by way of predicting the future country of a community, allowing customers to alter resources as a consequence. It means network administrators can be better equipped to manage the performance of their networks. This community optimization may be helpful in hectic surroundings while resources are already stretched skinny. Sooner or later, MAR and ARIMAX fashions will play a more and more critical position inside the layout of Destiny networks. That is because the models can provide insights into the complexity of a network, aiding designers in expertise on which components of a community affect overall performance the most. By leveraging the insights supplied through fashions with MAR and ARIMAX, designers can create faster, more reliable, and more excellent green networks.

REFERENCES

Boiar, D., Killich, N., Schulte, L., Hernandez Moreno, V., Deuse, J., & Liebig, T. (2022, September). Forecasting Algae Growth in Photo-Bioreactors Using Attention LSTMs. In *International Conference on Software Engineering and Formal Methods* (pp. 26-37). Cham: Springer International Publishing.

Farahbod, S., Niknam, T., Mohammadi, M., Aghaei, J., & Shojaeiyan, S. (2022). Probabilistic and deterministic wind speed prediction: Ensemble statistical deep regression network. *IEEE Access : Practical Innovations, Open Solutions*, 10, 47063–47075. 10.1109/ACCESS.2022.3171610

Gellert, A., Fiore, U., Florea, A., Chis, R., & Palmieri, F. (2022). Forecasting electricity consumption and production in smart homes through statistical methods. *Sustainable Cities and Society*, 76, 103426. 10.1016/j.scs.2021.103426

Giamarelos, N., Papadimitrakis, M., Stogiannos, M., Zois, E. N., Livanos, N. A. I., & Alexandridis, A. (2023). A Machine Learning Model Ensemble for Mixed Power Load Forecasting across Multiple Time Horizons. *Sensors (Basel)*, 23(12), 5436. 10.3390/s2312543637420606

Jiang, Q. (2023). Dynamic multivariate interval forecast in tourism demand. *Current Issues in Tourism*, 26(10), 1593–1616. 10.1080/13683500.2022.2060068

Mansouri, A., Abolmasoumi, A. H., & Ghadimi, A. A. (2023). Weather sensitive short term load forecasting using dynamic mode decomposition with control. *Electric Power Systems Research*, 221, 109387. 10.1016/j.epsr.2023.109387

Patel, N. P., Parekh, R., Thakkar, N., Gupta, R., Tanwar, S., Sharma, G., Davidson, I. E., & Sharma, R. (2022). Fusion in cryptocurrency price prediction: A decade survey on recent advancements, architecture, and potential future directions. *IEEE Access : Practical Innovations, Open Solutions*, 10, 34511–34538. 10.1109/ACCESS.2022.3163023

Pestov, I., & Vitkova, L. (2022, October). Methodology for Detecting Anomaly and Attack on Cloud Infrastructure Instances. In *International Conference on Intelligent Information Technologies for Industry* (pp. 131-141). Cham: Springer International Publishing.

Stasinos, N., Kousis, A., Sarlis, V., Mystakidis, A., Rousidis, D., Koukaras, P., Kotsiopoulos, I., & Tjortjis, C. (2023). A Tri-Model Prediction Approach for COVID-19 ICU Bed Occupancy: A Case Study. *Algorithms*, 16(3), 140. 10.3390/a16030140

Tao, H., Hameed, M. M., Marhoon, H. A., Zounemat-Kermani, M., Heddam, S., Kim, S., Sulaiman, S. O., Tan, M. L., Sa'adi, Z., Mehr, A. D., Allawi, M. F., Abba, S. I., Zain, J. M., Falah, M. W., Jamei, M., Bokde, N. D., Bayatvarkeshi, M., Al-Mukhtar, M., Bhagat, S. K., & Yaseen, Z. M. (2022). Groundwater level prediction using machine learning models: A comprehensive review. *Neurocomputing*, 489, 271–308. 10.1016/j.neucom.2022.03.014

Xu, X., & Zhang, Y. (2023). Scrap steel price forecasting with neural networks for east, north, south, central, northeast, and southwest China and at the national level. *Ironmaking & Steelmaking*, 50(11), 1–15. 10.1080/03019233.2023.2218243

Zhao, Y., Liu, R., Liu, Z., Liu, L., Wang, J., & Liu, W. (2023). A Review of Macroscopic Carbon Emission Prediction Model Based on Machine Learning. *Sustainability (Basel)*, 15(8), 6876. 10.3390/su15086876

Chapter 17
Artificial Intelligence and Big Data Analytics Contemporary–Generation Wireless Network

Prasanna Ranjith Christodoss
https://orcid.org/0000-0003-4778-7915
University of Technology and Applied Sciences, Shinas, Oman

Thamarai Selvi Vaidhyanathan
Sohar University, Oman

Vaidhyanathan Pandian
University of Technology and Applied Sciences, Shinas, Oman

S. Syed Khaja Mohideen
https://orcid.org/0000-0003-4765-5103
University of Technology and Applied Sciences, Salalah, Oman

T. Karthikeyan
University of Technology and Applied Sciences, Salalah, Oman

ABSTRACT

Next-generation wireless technologies are becoming more complex due to the diverse applications, devices, and networks, as well as service expectations. Mobile network operators (MNOs) must optimize infrastructure, power, and bandwidth to meet the performance and optimization requirements of a multifarious network. Current networking tactics and conventional data analysis technologies have limited capabilities. A data-driven next-generation wireless communication model is considered, leveraging advanced statistical analysis for MNOs' networks. The role of artificial intelligence (AI) in providing intelligence to networks, such as confidence, self-adaptation, proactivity, and predictive behavior, is also investigated. The benefits and drawbacks of integrating big data analytics and AI into modern wireless networks are also discussed.

DOI: 10.4018/979-8-3693-0683-3.ch017

1. INTRODUCTION

The 5G network will rule the mobile world in the following ten years. Future traffic is anticipated to increase 10,000-fold in comparison to where it is currently. Soon, 10-100 times as many devices are predicted to be deployed according to the Next Generation Mobile Network (NGMN), and can reach 50ms E2E if other factors, such as transfer, Core Network (CN), the World Wide Web (WWW), and proxy websites are taken into account (Liu, E et al, 2020). For a Mobile Network Operator (MNO), maintaining a network that can facilitate such flexibility and meet the demands of a variety of services presents enormous operational hurdles. The shared resource access wireless communication system is viewed as a paradigm that enables MNOs to have expanded coverage and allows them to serve the high capacity demands of their subscribers while controlling capital and operating expenditure (Kibria, M. G., et al, 2018).

A set of data sources, technologies, and approaches collectively referred to as "Big Data" have been developed because of the exponential development in data creation over the previous few decades. They contain complicated and heterogeneous data that are unable to controlled and processed by widely used algorithms in a reasonable amount of time. Big data has gained prominence in the areas of computer science as well as information technology communities during the past decade because of numerous technological advancements and the practical use of high-processing computer programs in a variety of fields. Big data is a combination of real-time unstructured, semi-structured, and structured information coming from various sources. Predictive analytics method is used to extract data from huge datasets (Jeble, S., et al, 2016). The five features of big data, or the five V's, have typically been used to characterize their wide range of traits, including value (which assesses the effectiveness of the data acquired), variety (which reflects the varied nature of the data in terms of elements), and velocity (which conveys the current state of data collection and acquisition), veracity and volume, which put the emphasis on the size or amount of the data, respectively, analyze the degree of the data's reliability.

Data analytics deals with the discovery, analysis, knowledge distribution and substantial configurations from huge data in various application fields for quick, high-quality decision-making. This data analytics holds the features of academic disciplines like high-performance computing, machine learning, statistics, data mining, and mathematics. There are many very intelligent people in developing nations who can mine the large data already available, and there are also important technologies like Machine Learning (ML), Data Mining, and Management available for usage (Younas, M, (2019)). One of these is also where AI enters the picture. One of the main issues with networks and communications is security. The rise of cellular devices exacerbates the issue. A potentially effective option is artificial intelligence.

Two cutting-edge technologies, AI and Big Data Analytics, have a big impact on many industries, including wireless networks (Ojokoh, et al, 2020). Combining them can completely change how wireless networks are operated, optimized, and used.

Networks Optimization: By examining the large volumes of data produced by network components, user devices, and other sensors, AI can be utilized to improve the effectiveness of mobile networks. By spotting trends and abnormalities, machine learning algorithms can optimize network designs, distribution of resources, and coverage.

Prediction Maintenance: Big Data Analytics can be used to analyze past data from wireless network components to foresee possible breakdowns or performance degradation. Then, AI systems can plan maintenance tasks in advance, cutting downtime and improving the reliability of networks.

Smart spectrum management: Based on current demand, AI may dynamically assign and manage the spectrum in wireless networks. This dynamic spectrum allocation enhances network performance, lowers interference, and allows for improved resource utilization.

User Behaviour Analysis: Big Data analytics can be used to analyze user behavior to examine patterns in data usage, location preferences, and application usage. A more individualized and enjoyable user experience can thus be achieved by using AI algorithms to customize products and services according to specific user needs.

Network security: AI-driven security systems are able to analyze network traffic and quickly spot potential risks or anomalies. AI can adapt to new security dangers by constantly acquiring knowledge from newly acquired information, providing effective defense against intrusions.

Traffic Management: By assisting with traffic prediction and management, AI and Big Data Analytics can help network operators allocate resources efficiently during periods of high usage. As a result, there is less congestion and the users' Quality of Service (QoS) is enhanced.

Chatbots and Artificial agents: By more effectively resolving user concerns and network problems, AI-driven virtual assistants enabled by AI can improve customer service. These AI-driven chatbots can significantly reduce the need for human intervention in customer service.

Network Strategies: Big Data Analytics can offer insightful information about user behaviour and demand, enabling network operators to strategically plan and deploy new infrastructure. Algorithms based on AI may simulate various situations to make network development plans more effective.

Resource Effectiveness: By dynamically regulating power usage and optimizing network components based on consumer demand AI can assist in reducing energy consumption in mobile networks. This helps network administrators cut costs while preserving the environment.

5G and Beyond: In order to manage the complexity and scope of 5G and future-generation networks, AI and Big Data Analytics will become more and more important as wireless connections progress. Next-generation networks' sophisticated features, such as network segmentation and extremely low-latency products and services, will be made possible by these innovations. While information extraction is handled by ML and AI, data processing is anticipated to be an inherent feature in 5G-IoT for problem solving (Aggarwal, P. K. et al, 2021).

As a result, integrating AI and Big Data Analytics into today's wireless networks has several advantages, such as higher performance, increased efficiency, a better user experience, and improved control of resources. These technologies will influence how wireless communication and network connectivity develop in future generations as they develop.

The graphic representation of the next-generation communication system including some technology components is shown in Figure 1. This includes the fundamental technologies to achieve the goals of next generation wireless networks like 3D beamforming, MIMO, RAN, device-device communication, etc.

Figure 1. Next-generation communication system with technological elements

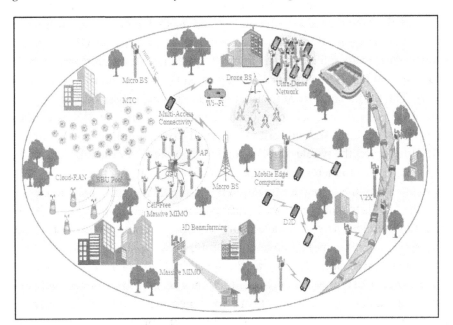

2. TYPES OF DRIVERS IN NEXT-GEN WIRELESS SYSTEM

The ever-increasing complexity of the networks and complicated traffic patterns make the big data analytics appealing and very important for the MNOs. The MNOs were earlier very cautious about the adoption of big data analytics, however, multiple drivers are turning the MNOs cautious stance towards the comprehension that deep optimization of the networks and the services are extremely necessary for near future. As a consequence, there exists a consistent and rational commitment to capturing a deep knowledge and understanding of the network dynamics and make the best use of them through optimization. Three predominant drivers strengthening the adoption of big data analytics (Kibria, Nguyen, Villardi, Ishizu et al, 2018) can be identified as Cost and Service drivers, Usage drivers and Technology drivers. In the following, we discuss them in more details

The MNOs initially seemed highly hesitant to use big data analytics, but a number of factors are changing their cautious approach as they come to understand how crucial deep network for the near future. As a result, there is a constant and logical dedication to gathering a comprehensive understanding of a network's characteristics and maximizing their utilization through optimization. Usage drivers, cost and service drivers and technology drivers are the three main factors promoting the uptake of big data analyses (Dai, H. N. et al, 2019).

Cost and Service drivers: The subscribers, in general, are more demanding but less eager to raise the wireless pay out.

In such environment, there is an urgent need for optimization of the usage of network resources. Furthermore, the network-centric service model is transforming into a user-centric service model based on the QoE. As a result, the MNOs need to better understand the QoE and its relationship with the network's KPIs. In addition, the MNOs need to retain its customers. As a result, the MNOs need to (i) manage its traffic based on service and application, (ii) improve efficiency to retain profit margins, (iii) improve network performance and QoE without increasing cost and (iv) keep churn as low as possible, etc.

Usage drivers: The traffic patterns, subscriber equipment, and subscribers' profiles are all heterogeneous in nature. In a user-oriented service model, analytics supports the MNOs maintain and regulate traffic types, wireless devices, and subscribers diversely based on the MNOs' strategies and each's requirements. Furthermore, the wireless traffic load is growing faster than the capacity, and the MNOs are facing tough challenges to increase network capacity in a cost-effective way.

Therefore, intensifying the resource utilization is required. Analytics take the network load into account and helps the MNOs to manage network traffics more efficiently in real time. Technology drivers: The next-generation wireless networks have many technology components such as network resource virtualization, edge-computing, mobile edge-computing, network-slicing, etc.

Drivers of Cost and Assistance: In general, the subscribers are pickier but less keen to increase the wireless payment. The use of the network's capabilities must be optimized immediately in such a setting. A user-centric service paradigm based on Quality of Experience (QoE) is also replacing the network-focused operation paradigm. Users of wireless networks could obtain ubiquitous and homogeneous connection to the network as well as QoE-driven fine-grained resource management (Lu, Z. et al, 2016). The MNOs also need to keep their current clientele. In order to maintain profit margins, MNOs must (i) control traffic based on service and usage, (ii) increase efficiency, (iii) enhance network reliability and QoE despite raising costs, (iv) maintain as low turnover rates as feasible, etc.

Usage factors: The subscriber's devices, subscriber profiles, and traffic dynamics are all varied in nature. Analytics helps the MNOs to manage and control different traffic types, mobile devices, and subscribers based on the MNOs' plans and each requirement. Statistics take into consideration the network's capacity and assist MNOs in managing network traffic more effectively in the present. MNOs are important in delivering IoT communications platforms since they control network traffic (Ogudo, K. A. et al, 2019).

Technology Drivers: Driving technologies of numerous technological elements for mobile devices, network slicing, etc., are present in contemporary WiFi networks (Shen, X. et al, 2020). It supports a variety of use-cases and incorporates multiple air-interface layers for the network. To effectively coordinate the automated network components, MNOs require an efficient analytics infrastructure. The MNOs can better balance dispersed and centralized capabilities with the use of analytics. The analysis of data helps MNOs determine the best way to divide the network's structure and traffic, including the number of slices, how traffic is divided among slices, etc., depending on traffic type and space.

3. TYPES OF ANALYTICS IN NEXT-GEN WIRELESS SYSTEMS

There exists a succession of evolution in big data analytics, starting from descriptive analytics to diagnostic analytics to predictive analytics, and excelling towards prescriptive analytics as shown in Fig. 3, out of which three (descriptive, predictive and prescriptive analytics) are dominant. The MNOs currently are in descriptive phase and use mainly the visualization tools to get insights on what has happened, the network performance, traffic profile, etc. The MNOs can make use of the diagnostic analytics to figure out the root-causes of the network anomalies and find out the faulty KPIs and network functions/ elements. In order to get the diagnostic analytics, the analytics tool employs techniques like drill-down, deep learning, data discovery, correlations, etc.

Predictive analytics is a great tool for making predictions. Note that it can never report or be certain about what will happen, however, predictive analytics can only produce forecasting about what might happen, for example, future locations of the subscribers, future traffic pattern and network congestion, etc. Predictive analytics deliver predictions about the future events based on the real-time and archived data by making use of various statistical techniques such as machine learning, data mining, modeling as some statistical process and game-theoretic analysis. Prescriptive analytics goes steps ahead of just predicting the future events by suggesting decision options for slicing (i.e., how to slice, how many slices), virtualization, edge-computing, etc., along with the implications of each decision option. Therefore, the prescriptive analytics need an efficient predictive model, actionable data and a feedback system for tracking down the results generated by the action taken. The decision options (e.g., for network expansion, resource usage) are produced considering the MNOs preferences, system constraints (backhaul, fronthaul, spectrum, transmission power), etc. Prescriptive analytics can also suggest the finest course of actions for any pre-defined target, for example, of a particular KPI.

The MNOs have access to large amounts of data which can be categorized into two classes such as internal data and external data as shown in Fig. 2. The internal data corresponds to data belonging to the MNOs and/or produced in the network, which is network related and subscriber related.

The external data is collected from the third parties. Both the internal and external data can be further classified into two categories, which are structured data and unstructured data.

The structured is stored in a relational database, i.e., each field in the database has a name and the relationship between the fields are well-defined. On the other hand, the unstructured data (for example, call center transcripts, messages, etc) is not usually saved in a relational database. A comprehensive coverage on the features and sources of mobile big data can be found in Aggarwal et al. (2021) and Sidhu and Krishan (n.d.).

C. Computational Intelligence

MNOs have access to a collection of data sets (i.e., these data can be highly dimensional, heterogeneous, complex, unstructured and unpredictable) that are so large and complex that the traditional data processing and analysis approaches cannot be employed due to their limited processing space and/or processing time. Computational intelligence, a set of nature-influenced computational techniques and approaches, play a very crucial role in the big data analysis (Lu et al., 2016). It enables the analytics agent to computationally process and analyze the historical and real-time data, and eventually finds out and explain the underlying patterns, correlations, as well as to

Big data analytics is the act of gathering, organizing, and analyzing huge data sets, also known as big data, to find patterns and other important information (Poornima, S., & Pushpalatha, M. (2016)). Big data analytics have undergone a series of evolutions, with three of them-descriptive, predictive, and prescriptive analytics-dominating. These include descriptive analytics, diagnosing analytics, prediction analytics, and prescriptive analytics, respectively. Presently in the descriptive phase, MNOs primarily rely on visualization tools to gain insights into what has occurred, the performance of the network, the traffic description, etc. These diagnostic analyses can be used by MNOs to identify the underlying causes of network anomalies and identify broken KPIs, which are key performance indicators, and networking functions/elements. The analytics tool uses methods like drill-down, AI, searching for data correlations, etc. to obtain the diagnostic analytics.

Developing predictions is a straightforward procedure developed with statistical analysis. A form of AI known as predictive analytics employing machine learning makes use of statistical methods to enable computers to "learn" from data without having to be specifically configured (Ongsulee, P. et al, 2018). Forecasting analytics, nevertheless, can only produce predictions about potential outcomes, such as subscriber positions soon, traffic patterns, congested networks, etc. A variety of statistical strategies, including ML, modeling, mining as a stochastic procedure, and game theory analysis, predictive analytics provides predictions about upcoming events that utilize real-time and archived information.

By offering decision-making alternatives for slicing, virtualization, computing on the edge, etc., predictive data analysis goes beyond merely forecasting future events. Prescriptive analytics consequently require an effective predictive model, relevant information, and a feedback mechanism for monitoring the outcomes of the action made. The standard of everyday wireless lifestyle is anticipated to be much improved with the integration of the upcoming fifth generation (5G) wireless networks with big data analytics (Zheng, K. et al, 2016).

Large volumes of data are available to MNOs, and these data can be divided into two categories such as internal and external data which is shown in Figure 2. Internal information relates to subscriber- and network-related data that is produced by the MNOs and/or owned by them. Third parties are used to gather the external data. The two categories of structured data and unstructured data can be used to further categorize both internal and external data. The organized information is kept in a relational database, where each field has an identifier and there is an apparent connection between them. However, unstructured info is not often stored in a relational database, such as call center documents, messages, etc. Detailed descriptions of the characteristics, uses, and sources associated with mobile big data are provided (Cheng, X. et al, 2017).

Figure 2. Data sources available to MNO for data analytics and AI

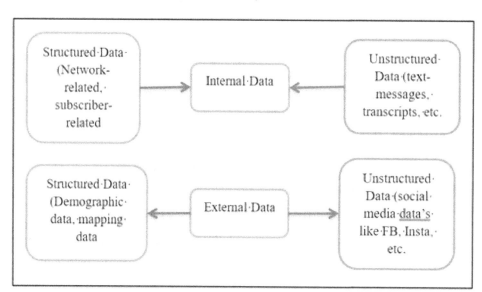

Computational Intelligence: MNOs could access a variety of collections of information that are so huge and intricate that conventional approaches of processing and analyzing the information cannot be used due to their constrained processing space and/or processing times. These data sets may be extensively dimensional, inconsistent, complicated unorganized, and unanticipated. The enormous amount of unstructured, organized, and unprocessed raw data from the MNOs is transformed into useful knowledge and data using computational analysis tools and procedures.

In general, the MNO can use either a top-down strategy or a bottom-up approach for big data analytics. In the top-down method, the MNOs specify the goals they must reach or the issues they must solve before determining which data sets are necessary. While under the bottom-up strategy, MNO's have access to large volumes of data and use that data to their advantage to gain insights. The transformation of the transportation architecture demands extensive scientific assessment of the problems, the order of importance, the dangers, and the unpredictability. A bottom-up strategy was utilized to illustrate the potential future of wireless communication distribution and implementation to deal with these difficulties (Cheng, X. et al, 2022).

4. MANAGING COMPLEXITIES USING AI OVER ML

The ML and AI are two very powerful tools that are emerging as solutions for managing large amounts of data, especially for making predictions and providing suggestions based on the data sets. They are, however, very often appear to be used interchangeably in spite of some parallels.

In particular, for producing predictions and offering proposals according to data sets, ML and AI constitute extremely powerful techniques that are emerging as solutions for handling massive volumes of data. The idea that humans can allow the computers learn on their own by giving them plenty of access to a lot of data has led to ML being mentioned occasionally as a subfield of AI. In contrast to ML models, AI models interact with the outside world, adapt to changes, and recreate themselves. AI goes beyond forecasts and recommends strategies or proposals that have consequences for achieving a beneficial outcome compared to ML. It becomes increasingly challenging to manage wireless networks as they expand in size and complexity since new components and technologies must be integrated in order to take advantage of technological advancements. Such massive and intricate networks generate an excessive amount of data. Both ML and AI are beneficial for analytics because they can extract significant details from the unprocessed information and produce illuminating recommendations and forecasts.

The use of ML and AI has an opportunity to assist MNOs in tackling problems that are either too complicated for conventional methods to handle or that are brand-new and lack precedent information. The ML and AI algorithms can connect data from many sources and identify what is pertinent. Due to the automated methods' ability to analyze and scrutinize data, they may potentially make connections and interconnections that were previously undetected more thoroughly and methodically. Human knowledge has a limited capacity for developing fresh ideas and insights, despite being beneficial in focusing attention to produce solutions and manage complicated challenges. Without any question, artificial intelligence will be essential to wireless communications in future generations.

5. COVERAGE AND CAPACITY OPTIMIZATION OF NEXT-GENERATION

All the subtleties that can influence service quality are outside the scope of the traditional network-oriented paradigm. Mobile operators require solutions that give them an analysis capability that gathers all the data about the network and subscribers into one corporate geo-location platform, removing the assumptions required in in-fault isolation and cutting down on mean time to repair. Due to their access to vast amounts of data, MNOs are well-positioned to benefit from big data analytics. The following analytics, which are mostly based on data from two different sources, such as subscriber's data and network statistics, can be produced by or predicted by the big data analytics engine/agent and used to design and optimize the network. The data analytics of next generation wireless communication system that consists of remote components is shown in figure 3.

Figure 3. Data analytics – Next gen wireless communication system

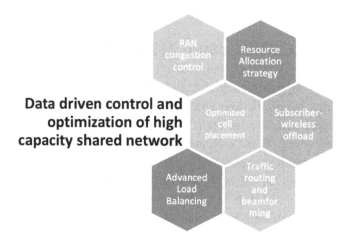

Subscriber Profile (SP): The subscriber profile in this situation includes information about the subscriber's equipment, Service Level Agreement (SLA), affordability (price per unit of data rate), QoS/policy, behavioural profile, etc. It is essential to the process of controlling and optimizing. When performing the distribution of resources, congestion mitigation, and traffic discharge, the subscriber's precedence inside the network is specified in the subscriber profile. Information on user behaviour in utilizing various applications and services is provided through behavioural data.

Subscriber Perspective (Sub-P): A subscription-centric view of the network is provided for analytics by the attribute or measure known as subscriber perspective, which links MNO network activity with the user's SLA, pricing, QoS, and QoE, among other things. The Cost over Quality Ratio, which in general describes the subscriber perspective, can be refined by a number of factors related to the requested service class and perceived friendliness of the service, such as QoS violation, latency violation, etc. It gives the MNO the ability to assess the RAN quality from the perspective of the subscriber and puts them in a better position to deliver high QoE. While considering the consumer's point of view and with the ultimate objective of giving them the greatest experience possible, also MNO perspective is considered for the most beneficial outcomes (Goncalves, L. C. B. D. S. (2020)).

RAN Perspective (RAN-P): The RAN perspective, or RAN performance from the standpoint belonging to the subscribers, is a measurement that gives the MNO the customer-centric RAN efficiency. The MNO's analytics can greatly benefit from the user equipment's perspective of signaling data such as signal strength, error codes, available networks, etc. The MNO may provide a heat map for coverage and assess the RAN quality using the user's projected trajectory, the spatial deployment of the BSs, and signaling metrics. The MNO can identify radio cell abnormalities and other negative symptoms via anomaly (i.e., SLA violation) analysis and trajectory investigation of the time sequence data, and regulate bandwidth and RAN congested issues, according to contemporary cell mining that systematically analyses the data effectiveness. The complete end-to-end subscription interaction can be assessed in terms of customer service Reliability and consequently correlated to the precise location throughout the network using RAN Perspective.

Mobility Pattern for Subscriber (MPS): Considering a user's mobility characteristics in advance is essential for ensuring QoS specifications, maintaining resource utilization, traffic offloading, and routing, and for routing. Measurements of human travel behaviors show that people follow particular routes with a fair amount of regularity. By considering a mobile user's current position, direction of movement, and overall SMP history, one can forecast their trajectory. It is feasible to forecast a spatiotemporal trajectories (trajectory containing both temporal as well as spatial variables), which means that in addition to the future position of the portable user; it is also able to determine the user's arrival time and length of stay. The majority of the time, a user's mobility profile is determined by their position, which may be determined using wireless system transmissions.

Radio Environment Map (REM): A REM for MNO is a specialized version of the REM that focuses on the specific needs and requirements of the operator's wireless network. In 4G/5G networks, base station energy levels are distributed using REM-based techniques while taking disruption from a licensed network into account (Kryszkiewicz, P. et al, 2018). The REM for an MNO typically includes data related to the MNO's base stations, coverage areas, signal strength, interference levels, and other relevant network parameters such as Network planning and Optimization, coverage analysis, Interference Management, capacity planning, spectrum management, Network security, data driven decision making and performance monitoring.

The creation and maintenance of a REM for an MNO involve a continuous process of data collection, analysis, and updates. Advanced technologies, such as AI and big data analytics, are often employed to handle the large volumes of data and derive actionable insights for network optimization and management.

Radio Access Network Congestion Control: Congestion in the RAN is inevitable due to the constrained network resources and ever increasing demand, which lowers the quality of the user experience. This issue can be resolved by expanding the current RAN, but doing so is expensive. Deploying a proactive policy surveillance system to avert a shortage of RAN resources is a flexible and economical option. Smart congestion control methods can provide perceptibility at a specific sub-cell level and prioritize some customers based on their tiers by taking into account location data, the load level of network elements, and users' contractual service levels. There are several approaches for managing RAN congestion, such as lowering the QoS for subscribers who belong to the lowest level of users, refusing to initiate new events, and dismissing certain transactions.

6. ADVANCED LOAD BALANCING USING AI

Advanced load balancing for next-generation wireless networks using AI is a powerful technique that leverages artificial intelligence to optimize the distribution of traffic and resources across the network. Load balancing is crucial in 5G and beyond networks, as they support a massive number of connected devices and diverse applications with varying quality-of-service requirements. AI-powered load balancing algorithms can dynamically adapt to changing network conditions and user demands, ensuring efficient utilization of network resources and providing an enhanced user experience. Here's how AI can be applied to achieve advanced load balancing in next-gen wireless networks such as Real-time Network Monitoring, Data-driven Decision Making, Dynamic Resource Allocation, User-centric Load Balancing, Proactive Network Optimization, Multi-dimensional Load Balancing, Edge Intelligence, Self Optimizing Networks (SON), Anomaly Detection and Fault Tolerance.

By integrating AI into load balancing strategies, next-gen wireless networks can adapt to dynamic and complex environments, handle diverse traffic patterns, and deliver a seamless and efficient user experience.

7. BENEFITS AND CHALLENGES

Despite using statistical analysis of big data to manage and improve wireless networks is very appealing to MNOs, there are certain difficulties involved. Managing and utilizing a large volume of data, building algorithms for the constantly changing and efficient interpretation of massive amounts of information, and then utilizing the networked insights from data analytics might present special obstacles. The loss of the MNOs' remaining primary authority over the wireless infrastructure, nevertheless, is more likely to be the biggest and hardest task. However, due to the enormous complexity of contemporary networks, automating is unavoidable, and it is essential to transfer that level of direct management (Kibria, M. G., et al, 2018).

The complete networking and service provisioning are made more efficient by big data analytics. Analytics enables MNOs to benefit from better planning, increased network resource utilization, effective maintenance of the network elements, and reduced operating costs. The MNOs now have the freedom to create and implement their own network utilization plan. It aids operators in developing new services and presenting plans that are appropriate for subscribers' needs. Even though MNOs currently provide these kinds of services, analytics offers deeper insights.

Implementing policies and managing subscribers are both improved by analytics. An independent support system can be improved with the help of the processing of natural languages and interacting with the smart digital assistants in the user devices.

In addition to the control and optimization scenarios already mentioned the MNOs frequently struggle with successfully and precisely maintaining network elements, backhaul tracking (potential obstacles in backhaul networks), fronthaul management and coordination, intelligent network segmentation, energy optimization, and monitoring crucial network performance factors. Analysis of big data can be used to do anticipatory preservation on network components. Using sensors, the system of predictive maintenance continuously examines the network components' operating status. Big data analytics makes it feasible to identify potential dangers, which leads to an early discovery of any possible vulnerability. This enables the MNO's service and operation team to develop a proactive approach to developing an anticipatory maintenance scheduling strategy.

8. CONCLUSION

Here, a data-driven approach for reviewing contemporary wireless networks is considered. In this model, MNOs use advanced data analytics and AI to operate, control, and optimize their networks effectively. The primary forces driving the widespread utilization of big data processing are highlighted, and it is additionally addressed below the way ML, and artificial intelligence play crucial roles in data analytics for next-generation wireless networks. Additionally, a collection of network design and optimization strategies for data analytics are offered.

One challenge of using data analytics in wireless networks is the difficulty in integrating data from various sources, such as cell towers, mobile devices, and backhaul networks. Techniques like data fusion and correlation analysis can help integrate data and provide a more comprehensive view of network performance.

Data analytics can improve wireless network performance by identifying areas with poor coverage or congestion, enabling targeted investments in new infrastructure, or improving existing performance. It can also optimize network traffic flow, improving network speeds and reducing latency.

REFERENCES

Aggarwal, P. K., Jain, P., Mehta, J., Garg, R., Makar, K., & Chaudhary, P. (2021). Machine learning, data mining, and big data analytics for 5G-enabled IoT. *Blockchain for 5G-Enabled IoT: The new wave for Industrial Automation,* 351-375.

Cheng, X., Fang, L., Yang, L., & Cui, S. (2017). Mobile big data: The fuel for data-driven wireless. *IEEE Internet of Things Journal,* 4(5), 1489–1516. 10.1109/JIOT.2017.2714189

Cheng, X., Hu, Y., & Varga, L. (2022). 5G network deployment and the associated energy consumption in the UK: A complex systems' exploration. *Technological Forecasting and Social Change,* 180, 121672. 10.1016/j.techfore.2022.121672

Goncalves, L. C. B. D. S. (2020). *Improved planning and resource management in next generation green mobile communication networks.* Academic Press.

Jeble, S., Kumari, S., & Patil, Y. (2016). Role of big data and predictive analytics. *International Journal of Automation and Logistics,* 2(4), 307–331. 10.1504/IJAL.2016.080336

Kibria, M. G., Nguyen, K., Villardi, G. P., Ishizu, K., & Kojima, F. (2018). Shared resource access high capacity wireless networks: A stochastic geometry framework. In *2018 IEEE Wireless Communications and Networking Conference (WCNC)* (pp. 1-6). 10.1109/WCNC.2018.8377415

Kibria, M. G., Nguyen, K., Villardi, G. P., Zhao, O., Ishizu, K., & Kojima, F. (2018). Big data analytics, machine learning, and artificial intelligence in next-generation wireless networks. *IEEE Access: Practical Innovations, Open Solutions,* 6, 32328–32338. 10.1109/ACCESS.2018.2837692

Kryszkiewicz, P., Kliks, A., Kułacz, Ł., Bogucka, H., Koudouridis, G. P., & Dryjański, M. (2018). Context-based spectrum sharing in 5G wireless networks based on radio environment maps. *Wireless Communications and Mobile Computing,* 2018, 1–15. 10.1155/2018/3217315

Liu, E., Effiok, E., & Hitchcock, J. (2020). Survey on health care applications in 5G networks. *IET Communications,* 14(7), 1073–1080. 10.1049/iet-com.2019.0813

Lu, Z., Lei, T., Wen, X., Wang, L., & Chen, X. (2016). SDN based user-centric framework for heterogeneous wireless networks. *Mobile Information Systems,* 2016, 2016. 10.1155/2016/9874969

Ogudo, K. A., Muwawa Jean Nestor, D., Ibrahim Khalaf, O., & Daei Kasmaei, H. (2019). A device performance and data analytics concept for smartphones' IoT services and machine-type communication in cellular networks. *Symmetry,* 11(4), 593. 10.3390/sym11040593

Ojokoh, B. A., Samuel, O. W., Omisore, O. M., Sarumi, O. A., Idowu, P. A., Chimusa, E. R., & Katsriku, F. A. (2020). Big data, analytics and artificial intelligence for sustainability. *Scientific African,* 9, e00551. 10.1016/j.sciaf.2020.e00551

Ongsulee, P., Chotchaung, V., Bamrungsi, E., & Rodcheewit, T. (2018). Big data, predictive analytics and machine learning. In *2018 16th IEEE international conference on ICT and knowledge engineering (ICT&KE)* (pp. 1-6). 10.1109/ICTKE.2018.8612393

Poornima, S., & Pushpalatha, M. (2016). A journey from big data towards prescriptive analytics. *ARPN J. Eng. Appl. Sci*, 11(19), 11465–11474.

Shen, X., Gao, J., Wu, W., Lyu, K., Li, M., Zhuang, W., & Rao, J. (2020). AI-assisted network-slicing based next-generation wireless networks. *IEEE Open Journal of Vehicular Technology*, 1, 45–66. 10.1109/OJVT.2020.2965100

Sidhu, R. K., & Krishan, R. (n.d.). Role of Big Data Analytics in Wireless Network Applications. *Advances in Wireless Communication and Mathematics*.

Younas, M. (2019). Research challenges of big data. *Service Oriented Computing and Applications*, 13(2), 105–107. 10.1007/s11761-019-00265-x

Zheng, K., Yang, Z., Zhang, K., Chatzimisios, P., Yang, K., & Xiang, W. (2016). Big data-driven optimization for mobile networks toward 5G. *IEEE Network*, 30(1), 44–51. 10.1109/MNET.2016.7389830

Chapter 18
Analysis of Object Recognition Using Back Propagation–Based Algorithms

Aruna S.

Department of Computational Intelligence, SRM Institute of Science and Technology, Kattankulathur, India

Maheswari M.

Department of Computational Intelligence, SRM Institute of Science and Technology, Kattankulathur, India

Charulatha G.

Selvam College of Technology, India

Lekashri S.

King Engineering College, India

Nivedha M.

Arasu Engineering College, India

Vijayalakshmi A.

http://orcid.org/0000-0003-3594-6691

Vels Institute of Science, Technology, and Advanced Studies, India

ABSTRACT

Lower back propagation-based algorithms (BPBA) use supervised gaining knowledge to understand items in photos. BPBAs are frequently called convolutional neural networks (CNNs) because they utilize filters to extract dense functions from input photos and construct larger, extra-strong models of objects. In this chapter, the authors discuss evaluating BPBAs for item reputation obligations. They compare BPBA models to conventional machine studying techniques (such as aid vector machines) and compare their overall performance. They use metrics that include accuracy, precision, recall, and F1 score to compare the fashions. The findings advise that BPBAs outperform traditional gadget-mastering procedures for object recognition obligations and impart advanced accuracy in photograph classification tasks. Additionally, they display that BPBAs have a bonus over traditional methods in that they require drastically less education time. Eventually, BPBAs represent a possible alternative to conventional methods for object popularity and other computer vision duties.

DOI: 10.4018/979-8-3693-0683-3.ch018

I. INTRODUCTION

Lower back propagation-based Algorithms (BPA) are the maximum popular algorithms utilized in item reputation. Those algorithms use a set of training samples, additionally called a mastering set. The schooling samples teach the object popularity set of rules and the distinguishing features of different objects (Zhao et al., 2023). BPA is based on a feed-forward neural community and uses pre-described enter, output, and hidden layers and backpropagation of the error across the layers to examine the traits of the objects inside the mastering set (Ding et al., 2023).BPA may be used in a selection of applications related to item popularity, including facial recognition, tracking, and object category. Some of the benefits of those algorithms include faster schooling speeds, excessive accuracy, and flexibility in which objects can be blanketed in the learning set (Singh et al., 2023). Usually, BPA affords a powerful tool that can be used to recognize and classify objects quickly and correctly. A careful evaluation of BPA while used for object popularity should be done to ensure that the algorithm is efficaciously learning the required features. Care must be taken to ensure that the studying set used is representative of all styles of items to be recognized, mainly in the case of facial reputation (Zhang et al., 2023). Additionally, the range of layers and neurons used within the community should be competently adjusted to offer the most appropriate schooling speed-accuracy tradeoff. It could ensure that the rules are educated quickly while offering accurate recognition. Lower back propagation-primarily based Algorithms for object recognition are artificial intelligence algorithms that allow computer systems to perceive gadgets in snapshots (Yu et al., 2023). This technology has become increasingly famous due to its accuracy and capacity to learn from information patterns. The returned propagation-primarily based algorithms can recognize objects from a spread of assets, together with coloration, form, size, and texture (Li et al., 2022). The manner of gaining knowledge is based totally on the concept of blunders lower back-propagating; this means that when wrong guesses are made, the feedback is used to regulate the parameters of the version to enhance the accuracy of the prediction (Nath & Mala., 2022). One of the maximum crucial innovations of the lower back propagation-based algorithms is the clever evaluation of parameters (Arumugam et al., 2022). This gadget has the potential to systematically examine which parameters are the maximum applicable to the mission at hand, after which to update them thus (VIKRUTHI et al., 2022). It means the model can optimize its performance by specializing in the most probable critical parameters to improve the popularity's accuracy. Any other innovation of again propagation-based algorithms uses deep learning (Guo et al., 2022). Deep mastering is a form of gadget studying that uses a couple of layers of neurons on the way to understanding complex patterns. The algorithms can apprehend items in actual time using this sort of deep getting-to-know, even though the photo incorporates state-of-the-art info (Phasinam & Kassanuk., 2022). Furthermore, the returned propagation-based total algorithms are notably green and can research snapshots quickly. It means the version can technique images with much less computational strength than other algorithms. The innovative assessment of Backpropagation-based total Algorithms for item recognition (SEBRO) is a groundbreaking innovation within item reputation (Chen et al., 2022). Figure 1 shows the presented human–device collaboration-primarily based object inspection.

Figure 1. Presented human–device collaboration-primarily based object inspection

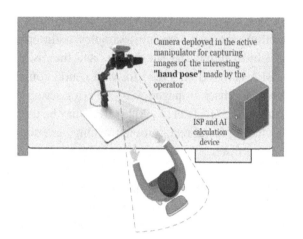

It applies a method of artificial intelligence called backpropagation, which uses neural networks to discover items in digital images. The SEBRO system is designed to be efficient and dependable – a vital gain in large-scale clever picture know-how packages. At its center, the SEBRO gadget uses the recursive backpropagation algorithm to "educate" the neural networks (Ma et al., 2022). It allows instant and correct popularity of items in virtual photographs, even under harsh conditions. The device combines characteristic-factor matching, multi-stage facts fusion, and choice-making stages to classify items in photographs. It also carries a rationality module, ensuring that the conclusions drawn from the photo analysis are correct and meaningful (Patel et al., 2022). This module is also able to perceive items in one-of-a-kind photos well. The SEBRO device is some distance more correct than conventional techniques and has tested a high diploma of accuracy in studying diverse styles of pix from exclusive sources. Moreover, it is also more excellent green than many existing object recognition systems – it is far more capable of handling massive datasets in a fragment of the time that might be required if they had been to be processed manually. Subsequently, its reliability assures users that the gadget's effects are trustworthy. The SEBRO system is an effective tool for spotting and reading items in virtual pix and films. Its accuracy, performance, and reliability make it an invaluable tool for any wise picture expertise application. By leveraging the abilities of backpropagation-based algorithms, the SEBRO machine provides users with a reliable, efficient, and accurate manner of recognizing objects in virtual pix. The main contribution of the research has the following,

- Assessment of deep studying-based total algorithms on fashionable datasets.
- Design an efficient technique to educate a convolutional neural community robotically.
- Evaluation of lower back propagation-primarily based algorithms on a given dataset.
- Analysis of the impact of function selection on object popularity accuracy.

II. RELATED WORKS

A lightweight community for SAR ship Detection primarily based on Multi-stage Laplacian Denoising is a community architecture designed to discover ships in Synthetic Aperture Radar (SAR) imagery (Zhao et al., 2023). The community uses multi-degree Laplacian denoising, which uses extra convolutional layers at one-of-a-kind scales using one-of-a-kind stride settings, kernel length, and dilation charge. This approach is intended to reduce noise in SAR images to facilitate better detection of delivery. Moreover, the community is designed to be lightweight, permitting it to be successfully used in actual-time programs.

A Human Manipulator Collaboration-based Scheme for Item Inspection is a new approach utilized in clever Factories to check out objects (Ding et al., 2023). This scheme leverages hand pose sensing photos of numeric symbols and non-numeric expressions blended with superior system studying strategies to allow sturdy and fast popularity of items. It is a collaborative method that allows people to manipulate objects in a safe and controlled manner, which, in flip, lets in for better and more efficient object inspections. The scheme additionally brings greater accuracy and productiveness to the inspection procedure, leading to stepped forward product best, decreased downtime, and extended customer delight.

Using artificial intelligence (AI) in harm evaluation for laminated composite structures is essential to enhancing protection and reliability (Singh et al., 2023). AI has been increasingly used within composite materials, supplying possibilities to discover and evaluate the harm because of various effects and hundreds. AI-primarily based methods may be used as they should be and hastily assess the severity of damage without the want for guide interpretation or reliance on traditional methods.IT evaluation aims to talk about AI's role in the harm assessment of laminated composite structures, highlighting the numerous existing algorithms used in this field.

The review additionally investigates the benefits and limitations of the numerous AI methods on this subject. The review begins using outlining the diverse forms of laminated composite systems (Zhang et al., 2023). It then explores the one-of-a-kind harm resulting from various loads and influences, providing an overview of the harm assessment techniques maximum usually utilized in laminated composite systems. Diverse AI strategies, image processing, and machine getting to know are then discussed. Examples of AI-based total harm detection techniques for composite systems are also supplied. Sooner or later, the evaluation discusses the advantages and limitations of AI for the harm evaluation of laminated composite systems, outlining pleasant practices for using AI on this subject and highlighting its capability in the future.

Adverse examples in visible object tracking in satellite tv for pc movies contain producing samples that can be used to deceive a deep getting-to-know-based total version used for visible object monitoring (Yu et al., 2023). Usually, those opposed examples are generated by cross-body momentum accumulation, a technique leveraging the successive frames in a video and biasing the version closer to a predefined goal region, even minimizing the output of the photo classifier. It will be performed by using the motion statistics from previous frames and growing a movement vector from them, which is then used to bias the found-out model toward the preferred region iteratively. This approach aims to make the item monitoring model less accurate and create situations with wrong detections or false labels that can lead to errors in the following video frames.

A novel deep feature-based classifier for the breast mass category is a device mastering a set of rules that uses a synthetic neural network to automatically classify a breast mass primarily based on its capabilities and characteristics (Li et al., 2022). It may be used to as it should be distinguished benign from malignant tumors, as well as different functions consisting of tumor size and vicinity. It could guide extra particular diagnosis and treatment of breast cancer. Table 1 shows the smart evaluation of back propagation-Based Algorithms for Object Recognition.

Table 1. The smart evaluation of Back propagation-Based Algorithms for Object Recognition

Model	Tecnology	Advandage	Drawbacks
SAR Ship Detection Based on Multi-Level Laplacian Denoising	Lightweight Network	The community uses multi-degree Laplacian denoising, which uses extra convolutional layers at one-of-a-kind scales using one-of-a-kind stride settings, kernel length, and dilation charge	This approach is intended to reduce noise in SAR images to facilitate better detection of delivery.
A Human Manipulator Collaboration-based Scheme for Object Inspection	Algorithms	A Human Manipulator Collaboration-based Scheme for Item Inspection is a new approach utilized in clever Factories to check out objects	It is a collaborative method that allows people to manipulate objects in a safe and controlled manner, which, in flip, lets in for better and more efficient object inspections
role of ai in damage assessment in laminated composite structures.	composite structures	AI has been increasingly used within composite materials, supplying possibilities to discover and evaluate the harm because of various effects and hundreds	The review begins using outlining the diverse forms of laminated composite systems.
Visual Object Tracking in Satellite Videos	Multimedia Tools	Usually, those opposed examples are generated by cross-body momentum accumulation, a technique leveraging the successive frames in a video and biasing	This approach aims to make the item monitoring model less accurate and create situations with wrong detections or false labels that can lead to errors in the following video frames
Multimedia Tools and Applications	Lightweight Network	A novel deep feature-based classifier for the breast mass category is a device mastering a set of rules that uses a synthetic neural network to automatically classify	It could guide extra particular diagnosis and treatment of breast cancer.

III. PROPOSED MODEL

This research paper proposes a novel approach for efficaciously comparing backpropagation-based algorithms for item recognition. This approach offers a manner to evaluate various capabilities related to the set of rules, along with accuracy, velocity, and scalability. First, the paper develops a detailed theoretical evaluation of the backpropagation-based algorithm and its associated capabilities. An example case study is then offered to demonstrate the effectiveness of this method. Figure 2 shows the Laplacian pyramid denoising version.

Figure 2. Laplacian pyramid denoising version

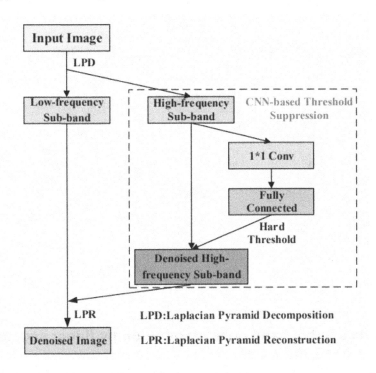

This example compares the performance of more than a few backpropagation-based total algorithms for object recognition on an intensive photograph dataset. Subsequently, the paper proposes a green approach for evaluating backpropagation-primarily based algorithms. This approach consists of an iterative feedback loop in which an evaluation metric is used to evaluate the overall performance of the algorithm and music its parameters. An extended-term aim of this evaluation method is that you want to spontaneously and proactively adapt to modifications in the dataset and optimize the algorithm's overall performance for this reason. Eventually, the paper offers a test that tests the proposed evaluation approach on a range of backpropagation-based algorithms for item popularity. The results display its effectiveness in accurately evaluating the overall performance of the algorithms. Figure 3 shows the BAM Yolox-tiny structure.

Figure 3. BAM Yolox-tiny structure

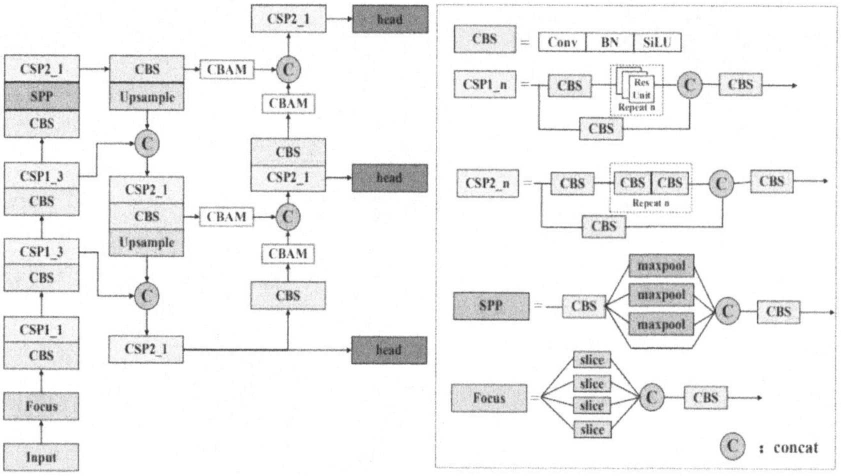

A. Fast numeric symbol hand pose recognition by finger segmentation.

Rapid numeric image hand pose reputation using finger segmentation of returned propagation-based totally algorithms for item recognition is a deep studying based totally method to quickly and appropriately apprehend and classify one-of-a-kind hand poses in 3-D area. The method uses a multi-layered convolutional neural network (CNN) to extract capabilities from a series of pics in a 3-d area. The functions are then labelled and segmented into distinct finger-like groups, further categorized consistent with various hands and their spatial arrangement. It requires much fewer schooling facts than different strategies due to its speedy schooling time and the fact that it may hastily and appropriately classify hand poses in a three-D area. The set of rules outperforms traditional hand gesture popularity algorithms by emulating the functioning of the human mind using device learning and synthetic intelligence. Table 2 shows the Comparison of maximum segment angle thresholds of confusing hand pose sets.

Table 2. Comparison of maximum segment angle thresholds of confusing hand pose sets

Conditions	Threshold (TH)	Θ max > TH	Θ max $\leq$ TH
1(three segments, thumb detected)	120	Pose RB	Pose 8
2(four segments, thumb detected)	140	Pose RE	Pose 9
3 (two segments, thumb detected)	110	Pose 6	Pose 5
4(two segments, no thumb)	60	Pose RC	Pose 2
5(four segments, no thumb)	70	Pose RD	Pose 4

B. Robust Finger Segmentation

The sturdy finger segmentation-based totally hand pose recognition with the elimination of noisy records of the pores and skin-like region that is not always a part of the operator's hand is based totally on a backpropagation-primarily based set of rules. This algorithm is used to photograph photographs received from a consumer's camera. The rules work in stages: First, the rules pre-process the picture records to separate the skin-like region from the operator's hand. That is finished thru a mean clear out, eliminating noisy data factors.

$$Solidity = \frac{contour\_area}{convexhull\_area}, \tag{1}$$

$$Circularity = \frac{4\pi \cdot contour\_area}{contour\_perimeter^2}, \tag{2}$$

$$Extent = \frac{contour\_area}{rec\tangleborder\_area}, \tag{3}$$

$$\theta_i = MaxPool(f_i * X_H + b_i) \tag{4}$$

$$D = ReLU(\varphi\theta + b) \tag{5}$$

$$ReLU(x) = \begin{cases} x, x)0 \\ 0, x \le 0 \end{cases} \tag{6}$$

$$\widehat{X}_H(x,y) = hard\_thresold(X_H(x,y))$$
$$= \begin{cases} 0.001 \times X_H(x,y), X_H(x,y) \le D \\ X_H(x,y), X_H(x,y))D \end{cases} \tag{7}$$

$$\mu_c(\lambda) = \sigma(MLP(AvgPool(\lambda)) + MLP(MaxPool(F))) \tag{8}$$

$$\mu_s(\lambda) = \sigma(f^{7\times7}([AvgPool(\lambda); MaxPool(\lambda)])) \tag{9}$$

It is then observed via convolutional layers that extract features from the photo and separate the hand regions from the background. In the 2nd degree, an assist vector gadget (SVM) classifier is used to classify hand areas according to the relative function of the distinctive arms and discover distinctive postures. The algorithm performs this with an accuracy of eighty-five-95%, relying on the specifics of the machine and statistics used. The output is a matrix representing the numerous finger postures within the photo, collectively with the indices that explain the beginning and end of every posture. ultimately, the segmentation output is analyzed to determine the relative region of the reference points and convey the hand pose. The proposed algorithm has shown in the following,

Algorithm.1: Object Recognition Algorithm

```
Load fis, trustFactor, training Vectors
For each r of fis.rules {
r.weight=r.weight*transFactor }
For each r of fis.rules {
If r.premise(LC2H2DivByC2H6, LC2H2DivByC2H4)>0,5 {
r.conclusion=(r.conculsion*r.weight+t.thermalFaultLowTemperature)/(r.weight+1)
r.weight-r.weight+1 } } }
trustFactor=0
For each r of fis.rules{
trustFactor=max(trustFactor, r.weight) }
For each r of fis.rules {
r.weight-r.weight/trustFactor }
Save fis, trustFactor
```

C. Two-Phase Recognition

The 2-phase popularity of numeric and non-numeric hand pose pictures for item identification and categorization is based on the backpropagation-primarily based object popularity algorithms. The algorithms recollect the item function values, texture kinds, and different information for recognition. The first segment of recognition goals to hit upon the item type of the hand pose photograph, while in the 2nd section, the set of rules detects the item first-rate of the operator's hand. The machine mainly uses superior Convolutional Neural network (CNN) models to classify the hand pose photograph to extract significant facts from the hand photos, generating a possibility of the object type. The accuracy of the item recognition is further advanced by using a variation of CNN called long brief period memory (LSTM). The LSTM model facilitates higher capture of the lengthy-time period relationships between item functions and lengthy-term dependencies inside the hand sequence pics. Primarily based on the chance generated by the CNN and LSTM fashions, the rules can better differentiate among gadgets of different sorts and appropriately categorize them. Similarly, numerous geometric and color functions are used to understand and classify objects lovely accurately. In the end, again-propagation strategies are used to optimize the weights in the layers of the networks. These techniques help to refine the classification accuracy and improve the overall machine.

IV. RESULTS AND DISCUSSION

The proposed algorithm getting-to-know fee, however, can reason the algorithm to converge on local minima rather than the worldwide minima, resulting in poorer classification accuracy.

$$Precision = \frac{AC}{AC + \lambda C} \tag{10}$$

$$\text{Re}call = \frac{AC}{AC| + \lambda N} \tag{11}$$

$$EC = \int_0^1 C(R) \cdot RdR \tag{12}$$

$$\lambda_1 = \frac{2.R.C}{R + C} \tag{13}$$

Table 3 shows the results of different methods on SSDD

Table 3. The results of different methods on SSDD

Methods	Recall	Precision	AP	F1	Params	FPS
SSD	67.42%	96.47%	92.81%	78.23%	85.65%	78.96%
Center Net	56.85%	81.65%	54.68%	56.85%	87.24%	65.28%
Yolo v7	51.69%	98.65%	96.21%	51.69%	73.28%	91.38%
Yolo v4-tiny	78.96%	78.96%	78.96%	96.47%	81.65%	78.23%
Yolox - tiny	85.65%	85.65%	85.65%	81.65%	98.65%	98.54%
Proposed	67.42%	84.57%	73.28%	98.65%	78.96%	84.57%
The Results of Different Methods on AIR SARShip-1.0						
SSD	96.45%	82.65%	54.68%	73.28%	78.96%	77.42%
Center Net	81.69%	98.65%	96.21%	81.65%	65.28%	86.85%
Yolo v7	98.96%	75.86%	78.96%	66.85%	91.38%	51.69%
Yolo v4-tiny	86.85%	81.65%	92.68%	41.69%	78.23%	78.96%
Yolox - tiny	61.69%	98.65%	96.21%	76.85%	68.54%	75.65%
Proposed	86.96%	98.86%	78.96%	91.69%	84.57%	67.42%

A. Sensitivity

Again propagation-primarily based algorithms are a type of supervised mastering method that can be used for object popularity. The algorithm uses an artificial neural network to propagate the entered signals backward through the network to replace weights with new values generated from the output mistakes. The final goal of backpropagation is to reduce the mistake between the discovered output and the goal output inside the training set. Figure 4 shows the PR curves of strategies with extraordinary thresholds.

Figure 4. PR curves of strategies with extraordinary thresholds

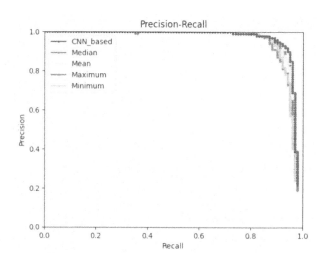

It is accomplished repeatedly by comparing the observed output with the goal output and calculating the mistakes, which can then be propagated backward in a layer-through-layer sequence. In each layer, the mistake is then used to replace the weights of the connections. Figure 5 shows the Precision-consider (PR) curves of various algorithms at the SSDD.

Figure 5. Precision-consider (PR) curves of various algorithms at the SSDD

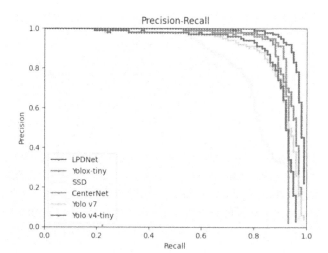

The performance of these algorithms is touchy to the learning charge used, the number of neurons inside the network, the range of training cycles, and the initial weights of the connections. A lower mastering rate generally results in greater accurate weights being calculated. In addition, the variety of neurons inside the community will affect the accuracy of the object's reputation. Increasing the number of neurons will deliver the community a more significant potential and potential to comprehend extra complex items. However, the specified number of neurons must be sufficient to stumble on the variations among the objects, no longer unnecessarily massive.

B. Specificity

Lower back propagation-primarily based algorithms are utilized in object recognition because of their capability to determine relationships between multiple inputs and outputs accurately. A again propagation algorithm includes two steps: first, the ahead skip, wherein inputs are propagated through some of the layers, and second, the backward bypass, where weights are adjusted to reduce a fee feature. Within the forward skip of a lower back propagation-based object recognition set of rules, inputs are handed via a sequence of layers to generate output ratings of ability gadgets in the image. Figure 6 shows the Precision-take into account (PR) curves of various algorithms at the AIR SARShip-1.zero

Figure 6. Precision-take into account (PR) curves of various algorithms at the AIR SARShip-1.zero

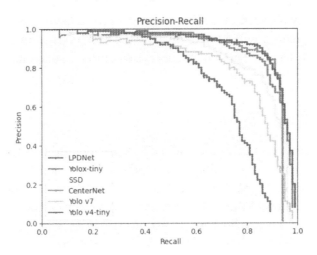

The output scores for each item are then correlated with their corresponding training labels within the backward pass. At this level, the layer weights are adjusted such that the value characteristic of the network is minimized through backpropagation, and the error related to the prediction made is minimized. The adjustment of weights is commonly finished using an optimizer. Using this method, returned propagation-based totally algorithms can learn the relationships among enter and output rankings for every item more than it should be, compared to just using a single layer for all object reputation applications. In the long run, a returned propagation-based set of rules can better recognize and classify gadgets in a picture compared to different item recognition algorithms.

C. True Negative Rate

The terrible price of returned propagation-based Algorithms for item reputation relies on the training facts and the complexity of the gadgets being diagnosed. Usually, a nicely-trained model can gain excessive genuine nasty fees between 95%-99%. It is usually executed by using an extensive dataset containing a couple of examples of each object's magnificence, and the items are quickly sufficient to be recognized with fundamental capabilities. However, if the gadgets are extra complicated, the actual terrible charge can pass down to 85%-90%. It is also possible to enhance the accurate poor price of these algorithms by using further education on the version and extra sophisticated functions.

V. CONCLUSION

This look believes that back propagation-based algorithms are powerful in classifying gadgets for recognition. With a growth in the length and complexity of data, the backpropagation algorithm can be adapted to recognize new gadgets correctly. These algorithms produce high-accuracy prices with one-of-a-kind datasets, making them a possible choice for item reputation obligations. Additionally, the algorithm can be similarly changed to tackle smaller gadgets, allowing the algorithms to predict item classes while an area of interest is identified. Because the backpropagation set of rules is pretty simple but effective, it stays a widely used option for supervised object reputation obligations.

VI. FUTURE SCOPE

The future scope of the clever evaluation of back propagation-primarily based Algorithms for item reputation is enormous. There is the ability to comprise a large number of different device-studying strategies inclusive of Convolutional Neural Networks (CNNs), Deep studying (DL), Generative antagonistic Networks (GANs), and aid Vector Machines (SVMs), to name a few. As information and research amplify, so does the opportunity to improve the set of rules. Additionally, enhancements can be made regarding the speed of operation, accuracy, and studying fee of the algorithms. It could lead to faster and more incredible correct item popularity. Furthermore, developing hybrid models combing diverse ML algorithms should result in more correct and reliable popularity.

REFERENCES

Arumugam, K., Swathi, Y., Sanchez, D. T., Mustafa, M., Phoemchalard, C., Phasinam, K., & Okoronk-wo, E. (2022). Towards applicability of machine learning techniques in agriculture and energy sector. *Materials Today: Proceedings*, 51, 2260–2263. 10.1016/j.matpr.2021.11.394

Chen, Z., Dai, R., Liu, Z., Chen, L., Liu, Y., & Sheng, K. (2022). An Interpretive Adversarial Attack Method: Attacking Softmax Gradient Layer-Wise Relevance Propagation Based on Cosine Similarity Constraint and TS-Invariant. *Neural Processing Letters*, 1–17.35495852

Ding, J., Hsieh, M. C., & Wu, Z. X. (2023). A Human Manipulator Collaboration-based Scheme for Object Inspection by Robust and Fast Recognition of Hand Pose Sensing Images of Numeric Symbols Combined with Non-numeric Expressions for Smart Factories. *Sensors and Materials*, 35(3), 35. 10.18494/SAM4236

Guo, Y., Gao, J., Tunio, M. H., & Wang, L. (2022). Study on the Identification of Mildew Disease of Cuttings at the Base of Mulberry Cuttings by Aeroponics Rapid Propagation Based on a BP Neural Network. *Agronomy (Basel)*, 13(1), 106. 10.3390/agronomy13010106

Li, Y., Gong, Y., & Zhang, Z. (2022). Few-shot object detection based on self-knowledge distillation. *IEEE Intelligent Systems*.

Ma, Y., Liu, Z., Shi, Q., Liu, J., Geng, X., & Xue, R. (2022). Interval prediction of ultimate strength for laminated composite structures using back-propagation neural network. *Archive of Applied Mechanics*, 92(4), 1–18. 10.1007/s00419-021-02097-8

Nath, S., & Mala, C. (2022). Thermal image processing-based intelligent technique for object detection. *Signal, Image and Video Processing*, 16(6), 1631–1639. 10.1007/s11760-021-02118-7

Patel, D., Patel, S., Patel, P., & Shah, M. (2022). Solar radiation and solar energy estimation using ANN and Fuzzy logic concept: A comprehensive and systematic study. *Environmental Science and Pollution Research International*, 29(22), 32428–32442. 10.1007/s11356-022-19185-z35178628

Phasinam, K., & Kassanuk, T. (2022). Supervised Machine Learning in Precision Agriculture. *International Journal of Mechanical Engineering*, 7(1), 1621–1625.

Singh, A. P., Asgar, M. E., Ranjan, R., Kaushik, Y., Reji, J., & Tyagi, T. (n.d.). A review on role of ai in damage assessment in laminated composite structures. *Composites, 17*(19), 70-71.

Vikruthi, S., Archana, D. M., & Chaithanya, D. R. (2022). Enhanced vehicle detection using pooling based dense-yolo model. *Journal of Theoretical and Applied Information Technology*, 100(24).

Yu, X., Ren, Z., Guttery, D. S., & Zhang, Y. D. (2023). DF-dRVFL: A novel deep feature based classifier for breast mass classification. *Multimedia Tools and Applications*, 83(5), 1–30. 10.1007/s11042-023-15864-238283725

Zhang, Y., Wang, L., Zhang, C., & Li, J. (2023). Adversarial Examples in Visual Object Tracking in Satellite Videos: Cross-Frame Momentum Accumulation for Adversarial Examples Generation. *Remote Sensing (Basel)*, 15(13), 3240. 10.3390/rs15133240

Zhao, C., Fu, X., Dong, J., Feng, C., & Chang, H. (2023). LPDNet: A Lightweight Network for SAR Ship Detection Based on Multi-Level Laplacian Denoising. *Sensors (Basel)*, 23(13), 6084. 10.3390/s2313608437447932

Chapter 19
A Collaborative System for Machine Learning–Based Final-Year Projects With Enhanced Dataset Accessibility

Razika Lounas

LIMOSE Laboratory, Faculty of Sciences, University of M'Hamed Bougara of Boumerdes, Algeria

Rachid Djerbi

http://orcid.org/0000-0003-1505-3415

LIMOSE Laboratory, Faculty of Sciences, University of M'Hamed Bougara of Boumerdes, Algeria

Hocine Mokrani

LIMOSE Laboratory, Faculty of Sciences, University of M'Hamed Bougara of Boumerdes, Algeria

Mohamed Tahar Bennai

LIMOSE Laboratory, Faculty of Sciences, University of M'Hamed Bougara of Boumerdes, Algeria

ABSTRACT

This chapter explores the transformative impact of information and communication technology (ICT) on pedagogy, specifically focusing on the integration of collaboration tools in final year projects (FYPs). Final year projects (FYPs) represent the ultimate activity in the student's curriculum. They are designed to use, test, and enhance the knowledge students have gained over the years by confronting them with real-world projects. Despite existing systems for FYPs, the chapter identifies gaps, particularly in covering the entire FYP process and in addressing different collaborative aspects. With a focus on the rise of machine learning-based FYPs, this research aims to propose a comprehensive solution based on a proposed collaboration architecture in response to various needs such as communication, coordination, production, and resource sharing. The application is designed for multiple user roles, including students, advisors, and administrative staff, each allocated a personalized workspace. The novelty of the proposed system is its comprehensive coverage of all collaborative aspects mentioned throughout the FYP process, including proposal processing, project assignment, project completion, and evaluation. The research contributes to fostering innovation in machine learning projects by effectively managing and sharing

DOI: 10.4018/979-8-3693-0683-3.ch019

datasets through collaboration tools. The results indicate good scores in improving collaborative aspects with a score of 98% for virtualization in coordination and 96% for communication. The results also showed that surveyed users are positively inclined to use the system as their final year project (FYP) management system, with an attention-to-use score of 90% of advisors and 92.8% of students.

INTRODUCTION

Recent years have witnessed a discernible upward trajectory in the utilization of Information and Communication Technology (ICT) as a means of facilitating collaboration (Jones, 2012). People are increasingly working together virtually in different domains. Notably, the field of pedagogy has encountered a profound influence from these technological tools, engendering a transformation akin to a veritable revolution. This paradigm shift has engendered a reconfiguration of the dynamics governing the interactions between educators and learners, leading to new modalities of pedagogical practice (Hüttel & Gnaur, 2019). These modes require using particular collaboration tools and their inclusion in work platforms (Shamir-Inbal & Blau, 2021). They are designed to accommodate several curriculum-related activities students must complete, such as courtyards (Tarazi & Akre, 2013) or assessments (Efu, 2019).

Final Year Projects (FYPs) constitute the culmination of a student's academic journey. These projects serve as a platform for students to apply, evaluate, and refine the knowledge they have amassed throughout their educational trajectory. By engaging with real-world challenges and endeavors, FYPs provide a practical dimension to their learning experiences (Beus-Dukic, 2011 ; Rozenes & Kukliansky, 2013; Bringula et al., 2016). Preparing students for FYP involves several tasks and actors, such as advisors and administrative staff. Projects are first reviewed and then assigned to students. A supervisor mentors a student for one semester to complete the project. At the end of the project, the student presents the results to a committee for evaluation. The orchestration of all the activities mentioned above and the involvement of the actors take advantage of collaborative tools. These tools address several aspects such as communication between students (Aiken et al., 2011) and their advisors, outlining projects, coordinating activities between advisors and administrative staff, sharing resources, or generating reports. Several studies have shown the use of online collaboration tools (Berthoud & Gliddon, 2018; Chu & Kennedy, 2011) or social media in FYP.

Final year project themes encompass a diverse range of application areas, reflecting the technological evolution and its intersection with real-world challenges. These projects relate to topics that are not only academically engaging but also have immediate practical relevance. As the practicality and effectiveness of artificial intelligence, particularly machine learning techniques, continue to extend their reach into various domains, many final-year projects align with this technological wave. These projects offer students the opportunity to delve into the dynamic field of AI and apply its principles to solve problems from diverse sectors such as healthcare diagnostics, sentiment analysis, or optimizing financial processes.

In response to the rising requirement of integrating collaboration tools in working platforms (Prinz et al., 2012), several researchers endeavored to provide systems for FYP that integrate tools for several collaboration functionalities. Some of the existing systems are intended for a specific step such as project assessment (Tiwari et al., 2019) or project allocation(Jailani et al., 2022), whereas others are deployed for several FYP steps (Leung et al., 2015 ; Bakar et al., 2011).

Despite the plethora of existing systems, this research topic is still exciting because several issues have been raised and motivated this work. First, the existing platforms do not cover the entire FYP process, including the preliminary exchanges between students and advisors and the processing of project proposals which are determinant in the students' academic pursuits. In addition, certain facets of collaborative work have been omitted from the purview of these systems, notably the aspects of collaborative decision-making and effective communication. Furthermore, with the rise of artificial intelligence and machine learning, many FYPs focus on these areas, raising crucial questions and pressing inquiries about the accessibility and sharing of data among the team members.

The objective of this research is to propose a solution based on a collaboration architecture that explores the benefits of collaboration tools in tackling the aforementioned concerns: the coverage of the whole FYP process from different actors' points of view, the availability of collaborative functions among students and advisors throughout the FYP journey; addressing the difficulties with dataset availability for machine learning based projects; and illustrating the advantages of deploying a robust collaboration platform. In order to fulfill these objectives, the proposed solution makes the following contributions:

- Complete process: The proposed framework covers the whole FYP management process by offering suitable tools for each step.
- Collaboration suite: The application provides coordination, communication, production, and sharing functionalities for students, professors, and administrative staff.
- Complete virtualization: The collaborative application for FYP is proposed in a Computer Science Department case study. The complete virtualization of the process makes the solution suitable for exceptional situations such as pandemic lockdowns.
- Collaboration framework: The proposed system is based on a layered architecture that follows the principle of distinguishing between aspects of the collaboration and the process.
- Machine learning projects: The proposed system fosters an environment of innovation and progress within the machine learning community by properly utilizing collaboration tools to manage and share datasets.

The remainder of the paper is organized as follows: Section 2 presents related work on the use of collaborative tools and platforms for FYP and machine learning projects; Section 3 is devoted to the methodology, including the presentation of the background and participants, the collection of data through the entire FYP process, and the description of the proposed system; Section 4 presents the application and discusses the results; Section 5 concludes this work and provides some future directions.

BACKGROUND

FYP Tools and Platforms

Communication is the foundation of collaboration (Buchem et al., 2012; Stevenson & Starkweather, 2017). In Final Year Projects, this is mostly discussed regarding advisor-to-advisee relationship (Wrench & Punyanunt, 2004). Indeed, this relationship involves regular meetings that are important for setting goals and discussing ideas about the project (Ashraf et al., 2012; De Kleijn, 2013). In addition to face-to-face meetings, several tools are used to communicate, such as email, chat, web conferencing, or social software (Gaines et al., 2019). In addition, these tools are necessary for communication between all parties involved, including administrative staff, during different stages of projects, such as project allocation (Bakar et al., 2011).

Coordination is related to the orchestration of tasks among different authors and considering several steps in time (Raposo et al., 2001). During the FYP process, students pass through several stages, including investigations, state-of-the-art methodology definitions, experiments, result interpretations, and conclusions. These steps are discussed with advisors to set goals and plan tasks and deadlines. Online shared agendas are used to schedule tasks and arrange meetings. These tools are essential, especially when an advisor supervises several student groups and has to keep track of their progress. In addition to agendas, tools for task management such as Gantt charts are used to record tasks to be completed and keep track of project progress (Deepamala & Shobha, 2018).

Collaboration is also strongly related to the functionality of production (Leung & Chu, 2009). During their FYP, students must produce documents such as project reports, codes, and entries. The supervisor's role is to guide them to understand and work around complex problems. The involvement of advisors requires tools that allow them to intervene directly in the students' work if necessary (Singh & Mayer, 2014; Roschelle & Teasley, 1995). With these tools, it is possible to share objects and environments, enabling the collaborative construction of outcomes and knowledge. Sharing knowledge and resources is also a major concern in the FYP framework. Sharing tools and mechanisms such as online libraries, blogs, and podcasts are used to enhance the outcomes of student projects. These tools provide better learning environments and enhance students' abilities to work in teams and apply learned skills (Gardner & Elliott, 2014).

Several research works have highlighted the importance of integrating communication, coordination, production, and sharing tools into a platform to provide a collaborative work environment (Prinz et al., 2012; Abdullah et al., 2018). Romdhani et al., 2011 presented the student project performance management system. It is student-centered and federates the efforts of several stakeholders: students, supervisors, administrators, and reviewers. The system relies on the project and supervised databases to specify each project and on the expertise profile of each supervisor to facilitate the supervisor assignment process: the supervisory system automatically suggests potential supervisors for a given project. The system provides a performance management subscription to define milestones, tasks, and deliverables and check project progress. Progress forms are produced and exported to the relevant actors. The system also provides communication tools, a record management system, evaluation forms, and academic and professional workshops database. It also provides training for students to consolidate and acquire new skills if supervisors indicate the necessary skills.

In (Bakar et al., 2011), the authors proposed a web-based supervision management system. The users of the system are students, supervisors, and the head of the department. The system is composed of three modules. The first module manages students' and supervisors' profiles and provides a function to assign supervisors to students. The second module manages time for meetings between students and supervisors. The third module is dedicated to monitoring the project's process in two aspects: system development and report writing. It uses a Gantt chart to monitor the evolution of the project in time and provides deadline reminders and notifications. The system also provides spaces for discussions and uploading documents and reports.

The system proposed by Leung et al., 2015 is for three users (FYP program organizer, supervisors, and students) and is based on five modules. The first module is used to perform project selection and assignment procedures. The second module provides communication tools such as chat and conferencing among students and between students and supervisors. The system provides a resource-sharing module for a secure, centralized location to share files, code, and produce results. The project management module tracks student schedules and checks on project progress. A submission scoring module allows students to submit their reports for scoring. Clement & Bounds, 2013 proposed a system that, in addition to communication, file sharing, and task management functions, provides tools to facilitate the connection between students and potential supervisors before the assignment process begins. This connection lets students learn about the supervisor's projects and helps administrative staff quickly generate a draft for project assignments. The system also provides tools for submitting evaluations.

The system proposed in (Awad, 2017) provides tools to manage proposals by implementing a call for proposals module. Students can search for projects and sign up for topics that interest them. Students upload their final reports, presentations, and other deliverables for evaluation at the end of their projects. In addition, a coordinator can create a schedule by defining dates, times, locations, and examiners for exams. The system provides reporting functionality on student and grade statistics and an analytics data module to discover patterns that can be used to adjust and improve learning activities. The framework presented in (Naeem et al., 2019) provides tools that support several activities such as supervisor selection, project assignment, and checking student progress through engagement checkpoints. The system also provides individual project sites for students. This functionality is used in several aspects: having a workspace, sharing documents, collaborating in real-time, submitting project documents, and managing the project. The site provides subscription tools to detail the activities and their start and expected completion dates. In addition, it inludes information on additional knowledge and skills that students need to acquire to achieve a successful outcome for their projects. An assessment module allows students to present posters and live presentations to be graded. In (Abdullah et al, 2018), the authors present a system consisting of two modules to manage the FYP. The first module is for enrollment. It allows assigning supervisors to students, recording supervisor approval, and providing student notifications. The second module relates to assessment and provides tools for the grading process as a co-decision between reviewers and supervisors.

The proposal in (Tuah et al., 2022) provides a dashboard-based system for the FYP course proposed for computing and information technology students. The dashboard and data analytics platform presents a collection of data, reports, and analysis about students and enables them to to self-monitor, track progress and manage important information related to their FYP. The proposed functionalities allow student form completion, student file submission through, and instructor remarks. It also provides consultation sessions for the students to allocate time for progress meetings with their supervisor and discuss ideas, issues, problems, and solutions related to their project. In (Kar et al., 2020), the authors present an Online Project Evaluation and Supervision System (oPENs) to manage the submission of project approval forms, weekly reporting process, and group registration process. The system is based on several modules. The profile module allows the coordinator, supervisors and students to access the system and update their profiles. The registration module provides functions to pre-registration and supervisor selection. The weekly reporting module allows supervisors to monitor the progress of their students. The system also provides an announcement corner to inform the user about recent information and an archive system that can be used to access all previous FYP projects.

Table 1 illustrates the positioning of the leading systems with respect to the stages of the FYP process. The FYP management process follows several stages (Yilmaz et al., 2018): proposal processing, project assignment, project completion, and project evaluation. In the proposal stage, project descriptions are discussed to standardize proposals against the students' curriculum, determine requirements, investigate complexity, and check alignment with the students' education and project originality. In the allocation stage, projects are assigned to students. This process is based on several allocation algorithms. Allocation algorithms are beyond the scope of this paper. During project completion, students perform hands-on actions to achieve the defined goals, communicate with their advisors to provide feedback, discuss ways to achieve them, and produce the required project outcomes. The final step is related to the evaluation of the project. Students submit their reports and results for evaluation by committees that are usually appointed by the administrative staff. Table 1 also indicates that the proposed systems do not cover the entire FYP process. Moreover, most systems do not consider the stepbefore the beginning of the allocation, including project validation and discussions between students and supervisors, although it is critical for student choice. Furthermore, in several covered steps, some collaboration functions are missing. For instance, in (Leung et al., 2015), the steps related to assessment and the grading module do not take into account communication between grading members, and in (Awad, 2017), the system does not provide tools for communication between students and advisors during projects processing neither coordination tools between administrative staff during projects processing or allocation. In comparison with the presented existing systems, this paper proposes a solution that covers the whole process of FYP and includes collaboration tools suitable for each step.

Table 1. Covered steps in FYP systems

The System Reference	Proposals Processing	Projects Allocation	Projects Realization	Projects Assessment
Bakar, M. A., Jailani, N., Shukur, Z., & Yatim, N. F. M. (2011)		✓	✓	
Leung, C. H., Lai, C. L., Yuan, T. K., Pang, W. M., Tang, J. K., Ho, W. S., & Wong, T. L. (2015)		✓	✓	✓
Clement, R., & Bounds, P. (2013)	✓	✓		✓
Naeem, U., Islam, S., & Siddiqui, A. (2019, April)		✓	✓	✓
Abdullah, N., Salleh, S. N. M., Mahdin, H., Darman, R., Daniel, B. D., & Surin, E. S. M. (2018, February)		✓		✓
Romdhani, I., Tawse, M., & Habibullah, S. (2011, January)		✓	✓	
Awad, M. (2017)	✓	✓		✓
Kar, S. C., Ismail, S. I., Abdullah, R., Mohamed, H., & Enzai, N. M. (2020, April)	✓	✓	✓	
Tuah, N. M., Yoag, A., Nizam, D., Mohd, N., & Chin, C. W. (2022)	✓		✓	✓

Machine Learning Projects

Machine learning constitutes a pivotal subfield within the domain of Artificial Intelligence, which is centered on formulating and refining operational models concerning pertinent parameters. These models derive their functionality from extensive datasets where model training serves as the bedrock for accurate outcomes generation. The progression of machine learning projects is structured around a series of well-defined steps (Hapke & Nelson, 2020). Figure 1 illustrates these principal phases. The initial step, known as data collection encompasses the systematic gathering, measurement, and meticulous analysis of pertinent insights tailored to the research objectives. Following this, the second phase, termed data preprocessing, takes center stage. This critical stage aims to ensure data quality and relevance by rectifying any discrepancies or missing data points within the dataset. Moreover, this phase involves the partitioning of the dataset into distinct training and test sets. Subsequently, in the third step, machine learning algorithms are engaged to construct and assess the performance of the models.

Figure 1. The process of a machine learning project

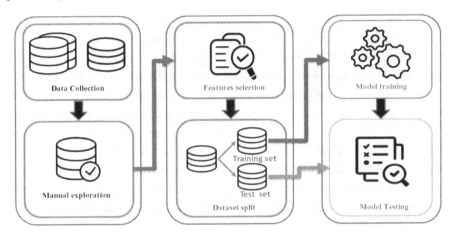

Dataset Collection and Preprocessing is the initial step in data analysis, where users explore large unstructured datasets to uncover initial patterns, characteristics, and points of interest. This process does not involve revealing every bit of information a dataset holds, but rather helps create a broad picture of trends and major points to study in more detail. Moreover, some critical features are not always directly available. The growing interest in applying machine learning across various application areas (Shinde & Shah, 2018 ; et al., 2023) has sparked an increasing demand and concern for datasets, which constitute a valuable and fundamental resource for such projects. Several studies have addressed dataset availability and sharing within domains such as healthcare research (Khan et al., 2021), system security (Goh et al., 2017), and economics (Azzarri et al., 2016). The more numerous and representative is the data, the better the model can learn to generalize from it. Data sharing can accelerate the development of systems, especially collaborative systems. Rather than collecting data from scratch, researchers and developers can use shared data to start developing integrative models more quickly. Also, data sharing can contribute to greater transparency and accountability in the development of integrative collaborative applications. It enables the community to verify and reproduce results, which is essential for ensuring fairness and ethics in the use of AI.

In (Kumbhare et al., 2011), the authors presented the design and implementation of Cryptonite, a secure data repository service for storing and sharing scientific and engineering datasets on public clouds. Cryptonite aims to tackle the challenges of data security, privacy, and integrity in cloud environments where data owners may be uncertain of the cloud provider's trustworthiness or the repository itself. To achieve this, It uses various cryptographic techniques, such as encryption, digital signatures, broadcast encryption, searchable encryption, and lazy revocation, to protect the data and metadata against unauthorized access, modification, or leakage. Moreover, it provides fine-grained access control and auditing capabilities for data owners and consumers. The authors of (Keerie et al., 2018), have implemented a practical solution for the anonymization process in the medical field. The anonymization process is applied to a set of patients to determine whether mercaptopurine can prevent or delay postoperative recurrence of Crohn's disease. To create anonymity, the authors followed several steps. From deciding on the sharing model, initial data collection, identification of direct identifiers, indirect identifiers and superfluous information, through to the application of anonymity by either deleting or coding the data for each information family, ending with the creation of the final dataset. The anonymization method proposed in this article is entirely manual, carried out by a group of medical experts. The more complex the anonymization process, the longer it takes and the greater the risk of error.

The authors of (Zuo et al., 2021) surveyed the strategies for sharing and reusing COVID-19 pandemic research data to help researchers develop and publish new datasets. The authors collected 128 unique COVID-19 dataset URLs. By analyzing the collected datasets in terms of content, accessibility, and citation, the authors observed significant heterogeneity in the way these datasets are referred to, shared, updated and cited. These findings on current practices in generating, sharing and citing datasets for COVID-19 research can provide valuable insights for future improvements in the data collection approach. The contribution by ((Aiken & Lewandowski, 2021), presented a model for sharing quantitative data in the field of physics education research. It is based on sharing recommendations from various fields such as psychology and physical education. The proposal is articulated in four steps. The first step, data collection, defines the collected data, the method of collection, and the different levels of data. The second step, called data schema, describes the relationships between the various components of data. Data anonymization is performed to remove identifying data related to students, instructors, and institutions. The last step, data sharing, refers to making data electronically available for download by researchers for its use. The entire framework uses the ECLASS dataset as an example of its implementation. The study published in (Stvilia & Gibradze, 2022) focused on the activities in which the community engages. The study identified three activities: answering questions, sharing data and creating a community. The results of this research provided a better understanding of activity structures, the data and information sources used, and the challenges and problems encountered when users search, share and make sense of datasets on the web. The authors proposed a meta-model of the community activity structure. The study focused solely on Reddit community discussions on dataset sharing, without scaling the results to other social networks.

The endeavors presented in this section demonstrate the significance of dataset availability and point out the fact that dataset sharing accelerates the development of systems and research endeavors. This importance becomes even more crucial when projects are constrained by limited time frames, such as student projects. Furthermore, research has highlighted the critical role of collaboration in the dataset-sharing process. In contrast to the systems presented, which offer thematic-based datasets (such as healthcare or physical education) or solutions focused on specific issues like anonymization, we propose a generic solution tailored to a broad range of topics of interest for final-year students in their projects. In the following sections, this paper will comprehensively explore the collaborative system, including dataset sharingwithin the context of Final Year Projects (FYPs). It will delve into the system's background, features, and implementation, offering a detailed understanding of its functionality and potential impact.

METHODOLOGY

Context of the Study

This article examines the case of FYP management in the Computer Science Department of the Algerian Boumerdes University. This project-based course is taught for postgraduate students throughout the second semester of the academic year. Figure 2 illustrates the stages of the FYP process with the users involved.

Figure 2. Steps of FYP process

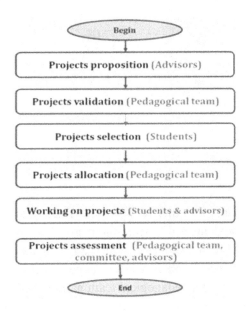

The process begins at the end of the first semester. The department head initiates the project proposal process and provides a timeline for each step. Supervisors (lecturers, professors, and associate professors) must propose projects including the following information: project title, description, keywords, initial subscription, and tools. These projects are then reviewed by a pedagogical team composed of the department head, assistant head, and specialty heads and then published to students. Students are grouped into teams of two or three and select their favorite projects. An allocation process is then initiated to assign the projects to students. At the beginning of the second semester, students and advisors work closely together to progress the project. The official course specifications state that a minimum of one and a half hours of weekly meetings is required. The rest of the work is done remotely using online tools.

The growing excitement about machine learning projects is a palpable reality that is observed every academic year both at the reception of the proposals by teachers, and at the reception of students' choices. Indeed, several projects related to this topic are submitted by teachers with regard to several application areas such as healthcare, sentiment analysis, and security issues, reflecting the growing relevance of this field. From a student's point of view, the observation of choices reveals a an increasing interest in working on those topics. Figure 3 represents insightful statistics about the number of machine learning projects.

The figure shows that for the academic year 2022/2023, the proportion of machine learning projects is (26 out of 66) 39.40%. As the Figure shows, it is the topic with the most significant proportion of projects.

Figure 3. Proportion of FYP projects by topic

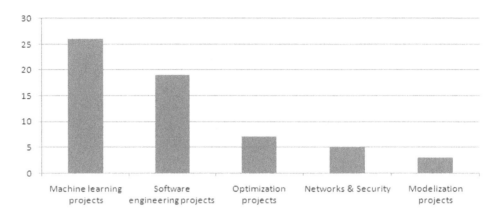

Data Collection

This study enrolled participants with different profiles (final- year students, professors, and administrative staff). The number of students is 42. All of them are between 21 and 25 years old. The number of professors (advisors) is 10. Five of them have more than 10 years of experience in conducting FYP, whereas the other five have between 5 and 10 years of experience. The number of administrative staff is two respondents. Two members of a pedagogical team participated in this study.

The study used two questionnaires: one for students and one for advisors. The questionnaires were administered to participants in Google forms. The student questionnaire was divided into three sections related to:

- Collaboration with advisors: include questions related to communication, coordination, resource sharing, and production activities between students and their advisors;
- Collaboration with teammates: include questions related to communication, coordination, resource sharing, and production activities;
- General collaboration: include aspects throughout the process.

The questionnaire intended for advisors contains items related to:

- Collaboration with their advisees: include questions related to communication, coordination, resources haring, and production activities;
- General collaboration aspects along the process.

The administrative staff and pedagogical team members are involved in the study, with live interviews conducted by the authors throughout the study.

Proposal Processing

During this stage, the pedagogical team reviews the proposed projects for verification. Members ensure that the projects are consistent with the proposed training, detailed project descriptions, methodologies, and tools. During this stage, the instructional team interacts with advisors to discuss issues such as: adding required details or bibliographic references for projects. The advisors improve their project descriptions based on this feedback. The verification step is manual and ends with an email to the departmental service to publish the list of projects. According to the team members interviewed, the main issues raised during this stage are the following:

- The progress of the verification stage depends on the advisors responding quickly to the required changes. The audit is not complete until all the necessary improvements have been made. In some cases, another validation meeting is needed.
- Enhancements are sent by email, which involves re-uploading the proposals a second time to finalize the verification step.

Students must form groups when the list of validated projects is published (by posting it manually via an official website or social network page). Each group can choose their preferred project topics. Each student group provides a list of its ten favorite projects. It is manually ranked to the departmental service. Before completing the top-ten list, students interact with advisors if they have questions about the proposed projects. These interactions are done face-to-face or through emails. This step is crucial for students to order their choices. Table 2 illustrates the data on issues raised by students.

Table 2. Proposal processing issues

Questions and Issues	Rates
Importance of discussions about proposed projects	95.2%
Challenges and difficulties during this step	61.9%
Change decision about top-ten list after discussions with professors about the proposals	64.3%
Join professors and discuss proposals before deadlines	39.4%
Challenges in joining and discussing with several professors	39.4%

Students agree on 95.2% about the importance of discussing proposed projects, and 64.3% of them state that they changed their decision about their top-ten list after discussing the proposed projects with professors. The table illustrates that 61.9% of students declared that they had met some challenges during this step. The main challenges raised by students are related to discussing proposals before the deadline of the top-ten list submission. Moreover, this challenge is accentuated when meetings with several professors are required. This happens when students feel interested in several proposed projects. On the other hand, advisors agree on 100% about the importance of this step and 60% of them pointed out that they receive several groups of students asking, in some cases, the same questions about the proposals.

Another issue is when students want to update the list (possibly before the deadline). According to the administrative staff, this update involves filing and providing another manual version.

Projects Allocation

After receiving all the top ten lists, the pedagogical team executes the allocation process. Allocation is based on student preferences. Conflicts in choices between groups are resolved by referring to a printed list of students' academic rankings calculated for the previous year. Each group is assigned a project proposal to work on at the beginning of the second semester. The administrative staff validates this assignment. The main problem with this step is that it is done manually and takes a long time. The allocation result is published by manual posting on the official website or social media page.

Projects Realization

During the project's realization, students must meet with supervisors to establish a working plan, steps, tasks, the required output of each step, and the deadlines. This intense exchange raises several issues from both students' and advisors' points of view as depicted in Table3.

Table 3. Project realization issues

Questions and Issues	Rates
Students' point of view	
Challenges in communication with the advisors	51.2%
Challenges in communication with teammates	12.2%
Challenges in coordination with advisors	56.1%
Challenges in coordination with teammates	31.7%
Issues related to means of resource sharing	47.1%
Issues related to means of version tracking	44.1%
Issues with data and information search	50%
Advisors' point of view	
Challenges in communication with advisees	30%
Challenges in coordination with advisees	60%
Challenges in keeping track of different groups' progress	80%
Challenges in keeping track of different versions of students reports	60%
Issues with data and information search through advisees' resources	50%
Issues related to resource sharing with advisees	40%

Table 3 illustrates the rates of students and advisors that raised issues related to several aspects of collaboration:

- Students and advisors communicate via face-to-face meetings, messaging, or conferencing tools. The use of various communication platforms leads to situations of scattered information. Indeed, crucial information, data, and files are shared during communication, and using several tools makes it difficult to search for the correct information if required.

- Advisors share resources and files with students. If an advisor shares the same resource with several students, he has to send it to several addresses, and the student has to manage resources in his email box. Some advisors share resources through online drives. This solution becomes tedious with the increase of advisees.
- Students produce reports and codes that have to be corrected and checked by advisors. The students' reports pass through several versions. These versions are sent by email to the advisor. The email storage of both sides becomes rapidly overloaded, making managing different versions difficult.
- Advisors supervise several FYPs in a semester. They use personal tools (manual or online lists and tracking files) to track all students' progress. Using various applications and platforms for each aspect of collaboration during the project realization leads to slowness or repetition as the user must open several windows to manage these aspects and post some information or data on several platforms.

Projects Assessment

By the end of the second semester, FYP defenses are planned and prepared. The department chair provides a schedule and materials for these events. The pedagogical team assigns committee members to each project. Advisors and students are informed of the composition of each project defense, its date, time, and location (published in the official medium). Students are required to provide their physical manuscripts to committee members. These reports are provided to the department. The members of the defense committee (lecturers, assistant professors, and professors) must review and evaluate the reports. The evaluation is given after the defense of the project by filling out evaluation forms. At the end of the defense sessions, administrative reports are produced for the statistics. These tasks are done manually and by traditional office applications.

System Overview

In response to the issues raised at each stage of the process, a collaborative solution is proposed in this section to provide a comprehensive working environment that covers all stages of the process and provides tools for each issue raised. The proposed system is structured into three layers as depicted in Figure 4. The layered collaborative architecture separates basic requirements, collaboration requirements, and process requirements. This separation of concerns is the foundation of collaboration architectures. The three layers of the system are:

Figure 4. Overview of the FYP system

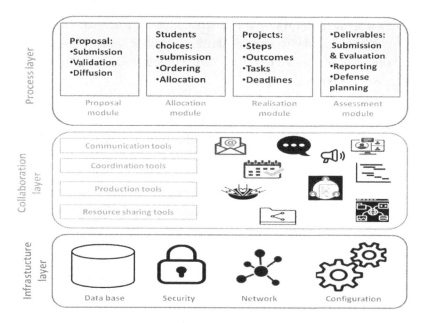

1. **Infrastructure layer:** This layer provides the execution platform for the system. It includes the database, networking resources, securing functionalities for user data and identities, and configuration functions. The system configuration allows defining the global calendar of the process: dates and deadlines for each step. The configuration also includes the definition of the different roles: students, advisors, pedagogical team members, or department head (from one year to another, the team members can change, and also the department head). Configuration is meant to be performed at the start of the second semester.

2. **Collaboration layer:** The study of the process and the raised issues has demonstrated the importance of collaboration tools to manage final year projects; hence, the proposed system contains a layer that provides a plethora of tools for every aspect of collaboration. This layer includes communication, coordination, production, and resource-sharing tools. Every module of the process uses these tools. Details about some tools will be presented in the following section.

3. **Process layer:** The FYP process layer is divided into four main modules: a proposal management module, an allocation module, a project delivery module, and an evaluation module. The proposal management module allows advisors to publish their projects. Before these projects are published for students, they are first validated by members of the pedagogical team. This module provides tools to view, discuss, and validate proposals. It also allows the modification of the proposals by the advisors if necessary. Once validated, students view the proposals and discuss the projects with advisors before filling out their top ten list forms. The assignment module provides forms for filling out student preferences. The system implements a feature to assign projects to students based on their choices and with reference to their academic records from the past year. Students are allowed to update their choices by a defined deadline. The tracking module will enable advisors and students to manage the development and progress of the project. Tools for defining milestones, timelines, and

outcomes are provided. This module also allows advisors to share different resources (documents, images, videos) and define access permissions to these resources. Students can produce documents on the platform. These documents can be viewed and modified by students and advisors. They can save different versions of the documents produced. This module allows advisors to manage the progress of several projects during the semester. The evaluation module allows students to upload their final reports or other documents. Students can view their deliverables. This module allows administrators to subscribe to defense sessions and committees. Committee members can view student evaluation reports and complete evaluation forms and defense reports.

PRESENTATION OF THE APPLICATION AND RESULTS

The proposed system was implemented as an online platform providing personal workspaces, collaboration tools, and FYP process functionality. The application is developed using PHP as the backend framework and MySQL as the database system. For the front-end development, HTML and CSS 3 were used. The GUI components are provided in a way that makes it easy to navigate between the different modules of the system and the most used features and data. Functions for all process steps and user categories are implemented. Each user has a profile with the corresponding tools and functions. Before the start of the second semester, the application administrator (department head or deputy) creates user accounts so that supervisors can submit their project proposals on the system and the pedagogical team can check them.

At the reception of all the proposals, the pedagogical team members access the platform to study the proposals. They interact online with the advisors with regard to proposals if necessary and with each other (via instant messaging) to provide a decision for every project. In the case of necessary improvement, advisors update their proposals. After the validation, the list of projects is published on the platform for students. The administrator adds it in a common shared resource space. The student users are then registered to access proposals and discuss them with advisors. Figure 5 represents a communication interface related to a proposal by a professor. The window provides, on the left side, an abstract of the project, its title, keywords, and used tools. The right side of the window provides a discussion space related to the project description.

Figure 5. Interface for student-advisor discussion about a proposal

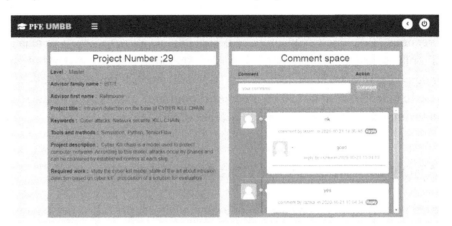

Figure 6 illustrates the overall satisfaction of the users (students and advisors) about the discussion of the proposals on both the old and the new systems. The user evaluation of the functionality is based on a 5-point scale such that: (1) Strong dissatisfaction; (2) Dissatisfaction ; (3) Neither satisfaction, nor dissatisfaction; (4) Satisfaction; (5) Strong satisfaction.

Figure 6. Proposal discussion scoring

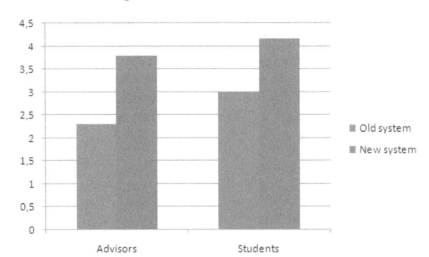

Students provide the list of their top ten projects on the platform. The pedagogical team uses this list to perform the allocation.The application automates the process of assignment. When the projects start, the application provides different functions to support students, advisors, and administrative staff. These functions are related to communication tools (chat, emails), file sharing, planning, writing, and task management.

The figure (Figure 7) illustrates an interface to track student's progress regarding different project tasks. Each task is given by its state (completed, pending, or late), its beginning date and deadline, and the progress percentage. The percentage progress of each task helps to calculate the percentage progress of the whole project. This tool is very useful for advisors who evaluated the functionality with the scores of 5 (50%) and 4 (50%). The application is also helpful for the Department head. At the approach of the end of the second semester, advisors are required to provide a report about the progress of their students. These reports are a file to be completed with information such as tasks completed, the percentage of tasks, and an estimated deadline.

Figure 7. Interface for tracking project progress

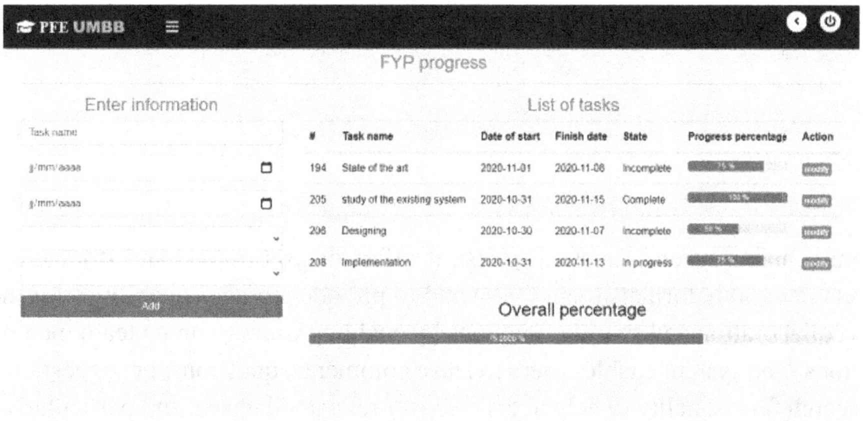

The application is designed to enhance the execution of final- year machine learning projects, offering robust functionalities for communication, coordination, and sharing of datasets among students and advisors. Figure 8 illustrates the principle features of this module.

Figure 8. Dataset sharing main interface

The system contains several functions. First, it offers dataset upload and storage to allow users to upload datasets in various formats (e.g., CSV) and to provide storage capabilities for these datasets. It also includes collaboration and sharing functions by enabling users to invite team members and control their permissions. The system enables users to leave comments, questions, or suggestions on datasets. It implements search functionality to help users discover relevant datasets and particularly allowing them to search for previous projects that used the dataset. Furthermore, the system comes with anotification system to keep theusersinformed about dataset updates, comments, and questions. It also offers the users the possibility to export and download the datasets in different formats for offline use.

The department head studies the submitted reports to get an insight into the projects' progress and plans the defense session accordingly. Instead of the manual process, the application provides visual tools for this concern. Figure 9 represents statistics on the progress of Master 2 students in the Department (the number of student groups that reach a given percentage). The department head publishes the agenda related to project defense on the platform, and the pedagogical team completes the remaining details (committee, date, and location). Students submit project reports for assessment on the platform. Defense committee members are then informed about the submissions and are provided with access the reports for evaluation.

Figure 9. An example of a reporting function

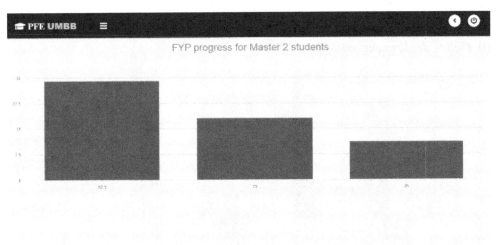

The evaluation of the system was performed in the Computer Science Department. The evaluation members included student delegates, advisors, and administrative staff. The presented system has obtained a satisfying official rate. The system was evaluated considering the following criteria: virtualization of the process steps, the ease of use, and response to collaboration requirements. Table 4 details the developed tools at each step of the FYP process. The development of these tools leads to the virtualization of the process. The advisors showed 90% attention to use. The rate of intention to use is 92.8% for students.

Table 4. Recapitulation of proposed tools

Process Step	Tools Proposed by the Application
Proposal processing	Online schedule on a common sharing space, projects submission forms, Online discussion space about proposals, Voting option for validation, Project top ten list forms.
allocation	Online top ten list form, Automatic allocation, Publication of the result of the allocation on the system
Project realization	For each project: a workspace containing: Shared resources function, Shared calendars, Redaction space, Progress bar tools & task states, Emails, discussions.
Defense preparation	Announcement space, statistics reporting functions, report submission, evaluation forms.

Figure 10 depicts the department's online tools before and after the deployment of the proposed system. Figure 10 also illustrates the usage rate of the online tools for each process step. The percentage of each step is calculated as follows: first, a detailed task list for each step is provided. Second, a score of the virtualization of each task is provided for the two cases: before the system development and after the installation of the proposed system. Finally, an average is calculated for each step in both cases. Figure 10 also shows that the production stage has the lowest percentage. This is because the current application does not consider the production of some results such as codes and does not provide advanced editing functions. The high degree of virtualization of the steps related to the processing, awarding, and evaluation of proposals has reduced the processing time related to each step. This additional time was estimated to be 4 weeks and is invested in the completion phase to allow for better student performance and knowledge acquisition.

Figure 10. Online deployment scores for FYP steps

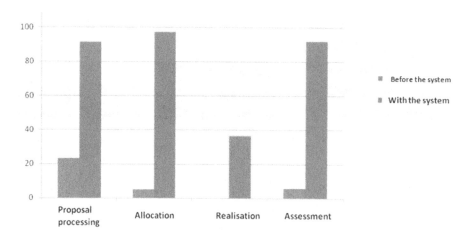

Figure 11 illustrates the improvement made by the application with respect to the aspects of online collaboration. The four aspects are presented in two cases: before the development of the system and aspects using the developed system. In the first case, the tools considered are the online tools used as an official means in each procedure by the department (official social networks, professional emails, online directories). The improvement study considers the four FYP steps. For example, communication is necessary throughout the process. Therefore, to improve, the ability to ensure communication between all users involved is considered in both directions. For example, prior to the development of the system, communication tools from students to administrative staff and from administrative staff to students did not have the same facilities and were considered as information dissemination. On the other hand, in the second case, with the new system, communication is accessible between all users. The scores of the other aspects are provided, for each of them, by citing all the activities that require it. For example, the production function is mostly required by the implementation phase; however, other activities require collaborative production, such as the production of an evaluation form by all members of the defense committee or the production of a final verification report for all projects at the end of the proposal processing stage. A score is assigned to each task based on the tools used to accomplish it, and then an average is calculated for the entire aspect.

Figure 11. Collaboration aspects improvement

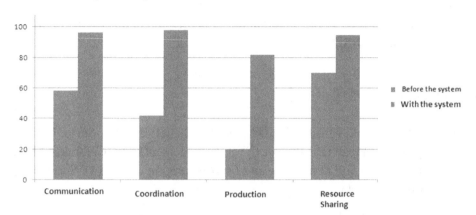

CONCLUSION

This paper introduced a collaborative application for machine learning based final -year projects. The presented system can significantly reduce the users' workload and introduce flexibility during the whole FYP management process. The modules provided address communication, sharing, coordination, and production needs. The modules related to the different user profiles, project proposals, validation, allocation, execution, and defense preparation have been successfully developed. The application provides several functions related to the dataset-sharing system, allowing greater collaboration and project management efficiency. The application is implemented considering a computer science department; however, it generalizes well since state-of-the-art has shown common steps for several disciplines. In the future, this work may benefit from several extensions. First, enhancements to the system's collaborationfunctionalities, such as advanced online editing functions, are planned. Additionally, student communities will be fostered by connecting individuals with similar project areas, facilitating knowledge exchange and mutual support. Finally, in order to enhance machine learning projects, the module for dataset sharing will benefit from advanced functions such as dataset versioning and the integration of existing tools.

ACKNOWLEDGMENT

This research was supported by the Algerian General Directorate for Scientific Research and Technological Development (DGRSDT).

REFERENCES

Abdullah, N., Salleh, S. N. M., Mahdin, H., Darman, R., Daniel, B. D., & Surin, E. S. M. (2018, February). Mitigating Manual Final Year Project (FYP) Management to Be Centralized Electronically. In *International Conference on Soft Computing and Data Mining* (pp. 105-114). Springer. https://doi.org/10.1007/978-3-319-72550-5_11

Aiken, J. M., & Lewandowski, H. J. (2021). Data sharing model for physics education research using the 70 000 response Colorado Learning Attitudes about Science Survey for Experimental Physics dataset. *Physical Review. Physics Education Research*, 17(2), 020144. 10.1103/PhysRevPhysEducRes.17.020144

Aiken, M., Wang, J., Gu, L., & Paolillo, J. (2011). An exploratory study of how technology supports communication in multilingual groups. *International Journal of e-Collaboration*, 7(1), 17–29. 10.4018/jec.2011010102

Awad, M. (2017). GPMS: An educational supportive graduation project management system. *Computer Applications in Engineering Education*, 25(6), 881–894. 10.1002/cae.21841

Azzarri, C., Bacou, M., Cox, C. M., Guo, Z., & Koo, J. (2016). Subnational socio-economic dataset availability. *Nature Climate Change*, 6(2), 115–116. 10.1038/nclimate2842

Bakar, M. A., Jailani, N., Shukur, Z., & Yatim, N. F. M. (2011). Final year supervision management system as a tool for monitoring Computer Science projects. *Procedia: Social and Behavioral Sciences*, 18, 273–281. 10.1016/j.sbspro.2011.05.039

Beus-Dukic, L. (2011, August). Final year project: A test case for requirements engineering skills. In *2011 6th International Workshop on Requirements Engineering Education and Training* (pp. 5-8). IEEE. 10.1109/REET.2011.6046272

Bringula, R. P., Balcoba, A. C., & Basa, R. S. (2016, May). Employable Skills of Information Technology Graduates in the Philippines: Do Industry Practitioners and Educators have the Same View? In *Proceedings of the 21st Western Canadian Conference on Computing Education* (pp. 1-6). 10.1145/2910925.2910928

Buchem, I., Cochrane, T., Gordon, A., Keegan, H., & Camacho, M. (2012). M-Learning 2.0: The potential and challenges of collaborative mobile learning in participatory curriculum development. In *Proceedings of the IADIS Mobile Learning Conference* (pp. 243-252). Academic Press.

Byrnes, K. G., Kiely, P. A., Dunne, C. P., McDermott, K. W., & Coffey, J. C. (2021). Communication, collaboration and contagion: "Virtualisation" of anatomy during COVID-19. *Clinical Anatomy (New York, N.Y.)*, 34(1), 82–89. 10.1002/ca.2364932648289

Chen, Y. M., Chen, T. Y., & Li, J. S. (2023). A Machine Learning-Based Anomaly Detection Method and Blockchain-Based Secure Protection Technology in Collaborative Food Supply Chain. *International Journal of e-Collaboration*, 19(1), 1–24. 10.4018/IJeC.315789

Chu, S. K. W., & Kennedy, D. M. (2011). Using online collaborative tools for groups to co-construct knowledge. *Online Information Review*, 35(4), 581–597. Advance online publication. 10.1108/14684521111161945

Clement, R., & Bounds, P. (2013). Making connections between final year students and potential project supervisors. *Proceedings of the HEA STEM annual learning and teaching conference 2013: Where practice and pedagogy meet.*

Craig, K., Humburg, M., Danish, J. A., Szostalo, M., Hmelo-Silver, C. E., & McCranie, A. (2020). Increasing students' social engagement during COVID-19 with Net. Create: Collaborative social network analysis to map historical pandemics during a pandemic. *Information and Learning Science*, 121(7/8), 533–547. Advance online publication. 10.1108/ILS-04-2020-0105

De Kleijn, R. A. M. (2013). *Master's Thesis Supervision: Feedback, interpersonal relationships, and adaptivity.* Utrecht University.

Deepamala, N., & Shobha, G. (2018). Effective approach in making Capstone project a holistic learning experience to students of undergraduate computer science engineering program. *JOTSE: Journal of Technology and Science Education*, 8(4), 420–438. 10.3926/jotse.427

Gaines, J., Akintewe, O., & Small, S. (2019). Engineering Design Instruction Using Slack for Project Support and Team-work. In *2019 ASEE Annual Conference & Exposition* (pp. 16-19). 10.18260/1-2--32721

Gardner, M., & Elliott, J. (2014). The Immersive Education Laboratory: understanding affordances, structuring experiences, and creating constructivist, collaborative processes, in mixed-reality smart environments. *EAI Endorsed Transactions on Future Intelligent Educational Environments, 14*(1). 10.4108/fiee.1.1.e6

Goh, J., Adepu, S., Junejo, K. N., & Mathur, A. (2017). A dataset to support research in the design of secure water treatment systems. In *Critical Information Infrastructures Security: 11th International Conference, CRITIS 2016, Paris, France, October 10–12, 2016, Revised Selected Papers 11* (pp. 88-99). Springer International Publishing. 10.1007/978-3-319-71368-7_8

Hapke, H., & Nelson, C. (2020). *Building machine learning pipelines.* O'Reilly Media.

Hüttel, H., & Gnaur, D. (2019). A Web-Based Platform for Competence Development in PBL Supervision. *International Journal of e-Collaboration*, 15(3), 20–33. 10.4018/IJeC.2019070102

Jailani, N. I. S. I., Ali, A. F. M., & Ngah, S. (2022, May). Final Year Project Allocation System Techniques: A Systematic Literature Review. In *2022 IEEE 12th Symposium on Computer Applications & Industrial Electronics (ISCAIE)* (pp. 99-104). IEEE. 10.1109/ISCAIE54458.2022.9794501

Jones, M. (2012). The Evolution of Digital Technologies–from Collaboration to eCollaboration–and the Tools which assist eCollaboration. *Issues in Informing Science and Information Technology*, 9, 209–219. 10.28945/1617

Kar, S. C., Ismail, S. I., Abdullah, R., Mohamed, H., & Enzai, N. M. (2020, April). Performance and Usability Testing for Online FYP System. In *Journal of Physics: Conference Series* (Vol. 1529, No. 2, p. 022029). IOP Publishing. 10.1088/1742-6596/1529/2/022029

Keerie, C., Tuck, C., Milne, G., Eldridge, S., Wright, N., & Lewis, S. C. (2018). Data sharing in clinical trials–practical guidance on anonymising trial datasets. *Trials*, 19(1), 1–8. 10.1186/s13063-017-2382-929321053

Khan, S. M., Liu, X., Nath, S., Korot, E., Faes, L., Wagner, S. K., Keane, P. A., Sebire, N. J., Burton, M. J., & Denniston, A. K. (2021). A global review of publicly available datasets for ophthalmological imaging: Barriers to access, usability, and generalisability. *The Lancet. Digital Health*, 3(1), e51–e66. 10.1016/S2589-7500(20)30240-533735069

Kumbhare, A. G., Simmhan, Y., & Prasanna, V. (2011, November). Designing a secure storage repository for sharing scientific datasets using public clouds. In *Proceedings of the second international workshop on Data intensive computing in the clouds* (pp. 31-40). 10.1145/2087522.2087530

Leung, C. H., Lai, C. L., Yuan, T. K., Pang, W. M., Tang, J. K., Ho, W. S., & Wong, T. L. (2015). The development of a final year project management system for Information Technology programmes. In *Technology in Education. Transforming Educational Practices with Technology* (pp. 86–97). Springer. 10.1007/978-3-662-46158-7_9

Leung, K., & Chu, S. K. W. (2009, December). Using wikis for collaborative learning: A case study of an undergraduate students' group project in Hong Kong. In *The International Conference on Knowledge Management* (pp. 1-14). https://web.edu.hku.hk/f/acadstaff/447/2009_wiki_learning.pdf

Naeem, U., Islam, S., & Siddiqui, A. (2019, April). An Effective Framework for Enhancing Student Engagement and Performance in Final Year Projects. In *2019 IEEE Global Engineering Education Conference (EDUCON)* (pp. 401-410). IEEE. https://doi.org/10.1109/EDUCON.2019.8725253

Prinz, W., Martínez-Carreras, M. A., & Pallot, M. (2012). From collaborative tools to collaborative working environments. In *Advancing Collaborative Knowledge Environments: New Trends in E-Collaboration* (pp. 1-10). IGI Global. 10.4018/978-1-61350-459-8.ch001

Raposo, A. B., Magalhães, L. P., Ricarte, I. L. M., & Fuks, H. (2001, September). Coordination of collaborative activities: A framework for the definition of tasks interdependencies. In *Proceedings Seventh International Workshop on Groupware. CRIWG 2001* (pp. 170-179). IEEE. 10.1109/CRIWG.2001.951845

Romdhani, I., Tawse, M., & Habibullah, S. (2011, January). Student project performance management system for effective final year and dissertation projects supervision. *London International Conference on Education*.

Roschelle, J., & Teasley, S. D. (1995). The construction of shared knowledge in collaborative problem solving. In *Computer supported collaborative learning* (pp. 69–97). Springer. 10.1007/978-3-642-85098-1_5

Rozenes, S., & Kukliansky, I. (2013). An Embedded Approach for Project Management Learning Process. *International Journal of Information Technology Project Management*, 4(3), 38–49. 10.4018/jitpm.2013070103

Sadik, A. (2017). Students' acceptance of file sharing systems as a tool for sharing course materials: The case of Google Drive. *Education and Information Technologies*, 22(5), 2455–2470. 10.1007/s10639-016-9556-z

Shamir-Inbal, T., & Blau, I. (2021). Characteristics of pedagogical change in integrating digital collaborative learning and their sustainability in a school culture: e-CSAMR framework. *Journal of Computer Assisted Learning*, 37(3), 825–838. Advance online publication. 10.1111/jcal.12526

Shinde, P. P., & Shah, S. (2018, August). A review of machine learning and deep learning applications. In *2018 Fourth international conference on computing communication control and automation (ICCUBEA)* (pp. 1-6). IEEE. 10.1109/ICCUBEA.2018.8697857

Singh, V., & Mayer, P. (2014). Scientific writing: Strategies and tools for students and advisors. *Biochemistry and Molecular Biology Education*, 42(5), 405–413. 10.1002/bmb.2081525052425

Stevenson, D., & Starkweather, J. A. (2017). IT project success: The evaluation of 142 success factors by it pm professionals. *International Journal of Information Technology Project Management*, 8(3), 1–21. 10.4018/IJITPM.2017070101

Stvilia, B., & Gibradze, L. (2022). Seeking and sharing datasets in an online community of data enthusiasts. *Library & Information Science Research*, 44(3), 101160. 10.1016/j.lisr.2022.101160

Tarazi, J., & Akre, V. L. (2013, December). Enabling e-Collaboration and e-Pedagogy at an Academic Institution in the UAE. In *2013 International Conference on Current Trends in Information Technology (CTIT)* (pp. 118-124). IEEE. 10.1109/CTIT.2013.6749489

Tiwari, G., Singh, R., Chandna, V. K., Shimi, S. L., & Jain, M. (2019). Outcome-Based Assessment of Engineering Undergraduate Final Year Projects for Tire-2 Institutes. In *Third International Congress on Information and Communication Technology* (pp. 211-221). Springer. 10.1007/978-981-13-1165-9_19

Tuah, N. M., Yoag, A., Nizam, D., Mohd, N., & Chin, C. W. (2022). A dashboard-based system to manage and monitor the progression of undergraduate it degree final year projects. *Pertanika Journal of Science & Technology*, 30(1). Advance online publication. 10.47836/pjst.30.1.13

Wrench, J. S., & Punyanunt, N. M. (2004). Advisee-advisor communication: An exploratory study examining interpersonal communication variables in the graduate advisee-advisor relationship. *Communication Quarterly*, 52(3), 224–236. 10.1080/01463370409370194

Yilmaz, M., Tasel, F. S., Gulec, U., & Sopaoglu, U. (2018). Towards a process management life-cycle model for graduation projects in computer engineering. *PLoS One*, 13(11), e0208012. 10.1371/journal.pone.020801230496242

Zuo, X., Chen, Y., Ohno-Machado, L., & Xu, H. (2021). How do we share data in COVID-19 research? A systematic review of COVID-19 datasets in PubMed Central Articles. *Briefings in Bioinformatics*, 22(2), 800–811. 10.1093/bib/bbaa33133757278

Chapter 20
Personality Prediction Based on Myers–Briggs Type Indicator Using Machine Learning

N. Krishnamoorthy
Vellore Institute of Technology, India

Vinoth Kumar Venkatesan
Vellore Institute of Technology, India

B. Swapna
https://orcid.org/0000-0002-7186-2842
Dr. MGR Educational and Research Institute, India

Deepakshi Rawal
Vellore Institute of Technology, India

Dakshita Dutta
Vellore Institute of Technology, India

S. Sushil
Vellore Institute of Technology, India

ABSTRACT

The personality indicator uses machine learning techniques to assess each person's personality in both the personal and professional lives. There are various types of indicators, but the two commonly used ones are Myers-Briggs type indicator (MTBI) and big five personality traits model. This work used MBTI personality indicator, and it can offer valuable insights. It attempted to use SVD, naive bayes, random forest, and logistic regression machine learning approaches for personality prediction. This model makes it simple for users to identify their personalities and technical abilities. This personality indicator is based on MBTI that categorizes individuals into one of 16 personality types. This approach has the potential to provide a more objective and scalable way of assessing personality, compared to traditional self-report measures. The use of MBTI type based on their online activity, such as their social media posts and communication habits, has gained popularity in recent years.

I. INTRODUCTION

The "Myers-Briggs Type Indicator (MBTI)" is a personality assessment tool that reflects and categorize a person's character into 16 individual personality types namely extraversion vs. introversion, sensing vs. intuition, thinking vs. feeling, and judging vs. perceiving. These traits change throughout time and

DOI: 10.4018/979-8-3693-0683-3.ch020

may vary depending on the situation. This prediction has led to the development of new tools that can provide individuals with accurate and personalized feedback on their personality traits (Amirhosseini, M. H., & Kazemian, H, 2020). There are numerous other personality models, but the MBTI is the most well-known and effective due to broader application in a variety of disciplines. Nowadays, automatic personality prediction from social networks has drawn growing interest from both the natural language processing and social science communities. (Bleidorn, W., & Hopwood, C. J, 2019) Social networks can also be used to learn more about a person's personality. There are many other ways to post something on social media, including using an image, a URL link, or music. In this research, we have used forum messages to categorize an individual into 16 MBTI types shown in Figure 1. (Mehta, Y et al., 2020) with the help of machine learning, it has become possible to gain valuable insights into human behaviour that was previously difficult to obtain. In this paper, we have used four models namely SVD (Singular Value Decomposition), Random Forest, Naive Bayes and logistic regression to predict MBTI personalities. With each model, we have tried to increase the prediction's accuracy. Then, we have used the model with highest accuracy to predict personality on a sample dataset and tell which type of people exists most in the world.

Figure 1. Shows all the 16 MBTI categories and what each category tells about the personality of a person from Creative Commons Attribution-ShareAlike 4.0 International

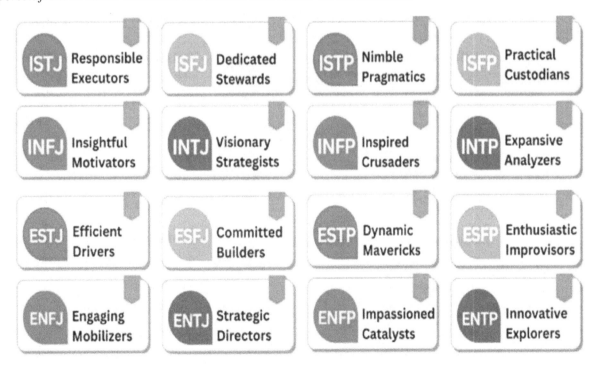

This personality indicator can be used in various streams like career development, team building and collaboration, leadership development, education and personality development. In career development, MBTI type can provide valuable guidance for career exploration and decision making. (Khan, A. S et al., 2020) for example, Extrovert people tend more likely to involve in jobs with maximum interaction and teamwork while it is opposite for introvert people. In team building and collaboration, MBTI can be used to understand strengths and weaknesses of team members and assign roles accordingly to get out maximum input from them.

In leadership development, thinking related people will prefer logical analysis and task-oriented jobs while feeling oriented types emphasize more on empathy and relation building. This depends upon the type of leadership needed for a particular type of team. In Education, MBTI can be used to identify various learning styles for different types of students. Educators can provide an inclusive and effective learning environment for students. In personality development, MBTI can provide person's strengths and weaknesses so that they can improve their skills, personal growth, better relationships and improved interactions shown in Figure 2.

Figure 2. Shows what each key of each personality type means (Mohammad Hossein et al., 2020)

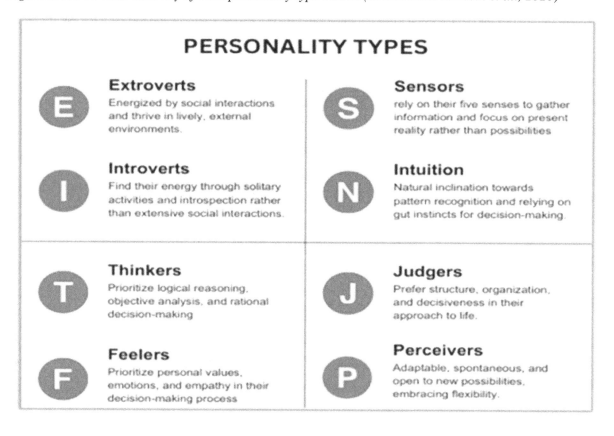

II. RELATED WORKS

The Myers-Briggs Type Indicator (MBTI) has been widely studied and researched leading to criticism, debates regarding its psychometric properties but still tend to remain one of the best personality indicators. (Mazza C et al., 2019) this method is used in this study to classify people into 16 different personality types based on a variety of personality traits, such as extraversion vs. introversion, sensing vs. intuition, thinking vs. emotion, and judging vs. perceiving. Studies using datasets of voice signals suggest that the speech was harder to understand than other datasets.

To the best of knowledge, they focused verbal characteristics classified by Support Vector Machine (SVM) with a focus on feature extraction and classification techniques. As an example, a personality prediction model based on the user's vocabulary was developed, which offered evidence that language-related (Tay L et al., 2020) evaluation might be a trustworthy way to assess personality. The linguistic inquiry and word count (LIWC) approach was developed by pioneering psychologists Pennebaker and King after they reliably linked writing style to personality. (Stachl C et al., 2020).Deep neural networks are mostly used in the most recent approach to study personality traits through semantic understanding. A thorough overview of the area is provided in some review articles (Abidin N. H. Z.et al., 2020).

In order to find more personality-related traits, they altered the BERT model. Then, each sentence is used as a vector representation and each word and token-level coding representation is encoded using a tuned BERT model (Ren Z et al., 2021). The Synthetic Minority Oversampling Technique (SMOTE) was created to lessen oversampling flaws by creating synthetic data (Wang Z. H. E et al.,2019) Despite SMOTE's success in many applications, some of the generated samples correlate with some of the original minority samples. (Rastogi R et al., 2020) examined recent research on (Krishnamoorthy N et al., 2022) deep learning-based automated personality systems with a focus on successful multimodal personality prediction (Hans C et al., 2021).

III. MATERIALS AND METHODS

A. Dataset as Material

The dataset is collected from Kaggle. The size of dataset used is Users (11187792, 5), ForumMessages (1727978, 8), mbti (8675,2).

There are three files in this dataset:

Users – It includes the users with data such as Id, name, DisplayName (name by which user uses the platform), RegisterDate and PerformanceTier (0 to 5).

Forum Messages – It consists of Id, ForumTop (top number list on forum), PostUserId(User who posted the message), ReplyToForumMessageId, Message, Medal, MedalAwardDate.

Mbti – It consists of only two columns namely type of personality (out of 16) and forum post related to that type.

B. Development Tools

The development approach made use of the distributed gradient boosting module for Python called XGBoost and the natural language processing toolkit (NLTK). NLTK is a potent natural language processing toolkit used to create Python program that process data in human language (Koti et al., 2022). Additionally, the Gradient Boosting framework's machine learning algorithms can be implemented using XGBoost. Other Python libraries utilised were matplotlib, sklearn, numpy, re, seaborn, and pandas (Natarajan, R et al., 2023).

IV. EXPERIMENTAL PROCEDURE

Matplotlib is a powerful Python 2D plotting library widely used for visualizing data and creating various types of graphs, including line plots, scatter plots, bar charts, histograms, and more. It provides a flexible and customizable interface to create publication-quality visualizations for data analysis and exploration (Kumar, V. V et al., 2021). On the other hand, Seaborn, a data visualisation library built on top of Matplotlib, makes it even easier to produce eye-catching statistical graphics. With Seaborn's higher-level interface, it's simpler to create intricate visualizations with short code. It is especially helpful for producing visually appealing statistical plots that can provide deeper insights into the dataset, such as violin plots, box plots, and joint plots.

Figure 3. Number of occurrences for all the 16 personality types

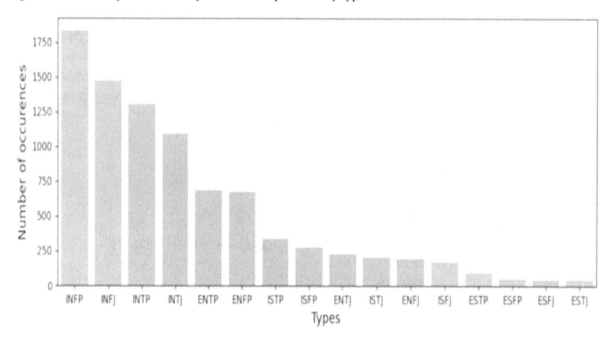

These two libraries Matplotlib and Seaborn complement one another in data analysis and exploration and together make up a vital toolkit for data scientists and analysts. Their combined functionalities enable a thorough and sophisticated analysis of the data, assisting in the discovery of significant patterns and relationships that might otherwise go undetected (Kumar, D et al., 2021). Figure 3, as depicted, showcases the distribution of all 16 MBTI (Myers- Briggs Type Indicator) personality types within the dataset. This visualisation offers preliminary insights into potential trends or patterns related to personality traits and offers useful information on the prevalence of each personality type (Jalaeian Zaferani E et al., 2022).

The first model we used to analyze the dataset is SVD (Singular Value Decomposition) which is a mathematical matrix factorization technique used to correlate certain words and phrases in written or spoken with specific personality traits (Ahmed, S. T et al., 2023). It is used to identify underlying patterns and relationships between words and personality of the user. The equation below represents

SVD where A is an m*n matrix, U is an m * m orthogonal matrix, V is an n*n orthogonal matrix and V is transpose of V.

A = UΣV   (1)

To compute the SVD of a given m x n matrix A, we first calculate the product of A and its transpose A to obtain matrix B. Next, we find the eigenvalues and corresponding eigenvectors of B. These eigenvalues are then sorted in descending order, and the first m eigenvectors are used to construct an orthogonal matrix U. The singular values are obtained by taking the square root of the sorted eigenvalues and used to create a diagonal matrix Σ. Finally, we compute the orthogonal matrix V by using the original matrix A, U, and the inverse of Σ. The resulting matrices U, Σ, and V constitute the Singular Value Decomposition of A, where U represents the left singular vectors, Σ contains the singular values, and V represents the right singular vectors. SVD allows us to express complex matrices as a product of simpler components, enabling a deeper understanding of the data's underlying structures and facilitating various applications like data compression and image processing.

For using this model, we first replace any NaN (Not a Number) values in the message column with text data that contains missing values. After this, the data is grouped by user id and all the messages for that particular user is concatenated with spaces separating each message. A learning technique called ExtraTreesClassifier fits numerous decision tree classifiers on various dataset samples and uses averaging to improve the accuracy (Krishnamoorthy N et al., 2016). TfidfVectorizer is a text feature extraction method that converts raw data into a matrix which can further be used for feeding data into a learning model. TruncatedSVD is a linear dimensionality reduction technique used for reducing the dimensions of text data and it works by performing SVD on the data matrix. An instance of all the three class is created from the scikit-learn library. These are then processed using pipeline in python and then StratifiedKFold class is used to evaluate the performance of the model by iterating over the folds. Finally, cross-validation is done and accuracy, F1-score and log loss for the SVD model is calculated. Table 1 shows all these parameters for SVD model technique applied on dataset.

Table 1. Accuracy, F1, and LogLoss for SVD model

SVD Model	
CV Accuracy	**0.2883(+/-0.0159)**
CV F1	0.2883(+/-0.0159)
CV Logloss	-2.1516(+/-0.0140)

The accuracy for SVD model was not satisfactory enough so we applied Random Forest model to increase the accuracy for prediction of the personality of a user. Random Forest is a machine learning algorithm that belongs to ensemble methods which combines multiple techniques for prediction (Krishnamoorthy N et al., 2021). It works by an ensemble of decision trees and uses majority voting for final prediction. Each tree is made of random subset of dataset with replacement. This randomness helps to reduce overfitting so that the model's generalization ability increases.

In this, forum messages post is the input variable while type of personality is the target variable. The textual data is converted into numerical data using countVectorizer function. The training split is taken as 80% while testing split is 20% which is done using tran_test_split function. The training set is used to train random forest model on the labelled examples. Here, the model learns to map the features of corresponding MBTI personality types. An instance of random forest classifier is created for classification of posts into different personality types. After training the data with the model then predictions are made on the testing data (Devi K. N et al., 2022). Finally, the accuracy, F1 and LogLoss is calculated for Random Forest model. This model has hyperparameters that control their behaviours such as number of trees, maximum depth of trees and number of features used at each split. Tuning of these parameters is performed like cross – validation to find the optimal set of hyperparameters and get the best performance for the random forest model. Table 2 shows all these parameters for random forest applied on dataset.

Table 2. Accuracy, F1, and LogLoss for random forest model

Random Forest Model	
CV Accuracy	**0.3914**
CV F1	0.3171
CV Logloss	2.4439

Random forest increased the accuracy of prediction but still satisfactory numbers were not obtained. Next, we tried to use Naïve Bayes algorithm to train and test the data. Naïve Bayes is a probabilistic classification algorithm used to calculate probability of a category and its features and then chooses the category with highest probability as the predicted one for the sample (Krishnamoorthy, N et al., 2021). This algorithm assumes that the features are conditionally independent given the class. This means that presence or absence of a particular feature does not affect the presence or absence of other features. The equation given below is the Bayes Theorem used here.

$$P(A|B) = P(B|A) * P(A) / P(B) \qquad (2)$$

Before proceeding with the next model, we decided to clean the posts column of mbti data using BeautifulSoup which removes all the HTML tags that are present in the text and the occurrences of various operators is also removed. MultinomialNB is a class that uses Naïve Bayes classifier for text classification. Also, handling the missing values is really important. This model takes the posts column data as input, converts them into a matrix of token counts using a CountVectorizer class and then trains a Naïve Bayes classifier on the resulting matrix. The training data is used to calculate the prior probabilities for each MBTI personality type. The likelihoods of each feature is also calculated using the Naïve Bayes assumption of conditional independence between features. The zero probabilities are handled using Laplace smoothing. For the testing set, Bayes Theorem is used to calculate the posterior probability of each MBTI personality type. The sample is assigned to that class with highest posterior probability. Here, the hyperparameter tuning is optional and not necessarily required. Thus, the resulting model can be used to classify on the basis of 16 MBTI categories. Finally, the accuracy, F1 and LogLoss is calculated for Naïve Bayes model. Table 3 shows all these parameters for Naïve Bayes model technique applied on dataset.

Table 3. Accuracy, F1, and LogLoss for naïve Bayes model

Naïve Bayes Model	
CV Accuracy	**0.5622(+/-0.0114)**
CV F1	0.5622(+/-0.0114)
CV Logloss	6.1920(+/-0.3672)

The results from Naïve Bayes model were better than SVD but we decided to use another model named Logistic Regression to further increase the accuracy of the model. Logistic Devi, K. N., et al (2022) Regression is a classification algorithm which works by fitting a logistic function to the data which maps the input features with output probability of a particular category. The logistic regression model starts with a linear combination of features weighted by coefficients. The linear model is given by the equation given below:

$$z = \beta_0 + \beta_1 * x \tag{3}$$

Here, z is the linear combination of the intercept β_0 and the coefficient β_1 multiplied by feature x. To convert the linear model's output into a probability between 0 and 1, the logistic function is applied. The logistic function is defined as:

$$p = 1 / (1 + \exp(-z)) \tag{4}$$

Here, p represents the probability of the positive class (e.g., belonging to a specific MBTI personality type), and exp() denotes the exponential function. The data here is first transformed to a vector using CountVectorizer and then the model is trained by already labelled personality types. The trained model can be used to predict new user's personality. The regularization strength of logistic regression model is set to 0.005. This model trains a logistic regression classifier on the resulting matrix. This model learns the relationship between the features and the binary target variable which is MBTI type and estimates the weights for each feature. After training, it is used to make predictions on the testing set (Krishnamoorthy N et al., 2021). The model will output probabilities of an individual belonging to each MBTI type, which can be thresholder to make binary predictions. Logistic regression models are interpretable, and you can analyse the learned coefficients to understand which features are most influential in predicting specific MBTI personality types. Finally, the accuracy, F1 and LogLoss is calculated for Logistic Regression model. Table 4 shows all these parameters for Logistic Regression model technique applied on dataset.

Table 4. Accuracy, F1, and LogLoss for logistic regression model

Logistic Regression Model	
CV Accuracy	**0.6522(+/-0.0134)**
CV F1	0.6522(+/-0.0134)
CV Logloss	1.3080(+/-0.0125)

V. RESULTS AND DISCUSSIONS

Amongst all the four models, Logistic Regression model proves to be the best amongst all as it gives the accuracy of 65.52%. A learning curve is generated for this model which is trained earlier. It is a plot that illustrates how a machine learning system performs better with more training data (Mahesh T. R et al., 2023). It helps to detect issues like underfitting and overfitting. Figure 4 shows the learning curve for Logistic Regression. It shows that as the size of training dataset increases, accuracy of model gradually decreases while the accuracy on test set gradually increases. Both the increase and decrease is not that significant here. In this case, the relatively stable and non-drastic changes in the accuracy signifies that the model is nether heavily underfitted nor overfitted and hence maintaining a balanced performance. Additional training data allows the model to understand more patterns in data helps to improve the performance of the test set. Availability of additional training data and the computational resources required for training is essential for improving the performance of the model. It aids in the fine-tuning of hyper parameters and the overall optimization of the model

Figure 4. Learning curve for logistic regression

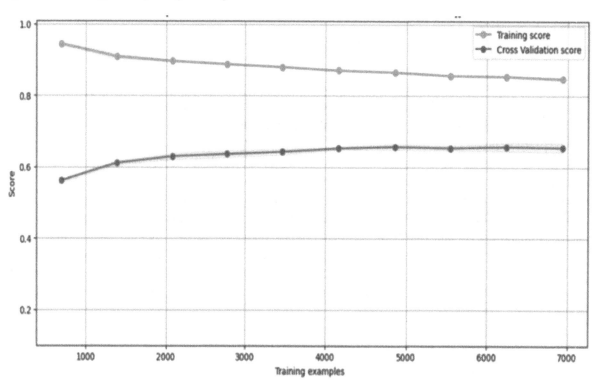

A bar plot is constructed that is used to visualize number of occurrences of each personality type in from logistic regression model's output. It determines easy identification of the most and the least common personality types in the model's predictions. ESFP (Extroverts Sensors Feelers Perceivers) which are often described as fun loving, warm and spontaneous individuals occur most in the test dataset. They enjoy engaging with others, seeking new experiences, and tend to be sensitive to the needs and emotions of those around them. INFJ (Introvert Intuition Feeling Judging) are insightful, empathetic and idealistic individuals. They have a deep understanding of human emotions and motivations and often seek to help and support others. This category occurs the least in the test dataset. The Figure 5 below shows the number of occurrences of each personality types from logistic regression model's output.

Figure 5. Number of occurrences of each type of personality in test dataset using logistic regression model

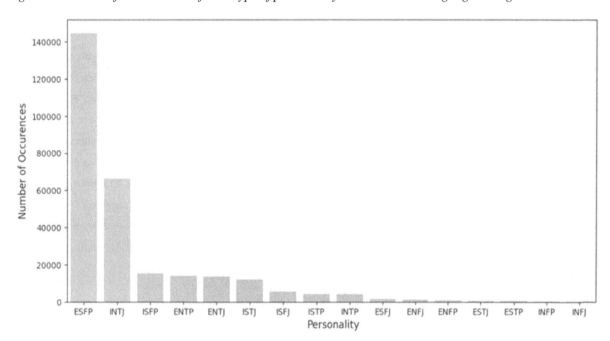

To determine each personality count and its percentage present in the dataset, we construct a data frame and sum the similar type of personality for count value. A new column named description is added to the data-frame by applying a lambda function to the values in the personality column. It contains the textual descriptions of each personality type based on the MBTI codes. The lambda function converts each value in personality to a string representation by joining the corresponding values from the mbti dataset. This can be helpful for providing more understandable and human-readable representations of the personality types in the Data-Frame. The descriptions can be used for further analysis or for better visualization of the results. The Figure 6 below shows the count and percentage of each personality type. The percentage of ESFP is maximum having percentage of 50.05% and a count of 144845 and INFJ has least percentage of 0.0995% with a count of just 285 individuals. The data frame consists of 4 columns namely personality, count, percentage and description for each of the 16 MBTI personality types.

Figure 6. Count and percentage of each personality type in dataset

	personality	count	percent	description
5	ESFP	144845	0.505798	Extroversion Sensing Feeling Perceiving
10	INTJ	66435	0.231991	Introversion Intutions Thinking Judging
13	ISFP	15302	0.053435	Introversion Sensing Feeling Perceiving
3	ENTP	14198	0.049579	Extroversion Intutions Thinking Perceiving
2	ENTJ	13814	0.048238	Extroversion Intutions Thinking Judging
14	ISTJ	12036	0.042030	Introversion Sensing Thinking Judging
12	ISFJ	5651	0.019733	Introversion Sensing Feeling Judging
15	ISTP	4302	0.015023	Introversion Sensing Thinking Perceiving
11	INTP	4238	0.014799	Introversion Intutions Thinking Perceiving
4	ESFJ	1471	0.005137	Extroversion Sensing Feeling Judging
0	ENFJ	1343	0.004690	Extroversion Intutions Feeling Judging
1	ENFP	901	0.003146	Extroversion Intutions Feeling Perceiving
6	ESTJ	650	0.002270	Extroversion Sensing Thinking Judging
7	ESTP	533	0.001861	Extroversion Sensing Thinking Perceiving
9	INFP	365	0.001275	Introversion Intutions Feeling Perceiving
8	INFJ	285	0.000995	Introversion Intutions Feeling Judging

Plotly library is used to create a pie chart representing the distribution of personality types based on the description column in the Data Frame. The pie chart displays the percentage of each personality type in the dataset. Each slice of the pie chart corresponds to a personality type, and its size represents the percentage of occurrences of that personality type in the dataset. The Figure 7 below shows the pie chart.

Figure 7. Pie chart for above percentage of personality types

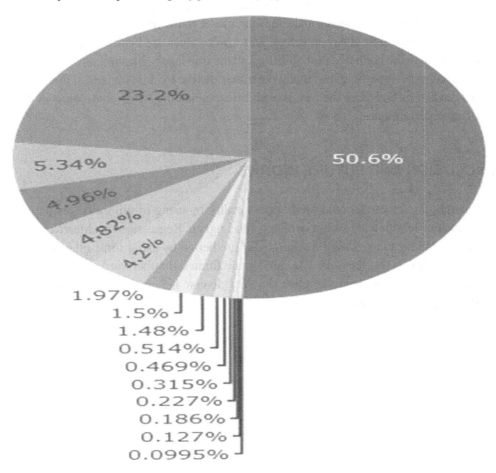

Table 5. Results

	Accuracy	F1 Score	Log Loss
SVD	28.83%	0.2883	-2.1516
Random Forest	39.14%	0.3171	2.4439
Naive Bayes	56.22%	0.5622	6.1920
Logistic Regression	65.52%	0.6552	1.3080

Accuracy, F1 score, and Log Loss are commonly used evaluation metrics in machine learning classification tasks. Each of these metrics serves a specific purpose in assessing the performance of a classification model. Accuracy measures the overall correctness of the model's predictions. F1 score provides a balance between precision and recall, making it useful for imbalanced datasets. Log Loss assesses the accuracy of predicted probabilities, making it suitable for probabilistic classification tasks. Highest accuracy tells that the model is best to be applied on the test dataset. An F1 score near 0 implies poor model performance, indicating a significant number of false positives and/or false negatives. An

F1 score near 1 indicates excellent model performance, suggesting that the model is making accurate predictions for the positive class with a good balance of precision and recall. A lower log loss value indicates that the model's predicted probabilities are closer to the true probabilities, which is desirable. In practice, log loss is almost always positive, and lower values are better. A log loss of 0 indicates a perfect match between the predicted probabilities and the true labels, meaning the model's confidence in its predictions aligns perfectly with the actual outcomes. As the log loss increases, the model's predicted probabilities deviate further from the true probabilities, indicating lower confidence in the predictions and less accurate performance.

VI. CONCLUSION AND FUTURE WORKS

In conclusion, this research could predict personality by using forum messages data, and the best model of a machine learning algorithm, which is the Logistic Regression machine learning algorithm.

In future, we can try to increase the accuracy of prediction by using some other model. The reason for accuracy being low is that the train data can contain limited English word samples but the actual test data consists a lot more than that as English is a very diverse language. Still, the improvement can be done by applying different models in future.

REFERENCES

Abidin, N. H. Z., Remli, M. A., Ali, N. M., Phon, D. N. E., Yusoff, N., Adli, H. K., & Busalim, A. H. (2020). Improving intelligent personality prediction using Myers-Briggs type indicator and random forest classifier. *International Journal of Advanced Computer Science and Applications*, 11(11). Advance online publication. 10.14569/IJACSA.2020.0111125

Ahmed, S. T., Kumar, V. V., & Kim, J. (2023). AITel: eHealth Augmented-Intelligence-Based Telemedicine Resource Recommendation Framework for IoT Devices in Smart Cities. *IEEE Internet of Things Journal*, 10(21), 18461–18468. 10.1109/JIOT.2023.3243784

Amirhosseini, M. H., & Kazemian, H. (2020). Machine learning approach to personality type prediction based on the myers–briggs type indicator®. *Multimodal Technologies and Interaction*, 4(1), 9. 10.3390/mti4010009

Bleidorn, W., & Hopwood, C. J. (2019). Using machine learning to advance personality assessment and theory. *Personality and Social Psychology Review*, 23(2), 190–203. 10.1177/1088868318772990029792115

Devi, K. N., Krishnamoorthy, N., Jayanthi, P., Karthi, S., Karthik, T., & Kiranbharath, K. (2022, January). Machine Learning Based Adult Obesity Prediction. In *2022 International Conference on Computer Communication and Informatics (ICCCI)* (pp. 1-5). IEEE.

Hans, C., Suhartono, D., Andry, C., & Zamli, K. Z. (2021). Text based personality prediction from multiple social media data sources using pre-trained language model and model averaging. *Journal of Big Data*, 8(68).

Jalaeian Zaferani, E., Teshnehlab, M., & Vali, M. (2022). Automatic personality recognition and perception using deep learning and supervised evaluation method. *Journal of Applied Research on Industrial Engineering, 9*(2), 197-211.

Khan, A. S., Hussain, A., Asghar, M. Z., Saddozai, F. K., Arif, A., & Khalid, H. A. (2020). Personality classification from online text using machine learning approach. *International Journal of Advanced Computer Science and Applications*, 11(3). Advance online publication. 10.14569/IJACSA.2020.0110358

Koti, M. S., Muthukumaran, V., Devi, A., Rajalakshmi, V., Kumar, S. S., & Kumar, V. V. (2022). Efficient Deep Learning Techniques for Security and Privacy in Industry. *Cyber Security and Operations Management for Industry 4.0, 2–32.*

Krishnamoorthy, N., Asokan, R., & Jones, I. (2016). Classification of malignant and benign micro calcifications from mammogram using optimized cascading classifier. *Current Signal Transduction Therapy*, 11(2), 98–104. 10.2174/1574362411666160614083720

Krishnamoorthy, N., Nirmaladevi, K., Kumaravel, T., Nithish, K. S., Sarathkumar, S., & Sarveshwaran, M. (2022, April). Diagnosis of Pneumonia Using Deep Learning Techniques. In *2022 Second International Conference on Advances in Electrical, Computing, Communication and Sustainable Technologies (ICAECT)* (pp. 1-5). IEEE. 10.1109/ICAECT54875.2022.9807954

Krishnamoorthy, N., Nirmaladevi, K., Shanth, S., & Karthikeyan, N. (2021, November). Investigation and comparison of different CNN architectures on tomato leaf disease prediction using deep learning. In *AIP Conference Proceedings* (Vol. 2387, No. 1). AIP Publishing. 10.1063/5.0068638

Krishnamoorthy, N., Prasad, L. N., Kumar, C. P., Subedi, B., Abraha, H. B., & Sathishkumar, V. E. (2021). Rice leaf diseases prediction using deep neural networks with transfer learning. *Environmental Research*, 198, 111275. 10.1016/j.envres.2021.11127533989629

Kumar, D., Swathi, P., Jahangir, A., Sah, N. K., & Vinothkumar, V. (2021). Intelligent speech processing technique for suspicious voice call identification using adaptive machine learning approach. In *Handbook of Research on Innovations and Applications of AI, IoT, and Cognitive Technologies* (pp. 372-380). IGI Global. 10.4018/978-1-7998-6870-5.ch025

Kumar, V. V., Raghunath, K. M. K., Muthukumaran, V., Joseph, R. B., Beschi, I. S., & Uday, A. K. (2021). Aspect based sentiment analysis and smart classification in uncertain feedback pool. *International Journal of System Assurance Engineering and Management*, 13(S1), 252–262.

Mahesh, T. R., Sivakami, R., Manimozhi, I., Krishnamoorthy, N., & Swapna, B. (2023). Early Predictive Model for Detection of Plant Leaf Diseases Using MobileNetV2 Architecture. *International Journal of Intelligent Systems and Applications in Engineering*, 11(2), 46–54.

Mazza, C., Monaro, M., Orrù, G., Burla, F., Colasanti, M., Ferracuti, S., & Roma, P. (2019). Introducing machine learning to detect personality faking-good in a male sample: A new model based on Minnesota multiphasic personality inventory-2 restructured form scales and reaction times. *Frontiers in Psychiatry*, 10, 389. 10.3389/fpsyt.2019.0038931275176

Mehta, Y., Fatehi, S., Kazameini, A., Stachl, C., Cambria, E., & Eetemadi, S. (2020, November). Bottom-up and top-down: Predicting personality with psycholinguistic and language model features. In *2020 IEEE International Conference on Data Mining (ICDM)* (pp. 1184-1189). IEEE. 10.1109/ICDM50108.2020.00146

Mehta, Y., Majumder, N., Gelbukh, A., & Cambria, E. (2020). Recent trends in deep learning based personality detection. *Artificial Intelligence Review*, 53(4), 2313–2339. 10.1007/s10462-019-09770-z

Natarajan, R., Lokesh, G. H., Flammini, F., Premkumar, A., Venkatesan, V. K., & Gupta, S. K. (2023). A Novel Framework on Security and Energy Enhancement Based on Internet of Medical Things for Healthcare 5.0. *Infrastructures*, 8(2), 22. 10.3390/infrastructures8020022

Rastogi, R., Chaturvedi, D. K., Satya, S., Arora, N., Trivedi, P., Singh, A. K., & Singh, A. (2020). Intelligent analysis for personality detection on various indicators by clinical reliable psychological TTH and stress surveys. *Computational Intelligence in Pattern RecognitionProceedings of CIPR*, 2019, 127–143.

Ren, Z., Shen, Q., Diao, X., & Xu, H. (2021). A sentiment-aware deep learning approach for personality detection from text. *Information Processing & Management*, 58(3), 102532. 10.1016/j.ipm.2021.102532

Stachl, C., Pargent, F., Hilbert, S., Harari, G. M., Schoedel, R., Vaid, S., & Bühner, M. (2020). Personality research and assessment in the era of machine learning. *European Journal of Personality*, 34(5), 613–631. 10.1002/per.2257

Tay, L., Woo, S. E., Hickman, L., & Saef, R. M. (2020). Psychometric and validity issues in machine learning approaches to personality assessment: A focus on social media text mining. *European Journal of Personality*, 34(5), 826–844. 10.1002/per.2290

Wang, Z. H. E., Wu, C., Zheng, K., Niu, X., & Wang, X. (2019). SMOTETomek-based resampling for personality recognition. *IEEE Access : Practical Innovations, Open Solutions*, 7, 129678–129689. 10.1109/ACCESS.2019.2940061

Compilation of References

5G. no llegaría a Costa Rica antes de fines de 2024. (2022, August 20). From BN Americas: https://www.bnamericas.com/es/noticias/5g-no-llegaria-a-costa-rica-antes-de-fines-de-2024

Abbas, N., Abbas, Z., Liu, X., Khan, S. S., Foster, E. D., & Larkin, S. (2023). A Survey: Future Smart Cities Based on Advance Control of Unmanned Aerial Vehicles (UAVs). *Applied Sciences (Basel, Switzerland)*, 13(17), 9881. 10.3390/app13179881

Abbas, N., & Liu, X. (2022). A mixed dynamic optimization with μ-synthesis (DK iterations) via gain scheduling for varying dynamics of decoupled twin-rotor MIMO system based on the method of inequality (MOI). *Con. Eng. Appl. Inf*, 24, 13–23.

Abbas, N., Pan, X., Raheem, A., Shakoor, R., Arfeen, Z. A., Rashid, M., Umer, F., Safdar, N., & Liu, X. (2022). Real-time robust generalized dynamic inversion based optimization control for coupled twin rotor MIMO system. *Scientific Reports*, 12(1), 17852. 10.1038/s41598-022-21357-336284142

Abdeldjouad, F. Z., Brahami, M., & Matta, N. (2020). A hybrid approach for heart disease diagnosis and prediction using machine learning techniques. *The Impact of Digital Technologies on Public Health in Developed and Developing Countries: 18th International Conference, ICOST 2020, Hammamet, Tunisia, June 24–26, 2020Proceedings*, 18, 299–306.

Abdullah, N., Salleh, S. N. M., Mahdin, H., Darman, R., Daniel, B. D., & Surin, E. S. M. (2018, February). Mitigating Manual Final Year Project (FYP) Management to Be Centralized Electronically. In *International Conference on Soft Computing and Data Mining* (pp. 105-114). Springer. https://doi.org/10.1007/978-3-319-72550-5_11

Abidin, N. H. Z., Remli, M. A., Ali, N. M., Phon, D. N. E., Yusoff, N., Adli, H. K., & Busalim, A. H. (2020). Improving intelligent personality prediction using Myers-Briggs type indicator and random forest classifier. *International Journal of Advanced Computer Science and Applications*, 11(11). Advance online publication. 10.14569/IJACSA.2020.0111125

Abukhzam, M., & Lee, A. (2010). Workforce attitude on technology adoption and Diffusion, *The Built & Human. Environmental Reviews*, 3, 60–72. https://www.semanticscholar.org/paper/

Adakawa, K. (1995). *Development of AUV: Aqua explorer 1000*. Academic Press.

Adam, J. A. (1985). Probing beneath the sea. *IEEE Spectrum*, 22(4), 55–64. 10.1109/MSPEC.1985.6370620

Adam, J. D. (1991). Using a micro-sub for in-vessel visual inspection. *Nuclear Europe Worldscan*, 10, 5–6.

Adhatrao, K., Gaykar, A., Dhawan, A., Jha, R., & Honrao, V. (2013). Predicting students' performance using ID3 and C4. 5 classification algorithms. arXiv preprint arXiv:1310.2071.

Aggarwal, P. K., Jain, P., Mehta, J., Garg, R., Makar, K., & Chaudhary, P. (2021). Machine learning, data mining, and big data analytics for 5G-enabled IoT. *Blockchain for 5G-Enabled IoT: The new wave for Industrial Automation,* 351-375.

Ahad, A., Tahir, M., Sheikh, M. A., Ahmed, K. I., Mughees, A., & Numani, A. (2020). Technologies trend towards 5g network for smart healthcare using IoT: A review. *Sensors (Basel)*, 20(14), 4047. 10.3390/s2014404732708139

Ahamad, S., Veeraiah, V., Ramesh, J. V. N., Rajadevi, R., Reeja, S. R., Pramanik, S., & Gupta, A. (2023). Deep Learning based Cancer Detection Technique. In *Thrust Technologies' Effect on Image Processing*. IGI Global.

Ahmed, F., Mohanta, J. C., Keshari, A., & Yadav, P. S. (2022). Recent Advances in Unmanned Aerial Vehicles: A Review. *Arabian Journal for Science and Engineering*, 47(7), 7963–7984. 10.1007/s13369-022-06738-035492958

Ahmed, S. T., Kumar, V. V., & Kim, J. (2023). AITel: eHealth Augmented-Intelligence-Based Telemedicine Resource Recommendation Framework for IoT Devices in Smart Cities. *IEEE Internet of Things Journal*, 10(21), 18461–18468. 10.1109/JIOT.2023.3243784

Ai, G., Zhang, Y., Wen, Y., Gu, M., Zhang, H., & Wang, P. (2023). Convolutional neural network-based lightweight hardware IP core design for EEG epilepsy prediction. *Microelectronics*, 137, 105810. 10.1016/j.mejo.2023.105810

Aiken, J. M., & Lewandowski, H. J. (2021). Data sharing model for physics education research using the 70 000 response Colorado Learning Attitudes about Science Survey for Experimental Physics dataset. *Physical Review. Physics Education Research*, 17(2), 020144. 10.1103/PhysRevPhysEducRes.17.020144

Aiken, M., Wang, J., Gu, L., & Paolillo, J. (2011). An exploratory study of how technology supports communication in multilingual groups. *International Journal of e-Collaboration*, 7(1), 17–29. 10.4018/jec.2011010102

Akhtar, M. W., Hassan, S. A., Ghaffar, R., Jung, H., Garg, S., & Hossain, M. S. (2020). The shift to 6g communications: Vision and requirements. *Human-centric Computing and Information Sciences.*, 10(1), 1. 10.1186/s13673-020-00258-2

Alaa, A. M., Bolton, T., Di Angelantonio, E., Rudd, J. H., & Van der Schaar, M. (2019). Cardiovascular disease risk prediction using automated machine learning: A prospective study of 423,604 UK Biobank participants. *PLoS One*, 14(5), e0213653. 10.1371/journal.pone.021365331091238

Alabama, N. R. T. C. (2022, February 22). Industry 4.0: Simulations, IOT, and AR in manufacturing - NRTC automation. From NRTC Automation: https://nrtcautomation.com/blog/industry-40-simulations-iot-and-ar-in-manufacturing

Albaqami, H., Hassan, G. M., & Datta, A. (2023). MP-SeizNet: A multi-path CNN Bi-LSTM Network for seizure-type classification using EEG. *Biomedical Signal Processing and Control*, 84, 104780. 10.1016/j.bspc.2023.104780

Alfaro, J. (2023, January 8). https://www.elfinancierocr.com/economia-y-politica/inversion- extranjera-directa-como-se-compara-costa/CPMMPU5HIZBORISU47VQZVMXCI/story/

Alfian, G., Syafrudin, M., Ijaz, M. F., Syaekhoni, M. A., Fitriyani, N. L., & Rhee, J. (2018). A Personalized Healthcare Monitoring System for Diabetic Patients by Utilizing BLE-Based Sensors and Real-Time Data Processing. *Sensors (Basel)*, 18(7), 2183. 10.3390/s1807218329986473

Al-Ghaith, W., Sanzogni, L., & Sandhu, K. (2010). Factors influencing the adoption and usage of online services in Saudi Arabia. *The Electric Journal on Information Systems in Developing Countries*, 40. https://citeseerx.ist.psu.edu/viewdoc/download?

Alli, A. A., & Alam, M. M. (2019). SecOFF-FCIoT: Machine learning based secure offloading in Fog-Cloud of things for smart city applications. *Internet of Things : Engineering Cyber Physical Human Systems*, 7, 100070. 10.1016/j.iot.2019.100070

Alrashdi, I., Alqazzaz, A., Aloufi, E., Alharthi, R., Zohdy, M., & Ming, H. (2019, January). Ad-iot: Anomaly detection of iot cyberattacks in smart city using machine learning. In *2019 IEEE 9th Annual Computing and Communication Workshop and Conference (CCWC)* (pp. 305-310). IEEE.

Alsamhi, S. H., Ma, O., Ansari, M. S., & Almalki, F. A. (2019). Survey on collaborative smart drones and internet of things for improving smartness of smart cities. *IEEE Access : Practical Innovations, Open Solutions*, 7, 128125–128152. 10.1109/ACCESS.2019.2934998

Al-Turjman, F., Nawaz, M. H., & Ulusar, U. D. (2020). Intelligence in the Internet of Medical Things era: A systematic review of current and future trends. *Computer Communications*, 150, 644–660. 10.1016/j.comcom.2019.12.030

Al-Turjman, F., Zahmatkesh, H., & Mostarda, L. (2019). Quantifying uncertainty in internet of medical things and big-data services using intelligence and deep learning. *IEEE Access : Practical Innovations, Open Solutions*, 7, 115749–115759. 10.1109/ACCESS.2019.2931637

Amirhosseini, M. H., & Kazemian, H. (2020). Machine learning approach to personality type prediction based on the myers–briggs type indicator®. *Multimodal Technologies and Interaction*, 4(1), 9. 10.3390/mti4010009

Anbazhagu, U. V., Koti, M. S., Muthukumaran, V., Geetha, V., & Munrathnam, M. (2024). Multi-Criteria Decision-Making for Energy Management in Smart Homes Using Hybridized Neuro-Fuzzy Approach. *Distributed Generation & Alternative Energy Journal*, 83–110.

Anbuselvan, P. (2020). Heart disease prediction using machine learning techniques. *International Journal of Engineering Research & Technology (Ahmedabad)*, 9, 515–518.

Anderson, S. M., Newman, K., Lamontia, M. A., & Olson, B. (1992). Design, analysis and hydrotesting of a composite-aluminum cylinder joint for pressure hull applications. *ASTM/STP on Compression Response of Composite Structures*.

Anshari, M., Syafrudin, M., & Fitriyani, N. L. (2022). Fourth industrial revolution between knowledge management and digital humanities. *Information (Basel)*, 13(6), 292. 10.3390/info13060292

Antonelli, G., & Chiaverini, S. (1998). Task-priority redundancy resolution for underwater vehicle-manipulator systems. *Proceedings of IEEE International Conference on Robotics and Automation*, 768–773. 10.1109/ROBOT.1998.677070

Anuar, N. N., Hafifah, H., Zubir, S. M., Noraidatulakma, A., Rosmina, J., Ain, M. N., ... Rahman, A. (2020). *Cardiovascular disease prediction from electrocardiogram by using machine learning*. Academic Press.

Arasteh, H., Hosseinnezhad, V., Loia, V., Tommasetti, A., Troisi, O., Shafie-khah, M., & Siano, P. (2016, June). Iot-based smart cities: A survey. In *2016 IEEE 16th international conference on environment and electrical engineering (EEEIC)* (pp. 1-6). IEEE. 10.1109/EEEIC.2016.7555867

Artavia, R. (2021, January 25). La verdad sobre las zonas francas. From Delfino: https://delfino.cr/2021/01/la-verdad-sobre-las-zonas-francas

Arumugam, K., Swathi, Y., Sanchez, D. T., Mustafa, M., Phoemchalard, C., Phasinam, K., & Okoronkwo, E. (2022). Towards applicability of machine learning techniques in agriculture and energy sector. *Materials Today: Proceedings*, 51, 2260–2263. 10.1016/j.matpr.2021.11.394

Asamblea Legislativa. (2012). Ley de Promoción de la Competencia y Defensa Efectiva del Consumidor.

Asamblea Legislativa. (2021). Ley de Promoción del Desarrollo Científico y Tecnológico.

Asamblea Legislativa. (2021). Ley para el fortalecimiento de la formación profesional para la empleabilidad, la inclusión social y la productividad de cara a la Revolución Industrial 4.0 y el empleo del futuro.

Asamblea Legislativa. (2022). Ley de Régimen de Zonas Francas.

Asghar, R., & Tamimy. (2020). The Fourth Industrial Revolution in the Developing Nations: Challenges and Road Map. *South Centre*, 4-33.

Ashley, S. (1993). Voyage to the bottom of the sea. *Mechanical Engineering (New York, N.Y.)*, 115(12), 52–57.

Aulia, T. F., & Wijaya, D. R. (2020). Poverty level prediction based on E-commerce data using K-nearest neighbor and information-theoretical-based feature selection. *ICOIACT*, 2020, 28–33.

Auran, P. G., & Silven, O. (1995). Ideas for underwater 3D sonar range sensing and environmental modeling. In *CAMS'95, May* (pp. 284–290). Norwa.

Awad, M. (2017). GPMS: An educational supportive graduation project management system. *Computer Applications in Engineering Education*, 25(6), 881–894. 10.1002/cae.21841

Aziz, S., & Dowling, M. (2019). Machine learning and AI for risk management. *Disrupting finance: FinTech and strategy in the 21st century*, 33-50. 10.1007/978-3-030-02330-0_3

Azzarri, C., Bacou, M., Cox, C. M., Guo, Z., & Koo, J. (2016). Subnational socio-economic dataset availability. *Nature Climate Change*, 6(2), 115–116. 10.1038/nclimate2842

Bag, S., Yadav, G., Dhamija, P., & Kataria, K. K. (2021). Key resources for industry 4.0 adoption and its effect on sustainable production and circular economy: An empirical study. *Journal of Cleaner Production*, 281, 125233. 10.1016/j.jclepro.2020.125233

Bairagi, R. N., Maniruzzaman, M., Pervin, S., & Sarker, A. (2021). Epileptic seizure identification in EEG signals using DWT, ANN and sequential window algorithm. *Soft Computing Letters*, 3, 100026. 10.1016/j.socl.2021.100026

Bakar, M. A., Jailani, N., Shukur, Z., & Yatim, N. F. M. (2011). Final year supervision management system as a tool for monitoring Computer Science projects. *Procedia: Social and Behavioral Sciences*, 18, 273–281. 10.1016/j.sbspro.2011.05.039

Banco Central de Costa Rica. (2023). Banco Central mantiene en 2,7% la proyección de crecimiento del PIB para el 2023 y para el 2024 lo estima en 3,5%. *Comunicado de Prensa*, 1-5.

Baradell, S. (2018) Understanding the long tail theory in media, marketing and E-commerce. *Idea Grove*.https://www.ideagrove.com/blog/understanding-the-long-tail-theory-of-media-fragmentation

Barquero, M. (2018, April 18). Atraso en aprobación de seis proyectos de ley frena acceso de Costa Rica a la OCDE. From La Nación: https://www.nacion.com/economia/politica- economica/atraso-en-aprobacion-de-seis-proyectos-de-ley/2GAQFYKWRNAKJE6MTPP424VXYQ/story/

Basheer, S., Anbarasi, M., Sakshi, D. G., & Vinoth Kumar, V. (2020). Efficient text summarization method for blind people using text mining techniques. *International Journal of Speech Technology*, 23(4), 713–725. 10.1007/s10772-020-09712-z

Berman, R., & Katona, Z. (2013). The Role of Search Engine Optimization in Search Marketing. *Marketing Science*, 32(4), 644–651. Advance online publication. 10.1287/mksc.2013.0783

Bernard, H. R., & Ryan, G. W. (2010). *Analyzing qualitative data: Systematic approaches*. Sage Publications.

Beus-Dukic, L. (2011, August). Final year project: A test case for requirements engineering skills. In *2011 6th International Workshop on Requirements Engineering Education and Training* (pp. 5-8). IEEE. 10.1109/REET.2011.6046272

Bhansali, S., Li, C.Z., & Kaushik, A. (2022). Towards hospital-on-chip supported by 2D MXenes-based 5th generation intelligent biosensors. *Biosens. Bioelectron.*, 220, 114847.

Bhattacharya, A., Ghosal, A., Obaid, A. J., Krit, S., Shukla, V. K., Mandal, K., & Pramanik, S. (2021). Unsupervised Summarization Approach with Computational Statistics of Microblog Data. In Samanta, D., Althar, R. R., Pramanik, S., & Dutta, S. (Eds.), *Methodologies and Applications of Computational Statistics for Machine Learning* (pp. 23–37). IGI Global. 10.4018/978-1-7998-7701-1.ch002

Bhinder, B., Gilvary, C., Madhukar, N. S., & Elemento, O. (2021). Artificial Intelligence in Cancer Research and Precision Medicine. *Cancer Discovery*, 11(4), 900–915. 10.1158/2159-8290.CD-21-009033811123

Bhuva, K., & Srivastava, K. (2018). Comparative study of the machine learning techniques for predicting the employee attrition. [IJRAR]. *IJRAR-International Journal of Research and Analytical Reviews*, 5(3), 568–577.

Bleidorn, W., & Hopwood, C. J. (2019). Using machine learning to advance personality assessment and theory. *Personality and Social Psychology Review*, 23(2), 190–203. 10.1177/108886831877299029792115

Boiar, D., Killich, N., Schulte, L., Hernandez Moreno, V., Deuse, J., & Liebig, T. (2022, September). Forecasting Algae Growth in Photo-Bioreactors Using Attention LSTMs. In *International Conference on Software Engineering and Formal Methods* (pp. 26-37). Cham: Springer International Publishing.

Bonifazi, G., Fiore, L., Gasbarrone, R., Palmieri, R., & Serranti, S. (2023). Hyperspectral Imaging Applied to WEEE Plastic Recycling: A Methodological Approach. *Sustainability (Basel)*, 15(14), 11345. 10.3390/su151411345

Breiman, L., Friedman, J., Olshen, R., & Stone, C. (1984). *Cart. Classification and regression trees.*. 10.1201/9781315139470

Breuker, D., & Matzner, M. (2016). Comprehensible predictive models for business processes. *Manag Inf Syst Q*. https://aisel.aisnet.org/misq/vol40/iss4/12

Bringula, R. P., Balcoba, A. C., & Basa, R. S. (2016, May). Employable Skills of Information Technology Graduates in the Philippines: Do Industry Practitioners and Educators have the Same View? In *Proceedings of the 21st Western Canadian Conference on Computing Education* (pp. 1-6). 10.1145/2910925.2910928

Brynjolfsson, E., Yu, J. H., & Simester, D. (2011). Goodbye Pareto Principle, Hello Long Tail: The Effect of Search Costs on the Concentration of Product Sales. *Management Science*, 57(8), 1373–1386. Advance online publication. 10.1287/mnsc.1110.1371

Buchem, I., Cochrane, T., Gordon, A., Keegan, H., & Camacho, M. (2012). M-Learning 2.0: The potential and challenges of collaborative mobile learning in participatory curriculum development. In *Proceedings of the IADIS Mobile Learning Conference* (pp. 243-252). Academic Press.

Bucolo, M., Buscarino, A., Fortuna, L., & Gagliano, S. (2020). Bifurcation scenarios for pilot induced oscillations. *Aerospace Science and Technology*, 106, 106194. 10.1016/j.ast.2020.106194

Budiharto W. (2021). Data science approach to stock prices forecasting in Indonesia during Covid-19 using Long Short-Term Memory (LSTM). *J Big Data*, 1–9.

Byrnes, K. G., Kiely, P. A., Dunne, C. P., McDermott, K. W., & Coffey, J. C. (2021). Communication, collaboration and contagion: "Virtualisation" of anatomy during COVID-19. *Clinical Anatomy (New York, N.Y.)*, 34(1), 82–89. 10.1002/ca.2364932648289

Castro, D. (2022, March 22). INA desarrollará prótesis craneales para pacientes del Hospital México. From Telediario: https://www.telediario.cr/nacional/ina-desarrollara-protesis- craneales-pacientes-hospital-mexico

Castro, J. (2022, April 28). Costa Rica subió tres puestos en ranking mundial de velocidades fijas a Internet. From La República: https://www.larepublica.net/noticia/costa-rica-subio-tres-puestos-en-ranking-mundial-de-velocidades-fijas-a-internet

Castro. (2018, May 8). Costa Rica lidera mercado de datacenters en el istmo. From La República: https://www.larepublica .net/noticia/costa-rica-lidera-mercado-de-datacenters-en-el-istmo

Celenta, R., Cucino, V., Feola, R., & Parente, R. (2024). Towards Innovation 5.0: The Role of Corporate Entrepreneurship. In *The International Research & Innovation Forum* (pp. 451–463). Springer.

Cerdas, M. (2023, April 12). Inflación de Costa Rica se aproxima a la meta, variación interanual de marzo fue de 4,42%. From El Financiero: https://www.elfinancierocr.com/finanzas/inflacion-de-costa-rica-se-aproxima-a-la- meta/SRQGG-3NGJV AK5PL2Y4PTQXL73A/story/

Chandan, R. R., Soni, S., Raj, A., Veeraiah, V., Dhabliya, D., Pramanik, S., & Gupta, A. (2023). Genetic Algorithm and Machine Learning. In *Advanced Bioinspiration Methods for Healthcare Standards, Policies, and Reform*. IGI Global. 10.4018/978-1-6684-5656-9

Chaudhary, V., Khanna, V., Awan, H. T. A., Singh, K., Khalid, M., & Mishra, Y. (2022). Towards hospital-on-chip supported by 2D MXenes-based 5th generation intelligent biosensors. *Biosensors & Bioelectronics*.36335709

Chaves, Gamboa, Hernández, & Sánchez. (2006). Balance de las Zonas Francas: Beneficio Neto del Régimen para Costa Rica. 2-111.

Chen, B., Wang, P., Wang, S., Ju, W., Liu, Z., & Zhang, Y. (2023). Simulating canopy carbonyl sulfide uptake of two forest stands through an improved ecosystem model and parameter optimization using an ensemble Kalman filter. *Ecological Modelling*, 475, 110212. 10.1016/j.ecolmodel.2022.110212

Cheng, X., Fang, L., Yang, L., & Cui, S. (2017). Mobile big data: The fuel for data-driven wireless. *IEEE Internet of Things Journal*, 4(5), 1489–1516. 10.1109/JIOT.2017.2714189

Cheng, X., Hu, Y., & Varga, L. (2022). 5G network deployment and the associated energy consumption in the UK: A complex systems' exploration. *Technological Forecasting and Social Change*, 180, 121672. 10.1016/j.techfore.2022.121672

Chen, S., Liang, Y. C., Sun, S., Kang, S., Cheng, W., & Peng, M. (2022). Vision, requirements, and technology trend of 6g: How to tackle the challenges of system coverage, capacity, user data-rate and movement speed. *IEEE Wireless Communications*, 217.

Chen, Y. M., Chen, T. Y., & Li, J. S. (2023). A Machine Learning-Based Anomaly Detection Method and Blockchain-Based Secure Protection Technology in Collaborative Food Supply Chain. *International Journal of e-Collaboration*, 19(1), 1–24. 10.4018/IJeC.315789

Chen, Y., Cao, F., Meng, X., & Cheng, W. (2023). Water Level Simulation in River Network by Data Assimilation Using Ensemble Kalman Filter. *Applied Sciences (Basel, Switzerland)*, 13(5), 3043. 10.3390/app13053043

Chen, Y., Jia, J., Wu, C., Ramirez-Granada, L., & Li, G. (2023). Estimation on total phosphorus of agriculture soil in China: A new sight with comparison of model learning methods. *Journal of Soils and Sediments*, 23(2), 998–1007. 10.1007/s11368-022-03374-x

Chen, Y., Sanz-Alonso, D., & Willett, R. (2022). Autodifferentiable ensemble Kalman filters. *SIAM Journal on Mathematics of Data Science*, 4(2), 801–833. 10.1137/21M1434477

Chen, Y., & Xie, J. (2008). Online consumer review: Word-of-mouth as a new element of marketing communication mix. *Management Science*, 54(3), 477–491. 10.1287/mnsc.1070.0810

Chen, Z., Dai, R., Liu, Z., Chen, L., Liu, Y., & Sheng, K. (2022). An Interpretive Adversarial Attack Method: Attacking Softmax Gradient Layer-Wise Relevance Propagation Based on Cosine Similarity Constraint and TS-Invariant. *Neural Processing Letters*, 1–17.35495852

Cho, S. (2021). Fault detection and diagnosis of a blade pitch system in a floating wind turbine based on Kalman flters and artifcial neural networks. *Renewable Energy*, 169, 1–13.

Chowdhury, M. Z., Shahjalal, M., Ahmed, S., & Jang, Y. M. (2020). 6G Wireless Communication Systems: Applications, Requirements, Technologies, Challenges, and Research Directions. *IEEE Open Journal of the Communications Society*, 1, 957–975. 10.1109/OJCOMS.2020.3010270

Chu, S. K. W., & Kennedy, D. M. (2011). Using online collaborative tools for groups to co-construct knowledge. *Online Information Review*, 35(4), 581–597. Advance online publication. 10.1108/14684521111161945

Clement, R., & Bounds, P. (2013). Making connections between final year students and potential project supervisors. *Proceedings of the HEA STEM annual learning and teaching conference 2013: Where practice and pedagogy meet.*

Coburn, E. (2015) The 7 Types of Digital Magazines, *Linkedin*, https://www.linkedin.com/pulse/7-types-digital-magazines-ed-coburn

Cole, K. A., Ijaz, H., Surrey, L. F., Santi, M., Liu, X., Minard, C. G., ... Weigel, B. J. (2023). *Pediatric phase 2 trial of a WEE1 inhibitor, adavosertib (AZD1775), and irinotecan for relapsed neuroblastoma, medulloblastoma, and rhabdomyosarcoma*. Cancer.

Comex. (2019, August 21). Boston Scientific se convierte en la empresa de dispositivos médicos más grande de Costa Rica. From Comercio Exterior Costa Rica: https://www.comex.go.cr/sala-de-prensa/comunicados/2019/agosto/cp-2401-boston- scientific-se-convierte-en-la-empresa-de-dispositivos-m%C3%A9dicos-m%C3%A1s- grande-de-costa-rica/

Cordero & Paus (2008). Foreign Investment and Economic Development in Costa Rica: The Unrealized Potential. Working Group on Development and Environment in the Americas, 1-29.

Costa Rica's commitment to developing talent in industry 4.0. (2022, August 31). From Investment Monitor: https://www.investmentmonitor.ai/sponsored/costa-ricas-commitment-to-developing-talent-in-industry-4-0/

Coursera and Costa Rica Launch a Joint Program to Strengthen Industry 4.0 Skills and Train - Free of Charge - 50,000 People to Confront the COVID-19 Crisis. (2020, June 15). From CINDE Invest in Costa Rica: https://www.cinde.org/en/essential-news/coursera-and-costa-rica-launch-a-joint-program-to-strengthen-industry-40-skills-and-train-free- of-charge-50000-people-to-confront-the-covid19-crisis

Coursera. (2020). Coursera Impact Report. 2-25. From Coursera.

Cover, T., & Hart, P. (1967). Nearest neighbor pattern classification. *IEEE Transactions on Information Theory*, 13(1), 21–27. 10.1109/TIT.1967.1053964

Craig, K., Humburg, M., Danish, J. A., Szostalo, M., Hmelo-Silver, C. E., & McCranie, A. (2020). Increasing students' social engagement during COVID-19 with Net. Create: Collaborative social network analysis to map historical pandemics during a pandemic. *Information and Learning Science*, 121(7/8), 533–547. Advance online publication. 10.1108/ILS-04-2020-0105

Cruz, J. A., & Wishart, D. S. (2006). Applications of Machine Learning in Cancer Prediction and Prognosis. *Cancer Informatics*, 2. 10.1177/117693510600200030194558758

Cucino, V., Dagnino, G. B., Ferrigno, G., Kaplan, A., Ritala, P., Higgins, C., & Liang, C. H. E. N. (2024). Special Issue Call for Papers NEW TECHNOLOGIES FOR BUSINESS AND SOCIETY: ACHIEVING MULTIPLE GOALS WITH MULTIPLE TYPES OF ORGANIZATIONS. Business & Society.

Cucino, V., Lungu, D. A., De Rosis, S., & Piccaluga, A. (2023). Creating value from purpose-based innovation: Starting from frailty. *Journal of Social Entrepreneurship*, •••, 1–29.

Cugurullo, F. (2021). *Frankenstein urbanism: Eco, smart and autonomous cities, artificial intelligence and the end of the city*. Routledge. 10.4324/9781315652627

Cui, Q., Yang, B., Liu, B., Li, Y., & Ning, J. (2022). Tea Category Identification Using Wavelet Signal Reconstruction of Hyperspectral Imagery and Machine Learning. *Agriculture*, 12(8), 1085. 10.3390/agriculture12081085

Dalal, S., Goel, P., Onyema, E. M., Alharbi, A., Mahmoud, A., Algarni, M. A., & Awal, H. (2023). Application of Machine Learning for Cardiovascular Disease Risk Prediction. *Computational Intelligence and Neuroscience*, 2023, 2023. 10.1155/2023/9418666

Dalenogare, L. S., Benitez, G. B., Ayala, N. F., & Frank, A. G. (2018). The expected contribution of Industry 4.0 technologies for industrial performance. *International Journal of Production Economics*, 204, 383–394. 10.1016/j.ijpe.2018.08.019

Dalzochio, J., & Kunst, R. (2020). Machine learning and reasoning for predictive maintenance in Industry 4.0: Current status and challenges. *Computers in Industry*.

Daniel, P., Sun, C., Koptyra, M., Drinkwater, C., Chew, N., Bradshaw, G., Loi, M., Shi, C., Tourchi, M., Parackal, S., Chong, W. C., Fernando, D., Adjumain, S., Nguyen, H., Habarakada, D., Sooraj, D., Crombie, D., Zhukova, N., Jones, C., & Firestein, R. (2022). MODL-17. The Childhood Brain Cancer Cell Line Atlas: A Resource for Biomarker Identification and Therapeutic Development. *Neuro-Oncology*, 24(Supplement_1), i172–i172. 10.1093/neuonc/noac079.640

Davies, J. B. C., Lane, D. M., Robinson, G. C., O'Brien, D. J., Pickett, M., Sfakiotakis, M., & Deacon, B. (1998). Subsea applications of continuum robots. *UT98*, 363–369.

De Kleijn, R. A. M. (2013). *Master's Thesis Supervision: Feedback, interpersonal relationships, and adaptivity*. Utrecht University.

Deepamala, N., & Shobha, G. (2018). Effective approach in making Capstone project a holistic learning experience to students of undergraduate computer science engineering program. *JOTSE: Journal of Technology and Science Education*, 8(4), 420–438. 10.3926/jotse.427

Del Sarto, N., Cesaroni, F., Di Minin, A., & Piccaluga, A. (2022). One size does not fit all. Business models heterogeneity among Internet of Things architecture layers. *Technology Analysis and Strategic Management*, 34(7), 787–802. 10.1080/09537325.2021.1921138

Del Vecchio, P., Di Minin, A., Petruzzelli, A. M., Panniello, U., & Pirri, S. (2018). Big Data For Open Innovation In Smes And Large Corporations: Trends, Opportunities, And Challenges. *Creativity and Innovation Management*, 27(1), 6–22. 10.1111/caim.12224

Deloitte. (2018). IoT para el Sector Empresarial en América Latina. cet. la, 1-249. ¿Hay buena cobertura de Internet de fibra óptica en Costa Rica? https://www.marketeroslatam.com/hay-buena-cobertura-de-internet-de-fibra-optica-en-costa-rica/

Devi, K. N., Krishnamoorthy, N., Jayanthi, P., Karthi, S., Karthik, T., & Kiranbharath, K. (2022, January). Machine Learning Based Adult Obesity Prediction. In *2022 International Conference on Computer Communication and Informatics (ICCCI)* (pp. 1-5). IEEE.

Dhamodaran, S., Ahamad, S., Ramesh, J. V. N., Sathappan, S., Namdev, A., Kanse, R. R., & Pramanik, S. (2023). *Fire Detection System Utilizing an Aggregate Technique in UAV and Cloud Computing. In Thrust Technologies' Effect on Image Processing*. IGI Global.

Dhiman, G., Vinoth Kumar, V., Kaur, A., & Sharma, A. (2021). Don: Deep learning and optimization-based framework for detection of novel coronavirus disease using x-ray images. *Interdisciplinary Sciences, Computational Life Sciences*, 13(2), 260–272. 10.1007/s12539-021-00418-733587262

Dhunmati, K., Nalini, C. N., Ramalakshmi, N., Niraimathi, V., & Amuthalakshmi, S. (2022). Synthesis, Molecular Docking and Invitro Evaluation of Nipecotic Acid-Flavone Hybrids as Anti Alzheimer Agents.–A Multi Target Directed Ligand Approach. *Journal of Pharmaceutical Negative Results*, 229–238.

Dileep, M. R., Navaneeth, A. V., & Abhishek, M. (2021, February). A novel approach for credit card fraud detection using decision tree and random forest algorithms. In *2021 Third International Conference on Intelligent Communication Technologies and Virtual Mobile Networks (ICICV)* (pp. 1025-1028). IEEE. 10.1109/ICICV50876.2021.9388431

Dinesh, K. G., Arumugaraj, K., Santhosh, K. D., & Mareeswari, V. (2018, March). Prediction of cardiovascular disease using machine learning algorithms. In *2018 International Conference on Current Trends towards Converging Technologies (ICCTCT)* (pp. 1-7). IEEE. 10.1109/ICCTCT.2018.8550857

Ding, J., Hsieh, M. C., & Wu, Z. X. (2023). A Human Manipulator Collaboration-based Scheme for Object Inspection by Robust and Fast Recognition of Hand Pose Sensing Images of Numeric Symbols Combined with Non-numeric Expressions for Smart Factories. *Sensors and Materials*, 35(3), 35. 10.18494/SAM4236

Diro, A. A., & Chilamkurti, N. (2018). Distributed attack detection scheme using deep learning approach for Internet of Things. *Future Generation Computer Systems*, 82, 761–768. 10.1016/j.future.2017.08.043

Dixon, M. F., Halperin, I., & Bilokon, P. (2020). *Machine learning in finance* (Vol. 1170). Springer International Publishing. 10.1007/978-3-030-41068-1

Dogan, A., & Birant, D. (2021). Machine learning and data mining in manufacturing. *Expert Systems with Applications*, 166, 114060.

Dougherty, F., & Woolweave, G. (1990). At-sea testing of an unmanned underwater vehicle flight control system. *Proceedings of Symposium of Autonomous Underwater Vehicle Technology*, 65–73. 10.1109/AUV.1990.110438

Drake, M. G. (2015) Past drive subscribers' attitudes and usage behaviors in regard to the publication's digital outlets: Thesis submitted to the Faculty of the Graduate College of the Oklahoma State University in partial fulfillment of the requirements for the Degree of Master of Science, https://shareok.org/bitstream/handle/

Duarte, F. (2023, April 3). Amount of Data Created Daily. From Exploding Topics: https://explodingtopics.com/blog/data-generated-per-day

Dunn, S. E., & Rae, G. J. S. (1992). On-line damage detection for autonomous underwater vehicles. *IEEE AUV'94*, 383–392.

Eberl, M. (2021, May 25). What is Industry 4.0? From Customodal: https://customodal.com/blog/what-is-industry-4-0/

EFE. (2018, November 15). Turismo aporta 8.2% del pib de forma directa e indirecta en costa rica. From El Economista: https://www.eleconomista.net/actualidad/Turismo-aporta- 8.2-del- PIB-de-forma-directa-e-indirecta-en-Costa-Rica-20181115-0032.html

Eisenhardt, K. M. (1989). Building theories from case study research. *Academy of Management Review*, 14(4), 532–550. 10.2307/258557

Eisenhardt, K. M., & Graebner, M. E. (2007). Theory building from cases: Opportunities and challenges. *Academy of Management Journal*, 50(1), 25–32. 10.5465/amj.2007.24160888

El-Hasnony, I. M., Elzeki, O. M., Alshehri, A., & Salem, H. (2022). Multi-label active learning-based machine learning model for heart disease prediction. *Sensors (Basel)*, 22(3), 1184. 10.3390/s2203118435161928

Enholm, I. M., Papagiannidis, E., Mikalef, P., & Krogstie, J. (2022). Artificial intelligence and business value: A literature review. *Information Systems Frontiers*, 24(5), 1709–1734. 10.1007/s10796-021-10186-w

Erboz, G. (2017). How to Define Industry 4.0: The Main Pillars Of Industry 4.0. Managerial Trends in the Development of Enterprises in Globalization Era, 761-767.

Esencial Costa Rica. (2022). *Procomer*. Guía Régimen Zonas Francas.

Esquivel, M. (2019, October 10). Costa Rica ranks 62 according to the Global Competitiveness Report. From INCAE: https://en.incae.edu/en/node/95858

Exterior, C. (2022, November 25). Exportaciones de costa rica crecieron 26,25% en 2021. From INEC: https://inec.cr/noticias/exportaciones-costa-rica-crecieron-2625- 2021

Factory, S. What is smart Manufacturing? (2022, December 7). From Team Viewer: https://www.teamviewer.com/en/info/what-is-smart-factory/

Fafoutis, X., Marchegiani, L., Elsts, A., Pope, J., Piechocki, R., & Craddock, I. (2018). Extending the battery lifetime of wearable sensors with embedded machine learning. *Proc. IEEE 4th World Forum Internet Things*. 10.1109/WF-IoT.2018.8355116

Faizan, M., & Zuhairi, M. F. (2020). *Challenges and use cases of process discovery in process mining* (Vol. 9). Int J Adv Trends Comput Sci Eng.

Fallucchi, F., Coladangelo, M., Giuliano, R., & William De Luca, E. (2020). Predicting employee attrition using machine learning techniques. *Computers*, 9(4), 86. 10.3390/computers9040086

Farahbod, S., Niknam, T., Mohammadi, M., Aghaei, J., & Shojaeiyan, S. (2022). Probabilistic and deterministic wind speed prediction: Ensemble statistical deep regression network. *IEEE Access : Practical Innovations, Open Solutions*, 10, 47063–47075. 10.1109/ACCESS.2022.3171610

Felli, E., Cinelli, L., Bannone, E., Giannone, F., Muttillo, E. M., Barberio, M., Keller, D. S., Rodríguez-Luna, M. R., Okamoto, N., Collins, T., Hostettler, A., Schuster, C., Mutter, D., Pessaux, P., Marescaux, J., Gioux, S., Felli, E., & Diana, M. (2022). Hyperspectral imaging in major hepatectomies: Preliminary results from the ex-machyna trial. *Cancers (Basel)*, 14(22), 5591. 10.3390/cancers1422559136428685

Feltes, B. C., Chandelier, E. B., Grisci, B. I., & Dorn, M. (2019). CuMiDa: An Extensively Curated Microarray Database for Benchmarking and Testing of Machine Learning Approaches in Cancer Research. *Journal of Computational Biology*, 26(4), 376–386. 10.1089/cmb.2018.023830789283

Fernández, A. (2020). Retos de la cuarta revolución industrial sobre el mercado laboral costarricense. 4-92.

Ferrigno, G., Crupi, A., Di Minin, A., & Ritala, P. (2023). 50+ years of R&D Management: a retrospective synthesis and new research trajectories. *R&D Management*.

Ferrigno, G., & Cucino, V. (2023). AI technologies and hospital blood delivery in peripheral regions: insights from zipline international. In *Impact of Artificial Intelligence in Business and Society. Opportunities and challenges*. Routledge.

Ferrigno, G., Del Sarto, N., Piccaluga, A., & Baroncelli, A. (2023). Industry 4.0 base technologies and business models: A bibliometric analysis. *European Journal of Innovation Management*, 26(7), 502–526. 10.1108/EJIM-02-2023-0107

Ferrigno, G., Zordan, A., & Di Minin, A. (2022). The emergence of dominant design in the early automotive industry: An historical analysis of Ford's technological experimentation from 1896 to 1906. *Technology Analysis and Strategic Management*, 1–12.

Fıçıcı, C., Telatar, Z., & Eroğul, O. (2022). Automated temporal lobe epilepsy and psychogenic nonepileptic seizure patient discrimination from multichannel EEG recordings using DWT based analysis. *Biomedical Signal Processing and Control*, 77, 103755. 10.1016/j.bspc.2022.103755

Financeonline.com. (2022) 8 Future Collaboration Trends & Forecasts for 2022 – A Look into What's Next, *Financeonline.com*, https://financesonline.com/collaboration-trends/

Fitrianto, A., Muhamad, W. Z. A. W., & Susetyo, B. (2022). Development of direct marketing strategy for the banking industry: The use of a Chi-squared Automatic Interaction Detector (CHAID) in deposit subscription classification. *Journal of Socioeconomics and Development*, 5(1), 64–75. 10.31328/jsed.v5i1.3420

Fix, E., & Hodges, J. L. (1951). *Discriminatory analysis, nonparametric discrimination: consistency properties.* US Air Force School of Aviation Medicine. Technical Report 4, (3).

Foleon.com. (2022) How to start your own online magazine in 2022, *Foleon.com*, https://www.foleon.com/topics/how -to-start-your-own-online-magazine-from-scratch

Furman, W. L., McCarville, B., Shulkin, B. L., Davidoff, A., Krasin, M., Hsu, C. W., Pan, H., Wu, J., Brennan, R., Bishop, M. W., Helmig, S., Stewart, E., Navid, F., Triplett, B., Santana, V., Santiago, T., Hank, J. A., Gillies, S. D., Yu, A., & Federico, S. M. (2022). Improved outcome in children with newly diagnosed high-risk neuroblastoma treated with chemoimmunotherapy: Updated results of a phase II study using hu14. 18K322A. *Journal of Clinical Oncology*, 40(4), 335–344. 10.1200/JCO.21.0137534871104

Gaines, J., Akintewe, O., & Small, S. (2019). Engineering Design Instruction Using Slack for Project Support and Team-work. In *2019 ASEE Annual Conference & Exposition* (pp. 16-19). 10.18260/1-2--32721

Gao, Q., Omran, A. H., Baghersad, Y., Mohammadi, O., Alkhafaji, M. A., Al-Azzawi, A. K., Al-Khafaji, S. H., Emami, N., Toghraie, D., & Golkar, M. J. (2023). Electroencephalogram signal classification based on Fourier transform and Pattern Recognition Network for epilepsy diagnosis. *Engineering Applications of Artificial Intelligence*, 123, 106479. 10.1016/j.engappai.2023.106479

Gardner, M., & Elliott, J. (2014). The Immersive Education Laboratory: understanding affordances, structuring experiences, and creating constructivist, collaborative processes, in mixed-reality smart environments. *EAI Endorsed Transactions on Future Intelligent Educational Environments, 14*(1). 10.4108/fiee.1.1.e6

Gasto público en educación, total (% del PIB) - Costa Rica. (2020). From Banco Mundial: https://datos.bancomundial .org/indicator/SE.XPD.TOTL.GD.ZS?locations=CR

Gebhardt, M., Kopyto, M., Birkel, H., & Hartmann, E. (2022). Industry 4.0 technologies as enablers of collaboration in circular supply chains: A systematic literature review. *International Journal of Production Research*, 60(23), 6967–6995. 10.1080/00207543.2021.1999521

Gellert, A., Fiore, U., Florea, A., Chis, R., & Palmieri, F. (2022). Forecasting electricity consumption and production in smart homes through statistical methods. *Sustainable Cities and Society*, 76, 103426. 10.1016/j.scs.2021.103426

Geniusproject.com. (2022) Types of Collaboration Tools, https://www.geniusproject.com/guide/project-collaboration -tools/types-collaboration-tools

George, S., Lakshmi, K. A., & Thomas, K. T. (2022, December). Predicting Employee Attrition Using Machine Learning Algorithms. In *2022 4th International Conference on Advances in Computing, Communication Control and Networking (ICAC3N)* (pp. 700-705). IEEE. 10.1109/ICAC3N56670.2022.10074131

Gerard, J. (2017) How to Publish a Magazine on a Kindle, *Pen and the Paper,* https://penandthepad.com/publish-magazine-kindle-8296149.html

Ghanem, S. S., Majbour, N. K., Vaikath, N. N., Ardah, M. T., Erskine, D., Jensen, N. M., Fayyad, M., Sudhakaran, I. P., Vasili, E., Melachroinou, K., Abdi, I. Y., Poggiolini, I., Santos, P., Dorn, A., Carloni, P., Vekrellis, K., Attems, J., McKeith, I., Outeiro, T. F., & El-Agnaf, O. M. (2022). α-Synuclein phosphorylation at serine 129 occurs after initial protein deposition and inhibits seeded fibril formation and toxicity. *Proceedings of the National Academy of Sciences of the United States of America*, 119(15), e2109617119. 10.1073/pnas.210961711935353605

Ghazali, S. M., Alizadeh, M., Mazloum, J., & Baleghi, Y. (2022). Modified binary salp swarm algorithm in EEG signal classification for epilepsy seizure detection. *Biomedical Signal Processing and Control*, 78, 103858. 10.1016/j.bspc.2022.103858

Ghazal, T. M., & Alzoubi, H. M. (2021). Modeling supply chain information collaboration empowered with machine learning technique. *Intelligent Automation & Soft Computing*, 29(3), 243–257. 10.32604/iasc.2021.018983

Giamarelos, N., Papadimitrakis, M., Stogiannos, M., Zois, E. N., Livanos, N. A. I., & Alexandridis, A. (2023). A Machine Learning Model Ensemble for Mixed Power Load Forecasting across Multiple Time Horizons. *Sensors (Basel)*, 23(12), 5436. 10.3390/s2312543637420606

Gobierno de Argentina. (2022, November 8). Argentina y España sellan acuerdo productivo estratégico para el desarrollo de la Industria 4.0. From Argentina. gob.ar: https://www.argentina.gob.ar/noticias/argentina-y-espana-sellan-acuerdo-productivo-estrategico-para-el-desarrollo-de-la-industria.

Goh, J., Adepu, S., Junejo, K. N., & Mathur, A. (2017). A dataset to support research in the design of secure water treatment systems. In *Critical Information Infrastructures Security: 11th International Conference, CRITIS 2016, Paris, France, October 10–12, 2016, Revised Selected Papers 11* (pp. 88-99). Springer International Publishing. 10.1007/978-3-319-71368-7_8

Gomez-Cravioto, D. A., & Diaz-Ramos, R. E. (2022). Supervised machine learning predictive analytics for alumni income. *Journal of Big Data*, 9(1), 1–31.

Goncalves, L. C. B. D. S. (2020). *Improved planning and resource management in next generation green mobile communication networks*. Academic Press.

Gong, S., & Wu, X. (2020). Research on Fault Diagnosis Method of Photovoltaic Array Based on Random Forest Algorithm. *Chinese Control Conference CCC, IEEE.,* https://ieeexplore.ieee.org/document/9362559/

Gong, C., Zhang, X., & Niu, Y. (2020). Identification of epilepsy from intracranial EEG signals by using different neural network models. *Computational Biology and Chemistry*, 87, 107310. 10.1016/j.compbiolchem.2020.10731032599460

Gopal, M. (2019). Applied machine learning. McGraw-Hill Education.

Gordon, J. (2011). The Case for Advertising in Interactive Digital Magazines: How the Next Generation of Digital Magazines is Succeeding as an Advertising Platform: Nextbook Media and VIVmag, http://pages.nxtbook.com/nxtbooks/NXTbook/

Gosala, B., Kapgate, P. D., & Jain, P. (2023). Wavelet transforms for feature engineering in EEG data processing: An application on Schizophrenia. *Biomedical Signal Processing and Control*, 85, 104811. 10.1016/j.bspc.2023.104811

GSMA. (2021). *El camino hacia una Costa Rica digital*. GSMA Latin America.

Guarneros-Nolasco, L. R., Cruz-Ramos, N. A., Alor-Hernández, G., Rodríguez-Mazahua, L., & Sánchez-Cervantes, J. L. (2021). Identifying the main risk factors for cardiovascular diseases prediction using machine learning algorithms. *Mathematics*, 9(20), 2537. 10.3390/math9202537

Guo, Y., Gao, J., Tunio, M. H., & Wang, L. (2022). Study on the Identification of Mildew Disease of Cuttings at the Base of Mulberry Cuttings by Aeroponics Rapid Propagation Based on a BP Neural Network. *Agronomy (Basel)*, 13(1), 106. 10.3390/agronomy13010106

Gupta, A., Fernando, X., & Das, O. (2021). *Reliability and Availability Modeling Techniques in 6G IoT Networks: A Taxonomy and Survey. In 2021 International Wireless Communications and Mobile Computing*. IWCMC. 10.1109/IWCMC51323.2021.9498628

Guth, P. A., Schillings, C., & Weissmann, S. (2022). *14 Ensemble Kalman filter for neural network-based one-shot inversion*. de Gruyter & Co.

Gutiérrez, T. (2023, February 9). Empresas multinacionales generaron 22 mil nuevos empleos en 2022. From La República: https://www.larepublica.net/noticia/empresas-multinacionales-generaron-22-mil-empleos-nuevos-el-ano-pasado

Habibzadeh, H., & Soyata, T. (2020). Toward uniform smart healthcare ecosystems: A survey on prospects, security, and privacy considerations. *Connected health in smart cities*, 75-112.

Haenlein, M., & Kaplan, A. (2019). A brief history of artificial intelligence: On the past, present, and future of artificial intelligence. *California Management Review*, 61(4), 5–14. 10.1177/0008125619864925

Hakeem, A. A., & Hussein, H. H. (2022, June). Hyung won, K.: Vision and research directions of 6G technologies and applications. *Journal of King Saud University. Computer and Information Sciences*, 34(6), 2419–2442. 10.1016/j.jksuci.2022.03.019

Hall, F. (2020) Creative Digital Collaboration in Publishing: How do digital collaborative partnerships work and how publishing companies adapt to facilitate them? A Doctoral thesis (Ph.D), Submitted to the University College London, https://discovery.ucl.ac.uk/id/eprint/10110283/

Hans, C., Suhartono, D., Andry, C., & Zamli, K. Z. (2021). Text based personality prediction from multiple social media data sources using pre-trained language model and model averaging. *Journal of Big Data*, 8(68).

Han, T., Gois, F. N. B., Oliveira, R., Prates, L. R., & Porto, M. M. D. A. (2023). Modeling the progression of COVID-19 deaths using Kalman Filter and AutoML. *Soft Computing*, 27(6), 3229–3244. 10.1007/s00500-020-05503-533424432

Hapke, H., & Nelson, C. (2020). *Building machine learning pipelines*. O'Reilly Media.

Haq, A. U., Li, J. P., Memon, M. H., Nazir, S., & Sun, R. (2018). A hybrid intelligent system framework for the prediction of heart disease using machine learning algorithms. *Mobile Information Systems*, 2018, 1–21. 10.1155/2018/3860146

Hassan, A.R, & Subasi, A. (2016). *Automatic identification of epileptic seizures from EEG signals using linear programming boosting. computer methods and programs in biomedicine*. Academic Press.

Hernandez, D. (2022, December 2). Costa Rica, el país que lleva 74 años sin ejército. From Voz de América: https://www.vozdeamerica.com/a/costa-rica-el-pa%C3%ADs-que-lleva-74-a%C3%B1os-de-vivir-sin-ej%C3%A9rcito/6860180.html#:~:text=Costa%20Rica%2C%20el%20pa%C3%ADs%20que%20lleva %2074%20a%C3%B1os%20sin%20ej%C3%A9rcito

Hesko, C., Liu, W., Srivastava, D. K., Brinkman, T. M., Diller, L., Gibson, T. M., Oeffinger, K. C., Leisenring, W. M., Howell, R., Armstrong, G. T., Krull, K. R., & Henderson, T. O. (2023). Neurocognitive outcomes in adult survivors of neuroblastoma: A report from the Childhood Cancer Survivor Study. *Cancer*, 129(18), 2904–2914. 10.1002/cncr.3484737199722

Hiley, C. (2022, March 10). Global Broadband Index. From Uswitch: https://www.uswitch.com/broadband/studies/global-broadband-index/

Howlader, N., Noone, A. M., Krapcho, M., Miller, D., Brest, A., Yu, M., Ruhl, J., Tatalovich, Z., Mariotto, A., Lewis, D. R., Chen, H. S., Feuer, E. J., & Cronin, K. A. (2023, July 10). *SEER Cancer Statistics Review 1975-2016.* National Cancer Institute. https://seer.cancer.gov/csr/1975_2016/

Hsieh, J. J., Purdue, M. P., Signoretti, S., Swanton, C., Albiges, L., Schmidinger, M., Heng, D. Y., Larkin, J., & Ficarra, V. (2017). Renal cell carcinoma. *Nature Reviews. Disease Primers*, 3(1), 17009. Advance online publication. 10.1038/nrdp.2017.928276433

Hssayeni, M. D., & Chala, A. (2021). The forecast of COVID-19 spread risk at the county level. *Journal of Big Data*, 8, 1–16.

Huang, S. H., Liu, P., Mokasdar, A., & Hou, L. (2013). Additive manufacturing and its societal impact: A literature review. *International Journal of Advanced Manufacturing Technology*, 67(5-8), 1191–1203. 10.1007/s00170-012-4558-5

Huda, N. (2023, February 16). The Rise of Industry 4.0 in Germany: A Journey of Innovation and Transformation. From Linkedin: https://www.linkedin.com/pulse/rise-industry-40- germany-journey-innovation-nazmul-huda#:~:text=The%20 German%20government%20has%20also,partnerships%20between%20industry%20and%20academia

Hussain, S. F., & Qaisar, S. M. (2022). Epileptic seizure classification using level-crossing EEG sampling and ensemble of sub-problems classifier. *Expert Systems with Applications*, 191, 116356. 10.1016/j.eswa.2021.116356

Hussein, H. H., & Abd El-Kader, S. M. (2017). Enhancing signal to noise interference ratio for device to device technology in 5G applying mode selection technique. In *2017 Intl Conf on Advanced Control Circuits Systems (ACCS) Systems & 2017 Intl Conf on New Paradigms in Electronics & Information Technology (PEIT)*. 10.1109/ACCS-PEIT.2017.8303040

Hüttel, H., & Gnaur, D. (2019). A Web-Based Platform for Competence Development in PBL Supervision. *International Journal of e-Collaboration*, 15(3), 20–33. 10.4018/IJeC.2019070102

Hu, X., Li, S., Huang, T., Tang, B., Huai, R., & Chen, L. (2023). How Simulation Helps Autonomous Driving: A Survey of Sim2real, Digital Twins, and Parallel Intelligence. *IEEE Transactions on Intelligent Vehicles*.

IMF Press Center. (2021, July 28). Five Things to Know about the Informal Economy. From International Monetary Fund: https://www.imf.org/en/News/Articles/2021/07/28/na-072821-five-things-to-know-about-the-informal-economy#:~:text=The%20informal%20economy%20consists%20of,lights%20all%20over%20the%20world

Information Resources Management Association. (2018) E-Planning and Collaboration: Concepts, Methodologies, Tools, and Applications (3 Volumes). https://www.igi-global.com/book/collaborative-distributed-research/5827210.4018/978-1-5225-5646-6

Inoue, S., Nay Win, K. H., Mon, C. Y., Fujikawa, T., Hyodo, S., Uemura, S., Ishida, T., Mori, T., Hasegawa, D., Kosaka, Y., Nishimura, A., Nakatani, N., Nino, N., Tamura, A., Yamamoto, N., Nozu, K., & Nishimura, N. (2023). Higher levels of minimal residual disease in peripheral blood than bone marrow before 1st and 2nd relapse/regrowth in a patient with high-risk neuroblastoma: A case report. *Oncology Letters*, 26(3), 1–5. 10.3892/ol.2023.1395537559575

Inteligente, M. (2023). From CINDE: https://www.cinde.org/es/sectores/manufactura-inteligente/manufactura

I-Scoop. (2023, April 11). Industry 4.0 and the fourth industrial revolution explained. From I- Scoop: https://www.i-scoop.eu/industry-4-0/

Jailani, N. I. S. I., Ali, A. F. M., & Ngah, S. (2022, May). Final Year Project Allocation System Techniques: A Systematic Literature Review. In *2022 IEEE 12th Symposium on Computer Applications & Industrial Electronics (ISCAIE)* (pp. 99-104). IEEE. 10.1109/ISCAIE54458.2022.9794501

Jain, P. K., Jain, M., & Pamula, R. (2020). Explaining and predicting employees' attrition: A machine learning approach. *SN Applied Sciences*, 2(4), 1–11. 10.1007/s42452-020-2519-4

Jain, R., & Nayyar, A. (2018, November). *Predicting employee attrition using xgboost machine learning approach. In 2018 international conference on system modeling & advancement in research trends (smart)*. IEEE.

Jakub, Z. (2015) Search Engine Optimization, *CBU International Conference Proceedings*, 3. 10.12955/cbup.v3.645

Jalaeian Zaferani, E., Teshnehlab, M., & Vali, M. (2022). Automatic personality recognition and perception using deep learning and supervised evaluation method. *Journal of Applied Research on Industrial Engineering, 9*(2), 197-211.

Janjua, M.B., Duranay, A.E., & Arslan, H. (2020). Role of Wireless Communication in Healthcare System to Cater Disaster Situations Under 6G Vision. *Frontiers in Communications and Networks, 1.*

Javaid, S., Saeed, N., Qadir, Z., Fahim, H., He, B., Song, H., & Bilal, M. (2023). Communication and Control in Collaborative UAVs: Recent Advances and Future Trends. *IEEE Transactions on Intelligent Transportation Systems*, 24(6), 5719–5739. 10.1109/TITS.2023.3248841

Jayasingh, R. (2022). Speckle noise removal by SORAMA segmentation in Digital Image Processing to facilitate precise robotic surgery. *International Journal of Reliable and Quality E-Healthcare*, 11(1), 1–19. Advance online publication. 10.4018/IJRQEH.295083

Jeble, S., Kumari, S., & Patil, Y. (2016). Role of big data and predictive analytics. *International Journal of Automation and Logistics*, 2(4), 307–331. 10.1504/IJAL.2016.080336

Jiang, Q. (2023). Dynamic multivariate interval forecast in tourism demand. *Current Issues in Tourism*, 26(10), 1593–1616. 10.1080/13683500.2022.2060068

Jiménez, G. (2019, November 13). Empresas, gobierno y academia: actores esenciales para implementar la industria 4.0 en Costa Rica. From Tecnológico de Costa Rica: https://www.tec.ac.cr/hoyeneltec/2019/11/13/empresas-gobierno-academia-actores- esenciales-implementar-industria-40-costa-rica

Jindal, H., Agrawal, S., Khera, R., Jain, R., & Nagrath, P. (2021). Heart disease prediction using machine learning algorithms. *IOP Conference Series. Materials Science and Engineering*, 1022(1), 012072. 10.1088/1757-899X/1022/1/012072

Jones, M. (2012). The Evolution of Digital Technologies–from Collaboration to eCollaboration–and the Tools which assist eCollaboration. *Issues in Informing Science and Information Technology*, 9, 209–219. 10.28945/1617

Joseph, R., Udupa, S., Jangale, S., Kotkar, K., & Pawar, P. (2021, May). Employee attrition using machine learning and depression analysis. In *2021 5th International Conference on Intelligent Computing and Control Systems (ICICCS)* (pp. 1000-1005). IEEE. 10.1109/ICICCS51141.2021.9432259

Joshi, M. (2017) A Study of Online Buying Behavior among Adults in Pune City, *SIES Journal of Management*, 13(1), 29-37. https://web.s.ebscohost.com/abstract

Juan, A. A. (2012) Collaborative and Distributed E-Research: Innovations in Technologies, Strategies and Applications. https://www.igi-global.com/book/collaborative-distributed-research/5827210.4018/978-1-4666-0125-3

Kaleem, M., Guergachi, A., & Krishnan, S. (2018). Patient-specific seizure detection in long-term EEG using wavelet decomposition. *Biomedical Signal Processing and Control*, 46, 157–165. 10.1016/j.bspc.2018.07.006

Kalnoskas, A. (2017, August 1). Industry 4.0: Interweaving Manufacturing and Technology for a Smart Factory. From EE World: https://www.eeworldonline.com/industry-4-0- interweaving-manufacturing-technology-smart-factory/

Kar, S. C., Ismail, S. I., Abdullah, R., Mohamed, H., & Enzai, N. M. (2020, April). Performance and Usability Testing for Online FYP System. In *Journal of Physics: Conference Series* (Vol. 1529, No. 2, p. 022029). IOP Publishing. 10.1088/1742-6596/1529/2/022029

Karim, S., Qadir, A., Farooq, U., Shakir, M., & Laghari, A. A. (2023). Hyperspectral imaging: A review and trends towards medical imaging. *Current Medical Imaging*, 19(5), 417–427. 10.2174/1573405618666220519144435835598236

Karthikeyan, T., Sekaran, K., Ranjith, D., & Balajee, J. M. (2019). Personalized content extraction and text classification using effective web scraping techniques. [IJWP]. *International Journal of Web Portals*, 11(2), 41–52. 10.4018/IJWP.2019070103

Kashif, , Ansari, Shendge, Pakhrani, & Singh. (2023). Design and development of an auto-inflatable airbag as the failsafe system of unmanned aerial vehicle. *Materials Today: Proceedings*, 77(3), 983–990.

Katarya, R., & Meena, S. K. (2021). Machine learning techniques for heart disease prediction: A comparative study and analysis. *Health and Technology*, 11(1), 87–97. 10.1007/s12553-020-00505-7

Katz, M., & Ahmed, I. (2020). *Opportunities and challenges for visible light commu- nications in 6g. 2020 2nd 6G wireless summit (6G SUMMIT.*

Kaul, V., Enslin, S., & Gross, S. A. (2020). History of artificial intelligence in medicine. *Gastrointestinal Endoscopy*, 92(4), 807–812. 10.1016/j.gie.2020.06.04032565184

Kaur, T, & Gandhi, T.K. (2023). Automated Diagnosis of Epileptic Seizures using EEG image representations and Deep Learning. *Neuroscience Informatics*, 100139.

Kaur, J., & Ramkumar, K. R. (2022). The recent trends in cyber security: A review. *Journal of King Saud University. Computer and Information Sciences*, 34(8), 5766–5781. 10.1016/j.jksuci.2021.01.018

Keerie, C., Tuck, C., Milne, G., Eldridge, S., Wright, N., & Lewis, S. C. (2018). Data sharing in clinical trials–practical guidance on anonymising trial datasets. *Trials*, 19(1), 1–8. 10.1186/s13063-017-2382-929321053

Khan, A. S., Hussain, A., Asghar, M. Z., Saddozai, F. K., Arif, A., & Khalid, H. A. (2020). Personality classification from online text using machine learning approach. *International Journal of Advanced Computer Science and Applications*, 11(3). Advance online publication. 10.14569/IJACSA.2020.0110358

Khan, A., Qureshi, M., Daniyal, M., & Tawiah, K. (2023). A Novel Study on Machine Learning Algorithm-Based Cardiovascular Disease Prediction. *Health & Social Care in the Community*, 2023, 2023. 10.1155/2023/1406060

Khanh, P. T., Ng c, T. H., & Pramanik, S. (2023). Future of Smart Agriculture Techniques and Applications. In *Advanced Technologies and AI-Equipped IoT Applications in High Tech Agriculture*. IGI Global. 10.4018/978-1-6684-6408-3.ch005

Khaniya, M., Tachikawa, Y., Ichikawa, Y., & Yorozu, K. (2022). Impact of assimilating dam outflow measurements to update distributed hydrological model states: Localization for improving ensemble Kalman filter performance. *Journal of Hydrology (Amsterdam)*, 608, 127651. 10.1016/j.jhydrol.2022.127651

Khan, S. M., Liu, X., Nath, S., Korot, E., Faes, L., Wagner, S. K., Keane, P. A., Sebire, N. J., Burton, M. J., & Denniston, A. K. (2021). A global review of publicly available datasets for ophthalmological imaging: Barriers to access, usability, and generalisability. *The Lancet. Digital Health*, 3(1), e51–e66. 10.1016/S2589-7500(20)30240-533735069

Khan, W., Rehman, M. H., Zangoti, H. M., Afzal, M. K., Armi, N., & Salah, K. (2019). Industrial Internet of Things: Recent Advances, Enabling Technologies, and Open Challenges. *Computers & Electrical Engineering*, 81, 106522. Advance online publication. 10.1016/j.compeleceng.2019.106522

Kholodenko, B. N., Kolch, W., & Rukhlenko, O. S. (2023). Reversing pathological cell states: The road less travelled can extend the therapeutic horizon. *Trends in Cell Biology*, 33(11), 913–923. 10.1016/j.tcb.2023.04.00437263821

Kibria, M. G., Nguyen, K., Villardi, G. P., Ishizu, K., & Kojima, F. (2018). Shared resource access high capacity wireless networks: A stochastic geometry framework. In *2018 IEEE Wireless Communications and Networking Conference (WCNC)* (pp. 1-6). 10.1109/WCNC.2018.8377415

Kibria, M. G., Nguyen, K., Villardi, G. P., Zhao, O., Ishizu, K., & Kojima, F. (2018). Big data analytics, machine learning, and artificial intelligence in next-generation wireless networks. *IEEE Access : Practical Innovations, Open Solutions*, 6, 32328–32338. 10.1109/ACCESS.2018.2837692

Klitou, D., Conrads, J., Rasmussen, M., Probst, L., & Pedersen, B. (2017). Germany: Industrie 4.0. Digital Transformation Monitor, 2-7.

Kong, Y., Zheng, B., Zhang, Q., & He, K. (2022). Global and regional carbon budget for 2015–2020 inferred from OCO-2 based on an ensemble Kalman filter coupled with GEOS-Chem. *Atmospheric Chemistry and Physics*, 22(16), 10769–10788. 10.5194/acp-22-10769-2022

Koti, M. S., Muthukumaran, V., Devi, A., Rajalakshmi, V., Kumar, S. S., & Kumar, V. V. (2022). Efficient Deep Learning Techniques for Security and Privacy in Industry. *Cyber Security and Operations Management for Industry 4.0*, 2–32.

Kozolanka, K. (2018, May 25). Think in three dimensions: Innovative Design and manufacturing find a home at IDEAWORKS. Mohawk College. From Mohawk College:http://web.archive.org/web/20210920082530/https:/www .mohawkcollege.ca/about/ne ws/blogs/think-three-dimensions-innovative-design-and-manufacturing-finds-a-home- at-0

Krishen, A., Kachen, S., & Haniff, Z. (2014) Are we Locked in Print? Exploring Consumer Perceptions of Digital Versus Print Magazines, *Developments in Marketing Science: Proceedings of the Academy of Marketing Science book series* (DMSPAMS) https://link.springer.com/chapter/10.1007/978-3-319-10951-0_102

Krishnamoorthy, N., & Parameswari, V. L. (2018). Rice leaf disease detection via deep neural networks with transfer learning for early identification. *Turkish Journal of Physiotherapy and Rehabilitation, 32*, 2.s (ICAECT) (pp. 1-5). IEEE.

Krishnamoorthy, N., Nirmaladevi, K., Shanth, S., & Karthikeyan, N. (2021, November). Investigation and comparison of different CNN architectures on tomato leaf disease prediction using deep learning. In *AIP Conference Proceedings* (Vol. 2387, No. 1). AIP Publishing. 10.1063/5.0068638

Krishnamoorthy, N., Asokan, R., & Jones, I. (2016). Classification of malignant and benign micro calcifications from mammogram using optimized cascading classifier. *Current Signal Transduction Therapy*, 11(2), 98–104. 10.2174/157 43624116661606140837 20

Krishnamoorthy, N., Nirmaladevi, K., Kumaravel, T., Nithish, K. S., Sarathkumar, S., & Sarveshwaran, M. (2022, April). Diagnosis of Pneumonia Using Deep Learning Techniques. In *2022 Second International Conference on Advances in Electrical, Computing, Communication and Sustainable Technologies (ICAECT)* (pp. 1-5). IEEE. 10.1109/ ICAECT54875.2022.9807954

Krishnamoorthy, N., Prasad, L. N., Kumar, C. P., Subedi, B., Abraha, H. B., & Sathishkumar, V. E. (2021). Rice leaf diseases prediction using deep neural networks with transfer learning. *Environmental Research*, 198, 111275. 10.1016/j.envres.2021.11127533989629

Krishnan, S., & Geetha, S. (2019, April). Prediction of heart disease using machine learning algorithms. In *2019 1st international conference on innovations in information and communication technology (ICIICT)* (pp. 1-5). IEEE.

Krishnani, D., Kumari, A., Dewangan, A., Singh, A., & Naik, N. S. (2019, October). Prediction of coronary heart disease using supervised machine learning algorithms. In *TENCON 2019-2019 IEEE Region 10 Conference (TENCON)* (pp. 367-372). IEEE. 10.1109/TENCON.2019.8929434

Krittanawong, C., Virk, H. U. H., Bangalore, S., Wang, Z., Johnson, K. W., Pinotti, R., Zhang, H. J., Kaplin, S., Narasimhan, B., Kitai, T., Baber, U., Halperin, J. L., & Tang, W. W. (2020). Machine learning prediction in cardiovascular diseases: A meta-analysis. *Scientific Reports*, 10(1), 16057. 10.1038/s41598-020-72685-132994452

Kryszkiewicz, P., Kliks, A., Kułacz, Ł., Bogucka, H., Koudouridis, G. P., & Dryjański, M. (2018). Context-based spectrum sharing in 5G wireless networks based on radio environment maps. *Wireless Communications and Mobile Computing*, 2018, 1–15. 10.1155/2018/3217315

Kuepper, J. (2022, May 5). What Is a Developing Country? From The Balance: https://www.thebalancemoney.com/what-is-a-developing-country-1978982

Kumar, D., Swathi, P., Jahangir, A., Sah, N. K., & Vinothkumar, V. (2021). Intelligent speech processing technique for suspicious voice call identification using adaptive machine learning approach. In Handbook of Research on Innovations and Applications of AI, IoT, and Cognitive Technologies (pp. 372-380). IGI Global. 10.4018/978-1-7998-6870-5.ch025

Kumar, N. K., Sindhu, G. S., Prashanthi, D. K., & Sulthana, A. S. (2020, March). Analysis and prediction of cardio vascular disease using machine learning classifiers. In *2020 6th International Conference on Advanced Computing and Communication Systems (ICACCS)* (pp. 15-21). IEEE. 10.1109/ICACCS48705.2020.9074183

Kumar, M., Kavita, , Verma, S., Kumar, A., Ijaz, M. F., & Rawat, D. B. (2022). ANAF-IoMT: A Novel Architectural Framework for IoMT-Enabled Smart Healthcare System by Enhancing Security Based on RECC-VC. *IEEE Transactions on Industrial Informatics*, 18(12), 8936–8943. 10.1109/TII.2022.3181614

Kumar, S. S., Muthukumaran, V., Devi, A., Geetha, V., & Yadav, P. N. (2023). A Quantitative Approach of Purposive Sampling Techniques for Security and Privacy Issues in IoT Healthcare Applications. In *Handbook of Research on Advancements in AI and IoT Convergence Technologies* (pp. 281–299). IGI Global. 10.4018/978-1-6684-6971-2.ch016

Kumar, V. V., Raghunath, K. M. K., Muthukumaran, V., Joseph, R. B., Beschi, I. S., & Uday, A. K. (2021). Aspect based sentiment analysis and smart classification in uncertain feedback pool. *International Journal of System Assurance Engineering and Management*, 13(S1), 252–262.

Kumbhare, A. G., Simmhan, Y., & Prasanna, V. (2011, November). Designing a secure storage repository for sharing scientific datasets using public clouds. In *Proceedings of the second international workshop on Data intensive computing in the clouds* (pp. 31-40). 10.1145/2087522.2087530

Lasi, H., Fettke, P., Kemper, H. G., Feld, T., & Hoffmann, M. (2014). Industry 4.0. *Business & Information Systems Engineering*, 6(4), 239–242. 10.1007/s12599-014-0334-4

Latif, S., & Zafar, N. A. (2017, November). A survey of security and privacy issues in IoT for smart cities. In *2017 Fifth International Conference on Aerospace Science & Engineering (ICASE)* (pp. 1-5). IEEE. 10.1109/ICASE.2017.8374288

Learned-Miller, E. G. (2014). *Introduction to supervised learning*. Department of Computer Science, University of Massachusetts.

Lee, J. (2021). Migration from the traditional to the smart factory in the die-casting industry: Novel process data acquisition and fault detection based on artifcial neural network. *Journal of Materials Processing Technology*.

Legislativa, A. (2011). *Ley de protección de la persona frente al tratamiento de sus datos personales*. La Gaceta.

Leung, K., & Chu, S. K. W. (2009, December). Using wikis for collaborative learning: A case study of an undergraduate students' group project in Hong Kong. In *The International Conference on Knowledge Management* (pp. 1-14). https://web.edu.hku.hk/f/acadstaff/447/2009_wiki_learning.pdf

Leung, C. H., Lai, C. L., Yuan, T. K., Pang, W. M., Tang, J. K., Ho, W. S., & Wong, T. L. (2015). The development of a final year project management system for Information Technology programmes. In *Technology in Education. Transforming Educational Practices with Technology* (pp. 86–97). Springer. 10.1007/978-3-662-46158-7_9

Li, Y., Sperrin, M., Ashcroft, D. M., & Van Staa, T. P. (2020). Consistency of variety of machine learning and statistical models in predicting clinical risks of individual patients: longitudinal cohort study using cardiovascular disease as exemplar. *BMJ, 371*.

Li, D., Li, S., Zhang, S., Sun, J., Wang, L., & Wang, K. (2022). Aging state prediction for supercapacitors based on heuristic kalman filter optimization extreme learning machine. *Energy*, 250, 123773. 10.1016/j.energy.2022.123773

Li, M., Chen, W., & Zhang, T. (2017). Classification of epilepsy EEG signals using DWT-based envelope analysis and neural network ensemble. *Biomedical Signal Processing and Control*, 31, 357–365. 10.1016/j.bspc.2016.09.008

Li, N., Xue, J., & Jia, S. (2022, January). Spectral context-aware transformer for cholangiocarcinoma hyperspectral image segmentation. In *Proceedings of the 2022 5th International Conference on Image and Graphics Processing* (pp. 209-213). 10.1145/3512388.3512419

Liu, Q., Levinson, S., Wu, Y., & Huang, T. (2000, February). Interactive and incremental learning via a mixture of supervised and unsupervised learning strategies. In *Proceedings of the Fifth Joint Conference on Information Sciences* (Vol. 1, pp. 555-558). Academic Press.

Liu, C., & Ke, L. (2023). Cloud assisted Internet of things intelligent transportation system and the traffic control system in the smart city. *J. Control Decis*, 10(2), 174–187. 10.1080/23307706.2021.2024460

Liu, E., Effiok, E., & Hitchcock, J. (2020). Survey on health care applications in 5G networks. *IET Communications*, 14(7), 1073–1080. 10.1049/iet-com.2019.0813

Liu, Z., & Wang, S.LIU. (2011). Improved linear discriminant analysis method. *Jisuanji Yingyong*, 31(1), 250–253. 10.3724/SP.J.1087.2011.00250

Li, W., Chai, Y., Khan, F., Jan, S. R. U., Verma, S., Menon, V. G., Kavita, , & Li, X. (2021). A comprehensive survey on machine learning-based big data analytics for IoT-enabled smart healthcare system. *Mobile Networks and Applications*, 26(1), 234–252. 10.1007/s11036-020-01700-6

Li, Y., Gong, Y., & Zhang, Z. (2022). Few-shot object detection based on self-knowledge distillation. *IEEE Intelligent Systems*.

Liyew, C. M., & Melese, H. A. (2021). Machine learning techniques to predict daily rainfall amount. *Journal of Big Data*, 8(1), 1–11.

Louridi, N., Amar, M., & El Ouahidi, B. (2019, October). Identification of cardiovascular diseases using machine learning. In *2019 7th mediterranean congress of telecommunications (CMT)* (pp. 1-6). IEEE. 10.1109/CMT.2019.8931411

Lu, Z., Lei, T., Wen, X., Wang, L., & Chen, X. (2016). SDN based user-centric framework for heterogeneous wireless networks. *Mobile Information Systems*, 2016, 2016. 10.1155/2016/9874969

Magplus (2019) Ten Benefits of Publishing Digital Magazines, https://www.magplus.com/blog/ten-benefits-of-publishing-digital-magazines/

Mahesh, T. R., Sivakami, R., Manimozhi, I., Krishnamoorthy, N., & Swapna, B. (2023). Early Predictive Model for Detection of Plant Leaf Diseases Using MobileNetV2 Architecture. *International Journal of Intelligent Systems and Applications in Engineering*, 11(2), 46–54.

Mahmoud, A., & El-Sharkawy, Y. H. (2023). Quantitative phase analysis and hyperspectral imaging for the automatic identification of veins and blood perfusion maps. *Photodiagnosis and Photodynamic Therapy*, 42, 103307. 10.1016/j.pdpdt.2023.10330736709016

Maiga, J., & Hungilo, G. G. (2019, October). Comparison of machine learning models in prediction of cardiovascular disease using health record data. In *2019 International Conference on Informatics, Multimedia, Cyber and Information System (ICIMCIS)* (pp. 45-48). IEEE. 10.1109/ICIMCIS48181.2019.8985205

Maithili, K., Vinothkumar, V., & Latha, P. (2018). Analyzing the security mechanisms to prevent unauthorized access in cloud and network security. *Journal of Computational and Theoretical Nanoscience*, 15(6-7), 2059–2063. 10.1166/jctn.2018.7407

Ma, L., Little, J. V., Chen, A. Y., Myers, L., Sumer, B. D., & Fei, B. (2022). Automatic detection of head and neck squamous cell carcinoma on histologic slides using hyperspectral microscopic imaging. *Journal of Biomedical Optics*, 27(4), 046501–046501. 10.1117/1.JBO.27.4.04650135484692

Malik, A. (2021) Instagram rolls out new tools for creators to collaborate and partner with brands. https://techcrunch.com/2021/10/22/

Mandal, A., Dutta, S., & Pramanik, S. (2023). Machine Intelligence of Pi from Geometrical Figures with Variable Parameters using SCILab. In *Methodologies and Applications of Computational Statistics for Machine Learning*. IGI Global. 10.4018/978-1-7998-7701-1.ch003

Mansouri, A., Abolmasoumi, A. H., & Ghadimi, A. A. (2023). Weather sensitive short term load forecasting using dynamic mode decomposition with control. *Electric Power Systems Research*, 221, 109387. 10.1016/j.epsr.2023.109387

Mao, B., Kawamoto, Y., & Kato, N. (2020). AI-Based Joint Optimization of QoS and Security for 6G Energy Harvesting Internet of Things. *IEEE Internet of Things Journal*, 7(8), 7032–7042. 10.1109/JIOT.2020.2982417

Marbaniang, I. A., Choudhury, N. A., & Moulik, S. (2020, December). Cardiovascular disease (CVD) prediction using machine learning algorithms. In *2020 IEEE 17th India Council International Conference (INDICON)* (pp. 1-6). IEEE.

Martinelli, Mina, & Moggi. (2021). The enabling technologies of industry 4.0: examining the seeds of the fourth industrial revolution. *Oxford University Press.*

Martinez-Vega, B., Tkachenko, M., Matkabi, M., Ortega, S., Fabelo, H., Balea-Fernandez, F., La Salvia, M., Torti, E., Leporati, F., Callico, G. M., & Chalopin, C. (2022). Evaluation of preprocessing methods on independent medical hyperspectral databases to improve analysis. *Sensors (Basel)*, 22(22), 8917. 10.3390/s2222891736433516

Mathew, D. (2022). An Improvised Random Forest Model for Breast Cancer Classification. *NeuroQuantology : An Interdisciplinary Journal of Neuroscience and Quantum Physics*, 20(5), 713–722. 10.14704/nq.2022.20.5.NQ22227

Ma, Y., Liu, Z., Shi, Q., Liu, J., Geng, X., & Xue, R. (2022). Interval prediction of ultimate strength for laminated composite structures using back-propagation neural network. *Archive of Applied Mechanics*, 92(4), 1–18. 10.1007/s00419-021-02097-8

Mazza, C., Monaro, M., Orrù, G., Burla, F., Colasanti, M., Ferracuti, S., & Roma, P. (2019). Introducing machine learning to detect personality faking-good in a male sample: A new model based on Minnesota multiphasic personality inventory-2 restructured form scales and reaction times. *Frontiers in Psychiatry*, 10, 389. 10.3389/fpsyt.2019.0038931275176

McCormick, M. (2017) Ecommerce: How to Effectively Price your Products, *BlackCurve,*https://blog.blackcurve.com/ecommerce-how-to-effectively-price-your-products

McGhin, T., Kim-Kwang, R. C., Charles, Z. L., & He, H. D. (2019). Blockchain in healthcare applications: Research challenges and opportunities. *Journal of Network and Computer Applications*, 135, 62–75. 10.1016/j.jnca.2019.02.027

McLaughin, S. (2022, August 17). Horizontal and Vertical Integration in Industry 4.0 for Pharmaceutical and Medical Device Manufacturers. From SL Controls: https://slcontrols.com/en/horizontal-and-vertical-integration-in-industry-4-0-for- pharmaceutical-and-medical-device-manufacturers/

Mehta, Y., Fatehi, S., Kazameini, A., Stachl, C., Cambria, E., & Eetemadi, S. (2020, November). Bottom-up and top-down: Predicting personality with psycholinguistic and language model features. In *2020 IEEE International Conference on Data Mining (ICDM)* (pp. 1184-1189). IEEE. 10.1109/ICDM50108.2020.00146

Mehta, Y., Majumder, N., Gelbukh, A., & Cambria, E. (2020). Recent trends in deep learning based personality detection. *Artificial Intelligence Review*, 53(4), 2313–2339. 10.1007/s10462-019-09770-z

Michael, G. (2014), *4 Important Digital Marketing Channels You Should Know About*, from https://www.digitaldoughnut.com/articles/2014/november/4-important-digital-marketing-channels-you-should/

MICITT. (2022). Estrategia de Transformación Digital hacia la Costa Rica del Bicentenario 4.0. 1-54.

MINAE. (2018). Resumen del Sexto Informe Nacional al Convenio de Diversidad Biológica NACIONAL COSTA RICA de Costa Rica. Programa de Naciones Unidas para el Desarrollo, 1-66.

Ministerio de Ciencias. (2019). *Tecnología y Telecomunicaciones*. Indice de Brecha Digital.

Ministerio delle Imprese. (2016). Piano Nazionale Industria 4.0. 2-18.

Mishra, N., Patel, D. P., & Jain, S. K. (n.d.). Hyperspectral imaging technique: A brief introduction for evaluating food quality of agro produce. *Exploration and Development of Agriculture in India,* 88.

Mogyorósi, F., Revisnyei, P., Pašić, A., Papp, Z., Törös, I., Varga, P., & Pašić, A. (2022). Positioning in 5G and 6G Networks—A Survey. *Sensors (Basel)*, 22(13), 4757. 10.3390/s2213475735808254

Mohajan, H. (2019). The First Industrial Revolution Brings Global Development. *Journal of Social Sciences and Humanities*, 2–27.

Mohajan, H. (2021). Third Industrial Revolution Brings Global Development. *Journal of Social Sciences and Humanities*, 2–33.

Mohan, S., Thirumalai, C., & Srivastava, G. (2019). Effective heart disease prediction using hybrid machine learning techniques. *IEEE Access : Practical Innovations, Open Solutions*, 7, 81542–81554. 10.1109/ACCESS.2019.2923707

Mohbey, K. K. (2020). Employee's attrition prediction using machine learning approaches. In *Machine Learning and Deep Learning in Real-Time Applications* (pp. 121–128). IGI Global. 10.4018/978-1-7998-3095-5.ch005

Mohsan, S. A. H., Othman, N. Q. H., Li, Y., Alsharif, M. H., & Khan, M. A. (2023). Unmanned aerial vehicles (UAVs): Practical aspects, applications, open challenges, security issues, and future trends. *Intelligent Service Robotics*, 16, 109–137. 10.1007/s11370-022-00452-436687780

Mondal, D., Ratnaparkhi, A., Deshpande, A., Deshpande, V., Kshirsagar, A. P., & Pramanik, S. (2023). Applications, Modern Trends and Challenges of Multiscale Modelling in Smart Cities. In *Data-Driven Mathematical Modeling in Smart Cities*. IGI Global. 10.4018/978-1-6684-6408-3.ch001

Monge, R. (2023, June 1). Preparación laboral para triunfar en la era de la automatización. From Academia de Centroamérica: https://www.academiaca.or.cr/opinion/preparacion- laboral-para-triunfar-en-la-era-de-la-automatizacion/

Moore, L. (2019, April 19). Augmented reality vs. virtual reality vs. mixed reality. From Tech Target: https://www.techtarget.com/searcherp/feature/AR-vs-VR-vs-MR-Differences-similarities-and-manufacturing-uses

Moral, M. (2022, June 8). La agricultura de precisión nos ha permitido ser más eficientes en la gestión de los envíos de piña en estos momentos complicados. From Fresh Plaza: https://www.freshplaza.es/article/9433882/la-agricultura-de-precision-nos-ha- permitido-ser-mas-eficientes-en-la-gestion-de-los-envios-de-pina-en-estos-momentos- complicados/

Morales, A. A. (2022, June 2). Panorama. Retrieved from https://www.panoramadigital.co.cr/la-agricultura-de-precision-en-costa-rica-el-futuro- ya-llego/

Motarwar, P., Duraphe, A., Suganya, G., & Premalatha, M. (2020, February). Cognitive approach for heart disease prediction using machine learning. In *2020 International Conference on Emerging Trends in Information Technology and Engineering (ic-ETITE)* (pp. 1-5). IEEE. 10.1109/ic-ETITE47903.2020.242

Mporas, I., Tsirka, V., Zacharaki, E. I., Koutroumanidis, M., Richardson, M., & Megalooikonomou, V. (2015). Seizure detection using EEG and ECG signals for computer-based monitoring, analysis and management of epileptic patients. *Expert Systems with Applications*, 42(6), 3227–3233. 10.1016/j.eswa.2014.12.009

Mucchi, L., Jayousi, S., Caputo, S., Paoletti, E., Zoppi, P., Geli, S., & Dioniso, P. (2020). *How 6G Technology Can Change the Future Wireless Healthcare. In 2020 2nd 6G Wireless Summit (6G SUMMIT).*, 10.1109/6GSUMMIT49458.2020.9083916

Mughees, A., Tahir, M., Sheikh, M.A., & Ahad, A. (n.d.). *Energy-efficient ultra-dense 5G networks: recent advances, taxonomy and future research directions*. IEEE.

Muñoz, D. (2014). Un acercamiento a la brecha digital en Costa Rica desde el punto de vista del acceso, la conectividad y la alfabetización digital. E-Ciencias de la Información, 1- 29.

Murillo, A. (2014, April 9). Intel deja a costa rica sin su mayor fábrica exportadora. From El País: https://elpais.com/economia/2014/04/09/actualidad/1397005915_851656.html

Muthukumaran, V., & Manimozhi, I. (2021). Public Key Encryption With Equality Test for Industrial Internet of Things Based on Near-Ring. *International Journal of e-Collaboration*, 17(3), 25–45. 10.4018/IJeC.2021070102

Muthukumaran, V., Vinoth Kumar, V., Joseph, R. B., Munirathnam, M., Beschi, I. S., & Niveditha, V. R. (2022, November). Efficient Authenticated Key Agreement Protocol for Cloud-Based Internet of Things. *International Conference on Innovative Computing and Communications Proceedings of ICICC*, 3, 365–373.

Muthukumar, V., Sivakami, R., Venkatesan, V. K., Balajee, J., Mahesh, T. R., Mohan, E., & Swapna, B. (2023). Optimizing Heterogeneity in IoT Infra Using Federated Learning and Blockchain-based Security Strategies. *International Journal of Computers, Communications & Control*, 18(6). Advance online publication. 10.15837/ijccc.2023.6.5890

Nadakinamani, R. G., Reyana, A., Kautish, S., Vibith, A. S., Gupta, Y., Abdelwahab, S. F., & Mohamed, A. W. (2022). Clinical data analysis for prediction of cardiovascular disease using machine learning techniques. *Computational Intelligence and Neuroscience*, 2022, 2022. 10.1155/2022/297332435069715

Naeem, U., Islam, S., & Siddiqui, A. (2019, April). An Effective Framework for Enhancing Student Engagement and Performance in Final Year Projects. In *2019 IEEE Global Engineering Education Conference (EDUCON)* (pp. 401-410). IEEE. https://doi.org/10.1109/EDUCON.2019.8725253

Nagarajan, S. M., Deverajan, G. G., Chatterjee, P., Alnumay, W., & Muthukumaran, V. (2022). Integration of IoT based routing process for food supply chain management in sustainable smart cities. *Sustainable Cities and Society*, 76, 103448. 10.1016/j.scs.2021.103448

Nanglia, P., Kumar, S., Mahajan, A. N., Singh, P., & Rathee, D. (2021). A hybrid algorithm for lung cancer classification using SVM and Neural Networks. *ICT Express*, 7(3), 335–341. 10.1016/j.icte.2020.06.007

Natale, G., Forte, S., Messina, G., Leonardi, B., Mirra, R., Leone, F., Di Filippo, V., Pica, D. G., Capasso, F., Bove, M., Noro, A., Opromolla, G., Martone, M., De Angelis, S., & Fiorelli, A. (2023). Intrathoracic neurogenic tumors (ITNs): Management of solid and cystic lesions. *Thoracic Cancer*, 14(19), 1824–1830. 10.1111/1759-7714.1492737201908

Natarajan, R., Lokesh, G. H., Flammini, F., Premkumar, A., Venkatesan, V. K., & Gupta, S. K. (2023). A Novel Framework on Security and Energy Enhancement Based on Internet of Medical Things for Healthcare 5.0. *Infrastructures*, 8(2), 22. 10.3390/infrastructures8020022

Nath, S., & Mala, C. (2022). Thermal image processing-based intelligent technique for object detection. *Signal, Image and Video Processing*, 16(6), 1631–1639. 10.1007/s11760-021-02118-7

Nayak, S., & Patgiri, R. (2021). *6G Communication Technology: A Vision on Intelligent Healthcare.* 10.1007/978-981-15-9735-0_1

Neves de Carvalho, T. A. (2014) Effects of Message Design and Content on the Performance of Email Marketing Campaigns: Dissertation submitted in partial fulfillment of the requirements for the degree of MSc in Business Administration at Católica-Lisbon School of Business & Economics, https://repositorio.ucp.pt/bitstream/10400.14/18224/1/Thesis%20Teresa%20%20Carvalho.pdf

Newaz, A. I., Sikder, A. K., Rahman, M. A., & Uluagac, A. S. (2019, October). Healthguard: A machine learning-based security framework for smart healthcare systems. In *2019 sixth international conference on social networks analysis, management and security (SNAMS)* (pp. 389-396). IEEE. 10.1109/SNAMS.2019.8931716

Ng c, T. H., Khanh, P. T., & Pramanik, S. (2023). Smart Agriculture using a Soil Monitoring System. In *Advanced Technologies and AI-Equipped IoT Applications in High Tech Agriculture.* 10.4018/978-1-6684-9231-4.ch011

Ngo, F. T., Govindu, R., & Agarwal, A. (2015). Assessing the predictive utility of logistic regression, classification, and regression tree, chi-squared automatic interaction detection, and neural network models in predicting inmate misconduct. *American Journal of Criminal Justice*, 40(1), 47–74. 10.1007/s12103-014-9246-6

Nguyen, D. C., Ding, M., Pathirana, P. N., Seneviratne, A., Li, J., Niyato, D., Dobre, O., & Poor, H. V. (2022). 6G Internet of Things: A Comprehensive Survey. *IEEE Internet of Things Journal*, 9(1), 359–383. 10.1109/JIOT.2021.3103320

Nikhar, S., & Karandikar, A. M. (2016). Prediction of heart disease using machine learning algorithms. International Journal of Advanced Engineering. *Management Science*, 2(6), 239484.

Noor-A-Rahim, M., Liu, Z., Lee, H., Khyam, M. O., He, J., Pesch, D., Moessner, K., Saad, W., & Poor, H. V. (2022). 6G for Vehicle-to-Everything (V2X) Communications: Enabling Technologies, Challenges, and Opportunities. *Proceedings of the IEEE*, 110(6), 712–734. 10.1109/JPROC.2022.3173031

Nova, S.N., Rahman, M.S., & Chakraborty, C. (2021). Patients' Health Surveillance Model Using IoT and 6G Technology. *Green Technological Innovation for Sustainable Smart Societies: Post Pandemic Era*, 191–209.

O'Leary, B. (2014). An architecture of collaboration. *Publishing Research Quarterly*, 30(3). www.researchgate.net

OCDE. (2020). *Estudios Económicos de la OCDE: Costa Rica*, 2020, 2–66.

OECD. (2020). Costa Rica: Assessment and Competition of Law and Policy 2020.

OECD. (2020). Digital Economy Policy in Costa Rica. 2-75.

OECD. (2022). Recommendation of the Council on Information and Communication Technologies and the Environment. OECD Legal Instruments, 3-6.

OECD. (n.d.). Growth in Latin America. From OECD: https://www.oecd.org/countries/ecuador/growth-in-latin-america .htm/

Oficina Económica y Comercial de España en Panamá. (2021). Informe Económico y Social: Costa Rica. Secretaria de estado de Comercio, 1-45.

Ogudo, K. A., Muwawa Jean Nestor, D., Ibrahim Khalaf, O., & Daei Kasmaei, H. (2019). A device performance and data analytics concept for smartphones' IoT services and machine-type communication in cellular networks. *Symmetry*, 11(4), 593. 10.3390/sym11040593

Ojokoh, B. A., Samuel, O. W., Omisore, O. M., Sarumi, O. A., Idowu, P. A., Chimusa, E. R., & Katsriku, F. A. (2020). Big data, analytics and artificial intelligence for sustainability. *Scientific African*, 9, e00551. 10.1016/j.sciaf.2020.e00551

Okamoto, N., Rodríguez-Luna, M. R., Bencteux, V., Al-Taher, M., Cinelli, L., Felli, E., Urade, T., Nkusi, R., Mutter, D., Marescaux, J., Hostettler, A., Collins, T., & Diana, M. (2022). Computer-assisted differentiation between colon-mesocolon and retroperitoneum using hyperspectral imaging (HSI) technology. *Diagnostics (Basel)*, 12(9), 2225. 10.3390/diagnostics1209222536140626

Ongsulee, P., Chotchaung, V., Bamrungsi, E., & Rodcheewit, T. (2018). Big data, predictive analytics and machine learning. In *2018 16th IEEE international conference on ICT and knowledge engineering (ICT&KE)* (pp. 1-6). 10.1109/ICTKE.2018.8612393

Padala, S. A., & Kallam, A. (2023, July 13). *Clear Cell Renal Carcinoma*. StatPearls Publishing. https://www.ncbi.nlm .nih.gov/books/NBK557644/

Padmanabhan, M., Yuan, P., Chada, G., & Nguyen, H. V. (2019). Physician-friendly machine learning: A case study with cardiovascular disease risk prediction. *Journal of Clinical Medicine*, 8(7), 1050. 10.3390/jcm807105031323843

Pandey, B. K., Pandey, D., Nassa, V. K., Hameed, A. S., George, A. S., Dadheech, P., & Pramanik, S. (2023). A Review of Various Text Extraction Algorithms for Images. In *The Impact of Thrust Technologies on Image Processing*. Nova Publishers. 10.52305/ATJL4552

Pangestu, A., & Wijaya, D. R. (2020). *Wrapper feature selection for poverty level prediction based on E-commerce dataset, ICoDSA*. IEEE.

Patangia, S. (2020). Sales Prediction of Market using Machine Learning. *International Journal of Engineering Research & Technology (Ahmedabad)*, V9(09). Advance online publication. 10.17577/IJERTV9IS090345

Patel, D., Patel, S., Patel, P., & Shah, M. (2022). Solar radiation and solar energy estimation using ANN and Fuzzy logic concept: A comprehensive and systematic study. *Environmental Science and Pollution Research International*, 29(22), 32428–32442. 10.1007/s11356-022-19185-z35178628

Patel, N. P., Parekh, R., Thakkar, N., Gupta, R., Tanwar, S., Sharma, G., Davidson, I. E., & Sharma, R. (2022). Fusion in cryptocurrency price prediction: A decade survey on recent advancements, architecture, and potential future directions. *IEEE Access : Practical Innovations, Open Solutions*, 10, 34511–34538. 10.1109/ACCESS.2022.3163023

Pérez, J. C. (2022, October 17). Pymes del sector tecnología en Costa Rica y cuarta revolución industrial. From Disruptiva: https://www.disruptiva.media/pymes-del-sector-tecnologia-en-costa-rica-y-cuarta-revolucion-industrial

Pestov, I., & Vitkova, L. (2022, October). Methodology for Detecting Anomaly and Attack on Cloud Infrastructure Instances. In *International Conference on Intelligent Information Technologies for Industry* (pp. 131-141). Cham: Springer International Publishing.

Petaling, J. (2017, October 12). Low awareness, and adoption of Industry 4.0 among Malaysian Manufacturers. From Sun Daily: https://www.thesundaily.my/archive/low-awareness-adoption-industry-40-among-malaysian-manufacturers-FTARCH492369

Pettigrew, A. M. (1990). Longitudinal field research on change: Theory and practice. *Organization Science*, 1(3), 267–292. 10.1287/orsc.1.3.267

Phasinam, K., & Kassanuk, T. (2022). Supervised Machine Learning in Precision Agriculture. *International Journal of Mechanical Engineering*, 7(1), 1621–1625.

Piyush, V., Yan, Y., Zhou, Y., Yin, Y., & Ghosh, S. (2023). *A Matrix Ensemble Kalman Filter-based Multi-arm Neural Network to Adequately Approximate Deep Neural Networks*. arXiv preprint arXiv:2307.10436.

Polu, S. K. (2019). Modeling of telemonitoring system for remote healthcare using ontology. *International Journal for Innovative Research in Science & Technology*, 5(9), 6–8.

Poornima, S., & Pushpalatha, M. (2016). A journey from big data towards prescriptive analytics. *ARPN J. Eng. Appl. Sci*, 11(19), 11465–11474.

Pramanik, S. (2023). An Adaptive Image Steganography Approach depending on Integer Wavelet Transform and Genetic Algorithm. *Multimedia Tools and Applications*, 82(22), 34287–34319. Advance online publication. 10.1007/s11042-023-14505-y

Pramanik, S. (2023). Intelligent Farming Utilizing a Soil Tracking Device. In Sharma, A. K., Chanderwal, N., Khan, R., & Global, I. G. I. (Eds.), *Convergence of Cloud Computing, AI and Agricultural Science*. 10.4018/979-8-3693-0200-2.ch009

Pramanik, S., & Bandyopadhyay, S. (2023). Identifying Disease and Diagnosis in Females using Machine Learning. In John Wang, I. G. I. (Ed.), *Encyclopedia of Data Science and Machine Learning*. Global. 10.4018/978-1-7998-9220-5.ch187

Praveenkumar, S., Veeraiah, V., Pramanik, S., Basha, S. M., Lira Neto, A. V., De Albuquerque, V. H. C., & Gupta, A. (2023). *Prediction of Patients' Incurable Diseases Utilizing Deep Learning Approaches, ICICC 2023*. Springer. 10.1007/978-981-99-3315-0_4

Prinz, W., Martínez-Carreras, M. A., & Pallot, M. (2012). From collaborative tools to collaborative working environments. In *Advancing Collaborative Knowledge Environments: New Trends in E-Collaboration* (pp. 1-10). IGI Global. 10.4018/978-1-61350-459-8.ch001

Prococomer; Esencial Costa Rica. (2022). Guía Régimen Zona Franca. 4-25.

PROCOMER. (2020). Costa Rica and Industry 4.0. Business Intelligence Department, 3-12.

PROCOMER. (2022, March 3). 22% del parque empresarial TIC de Costa Rica ofrece tecnologías vinculadas a la cuarta revolución industrial. From Esencial Costa Rica & PROCOMER: https://www.procomer.com/noticia/exportador-noticia/22-del-parque- empresarial-tic-de-costa-rica-ofrece-tecnologias-vinculadas-a-la-cuarta-revolucion- industrial/

Producción mundial de piña por país. (2021). From Atlas Big: https://www.atlasbig.com/es- es/paises-por-produccion-de-pina

Pruitt, K., Johnson, B., Gahan, J., Ma, L., & Fei, B. (2023, April). A high-speed hyperspectral laparoscopic imaging system. *Image-Guided Procedures, Robotic Interventions, and Modeling*, 12466, 49–61.

Puustinen, S., Vrzáková, H., Hyttinen, J., Rauramaa, T., Fält, P., Hauta-Kasari, M., Bednarik, R., Koivisto, T., Rantala, S., von und zu Fraunberg, M., Jääskeläinen, J. E., & Elomaa, A. P. (2023). Hyperspectral Imaging in Brain Tumor Surgery—Evidence of Machine Learning-Based Performance. *World Neurosurgery*, 175, e614–e635. 10.1016/j.wneu.2023.03.14937030483

Quinlan, J. R. (1996). Improved use of continuous attributes in C4. 5. *Journal of Artificial Intelligence Research*, 4, 77–90. 10.1613/jair.279

Quinlan, J. R. (2014). *C4. 5: programs for machine learning*. Elsevier. 10.1016/j.procs.2016.04.224

Quinn, A. (2016) A History of British Magazine Design, https://www.amazon.com/History-British-Magazine-Design/dp/1851777865

Raghu, S., Sriraam, N., Temel, Y., Rao, S. V., Hegde, A. S., & Kubben, P. L. (2019). Performance evaluation of DWT based sigmoid entropy in time and frequency domains for automated detection of epileptic seizures using SVM classifier. *Computers in Biology and Medicine*, 110, 127–143. 10.1016/j.compbiomed.2019.05.01631154257

Raj, A., Dwivedi, G., Sharma, A., de Sousa Jabbour, A. B. L., & Rajak, S. (2020). Barriers to the adoption of industry 4.0 technologies in the manufacturing sector: An inter-country comparative perspective. *International Journal of Production Economics*, 224, 107546. 10.1016/j.ijpe.2019.107546

Rajeswari, G. R., Murugesan, R., Aruna, R., Jayakrishnan, B., & Nilavathy, K. (2022, October). Predicting Employee Attrition through Machine Learning. In *2022 3rd International Conference on Smart Electronics and Communication (ICOSEC)* (pp. 1370-1379). IEEE. 10.1109/ICOSEC54921.2022.9952020

Raposo, A. B., Magalhães, L. P., Ricarte, I. L. M., & Fuks, H. (2001, September). Coordination of collaborative activities: A framework for the definition of tasks interdependencies. In *Proceedings Seventh International Workshop on Groupware. CRIWG 2001* (pp. 170-179). IEEE. 10.1109/CRIWG.2001.951845

Rastogi, R., Chaturvedi, D. K., Satya, S., Arora, N., Trivedi, P., Singh, A. K., & Singh, A. (2020). Intelligent analysis for personality detection on various indicators by clinical reliable psychological TTH and stress surveys. *Computational Intelligence in Pattern RecognitionProceedings of CIPR*, 2019, 127–143.

Ratanamahatana, C., & Gunopulos, D. (2003). Feature selection for the naive bayesian classifier using decision trees. *Applied Artificial Intelligence*, 17(5–6), 475–487. 10.1080/713827175

Raza, M. A., Aziz, S., Noreen, M., Saeed, A., Anjum, I., Ahmed, M., & Raza, S. M. (2022). Artificial Intelligence (AI) in Pharmacy: An Overview of Innovations. *Innovations in Pharmacy*, 13(2), 13. Advance online publication. 10.24926/iip.v13i2.483936654703

Rebública, L. (2020, May 6). Nuevas becas para capacitación y certificación en áreas tecnológicas. From La República: https://www.larepublica.net/noticia/nuevas-becas-para-capacitacion-y-certificacion-en-areas-tecnologicas

Red Reply. (2018). How to Take Advantage of Cloud Computing for Industrie 4.0 and Enterprise 4.0. International Journal of Interactive Mobile Technologies, 3-14.

Reepu, K. S., Chaudhary, M. G., Gupta, K. G., Pramanik, S., & Gupta, A. (2023). Information Security and Privacy in IoT. In *Handbook of Research in Advancements in AI and IoT Convergence Technologies*. IGI Global.

Renee, K. (2018) How to start a magazine online in 15 steps, *Lucidpress.com,*https://www.lucidpress.com/blog/how-to-start-magazine-online

Ren, Z., Shen, Q., Diao, X., & Xu, H. (2021). A sentiment-aware deep learning approach for personality detection from text. *Information Processing & Management*, 58(3), 102532. 10.1016/j.ipm.2021.102532

Rieke, N. (n.d.). The future of digital health with federated learning. *NPJ Digital*. 10.1038/s41746-020-00323-1

Robot asiste a ortopedistas en cirugía de reemplazo de rodilla. (2021, June 21). From El País: https://www.elpais.cr/2021/06/21/robot-asiste-a-ortopedistas-en-cirugia-de-reemplazo- de-rodilla/

Rodrigues, E. M., & Hemmer, E. (2022). Trends in hyperspectral imaging: From environmental and health sensing to structure-property and nano-bio interaction studies. *Analytical and Bioanalytical Chemistry*, 414(15), 4269–4279. 10.1007/s00216-022-03959-y35175390

Rogerson, Hankins, Fuentes, & Rahim. (2022). Government AI Readiness Index 2022. Oxford Insights, 3-59.

Rojko, A. (2017). Industry 4.0 Concept: Background and Overview. ECPE European Center for Power Electronics, 77-90.

Romdhani, I., Tawse, M., & Habibullah, S. (2011, January). Student project performance management system for effective final year and dissertation projects supervision. *London International Conference on Education*.

Roschelle, J., & Teasley, S. D. (1995). The construction of shared knowledge in collaborative problem solving. In *Computer supported collaborative learning* (pp. 69–97). Springer. 10.1007/978-3-642-85098-1_5

Rowland, B. (2013) The fall and rise of magazines from print to digital, *The Guardian,*https://www.theguardian.com/media-network/media-network-blog/2013/mar/07/fall-rise-magazines-print-digital

Rozenes, S., & Kukliansky, I. (2013). An Embedded Approach for Project Management Learning Process. *International Journal of Information Technology Project Management*, 4(3), 38–49. 10.4018/jitpm.2013070103

Sadik, A. (2017). Students' acceptance of file sharing systems as a tool for sharing course materials: The case of Google Drive. *Education and Information Technologies*, 22(5), 2455–2470. 10.1007/s10639-016-9556-z

Saeidi, T., Mahmood, S. N., Alani, S., Ali, S. M., Ismail, I., & Alhawari, A. R. H. (2020). Sub-6G Metamaterial-Based Flexible Wearable UWB Antenna for IoT and WBAN. *Proceedings - IEEE 18th International Conference on Dependable, Autonomic and Secure Computing, IEEE 18th International Conference on Pervasive Intelligence and Computing, IEEE 6th International Conference on Cloud and Big Data Computing and IEEE 5th Cybe*, 7–13.

Sahin, E., Dagdeviren, O., & Akkas, M. A. (2021). An Evaluation of Internet of Nano-Things Simulators. *2021 6th International Conference on Computer Science and Engineering (UBMK)*, 670–675. 10.1109/UBMK52708.2021.9558990

Säily, M., Yilmaz, O. N. C., Michalopoulos, D. S., Pérez, E., Keating, R., & Schaepperle, J. (2021). Positioning Technology Trends and Solutions Toward 6G. *2021 IEEE 32nd Annual International Symposium on Personal, Indoor and Mobile Radio Communications (PIMRC)*, 1–7. 10.1109/PIMRC50174.2021.9569341

Sajja, G. S., Mustafa, M., Phasinam, K., Kaliyaperumal, K., Ventayen, R. J. M., & Kassanuk, T. (2021, August). Towards application of machine learning in classification and prediction of heart disease. In *2021 Second International Conference on Electronics and Sustainable Communication Systems (ICESC)* (pp. 1664-1669). IEEE. 10.1109/ICESC51422.2021.9532940

Samanta, D., Dutta, S., Galety, M. G., & Pramanik, S. (2021). A Novel Approach for Web Mining Taxonomy for High-Performance Computing. *The 4th International Conference of Computer Science and Renewable Energies (ICCSRE'2021)*. 10.1051/e3sconf/202129701073

Samper, & González. (2020). Caracterización de los espacios rurales en Costa Rica y propuestas de alternativas metodológicas para su medición. Documentos de proyectos, 3-79.

Samuel, A. L. (1959). Some studies in machine learning using the game of checkers. *IBM Journal of Research and Development*, 3(3), 210–229. 10.1147/rd.33.0210

San Segundo-Val, I., & Sanz-Lozano, C. S. (2016). Introduction to the Gene Expression Analysis. *Molecular Genetics of Asthma*, 29–43. 10.1007/978-1-4939-3652-6_3

Santos-Silva, D. (2012) The future of digital magazine publishing· Presented at 16th International Conference on Electronic Publishing – ELPUB 2012 – Social Shaping of Digital Publishing: Exploring the Interplay between Culture and Technology, https://content.iospress.com/articles/information-services-and-use/isu661

Sarieddeen, H., Saeed, N., Al-Naffouri, T. Y., & Alouini, M.-S. (2020). Next Generation Terahertz Communications: A Rendezvous of Sensing, Imaging, and Localization. *IEEE Communications Magazine*, 58(5), 69–75. 10.1109/MCOM.001.1900698

Sawada, Y., & Duc, L. (2023). *An efficient estimation of spatio-temporally distributed parameters in dynamic models by an ensemble Kalman filter.* arXiv preprint arXiv:2305.07798.

Scandling, J. D. (2007). Acquired Cystic Kidney Disease and Renal Cell Cancer after Transplantation. *Clinical Journal of the American Society of Nephrology; CJASN*, 2(4), 621–622. 10.2215/CJN.0200050717699473

Schwab, K. (2019). The Global Competitiveness Report 2019. World Economic Forum.

Shah, D., Patel, S., & Bharti, S. K. (2020). Heart disease prediction using machine learning techniques. *SN Computer Science*, 1(6), 1–6. 10.1007/s42979-020-00365-y

Shahrubudin, Lee, & Ramlan. (2019). An Overview on 3D Printing Technology: Technological, Materials, and Applications An Overview on 3D Printing Technology: T. *Procedia Manufacturing*, 1287–1296.

Shameer, K., Johnson, K. W., Glicksberg, B. S., Dudley, J. T., & Sengupta, P. P. (2018). Machine learning in cardiovascular medicine: Are we there yet? *Heart (British Cardiac Society)*, 104(14), 1156–1164. 10.1136/heartjnl-2017-31119829352006

Shamir-Inbal, T., & Blau, I. (2021). Characteristics of pedagogical change in integrating digital collaborative learning and their sustainability in a school culture: e-CSAMR framework. *Journal of Computer Assisted Learning*, 37(3), 825–838. Advance online publication. 10.1111/jcal.12526

Shanthakumari, S., & Priyadarsini, K. (2013) A study on E- Promotional strategies for e-marketing *International Journal of scientific research and management, Volume1 Issue 8 Pages 426-434* www.ijsrm.in

Sharada, K. A., Sushma, K. S. N., Muthukumaran, V., Mahesh, T. R., Swapna, B., & Roopashree, S. (2023). High ECG diagnosis rate using novel machine learning techniques with Distributed Arithmetic (DA) based gated recurrent units. *Microprocessors and Microsystems*, 98, 104796. 10.1016/j.micpro.2023.104796

Sharma, R., Pachori, R. B., & Sircar, P. (2020). Seizures classification based on higher order statistics and deep neural network. *Biomedical Signal Processing and Control*, 59, 101921. 10.1016/j.bspc.2020.101921

Shen, M., Wen, P., Song, B., & Li, Y. (2023). Real-time epilepsy seizure detection based on EEG using tunable-Q wavelet transform and convolutional neural network. *Biomedical Signal Processing and Control*, 82, 104566. 10.1016/j.bspc.2022.104566

Shen, X., Gao, J., Wu, W., Lyu, K., Li, M., Zhuang, W., & Rao, J. (2020). AI-assisted network-slicing based next-generation wireless networks. *IEEE Open Journal of Vehicular Technology*, 1, 45–66. 10.1109/OJVT.2020.2965100

Shinde, P. P., & Shah, S. (2018, August). A review of machine learning and deep learning applications. In *2018 Fourth international conference on computing communication control and automation (ICCUBEA)* (pp. 1-6). IEEE. 10.1109/ICCUBEA.2018.8697857

Shitharth, S., Manoharan, H., Alshareef, A. M., Yafoz, A., Alkhiri, H., & Mirza, O. M. (2022). Hyper spectral image classifications for monitoring harvests in agriculture using fly optimization algorithm. *Computers & Electrical Engineering*, 103, 108400. 10.1016/j.compeleceng.2022.108400

Shorthand.com. (2022) The definitive guide to making a digital magazine, *Shorthand.com,* https://shorthand.com/the-craft/how-to-make-a-digital-magazine/index.html

Sidhu, R. K., & Krishan, R. (n.d.). Role of Big Data Analytics in Wireless Network Applications. *Advances in Wireless Communication and Mathematics*.

Siggelkow, N. (2007). Persuasion with case studies. *Academy of Management Journal*, 50(1), 20–24. 10.5465/amj.2007.24160882

Siles, A. (2022, December 7). Falta de inversión y desconocimiento ponen en jaque a Pymes ante ciberataques. From DPL News: https://dplnews.com/costa-rica-falta-de-inversion- y-desconocimiento-ponen-en-jaque-a-pymes-ante-ciberataques/

Siles, A. (2022, October 13). Costa Rica | IA lleva a ganaderos ticos a un nuevo nivel. From DPL News: https://dplnews.com/costa-rica-ia-lleva-a-ganaderos-ticos-a-un-nuevo- nivel/

Singh, A. P., Asgar, M. E., Ranjan, R., Kaushik, Y., Reji, J., & Tyagi, T. (n.d.). A review on role of ai in damage assessment in laminated composite structures. *Composites, 17*(19), 70-71.

Singh, Y. K., Sinha, N., & Singh, S. K. (2017). Heart disease prediction system using random forest. In *Advances in Computing and Data Sciences:First International Conference, ICACDS 2016,Ghaziabad, India,November 11-12, 2016, Revised Selected Papers 1* (pp. 613-623). Springer Singapore. 10.1007/978-981-10-5427-3_63

Singh, V., & Mayer, P. (2014). Scientific writing: Strategies and tools for students and advisors. *Biochemistry and Molecular Biology Education*, 42(5), 405–413. 10.1002/bmb.2081525052425

Sitar-tăut, A., Zdrenghea, D., Pop, D., & Sitar-tăut, D. (2009). Using machine learning algorithms in cardiovascular disease risk evaluation. *Age (Dordrecht, Netherlands)*, 1(4), 4.

Sivek, S. C. (2013). City Magazines and Social Media: Moving Beyond the Monthly. *Journal of Magazine Media*, 14(2). Advance online publication. https://muse.jhu.edu/article/773658/pdf. 10.1353/jmm.2013.0001

Sodhro, A. H., Pirbhulal, S., Luo, Z., Muhammad, K., & Zahid, N. Z. (2021). Towards 6G Architecture for Energy Efficient Communication in IoT-Enabled Smart Automation Systems. *IEEE Internet of Things Journal*, 8(7), 5141–5148. 10.1109/JIOT.2020.3024715

Song, J. L., Hu, W., & Zhang, R. (2016). Automated detection of epileptic EEGs using a novel fusion feature and extreme learning machine. *Neurocomputing*, 175, 383–391. 10.1016/j.neucom.2015.10.070

Soto, T. (2023, May 3). Cinde: qué es y para qué sirve la coalición con la que rompió el gobierno de Rodrigo Chaves. From El Financiero: https://www.elfinancierocr.com/economia-y-politica/cinde-que-es-y-para-que-sirve-la-coalicion-conla/R5IN5DOJZFHMXOCO3YQNZTHPMY/story/

Srinivasu, P. N., JayaLakshmi, G., Jhaveri, R. H., & Praveen, S. P. (2022). JayaLakshmi, G., Jhaveri, R.H., Praveen, S.P.: Ambient Assistive Living for Monitoring the Physical Activity of Diabetic Adults through Body Area Networks. *Mobile Information Systems*, 2022, e3169927. 10.1155/2022/3169927

Stachl, C., Pargent, F., Hilbert, S., Harari, G. M., Schoedel, R., Vaid, S., & Bühner, M. (2020). Personality research and assessment in the era of machine learning. *European Journal of Personality*, 34(5), 613–631. 10.1002/per.2257

Stahl, F., Maass, W., & Schefer, M. (2004) Strategies for Selling Paid Content on Newspaper and Magazine Websites: An Empirical Analysis of Bundling and Splitting of News and Magazine Articles, https://www.tandfonline.com/doi/abs/10.1080/14241277.2004.9669382

Stasinos, N., Kousis, A., Sarlis, V., Mystakidis, A., Rousidis, D., Koukaras, P., Kotsiopoulos, I., & Tjortjis, C. (2023). A Tri-Model Prediction Approach for COVID-19 ICU Bed Occupancy: A Case Study. *Algorithms*, 16(3), 140. 10.3390/a16030140

Stein, N. R., & VanHouwelingen, L. (2023). Making good use of ultrasound for abdominal tumors in children. *Jornal de Pediatria, 99*, 1-3.

Steinberg, D., & Colla, P. (2009). CART: classification and regression trees. *The top ten algorithms in data mining, 9*, 179.

Stevenson, D., & Starkweather, J. A. (2017). IT project success: The evaluation of 142 success factors by it pm professionals. *International Journal of Information Technology Project Management*, 8(3), 1–21. 10.4018/IJITPM.2017070101

Strauss, J., Frost, R., & Sinha, N. (2014) *E-marketing*, Upper Saddle River, NJ: Pearson, https://www.scirp.org/

Strinati, E. C., Barbarossa, S., Gonzalez-Jimenez, J. L., Ktenas, D., & Cassiau, N. (2019). 6g: the next frontier: from holographic messaging to artificial intelligence using subterahertz and visible light communication. *IEEE Vehicular Technology Magazine*, 14.

Studier-Fischer, A., Seidlitz, S., Sellner, J., Bressan, M., Özdemir, B., Ayala, L., Odenthal, J., Knoedler, S., Kowalewski, K.-F., Haney, C. M., Salg, G., Dietrich, M., Kenngott, H., Gockel, I., Hackert, T., Müller-Stich, B. P., Maier-Hein, L., & Nickel, F. (2023). HeiPorSPECTRAL - the Heidelberg Porcine HyperSPECTRAL Imaging Dataset of 20 Physiological Organs. *Scientific Data*, 10(1), 414. 10.1038/s41597-023-02315-837355750

Stvilia, B., & Gibradze, L. (2022). Seeking and sharing datasets in an online community of data enthusiasts. *Library & Information Science Research*, 44(3), 101160. 10.1016/j.lisr.2022.101160

Sujlana, A. (2018). 10 Reasons to Create a digital magazine, https://www.clavistechnologies.com/blog/

Sunaryono, D., Sarno, R., & Siswantoro, J. (2022). Gradient boosting machines fusion for automatic epilepsy detection from EEG signals based on wavelet features. *Journal of King Saud University. Computer and Information Sciences*, 34(10), 9591–9607. 10.1016/j.jksuci.2021.11.015

Świętoń, D., Szarmach, A., & Kosiak, W. (2022). Contrast-enhanced ultrasound of adrenal hemorrhage: A helpful problem solving tool. *Medical Ultrasonography*, 24(3), 284–289.35437529

Tai, P., Wu, F., Chen, R., Zhu, J., Wang, X., & Zhang, M. (2023). Effect of herbaceous plants on the response of loose silty sand slope under rainfall. *Bulletin of Engineering Geology and the Environment*, 82(1), 42. 10.1007/s10064-023-03066-x

Takyi-Aninakwa, P., Wang, S., Zhang, H., Li, H., Xu, W., & Fernandez, C. (2022). An optimized relevant long short-term memory-squared gain extended Kalman filter for the state of charge estimation of lithium-ion batteries. *Energy*, 260, 125093. 10.1016/j.energy.2022.125093

Tao, H., Hameed, M. M., Marhoon, H. A., Zounemat-Kermani, M., Heddam, S., Kim, S., Sulaiman, S. O., Tan, M. L., Sa'adi, Z., Mehr, A. D., Allawi, M. F., Abba, S. I., Zain, J. M., Falah, M. W., Jamei, M., Bokde, N. D., Bayatvarkeshi, M., Al-Mukhtar, M., Bhagat, S. K., & Yaseen, Z. M. (2022). Groundwater level prediction using machine learning models: A comprehensive review. *Neurocomputing*, 489, 271–308. 10.1016/j.neucom.2022.03.014

Tarazi, J., & Akre, V. L. (2013, December). Enabling e-Collaboration and e-Pedagogy at an Academic Institution in the UAE. In *2013 International Conference on Current Trends in Information Technology (CTIT)* (pp. 118-124). IEEE. 10.1109/CTIT.2013.6749489

Tasci, I., Tasci, B., Barua, P. D., Dogan, S., Tuncer, T., Palmer, E. E., Fujita, H., & Acharya, U. R. (2023). Epilepsy detection in 121 patient populations using hypercube pattern from EEG signals. *Information Fusion*, 96, 252–268. 10.1016/j.inffus.2023.03.022

Tay, L., Woo, S. E., Hickman, L., & Saef, R. M. (2020). Psychometric and validity issues in machine learning approaches to personality assessment: A focus on social media text mining. *European Journal of Personality*, 34(5), 826–844. 10.1002/per.2290

Technologies, V. (2019, May 13). Integrating IoT into Healthcare, Agriculture and Transportation Applications. From IoT For All: https://www.iotforall.com/integrating- machine-learning-ml-iot-applications

Thatcher, J. E., Yi, F., Nussbaum, A. E., DiMaio, J. M., Dwight, J., Plant, K., Carter, J. E., & Holmes, J. H.IV. (2023). Clinical Investigation of a Rapid Non-invasive Multispectral Imaging Device Utilizing an Artificial Intelligence Algorithm for Improved Burn Assessment. *Journal of Burn Care & Research; Official Publication of the American Burn Association*, 44(4), 969–981. 10.1093/jbcr/irad05137082889

The Nielsen Company. (2010). *Changing Models: A Global Perspective on Paying for Content Online*. Available: http://blog.nielsen.com/nielsenwire/global/

Tian, J. X., & Zhang, J. (2022). Breast cancer diagnosis using feature extraction and boosted C5. 0 decision tree algorithm with penalty factor. *Mathematical Biosciences and Engineering*, 19(3), 2193–2205. 10.3934/mbe.202210235240781

Tingson, A. (2015) 7 Content Marketing Trends You Need To Focus On This 2015, https://www.linkedin.com/pulse/7-content-marketing-trends-you-need-focus-2015-arlene-tingson-mba?trk=portfolio_article-card_title

Tiwari, G., Singh, R., Chandna, V. K., Shimi, S. L., & Jain, M. (2019). Outcome-Based Assessment of Engineering Undergraduate Final Year Projects for Tire-2 Institutes. In *Third International Congress on Information and Communication Technology* (pp. 211-221). Springer. 10.1007/978-981-13-1165-9_19

Tonge, A. M., Kasture, S. S., & Chaudhari, S. R. (2013). Cyber security: Challenges for society-literature review. *IOSR Journal of Computer Engineering*, 2(12), 67–75. 10.9790/0661-1226775

Topol, E. J. (2019). High-performance medicine: The convergence of human and artificial intelligence. *Nature Medicine*, 25(1), 44–56. 10.1038/s41591-018-0300-730617339

Treviño-Elizondo, B. L., & García-Reyes, H. (2020). Industry 4.0 Adoption in Latin America: A Systematic Literature Review. In IIE Annual Conference. Proceedings (pp. 174-179). Institute of Industrial and Systems Engineers (IISE).

Truong, D. (2021). *Using causal machine learning for predicting the risk of flight delays in air transportation*. JATM.

Tsai, M. F., & Chu, Y. C. (2021). *Smart machinery monitoring system with reduced information transmission and fault prediction methods using industrial internet of things* (Vol. 9). MDPI AG. https://www.mdpi.com/2227-7390/9/1/3

Tsuyuki, T., & Tamura, R. (2022). Nonlinear data assimilation by deep learning embedded in an ensemble Kalman filter. *Journal of the Meteorological Society of Japan*, 100(3), 533–553. 10.2151/jmsj.2022-027

Tuah, N. M., Yoag, A., Nizam, D., Mohd, N., & Chin, C. W. (2022). A dashboard-based system to manage and monitor the progression of undergraduate it degree final year projects. *Pertanika Journal of Science & Technology*, 30(1). Advance online publication. 10.47836/pjst.30.1.13

Tuli, S., Basumatary, N., Gill, S. S., Kahani, M., Arya, R. C., Wander, G. S., & Buyya, R. (2020). HealthFog: An ensemble deep learning based Smart Healthcare System for Automatic Diagnosis of Heart Diseases in integrated IoT and fog computing environments. *Future Generation Computer Systems*, 104, 187–200. 10.1016/j.future.2019.10.043

UNESCO. (2021). Tasa de alfabetización, total de adultos (% de personas de 15 años o más) - Costa Rica. From Banco Mundial: https://datos.bancomundial.org/indicator/SE.ADT.LITR.ZS?locations=CR

United Nations. (2018). Industry 4.0 – the opportunities behind the challenge. Department of Trade, Investment, and Innovation (TII), 2-31.

United Nations. (2022). Industry 4.0 for inclusive development. Commission on Science and Technology for Development, 2-18.

Vennira Selvi, G., Muthukumaran, V., Kaladevi, A. C., Satheesh Kumar, S., & Swapna, B. (2022). Integrated dominating and hit set-inspired unequal clustering-based data aggregation in wireless sensor networks. *International Journal of Intelligent Computing and Cybernetics*, 15(4), 642–655. 10.1108/IJICC-10-2021-0225

Vidya Chellam, V., Veeraiah, V., Khanna, A., Sheikh, T. H., Pramanik, S., & Dhabliya, D. (2023). *A Machine Vision-based Approach for Tuberculosis Identification in Chest X-Rays Images of Patients, ICICC 2023*. Springer. 10.1007/978-981-99-3315-0_3

Vikruthi, S., Archana, D. M., & Chaithanya, D. R. (2022). Enhanced vehicle detection using pooling based dense-yolo model. *Journal of Theoretical and Applied Information Technology*, 100(24).

Vural, O., Aydos, U., Okur, A., Pinarli, F. G., & Atay, L. Ö. (2023). Prognostic Values of Primary Tumor Textural Heterogeneity and Blood Biomarkers in High-risk Neuroblastoma. *Journal of Pediatric Hematology/Oncology*, 45(7), 10–1097. 10.1097/MPH.0000000000002662 37027243

Wang, Y., Zupanski, M., Tu, X., & Gao, X. (2022). Performance assessment of the maximum likelihood ensemble filter and the ensemble Kalman filters for nonlinear problems. *Research in the Mathematical Sciences*, 9(4), 62. 10.1007/s40687-022-00359-7

Wang, Z. H. E., Wu, C., Zheng, K., Niu, X., & Wang, X. (2019). SMOTETomek-based resampling for personality recognition. *IEEE Access : Practical Innovations, Open Solutions*, 7, 129678–129689. 10.1109/ACCESS.2019.2940061

Wang, Z., Du, Y., Wei, K., Han, K., Xu, X., Wei, G., Tong, W., Zhu, P., Ma, J., Wang, J., Wang, G., Yan, X., Xiang, J., Huang, H., Li, R., Wang, X., Wang, Y., Sun, S., Suo, S., & Su, X. (2022). Vision, application scenarios, and key technology trends for 6G mobile communications. *Science China. Information Sciences*, 65(5), 1. 10.1007/s11432-021-3351-5

Ward, A., Sarraju, A., Chung, S., Li, J., Harrington, R., Heidenreich, P., Palaniappan, L., Scheinker, D., & Rodriguez, F. (2020). Machine learning and atherosclerotic cardiovascular disease risk prediction in a multi-ethnic population. *NPJ Digital Medicine*, 3(1), 125. 10.1038/s41746-020-00331-1 33043149

Wear, D., Bhagirath, E., Balachandar, A., Vegh, C., & Pandey, S. (2023). Autophagy Inhibition via Hydroxychloroquine or 3-Methyladenine Enhances Chemotherapy-Induced Apoptosis in Neuro-Blastoma and Glioblastoma. *International Journal of Molecular Sciences*, 24(15), 12052. 10.3390/ijms24151205237569432

Weng, S. F., Reps, J., Kai, J., Garibaldi, J. M., & Qureshi, N. (2017). Can machine-learning improve cardiovascular risk prediction using routine clinical data? *PLoS One*, 12(4), e0174944. 10.1371/journal.pone.017494428376093

Wijaya, D. R., & Paramita, N. L. P. S. P. (2020). *Estimating city-level poverty rate based on e-commerce data with machine learning*. ECR.

Williamson, B., & Eynon, R. (2020). Historical threads, missing links, and future directions in AI in education. *Learning, Media and Technology*, 45(3), 223–235. 10.1080/17439884.2020.1798995

Wimmer, R., & Dominick, T. (2011). *Mass Media Research: An Introduction*. Wadsworth Cengage Learning.

Wrench, J. S., & Punyanunt, N. M. (2004). Advisee-advisor communication: An exploratory study examining interpersonal communication variables in the graduate advisee-advisor relationship. *Communication Quarterly*, 52(3), 224–236. 10.1080/01463370409370194

Wu, G., Li, H., Hu, X., Bi, Y., Zhang, J., & Wu, X. (2009, August). MReC4. 5: C4. 5 ensemble classification with MapReduce. In *2009 fourth ChinaGrid annual conference* (pp. 249-255). IEEE. 10.1109/ChinaGrid.2009.39

Wu, T., Redoute, J.-M., & Yuce, M. R. (2018). A wireless implantable sensor design with subcutaneous energy harvesting for long-term IoT healthcare applications. *IEEE Access : Practical Innovations, Open Solutions*, 6, 35801–35808. 10.1109/ACCESS.2018.2851940

Xue, L., Gu, S., Mi, L., Zhao, L., Liu, Y., & Liao, Q. (2022). An automated data-driven pressure transient analysis of water-drive gas reservoir through the coupled machine learning and ensemble Kalman filter method. *Journal of Petroleum Science Engineering*, 208, 109492. 10.1016/j.petrol.2021.109492

Xu, X., & Zhang, Y. (2023). Scrap steel price forecasting with neural networks for east, north, south, central, northeast, and southwest China and at the national level. *Ironmaking & Steelmaking*, 50(11), 1–15. 10.1080/03019233.2023.2218243

Yadav, S., Jain, A., & Singh, D. (2018, December). Early prediction of employee attrition using data mining techniques. In *2018 IEEE 8th international advance computing conference (IACC)* (pp. 349-354). IEEE. 10.1109/IADCC.2018.8692137

Yang, C., Huang, Q., Li, Z., Liu, K., & Hu, F. (2017). Big Data and cloud computing: Innovation opportunities and challenges. *International Journal of Digital Earth*, 10(1), 13–53. 10.1080/17538947.2016.1239771

Yang, S., Guo, J. Z., & Jin, J. W. (2018). An improved Id3 algorithm for medical data classification. *Computers & Electrical Engineering*, 65, 474–487. 10.1016/j.compeleceng.2017.08.005

Yedida, R., Reddy, R., Vahi, R., & Jana, R. GV, A., & Kulkarni, D. (2018). Employee attrition prediction. *arXiv preprint arXiv:1806.10480*.

Yilmaz, M., Tasel, F. S., Gulec, U., & Sopaoglu, U. (2018). Towards a process management life-cycle model for graduation projects in computer engineering. *PLoS One*, 13(11), e0208012. 10.1371/journal.pone.020801230496242

Yin, R. K. (2009). How to do better case studies. The SAGE handbook of applied social research methods, 2(254-282).

Yin, H., Li, B., Zhang, F., Su, C. T., & Ou-Yang, A. G. (2022). Detection of early bruises on loquat using hyperspectral imaging technology coupled with band ratio and improved Otsu method. *Spectrochimica Acta. Part A: Molecular and Biomolecular Spectroscopy*, 283, 121775. 10.1016/j.saa.2022.12177536007346

Younas, M. (2019). Research challenges of big data. *Service Oriented Computing and Applications*, 13(2), 105–107. 10.1007/s11761-019-00265-x

You, X., Wang, C.-X., Huang, J., Gao, X., Zhang, Z., Wang, M., Huang, Y., Zhang, C., Jiang, Y., Wang, J., Zhu, M., Sheng, B., Wang, D., Pan, Z., Zhu, P., Yang, Y., Liu, Z., Zhang, P., Tao, X., & Ma, X. (2020). Towards 6G wireless communication networks: vision, enabling technologies, and new paradigm shifts. *Science China. Information Sciences*, 64(1), 110301. 10.1007/s11432-020-2955-6

Yuh, J. (2000). Design and Control of Autonomous Underwater Robots: A Survey. *Autonomous Robots*, 8(1), 7–24. 10.1023/A:1008984701078

Yüksel, H. (2020). An empirical evaluation of industry 4.0 applications of companies in Turkey: The case of a developing country. *Technology in Society*, 63, 101364. 10.1016/j.techsoc.2020.101364

Yu, X., Ren, Z., Guttery, D. S., & Zhang, Y. D. (2023). DF-dRVFL: A novel deep feature based classifier for breast mass classification. *Multimedia Tools and Applications*, 83(5), 1–30. 10.1007/s11042-023-15864-238283725

Zacharis, N. Z. (2018). Classification and regression trees (CART) for predictive modeling in blended learning. *International Journal of Intelligent Systems and Applications*, 3(3), 1–9. 10.5815/ijisa.2018.03.01

Zack, C. J., Senecal, C., Kinar, Y., Metzger, Y., Bar-Sinai, Y., Widmer, R. J., Lennon, R., Singh, M., Bell, M. R., Lerman, A., & Gulati, R. (2019). Leveraging machine learning techniques to forecast patient prognosis after percutaneous coronary intervention. *JACC: Cardiovascular Interventions*, 12(14), 1304–1311. 10.1016/j.jcin.2019.02.03531255564

Zhang, C., & Hu, C. (2021). Research on the application of Decision Tree and Random Forest Algorithm in the main transformer fault evaluation. *JPCS*. https://doi.org/10.1088/1742-6596/1732/1/012086

Zhang, L., Liao, J., Wang, H., Zhang, M., Liu, Y., Jiang, C., Han, D., Jia, Z., Qin, C., Niu, S. Y., Bu, H., Yao, J., & Liu, Y. (2023). Near-infrared II hyperspectral imaging improves the accuracy of pathological sampling of multiple cancer types. *Laboratory Investigation*, 103(10), 100212. 10.1016/j.labinv.2023.10021237442199

Zhang, Q., Bai, C., Chen, Z., Li, P., Yu, H., Wang, S., & Gao, H. (2021). Deep learning models for diagnosing spleen and stomach diseases in smart Chinese medicine with cloud computing. *Concurrency and Computation*, 33(7), 1–1. 10.1002/cpe.5252

Zhang, Y., Wang, L., Zhang, C., & Li, J. (2023). Adversarial Examples in Visual Object Tracking in Satellite Videos: Cross-Frame Momentum Accumulation for Adversarial Examples Generation. *Remote Sensing (Basel)*, 15(13), 3240. 10.3390/rs15133240

Zhao, J., & Kumar, V. (2022) Technologies and Systems for E-Collaboration during Global Crises. www.researchgate.net10.4018/978-1-7998-9640-1

Zhao, J., & Richards, J. (2021) E-Collaboration Technologies and Strategies for Competitive Advantage amid Challenging Times. www.researchgate.net10.4018/978-1-7998-7764-6

Zhao, C., Fu, X., Dong, J., Feng, C., & Chang, H. (2023). LPDNet: A Lightweight Network for SAR Ship Detection Based on Multi-Level Laplacian Denoising. *Sensors (Basel)*, 23(13), 6084. 10.3390/s2313608437447932

Zhao, Y., Liu, R., Liu, Z., Liu, L., Wang, J., & Liu, W. (2023). A Review of Macroscopic Carbon Emission Prediction Model Based on Machine Learning. *Sustainability (Basel)*, 15(8), 6876. 10.3390/su15086876

Zheng, K., Yang, Z., Zhang, K., Chatzimisios, P., Yang, K., & Xiang, W. (2016). Big data-driven optimization for mobile networks toward 5G. *IEEE Network*, 30(1), 44–51. 10.1109/MNET.2016.7389830

Zhou, Y., Ling, L., Wang, L., Hui, N., Cui, X., Wu, J., Peng, Y., Qi, Y., & Xing, C. (2020). Service aware 6G: An intelligent and open network based on convergence of communication, computing and caching. *Digital Communications and Networks*, 6(3), 253–260. Advance online publication. 10.1016/j.dcan.2020.05.003

Zuo, X., Chen, Y., Ohno-Machado, L., & Xu, H. (2021). How do we share data in COVID-19 research? A systematic review of COVID-19 datasets in PubMed Central Articles. *Briefings in Bioinformatics*, 22(2), 800–811. 10.1093/bib/bbaa33133757278

About the Contributors

Jingyuan Zhao obtained her PhD in Management Science and Engineering from University of Science and Technology of China. She completed postdoctoral programs respectively in Technological Economics with Harbin Institute of Technology, in Management of Technology with Université du Québec à Montréal, in Innovation and Governance with University of Toronto, in Mathematical and Computational Science with University of Toronto Mississauga. Dr. Zhao's research expertise includes management of technology innovation, behavior and information technology, high-tech industries, multinational governance, and science and technology policy. Dr. Zhao also has extensive industry experience and provides consulting services to major corporations such as China Mobile. She serves as editor-in-chief of International Journal of e-Collaboration(IJeC).

V. Vinoth Kumar is an Associate Professor in the Department of Computer Science and Engineering in MVJ College of Engineering, Bangalore, India. He is a highly qualified individual with around 8 years of rich expertise in teaching, entrepreneurship, and research and development with specialization in computer science engineering subjects. He has been a part of various seminars, paper presentations, research paper reviews, and conferences as a convener and a session chair, a guest editor in journals and has co-authored several books and papers in national, international journals and conferences. He is a professional society member for ISTE, IACIST and IAENG. He has published more than 15 articles in National and International journals, 10 articles in conference proceedings and one article in book chapter. He has filed Indian patent in IoT Applications. His Research interest includes Mobile Adhoc Networking and IoT.

* * *

Jyoti Agarwal is an Associate Professor - Department of CSE, Graphic Era (Deemed to be University), Dehradun. She has 12 years of rich experience in teaching, research experience.

Pratham Aggarwal is currently doing his B.Tech. in Information Technology at School of Information and Technology, Vellore Institute of Technology, Vellore, India. His research interests include machine learning and deep learning techniques for solving various real-world problems.

Bhuvaneswari Amma N. G. obtained her degree in Information Technology with Distinction in 2004 from Manonmaniam Sundaranar University, Tirunelveli, Tamil Nadu and Postgraduate degree in Computer Science and Engineering in 2009 from College of Engineering, Anna University Guindy Campus, Chennai, Tamil Nadu. She was awarded Ph.D. degree by the National Institute of Technology Tiruchirappalli, Tamil Nadu in 2020. Since 2004, she has been in the teaching profession and currently, she is an Assistant Professor (Senior) in the School of Computer Science and Engineering, Vellore Institute of Technology (VIT), Chennai, Tamil Nadu. She has 11 years of teaching experience and 7 years of research experience. Her research interests include data science and cyber security. She received awards such as, Best Paper Award, Best Poster Award, and CSIR Travel Grant. She has visited Nanyang Technological University Singapore and South Korea.

Suresh Kumar Arumugam is working as a Professor, Jain (Deemed to-be University) and is also Independent Researcher.

Tharun Ashwin B. is currently pursuing his B.Tech. Computer Science and Engineering with Specialization in Artificial Intelligence and Machine Learning from Vellore Institute of Technology, Chennai, Tamil Nadu-600127. He constantly seeks to improve his abilities and expand his knowledge in various fields which includes Machine Learning, Data Science, Computer Vision and Deep Learning. His primary areas of research include Machine Learning Algorithms and Explainable AI.

Mohamed T. Bennai is a Lecturer in the Department of Computer Science at the University of Boumerdes in Algeria. He is also a researcher at the LIMOSE laboratory (Laboratory of Computer Science, Modeling and Optimization of Systems). Dr. Bennai received his Ph.D. in 2022 and a Magister Diploma and Engineering Diploma in Computer Science from the University of Boumerdes. His main research interests include multi-agent systems, medical image processing, and the Internet of Things. He has over a decade of teaching experience at the University of Boumerdes, where he has supervised numerous undergraduate and graduate student projects. Before joining the university, Dr. Bennai worked for several years as a software engineer in the industry.

Sharon Christa is working as an Associate Professor in School of Computing, MIT ADT University, India.

Valentina Cucino is Assistant Professor at Scuola Superiore Sant'Anna, Pisa. She received her PhD in Management Innovation, Sustainability and Healthcare from Scuola Superiore Sant''Anna, Pisa. Her main research interest are technology transfer, purposedriven organization and entrepreneurship. She has published in European Journal of Innovation Management, Journal of Knowledge Management, R&D Management, Studies in Higher Education and The TQM Journal.

Amandeep Dhaliwal has been part of School of Leadership & Management, Manav Rachna International University, India since 2010. Her research interest areas include Entrepreneurship, Marketing and IT. She completed her Master's in Business Administration and then her Doctoral studies doctoral research in the area of Women Entrepreneurship from BIMTECH, G.Noida. She has been in Academics for almost a decade taking up courses related to areas of Marketing, IT and Entrepreneurship for management students. Prior to academics; she was working for numerous years with Agro-food Industry and IT sector specializing in marketing domain. She has published many research papers and Chapters in National and International Journals and Books (Indexed in UGC Care, SCOPUS, EBSCO, PUBMED etc) . Her special interest lies in Case Study writing and her case was published at International Case Centre (formerly ECCH). She has won Young Scholars Award for the same.

Rachid Djerbi is an associate professor at the department of computer science of the Boumerdes university (Algeria) and a researcher at the LIMOSE laboratory (Laboratory of Computer Science, Modeling and Optimization of Systems). He received his Ph.D. degree from Boumerdes University, (Algeria) in 2021. His main research interests are System Social Networks, Internet of Things, and Data Science. He has seven years experience in teaching the design and development of software systems, Networking and security of systems for MCS students at Boumerdes University (Algeria).

Giulio Ferrigno is a Senior Assistant Professor at Sant'Anna School of Advanced Studies of Pisa. He has held visiting positions at the University of Cambridge, Tilburg University, and the University of Umea. His main research themes include strategic alliances, big data, and Industry 4.0. His works have been published in Small Business Economics, Technological Forecasting and Social Change, International Journal of Management Reviews, R&D Management, Technology Analysis & Strategic Management, Review of Managerial Science, European Journal of Innovation Management, International Journal of Entrepreneurial Behavior & Research. He is an Associate Editor of Technology Analysis & Strategic Management.

Ankur Gupta has received the B.Tech and M.Tech in Computer Science and Engineering from Ganga Institute of Technology and Management, Kablana affiliated with Maharshi Dayanand University, Rohtak in 2015 and 2017. He is an Assistant Professor in the Department of Computer Science and Engineering at Vaish College of Engineering, Rohtak, and has been working there since January 2019. He has many publications in various reputed national/ international conferences, journals, and online book chapter contributions (Indexed by SCIE, Scopus, ESCI, ACM, DBLP, etc). He is doing research in the field of cloud computing, data security & machine learning. His research work in M.Tech was based on biometric security in cloud computing.

Rajaguru Harikumar received the Ph.D. degree in bio-signal processing from Anna University. He is currently a Professor with the Bannari Amman Institute of Technology, Sathyamangalam, India. His research interests include machine learning and deep learning.

Rose Bindu Joseph is currently working as an Assistant Professor in the Department of Mathematics at Dayanand Sagar College of Engineering. She received her Ph.D in Mathematics from VIT University, Vellore in the field of Fuzzy Theory. She has qualified NET for lectureship by CSIR-UGC. She holds a Master's degree and bachelor's degree in Mathematics from Mahatma Gandhi University, Kerala. She has more than 15 years of experience in academia and research. She has published more than 20 research papers along with book chapters and 2 published patent applications. Her research interests include Fuzzy Theory, Soft Computing, Applications of Soft Computing Methods In Computer Vision, Biometrics and Data Analytics.

Hulya Kocyigit is a postdoctoral fellow at the Icahn School of Medicine at Mount Sinai, New York, NY, USA. Her research focuses on the intersection of causal inference, machine learning, and biomarker methods in medicine, particularly in cancer data analysis and simulation studies.

Razika Lounas is a lecturer at the Computer Science Department and a researcher at LIMOSE Laboratory at the University of Boumerdes. She received her PhD from Boumerdes University, Algeria and Limoges University, France in 2018. Before that, she received her Magister Diploma form the Boumerdes University and her Diploma of Computer Engineering at the Tizi Ouzou University, Algeria. Her main research interests are dynamic software updating, formal methods and Internet of things. She has a ten years of experience in teaching the design and development of collaborative applications for MCS students at Boumerdes University. She supervised more than ten final year projects about collaborative applications from both academia and industry.

Hocine Mokrani is an associate professor at the department of computer science of the Boumerdes university (Algeria) and a researcher at the LIMOSE laboratory (Laboratory of Computer Science, Modeling and Optimization of Systems). He received his Ph.D. degree from Telecom Paris School (France) in 2014. His main research interests are System on Chip specification, Internet of Things, and the use of formal methods to prove the correctness of these systems. He has nine years experience in teaching the design and development of software systems, formal methods, and computer architectures for MCS students at Boumerdes University (Algeria).

Sujatha Moorthy has completed her doctorate in Wireless Communication, department of ECE in the Year 2017 at Sathyabama University, Chennai, Tamil Nadu, India. She has completed her Postgraduate in the year 2007 in M.E, Applied Electronics in the year 2006 at Sathyabama University, Chennai, Tamil Nadu, India and her Undergraduate in Electronics and Communication Engineering at Madras University in the year 1999. She has 23 years of teaching experience and 6 years of Research. She has held various position such as Head of the department, NAAC and NBA coordinator, Research Chairperson. Currently She is working as a Professor in KL University (Koneru Lakshmaiah Education Foundation) in the department of ECE.

Meram Munirathnam completed his Ph.D in 2013 from Sri Venkateswara University, Tirupati, Andhra Pradesh, India, under supervision of Prof. D. Bharathi. His research work is on Non-Associative Rings and also he did research on Derivations on Rings and published some papers. He published 3 Patents, 1 Book Chapter and 24 papers in various International journals and attended 14 National and International conferences and presented papers. He also organized 3 online National webinars. He was the member of various committees at the University level like Mathematics syllabus for Rajiv Gandhi University of Knowledge Technologies for the year 2021 & 2022. He has 12 years of teaching experience in Mathematics for B. Tech Students. Also he has experience in non-teaching positions also like Mathematics Subject coordinator, Assistant Placements coordinator and Warden for students.

Bharanidharan N. received the Ph.D. degree from the Faculty of Information and Communication Engineering, Anna University, Chennai, in 2020. He is currently an Assistant Professor with the School of Information and Technology, Vellore Institute of Technology, Vellore, India. His research interests include machine learning and deep learning techniques for solving various real-world problems.

Thillaiarasu Nadesan is currently working as an Associate Professor from Jan 2021 in the School of Computing and Information Technology, REVA University, Bengaluru, He has also served as an Assistant Professor at Galgotias University, Greater Noida from July 2019 to December 2020. He worked from April 2012 to Jun 2019 as an Assistant Professor in the Department of Computer Science and Engineering, SNS College of Engineering, Coimbatore. Obtained his B.E., in Computer Science and Engineering from Selvam College of Technology in 2010 and received his M.E., in Software Engineering from Anna University Regional Center, Coimbatore in 2012. He received his Ph.D., Degree from Anna University, Chennai in 2019, he has published more than 25 research papers in refereed, Springer, and IEEE Xplore conferences. he has organized several workshops, summer internships, and expert lectures for students. He has worked as a session chair, conference steering committee member, editorial board member, and reviewer in Springer Journal and IEEE Conferences. he is an Editor board Member of editing books titled "Machine Learning Methods for Engineering Application Development" Bentham Science. He is also working as editor for the title, "Cyber Security for Modern Engineering Operations Management: Towards Intelligent Industry", Design Principle, Modernization and Techniques in Artificial Intelligence for IoT: Advance Technologies, Developments, and Challenges" CRC Press Tylor and Francis, His area of interest includes Cloud Computing, Security, IoT, and Machine Learning.

Aditya Pai H (Senior Member - IEEE) is an Associate Professor and Program Head -Department of CSE - AIDE, Jain (Deemed to be University), Bengaluru. He has 12 years of rich experience in teaching, research and administrative experience.

Sabyasachi Pramanik is a professional IEEE member. He obtained a PhD in Computer Science and Engineering from Sri Satya Sai University of Technology and Medical Sciences, Bhopal, India. Presently, he is an Associate Professor, Department of Computer Science and Engineering, Haldia Institute of Technology, India. He has many publications in various reputed international conferences, journals, and book chapters (Indexed by SCIE, Scopus, ESCI, etc). He is doing research in the fields of Artificial Intelligence, Data Privacy, Cybersecurity, Network Security, and Machine Learning. He also serves on the editorial boards of several international journals. He is a reviewer of journal articles from IEEE, Springer, Elsevier, Inderscience, IET and IGI Global. He has reviewed many conference papers, has been a keynote speaker, session chair, and technical program committee member at many international conferences. He has authored a book on Wireless Sensor Network. He has edited 8 books from IGI Global, CRC Press, Springer and Wiley Publications.

Sannasi Chakravarthy S. R. received a B.E. degree in ECE from P. T. Lee CNCET, Kanchipuram, India, in 2010, M.E. degree in Applied Electronics from Thanthai Periyar Government Institute of Technology, Vellore, India, in 2012, and Ph.D. degree in Machine Learning from Anna University, Chennai, in 2020. Currently, he is an Associate Professor at Bannari Amman Institute of Technology, Sathyamangalam, India. His research interests include machine learning and deep learning approaches in Signal and Image Processing.

Mahesh T.R. is an Associate Professor and Program Head -Department of CSE - General, Jain (Deemed to be University), Bengaluru.

R. Udhayakumar currently works at the Department of Mathematics, School of Advanced Sciences, Vellore Institute of Technology, Vellore, TamilNadu, India. He did postdoctoral studies at Institute Technology Bandung, Bandung, Indonesia. He completed his PhD degree at Periyar University in the year 2015. Udhayakumar does research in Differential equations and Homological Algebra. He published more than 100 SCI/SCIE research articles.

Muthukumaran V. was born in Vellore, Tamilnadu, India, in 1988. He received the B.Sc. degree in Mathematics from the Thiruvalluvar University Serkkadu, Vellore, India, in 2009, and the M. Sc. degrees in Mathematics from the Thiruvalluvar University Serkkadu, Vellore, India, in 2012. The M. Phil. Mathematics from the Thiruvalluvar University Serkkadu, Vellore, India, in 2014 and Ph.D. degrees in Mathematics from the School of Advanced Sciences, Vellore Institute of Technology, Vellore in 2019. He has 4.5 years of teaching experience and 8 years of research experience, and he has published various research papers in high-quality journals Springer, Elsevier, IGI Global, Emerald, River, etc. At present, he has a working Assistant Professor in the Department of Mathematics, SRM Institute of Science and Technology, Kattankulathur, Tamil Nadu, India. Dr. V. Muthukumaran is a Fellow of the International Association for Cryptologic Research (IACR), India; He is a Life Member of the IEEE. He has published more than 80 research articles and 10 book chapters in peer-reviewed international journals. He has published 10 IPR patents in algebraic with IoT applications. He also presented 25 papers presented at national and international conferences. He has also been a reviewer of several international journals including, Journal of Intelligent Manufacturing (Springer), International Journal of Intelligent Computing and Cybernetics, International Journal of e-Collaboration (IJeC), International Journal of Pervasive Computing and Communications (IJPCC), International Journal of System of Assurance Engineering(IJSA), International Journal Speech Technology (IJST)-Springer, Journal of Reliable Intelligent Environments (JRIE), International Journal of Information Technology and Web Engineering (IJITWE), Applied Science, Symmetry, Mathematics, Computers in Biology and Medicine, Microprocessors and Microsystems. His research interests include Machine learning, Data Science, Block chain, IoT, Data Mining, and Algebraic Cryptography.

Vinoth Kumar V. (Member, IEEE) is currently an Associate Professor with the School of Information Technology and Engineering, Vellore Institute of Technology, India.

Index

Symbols

E

E-Commerce 47, 48, 97, 98, 100, 103, 104, 105, 106, 107, 108, 109, 111

EEG 200, 201, 202, 203, 204, 207, 208, 209, 210, 211, 212

Employee Attrition 79, 80, 81, 87, 89, 94, 95, 96

Ensemble 19, 24, 86, 159, 165, 185, 200, 201, 203, 204, 205, 206, 207, 211, 212, 223, 267, 268, 269, 270, 271, 272, 273, 274, 275, 276, 277, 279, 280, 281, 285, 297, 358

Ensemble Kalman 267, 268, 269, 270, 271, 272, 274, 275, 276, 277, 279, 280, 281

Epilepsy 200, 201, 202, 203, 208, 210, 211, 212

E-Pricing 97, 98, 100, 103, 104, 105, 106, 107, 109

E-Promotion 98, 100, 104, 105, 106, 108, 110

Evaluation 48, 50, 77, 81, 86, 90, 91, 94, 122, 126, 130, 131, 135, 141, 143, 144, 149, 150, 151, 152, 153, 154, 156, 160, 182, 212, 214, 218, 221, 241, 268, 269, 274, 278, 283, 284, 285, 286, 287, 290, 293, 294, 295, 296, 314, 315, 316, 317, 318, 325, 328, 329, 331, 332, 333, 340, 341, 342, 343, 346, 347, 352, 356, 364, 366

Examinations 119, 128

F

F1-Score 161, 170, 171, 172, 178, 179, 200, 204, 209, 358

Feature Selection 7, 19, 47, 183, 184, 186, 187, 188, 190, 191, 192, 193, 195, 196, 197, 198, 199, 202

Final Year Projects 328, 329, 330, 335, 341, 351, 352

Frequently 3, 5, 6, 18, 19, 20, 27, 79, 87, 94, 145, 163, 206, 214, 215, 227, 309, 313

G

Gradient Boosting 167, 169, 170, 171, 172, 185, 200, 204, 205, 206, 212, 228, 356

H

Healthcare 52, 60, 61, 69, 77, 115, 116, 117, 118, 119, 120, 121, 122, 123, 124, 125, 126, 129, 131, 132, 158, 185, 213, 214, 215, 216, 218, 219, 220, 222, 223, 235, 246, 248, 270, 329, 334, 335, 336, 367

Hyper Spectral 128, 129, 132, 133, 136, 137, 142

I

ICA 186, 194, 195, 197

Implications 50, 51, 56, 65, 69, 145, 208, 215, 304

Industry 4.0 47, 49, 50, 51, 52, 53, 54, 56, 57, 58, 59, 60, 61, 62, 63, 64, 65, 66, 67, 68, 69, 70, 71, 72, 73, 74, 75, 76, 77, 78, 366

Investigates 27, 200, 267, 316

IoT 49, 52, 59, 70, 71, 77, 96, 116, 117, 119, 120, 121, 122, 123, 124, 125, 126, 160, 213, 215, 216, 218, 219, 221, 222, 223, 248, 249, 301, 303, 311, 366, 367

K

KNN 1, 2, 20, 79, 81, 86, 87, 89, 94, 159, 166, 178, 206, 209, 228, 230, 241, 243, 272

L

Logistic Regression 19, 24, 80, 81, 91, 94, 147, 159, 163, 164, 165, 166, 170, 171, 225, 229, 243, 353, 354, 360, 361, 362, 364, 365

M

Machine Learning 1, 2, 3, 4, 5, 6, 18, 23, 24, 27, 28, 29, 34, 35, 43, 44, 46, 47, 48, 79, 80, 81, 86, 87, 95, 96, 104, 105, 108, 116, 120, 124, 130, 141, 142, 158, 159, 161, 162, 163, 164, 166, 167, 170, 180, 181, 182, 184, 185, 199, 201, 204, 205, 206, 207, 208, 209, 213, 215, 216, 218, 220, 221, 222, 223, 224, 225, 227, 228, 230, 231, 232, 236, 237, 240, 246, 247, 248, 249, 281, 285, 297, 298, 300, 304, 305, 311, 326, 328, 329, 330, 333, 334, 336, 337, 344, 348, 350, 352, 353, 354, 356, 358, 361, 364, 365, 366, 367, 368

Marketing Strategies 110

Medical Instrumentation 128, 129, 132

Medical Services 115

Microarray Gene Expression 183, 187, 197

Myers-Briggs Type Indicator 353, 355, 366

N

Naive Bayes 1, 2, 21, 27, 80, 159, 167, 169, 170, 171, 206, 209, 353, 354, 364

Naïve Bayes 5, 8, 21, 26, 28, 29, 36, 42, 44, 45, 46, 185, 187, 359, 360

Network Optimization 288, 308, 309

Neuroblastoma 143, 144, 145, 146, 147, 149, 150, 153, 154, 156, 157

Next-Generation Wireless Technologies 299

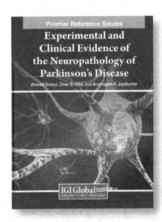
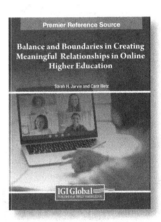

www.igi-global.com

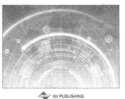

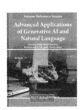

Printed in the United States
by Baker & Taylor Publisher Services